Luckey's Hummel®

12th Edition

Figurines & Plates

IDENTIFICATION AND PRICE GUIDE

D1504860

Carl F. Luckey   Updated by Dean

Published by

krause publications
An F&W Publications Company

**700 East State Street • Iola, WI 54990-0001
715-445-2214 • 888-457-2873
www.krause.com**

Please call or write for our free catalog of publications.
Our toll-free number to place an order or obtain a free catalog is (800) 258-0929.

Library of Congress Catalog Number: 2002107598
ISBN: 0-87349-472-5

The illustrations of M.I. Hummel art are printed in this collectors' guide under license by ARS AG, Zug/Switzerland. Neither ARS AG nor W. Goebel Porzellanfabrik are responsible for any information contained in this guide, in particular with regard to all quotations of prices.

M.I. Hummel®, Hummel®, and M.I. Hummel Club®, in signature and/or block forms, are registered trademarks of W. Goebel Porzellanfabrik GmbH & Co. KG, Germany.

M.I. Hummel figurines, plates, bells, and other collectibles are copyrighted products. ©Goebel.

The collector values in this book are meant to be used only as guidelines. They are not intended to set prices, influence the market or be the last word in value. They are derived by analysis of various known sales, sales lists, auction results, expert opinions, and other related data. They are greatly affected by condition as well as current demand. Neither the author nor the publisher assumes any responsibility for transactions based upon the values placed in this guide.

Dedication

This book is dedicated to Sister Maria Innocentia (Berta) Hummel, who lived from 1909 to 1946. Although her life was relatively short, she left behind the legacy of love and joy.

Millions of people around the world have delighted in the artistic genius and love of this extraordinary woman.

As one well-known obituary stated: "The gift of her art was the priceless endowment of Joy…."

Table of Contents

Chapter Two: Collectors' Guide (continued)

Chapter Three: The M.I. Hummel Collection

Chapter Four: Other Hummel Collectibles

Chapter Five: The Rare and The Unusual

Chapter Six: Hummel Collectibles by Others

Appendices

Index

Acknowledgments

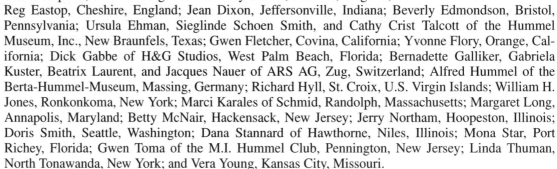

In the 20 years that Carl Luckey wrote about M.I. Hummel collectibles, he met an enormous number of very helpful people in the ongoing task of taking pictures and gathering data. There were so many who have helped, in fact, that it is not practical to attempt naming them all. There are some, however, who gave Carl so much, including their friendship, that it would be unforgivable not to name them.

Carl Luckey's Acknowledgments

Extra special thanks to Rue Dee and Judy Marker and to Pat and Carol Arbenz for their unselfish sharing, patience, and hospitality over all these years.

Thank you Donald Stephens and the Village of Rosemont, Illinois, for allowing me to photograph your extraordinary collection for this book. A special thanks with a laurel wreath goes to Betty Rossi, director of the museum housing this collection, for putting up with me, a bunch of equipment, and various photographers, publishers, and others underfoot on more than one occasion. You graciously accepted an inconvenient intruder.

Others who directly contributed to this and previous editions in some way are: Margaret Caddis, Prestwick, Scotland; Nancy M. Campbell of Lerner Publications, Minneapolis, Minnesota; C.C. Campbell; Dona Danziger of The Clay Works, Exmore, Virginia; Reg Eastop, Cheshire, England; Jean Dixon, Jeffersonville, Indiana; Beverly Edmondson, Bristol, Pennsylvania; Ursula Ehman, Sieglinde Schoen Smith, and Cathy Crist Talcott of the Hummel Museum, Inc., New Braunfels, Texas; Gwen Fletcher, Covina, California; Yvonne Flory, Orange, California; Dick Gabbe of H&G Studios, West Palm Beach, Florida; Bernadette Galliker, Gabriela Kuster, Beatrix Laurent, and Jacques Nauer of ARS AG, Zug, Switzerland; Alfred Hummel of the Berta-Hummel-Museum, Massing, Germany; Richard Hyll, St. Croix, U.S. Virgin Islands; William H. Jones, Ronkonkoma, New York; Marci Karales of Schmid, Randolph, Massachusetts; Margaret Long, Annapolis, Maryland; Betty McNair, Hackensack, New Jersey; Jerry Northam, Hoopeston, Illinois; Doris Smith, Seattle, Washington; Dana Stannard of Hawthorne, Niles, Illinois; Mona Star, Port Richey, Florida; Gwen Toma of the M.I. Hummel Club, Pennington, New Jersey; Linda Thuman, North Tonawanda, New York; and Vera Young, Kansas City, Missouri.

Dean A. Genth's Acknowledgments

Upon the publication of this 12th edition, I would like to gratefully acknowledge my father-in-law and mentor Robert L. Miller who has been a lifelong inspiration and knowledge-giver of a wealth of details regarding the variations and rarities of the M.I. Hummel Figurines.

Special thanks must also go to Maria Turner whose late-night editing expertise has made this new edition one generation better.

Thanks to Carl F. Luckey whose own legacy of providing the collecting public with a price and identification guide for M.I. Hummel figurines, plates, and other pieces lives on even though he passed away Nov. 2, 1998. I, along with the staff at Krause Publications, thank him for laying the foundation for this, the 12th edition, of his well-known and respected collectors' book.

And finally, I would be remiss in not expressing a word of gratitude to Gerhard Skrobek, longtime Hummel master sculptor. After years of sculpting followed by more years of serving as a Goebel ambassador and traveling the world to talk about his love for his work, Gerhard celebrated his 80th birthday this year and also gave his "Farewell Tour." I and other M.I. Hummel collectors are truly grateful for Gerhard's ability to bring Sister Maria Innocentia's art to life in homes around the world.

Author's Note

Carl F. Luckey spent more than 20 years writing about M.I. Hummel figurines and related M.I. Hummel items. Sadly, on Nov. 2, 1998, after the publication of the 11th edition of this book, Carl died.

Carl steadfastly tried to ferret out all the correct data through the years in his attempt to present it to you, the collector, so that you could enjoy the world of Hummel through the fun and excitement of new finds and additions to your collections.

Dean A. Genth

Over the years, Carl Luckey researched, traveled, and photographed many collections and rare finds, and picked the brains of many dealers and leading collectors. Carl noted that there are many collectible items related to M.I. Hummel beyond the realm of figurines. Thus, he expanded the book to include a selection of items, which includes the M.I. Hummel calendars, postcards, bells, plates, cups, thimbles, wall plaques, music boxes, and numerous other Hummel-related items.

Much of Carl's information came directly from the collectors who have bought, read, and used this book. Collectors all over the world have been an important part in making this book the resounding success it has been over the years.

In keeping with Carl's ever-expanding spirit of collector participation, I would encourage all collectors and dealers of M.I. Hummel items to relay any new or interesting information to the address listed below. I have accepted the challenge from Krause Publications to update the Luckey Hummel book and would invite your help in adding to my bulging research files. As Carl stated in the 11th edition of this book, "If you have boxes or overflowing file cabinets with old literature and catalogs, ship them to me. I am interested in anything connected to Goebel, Hummel, or not. Good quality photos are preferred, but snapshots are welcome. Please see Appendix A for directions on describing and photographing your Hummel items. By all means try it. You may be surprised at the results."

The body of knowledge regarding M.I. Hummel art, figurines, and related collectibles has grown steadily through the years due to the dedication and vigilance of both collectors and writers willing to share new bits of information about new finds, variations, and unique observations. Through the years, many of the newly published revela-

Carl F. Luckey, the man for whom this volume is named and its author for 11 editions. Carl died in 1998, leaving Dean Genth to continue his legacy of bringing collectors invaluable Hummel pricing and collecting tips.

tions have been just as surprising to the executives and production workers at the Goebel factory in Rodental, Germany, where the M.I. Hummel figurines are produced.

In the early days of production, the Goebel factory did not keep precise records of every change in coloration or style. This has allowed collectors of M.I. Hummel to help write the history of the production of M.I. Hummel figurines by uncovering many previously unknown variations of color and style.

Should you have an important discovery to share or need guidance with your own collection, feel free to write or call me.

Happy Collecting!
Dean A. Genth
12th Edition, Revisions Author
M.I. Hummel Specialist
Miller's Hallmark & Gift Gallery
1328 N. Barron St.
Eaton, OH 45320
(937) 472-4072 (9 a.m.-5 p.m. EST weekdays)
(937) 456-4151 (9 a.m.-9 p.m. weekdays,
9 a.m.-6 p.m. Saturdays, and noon-5 p.m. Sundays)

Introduction

The interest in M.I. Hummel figurines continues to grow with every passing year. Of course, there have been collectors of Hummel figurines and related articles since very soon after they were first offered by Goebel at the Leipzig Trade Fair in March of 1935, but the past 30 years have seen an incredible surge of interest.

Values skyrocketed for the first 10 or 12 of those years, but settled down in the mid-1990s. Indeed, some values have decreased, but M.I. Hummel figurines still remain one of the premier figurine collectibles in the world.

This book is for anyone with an interest in the world of Hummel: the dealer, the collector, anyone owning one or two figurines, or someone just contemplating beginning a collection. It is important to state that even though every effort is made to ensure its completeness and accuracy, neither this book nor any other can be an absolute authority at this time. Too much is still unknown. There are too many diverse opinions and too many unknown circumstances surrounding the history of the development, production, and marketing of the early Hummel pieces, new variations still being found, pieces not yet uncovered but known to have been produced at least in prototype, and last but not least, unquestionably genuine M.I. Hummel figurines showing up that were never believed to exist.

This is a collector's guide—just that and no more. It is a *guide*, to be used in conjunction with every bit of other information you may be able to obtain. To that end, I not only recommend that you obtain all the other books and publications you can, but list the titles and brief descriptions of them and, when possible, an address where you might obtain them.

The information in this book was obtained from many of the same sources available to collectors, dealers, and other writers. It is a compendium of information gleaned from historians, old company and dealer pamphlets, brochures, publications, dealers, collectors, shows/conventions, distributors, and writers, and the hope is that it will prove useful to all such contributors.

The book contains a short history of W. Goebel Porzellanfabrik, the company that makes Hummel figurines; a biographical sketch of Sister Maria Innocentia Hummel (the artist from whose works virtually all the designs are taken); an explanation of the trademark system and other markings found on the figurines; a glossary of terminology; a description of production techniques; and most important of all, a comprehensive listing of all the pieces themselves.

In the 11th edition and this 12th edition the listings have been considerably expanded to include much information that was not in the first 10 editions. Each listing contains a photograph of each piece when possible, detailed descriptions of color and mold variations and photos of them when available, current production status, sizes found and available, other remarks of interest, cross-references when of interest, a current market value range, and the latest Goebel factory recommended retail price list at the back of the book.

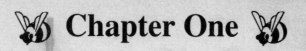

🐝 Chapter One 🐝

History and Preservation

Historical Overview

Sister of the Third Order of Saint Francis
Siessen Convent, Saulgau, Germany

Berta Hummel, who later became known as Sister Maria Innocentia, as portrayed in a self-portrait.

The story of the Hummel figurines is unique. It is practically required reading for those with an interest in the artist, her work, and the resulting three-dimensional fine earthenware renditions—the famous Hummel figurines.

These charming but simple figurines of boys and girls easily capture hearts. In them we see, perhaps, our son or daughter, sister or brother, or even ourselves when we were racing along the paths of happy childhood. When you see the School Boy or School Girl you may be taken back to your own school days. Seeing the figurine Culprits could bring back the time when you purloined your first apple from a neighbor's tree and were promptly chased away by his dog. You will delight in the beauty of the Flower Madonna or Shepherd's Boy. You will love them all with their little round faces and big questioning eyes. These figurines will collect you, and if you have the collecting tendency, you will undoubtedly want to collect them.

You may ask yourself what artist is behind these beguiling figurines. Who is the person with the talent to portray beauty and innocence with such simplicity? The answer is Berta Hummel, a Franciscan sister called Maria Innocentia.

Berta Hummel was born on May 21, 1909, in Massing in lower Bavaria, which was located about 40 miles northeast of Munich, Germany. She grew up

School Boy.

in a family of two brothers and three sisters in a home where music and art were part of everyday life. In this environment, her talent for art was encouraged and nourished by her parents.

Hummel attended primary school between 1915 and 1921. During these early years, she demonstrated the great imagination so necessary for an artist. She created delightful little cards and printed verses for family celebrations, birthdays, anniversaries, and Christmas. Her subjects were almost always the simple objects with which she was familiar: flowers, birds, animals, and her friends. In her simple child's world, she saw only the beautiful things around her.

When she finished primary school, Hummel was enrolled in the Girls Finishing School in Simbach in 1921, in order to nurture and train her talent further and to give her a wider scope of education and experience. Here again, her artistic talent was recognized and upon finishing, it was decided that she should go to a place where she could further cultivate that talent and realize her desire to pursue art as a vocation. In 1927, Hummel moved to Munich, where she entered the Academy of Fine and Applied Arts. There she lived the life of an artist, made friends, and painted to her heart's content. At the academy, she acquired full mastery of art history, theory, and technique. It was here also that she met two Franciscan sisters who, like herself, attended the academy.

There is an old adage that art and religion go together. Berta Hummel's life was no exception. She became friends

Flower Madonna.

Shepherd's Boy.

School Girl.

![M.I. Hummel signature facsimile]

Facsimile of the well-known M.I. Hummel signature.

with the two sisters and began to think that this might be the best way to serve. Over time, she decided to join the sisters in their pilgrimage for art and God, in spite of the fact that she had been offered a position at the academy.

For a time, Hummel divided her days between her talent for art and her love for humanity and hours of devotion and worship. Then she took the first step into a new life of sacrifice and love. After completing her term as a novice, the 25-year-old took the first vows in the Convent of Siessen on August 30, 1934.

Although Berta Hummel (now Sister Maria Innocentia) gave her life over to an idea she thought greater than any worldly aspiration, the world became the recipient of her wonderful works. Within the walls and the beautiful surroundings of the centuries-old convent, she created the paintings and drawings that were to make her famous. Within these sacred confines, her artistic desires enjoyed unbounded impetus.

Little did her superiors dream that this modest blue-eyed artist who had joined their community would someday win worldwide renown. Much less did they realize what financial assistance Hummel's beloved convent would derive from her work as an artist.

During World War II, in 1945, after the French had occupied the region, the noble-minded artist's state of health was broken. On November 6, 1946, at age 37, despite the best care, God summoned her to His eternal home, leaving all her fellow sisters in deep mourning.

Today, the M.I. Hummel figurines, modeled according to Sister Maria Innocentia's work, are known all over the world. They are her messengers, bringing pleasure to many, many people.

W. Goebel Porzellanfabrik

In an area very near Coburg in northern Bavaria, Franz Detleff Goebel and his son William Goebel founded the company in 1871. Once known as Oeslau, the village is now known as Rodental.

Initially, the company manufactured slates, pencils, and marbles, and after 1879, it was well into the production of porcelain dinnerware and beer steins.

By the mid-1910s, a third generation, Max Louis Goebel, had taken the helm of the company and it began manufacturing fine earthenware products. His son, Franz Goebel, became active in the company, and the two of them developed a line of porcelain figurines that was well accepted on the international market.

Upon Max Louis' death in 1929, Franz took over the running of the company along with his brother-in-law Dr. Eugen Stocke, a trained economist, who was the financial manager of the operation.

By the early 1930s, Goebel had gained considerable experience and expertise in fashioning products of porcelain and fine earthenware.

Sister Maria Innocentia's art came to the attention of Franz in December 1933 in the form of religious note cards for the Christmas and New Year seasons. These cards were brand-new publications of her art by Ars Sacra Josef Muller Verlag. (This company has since evolved into ArsEdition, well known to collectors of prints and postcards of Hummel art.)

Remarkably, it was in March of the same year that the Siessen Convent had made an unsolicited inquiry of the Josef Muller firm regarding the possibility of reproducing their Sister Maria Innocentia's art.

Once Franz Goebel saw the cards in Munich, he conceived the idea of translating them into three-dimensional figurines. He sought and gained permission from the convent and Sister Maria Innocentia Hummel. The original letters rest in the Goebel archives. The letter granting Goebel permission stated plainly that all proposed designs must be preapproved before the product could be manufactured. This is true to this day: The convent still has the final say as to whether a proposed design stays within the high standards insisted upon by M.I. Hummel.

After Franz Goebel gained permission for the company to produce the figurines, it took about a year to model the first examples, make the first molds, experiment with media, and make the first models of fine earthenware. The company presented the first figurines at the Leipzig Fair in 1935. They were a great success, and by the end of 1935, there were 46 models in the new line of Hummel figurines.

Production of Hummel figurines—and practically everything else in the Goebel lines—slowly dwindled during the years of World War II, and toward the end of the war, production had ceased completely. During the American Occupation, the United States Military Occupation Government allowed Goebel to resume operation. This, of course, included the

Merry Wanderer (Hum 7), one of the original 46 figurines released by Goebel in 1935, and one of the most-valuable figurines today.

production of Hummel figurines. During this period, the figurines became quite popular among U.S. servicemen in the occupation forces, and upon their return to the states, many brought them home as gifts. This activity engendered a new popularity for Hummel figurines.

Today, W. Goebel Porzellanfabrik maintains a large factory complex in Rodental, where it manufactures, among many other things, M.I. Hummel figurines and related articles. The company maintains a very nice visitor center where it welcomes collectors. Visitors are shown a film and then taken on a short tour to view the manufacturing process in a special demonstration room.

Museums and Institutions

The Donald E. Stephens Museum of Hummels

The Donald E. Stephens Museum of Hummels was opened in 1986 in the Rosemont Exposition Center. Stephens, longtime mayor of Rosemont, Illinois, donated his magnificent Hummel collection to the village in 1984 for the purpose of establishing a museum.

The 15,000-square-foot museum, located just five minutes from Chicago's O'Hare International Airport, is probably the largest public display in the world of both the current-production M.I. Hummel items and the old, rare pieces. The collection does not stop there, however. It is constantly expanding. With guidance from the board of directors and with Stephens' expert consulting, the museum continues to seek out and acquire rare pieces.

The museum is large enough to accommodate the Stephens Collection, a display of all current M.I. Hummel products, a facsimile Goebel factory that demonstrates the fashioning of the figurines, a display of other Goebel products, a display of ANRI figurines, special exhibits and shows, a retail store (known as The Village Gift Shop), and an auditorium.

The Donald E. Stephens Museum of Hummels is open to the public with free admission and parking. The address is:

Exterior view of the Donald E. Stephens Museum of Hummels in Rosemont, Illinois.

Interior view of the Donald E. Stephens Museum of Hummels.

Donald E. Stephens Convention Center—Lobby, 5555 North River Road, Rosemont, Illinois 60018. It is advisable to call for hours and/or to arrange a group visit: (847) 692-4000. The museum's Web site is: www.stephenshummelmuseum.com.

Das Berta-Hummel-Museum im Hummelhaus

This museum was opened in July 1994. It is located in the Hummel home in Massing, Bavaria, and was the birthplace of Berta Hummel and her home, before she took her vows to become a nun.

The museum, directed by her nephew Alfred Hummel, houses the largest exhibit of Hummel figurines in Europe. More important is the large collection of paintings and drawings the artist accomplished before entering the convent. The museum and a related pre-existing company have been responsible for the production of several M.I. Hummel collectibles, which are listed elsewhere in this volume.

The museum address is: Das Berta-Hummel-Museum im Hummelhaus, Strasse 2, D - 84323 Massing, Germany. The museum hours are: 9 a.m. to 5 p.m. Monday through Saturday and 10 a.m. to 5 p.m. Sunday.

A view of the entry to the Berta-Hummel-Museum in Massing, Germany.

An interior view showing some of Berta Hummel's artwork.

An interior view showing childhood and family photos of Berta Hummel.

The Siessen Convent-Hummelsaal (Hall of Hummels)

Sister Maria Innocentia's convent maintains an exhibit of many of her original drawings and paintings. If you are lucky, you may be able to see her renderings of the Stations of the Cross in the adjacent chapel. A selection of Hummel postcards and small prints is offered for sale. There is also the opportunity to see her final resting place in the convent cemetery. The convent is a regular stop on the annual club-sponsored tours.

The convent is located just 3 kilometers out of Saulgau in southern Germany. The address is Kloster Siessen, D-88348 Saulgau, Germany. The hours of operation are: closed Monday; 2 to 4 p.m. Tuesday through Friday; 10 a.m. to noon and 2 to 4 p.m. Saturday; and 1:30 to 4 p.m. Sunday. It is best to phone ahead in case of religious celebrations or other unscheduled closings.

🐝 Chapter Two 🐝

Collectors' Guide

Buying and Selling

Finding and Buying M.I. Hummel Collectibles

The single, most important factor in any collecting discipline is knowledge. Before you spend your hard-earned funds to start or expand a collection, it is incumbent upon you to arm yourself with knowledge. If you've bought this book, you have made a good start. Now you must study it, learn from it, and refer to it often when you're on your hunt.

But don't stop there.

In Appendix C is a list of other books and publications dealing with the subject. Some are out of print and no longer readily available, but others are easy to obtain. Get them and study them as well. Be sure you get the latest edition.

In today's market, there are many sources, some quite productive and some not so productive, as is true of any collectibles field. Supply and demand is a very important factor in the world of Hummel collecting. We have been through some extraordinary times. Nearly three decades ago, retailers had a

Sometimes there would be 40 or 50 tables like this at a show, all practically empty by the last day.

very difficult time obtaining Hummel figurines and plates in any quantity, never had a choice of pieces, and often went for weeks with none in stock. They often had to order an assortment, and there were three monetary levels of assortments. In addition, it was often two to three months between ordering them and taking delivery. This was true for almost every retail Hummel dealer in the country. Although the rule is still generally no choice for the smaller dealers, production increases have improved over the years to where the number you have to select from at your local dealer is usually pretty good.

In those years of limited supply, even small dealers would see their shipments gone in a matter of days. There was a time in the late-1970s and early 1980s that dealers not only couldn't meet collectors' demands, but kept lists of collectors and what each collector was looking for. The result was most of their stock was presold, and what was left would sometimes literally be fought over.

The shows and conventions that featured Hummel saw great crowds in those early years of the surge in Hummel popularity. Frequently, the dealers would literally be cleaned out before half the show was over, leaving booths empty of all but tables and display fixtures. Even this book was snatched up so rapidly at one show, that original author Carl Luckey was left with none to sell after the first day.

Our economic times have changed all that, but the good news is that the collector now has many sources from which to choose. This is particularly true if you are not

specializing in the older trademark pieces. These can be readily found in gift shops, jewelry stores, galleries, and shops specializing in collectibles. Even the popular new television shopping programs feature Hummel figurine sales from time to time. They are also available by mail-order from various dealers around the country, many of whom also deal in the old trademark pieces.

A great way to find them is by looking in the various antique and collectible publications (names and addresses of these are listed elsewhere in the book). Many of them have a classified ad section where dealers and collectors alike offer Hummel figurines and related pieces such as plates.

Productive sources, if you can get to them, are the large annual gatherings of dealers and collectors held around the country. Especially if you're trying to find the older-marked pieces, these shows can be a goldmine. But even if you're a collector of the new pieces, attending the shows is fun and a good learning experience. They usually offer lectures and seminars by experts and dealers, all of whom are subject to much "brain-picking" by crowds of collectors. You also have the opportunity to meet other collectors and learn from them. Just be sure to pick the ones with this book under their arm: they are obviously the smartest!

Of course, the age of technology has brought forth another new venue for finding and selling pieces. The Internet has provided collectors of all sorts of Hummel-related pieces with a place not only to shop, but also to interact in chat rooms or online discussion panels with other collectors. There are even appraisal services on the 'Net where trained appraisers can give you a value to your collection for a fee.

Using the Internet, the possibilities for expanding a collection (or selling one) now seem endless. Take, for example, the number of Hummel-related collectibles on auction Web sites; on eBay.com, a search under the word "Hummel" will bring forth an average of more than 4,000 choices every day. The one caution about using the Internet for buying, however, is to beware of potential fraud. Without the opportunity to actually pick up and inspect a piece, it is sometimes difficult to legitimize authenticity. See "More About E-Buying" for a bit more detail on Internet buying.

Other than at shows, by mail-order, or on the 'Net, you can find old trademark pieces in those shops that sell both new and old pieces. There are a few around the country. With the increased awareness of the value of the older-marked pieces, it is very unlikely—but still possible—that some smaller, uninformed shops could have a few pieces bearing older trademarks, bought some years ago for sale at whatever the current retail price is for the newer ones.

Bargains? Yes, there are bargains to be found. Sometimes you get lucky at auctions if no one else is looking for the particular figurine you have picked out. That would be a rare occurrence at an all-Hummel auction. Estate auctions and sales and country auctions would be your best bet. Flea markets (especially in Europe), junk shops, attics, basements, relatives, friends, acquaintances, and neighbors are by far the best sources for bargains. In short, anywhere one might find curious old gifts, castaways, etc.

These engaging little figurines have, for more than 65 years now, been considered a wonderful gift or souvenir. There are so many motifs that you can almost always find one that fits a friend's or relative's particular personality, profession, or avocation. Until recently, they were also relatively inexpensive. So "bone up," and start looking and asking. You may find a real treasure.

More About E-Buying

People today are flocking to online Internet sites to shop for a wide array of collectibles. As more opportunities develop for making the best deal, collectors need to educate themselves on the proper methods of buying online, and by doing so, reduce the risk of possible abuse by an unscrupulous merchant.

In 1999, auction sales amounted to $2 billion, and the figures continued to grow into the new century. Although online auctions have tapered somewhat in today's tough economy, I interviewed Federal Trade Commission staff attorney Lisa Hone for the April 2000 edition of Collector's Mart magazine and quoted her as saying auctions are popular because they give buyers and sellers wonderful opportunities to find each other.

"If I'm in Alaska, I can reach out all over the world and find a particular piece of Mission furniture or even a Beanie Baby," Hone said. "The vast majority of the times, it works out fine."

In the first half of 1998, the FTC's Bureau of Consumer Protection received about 300 complaints involving online auction fraud, according to Hone. In the first half of 1999, about 6,000 such complaints were recorded. The growth of exploitation is not surprising, given the phenomenal expansion of one-on-one trading through the Internet.

Collectors need to be aware of potential risks and apply a full measure of common sense precautions to ensure the safety and reliability of any transaction. Some test of basic principles must be utilized: What is the seller's reputation? Is the seller willing to give me a valid street address where I can find him should something go wrong? Do I get a warranty? Do I have return privileges?

In order to finesse your collectibles buying online, review the "E-Buying Tips" below for important considerations when you are shopping the 'Net.

With a few common sense precautions, you should be ready to e-shop until your fingers drop.

E-Buying Tips

- Understand how the auction works.
- Check out the seller. For company information, contact the state or local consumer protection agency and Better Business Bureau.
- Be especially careful if the seller is a private individual.
- Get the seller's name, street address, and telephone number to check him/her out or follow up if there is a problem.
- Ask about returns, warranties and service.
- Be wary of claims about collectibles.
- Use common sense and ask yourself: Is this the best way to buy this item? What is the most I am willing to bid?
- Get free insurance through the auction sites whenever possible.
- For assistance, check out these Web sites: www.fraud.com, www.ftc.gov and www.bbbonline.com.

The Price to Pay

The province of this book is primarily Hummel figurines and related articles. The preponderance of these collectibles are made by W. Goebel Porzellanfabrik (hereinafter called Goebel) and most of those covered here bear trademarks other than the one currently being used by the company. It is always nice to have a listing of what is currently being produced by Goebel, along with the suggested retail prices. There is one printed in the back of the book, but a more portable version printed by Goebel should be available at your nearest dealer.

Licenses have been granted to companies other than Goebel to produce various other items. Most, but not all, of these items utilize a two-dimensional Hummel design motif. The first and earliest were those who were licensed to produce prints and postcards. Many companies used these prints by applying them to such things as framed pictures, wall plaques, and music boxes. These and the more recent releases have yet to develop much of a secondary collector market. For this reason, you will see few of them in this book with a quoted collector value.

There are several factors that influence the actual selling price of the old and the new. The suggested retail price list, released by the company periodically, addresses those pieces bearing the current production trademark. Each time the list is released, it reflects changes in the retail price. These changes (usually increases) are due primarily to the basic principle of supply and demand, economic influences of the world money market, ever-increasing material and production costs, the American market demand, and last, but certainly not least, an expanding interest in Germany and the rest of the European market.

The list does not necessarily reflect the actual price you may have to pay. Highly popular pieces in limited supply can go higher and some of the less popular pieces can go for less. This has been the case more in the recent past than now, but the phenomenon still occurs.

The value of Hummel figurines, plates, and other collectibles bearing trademarks other than the one currently being used in production is influenced by some of the same factors discussed earlier, to a greater or lesser extent. The law of supply and demand comes into even more prominent light with regard to pieces bearing the older trademarks, for they are no longer being made and the number on the market is finite. More simply, there are more collectors desiring them than there are available pieces. Generally speaking, the older the trademark, the

When looking to buy Hummels to start a new collection, it's a good idea to start with your local retailer. Not only will retailers carry the latest releases, but they often are aware of other collectors in the area and can perhaps direct you to someone who would be willing to sell some of the rarer pieces on the secondary market.

more valuable or desirable the piece. One must realize, however, that this is not a hard and fast rule. In many instances there are larger numbers available of pieces bearing an older mark than there are of pieces bearing later trademarks. If the latter is a more desirable figure and is in much shorter supply, it is perfectly reasonable for it to be more valuable.

Another factor must be considered. The initial find of the rare International Figurines (see Chapter 5) saw values shoot up as high as $20,000 each. At first, the figurines were thought to exist in just eight designs and in only one or two prototypes of each. Over the years, several more designs and multiples of the figurines have surfaced. Although they are still quite rare, most bring less than half of the original inflated value. So you see, values can fall as the result of an increase in supply of a rare or uncommon piece. This situation can be brought about artificially as well. If someone secretly buys up and hoards a large quantity of a popular piece for a period of time, the short supply will drive the value up. If that supply is suddenly dumped on the market, demand goes down. This has happened more than once in the past, but not so much today.

Yet another circumstance that may influence a fall in pricing is the reissue of a piece previously thought by collectors to be permanently out of production. This has happened because of collectors' past confusion over company terminology with regard to whether a piece was permanently or temporarily withdrawn from production. Many collectors wish to possess a particular item simply because they like it and have no interest in an older trademark version. These collectors will buy the newer piece simply because they can purchase it for less, although recent years have seen the last of the older trademarked pieces go for about the same. It follows naturally that demand for an even older trademark version will lessen under those circumstances.

You may find it surprising that many of the values in the old trademark listing are less than the values reflected in the current Goebel suggested retail price list. You have to realize that serious collectors of old mark Hummel collectibles have very little interest in the price of or the collecting of those pieces currently being produced, except where the list has an influence on the pricing structure of the secondary market. As we have seen, demand softens for some of the later old trademark pieces. That is not to say that those and the current production pieces are not valuable—quite the contrary. They will be collectible on the secondary market eventually. Time must pass. Make no bones about it, with the changing of the trademarks and the passing of time will come the logical step into the secondary market. The principal market for the last two trademarks is found in the general public, not the seasoned collector. The heaviest trading in the collector market in the past couple of years has been in the Crown and Full Bee trademark pieces. The Stylized Bee and Three Line trademark pieces are currently remaining stable and the Last Bee trademark pieces are experiencing a stagnant market.

Selling M.I. Hummel Items

There is an old saying in the antique and collectibles world that goes like this: "You buy at retail and sell at wholesale." Although this is true in some cases, it is most assuredly (and thankfully) not the rule. The axiom can be true if you must sell and the only ready buyer is a dealer whose percent discount equals or exceeds the amount your item has appreciated in value. This can also be true if you have consigned your piece to an auction, although auctions usually allow you to set a reserve. A reserve is the lowest price you will sell at. If bidding doesn't reach your reserve, you still owe the auctioneer his fee, but you get your item back. This is the case whether you are dealing with a traditional auctioneer or an online auction site.

There are several other methods of selling, each of which has its own set of advantages and disadvantages.

Selling to a Dealer

The have-to-sell scenario above is an obvious disadvantage, but selling to a dealer will in most cases, be a painless experience. If you have been fortunate in your acquisitions and the collection has appreciated considerably, it may also be a profitable encounter. If you are not near the dealer and have to ship, then you run the risk of damage or loss.

Running Newspaper Ads

Selling to another collector in your local area is probably one of the easiest and most profitable ways to dispose of your piece(s). There is the advantage of personal examination and no shipping risks.

Running Collector Publication Ads

This is another fine way to get the best price, as long as the sale is to another collector. The same shipping risks exist here also, and you do have to consider the cost of the ad.

Answering Wanted Ads in Collector Publications

The only risk beyond the usual shipping risks is the possibility of the buyer being disappointed and wishing to return the pieces for a refund.

Selling Through a Local Dealer

If you are fortunate enough to have a dealer near you, he/she may take consignments for a percentage.

Selling on the Internet

Although shipping risks and those related to dissatisfied buyers also apply to Internet sales, one advantage over traditional advertisements is not having to pay to publicize your piece (if you have the computer savvy to set up your own Web site). Web sites also offer an opportunity to showcase not only the basic description of a piece, but also a display of a photo of it.

If you are not so technologically advanced that you can run your own Web site, selling via auction Web sites is relatively inexpensive as well. Such Web sites also offer a wide range of services, most notably for billing, which helps the seller lessen his/her risks of a fraudulent sale (buyers using bad checks, stolen credit cards, etc.).

Another advantage to selling on the Internet involves the Web's far-reaching capabilities. It is not called the World Wide Web for nothing! While some collector publications may only be accessible to people living in the United States, for example, the Internet provides worldwide exposure.

Utilize Collector Club Services

The M.I. Hummel Club runs a Collector's Market for members, where items wanted and items for sale are matched by a computer program. There is no charge for this service beyond membership dues. The club also periodically conducts mail auctions. The address is Dept. CM, M.I. Hummel Club, Goebel Plaza, P.O. Box 11, Pennington, NJ 08534. You must be a member, so if you need the enrollment forms call toll-free at (800) 666-2582.

The Hummel Collector's Club, Inc. publishes a quarterly newsletter in which it runs sales and wanted ads, free of charge to members. You respond to these ads by mailing your response to the club. They then forward the response, unopened, to the individuals running the ad. The address for

Possible Pitfalls

The determination of the authenticity of the piece in question is fairly easy in the greatest majority of instances. If you have no reason to suspect the piece of being a fake or forgery and it somewhere bears the incised M.I. Hummel signature, it is probably genuine. In a few instances, the pieces were simply too small for the incised signature to be placed on them without defacing them. Under these circumstances, the company usually places a paper or foil sticker where it is least obtrusive. Often these are lost from the piece over the years, but these small items are few in number and usually readily identifiable by the use of the incised mold number and trademark.

By carefully studying the section on how Goebel utilizes mold numbers on the M.I. Hummel pieces, you will gain much more insight into correct identification.

Be ever-alert to the trademarks found on pieces and how to interpret them (see "History and Explanation of Trademarks" later in this chapter). It is a complicated and sometimes confusing system, and you must know how marks are used and what they mean in order to know what you are buying.

Variations are rampant (see individual listings) in both size, coloration, and mold, and you may think you are buying one thing when you're actually getting something quite different.

When it comes to determining the value of broken but expertly restored pieces, they are generally worth one-half or less than the current value of the unbroken "mint" pieces. This value is entirely dependent upon the availability of unbroken mint pieces bearing the same mold number, size designator, and trademark. In the case of a rare piece, however, it is often worth almost as much as the mint piece if expertly restored, due simply to its scarcity. (See the list of restorers in "Care, Protection, and Display.")

Crazing is another important factor to keep in mind. Please refer to "Care, Protection, and Display" for further discussion of this matter.

Detecting Restored Pieces

It is sometimes difficult—or impossible—for the average collector to detect an expert restoration of a Hummel figurine or article. The two most reliable methods are: 1) examination by long-wave ultraviolet light, and 2) examination by X-ray. Until very recently, one could rely almost 100 percent on ultraviolet light examination, but some restorative techniques have been developed in the past few years that are undetectable except by X-ray examination.

Examination by X-ray

Access to X-ray equipment might prove difficult. If you have a good friend who is a doctor or dentist with his/her own equipment, you might be able to get your X-ray by reimbursing expenses. A crack otherwise invisible to the naked eye may appear where the piece has been restored. If the piece does exhibit such a feature, it is safe to assume it is a restored piece. There are some restoration marks, however, that may not show up, so the X-ray examination is not foolproof. The latter represents state-of-the-art restoration.

Examination by Ultraviolet Light

When an undamaged piece is exposed to long-wave ultraviolet light, it will appear uniformly light purple in color; the value of the purple will vary with color on the piece. A crack or fracture with glue in it will appear a lighter color (usually orange or pink), patches will appear almost white, and most new paint will appear a much, much darker purple.

Non-Hummel Items by Goebel

You need to be aware that from 1871, when the company was founded, until 1991, Goebel used the same trademarking system on just about all of its products. In 1991, the company changed the system so that now there is a special trademark that is used exclusively on M.I. Hummel items. The older Goebel trademark found on an item is, therefore, not necessarily an indication that it is a Hummel design, only that it *might be*. For further identification, use the guidelines

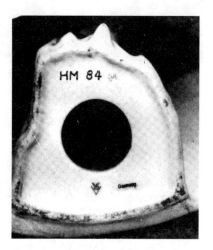

Base marking found on a non-Hummel Madonna made by Goebel. Note the "HM" letter prefix (enhanced here for reproduction with pen and ink).

described earlier in this chapter. You would not believe how many experts receive inquiries from folks who think they have a rare Hummel item only to find that they have another of Goebel's many other products.

With Goebel's M.I. Hummel products, it is the rule that letter prefixes are not used. When a letter or letters are used, they are almost invariably a suffix, placed after the incised mold number.

The Seven Dwarfs from the Walt Disney series by Goebel called Snow White and the Seven Dwarfs. They bear various trademarks from Stylized (TMK-3) through the Last Bee (TMK-5) and measure from 2-3/4" to 3".

A Norman Rockwell piece from Goebel. It bears the "ROCK 217" mold number, the Three Line Mark (TMK-4), and measures 3-5/8" x 5-1/2".

Two examples of Shrine by Janet Robson. Each bears the Three Line Mark (TMK-4) and the mold number ROB 422 incised and inked in, indicating they are Mother Mold pieces. Both have the incised 1961 copyright date and measure 5-1/4".

When Goebel marks a non-Hummel item, the mold number usually has a one-, two-, or three-letter prefix associated. Following are a few examples of the many prefixes and what they mean:

- Byj ... Taken from designs by Charlot Byj.
- Dis ... Taken from Walt Disney characters.
- FF ... Freestanding figure.
- HM ... Madonna.
- HX ... Religious figurine.
- KF ... Whimsical figure.
- Rob ... Taken from designs by Janet Robson.
- Rock ... Taken from Norman Rockwell art.
- Spo ... Taken from designs by Maria Spotl.

There are many more prefix examples than listed here, and the pieces are just as well-made as are the Hummel items and are themselves eminently collectible. They are not Hummel art, however, so be sure before you buy.

There seems to be a developing market for some non-Hummel Goebel products, such as the Charlot Byj "Red

This display plaque for the Charlot Byj Red Head series from Goebel bears the mold number "Byj 47," the Three-Line Mark (TMK-4), a 1966 copyright date, and 4-5/8" size.

Display plaque for the Goebel Friar Tuck series. The mold number "WZ 2" is incised and inked in, indicating it is a Mother Mold piece. It bears the Stylized Bee (TMK-3), a 1959 copyright date, and measures 4-3/4" x 3-7/8".

Heads" (as they are known) and the Little Monk or "Friar Tuck" pieces. There is already a well-developed secondary market for the Norman Rockwell and Walt Disney character figurines.

Fakes and Forgeries

Though not widespread in number, there have been a few rather obvious alterations to the trademarks and to the figurines themselves, making them appear older or different from the norm and therefore more valuable. There have been additions or deletions of small parts (i.e. birds, flowers, etc.) to figures. Worse, one or two unscrupulous individuals have been reglazing colored figurines and other articles with a white overglaze to make them appear to be the relatively uncommon to rare all-white pieces. The serious collector can sometimes detect these imposters, but it is best left to the experts. Should you purchase a piece that is ultimately proven to be one of these fakes, any reputable dealer would replace your figurine if possible. At the very least, the dealer would refund your money.

Imitations, Copies, and Reproductions of Original Hummel Pieces

Anyone interested in copies should consult the excellent book *Hummel Copycats* by Lawrence L. Wonsch (see Appendix C). Wonsch shows that the collecting of copycat M.I. Hummels can be fascinating and fun.

There are many reproductions and imitations of the original Hummel pieces, some better than others, but so far, all are easily detectable upon the most casual examination if one is reasonably knowledgeable about what constitutes an original.

The most common of these imitations are those produced in Japan. They are similar in design motif but obviously not original when one applies the simplest of rules. See "History and Explanation of Trademarks" later in this chapter.

This 3" imitation appears to be a combination of Easter Time (Hum 384) and Playmates (Hum 58). No markings.

Take note of the photo here of Retreat to Safety (Hum 201). To look at the photo is disconcerting because the figure appears to be genuine. When you hold this particular copy in your hand, however, it feels very light and is obvi-

Plastic imitation of Hum 201, Retreat to Safety. Made in Hong Kong, it appears the mold for this piece was taken directly from a genuine Hummel figurine.

ously inferior. Beneath the base is the phrase "Made in Hong Kong." Carl Luckey purchased this plastic copy in a truck stop gift shop in a Midwestern state in 1979 for $3.95. It was probably worth about 50 cents at the time. Over the years, many others have surfaced. In fact, there is a whole series of these plastic copies.

Many other figurines and articles make obvious attempts at copying the exact design of the genuine article. In every single instance, the falseness becomes immediately detectable as being made of materials and paints severely inferior to the quality exhibited by the real thing. Most are manufactured from a material similar to the plaster or plaster-like substance used in the manufacture of the

Plastic imitations of Hum 197, Be Patient. A variation with articulating arms is rather uncommon.

various prizes one wins at the carnival game booth. Some of these actually bear a sticker proclaiming that they are genuine, authentic, or original Hummel pieces.

These two 4-1/4" figures replicating Apple Tree Boy and Apple Tree Girl are made of plastic and are decidedly inferior. No markings found.

A 7" imitation of Hum 5, Strolling Along.

Six Herbert Dubler Figures.

The Dubler Figures

During World War II, the Nazi government did not allow the Goebel company to carry on production of Hummel figurines. At that time, a New York firm known as Ars Sacra (a subsidiary of today's Ars Edition in Munich) produced a small collection of figurines very much like the original designs and others in the Hummel style, but not copying any particular design. Those that were Hummel copies usually bore a 5/8" x 1" foil sticker, as reproduced here. They often also had "B. Hummel" and either "ARS SACRA" or "Herbert Dubler, Inc." associated with the signature. Either version was usually incised into the top or side of the base of the figurine. Frequently a copyright date also appears in the same area. In Wonsh's guide, Hummel Copycats, more than 20 of these Dubler figures are pictured. His research indicates the possibility that 61 of these figures were designed and perhaps made.

Most Dubler pieces were made of a chalk-like or plaster of Paris-type substance, but a few were rendered in bronze, and some have even been found cast in silver. The Crestwick Company of New York ostensibly distributed them in the United States. Crestwick later became Hummelwerk, an old U.S. distributing company owned by Goebel. It eventually evolved to the present Goebel operations in the U.S.

> AUTHENTIC
> **HUMMEL FIGURE**
> PRODUCED BY ARS SACRA
> MADE IN USA

Reproduction of ARS SACRA sticker.

Large and heavy bronze figures on marble. The one on the left measures 7" and the other 6-1/2". Incised at the rear of the figures is "Copyright 1942 Herbert Dubler, Inc."

These rather pitiful Hummel-like figures bear the inscription "Copyright 1947 Decorative Figurines Corp., the Dubler company."

Another name associated with Dubler was "Decorative Figurines, Inc." These figurines, also made of plaster of Paris, were almost exact copies.

The English or Beswick Pieces

These interesting pieces are intriguing in that some mystery surrounds their origin. Collectors usually know them together as "The English

English/Beswick backstamp.

Pieces." There has been speculation in the past that they have some claim to legitimacy, but there has never been any hard evidence found to support that notion. The backstamp "BESWICK-ENGLAND" indicates they were made by an old and respected English porcelain manufacturer that was later bought out by Royal Doulton. Royal Doulton finds no reference to the pieces in what records of Beswick that were obtained when they bought the company.

There have been 12 different designs identified with or without the Beswick backstamp, M.I. Hummel incised signature, and other markings. The mold numbers are 903 through 914. The number 907 model has never been found. The list follows:

- 903 Trumpet Boy
- 904 Book Worm
- 905 Goose Girl
- 906 Strolling Along

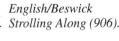

English/Beswick Strolling Along (906).

Two English/Beswick pieces, from left: Shepherd's Boy (914) and Farm Boy (912).

- 907 (No known name)
- 908 Stormy Weather
- 909 Puppy Love
- 910 Meditation
- 911 Max and Moritz
- 912 Farm Boy
- 913 Globe Trotter
- 914 Shepherd's Boy

The figurines are shiny and brightly colored in the faience tradition. Most of them bear the inscription "Original Hummel Studios Copyright" in script letters (see drawings on this page) and some version of the Beswick backstamp. Most, but not all, also bear an incised M.I. Hummel signature along with the base inscriptions described above, and there have been some found with no markings at all. All are sought eagerly by many serious collectors. The collector value range of those bearing the signature is $900-1,200.

English/Beswick pieces. Left to right with their incised mold numbers: Meditation (910), Trumpet Boy (903), and Puppy Love (909).

Various base markings from the 1940s.

Understanding Trademarks

Since 1935, there have been several changes in the trademarks used by Goebel on M.I. Hummel items. In later years of production, each new trademark design merely replaced the old one, but in the earlier years, frequently the new design trademark would be placed on a figurine that already bore the older style trademark. In some cases, a change from an incised trademark to a surface stamped version of the same mark would result in both appearing on the figure. The former represents a transition period from older to newer, and the latter resulted in what are called "Double Crown." This section is meant to give you an illustrated guide to the major trademarks and their evolution to the trademark presently used on Goebel-produced M.I. Hummel items.

Many subtle differences will not be covered because they serve no significant purpose in identifying the era in which an item was produced. There are, however, a few that do help to date a piece. These will be discussed and illustrated. The dates of the early trademark changes are approximate in some cases, but probably accurate to within five years or so. Please bear in mind that the dates, although mostly derived from company records, are not necessarily as definite as they appear. There are documented examples where pieces vary from the stated years, both earlier and later. A number of words and phrases associated with various trademarks can, in some cases, help to date a piece.

Note: It is imperative that you understand that the various trademarks illustrated and discussed here have been used by Goebel on *all* of its products, not just Hummel items, until about mid-1991, when a new mark was developed exclusively for use on M.I. Hummel items.

The Crown Mark (TMK-1): 1934-1950

Incised Crown Mark

Stamped Crown Mark

Wide Ducal Crown Mark

The Crown Mark (TMK-1 or CM), sometimes referred to as the "Crown-WG," was used by Goebel on all of its products in 1935, when M.I. Hummel figurines were first made commercially available. Subtle variations have been noted, but the illustration above is all you need to identify the trademark. Those subtle differences are of no important significance to the collector. The letters WG below the crown in the mark are the initials of William Goebel, one of the founders of the company. The crown signifies his loyalty to the imperial family of Germany at the time of the mark's design, around 1900. The mark is sometimes found in an incised circle.

Another Crown-type mark is sometimes confusing to collectors; some refer to it as the "Narrow Crown" and others the "Wide Ducal Crown." This mark was introduced by Goebel in 1937 and used on many of its products. Goebel calls it the Wide Ducal Crown mark, so we shall adopt this

M.J. Hummel © ♥

The Hummel signature as a base rim marking.

The base of Hum 163 illustrating the incised Crown Mark and the stamped Full Bee trademark. Note also the use of the decimal designator with the incised mold number.

name as well to alleviate confusion. To date, most dealers and collectors have thought this mark was never found on a M.I. Hummel piece. Goebel, however, in its newsletter Insights (Vol. 14, No. 3, pg. 8) states that the mark was used "...rarely on figurines," so we will defer to the company and assume there might be some out there somewhere.

Often, as stated earlier, the Crown Mark will appear twice on the same piece, more often one mark incised and the other stamped. This is, as we know, the "Double Crown."

When World War II ended and the United States Occupation Forces allowed Goebel to begin exporting, the pieces were marked as having been made in the occupied zone. The various forms and phrases to be found in this regard are illustrated below.

These marks were applied to the bases of the figurines, along with the other markings, from 1946 through 1948. They were sometimes applied under the glaze and often over the glaze. The latter were easily lost over the years through wear and cleaning if the owner was not careful. Between 1948 and 1949, the U.S. Zone mark requirement was dropped, and the word "Germany" took its place. With the partitioning of Germany into East and West, "W. Germany," "West Germany," or "Western Germany" began to appear most of the time instead.

Until the early 1950s the company occasionally used a WG or a WG to the right of the incised M.I. Hummel signature. When found, the signature is usually placed on the edge of, or the vertical edge of, the base. Some have been known to confuse this with the Crown Mark (TMK-1) when in fact it is not.

The Full Bee Mark (TMK-2): 1940-1959

In 1950, the Goebel company made a major change in its trademark. The company incorporated a bee in a V. It is thought that the bumblebee part of the mark was derived from a childhood nickname of Sister Maria Innocentia Hummel, meaning bumblebee. The bee flies within a V, which is the first letter of the German word for distributing com-

Incised Full Bee   *Stamped Full Bee*

The High Bee   *Small Bee - Note that the bee's wingtips are level with the top of the V.*

Baby Bee

Vee Bee

pany, Verkaufsgesellschaft. The mark was to honor M.I. Hummel, who died in 1946.

There are actually 12 variations of the Bee marks to be found on Goebel-produced M.I. Hummel items, but some are grouped together, as the differences between them are not considered particularly significant. They will be detailed as a matter of interest.

The Full Bee mark, also referred to as TMK-2 or abbreviated FB, is the first of the Bee marks to appear. The mark evolved over almost 20 years until the company began to modernize it. It is sometimes found in an incised circle. The history of the transition and illustrations of each major change follows. Each of them is still considered to be the Full Bee (TMK-2).

The very large bee flying in the V remained until around 1956, when the bee was reduced in size and lowered into the V. It can be found incised, stamped in black, or stamped in blue, in that order, through its evolution.

The Stylized Bee (TMK-3): 1958-1972

A major change in the way the bee is rendered in the trademark made its appearance in 1960. The Stylized Bee (TMK-3), sometimes abbreviated as Sty-Bee when written, as the major component of the trademark appeared in three basic forms through 1972. The first two are both classified as the Stylized Bee (TMK-3), but the third is considered a fourth step in the evolution, the Three Line Mark (TMK-4). It might interest you to know that Goebel reused the Crown-WG backstamp from 1969 until 1972. It is not always there, but when it shows, it is a small blue decal application. This was done to protect Geobel's copyright of the mark. It otherwise would have run out.

The Large Stylized Bee: This trademark was used primarily from 1960 through 1963. Notice in the illustration that the "W. Germany" is placed to the right of the bottom of the V. The color of the mark will be black or blue. It is sometimes found inside an incised circle. When you find the Large Stylized Bee mark, you will normally find a stamped "West" or "Western Germany" in black elsewhere on the base, but not always.

Large Stylized Bee

The Small Stylized Bee: This mark is also considered to be TMK-3. It was used concurrently with the Large Stylized

Bee from about 1960 and continued in this use until about 1972. Note in the illustration that the "W. Germany" appears centered beneath the V and bee. The mark is usually rendered in blue, and it too is often accompanied by a stamped black "West" or "Western Germany." Collectors and dealers sometimes refer to the mark as the One Line Mark.

Small Stylized Bee

The Three Line Mark (TMK-4): 1964-1972

Three Line Mark

This trademark is sometimes abbreviated 3-line or 3LM in print. The trademark used the same stylized V and bee as the others, but also included three lines of wording beside it, as you can see. This major change appeared in blue color.

The Last Bee Mark (TMK-5): 1972-1979

Actually developed and occasionally used as early as 1970, this major change was known by some collectors as the Last Bee Mark because the next change in the trademark no longer incorporated any form of the V and the bee. However, with the reinstatement of a bee in TMK-8 with the turn of the new century, TMK-5 is not technically the "Last Bee" any longer. The mark was used until about mid-1979, when Goebel began to phase it out, completing the transition to the new trademark in 1980. There are three minor variations in the mark shown in the illustration. Generally, the mark was placed under the glaze from 1972 through 1976 and is found placed over the glaze from 1976 through 1979.

Last Bee Mark

The Missing Bee Mark (TMK 6): 1979-1991

Missing Bee Mark

The transition to this trademark began in 1979 and was complete by mid-1980. As you can see, Goebel removed the V and bee from the mark altogether. Many dealers and collectors lamented the passing of the traditional stylized V and bee, and for a while, called the mark the Missing Bee.

In conjunction with this change, the company instituted the practice of adding to the traditional artist's mark the date the artist finished painting the piece. Because the white overglaze pieces are not usually painted, it would be reasonable to assume that the date is omitted on them.

The Hummel Mark (TMK-7): 1991-1999

Hummel Mark

In 1991, Goebel made a move of historical importance. The company changed the trademark once again. This time, the change was not only symbolic of the reunification of the two Germanies by removal of the "West" from the mark, but very significant in another way. Until then, Goebel used the same trademark on virtually all of its products. The mark illustrated here was for exclusive use on Goebel products made from the paintings and drawings of M.I. Hummel.

The Millennium Bee (TMK-8): 2000-Present

Millennium Bee Mark

Goebel decided to celebrate the beginning of a new century with a revival in a bee-adorned trademark. Seeking once again to honor the memory of Sister Maria Innocentia Hummel, a bumblebee, this time flying solo without the V, was reinstated into the mark in 2000 and continues today.

Other Base Marks

There are marks in addition to the U.S. Zone marks already covered that can be found on the bases and backs of Goebel Hummel items.

First of all, there are several colors of marks that you may encounter. The colors found to date are black, purple, red, brown, green, and blue.

The color blue has been used exclusively since 1972. There also have been several combinations of colors found.

The following list contains various words and marks found associated with the trademarks. There are probably more to be discovered, but these are representative.

- W. Germany – by W. Goebel (in script)
- W. Germany – W. Goebel (in script)
- GERMANY - Copr. W. Goebel
- Germany - by W. Goebel, Oeslau 1957
- WEST GERMANY - *II Gbl. 1948
- West Germany - OCCUPIED GERMANY
- WESTERN GERMANY - Western Germany

Anniversary backstamp.

Final Issue and First Issue stamps.

W. Goebel mark in script.

First Issue, Final Issue, and 125th Anniversary Backstamps

Starting in 1990, Goebel began stamping any newly issued piece with the words "First Issue," during the first year of production only. In 1991, the company began doing the same thing during the last year before retiring a piece, by marking each with the words "Final Issue." The words are also accompanied by the appropriate year date. The stamps are illustrated for you here. The first piece to bear the Final Issue backstamp was Hum 203, Signs of Spring, in both sizes. The Final Issue pieces will also be sold with a commemorative retirement medallion hung around them.

Goebel's 125th anniversary was in 1996, and all figures produced in that year bear the special backstamp.

Mold Numbers and Size Designators

Mold Numbers

All Goebel-made Hummel items are made by the use of molds and each unique mold is assigned a number. The number is part of the mold and it, along with the size designator, becomes a part of the finished piece. It is generally incised on the underside of the base, but for practical reasons may appear elsewhere on the item.

Issued in 2002, The Final Sculpt (Hum 2180) carries the highest mold number for a regular M.I. Hummel figurine to date.

Until the mid-1980s, it was thought by most collectors that the highest mold number normally used in production was in the mid-400s. Time and extensive research by writers, dealers, and serious collectors revealed, among other things, that the number in the Goebel design pool most likely exceeds 1,000 by a great deal. A large number of these have not yet been put into production, and those planned are designated Possible Future Editions (PFE) by Goebel. A few of these (presumably in sample form) have somehow found their way into the collector market, but the occurrence is exceedingly rare. When a PFE becomes a production piece, the earlier PFE example almost always bears an earlier trademark than the mark found on the production piece. It, therefore, retains its unique status. Of the remaining designs, some may be PFEs and some may never make it into the collection. The highest mold number used to date is 2180 for a regular figurine, but there are many gaps in numerical sequence and not every number between 1 and 2180 is currently designated for a figurine now or in the future. Additionally, there are several ball ornaments not produced by Goebel that have Hum numbers ranging from 3012 on up to 3021.

Note: Before we get into the explanation of the mold number system, let's eliminate the source of one area of confusion. Some price lists (including the one from Goebel) show an odd letter or

Flower Madonna (Hum 10).

number preceded by a slash mark associated with some Hummel mold numbers. Example: Flower Madonna, 10/l/ W. The "W" and the slash are price list indications that this piece is finished in all white. The actual mold number found incised on the piece is "10/1" only. The "/W," meaning white overglaze finish, and the "/11" or "/6," meaning the normal color finish, are the decor indicators found in some of today's price lists. Remember that they are not part of the mold number itself.

The Size Designator Portion of the Mold Number

While the mold number as discussed earlier in this section was treated as separate from the size designator system, in reality, the two comprise what is sometimes called the Hummel number (Hum number), but more commonly, the mold number. It seems complicated, but isn't really if you factor out Goebel's occasional departure from the rules.

The system has changed little over the years, but has been modified once or twice.

Beginning with the first commercial piece in 1935 and continuing to about 1952, the first size of a particular piece produced was considered by the factory to be the "standard" size. If plans were to produce a smaller or larger version, the factory would place a "0" (zero) or a decimal point after the model or mold number. Frequently, but not always, the "0" would be separated from the mold number by placing a slash mark (/) between them. There are many cases where the "0" or the decimal point did not appear. Apparently, this signified that at the time, there were no plans to produce other sizes of the same piece.

In the case of Hum 1, Puppy Love, there exists only one "standard" size and no size designator has ever been found on the figure. It is reasonable to assume, however, that subsequent changes in production plans would result in other sizes being produced. Therefore, the absence of the "0" or decimal point is not a reliable indicator that there exists only one standard size of the particular piece. In fact, there are some instances where later versions of a piece have been found bearing the "/ 0," decimal point, and even a "/I," which are smaller than the "standard" for that piece. In some cases, the decimal point appears along with the slash mark. The figurine Village Boy (Hum 51), for example, has been seen marked as: "51./0." It could be that when Goebel changed to the slash designator, it just didn't remove the decimal from the mold, but how do you explain the decimal point following the "0"?

The factory used Roman numerals or Arabic numbers

Puppy Love (Hum 1).

in conjunction with the mold numbers to indicate larger or smaller sizes than the standard.

The best way for the collector to understand the system is by example. The figure Village Boy (Hum 51) has been produced in four different sizes.

Example 51/0: The number 51 tells us that this is the figurine Village Boy and the "/0" indicates that it is the first size produced, therefore the standard size. In this case, the size of the piece is roughly 6". The presence of the "/0" (or of a decimal point) is also an indication that the figurine was produced sometime prior to 1952.

As discussed earlier, not all the figures produced before 1952 were designated with the "/0" or decimal point, but if present, it is a great help in beginning to date a figure. The one exception currently known is the discontinuance of the use of the "/0" designator on Hum 353, Spring Dance. It was produced with the 353/0 mold and size designator about 1963, taken out of current production later and recently reinstated once more.

Village Boy (Hum 51/0).

By checking the reference for Hum 51, you will note there exist three more sizes: Hum 51/I/0, Hum 51/3/0, and Hum 51/ 1. Roman numerals are normally used to denote sizes larger than the standard and Arabic numbers indicate sizes smaller than the standard. When utilized in the normal manner, the Arabic number is always found to the left of the "0" designator. There are two exceptions to this norm: one specific, the other general. The specific known exception is Heavenly Angel, Hum 21/0/1/2. This is one of only two known instances of the use of a fractional size designator. The last two numbers are incised and read as one-half (1/2). The general exception is the occasional use of an Arabic number in the same manner as the Roman numeral. The Roman numeral size indicator is never used with the "0" designator present, and the Arabic number is never normally used without the "0" designator. Therefore, if you were to find a mold number 51/2, you would know to read it 51/II, and that it represents a piece larger than the standard.

Spring Dance (Hum 353).

Note: After the mold for Hum 218 (Birthday Serenade), the use of the "/0" size designator was eliminated. The mold number (51/II) does not exist. It is used here for illustrative purposes only.

Example 51/1

As before, the number 51 identifies the piece for us. The addition of the "/1" tells us that this is a larger figure than the standard. In this case, it is about 1" larger.

Example 51/2/0 and 51/3/0

Once again, we know the identity of the piece is Hum 51, Village Boy. In both cases, there is an Arabic number, the mold number, and the "/0," therefore we can assume both are smaller than the standard. The 51/2/0 is smaller than 5" and the 51/3/0 is even smaller still.

The "0" and decimal point size designators are no longer in use. Keeping in mind the cited exceptions, we can usually assume that a figure with the mold number and no accompanying Arabic or Roman numerals is the standard size for that model. If the mold number is accompanied by Roman numerals the figure is a larger size, ascending to larger sizes the higher the numeral.

There seems to be no set standard size or set increase in size for each of the Arabic or Roman numeral size designators used in the collection. The designators are individually specific to each model and bear no relation to the designators on other models.

Note how this variation of Village Boy (Hum 51/2/0) differs from the 51/0 version shown on the previous page.

Additional Designators

There are a number of pieces in the collection—table lamps, candy boxes, bookends, ashtrays, fonts, plaques, music boxes, candleholders, plates, and sets of figures—that may have additional or different designators. A list follows, with explanations of how each is marked.

Table Lamps are numbered in the traditional manner. Some later price lists show the number preceded by an "M." Example: M/285.

Candy Boxes (Candy Bowls) are covered cylindrical deep bowls, the cover being topped with one of the Hummel figures. They are numbered with the appropriate mold number for the figure and preceded with the Roman numeral "III." Example: "III/57" is a candy box topped with Hum 57, Chick Girl.

Hum 61/A and Hum 61/B: A set of bookends that utilizes the figurines Playmates (Hum 58) and Chick Girl (Hum 47) as part of their design.

Bookends are both large figures with provisions for weighting with sand and smaller figures placed on wooden bookend bases. The only sand-weighted bookends are the Book Worms. The designation for a bookend is accomplished by placing an "A" and "III" after the assigned Hummel mold number for the bookends. Example: Hum 61/A and Hum 61/B are a set of bookends utilizing Hum 58 and Hum 47, Playmates and Chick Girl. These are the current designations. In some cases if the figurines are removed from the bookend bases they are indistinguishable from a regular figurine.

Ashtrays are numbered in the traditional manner.

Fonts are numbered in the traditional manner. Exception: There is a font, Hum 91 (Angel at Prayer), in two versions. One faces left; the other right. They are numbered 91/A and 91/B respectively.

Plaques are numbered in the traditional manner.

Music Boxes are round wooden contain-

Chick Girl candy box (Hum III/57).

Little Band music box.

ers in which there is a music box movement, topped with a traditional Hummel model that rotates as the music plays. The catalog and price list number for the music box is the Hummel number for the piece on the box followed by the letter "M." If the figure is removed from the top it will not have the "M" but will be marked in the traditional manner.

Candleholders are numbered in the traditional manner. They sometimes have Roman numerals to the left of the model designator in price lists. These indicate candle size: I = 0.6 cm, II = 1 cm.

Plates are numbered in the traditional manner. To date, none have been produced with the size designator, only the mold number.

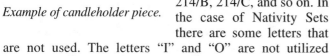

Example of candleholder piece.

Sets of figures are numbered with one model number sequence and followed by the designation / A, /B, /C ... /Z, to indicate each figure is part of one set. Example: The Nativity Set 214 contains 15 Hummel figures, numbers 214/A, 214/B, 214/C, and so on. In the case of Nativity Sets there are some letters that are not used. The letters "I" and "O" are not utilized because of the possibility of confusing them with the Roman numeral "I" or Arabic "I" and "0."

Additional Notes on Special Markings

Sets

Any time there have been two or more pieces in the collection that were meant to be matched as a pair or set, the alphabetical listings A through Z are respectively applied

Sets are sometimes referred to by names that describe the set as a whole, but do not actually reflect the names of each individual piece. Such is the case with the three figurines that are often referred to as the "Little Band" (shown bottom of left column). These are actually Hum 389, 390, and 391. The actual Little Band is Hum 392 (shown below) in which all three pieces are attached to a single base thereby creating a single figurine.

to the Hummel mold numbers in some way. Exception: Sometimes called the "Little Band" are the three figures: Hum 389, Hum 390, and Hum 391. They do not bear the A, B, C designating them as a set. The piece actually entitled "Little Band" is Hum 392, an incorporation of these three figures on one base together. References to the "Little Band" and the "Eight-Piece Orchestra" are occasionally found in price lists that include Hummel numbers 2/0, 1/I, 89/I, 89/II, 129, 389, 390, and 391. It's a charming group, but not officially a set.

Copyright Dates

The year date incised on the base of many M.I. Hummel pieces is the source of much confusion to some collectors. The year date is the copyright date. The copyright date is the date the original mold for that particular piece was made and not the date the piece was made. It bears no relationship whatsoever with the date of making the item, only the mold. As a matter

Example of a copyright.

of fact, there are many molds that are years old and still being used to make figures today. The copyright date doesn't always appear on the older pieces, but all those currently being made will have it.

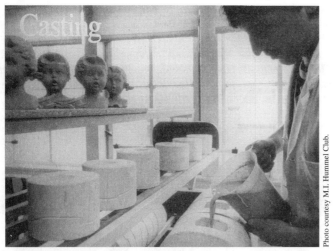

Pouring the slip into the mold.

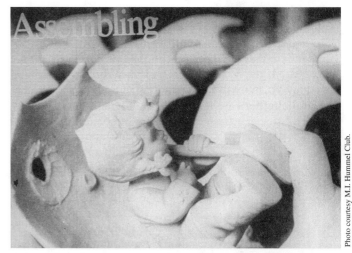

Assembling the cast parts prior to drying and bisque firing. These happen to be the parts for Umbrella Girl, Hum 152/B.

Refining the assembled pieces prior to the first firing.

Several hundred assembled figurines just before bisque firing. The various racks and shelves upon which they rest are called "furniture."

The Making of M.I. Hummel Figurines and Plates by Goebel

The question most asked by those uninitiated to the Hummel world is: "Why do they cost so much?" It is not an unreasonable question, and the answer can be simply that they are handmade. That, however, really doesn't do justice to the true story. The making of Hummel pieces is immensely complex—truly a hand operation from start to finish. The process requires no less than 700 steps! Those few of you who have been fortunate enough to visit Goebel's northern Bavaria facility know how complicated the operation is. Others of you who have seen the Goebel film and/or visited the facsimile factory on its 1985 U.S. tour have a pretty good idea.

A row of kilns at the factory.

To call the facility a factory is misleading, for the word "factory" causes the majority of us to conjure up an image of machinery and automated assembly lines. It is not that at all. It is an enormous artists' and artisans' studio and workshop complete with friendly relaxed surroundings, including good music, hanging baskets, and potted plants. In short, it is a pleasant place to create and work. It is packed with highly trained and skilled artists and craftspeople. Each of them must undergo a full three-year apprenticeship before actually taking part in the fashioning of the figurines and other items that are made available to the collector. This apprenticeship is required no matter whether the worker is a mold-maker or painter. Each specialist in the process must understand the duties of the others.

There is insufficient space to elaborate on all 700 steps involved, so they have been grouped into six basic areas: Sculpting the Master Model, Mother or Master Mold-Making, Molding the Pieces, Bisque Firing, Glaze Firing, and Painting and Decorating (décor firing).

Photo courtesy M.I. Hummel Club.

Master Sculptor Gerhard Skrobek sculpting the figurine Ring Around the Rosie, Hum 348.

1. Sculpting the Master Model

It is estimated that there are 1,200 to 1,500 M.I. Hummel artworks from which Goebel may choose to render into a three-dimensional figurine or other item. Once a piece of art is chosen, a master sculptor fashions a model in a water-based Bavarian black clay. This is a long process during which the artists must not just reproduce the art but interpret it. They must visualize, for instance, what the back of the piece must look like and sculpt it as they think M.I. Hummel would have rendered it. Once the wax model is deemed acceptable, it is taken to the Siessen Convent, where it is presented for approval or disapproval. If the preliminary model is approved, it is then taken back to Goebel for the next step.

2. Master or Mother Mold-Making

A figurine cannot be made from a single mold because of its complexity. Therefore, after a very careful study of the model, it is strategically cut into several pieces. Some figurines must be cut into as many as 30 pieces for molding. For example, Hum 396 (Ride into Christmas) had to be cut into 12 separate pieces and Hum 47 (Goose Girl) into seven.

Using the Goose Girl's seven pieces, we continue. Each of the seven are placed on a round or oval base and secured with more clay.

The Master Mold, also known as the Mother Mold.

The base is then surrounded by a piece of flexible plastic that extends above the piece to be molded. Liquid plaster of Paris is then poured into it. The dry plaster of Paris is removed, resulting in an impression of the part. This process must be repeated for the other six parts. After each of the seven parts is molded, the result is 14 separate mold halves. From these, the mother molds (sometimes called the master molds) are made. These are made from an acrylic resin. The mother molds are cream-colored and very durable. It is from the mother molds that the working molds are made. The plaster of Paris working molds can be used only about 20 times, at which time a new set

At left is the body of Goose Girl embedded in wax on an oval base in preparation for pouring. The result of the pouring of plaster of Paris is shown at right. The wax body has not yet been removed. Note the key slots.

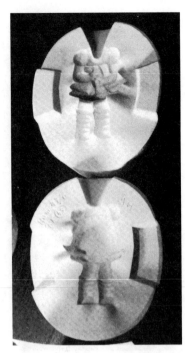

The two halves of a plaster of Paris working mold. Note the keys left and right. These ensure accuracy of fitting the two halves together for pouring the piece.

must be made from the mother molds.

Before full production of a new figure is commenced, a few samples are made. The figure must again be carried to the Siessen Convent for approval, rejection, or recommendations for changes. Once final approval is given, the piece is ready for production. That could be immediately or years later.

3. Molding and Assembly

All the pieces in the collection are made of fine earthenware, consisting of a mixture of feldspar, kaolin, and quartz. It is the finest earthenware available. Both porcelain and earthenware come under the definition of ceramic. Add just a bit more kaolin, and the earthenware would become porcelain. Goebel chooses to use earthenware because of its inherent softness. That softness is considered best for Hummel items.

The liquid mixture of the three ingredients plus water is called slip. The slip is poured into the working molds and left for a period of time. The porous character of the plaster of Paris acts like a sponge and draws moisture out of the slip. After a carefully monitored time, the remaining slip is poured out of the mold, leaving a hollow shell of the desired thickness. The parts are removed from the molds and while still damp, they are assembled, using the slip

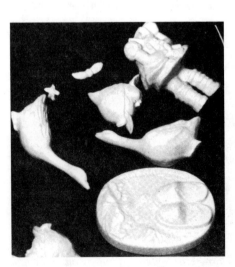

The seven pieces of a Goose Girl figurine, after removal from the molds and prior to assembly.

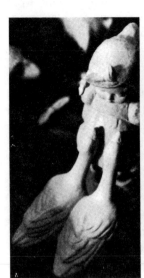

The photo at left shows the Goose Girl piece once it has been assembled and refined but before bisque firing. At right is the same figurine after bisque firing.

as a sort of glue. The assembled piece is then refined: all seams and imperfections are removed and the more subtle areas are detailed. The piece is then set aside to dry for about a week.

4. The Bisque Firing

Bisque is fired, unglazed ceramic. The dry assembled pieces are gathered together and fired in a kiln for 18 hours at 2,100 degrees Fahrenheit. This results in a white, unglazed bisque figurine.

5. The Glaze Firing

The bisque-fired pieces are then dipped into a tinted glaze mixture. The glaze is tinted to assure that the whole piece is covered with the mixture. The tint is usually green so that any uncovered area will show up white. The dipped pieces are then fired at 1,872 degrees Fahrenheit. When removed from the kiln after cooling, they are a shiny white.

The tinted piece prior to glaze firing.

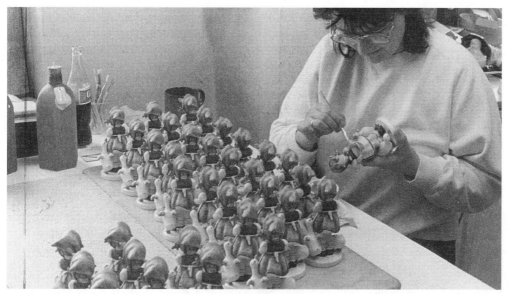

One of the final steps of
decorating prior to decor firing.

6. The Painting and Decorating

The colors are mixed in small amounts and given to the
painters only as needed. Some of the colors react to each other
upon firing, so oftentimes, the item must be painted with one
or a few colors and fired before others can be applied. This
results in multiple decor firings before the pieces are finished.
In some cases, up to 10 separate firings are required before
they are finished and ready for distribution.

As you can see now, the making of the pieces is a long,
involved, and painstaking operation. As noted earlier there are
700 separate operations, the workers are highly trained and
experienced, and there are 25 different quality-control inspection points. In spite of this, each figure is unique because it is
the result of a manual operation. No matter how a piece is
assembled or painted, no matter how experienced a worker is,
he or she is still a human being, inherently incapable of creating identical copies. That is part of the magic. Each piece is a
joy, each unique, each a handmade work of art.

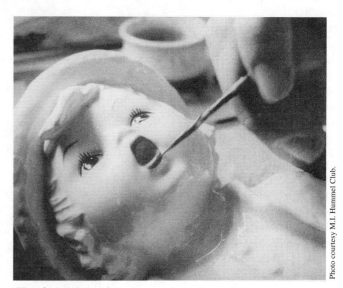

Photo courtesy M.I. Hummel Club.

Hand-painting a face.

One of the light and
cheerful studios where
artists paint the
figurines.

Care, Display, and Protection

Caring for Your Collection

Direct sunlight

The first consideration is the potential damage from direct sunlight. It can wreak havoc on just about any type of collectible, including kiln-fired colors on the pieces and the decals under the glaze. Once this occurs, the damage is irreversible. Some of the older figurines are much more susceptible to this than the newer ones. A few have discolored somewhat due to environmental and atmospheric pollution. In the early years, the pigments used in the paints, while the finest available at the time, were not as durable and lasting as those used today and were more sensitive to the caustic elements of air pollution.

Crazing

Crazing is defined as fine cracks in the glaze of ceramics, normally unintentional, resulting from the unequal shrinking of the glaze and the body of the object. It is manifest as a "crackle-look" finish or a fine, intricate web of what appear to be cracks in the glaze of a ceramic piece. This phenomenon is apparently inherent in the ceramic arts and is most likely to occur in older pieces, but can occur in newer ones as well.

In the introduction of *World Ceramics* (1968, Hamlyn Publishing Group, Ltd.), editor Robert J. Charleston says: "A glaze must be suited to the body of the pot which it covers, or it may crack..." Fired earthenware is quite porous and can absorb moisture if not *completely* covered by a suitable glaze. It is of paramount importance that the earthenware body and its glaze expand and contract uniformly. If they don't, crazing may result.

Caring for your collection involves many things, including displaying pieces where they are not susceptible to direct sunlight. The display shown here, although aesthetically pleasing, is perhaps not the best choice as the positioning so close to a window with somewhat sheer curtains may result in an irreversible discoloration of the figurines.

Heretofore, it had been thought that crazing was irreversible, so some accept its presence as an aesthetic charm. In fact, in some circles it is accepted as proof of antiquity. Most all ancient Chinese ceramics exhibit crazing.

In recent years, ceramicists have been studying crazing to discover whether it might be reversible after all. It now seems that the malady is curable. Those of you who are members of the Hummel Collector's Club, Inc. are already aware of this. In 1996, the club announced in its newsletter that they had found a company that had developed a procedure for the reversal of crazing, for whom the club is presently acting as an agent. This reversal company and one other company claiming successful reversal of crazing are listed later in this chapter under "Restorers." If you wish to use the club's services, be sure to understand the terms, conditions, guarantees, and cost before proceeding.

Crazing and Its Effect on Collector Values: Another very important aspect to crazing is how it can affect the collector value of a piece. As stated before, some collectors don't mind crazing unless it is apparent to the extent that it detracts from the inherent beauty or appeal of the figurine. In 1996, Dorothy Dous of the Hummel Collector's Club, Inc. published in the club newsletter a chart that is a subjective quantification of the amount of crazing and the corresponding percentage devaluation of a Hummel figurine. An informal survey of dealers revealed that they felt the Dous chart is a realistic evaluation of a crazed piece. It is predicated upon an observation of the piece in question with normal vision (presumably the naked eye or with corrected vision) from a distance of 18". There are three levels of condition:

None: No apparent crazing.

Light: No crazing visible from a distance of 18".

Severe: Crazing visible to the naked eye from a distance of 18".

These conditions are further defined as to the percent of devaluation according to the following criteria:

Crazing Location	Percent Devaluation	
	Light	Severe
Beneath base only	25%	30%
On top of base only	35%	40%
Beneath and top of base only	45%	50%
Figurine only, excluding face	50%	55%
Figurine only, including face	60%	65%
Total figurine excluding face	70%	75%
Total figurine including face	75%	80%

Example: Viewing a figurine worth $450 from 18", you observe that crazing is not apparent anywhere on it. When you examine it more closely, however, you detect some crazing beneath and on top of the base. Under this system, the piece would be considered to have *light* crazing and be devalued by 45 percent. If it is devalued by 45 percent, it is, therefore, worth 55 percent of its value in uncrazed condition. Collector Value = .55 x $450 = $247.50.

Some Display Tips to Help Prevent Crazing: Although no one can guarantee the prevention of crazing, nor of its reoccurrence after craze reversal, there are some precautions that you should be aware of.

1. Heat or cold can exacerbate crazing tendency, so avoid any circumstances where your pieces would be subject to heat or cold extremes.

2. A sudden change in temperature can also make worse the tendency toward crazing.

3. Avoid air pollution if possible.

4. Avoid excessive handling.

5. When cleaning by immersion in water or any other solution, try to prevent entry through airholes. Tape them or otherwise block them. If you do get liquid inside, allow the pieces to air dry for a long time before placing them back on display. Be sure to remove whatever you used to block the airholes.

Cleaning

A simple periodic dusting of earthenware or ceramic pieces is always a good idea, but occasionally, they may need a little freshening up. Through the M.I. Hummel Club, Goebel sells an M.I. Hummel Care Kit that consists of two specially formulated cleaning solutions and some brushes, all designed specifically with earthenware, ceramic, and porcelain collectibles in mind. It also includes an instruction booklet.

Should you not wish to order the kit, you can still clean your items. Use your kitchen sink or a similar large vessel. Line it with a towel or other soft material to minimize the possibility of breakage when handling your figures. Make up a solution of barely warm water and a mild soap, such as baby shampoo. Cover the airhole(s) with tape or by some other method. Dip the piece in the solution and scrub gently with a very soft toothbrush or similar soft-bristle brush, all the while holding it over the towel-lined sink.

To help keep your collectibles looking nice, dust them regularly, especially when they are displayed on a table as above. Occasionally, you may also clean them with a soft toothbrush, mild soap (baby shampoo, for example), and water. When in doubt about cleaning, consult an expert.

Rinse it off here also. It may take more than one washing if the piece is heavily soiled. Dab it with a soft, absorbent cloth and place on the same type of surface to air dry. Should you be unable to avoid getting water inside the figure, it may take quite some time to dry out.

Many knowledgeable dealers and collectors use strong detergents without harm, but it's probably best to be reluctant to use them as they may contain chemicals or other harsh additives that could be incompatible with the finish. At the very least, you may lose some of the base markings.

If while handling your figures, you notice a tinkling or rattling sound, don't worry. When the figure is being made sometimes a small piece comes loose inside the figure and rattles around. Sometimes, depending on the shape and design of the figure, you can stop this by injecting a little household glue into the interior of the figure through the airhole(s) and shaking it until the rattle stops. Place it on its side until it dries. Presto! No more rattle.

Cleaning paper collectibles beyond dusting is not recommended. If you are fortunate enough to own an original drawing or painting, proper archival framing and care of the frame is recommended. Best advice? Don't touch it. Leave the cleaning of such things to the professionals.

Displaying Your Collection

The display of your collection is limited only by your imagination. This section is not meant to help you with dis-

Remember that display is only limited by your imagination. Don't be afraid to mix your Hummel figurines in with a variety of other collectibles as shown here.

collection safely. Remember, a large group of earthenware figurines can be very heavy.

Remember also the severe damage that direct sunlight can inflict on just about any type of collectible. Try to avoid displaying on a mantle if there is ever a fire in the fireplace. You can cause severe damage to any framed artwork placed there.

Protecting Your Collection

Safeguards

We have discussed the strength factor with regard to the display fixture. Another consideration should be security. Certainly if there are any innocent—but mischievous—little hands about, keep the displays out of their reach and cabinets latched or locked. The most important consideration should be security. This is especially true if you have a significant and/or large collection.

After you have given the usual attention to normal home security, there are some things you need to consider with respect to your collection. No matter how tempting or flattering, turn down any media attention to your collection. This is a red alert to thieves, and yes, there are Hummel thieves. Most thefts take place from display tables set at shows and vehicles used to transport them to and from such events, but there have been instances of home burglary and armed robbery in the home. Keep knowledge of your collection among family and friends. If you don't have a home security system, consider installing one. Fairly inexpensive do-it-yourself systems have been developed. Some are even wireless, eliminating the need to run wires all over the house. Whether you are handy with this sort of thing, the best route may be a professionally installed system. It's your call.

What To Do When It's Broken

How you react to breakage depends upon the nature of the item and its value, intrinsic or sentimental. If you attach great meaning to the piece, but it is a relatively inexpensive item, you could simply glue it back together. If it

play ideas, but to give you some practical information and guidance for displaying your collection safely and securely.

One of the first considerations is the strength of the display case, if you choose to go that route. You should be sure that your display unit is strong enough to hold your

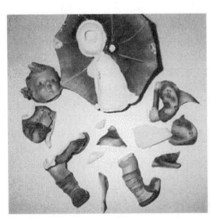
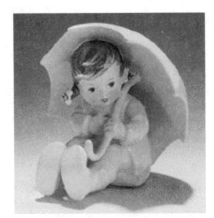

These photos show the before, during, and after stages of restoration of a seriously broken Umbrella Girl figurine (Hum 152/B). This piece was restored by Fredi W. Boese, a Goebel master artist with nearly 40 years experience who operates his own restoration business in Harriman, New York (see list of Restorers that follows for contact information).

has great sentimental value and you have the wherewithal, by all means, have it professionally restored. If you have damaged a very rare or valuable piece, it might be worth having it professionally restored. Restoration can be expensive and take quite some time, so you must first decide whether it is worth the trouble, and more importantly, whether the piece will be worth as much or more than the cost.

There are three types of restoration: cold repairing, firing, and bracing. The method used in the greatest majority of cases where Hummel figures are concerned is cold repairing (except in the case of craze reversal). Cold repairing is the least expensive of the three, and the results are very good. You will probably not be able to detect the repairs with the naked eye. Examination by X-ray and/or long-wave ultraviolet light is the only way to detect a professionally restored piece of earthenware or porcelain.

In selecting a restorer, a personal visit to the shop is advisable. There, you can look over work that is in process and maybe even see a few finished restorations. Many professionals keep a photo album of their work as well. Ask for some references, get an estimate for the job, and find out how long of a wait there is. In most cases, a long wait (we can be talking months here, folks) means many people on the list, and that is usually an indication of a good reputation. The best way to be sure is to get a recommendation from a friend or trusted dealer.

The following list of general restorers is a combination of the list provided by the M.I. Hummel Club and a list developed over the 25 years this book has existed. It is by no means complete, for there are dozens more around the country doing competent, professional restorations. Over the years, there have been dealers and collectors who have not been satisfied with the work or service of some of them, while on the other hand, there has been praise from others regarding the same restorers. In fairness to all of them, I cannot be responsible for recommendations and therefore offer only the list. The general restorers are listed alphabetically by the state in which they are located.

Restorers

Arizona

CHINA AND CRYSTAL CLINIC
Victor Coleman
1808 North Scottsdale Road
Tempe, AZ 85203
(480) 945-5510
(800) 658-9197

California

ATTIC UNLIMITED
22435 La Palma Avenue
Yorba Linda, CA 92887
(714) 692-2940

CERAMIC RESTORATION
Gene Gomas
Manteca, CA 95336
(209) 823-3922

MARK R. DURBAN
P.O. Box 4084
Big Bear Lake, CA 92315
(714) 585-9989

FOSTER ART RESTORATION
711 West 17th Street
Suite C-12
Costa Mesa, CA 92627
(800) 824-6967

GEPPETTO IMPORTS & RESTORATION
Barry J. Korngiebel
31121 Via Colinas, No. 1003
Westlake Village, CA 91362
(818) 889-0901

HOUSE OF RENEW
27601 Forbes Road, Unit 55
Laguna Niguel, CA 92677
(949) 582-3117

JOAN WALTON
San Diego, CA
(619) 291-6539

JUST ENTERPRISES
2790 Sherwin Avenue, No. 10
Ventura, CA 93003
(805) 644-5837

VENERABLE CLASSICS
645 Fourth Street, Suite 208
Santa Rosa, CA 95404
(707) 575-3626

Colorado

HERBERT F. KLUG CONSERVATION
2270 South Zang Court
Lakewood, CO 80228
(303) 985-9261

Connecticut

WALTER C. KAHN
76 North Sylvan Road
Westport, CT 06880

Florida

ROBERT E. DiCARLO RESTORATION
P.O. Box 616222
Orlando, FL 32861
(407) 886-7423

RESTORATIONS OBJECTS D'ART
Eric W. Idstrom Company
12500 Southeast U.S. Highway 301
Belleview, FL 32620
(352) 245-8862

MAISON GINO, INC.
Ginette or Irving Sultan
2021 North Bay Road
Miami Beach, FL 33140
(305) 532-2015

Illinois

J.B. SERVICES
John and Betty Bazar
2302 Sudbury Lane
Geneva, IL 60134

WAYNE WARNER
Route 16, Box 557
Bloomington, IL 61704
(309) 828-0994

Iowa

MAXINE'S LTD. GIFT GALLERY
7144 University Avenue
Des Moines, IA 50311
(515) 255-3197

Massachusetts

ROSINE GREEN ASSOCIATES
89 School Street
Brookline, MA 02446
(617) 277-8368

SHROPSHIRE GALLERY
J. Kevin Samara
274 South Street
Shrewsbury, MA 01545
(508) 842-5001

SHROPSHIRE GALLERY
600 Main Street
Shrewsbury, MA 01545
(508) 845-6317

New Jersey

BAER SPECIALTY SHOP
259 East Browning Road
Bellmawr, NJ 08031
(856) 931-0696

RESTORATIONS BY VALERIE
Valerie Schleifer
4 Country Club Court
Livingston, NJ 07039
(973) 992-9270
(973) 887-7326
Fax: (973) 992-8509

New York

CHINA AND GLASS REPAIR STUDIOS
282 Main Street
Eastchester, NY 10709
(914) 337-1977

FREDI W. BOESE M.I. HUMMEL RESTORATION
P.O. Box 933
309 Route 17 M
Harriman, NY 10926
(845) 783-4438
www.frediboese.com

IMPERIAL CHINA
22 North Park Avenue
Center, NY 11570
(516) 764-7311

RESTORATIONS UNLIMITED
Donna Curtin
1209 Milton Avenue
Syracuse, NY 13204
(315) 488-7123

CERAMIC RESTORATION OF WESTCHESTER, INC.
Hans-Jurgen Schindhelm
81 Water Street
Ossining, NY 10562
(914) 762-1719

Ohio

COLONIAL HOUSE OF COLLECTIBLES
182 Front Street, Terrace Park
Berea, OH 44017
(440) 826-4169

OLD WORLD RESTORATIONS, INC.
5729 Dragon Way, Suite 6
Cincinnati, OH 45227
(513) 271-5459

WIEBOLD ART CONSERVATION LAB
413 Terrace Place
Cincinnati, OH 45174
(513) 831-2541

Pennsylvania

HARRY A. EBERHARDT AND SON, INC.
2010 Walnut Street
Philadelphia, PA 19103
(215) 568-1877

A. LUDWIG KLEIN AND SONS, INC.
683 Sunnytown Pike
P.O. Box 145
Harleysville, PA 19438
(215) 256-9004

KRAUSE'S
97 West Wheeling Street
Washington, PA 15301
(724) 228-5034

CRAZEMASTERS
c/o Hummel Collectors Club, Inc.
1261 University Drive
Yardley, PA 19067-2857
(215) 493-6204

South Dakota

D & J GLASS CLINIC, INC.
Route 3, Box 330
Sioux Falls, SD 57106
(605) 361-7524

Texas

SHARON LEWIS HOBBY
8902 Deer Haven Road
Austin, TX 78737
(512) 301-2294

Virginia

CLAY WERKS LTD.
4058 Main Street
P.O. Box 353
Exmore, VA 23350
(757) 414-0567

Canada

J&H CHINA REPAIR
8296 Saint George Street
Vancouver, BC
Canada V5X 3S5
(604) 321-1093

ARTWORK RESTORATION
30 Hillhouse Road
Winnipeg, MB
Canada R2V 2V9
(204) 334-7090

CLASSIC ART RESTORATION
1260 Yonge Street
Toronto, ON
Canada M4T 1W5
(416) 968-9000

Insuring and Cataloguing Your Collection

"Insurance after a theft is like taking medicine after death."

This adage speaks pointedly to the problems that can occur when collectors fail to take the time to get their valuable collections properly insured and protected.

I know many collectors who have spent countless hours making weekend trips all over the country in pursuit of special items to add to their collections, yet they have not invested a few hours of time to adequately protect that same collection. Many collectors are also ignorant of the increased replacement value of their entire collection.

Collections by their very nature generally appreciate over time, with the collector not always aware of the inflation factor or the secondary market quotations for the pieces they have acquired. None of us care to dwell on the prospect of having our treasures stolen, broken or lost in transit, but a few logical precautions can properly protect the collection that you have so lovingly assembled.

Take the time necessary to review the options available regarding insurance for your collectibles. Several years of speaking on the subject of appraising and insuring collectibles has made me keenly aware of the lack of experience and understanding among collectors regarding insurance policy options for protecting their valuables.

One of the most important aspects of shopping for a good policy is to make a date with yourself to get the project started and stick to it. Don't procrastinate!

Insurance agents are generally accommodating and eager to help you obtain a good policy to protect your collectibles. Still, the buyer must truly beware.

It is always a good idea to get quotes from two or three different insurance companies because some specialize in certain types of policies. Be sure to find out exactly what is covered in the policy being quoted. For example, will it cover breakage, burglary, loss, damage, fire, etc.?

There are several types of coverage available today: valuable articles coverage (VAC); homeowner's or renter's; a separate endorsement to an existing policy; an endorsement to a business policy; or a completely separate policy.

Rates for insurance policies vary widely from company to company. Your best bet is to talk with other collectors to find out what companies they have dealt with, how pleased they have been with their coverage, and how their rates compare to what you have been quoted.

Because the insurance sales system works like any other free enterprise, agents are competing with others for your business. They may not want to burden you with too many details about insuring your collection, lest they drive you toward another agency. Therefore, it is up to you, the collector, to retain proper documentation regarding your collection's value.

Insurance agents will usually allow you to place the values on your items by using various reliable publications, such as this book, the *Collector's Mart Price Guide to Limited Edition Collectibles*, the *Collectibles Market Guide & Price Index* by Collector's Information Bureau, or various line-specific editions of *The Greenbook*.

If you already have a homeowner's policy, the best place to begin your insurance search is with your existing agent. Ask him to check your policy's fine print to see if

Reliable pricing sources, such as Collector's Mart Price Guide to Limited Edition Collectibles or this book, are essential tools when cataloguing your collection for insurance purposes.

tracting the services of a professional appraiser. Two outstanding appraisal organizations exist in the United States with members that are experts in various areas of collectibles: The American Society of Appraisers (ASA), P.O. Box 17265, Washington, DC 20041, and The International Society of Appraisers (ISA), 16040 Christensen Road, Suite 320, Seattle, WA 98188-2929. These organizations can give you the names of experts in various fields of interest in your respective area.

Appraisals

An appraiser is a person who determines the value of an item or items for insurance purposes and supplies the necessary information for the settlement of damage claims. The professional appraiser is also the person who determines the value of the collection at the time it is donated to a tax-exempt institution or charity.

Remember that appraising is not a casual matter. All expert appraisals must be accurate and precise, and should be updated annually to reflect market changes. Often an appraiser must be able to stand up in court if litigation arises from a dispute over valuation of the property.

Select an appraiser in the same manner you would select your family physician or attorney. Don't be afraid to ask for credentials and what type of experience the individual has acquired. Be careful not to rely solely on a shop owner purporting to be an "appraiser." It is also wise to check with collector friends as to whom they trust and feel confident with for appraisal opinions.

- Choose an appraiser based on these criteria:
- Documented accomplishments (experience)
- Professional certification (education)
- Reputation
- Personal interview (ask for credentials)
- Professional memberships (member of ASA or ISA)

your collection is indeed covered as part of the policy. It is important that you know exactly what is covered and what value will be paid in case you have a claim.

Replacement Value or Fair Market Value

Generally, most collectors will want to insure their collections for "current replacement value." Replacement value is the stated amount that it would take to replace the items if they were damaged, stolen, or lost.

Fair market value is the value of the collection if it were sold suddenly at auction or by any other willing seller/willing buyer arrangement. The fair market value is usually used for reports to the Internal Revenue Service when a collection is donated to a museum or charity. However, some collectors may feel that if their collection were completely lost, current fair market value would make the most sense for a "cash settlement" by the insurance company. A collector of advance years, who may not consider adding to his collection after a loss, may opt for fair market value coverage.

Cataloguing/Documentation

Cataloguing or documentation of your collection is a must when a claim is filed with an insurance company. Here are some possibilities that can make this task much easier.

You can free yourself from the burden of having to complete the documentation of your collection by con-

Detailed Inventory

Complete a list or cataloguing system of all the items in your collection. Although some insurance companies may not request such a list, you should have an inventory for your own use to determine your collection's value. With some policies, it may not be possible to receive reimbursement for the full value of your collection without a list.

Record the following basic information for each item:
- Item name
- Series name
- Year of issue
- Artist's name
- Manufacturer's name
- Edition limit/edition number (Hum number)
- Size/dimensions
- Your original cost
- Added expenses (shipping, framing, restoration, etc.)
- Special markings (artist's signatures, etc.)

- Date of purchase
- Secondary market history (if purchased on secondary market)
- Location in your home (for burglary or loss)
- Insurance company/policy or rider number

Record each new item you buy at the time of purchase so as not to get behind on your cataloguing. Make a date with yourself to update this material periodically, possibly after you complete your income taxes for the year. The pleasure of seeing how your collection is growing may offset the chores of preparing tax returns!

Large index cards will handle the pertinent information, or you may prefer to invest in one of the published record books, such as:

- *The Kovels' Organizer for Collectors* by Ralph and Terry Kovel (Crown Publishers, 1 Park Avenue, New York, NY 10016)
- *The Official Collector's Journal* (The House of Collectibles Inc., 201 East 50th Street, New York, NY 10022)
- *Collectors Inventory File* (Collectors News, Grundy Center, IA 50638)

These books may also be available in your local bookstore.

Depending on how technologically advanced you are, you may also develop a cataloguing system on your home computer. There are few software packages available, like The Collectible Dealers FastTrack Inventory and Business Management System 2002 TM available through the Antique and Art Information Network, Inc. Web site at www.aain.com. Though the name of the software makes it sound as though it is exclusive for dealers, it is also useful for individual collector use.

If you prefer not to invest in someone else's software system, it is quite simple to establish your own electronic inventory cataloguing system simply with the help of any spreadsheet program such as Microsoft Excel. Each needed piece of information can be entered into cells with the appropriate column headers, and suddenly you've got a nice electronic catalog.

Photo and Video Documentation

One extra backup to any cataloguing process is to show actual photographs or video of the pieces contained within your collection.

Refer to Appendix A of this book for instructions on photographing your collection. You can take the pictures and attach them to a written description of each piece including trademarks and any other marks found on the base. These will not usually be visible in the photos. Record the exact size and any other characteristic unique to your piece. Some put this information on the back of the photo itself.

If you choose to go the electronic cataloguing route, digital cameras will also allow you to visually inventory your collection and keep the images on a disc. Or, you can take photos the traditional way and scan the images with a computer scanner for storage as digital images on a disc.

A third option for establishing a pictorial record of your collection is to record everything on videotape with a personal camcorder. Begin with a general overview of the entire collection so the viewer can get a feel for its size and where it is displayed. After the introductory shots, detailed looks at each piece constitute a complete video document. Again refer to Appendix A for instructions on how to record your collection on video.

Inventory Safe-Keeping

Whatever method you use to inventory, catalogue, or document your collection, be sure to make a duplicate list, video, set of photographs, compact disc, etc. to be kept in

Photo courtesy Goebel of North America.

When cataloguing your collection, be sure to provide detailed information. This is especially important in reference to sets such as the Nativity Set shown here. It is important to not only list the name of the set, but also provide details (sizes, markings, etc.) for each piece within that set.

a safe deposit box or some other secure location away from your home or where you keep your collection. You don't want your catalog stolen or burned up with your collection. Your insurance company will very likely require an itemized list with description and value. Your safely stored catalog will be a big help to you and them in the case of a disaster.

Glossary

The following is an alphabetical listing of terms and phrases you will encounter in this book as well as other related books, references, and literature during the course of collecting Hummel items. In some cases, they are specific and unique to Hummel collecting and others are generic in nature, applying to other earthenware, ceramic, and porcelain as well. Refer to this glossary whenever you read or hear something you don't understand. Frequent use of it will enable you to become well versed in collecting Hummel figurines and other related items.

Airholes: Small holes under the arms or other unobtrusive locations to vent the hollow figures during the firing stage of production. This prevents them from exploding as the interior air expands due to intense heat. Many pieces have these tiny little holes, but often they are difficult to locate. Those open at the bottom usually have no need for these holes.

Anniversary Plate: In 1975 a 10" plate bearing the Stormy Weather motif was released. Subsequent anniversary plates were released at five-year intervals. 1985 saw the third and last in the series released.

Annual Plate: Beginning in 1971, the W. Goebel firm began producing an annual Hummel plate. Each plate con-

tains a bas-relief reproducing one of the Hummel motifs. The first was originally released to the Goebel factory workers in 1971, commemorating the hundredth anniversary of the firm. This original release was inscribed, thanking the workers. At the same time, the first in a series of 25 was released to the public. That series is complete and a new series began in 1997.

ARS: Latin word for "art."

ARS AG: ARS AG, Zug, Switzerland, holds the two-dimensional rights for many of the original M.I. Hummel drawings as well as the two-dimensional rights for reproductions of M.I. Hummel products made by Goebel.

Ars Edition: Ars Edition was formerly known as Ars Sacra Josef Mueller Verlag, the German publishing house that first published Hummel art, producing and selling postcards, postcard-calendars, and prints of M.I. Hummel. Today, Ars Edition GmbH is the exclusive licensee for publishing Hummel (books, calendars, cards, stationery, etc.) Owner: Marcel Nauer (grandson of Dr. Herbert Dubler).

Ars Sacra: Trademark on a gold foil label sometimes found on Hummel-like figurines produced by Herbert Dubler. This was a New York firm that produced these figurines during the years of World War II when Goebel was forbidden by the Nazi government to produce Hummel items. Ars Sacra is also the original name of the Ars Edition firm in Munich. Dubler was a son-in-law of Mr. and Mrs. Mueller, the owners of Ars Edition, formerly Ars Sacra, Munich. Although there was some corporate connection for a very short time between Mueller and Dubler, there is no connection between the Mueller Ars Sacra firm and the Hummel-like figurines produced by Dubler under the name "House of Ars Sacra" or the statement "Produced by Ars Sacra." Please see the discussion on the Dubler figures elsewhere in this volume.

Artist's Sample: See Master Sample.

Baby Bee: Describes the trademark of the factory used in 1958—a small bee flying in a V.

Backstamp: Backstamp is usually the trademark and any associated special markings on the underside of the base, the reverse, or backside of an item.

Basic Size: This term is generally synonymous with standard size. However, because the sizes listed in this book are not substantiated initial factory released sizes, it was felt that it would be misleading to label them "standard." "Basic size" was chosen to denote only an *approximate* standard size.

Bas-relief: A raised or sculpted design, as on the Annual Bells and the Annual Plates, as opposed to a two-dimensional painted design or decal.

Bee: A symbol used since about 1940 in various forms, as a part of or along with the factory trademark on Hummel pieces until 1979, when the bee was dropped. It was reincorporated in the special backstamp used on the M.I. Hummel exclusive pieces and a bee variation was again reinstated with new trademark (TMK-8) introduced in 2000.

Bisque: A fired but unglazed condition. Usually white but sometimes colored.

Black Germany: Term used to describe one of the various wordings found along with the Hummel trademarks on the underside of the pieces. It refers to the color used to stamp the word "Germany." Many colors have been used for the trademarks and associated marks, but black generally indicates the figure is an older mode; however, this is not an absolutely reliable indicator.

Bookends: Throughout the collection of Goebel-made Hummel items are bookends. Some are the regular figurines merely attached to wooden bookends with some type of adhesive. Some, however, are different. The latter are made without the customary base and then attached. The regular

pieces, when removed from the wood, have the traditional markings. Those without the base may or may not exhibit those markings.

Candleholder: Some Hummel figurines have been produced with provisions to place candles in them.

Candy Bowl/Candy Box/Candy Dish: Small covered cylindrical box with a Hummel figurine on the top. Design changes have been made in the shape of the box/bowl/dish over the years, as well as in the manner in which the cover rests upon the bowl. See individual listings.

Closed Edition (CE): A term used by the Goebel factory to indicate that a particular item is no longer produced and will not be placed in production again.

Closed Number (CN): A term used by the Goebel factory to indicate that a particular number in the Hummel Mold Number sequence has never been used to identify an item and never will be used. A caution here: Several unquestionably genuine pieces have been found over the years bearing these so-called closed numbers.

Club Exclusive: This refers to the products made for membership premiums and sale exclusively to members of the M.I. Hummel Club. Each of these bears a special club backstamp to identify it as such.

Collector's Plaque: Same as the dealer plaque except it does not state "authorized dealer," as most later dealer plaques do. Frequently used for display with private collections (see Dealer Plaque).

Copyright Date: The actual year the original mold was made. Often the mold is made, but figures are not produced for several years afterward. The copyright date is sometimes found along with other marks on older pieces but not always. All pieces currently being produced bear a copyright date.

Crazing: A fine web-like cracked appearance in the overglaze of older porcelain and earthenware. It occurs on Hummel figurines from time to time, mostly on older pieces. See earlier section on crazing.

Crown Mark (TMK-1): One of the early W. Goebel firm trademarks. Has not been used on Hummel figurines and related pieces since sometime between 1949 and 1950.

Current Mark: For many years, this was a term describing the trademark being used at the present time. It has become a somewhat confusing term, for what is current today may not be tomorrow. Most collectors and dealers have come to use a descriptive term such as the "Crown Mark" or the use of trademark number designations such as Trademark No. 1 (TMK-1) for the Crown Mark, for instance. The number designation is usu-

ally shortened to "trademark one" when spoken or "TMK-1" when written.

Current Production: Term describing figurines, plates, candy boxes, etc. supposedly being produced at the present time. They are not necessarily readily available, because the factory maintains the molds, but doesn't always produce the figure with regularity.

Dealer Plaque: A plaque made and distributed by the

Goebel firm to retailers for the purpose of advertising the fact that they are authorized dealers in Hummel figurines and related articles. The plaques always used to have the Merry Wanderer figure incorporated into them. Earlier models have a bumblebee perched on the top edge (see Collector's Plaque). In recent years, the figurine associated has not always been the Merry Wanderer. For more detailed information, see the listing for Hum 187.

Decimal Designator: Many earlier Goebel Hummel figurines exhibit a decimal point after the mold number, i.e.: "154." This is ostensibly to mean the same thing as the "slash" mark (/). The use of the slash mark means that there is another, smaller size of the piece either in existence, planned, or at least in prototype. There is another theory that the decimal is to make it easier to clarify the incised mold numbers and to help determine whether a number is, for instance, a 66 rather than a 99. The decimal is not always found alone with the number. Some examples the author has observed are "49./0.", "51./0.", and "84./5."

Display Plaque: See Collector's Plaque and Dealer Plaque.

Doll Face: See Faience.

Doughnut Base: Describes a type of base used with some figures. Looking at the bottom of the base, the outer margin of the base forms a circle or oval, and a smaller circle or oval within makes the base appear doughnut-like.

Doughnut Halo: The only figures on which these appear are the Madonnas. They are formed as a solid cap type, or molded so that the figure's hair protrudes through slightly. The latter are called "Donut Halos."

Double Crown: From 1934 to 1938, there were many figures produced with two Crown WG marks. This is known as the Double Crown. One of the crowns may be a stamped crown and the other incised. Pieces have been found with both trademarks incised (see earlier section on trademarks). Thereafter, only a single Crown Mark is found.

Embossed: An erroneous term used to describe incised (see Incised).

Faience (Doll Face): Faience is defined as brilliantly glazed, bright-colored fine earthenware. More commonly called "Doll Face" pieces by collectors, this describes the few Hummel figurines that were made by Goebel in the early days of paint and finish experimentation. Several have made it into collectors' hands. Refer to the color section in the center of this book for illustrations of a few.

Fink, Emil: Publisher of a limited number of postcards and greeting cards bearing the art of M.I. Hummel. All U.S. copyrights of cards published by Fink Verlag are owned by ARS AG, Zug, Switzerland.

Font: A number of pieces have been produced with a provision for holding a small portion of holy water. They can be hung on the wall. Often referred to as Holy Water Fonts.

Full Bee (TMK-2): About 1940, the W. Goebel firm began using a bee as part of its trademark. The Full Bee trademark has been found along with the Crown trademark. The Full Bee is the first bee to be utilized. There were many versions of the Full Bee trademark. The first Full Bee is sometimes found with (R) stamped somewhere on the base.

Germany (W. GERMANY, West Germany, Western Germany): All have appeared with the trademark in several different colors.

Goebelite: This is the name the Goebel firm gives to the patented mixture of materials used to form the slip used in pouring and fashioning the earthenware Hummel figurines and other related Hummel pieces. Not often heard.

High Bee: A variation of the early Bee trademarks wherein the bee is smaller than the original bee used in the mark and flies with its wings slightly higher than the top of the V in the trademark.

Hollow Base: A base variation. Some bases for figures are solid and some are hollowed out and open into a hollow figure.

Hollow Mold: An erroneous term actually meaning Hollow Base, as above. All Hummel pieces are at least partially hollow in finished form.

Holy Water Font: See Font.

Hummel Mark (TMK-7): This mark was introduced in 1991. It is the first trademark to be used exclusively on Goebel products utilizing M.I. Hummel art for its design.

Hummel Number or Mold Number: A number or numbers incised into the base or bottom of the piece, used to identify the mold motif and sometimes the size of the figure or article. This designation is sometimes inadvertently omitted, but rarely.

Incised/Indented: Describes a mark or wording that has actually been pressed into the surface of a piece, rather than printed or stamped on the surface. It is almost always found beneath the base.

Jumbo: Sometimes used to describe the few Hummel figurines that have been produced in a substantially larger

size than the normal range—usually around 30". (See Hum 7, 141, and 142.)

Light Stamp: See M.I. Hummel. It is thought that every Hummel figurine has Sister M.I. Hummel's signature stamped somewhere on it, but some apparently have no signature. In some cases, the signature may have been stamped so lightly that in subsequent painting and glazing all but unidentifiable traces are obliterated. In other cases, the signature may have been omitted altogether. The latter case is rare. The same may happen to the mold number.

Limited Edition: An item that is limited in production to a specified number or limited to the number produced in a defined period of time.

Master Sample/Mahlmuster/Master Zimmer: This is a figurine or other item that is the model from which Goebel artists paint the newly fashioned piece. The Master Sample figurines usually have a red line painted around the flat vertical portion of the base. It is known variously in German as the Mahlmuster, Master Zimmer, Muster Zimmer, or Originalmuster. There is another notation sometimes found on the base: "Orig Arbt Muster." These are abbreviations for the German words "Original Working Model."

M.I. Hummel (Maria Innocentia Hummel): This signature, illustrated below, is  supposed to be applied to every Hummel article produced. However, as in Light Stamp above, it may not be evident. It is also reasonable to assume that because of the design of a particular piece or its extremely small size, it may not have been practical to place it on the piece. In such cases, a small sticker is used in its place. It is possible that these stickers became loose and were lost over the years. The signature has been found painted on in some instances but rarely. It is also possible to find the signature in decal form, brown in color. From the late-1950s to early 1960s, Goebel experimented with placing the signature on the figurines by the decal method, but abandoned the idea. A few of the pieces the company tried it on somehow found their way into the market. Collectors should also take note of the fact that sometimes the signature appears as "Hummel" without the initials. This is also seldom found.

Mel: There are a few older Hummel figurines made by Goebel that bear this incised three-letter group along with a number. It is supposed that they were prototype pieces that were never placed in production, but at least three were.

Mold Induction Date: See Copyright Date.

Missing Bee Mark (TMK-6): In mid-1980, the Goebel company changed the trademark by removing the familiar "bee" mark collectors had grown accustomed to associating with M.I. Hummel items. It came to be known as the "Missing Bee" mark (TMK-6) for a while.

Model Number: See Mold Number.

Mold Growth: There have been many theories in the past to explain the differences in sizes of figurines marked the same and with no significant differences other than size. The explanation from Goebel is that in the earlier years of molding, the molds were made of plaster of Paris and had a tendency to wash out and erode with use. Therefore, successive use would produce pieces each being slightly larger than the last. Another possible explanation is that the firm has been known to use more than one mold simultaneously in the production of the same figure and market them with the same mold number. The company developed a synthetic resin to use instead of plaster of Paris in 1954. Although this is a vast improvement, the new material still has the same tendencies but to a significantly smaller degree.

Mold Induction Date (Copyright Date): An incorrectly used term in reference to what is actually the copyright date. See Copyright Date.

Mold Number: The official mold number used by Goebel that is unique to each Hummel item or motif used. See section on the explanation of the mold number system earlier in this chapter for an in-depth discussion.

Mother Mold Sample: When Goebel proposes a new figurine, the piece is modeled, a mother mold made, and usually three to six sample figures are produced and then painted by one of Goebel's master painters. These are for the convent and others to examine and either approve for production, suggest changes, or reject completely, as the case may be. Typically, never more than six to eight of these are produced. Sometimes the final approved models are marked with a red line and placed into service as a master sample for the artists. Although the mother mold samples do not necessarily have the red line, they are identifiable by the black ink within the incised mold number.

Mould: European spelling of Mold.

Muster Zimmer: See Master Sample.

Narrow Crown: Trademark used by the W. Goebel firm from 1937 to the early 1940s. To date, this trademark has never been found on an original Hummel piece.

One-Line Mark: See Stylized Bee.

Open Edition: Designates the Hummel figurines presently in production or in planning. It does not mean all are in production, only that it is "open" for production. Not necessarily available.

Open Number: A number in the numerical sequence of factory-designated Hummel model numbers that has not been used to identify a piece but may be used when a new design is released.

Out of Production: A confusing term sometimes used to indicate that an item is not of current production but may be placed back in production at some later date. The confusion results from the fact that some with this designation have been declared closed editions, and others have been returned to production, thus leaving all the others in the classification in limbo.

Orig Arbt Muster: A marking sometimes found beneath the base of a figurine. It is the abbreviation for the German words roughly translated to mean "Original Working Model."

Overglaze: See White Overglaze.

Oversize: A term sometimes used to describe a Hummel piece larger than that which is currently being produced. These variations could be due to mold growth (see Mold Growth).

Painter's Sample: See Master Sample.

Possible Future Edition (PFE): A term applied to Hummel mold design that does exist, but has not yet been released.

Production Mold Sample: A piece that is cast out of the first production mold.

Prototype: This is a proposed figurine or other item that must be approved by those with the authority to do so. As used by Goebel, it is further restricted to mean "the one and only sample," the first out of the mother mold. This is the one presented to the Siessen Convent for its approval/disapproval. See Mother Mold Sample.

Quartered Base: As it sounds, this is descriptive of the underside of the base of a piece being divided into four more or less equal parts.

Red Line: A red line around the outside edge of the base of a figurine means that the piece may have once served as the model for the painters.

Reinstated: A piece that is back in production after having been previously placed in a non-production status for some length of time.

Sample Model: A prototype piece modeled for the approving authorities. May or may not have gained approval. See Mother Mold Sample.

Secondary Market: When an item is bought and sold after the initial purchase, it is said to be traded on the secondary market.

Size Designator: Method of identifying the size of a figure. It is found in conjunction with the Hummel mold number on the bottom of the figure.

Slash-Marked: From time to time, a figure or a piece will be found with a slash or cut through the trademark. There are two theories as to the origin of this mark. Some think it is used to indicate a figure with some flaw or imperfection, although several figures with slash marks are, upon close examination, found to be in excellent, flawless condition. The other theory is that some figures are slash-marked to discourage resale of pieces given to or sold at a bargain price to factory workers.

Small Bee: A variation of the early Full Bee trademark wherein the bee is about half the size of the original bee.

Split Base: When viewing the bottom of the base of a piece, it appears to be split into sections. Generally refers to a base split into two sections, but could readily be used to describe more than two sections.

Stamped: A method of placing marks on the bottom of a figure wherein the data is placed on the surface rather than pressed into it (see Incised).

Standard Size: As pointed out in the section on size designators, this is a general term used to describe the size of the first figure to be produced, when there are more sizes of the same figure to be found. It is not the largest, nor the smallest, only the first. Over the years, as a result of mold design changes and possibly mold growth, all figures marked as standard are not necessarily the same size (see Basic Size).

Stylized Bee (TMK-3): About 1955, the traditional bee design in the trademark was changed to reflect a more modern "stylized" version. Also sometimes called the "One-Line Mark."

Temporarily Withdrawn: Similar to Out of Production, but in this case, it would be reasonable to assume that the piece so described will be put back into production at some future date.

Terra Cotta: Literally translated from the Latin it means "baked earth"; a naturally brownish-orange earthenware.

Three Line Mark (TMK-4): A trademark variation used in the 1960s and 1970s.

Underglaze: A term describing anything that is found underneath the glaze as opposed to being placed after the glazing.

U.S. Zone or U.S. Zone Germany: During the American occupation of Germany after World War II, the Goebel company was required to apply these words to its products. After the country was divided into East Germany and West Germany in 1948, they began using "West Germany" or "Western Germany." The various configurations in which these words are found are illustrated in the above section on trademarks.

White Overglaze: After a piece has been formed a clear glaze is applied and fired, resulting in a shiny, all-white finish.

Chapter Three

The M.I. Hummel Collection

Hummel Listing

The following list of Hummel pieces is arranged by the appropriate Hummel mold number in ascending order. To fully understand all of the notations you must read and study the first two chapters of this book very carefully.

You will find the price listings almost complete, but it is impossible to conscientiously assign a value to each and every model that exists today. (Please refer to the introduction and to the beginning of Chapter 2 for a discussion of value determination). There are more than 1,500 pieces identified in this chapter; this number does not take into consideration variations due to mold size variation, color variation and model design differences. When it was impossible to obtain pricing information on a particular figure size or variation, the appropriate space is left blank or the listing is omitted altogether. In the latter case, it was not possible to ascertain and document all existing models. From time to time it is possible to establish the existence of a piece but without sure information as to size or trademark. In these cases, the corresponding space is left blank.

As evidenced by this revised 12th edition, this book is periodically updated and improved, and these values and other information will be incorporated in subsequent editions.

As stated earlier, the sizes are approximate but as accurate as possible. Almost all lists are contradictory, but in most cases within reasonable agreement. The sizes listed are those most frequently encountered in those listings and notated as the "Basic Size." (See definition in glossary). Most of the time, this is the smallest size for each figure. Frequently, however, there would be one smaller size listed, but the preponderance of other listings would indicate a 1/4" or 1/2" larger size. In these cases, the larger size was assumed the more representative. Any sizes given in captions are actual hands-on measurements.

For purposes of simplification the various trademarks have been abbreviated in the list. Should you encounter any trouble interpreting the abbreviations, refer to the list below or to the glossary.

Trademark	Abbreviations	Dates
Crown	TMK-1	1934-1950
Full Bee	TMK-2	1940-1959
Stylized Bee	TMK-3	1958-1972
Three Line Mark	TMK-4	1964-1972
Last Bee	TMK-5	1972-1979
Missing Bee	TMK-6	1979-1991
Hummel Mark	TMK-7	1991-1999
Millennium Bee (Current)	TMK-8	2000-present

Hum 1: Puppy Love

Part of the original 46 pieces offered in 1935, Puppy Love was first known as the "Little Violinist." It was first modeled by master sculptor Arthur Moeller in 1935 and can be found in Crown Mark (TMK-1) through TMK-6. It was retired in 1988, never to be produced again.

Many of the original group of 46 have been found ren-

Puppy Love, Hum 1. Left: Decimal designator in the mold number (1.), incised Crown Mark (TMK-1), doughnut base, and black "Germany," and 5" tall. Center: Full Bee Mark (TMK-2) in an incised circle, black "Germany," 5-1/2" tall. Right: Last Bee (TMK-5), doughnut base, 4-7/8" tall.

dered in terra cotta, and Puppy Love is no exception, although so far, only one is known to exist in any private collection. It has an incised Crown Mark and incised number "T-1." It is valued at $4,000-$5,000.

The most significant variation occurs in Crown pieces only. In this variation, the head is tilted slightly to the right instead of the typical left, he wears a black hat, and there is no necktie. This very rare variation can bring $4,000-$5,000 on the collector market.

It is possible, though unlikely, that you may encounter a mold number variation of this piece. It seems that in the initial stages of planning and modeling the figurines, there was no formal designation of the mold number, and Puppy Love has been found with the mold number FF 15. If

found, this early sample with the original number is worth $5,000-$10,000.

A third early sample was produced in 1935 by Arthur Moeller and is similar to Little Hiker (Hum 16/I) with an attached pot. If found, this piece would be worth $5,000-$10,000.

Hum No.	Basic Size	Trademark	Current Value
1	5"	TMK-1	$755-$1,000
1	5"	TMK-2	$550-$600
1	5"	TMK-3	$510-$550
1	5"	TMK-4	$400-$510
1	5"	TMK-5	$350-$400
1	5"	TMK-6	$305-$350

Hum 2: Little Fiddler

Originally known as the "Violinist" and then "The Wandering Fiddler," this little fellow is almost always wearing a brown derby with an orange hatband. Modeled by master sculptor Arthur Moeller in 1935, the figure has been made in five sizes since its initial introduction as part of the original 46.

The two largest sizes were temporarily withdrawn from production in 1989. The smallest, Hum 2/4/0, was introduced into the line in 1984 and was temporarily withdrawn from the North American market on December 31, 1997.

A few Little Fiddlers with the Crown Mark (TMK-1) have been found in doll face or faience finish. These are valued at about 20% more than the regular Crown pieces, or $5,000-$6,000.

A mold number variation has been found with the mold number FF 16. In the days before the figurines were given the official "Hum" designation, the "FF" was used (on the first three models). It is possible, but not likely, that you will encounter this variation. If found, it would be worth $5,000-$10,000.

Goebel produced a limited edition of 50 Hum 2/I pieces in 1985 for a company-sponsored contest in Europe to celebrate 50 years of M.I. Hummel figurines. The limited edition had a gold painted base and special backstamp that

Little Fiddler, Hum 2. Left: This 2/II variation has an incised Crown Mark (TMK-1) that is colored in green. Note the unusually pale face. This black-and-white photo doesn't show it well, but this is an example of what collectors refer to as a "doll face" or faience piece (see color section and Chapter Five). It has a doughnut base and measures nearly 11". Right: Another with mold 2/II, but with Last Bee Mark (TMK-5) and incised 1972 copyright date.

Little Fiddler, Hum 2/0. The left piece has a small Stylized Bee (TMK-3), a brown derby hat with an orange hatband, and measures 5-3/4". The figure on the right is of the older Full Bee (TMK-2) era. It has a black hat, a black "Germany" beneath the base, and is 5-1/4" tall. Both figurines have a doughnut base.

The limited-edition gold-gilt base Little Fiddler, Hum 2/I. See Chapter Five.

The underside of the base of the gold-gilt base Hum 2/I Little Fiddler, showing the trademark and the German language Golden Jubilee backstamp. It reads: "50 JAHRE M.I. HUMMEL-FIGUREN 1935-1985."

Doll face Little Fiddler, Hum 2. This unusual example of the Little Fiddler bears an incised Crown Mark (TMK-1) that is colored in green. It has a doughnut base and measures nearly 11".

Photo courtesy Goebel of North America.

Still fiddlin' today, Little Fiddler as 2/0 continues in production at 6" with TMK-8.

read, "50 Jahre M.I. Hummel-Figuren 1935-1985." These are worth $1,500-$2,000.

Recently, a 12-1/4" version of Little Fiddler was introduced as part of the "Millennium Love" series, which also included Sweet Music (Hum 186/III), Serenade (Hum 85/III), Band Leader (Hum 129/III), and Soloist (Hum 135/III). These oversized pieces (Hum 85/III) were in limited supply and had to be special-ordered through an authorized M.I. Hummel retailer.

Hum No.	Basic Size	Trademark	Current Value
2/0	6"	TMK-5	$275-$300
2/0	6"	TMK-6	$260-$275
2/0	6"	TMK-7	$260-$275
2/0	6"	TMK-8	$260
2/I	7-1/2"	TMK-1	$1,110-$1,500
2/I	7-1/2"	TMK-2	$650-$930
2/I	7-1/2"	TMK-3	$565-$650
2/I	7-1/2"	TMK-4	$460-$560
2/I	7-1/2"	TMK-5	$425-$435
2/I	7-1/2"	TMK-6	$415-$420
2/II	11"	TMK-1	$2,500-$3,500
2/II	11"	TMK-2	$1,800-$2,300
2/II	11"	TMK-3	$1,515-$1,600
2/II	11"	TMK-4	$1,300-$1,515
2/II	11"	TMK-5	$1,200-$1,300
2/II	11"	TMK-6	$1,110-$1,200
2/III	12-1/4"	TMK-1	$3,500-$4,000
2/III	12-1/4"	TMK-2	$2,310-$2,800
2/III	12-1/4"	TMK-3	$1,600-$1,800
2/III	12-1/4"	TMK-4	$1,400-$1,600
2/III	12-1/4"	TMK-5	$1,300-$1,400
2/III	12-1/4"	TMK-6	$1,205-$1,300
2/III	12-1/4"	TMK-8	$1,550

Hum No.	Basic Size	Trademark	Current Value
2/4/0	3-1/2"	TMK-6	$130-$140
2/0	6"	TMK-1	$700-$850
2/0	6"	TMK-2	$430-$500
2/0	6"	TMK-3	$350-$400
2/0	6"	TMK-4	$325-$350

Hum 3: Book Worm

One of the original 46 released in 1935, the piece was modeled by master sculptor Arthur Moeller in 1935. This figure (a girl reading a book) appears more than once in the collection and was originally called "Little Book Worm." It is also found in a smaller size as Hum 8 and in the Hum 14/A and 14/B bookends with a companion figure of a boy reading (Book Worms).

The larger Hum 3/II and Hum 3/III have been out of current production for some time.

The Hum 3/III with older trademarks is avidly sought by collectors.

The numbers 3/II and 3/III are occasionally found with the Arabic number size designator (3/2 and 3/3 respectively).

The two larger sizes (8" and 9-1/2") have been temporarily withdrawn from current production.

There is a mold number variation. Before the figurines were given "Hum" mold numbers this figure was given the incised mold number FF 17. It is possible, but not likely, that you will encounter this variation. If found, it is worth $5,000-$10,000.

Additionally, a few faience pieces have surfaced. These are valued at $3,000-$5,000.

Hum No.	Basic Size	Trademark	Current Value
3/I	5-1/2"	TMK-1	$900-$1,110
3/I	5-1/2"	TMK-2	$600-$700
3/I	5-1/2"	TMK-3	$475-$500
3/I	5-1/2"	TMK-4	$400-$475
3/I	5-1/2"	TMK-5	$380-$400
3/I	5-1/2"	TMK-6	$370-$380
3/I	5-1/2"	TMK-7	$365-$370
3/I	5-1/2"	TMK-8	$370

Hum No.	Basic Size	Trademark	Current Value
3/II	8"	TMK-1	$2,500-$3,500
3/II	8"	TMK-2	$1,800-$2,300
3/II	8"	TMK-3	$1,500-$1,600
3/II	8"	TMK-4	$1,300-$1,500
3/II	8"	TMK-5	$1,200-$1,300
3/II	8"	TMK-6	$1,110-$1,200
3/III	9-1/2"	TMK-1	$3,500-$4,000
3/III	9-1/2"	TMK-2	$2,300-$2,800
3/III	9-1/2"	TMK-3	$1,600-$1,800
3/III	9-1/2"	TMK-4	$1,460-$1,600
3/III	9-1/2"	TMK-5	$1,360-$1,460
3/III	9-1/2"	TMK-6	$1,250-$1,360

Bookworm, Hum 3. Left: Crown Mark (TMK-1), 5-1/2". Right: Mold number 3/I with TMK-6 at 5-1/2".

Bookworm, Hum 3. There is no apparent trademark on either of these. There are, however, the regular incised mold numbers, 3/3. The left one is a doll face or faience piece (see color section and Chapter Five). It is rather gaudily painted, and it appears as if some of the paint ran before drying or during the firing of this experimental piece. It measures 9-1/2". The white overglaze piece measures 10".

Today's version (TMK-8) of Bookworm, Hum 3/I.

Hum 4: Little Fiddler

This is the same design as the Hum 2, Little Fiddler. The difference is, of course, that this is a smaller size than any of the original three sizes of the Hum 2. It too was modeled by master sculptor Arthur Moeller in 1935. One wonders why the company used two different mold numbers for the same basic piece in the original 46 released in 1935.

Another difference is that this variation (Hum 4) wears a black hat.

There is a significant variation found in some of the Crown Mark (TMK-1) pieces. The head is tilted to his right instead of the usual tilt to his left and he wears no tie. This variation can fetch up $3,000-$4,000 on the collector market. Refer to the color section to see a photo of a Hum 4 with this variation that is also in the faience finish.

The mold number is sometimes found with the decimal point (4.) designator, which can increase its value by up to 10%.

Little Fiddler, Hum 4. The left piece is the doll face. Note the very pale face and hands, the completely different head position, and the lack of a neckerchief. Each has the decimal point mold number designation (4.), the Crown Mark, and measures 5-1/8".

Hum No.	Basic Size	Trademark	Current Value
4	4-3/4"	TMK-1	$650-$800
4	4-3/4"	TMK-2	$400-$500
4	4-3/4"	TMK-3	$325-$375
4	4-3/4"	TMK-4	$300-$325
4	4-3/4"	TMK-5	$270-$300
4	4-3/4"	TMK-6	$250-$270
4	4-3/4"	TMK-7	$245-$250
4	4-3/4"	TMK-8	$240

Little Fiddler, Hum 4, is still in production today with a value of $240.

Photo courtesy Goebel of North America.

Hum 5: Strolling Along

One of the first 46 figures released in 1935, Hum 5 appears in only one basic size, 4-3/4". This figure, which is similar to Merry Wanderer (Hum 7), was modeled by Arthur Moeller in 1935.

The most notable variation found in Hum 5 is that TMK-6 figures have the boy looking straight ahead, while the older ones have him looking to the side. There is also evidence that a sample was produced with an attached pot, similar to Little Hiker (Hum 16/I) and if found, that piece is worth $5,000-$10,000.

Strolling Along was removed from production at the end of 1989, never to be made again.

Hum No.	Basic Size	Trademark	Current Value
5	4-3/4"	TMK-1	$700-$950
5	4-3/4"	TMK-2	$500-$600
5	4-3/4"	TMK-3	$450-$500
5	4-3/4"	TMK-4	$350-$450
5	4-3/4"	TMK-5	$300-$350
5	4-3/4"	TMK-6	$275-$300

Strolling Along, Hum 5. Left: Mold number is 5., has a Double Crown Mark (TMK-1), a black "Germany," and measures 5". Right: Last Bee Mark (TMK-5) at 4-7/8".

Hum 6: Sensitive Hunter

Called "The Timid Hunter" when first released among the original 46, this figure has remained in production ever since. Like the other originals, it was modeled by Arthur Moeller in 1935.

The most notable variation is the "H" shape of the suspenders used with the lederhosen. This variation is associated with all of the Crown Mark (TMK-1) figures and most of those with the Full Bee (TMK-2). The "H" variation will generally bring about 30% more than the value for the "X" pieces.

The later models have an "X" shape configuration. Crown Mark pieces have been found having the "X" shape suspenders. The color of the rabbit was usually orange, until 1981 when the company changed it to brown for all newly produced pieces.

Sensitive Hunter can also be found with the decimal (6.) designator. This can add up to 10% to its collector value.

The smallest of the sizes listed here, Hum 6/2/0, was added in 1985 as the second in a series of new smaller figurines matching mini-plates of the same design.

On December 31, 1984, Goebel announced the 7-1/2" size (Hum 6/II) was temporarily withdrawn from production status. In January 1999, the smallest size (6 2/0) was temporarily withdrawn. And as of June 15, 2002, the 4-3/4" size (6/0) also was temporarily withdrawn.

Hum No.	Basic Size	Trademark	Current Value
6/2/0	4"	TMK-6	$175-$180
6/2/0	4"	TMK-7	$170-$175
6	4-3/4"	TMK-1	$850-$1,000
6/0	4-3/4"	TMK-1	$650-$800
6/0	4-3/4"	TMK-2	$400-$500
6/0	4-3/4"	TMK-3	$325-$350
6/0	4-3/4"	TMK-4	$300-$325
6/0	4-3/4"	TMK-5	$275-$300
6/0	4-3/4"	TMK-6	$250-$275

Hum No.	Basic Size	Trademark	Current Value
6/0	4-3/4"	TMK-7	$245-$250
6/0	4-3/4"	TMK-8	$240
6/I	5-1/2"	TMK-1	$850-$1,000
6/I	5-1/2"	TMK-2	$500-$600
6/I	5-1/2"	TMK-3	$375-$425
6/I	5-1/2"	TMK-4	$350-$375
6/I	5-1/2"	TMK-5	$325-$350
6/I	5-1/2"	TMK-6	$300-$325
6/II	7-1/2"	TMK-1	$1,500-$2,000
6/II	7-1/2"	TMK-2	$955-$1,255
6/II	7-1/2"	TMK-3	$550-$650
6/II	7-1/2"	TMK-4	$475-$550
6/II	7-1/2"	TMK-5	$425-$475
6/II	7-1/2"	TMK-6	$350-$425

Continuing in the line today, Sensitive Hunter, Hum 6/0, now measures 4-3/4" and carries TMK-8.

Photo courtesy Goebel of North America.

Sensitive Hunter, Hum 6. Left: Decimal point designator in the mold number (6.), Double Crown Mark (TMK-1), doughnut base, black "Germany," red rabbit, and 4-3/4". Center: 6/0 mold number, Full Bee (TMK-2), doughnut base, black "Germany," red rabbit, and 4-3/4". Right: Another 6/0, but with TMK-6, brown rabbit, and at nearly 5".

Rear view of Sensitive Hunter, showing the "H" and "X" suspenders configuration discussed in the text.

Hum 7: Merry Wanderer

One of the original 46 figurines released in 1935, the same design also appears as Hum 11. Originally modeled by master sculptor Arthur Moeller, the Merry Wanderer is probably found in more sizes and variations than any other single figure in the collection. There are at least 12 different sizes known to exist. There is even a huge 6-foot concrete replica of the figure on the factory grounds in Germany. An 8-foot-high Merry Wanderer was displayed on the grounds of the former location of the M.I. Hummel Club in Tarrytown, New York, and subsequently was placed in storage for several years. It is now displayed at the Donald E. Stephens Museum of Hummels in Rosemont, Illinois.

It is also part of every dealer and collector's display plaque made prior to the 1986 introduction of the Tally display plaque, Hum 460. In 1990, the Merry Wanderer display plaque was reintroduced.

The rarest of sizes is the Hum 7/III, which was temporarily withdrawn from production in 1991.

The rarest of the base variations is illustrated in the accompanying photograph. Collectors refer to it variously as the "double step base," "stepped-up base," or the "stair step base." It is found on the Hum 7/I size of all the Crown Mark (TMK-1) and Full Bee (TMK-2) 7/I pieces, but only on the older Stylized Bee (TMK-3) pieces.

The 7/III size has been found in the faience finish. These can bring up to 20% to 50% more than the top value for the Crown Mark pieces.

The 2002 Goebel Suggested Retail Price List places a $26,550 value on the 32" "Jumbo" Merry Wanderer. The few "Jumbo" figures in private collectors' hands are generally used as promotional figures in showrooms and shops. They rarely bring full retail price. Few, if any, collectors paid the full recommended retail price. The dealers purchase at wholesale and often will sell at little or no profit after a period of time to put the money back into their business.

Hum No.	Basic Size	Trademark	Current Value
7/0	6-1/4"	TMK-1	$750-$1,000
7/0	6-1/4"	TMK-2	$475-$650
7/0	6-1/4"	TMK-3	$430-$455
7/0	6-1/4"	TMK-4	$375-$410
7/0	6-1/4"	TMK-5	$350-$370
7/0	6-1/4"	TMK-6	$335-$340
7/0	6-1/4"	TMK-7	$330-$335
7/0	6-1/4"	TMK-8	$330

Merry Wanderer, Hum 7/I. This Stylized Bee-marked figurine shows the rare stepped-up base.

Size certainly matters when pricing the Merry Wanderer. This "jumbo" variation at 32" and bearing the current-use trademark (TMK-8) is worth $15,000-$25,750.

Photo courtesy Goebel of North America.

Hum No.	Basic Size	Trademark	Current Value
7/I (double step base)	7"	TMK-1	$1,510-$1,750
7/I (double step base)	7"	TMK-2	$1,310-$1,500
7/I (double step base)	7"	TMK-3	$1,210-$1,300
7/I (plain base)	7"	TMK-3	$600-$750
7/I	7"	TMK-4	$500-$600
7/I	7"	TMK-5	$475-$500
7/I	7"	TMK-6	$450-$475
7/I	7"	TMK-7	$425-$450
7/II	9-1/2"	TMK-1	$3,000-$3,500
7/II	9-1/2"	TMK-2	$1,900-$2,750

Hum No.	Basic Size	Trademark	Current Value
7/II	9-1/2"	TMK-3	$1,700-$1,800
7/II	9-1/2"	TMK-4	$1,500-$1,700
7/II	9-1/2"	TMK-5	$1,250-$1,275
7/II	9-1/2"	TMK-6	$1,225-$1,250
7/II	9-1/2"	TMK-7	$1,200-$1,225
7/III	11-1/4"	TMK-1	$3,300-$4,000
7/III	11-1/4"	TMK-2	$2,500-$3,000
7/III	11-1/4"	TMK-3	$1,700-$2,000
7/III	11-1/4"	TMK-4	$1,400-$1,500
7/III	11-1/4"	TMK-5	$1,300-$1,350
7/III	11-1/4"	TMK-6	$1,250-$1,300
7/X	32"	TMK-5	$20,000-$25,750
7/X	32"	TMK-6	$15,000-$25,750
7/X	32"	TMK-7	$15,000-$25,750
7/X	32"	TMK-8	$15,000-$25,750

Hum 8: Book Worm

This figure is the same as Hum 3, except much smaller. First modeled by master sculptor Reinhold Unger in 1935, it was one of the original 46 to be offered at the Leipzig Fair that same year. It is found in only one size and remains in production today. At least one terra cotta Book Worm is known to be in collectors' hands, and if one exists, more may be out there.

Hum No.	Basic Size	Trademark	Current Value
8	4"	TMK-1	$700-$850
8	4"	TMK-2	$425-$500
8	4"	TMK-3	$350-$400
8	4"	TMK-4	$325-$350
8	4"	TMK-5	$290-$300
8	4"	TMK-6	$270-$290
8	4"	TMK-7	$255-$260
8	4"	TMK-8	$255

Bookworm, Hum 8, in today's TMK-8.

Bookworm, Hum 8. A comparison between the normal skin coloration (left) and the pale coloration on the doll face piece. Both measure 4-1/4". The left bears a Stylized Bee Mark (TMK-3). The one on the right is a doll face piece with a Double Crown Mark (TMK-1).

Hum 9: Begging His Share

There are two notable variations of this piece. Although originally designed by master sculptor Arthur Moeller in 1935 to be a candleholder, until 1964, it can be found with and without the candle-holding hole in the cake. In 1964, the hole was eliminated when the figurine was remodeled. The Stylized Bee (TMK-3) pieces seem to be those found most often without the hole. The Crown Mark (TMK-1) is the rarest occurrence of the no-hole variation.

Although not a major variation in terms of value, the fact that the earliest of the TMK-1 pieces have brightly colored striped socks is worth mentioning. Also, the earliest of these are the ones more likely to be found without the hole in the cake.

A very rare variation is illustrated by the left figure in the photo here. This no-base, large-shoes figure may have been intended to be utilized as a bookend piece, or it may have been simply an experiment. Whatever the case, if found it would command a low five-figure sum.

The piece was temporarily withdrawn in January 1999.

Hum No.	Basic Size	Trademark	Current Value
9	5-1/2"	TMK-1	$750-$900
9	5-1/2"	TMK-2	$450-$600
9 (hole)	5-1/2"	TMK-3	$400-$450
9 (without hole)	5-1/2"	TMK-3	$350-$400
9	5-1/2"	TMK-4	$325-$350
9	5-1/2"	TMK-5	$300-$325
9	5-1/2"	TMK-6	$290-$300
9	5-1/2"	TMK-7	$280-$290

Begging His Share candleholder, Hum 9. The doll face piece is on the left. Note the much paler face. Both have the decimal point designator in the mold number (9.), Double Crown Marks (TMK-1), doughnut bases, and measure 5-5/8".

Begging His Share candleholder, Hum 9. Left: Stamped with Crown Mark (TMK-1), and measuring 5-1/4". A very unusual piece; note the lack of the traditional base. The oversize shoes are utilized as a base. This piece was probably a prototype that never went into regular production. Right: Stylized Bee (TMK-3) in the incised circle, black "Western Germany," and 5-1/4".

Hum 10: Flower Madonna

Created in 1935 by master sculptor Reinhold Unger, this piece was listed in early catalogs as "Virgin With Flowers" and "Sitting Madonna with Child."

Several color and mold variations are known for this figure. In both sizes, it appears in color and in white overglaze. There have been reports of the figure occurring in tan, beige or brown, and in a royal blue, as well as in terra cotta in 10/III (13") and in 10/I size (9-1/2") with the Crown Mark (TMK-1).

The Crown Mark pieces all have the open-style or "doughnut" type halo. The figure was remodeled in the mid-1950s, eliminating the hole in the halo (closed halo). Because this took place during a trademark transition from

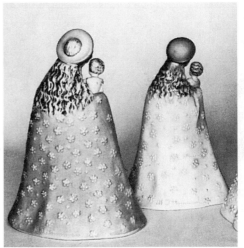

Open and closed halo variations of the Flower Madonna.

Flower Madonna, Hum 10. Left to right (A through D): A) The mold number has decimal designator (10./1.), incised Crown Mark (TMK-1), a stamped Crown Mark green in color, and measures 8-3/8". The overall color is beige, and the robe has no piping. B) Mold number is the regular 10/1. It has a large Stylized Bee (TMK-3) in an incised circle, is beige with orange piping, measures 8", and has a green "Western Germany" beneath. C) The mold number is rendered in pencil (10/1/11) and incised as 10. There is a green "Germany" stamped beneath. There are no other apparent markings. The color is blue cloak over a green gown. D) The mold number is 10/1. It has white overglaze finish, large Stylized Bee (TMK-3), and measures 9-3/8".

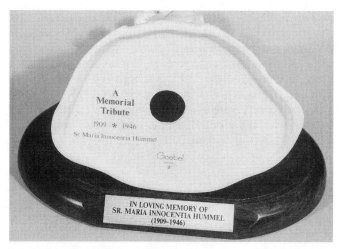

Base of a special-edition white overglaze Flower Madonna and wood display stand.

the Crown to the Full Bee marks, the Full Bee figures (TMK-2) are the pieces in which both types of halos are found. The Full Bee pieces with open halo bring about 20% more than those with closed halos. This variation has no significant influence on the white overglaze pieces.

The values of the significantly early color variations are $2,500 to $3,000 for the 10/I size and $3,000 to $3,500 for the 10/III size.

In 1996, the 50th anniversary of M.I. Hummel's death, Goebel issued a special edition of this piece in the 8-1/4" size for $225. The figure was on a hardwood base with a brass plaque (see photo).

Both the 10/I and 10/III sizes were temporarily withdrawn during TMK-6 period.

Hum No.	Basic Size	Trademark	Current Value
10/I (white)	9-1/2"	TMK-1	$500-$600
10/I (white)	9-1/2"	TMK-2	$300-$475

Hum No.	Basic Size	Trademark	Current Value
10/I (white)	8-1/4"	TMK-3	$275-$300
10/I (white)	8-1/4"	TMK-5	$230-$255
10/I (color)	9-1/2"	TMK-1	$800-$950
10/I (color)	9-1/2"	TMK-2	$700-$800
10/I (color)	8-1/4"	TMK-3	$575-$675
10/I (color)	8-1/4"	TMK-5	$500-$525
10/I (color)	8-1/4"	TMK-6	$475-$500
10/III (white)	13"	TMK-1	$450-$750
10/III (white) open halo	13"	TMK-2	$450-$650
10/III (white) closed halo	13"	TMK-2	$450-$650
10/III (white)	11-1/2"	TMK-3	$400-$470
10/III (white)	11-1/2"	TMK-5	$325-$350
10/III (white)	11-1/2"	TMK-6	$300-$325
10/III (color) open halo	13"	TMK-2	$800-$900
10/III (color) closed halo	13"	TMK-2	$800-$900
10/III (color)	11-1/2"	TMK-3	$600-$650
10/III (color)	11-1/2"	TMK-5	$525-$550
10/III (color)	11-1/2"	TMK-6	$500-$525

Hum 11: Merry Wanderer

This is the same design as the Hum 7, Merry Wanderer, and it too was first modeled by master sculptor Arthur Moeller in 1935.

Although most of these figures have five buttons on their vest, there are six- and seven-button versions of the 11/2/0 size. These bring a bit more than the five-button version of the 11/2/0 size, but it is not significant (about 10%).

The Hum 11 model of the Merry Wanderer has been found with faience finish.

In 1993, as part of a special Disneyland and Disney World promotion, an unknown number of the small Merry Wanderers were given a special decal transfer mark beneath the base to commemorate the occasion. The piece was supposed to be sold along with a similar-sized limited-edition Mickey Mouse. The Mickey Mouse has an incised mold number of 17322, a limited-edition indicator, and TMK-7. The Merry Wanderer is a regular production 11/2/0.

The problem was that the Merry Wanderers did not make it to the theme parks in time for the promotion. The edition for the pair on a wooden base was 1,500. The first sales of them on the secondary market apparently took place at the site of the M.I. Hummel Club Member Convention in Milwaukee, Wisconsin, in May 1993. Some private individuals were selling the figures out of their hotel room for $650 per set. They have been advertised for as high as $1,000 since then.

Hum No.	Basic Size	Trademark	Current Value
11	4-3/4"	TMK-1	$600-$750
11/2/0	4-1/4"	TMK-1	$450-$550
11/2/0	4-1/4"	TMK-2	$250-$325
11/2/0	4-1/4"	TMK-3	$225-$250
11/2/0	4-1/4"	TMK-4	$190-$225
11/2/0	4-1/4"	TMK-5	$175-$190
11/2/0	4-1/4"	TMK-6	$170-$175
11/2/0	4-1/4"	TMK-7	$165-$170
11/2/0	4-1/4"	TMK-8	$170
11/0	4-3/4"	TMK-1	$550-$700
11/0	4-3/4"	TMK-2	$400-$500
11/0	4-3/4"	TMK-3	$325-$375
11/0	4-3/4"	TMK-4	$300-$325
11/0	4-3/4"	TMK-5	$275-$300
11/0	4-3/4"	TMK-6	$250-$275
11/0	4-3/4"	TMK-7	$225-$230

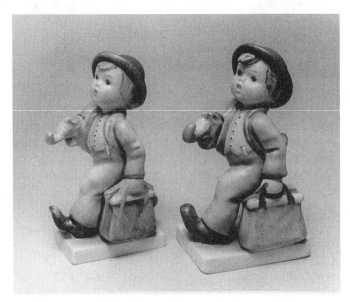

Left: Double Crown Mark, split base (quartered), and 4-7/8". Right: Carries mold number 11., Crown Mark (TMK-1), "Made in U.S. ZONE," black "Germany," split base (quartered), and 5-1/4".

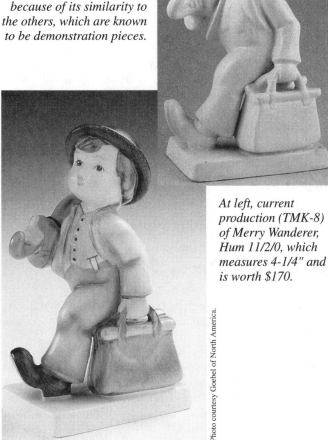

Merry Wanderer, Hum 11. Bears the decimal mold number designator 11., a Double Crown Mark, and a split (quartered) base. It is not likely to be a demonstration piece, due to its age. It is placed here because of its similarity to the others, which are known to be demonstration pieces.

At left, current production (TMK-8) of Merry Wanderer, Hum 11/2/0, which measures 4-1/4" and is worth $170.

Photo courtesy Goebel of North America.

Left: Carries mold number 11/2/0, Full Bee in an incised circle, black "Germany," seven buttons on vest, and 4-3/8". Right: 11/0, Stylized Bee, five vest buttons, and 4-5/8".

Hum 12: Chimney Sweep

When first introduced in 1935 as part of the original group displayed at the Leipzig Fair, this figure was called "Smoky." It was first designed by master sculptor Arthur Moeller in 1935 with several restylings through the years.

The small 4" size was not added to the line until well into the 1950s, and consequently, no Crown Mark (TMK-1) pieces are found in that size. There are many variations in size, but none are significant. Examples found in sales lists are 4", 5-1/2", 6-1/4", and 6-3/8".

There was a surprise in store for those who bought the 1992 Sampler (a Hummel introductory kit). In it was the usual club membership discount and that year's figurine, Chimney Sweep. Along with the figure came a special display base of a rooftop and chimney.

In 1995, Goebel produced for German retail promotion a special edition of the Chimney Sweep with a gilded base. The edition was limited to 500 pieces.

Hum No.	Basic Size	Trademark	Current Value
12/2/0	4"	TMK-2	$250-$325
12/2/0	4"	TMK-3	$175-$200
12/2/0	4"	TMK-4	$160-$175
12/2/0	4"	TMK-5	$150-$160
12/2/0	4"	TMK-6	$145-$150
12	5-1/2"	TMK-1	$700-$850
12	5-1/2"	TMK-2	$425-$500
12/I	5-1/2"	TMK-1	$700-$850
12/I	5-1/2"	TMK-2	$425-$500
12/I	5-1/2"	TMK-3	$350-$410
12/I	5-1/2"	TMK-4	$325-$350
12/I	5-1/2"	TMK-5	$270-$300
12/I	5-1/2"	TMK-6	$260-$270
12/I	5-1/2"	TMK-7	$255-$260
12/I	5-1/2"	TMK-8	$260

From left, Chimney Sweep, Hum 12, with 12/I mold number, Full Bee mark, and doughnut base, and another 12/I variation but with Stylized Bee, and doughnut base.

The 4" variation of Chimney Sweep, Hum 12/2/0, last appeared in TMK-6.

Photo courtesy Goebel of North America.

Hum 13: Meditation

The Hum 13/0 and the Hum 13/II sizes were the first to be released in 1935 and were first modeled by Reinhold Unger.

The most significant variations are with regard to the flowers in the baskets. When first released, the 13/II had flowers in the basket, but sometime in the Last Bee (TMK-5) era, the piece was restyled by master sculptor Gerhard Skrobek to reflect no flowers in the basket, and the style remains so today.

Variations in the Hum 13/0 are with regard to the pigtails. The first models of the figure in the Crown Mark (TMK-1) era sported short pigtails with a painted red ribbon. By the time the Full Bee (TMK-2) was being utilized, the ribbon had disappeared and the pigtails had grown longer.

The larger Hum 13/V was copyrighted in 1957 and has a basket filled with flowers. It is scarce in the older trademarks and hardly ever found for sale. It was temporarily withdrawn from production on December 31, 1989. Also temporarily withdrawn were 13/2/0 and 13/0 pieces in January 1999.

There is a very unusual and probably unique Meditation that has a bowl attached to its side. There have been three different figurines found with bowls attached. The other two are Goose Girl and Congratulations.

Meditation, Hum 13. Left: The old style 13/2, 7" size with flowers in the basket, Double Crown Mark, and "Made in Germany" beneath the base. Right: The newer style 13/II, 7" size without any flowers in the basket. The latter has TMK-6.

Hum No.	Basic Size	Trademark	Current Value
13/2/0	4-1/4"	TMK-2	$250-$350
13/2/0	4-1/4"	TMK-3	$225-$250
13/2/0	4-1/4"	TMK-4	$190-$225
13/2/0	4-1/4"	TMK-5	$175-$190
13/2/0	4-1/4"	TMK-6	$160-$170
13/0	5-1/4"	TMK-1	$700-$850
13/0	6"	TMK-2	$425-$500
13/0	5-1/4"	TMK-3	$350-$400
13/0	5"	TMK-4	$325-$350
13/0	5"	TMK-5	$270-$300
13/0	5"	TMK-6	$260-$270

Hum No.	Basic Size	Trademark	Current Value
13/0	5"	TMK-7	$245-$260
13/II (13/2) with flowers	7"	TMK-1	$4,000-$5,000
13/II (13/2) with flowers	7"	TMK-2	$3,500-$4,000
13/II (13/2) with flowers	7"	TMK-3	$3,000-$3,500
13/II	7"	TMK-5	$410-$455
13/II	7"	TMK-6	$350-$410
13/V	13-3/4"	TMK-1	$4,000-$5,000
13/V	13-3/4"	TMK-2	$3,000-$3,500
13/V	13-3/4"	TMK-3	$1,700-$2,200
13/V	13-3/4"	TMK-4	$1,350-$1,500
13/V	13-3/4"	TMK-5	$1,300-$1,350
13/V	13-3/4"	TMK-6	$1,200-$1,300

Hum 14/A and Hum 14/B: Book Worms (Bookends)

These are two figures, a boy and a girl (see Hum 3 and Hum 8). As far as is known to date, there is no other occurrence of the boy Book Worm anywhere else in the collection. It occurs only in conjunction with the bookends (Hum 14/A and Hum 14/B) in only one size. Early marketed boy pieces were titled "Learned Man."

These bookends do not have wooden bases. (Other bookends in the collection typically do have wooden bases.) There are holes on the bottom where the figures are weighted with sand, etc., and usually sealed with cork, a plastic plug, or a factory sticker, gold in color.

These bookends were temporarily withdrawn on December 31, 1989, but in 1993, they could be purchased by mail-order from Danbury Mint, thus the existence of the TMK-7 pieces.

Bookworms bookends, Hum 14 A and Hum 14 B. Both have TMK-3 in an incised circle and black "Western Germany."

Hum No.	Basic Size	Trademark	Current Value		Hum No.	Basic Size	Trademark	Current Value
14	5-1/2"	TMK-1	$600-$800		14/A&B	5-1/2"	TMK-4	$550-$600
14/A&B	5-1/2"	TMK-1	$1,200-$1,600		14/A&B	5-1/2"	TMK-5	$500-$550
14/A&B	5-1/2"	TMK-2	$650-$750		14/A&B	5-1/2"	TMK-6	$450-$500
14/A&B	5-1/2"	TMK-3	$600-$650		14/A&B	5-1/2"	TMK-7	$400-$450

Hum 15: Hear Ye, Hear Ye

Among the first 46 to be released by Goebel at the Leipzig Fair, this figure was first called "Night Watchman" and remained so until around 1950. It was first modeled by master sculptor Arthur Moeller in 1935.

Serious collectors seek out the larger 7-1/2" size with the Arabic size designator "15/2," for it represents the oldest of Crown Mark (TMK-1) figures and is worth up to $1,700.

Also sought-after—but very rare—are a few early samples in the faience style, which are valued at $3,000-$5,000.

In January 2002, the QVC offered a special 1,000-piece limited edition Hear Ye! Hear Ye! Progression Set (Hum 15/0). The set consisted of three figurines—one in whiteware, one partially painted, and one completed—along with a wooden display stand with commemorative porcelain plaque and authentic Goebel painter's brush. On Holiday (Hum 350) was offered in the same type of progression set later in the year.

Both the 15/I and 15/II sizes have been temporarily withdrawn, while the 15/0 variation remains in production today.

Photo courtesy Goebel of North America.

The most recent variation of Hear Ye, Hear Ye, Hum 15/2/0, which is in production today and is valued at $185.

Hear Ye, Hear Ye, Hum 15. Left: Carries 15/0 mold number, stamped Crown Mark (TMK-1), and has doughnut base. Right: Another 15/0 mold number, but with Full Bee (TMK-2), doughnut base, and black "Germany."

Hum No.	Basic Size	Trademark	Current Value
15/2/0	4"	TMK-6	$185-$190
15/2/0	4"	TMK-7	$180-$185
15/2/0	4"	TMK-8	$185
15/0	5"	TMK-1	$600-$750
15/0	5"	TMK-2	$350-$450
15/0	5"	TMK-3	$300-$325
15/0	5"	TMK-4	$275-$300
15/0	5"	TMK-5	$250-$270
15/0	5"	TMK-6	$240-$250
15/0	5"	TMK-7	$230-$240
15/0	5"	TMK-8	$240
15/I	6"	TMK-1	$700-$900
15/I	6"	TMK-2	$450-$600
15/I	6"	TMK-3	$375-$400
15/I	6"	TMK-4	$350-$375
15/I	6"	TMK-5	$310-$340
15/I	6"	TMK-6	$290-$310

Hum No.	Basic Size	Trademark	Current Value	Hum No.	Basic Size	Trademark	Current Value
15/I	6"	TMK-7	$280-$285	15/II	7-1/2"	TMK-4	$550-$650
15/II	7-1/2"	TMK-1	$1,200-$1,500	15/II	7-1/2"	TMK-5	$500-$525
15/II	7-1/2"	TMK-2	$750-$1,000	15/II	7-1/2"	TMK-6	$475-$500
15/II	7-1/2"	TMK-3	$650-$750	15/II	7-1/2"	TMK-7	$450-$475
				15	7-1/2"	TMK-1	$1,400-$1,700

Hum 16: Little Hiker

Modeled by master sculptor Arthur Moeller, Little Hiker is one of the original 46 released in the 16/I and 16/2/0 sizes and was originally referred to as "Happy-Go-Lucky."

The only significant variation is with the mold number. The mold number is sometimes found with only the 16 and sometimes with the decimal designator "16." in the 5-1/2" to 6" size. These are found with the Crown (TMK-1) and the Full Bee (TMK-2) trademarks and will bring about 15% more than comparably trademarked 16/I figures.

Early painting samples have been found with a green jacket and blue hat. These are worth $1,500-$2,000. And if found with an attached pot as shown in an old company product book, the piece would be worth $5,000-$10,000.

The 16/I size has been temporarily withdrawn from production, and the 16/2/0 variation was permanently retired on December 31, 2002. Those made in 2002 bear a "Final Issue 2002" backstamp and came with a "Final Issue" medallion.

Hum No.	Basic Size	Trademark	Current Value
16/2/0	4-1/4"	TMK-1	$350-$450
16/2/0	4-1/4"	TMK-2	$250-$300
16/2/0	4-1/4"	TMK-3	$175-$200
16/2/0	4-1/4"	TMK-4	$160-$175
16/2/0	4-1/4"	TMK-5	$150-$160
16/2/0	4-1/4"	TMK-6	$145-$150
16/2/0	4-1/4"	TMK-7	$140-$145
16/2/0	4-1/4"	TMK-8	$145
16/I	5-1/2"	TMK-1	$600-$700
16/I	5-1/2"	TMK-2	$400-$500
16/I	5-1/2"	TMK-3	$350-$400
16/I	5-1/2"	TMK-4	$300-$350
16/I	5-1/2"	TMK-5	$275-$300
16/I	5-1/2"	TMK-6	$260-$275
16/I	5-1/2"	TMK-7	$245-$250

Little Hiker, Hum 16. Left is a Double Crown Marked (TMK-1) piece measuring 5-1/2" with black "Made in Germany" beneath the base. The one on the right has an incised Full Bee (TMK-2) and a stamped Full Bee mark as well. It measures 5-7/8" and has a black "Germany" beneath the base.

In production today (TMK-8) is Little Hiker, Hum 16/2/0, at 4-1/4" and worth $145.

Photo courtesy Goebel of North America.

Hum 17: Congratulations

One of the original 1935 releases, Congratulations was first modeled by master sculptor Reinhold Unger.

There is a very unusual, perhaps unique, version of this piece where a bowl is attached to the figurine's right rear. The figurine in this version does not have the normal base.

When first modeled, the girl had no socks. Later versions (after 1970) have a new hairstyle that appears to be a little longer. The flowers in the pot are larger, and the girl wears socks. This change was made during the Three Line Mark (TMK-4) and Stylized Bee (TMK-5) eras, so you can find either version with these marks. Obviously, the no-socks piece would be the more desirable one.

Once again, an early product book shows a sample with an attached pot. If found, that piece is worth $5,000-$10,000.

The final issue of this figurine was produced in 1999.

Hum No.	Basic Size	Trademark	Current Value
17/0 (no socks)	6"	TMK-1	$600-$750
17/0 (no socks)	6"	TMK-2	$350-$450
17/0 (no socks)	6"	TMK-3	$300-$325
17/0 (no socks)	6"	TMK-4	$275-$300
17/0 (socks)	6"	TMK-5	$250-$275
17/0 (socks)	6"	TMK-6	$240-$250
17/0	6"	TMK-7	$230-$235
17/2 or 17/II	8-1/4"	TMK-1	$6,500-$8,000
17/2 or 17/II	8-1/4"	TMK-2	$5,500-$6,500
17/2 or 17/II	8-1/4"	TMK-3	$4,500-$5,500

Congratulations, Hum 17. Left: With 17/0 mold number and Double Crown Mark (TMK-1), 3-3/4". Right: With 17/0 mold number and Small Stylized Bee (TMK-3).

The latest variation of Congratulations, Hum 17/0, occurred in TMK-7.

Hum 18: Christ Child

Originally called "Christmas Night," this figure is very similar to the Christ Child figure used in the Nativity Sets, Hum 214 and 260.

First modeled by master sculptor Reinhold Unger in 1935, it has been produced in a solid white overglaze and sold in Belgium. This white overglaze piece is rare.

Christ Child was temporarily withdrawn from production at the end of 1990, was reinstated in 1997, and again temporarily withdrawn in January 1999.

Hum No.	Basic Size	Trademark	Current Value
18	3-3/4" x 6-1/2"	TMK-1	$400-$550
18	3-3/4" x 6-1/2"	TMK-2	$250-$300
18	3-3/4" x 6-1/2"	TMK-3	$225-$250
18	3-1/4" x 6"	TMK-4	$200-$225
18	3-1/4" x 6"	TMK-5	$175-$200
18	3-1/4" x 6"	TMK-6	$170-$175
18	3-1/4" x 6"	TMK-7	$165-$170

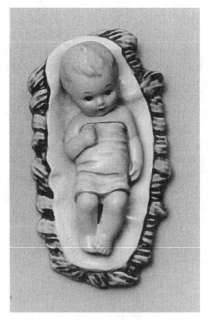

Christ Child, Hum 18, with Stylized Bee mark (TMK-3).

Hum 19: Prayer Before Battle (Ashtray, Closed Number)

Until 1986, when one of these surfaced in the United States, it was thought this was a closed number and the piece was never produced.

Even though one was found (temporarily), it may well be the only one ever made. The reason the term "temporarily" is used is as follows: It seems that a lady brought the piece to the Goebel Collectors' Club in Tarrytown, New York, for identification. The paint finish was badly damaged as a result of her having put it in a dishwasher to clean it. Goebel master sculptor Gerhard Skrobek coincidentally was there. He speculated that the reason the paint was damaged was because it was probably a sample piece, painted but never fired so that the paint had not bonded to the figurine.

Subsequent investigation of Goebel records revealed that the design was rejected by the Siessen Convent, and therefore never placed in production. Furthermore, there is no example in the company archives. How it got out of the factory and to the U.S. remains a mystery. It seems the lady left, taking her piece with her, and no one present could remember her name or where she was from.

The most recent footnote to this story: A noted and very serious collector pursued the search until he finally did find the ashtray and its owner. His attempt to purchase it, however, was rebuffed due to a sentimental attachment to the piece.

Hum No.	Basic Size	Trademark	Current Value
19	5-1/2"	TMK-1	$5,000-$10,000

Hum 20: Prayer Before Battle

First made by master sculptor Arthur Moeller, few changes of any significance have affected the collector value of this piece since its initial release in 1935. It has been listed at 4" and 4-1/2" in the price lists over the years.

There has been one most unusual figure uncovered, which exhibits peculiar color variations (see accompanying photographs). The horse is gray, black, and white instead of the normal tan, the wagon is a dark green with red wheels, the socks are the same green color, and his clothes are dark green and brown. The horn is a shiny gold. This may be a one-of-a-kind experimental piece that somehow made it out of the factory, but who knows? It is from the late Ed Wunner's collection.

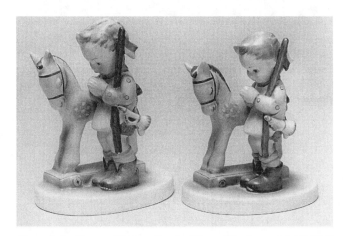

From left, Prayer Before Battle, Hum 20, first with TMK-2 and black "Germany," and then with TMK-5.

Prayer Before Battle, Hum 20, with peculiar color variations.

Another view of the Prayer Before Battle with the unusual paint colors.

Today's rendition (TMK-8) of Prayer Before Battle, Hum 20, which is worth $200.

Hum No.	Basic Size	Trademark	Current Value	Hum No.	Basic Size	Trademark	Current Value
20	4-1/4"	TMK-1	$500-$650	20	4-1/4"	TMK-6	$225-$250
20	4-1/4"	TMK-2	$350-$400	20	4-1/4"	TMK-7	$200-$225
20	4-1/4"	TMK-3	$300-$350	20	4-1/4"	TMK-8	$200
20	4-1/4"	TMK-4	$275-$300				
20	4-1/4"	TMK-5	$250-$275				

Hum 21: Heavenly Angel

First known as the "Little Guardian" or "Celestial Messenger," this figure was among the 46 original releases in 1935 and was first modeled by master sculptor Reinhold Unger.

This is the same motif used on the famous 1971 annual plate by Goebel and the Schmid company—the first-ever annual Hummel plate.

The 21/0 size was the first to be introduced. It was followed by the larger sizes soon after.

The only variation of any significance in terms of value is the white overglaze model. It has not been found, but factory records indicate that it was produced.

Both the 21/I and 21/II sizes have been temporarily withdrawn, but 21/0 and 21/0/1/2 variations remain in production today.

Hum No.	Basic Size	Trademark	Current Value
21/0	4-1/4"	TMK-1	$400-$500
21/I	4-1/4"	TMK-2	$225-$275
21/0	4-1/4"	TMK-3	$190-$210
21/0	4-1/4"	TMK-4	$170-$180
21/0	4-1/4"	TMK-5	$160-$170
21/0	4-1/4"	TMK-6	$155-$160
21/0	4-1/4"	TMK-7	$150-$155

From left, Heavenly Angel, Hum 21, with TMK-3 and TMK-5. Both have the mold numbers rendered as 21/0.

Hum No.	Basic Size	Trademark	Current Value
21/0	4-1/4"	TMK-8	$150
21/0/1/2*	6"	TMK-1	$700-$800
21/0/1/2*	6"	TMK-2	$425-$500
21/0/1/2*	6"	TMK-3	$350-$400
21/0/1/2*	6"	TMK-4	$325-$350
21/0/1/2*	6"	TMK-5	$280-$300
21/0/1/2*	6"	TMK-6	$270-$280
21/0/1/2*	6"	TMK-7	$260-$270
21/0/1/2*	6"	TMK-8	$260
21/I	6-3/4"	TMK-1	$750-$1,000
21/I	6-3/4"	TMK-2	$450-$550
21/I	6-3/4"	TMK-3	$400-$450
21/I	6-3/4"	TMK-4	$325-$375
21/I	6-3/4"	TMK-5	$320-$325
21/I	6-3/4"	TMK-6	$320-$325
21/I	6-3/4"	TMK-7	$310-$320
21/II	8-3/4"	TMK-1	$1,200-$1,600
21/II	8-3/4"	TMK-2	$700-$1,000
21/II	8-3/4"	TMK-3	$600-$700
21/II	8-3/4"	TMK-4	$500-$600
21/II	8-3/4"	TMK-5	$450-$475
21/II	8-3/4"	TMK-6	$430-$450
21/II	8-3/4"	TMK-7	$425-$430

Photo courtesy Goebel of North America.

The 21/I variation of Heavenly Angel, which measures 6-3/4" and last appeared in TMK-7, is worth $310-$320.

*One of the only two pieces in the Goebel collection where this "1/2" (one-half) designator is used. The other is Blessed Child, Hum 78.

Hum 22: Angel With Bird (Holy Water Font)

TMK-3 variation of Angel With Bird font, Hum 22/0.

A figure sometimes known as "Seated Angel With Bird" or "Sitting Angel," this piece was modeled by master sculptor Reinhold Unger. This font has variations in bowl design and appears in two basic sizes. The mold number 22 has been known to appear with the decimal point size designator (22.). The latter will bring about 15% more than the 22/0 counterpart in the Crown Mark (TMK-1). The 22/I size is a closed edition.

Hum No.	Basic Size	Trademark	Current Value
22	3-1/8" x 4-1/2"	TMK-1	$300-$325
22/0	2-3/4" x 3-1/2"	TMK-1	$250-$300
22/0	2-3/4" x 3-1/2"	TMK-2	$125-$150
22/0	2-3/4" x 3-1/2"	TMK-3	$75-$85
22/0	2-3/4" x 3-1/2"	TMK-4	$70-$75
22/0	2-3/4" x 3-1/2"	TMK-5	$65-$70
22/0	2-3/4" x 3-1/2"	TMK-6	$60-$65
22/0	2-3/4" x 3-1/2"	TMK-7	$55-$60
22/0	2-3/4" x 3-1/2"	TMK-8	$55
22/I	3-1/4" x 4-7/8"	TMK-1	$500-$600
22/I	3-1/4" x 4-7/8"	TMK-2	$400-$500
22/I	3-1/4" x 4-7/8"	TMK-3	$300-$400

Hum 23: Adoration

Known in the early years as "Ave Maria" and "At the Shrine," this member of the 1935 group was first modeled by master sculptor Reinhold Unger and originally released in the smaller size. Soon after came the 23/III variation.

Both sizes have been produced in white overglaze, but they are quite scarce. When found for sale, the white overglaze pieces usually go for about $1,500-$2,000 for the 6-1/4" size and $3,000-$4,000 for the 9" variation.

The 23/III size was temporarily withdrawn from production in January 1999.

Hum No.	Basic Size	Trademark	Current Value
23/I	6-1/4"	TMK-1	$1,000-$1,300
23/I	6-1/4"	TMK-2	$600-$800
23/I	6-1/4"	TMK-3	$500-$575
23/I	6-1/4"	TMK-4	$400-$500
23/I	6-1/4"	TMK-5	$425-$450
23/I	6-1/4"	TMK-6	$410-$420
23/I	6-1/4"	TMK-7	$400-$410
23/I	6-1/4"	TMK-8	$400
23/III	9"	TMK-1	$1,600-$2,100
23/III	9"	TMK-1	$1,500-$2,000
23/III	9"	TMK-2	$900-$1,250
23/III	9"	TMK-3	$800-$900
23/III	9"	TMK-4	$675-$775
23/III	9"	TMK-5	$625-$675
23/III	9"	TMK-6	$600-$625
23/III	9"	TMK-7	$595-$600

Adoration, Hum 23. Left: 23/I mold number, TMK-3 in an incised circle, black "Western Germany," and measuring 6-1/2". Right: 23/III mold number, TMK-5, split base (diagonally), and measuring 9".

The present-day variation of Adoration, 23/I, measuring 6-1/4" and bearing TMK-8.

Photo courtesy Goebel of North America.

Hum 24: Lullaby (Candleholder)

This piece, which was modeled by both master sculptors Arthur Moeller and Reinhold Unger, is quite similar to Hum 262, except that this one is a candleholder.

The larger 24/III was temporarily withdrawn from production for some time and reinstated in the early 1980s. It disappeared once again, however, from the Goebel price lists in 1982 and has remained withdrawn for several years.

The other size, 24/I, was listed as temporarily withdrawn at the end of 1989. By 1995, it was back on the suggested retail price list, only to be temporarily withdrawn again in January 1999.

The larger (24/III) was out of production for some time, but has recently been reissued. The 24/III bearing older marks command premium prices. The 24/III is sometimes found as 24/3.

Both sizes are known to have been made in white overglaze in the Full Bee (TMK-2) era. When found, they are worth $2,000-$4,000 apiece today.

Back in 1992, Carl Luckey received a letter from a collector describing a "Lullabye" candleholder with a "music box attached." It was purchased in 1951 in Hawaii. Carl was unable to confirm this and has no photo, but as he wrote in the last edition of this book, "it may be out there."

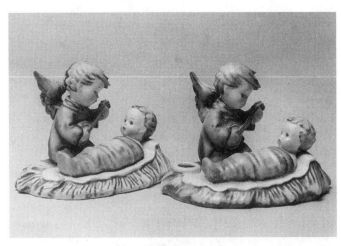

Lullaby candleholder, Hum 24. Left: Bears the mold number 24/1 and a small Stylized Bee (TMK-3). Right: Bears the mold number 24/I and the Last Bee (TMK-5). Note the candle hole variation. The older one is molded so the hole is not obvious without the candle in it.

Hum No.	Basic Size	Trademark	Current Value
24/I	3-1/4" x 5"	TMK-1	$550-$700
24/I	3-1/4" x 5"	TMK-2	$350-$430
24/I	3-1/4" x 5"	TMK-3	$275-$300
24/I	3-1/4" x 5"	TMK-4	$250-$275
24/I	3-1/4" x 5"	TMK-5	$230-$250
24/I	3-1/4" x 5"	TMK-6	$220-$230
24/I	3-1/4" x 5"	TMK-7	$210-$220
24/III	6" x 8-3/4"	TMK-1	$1,500-$1,900
24/III	6" x 8-3/4"	TMK-2	$950-$1,250
24/III	6" x 8-3/4"	TMK-3	$600-$700
24/III	6" x 8-3/4"	TMK-4	$525-$600
24/III	6" x 8-3/4"	TMK-5	$500-$525
24/III	6" x 8-3/4"	TMK-6	$475-$500

Hum 25: Angelic Sleep (Candleholder)

This candleholder is one of the original 46 figures displayed at the Leipzig Fair in 1935 and was called "Angel's Joy" in some early company literature. The design is credited to both master sculptors Arthur Moeller and Reinhold Unger.

It was made in white overglaze for a short period, but not for export to the U.S. The white overglaze pieces are considered rare and can bring $1,500-$2,000 when sold.

It was temporarily withdrawn on December 31, 1989.

From left, Angelic Sleep, Hum 25, with TMK-2 and black "Germany," and with TMK-3.

Hum No.	Basic Size	Trademark	Current Value
25	3-1/2" x 5"	TMK-1	$550-$700
25	3-1/2" x 5"	TMK-2	$350-$425
25 (white)	3-1/2" x 5"	TMK-2	$1,500-$2,000
25	3-1/2" x 5"	TMK-3	$260-$280
25	3-1/2" x 5"	TMK-4	$225-$260
25	3-1/2" x 5"	TMK-5	$215-$225
25	3-1/2" x 5"	TMK-6	$200-$215

Angelic Sleep, Hum 25, rear view TMK-2 and TMK-3 variations in the other photo, this time showing the hole variations between the two.

Hum 26: Child Jesus (Holy Water Font)

This font is one of the original 1935 releases and was first modeled by master sculptor Reinhold Unger.

The color of the robe is normally a deep orange-red. A very significant variation has appeared in the Stylized Bee (TMK-3) 26/0 size in which the robe has also been found as either light blue or green.

The font has been produced in two sizes all along, although the larger size has not appeared in the Goebel price list since the TMK-3 era, and the other size was temporarily withdrawn from production in January 1999.

TMK-3 version of Child Jesus font, Hum 26/0.

Hum No.	Basic Size	Trademark	Current Value
26/0	2-3/4" x 5"	TMK-1	$225-$275
26/0	2-3/4" x 5"	TMK-2	$125-$150
26/0	2-3/4" x 5"	TMK-3	$75-$85
26/0	2-3/4" x 5"	TMK-4	$60-$75
26/0	2-3/4" x 5"	TMK-5	$55-$60
26/0	2-3/4" x 5"	TMK-6	$50-$55
26/0	2-3/4" x 5"	TMK-7	$50-$52
26	3" x 5-3/4"	TMK-1	$350-$550
26/I	3-1/4" x 6"	TMK-1	$350-$550
26/I	3-1/4" x 6"	TMK-2	$250-$300
26/I	3-1/4" x 6"	TMK-3	$200-$250

Hum 27: Joyous News

First modeled by master sculptor Reinhold Unger in 1935, this piece is considered to be fairly scarce in the first three trademarks. As far as is presently known, there are probably less than 100 in collectors' hands.

The 27/III, which has been temporarily withdrawn from production, is sometimes found as 27/3 in the TMK-5 era.

Older marked figures command a premium price. There is a smaller size (27/I), but it is rare. This 2-3/4" version is a candleholder. There are only a few presently known to exist.

Hum No.	Basic Size	Trademark	Current Value
27/I	2-3/4"	TMK-1	$300-$500
27/I	2-3/4"	TMK-2	$250-$400
27/III	4-1/4" x 4-3/4"	TMK-1	$1,500-$2,000
27/III	4-1/4" x 4-3/4"	TMK-2	$1,000-$1,500
27/III	4-1/4" x 4-3/4"	TMK-3	$750-$1,000
27/III (27/3)	4-1/4" x 4-3/4"	TMK-5	$265-$280

Hum No.	Basic Size	Trademark	Current Value
27/III	4-1/4" x 4-3/4"	TMK-6	$250-$265
27/III	4-1/4" x 4-3/4"	TMK-7	$245-$250

Joyous News, Hum 27/3, with TMK-3 in an incised circle and black "Western Germany."

Hum 28: Wayside Devotion

This figurine is one of the initial 1935 designs displayed at the Leipzig Fair and has been called "The Little Shepherd" and "Evensong" over the years. It was first modeled by master sculptor Reinhold Unger.

Both sizes have been found with the Arabic size designator 28/2 and 28/3. The larger, 8-1/2" size also appears without the designator on all on the Crown Mark (TMK-1) figurines. These are valued at roughly 20% above the regularly marked counterpart.

The figure was produced for a short time in white overglaze. These are considered rare and are valued at about $3,000.

The 28/III size was temporarily withdrawn from production on June 15, 2002.

Hum No.	Basic Size	Trademark	Current Value
28/II	7" to 7-1/2"	TMK-1	$1,200-$1,500
28/II	7" to 7-1/2"	TMK-2	$750-$900
28/II	7" to 7-1/2"	TMK-3	$600-$700
28/II	7" to 7-1/2"	TMK-4	$550-$600
28/II	7" to 7-1/2"	TMK-5	$500-$550
28/II	7" to 7-1/2"	TMK-6	$485-$500
28/II	7" to 7-1/2"	TMK-7	$475-$485
28/II	7" to 7-1/2"	TMK-8	$475
28	8-3/4"	TMK-1	$1,700-$1,900
28/III	8-3/4"	TMK-1	$1,400-$1,700

From left, Wayside Devotion, Hum 28/II, first with TMK-3 and then with TMK-5.

Hum No.	Basic Size	Trademark	Current Value
28/III	8-3/4"	TMK-2	$1,000-$1,200
28/III	8-3/4"	TMK-3	$800-$900
28/III	8-3/4"	TMK-4	$700-$800
28/III	8-3/4"	TMK-5	$650-$700
28/III	8-3/4"	TMK-6	$625-$650
28/III	8-3/4"	TMK-7	$600-$615

Hum 29: Guardian Angel (Holy Water Font, Closed Edition)

This figure, which was first modeled in two sizes by master sculptor Reinhold Unger in 1935, is not in current production (closed edition) and is highly sought by collectors. A similar piece (Hum 248) exists and is considered to be a redesign of Hum 29. Hum 29 is, therefore, unlikely to ever be reissued. It has been found with the decimal point designator (29.).

Guardian Angel font, Hum 29, with incised Crown Mark.

Hum No.	Basic Size	Trademark	Current Value
29.	2-3/4" x 6"	TMK-1	$1,300-$1,500
29/0	2-1/2" x 5-5/8"	TMK-1	$1,300-$1,500
29/0	2-1/2" x 5-5/8"	TMK-2	$1,000-$1,250
29/0	2-1/2" x 5-5/8"	TMK-3	$900-$1,000
29/I	3" x 6-3/8"	TMK-1	$1,750-$2,000
29/I	3" x 6-3/8"	TMK-2	$1,500-$1,750

Hum 30/A and Hum 30/B: Ba-Bee Rings (Wall Plaques)

Part of the original collection released in 1935, these wall plaques were first called "Hummel Rings" and were modeled by master sculptor Reinhold Unger. They are found in two basic sizes.

Figures with the rings painted red in the Crown (TMK-1) era are found in both sizes and there has been at least one reported in bisque finish in the 30/0 size. Both of these are considered rare. They are also possibly found in the white overglaze finish. Value in red rings: $6,000-$9,000.

The figure remains in production in a buff color (rings) in the smaller size only.

Hum No.	Basic Size	Trademark	Current Value
30/A&B	4-3/4" x 5"	TMK-1	$550-$700
30/A&B	4-3/4" x 5"	TMK-2	$350-$450
30/0 A&B	4-3/4" x 5"	TMK-3	$290-$310
30/0 A&B	4-3/4" x 5"	TMK-4	$260-$280
30/0 A&B	4-3/4" x 5"	TMK-5	$250-$260
30/0 A&B	4-3/4" x 5"	TMK-6	$240-$250
30/0 A&B	4-3/4" x 5"	TMK-7	$236-$240
30/0 A&B	4-3/4" x 5"	TMK-8	$236
30/I A&B	5-1/4" x 6"	TMK-1	$2,000-$3,500
30/0 A&B (red rings)		TMK-1	$6,000-$7,000
30/1 A&B (red rings)		TMK-1	$8,000-$9,000

Ba-Bee Rings. Left: Mold number 30/0/B with Crown Mark and red in color. Right: With 30/1. mold number, Double Crown Mark and also red in color.

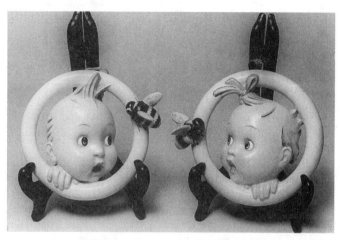

Ba-Bee Rings. Left: With 30/1., Double Crown Mark, and light tan color. Right: With 30/1/B mold number, incised Crown Mark, and light tan color.

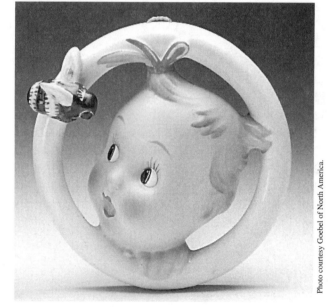

Today's version (TMK-8) of Ba-Bee Rings wall plaques, Hum 30/A and 30/B.

Photo courtesy Goebel of North America.

Hum 31: Advent Group (Candleholder)

This candleholder, which was first modeled by master sculptor Arthur Moeller in 1935, was often called "Advent Group" or "Silent Night with Black Child" until several of the same mold numbers began showing up with a white child in the left where the black child had ordinarily been. It is thought by some that, in fact, the white child version may be the more rare of the two. Whatever the case, both are quite rare.

Very similar to Silent Night (Hum 54), Hum 31 was produced first in 1935 with the other original 45. Both versions have been found in the Crown Mark (TMK-1) only. (See also Hum 54, Hum 113, and Hum 754.)

Hum No.	Basic Size	Trademark	Current Value
31	3-1/2" x 5"	TMK-1	$20,000-$25,000 (black child)
31	3-1/2" x 5"	TMK-1	$20,000-$25,000 (white child)

Two Crown Mark examples of Advent Group, Hum 31.

Hum 32: Little Gabriel

When first released in 1935, this figure was called "Joyous News." Master sculptor Reinhold Unger is responsible for the first design.

Only the 5" size (Hum 32 without the "/I" designator) continued in production into the 1990s, but has now been temporarily withdrawn.

Little Gabriel was redesigned in 1982. The older pieces have the arms that are attached to each other up to the hands. The newer design has the arms separated.

Hum No.	Basic Size	Trademark	Current Value
32/0	5"	TMK-1	$450-$550
32/0	5"	TMK-2	$300-$375
32/0	5"	TMK-3	$225-$250
32/0	5"	TMK-4	$200-$225
32/0	5"	TMK-5	$180-$200
32/0	5"	TMK-6	$125
32	5"	TMK-5	$180-$200
32	5"	TMK-6	$170-$180
32	5"	TMK-7	$165-$170
32	6"	TMK-1	$2,000-$2,500
32	6"	TMK-2	$1,500-$2,000
32/I	6"	TMK-1	$2,000-$2,500
32/I	6"	TMK-2	$1,500-$2,000
32/I	6"	TMK-3	$1,200-$1,500

Little Gabriel, Hum 32. Left: figure is a Hum 32/0 with a Full Bee (TMK-2) mark. On the right is a TMK-6 piece with mold number 32.

Hum 33: Joyful (Ashtray)

This is an ashtray, first modeled by master sculptor Reinhold Unger in 1935, that utilizes a figure very similar to Hum 53 (Joyful figurine), with the addition of a small bird on the edge of the tray next to the boy. This piece was temporarily removed from production December 31, 1984, and numerous Hummel experts predict it will never be produced again.

The piece has been found in the faience finish, which yields a value of $3,000-$5,000.

Typically the figure wears a blue dress and orange shoes, but a variation with the colors switched—orange dress and blue shoes—has surfaced. It is worth $2,000-$3,000.

Hum No.	Basic Size	Trademark	Current Value
33	3-1/2" x 6"	TMK-1	$400-$650
33	3-1/2" x 6"	TMK-2	$300-$350
33	3-1/2" x 6"	TMK-3	$220-$250
33	3-1/2" x 6"	TMK-4	$200-$220
33	3-1/2" x 6"	TMK-5	$190-$200
33	3-1/2" x 6"	TMK-6	$175-$190

Joyful ashtray, Hum 33. Both bear the Crown Mark (TMK-1) and measure 3-3/4". The one on the left is an example of the faience pieces. This one is rather poorly and gaudily painted. See color section and Chapter Five.

Hum 34: Singing Lesson (Ashtray)

Master sculptor Arthur Moeller is credited with the design of this ashtray, which utilizes a figure very similar to Hum 64, with a small bird perched on the edge of the tray instead of the boy's shoes.

This ashtray was listed as temporarily withdrawn from production at the end of 1989.

Hum No.	Basic Size	Trademark	Current Value
33	3-1/2" x 6"	TMK-1	$450-$650
33	3-1/2" x 6"	TMK-2	$300-$350
33	3-1/2" x 6"	TMK-3	$220-$250
33	3-1/2" x 6"	TMK-4	$200-$220
33	3-1/2" x 6"	TMK-5	$190-$200
33	3-1/2" x 6"	TMK-6	$175-$190

Singing Lesson ashtray, Hum 34. Left: Full Bee mark (TMK-2). This is an oversize ashtray measuring 4" x 6-1/2". Right: Stylized Bee (TMK-3), 3-7/8" x 6-3/16".

Hum 35: Good Shepherd (Holy Water Font)

Part of the original collection released in 1935, this figurine, which was designed by master sculptor Reinhold Unger, has had only minor modifications over the years. It remains in production today in the 35/0 size with no significant variations affecting collector value.

Good Shepherd font, Hum 35. Left: Double Crown mark, 5-1/2". Right: No apparent mark other than the mold number, 4-5/8".

Hum No.	Basic Size	Trademark	Current Value
35/0	2-1/4" x 4-3/4"	TMK-1	$225-$275
35/0	2-1/4" x 4-3/4"	TMK-2	$125-$150
35/0	2-1/4" x 4-3/4"	TMK-3	$75-$85
35/0	2-1/4" x 4-3/4"	TMK-4	$70-$75
35/0	2-1/4" x 4-3/4"	TMK-5	$65-$70
35/0	2-1/4" x 4-3/4"	TMK-6	$60-$65
35/0	2-1/2" x 4-3/4"	TMK-7	$55-$60
35/0	2-1/2" x 4-3/4"	TMK-8	$55
35	2-1/4" x 4-3/4"	TMK-1	$400-$450
35/I	2-3/4" x 5-3/4"	TMK-1	$375-$425
35/I	2-3/4" x 5-3/4"	TMK-2	$275-$375
35/I	2-3/4" x 5-3/4"	TMK-3	$175-$225

Good Shepherd font with 35/0 mold number and Stylized Bee (TMK-3).

Hum 36: Child With Flowers (Holy Water Font)

Child With Flowers font, Hum 36/0 with TMK-5 at 4-1/4".

Designed by master sculptor Reinhold Unger, this font is one of the original 46 released in 1935. It also has been called "Flower Angel" and "Angel With Flowers."

There have been only minor modifications over the years, other than that it has been found with the decimal point designator (36.) in the Crown Mark, 36/I size. The piece remains in production today as 36/0.

Hum No.	Basic Size	Trademark	Current Value
36/0	2-3/4" x 4"	TMK-1	$225-$275
36/0	2-3/4" x 4"	TMK-2	$125-$150
36/0	2-3/4" x 4"	TMK-3	$75-$85
36/0	2-3/4" x 4"	TMK-4	$70-$75
36/0	2-3/4" x 4"	TMK-5	$65-$70
36/0	2-3/4" x 4"	TMK-6	$60-$65
36/0	3-1/4" x 4-1/2"	TMK-7	$55-$60
36/0	3-1/4" x 4-1/2"	TMK-8	$55
36.	3-1/2" x 4-1/2"	TMK-1	$400-$450
36/I	3-1/2" x 4-1/2"	TMK-1	$375-$425
36/I	3-1/2" x 4-1/2"	TMK-2	$275-$375
36/I	3-1/2" x 4-1/2"	TMK-3	$175-$225

Hum 37: Herald Angels (Candleholder)

This piece, which was designed by master sculptor Reinhold Unger, is a group of figures very similar to Hum 38, 39, and 40, placed together on a common round base with a candle receptacle in the center. There are two versions: low and high candleholder. The higher holder is found on the older pieces.

A faience variation also exists and is valued at $3,000-$5,000.

This candleholder was temporarily withdrawn from current production in 1989.

Herald Angels candleholder, Hum 37, with small Stylized Bee (TMK-3).

Hum No.	Basic Size	Trademark	Current Value	Hum No.	Basic Size	Trademark	Current Value
37	2-1/4" x 4"	TMK-1	$600-$800	37	2-1/4" x 4"	TMK-4	$225-$250
37	2-1/4" x 4"	TMK-2	$400-$450	37	2-1/4" x 4"	TMK-5	$200-$225
37	2-1/4" x 4"	TMK-3	$250-$275	37	2-1/4" x 4"	TMK-6	$180-$200

Hum 38, Hum 39, and Hum 40: Angel Trio (Candleholders)

These three figures—Joyous News Angel With Lute, Joyous News Angel With Accordion, and Joyous News Angel With Trumpet—are presented as a set of three and are usually sold as a set. First modeled by master sculptor Reinhold Unger in 1935, these pieces have been called "Little Heavenly Angels" and "Angel Trio" in old company literature.

They each come in three versions according to size and candle size. The I/38/0, I/39/0, and I/40/0 versions are 2" tall and has 0.6-cm candle diameter. The III/38/0, III/39/0, and III/40/0 versions are 2" tall and have 1.0-cm candle diameters. The III/38/I, III/39/I, and III/40/I versions are 2-3/4" tall, with 1.0-cm candle diameters. Early pieces do not carry a size designator and because the pieces are so small, the signature on the back or leg of the angel may simply read "Hum." Another variation is that Hum 38/0, Angel With Lute, has been found with green shoes.

Both Angel With Lute (I/38/0) and Angel With Trumpet (I/40/) were listed as temporarily withdrawn as of June 24, 2000.

Hum No.	Basic Size	Trademark	Current Value
I/38/0	2" x 2-1/2"	TMK-1	$150-$200
I/38/0	2" x 2-1/2"	TMK-2	$100-$125
I/38/0	2" x 2-1/2"	TMK-3	$95-$100
I/38/0	2" x 2-1/2"	TMK-4	$85-$95
I/38/0	2" x 2-1/2"	TMK-5	$80-$85
I/38/0	2" x 2-1/2"	TMK-6	$75-$80

Hum No.	Basic Size	Trademark	Current Value
I/38/0	2" x 2-1/2"	TMK-7	$70-$75
I/38/0	2" x 2-1/2"	TMK-8	$70
III/38/0	2" x 2-1/2"	TMK-1	$150-$200
III/38/0	2" x 2-1/2"	TMK-2	$100-$125
III/38/0	2" x 2-1/2"	TMK-3	$90-$100
III/38/0	2" x 2-1/2"	TMK-4	$80-$90
III/38/0	2" x 2-1/2"	TMK-5	$70-$80
III/38/0	2" x 2-1/2"	TMK-6	$60-$70
III/38/1	2-1/2" x 2-3/4"	TMK-1	$300-$350
III/38/1	2-1/2" x 2-3/4"	TMK-2	$250-$300
III/38/1	2-1/2" x 2-3/4"	TMK-3	$200-$250
I/39/0	2" x 2-1/2"	TMK-1	$150-$200
I/39/0	2" x 2-1/2"	TMK-2	$105-$125
I/39/0	2" x 2-1/2"	TMK-3	$95-$105
I/39/0	2" x 2-1/2"	TMK-4	$85-$95
I/39/0	2" x 2-1/2"	TMK-5	$80-$85
I/39/0	2" x 2-1/2"	TMK-6	$75-$80
I/39/0	2" x 2-1/2"	TMK-7	$70-$75
I/39/0	2" x 2-1/2"	TMK-8	$70
III/39/0	2" x 2-1/2"	TMK-1	$150-$200
III/39/0	2" x 2-1/2"	TMK-2	$100-$125
III/39/0	2" x 2-1/2"	TMK-3	$90-$100
III/39/0	2" x 2-1/2"	TMK-4	$80-$90
III/39/0	2" x 2-1/2"	TMK-5	$70-$80

Angel Trio candleholders. Left: Angel with Lute, Hum 38, Full Bee (TMK-2), and black "Germany." Center: Angel With Accordion, Hum 39, with Full Bee mark and black "Germany." Right: Angel With Horn, Hum 40, with Full Bee and black "Germany."

Hum No.	Basic Size	Trademark	Current Value
III/39/0	2" x 2-1/2"	TMK-6	$60-$70
III/39/1	2-1/2" x 2-3/4"	TMK-1	$300-$350
III/39/1	2-1/2" x 2-3/4"	TMK-2	$250-$300
III/39/1	2-1/2" x 2-3/4"	TMK-3	$200-$250
I/40/0	2" x 2-1/2"	TMK-1	$150-$200
I/40/0	2" x 2-1/2"	TMK-2	$105-$125
I/40/0	2" x 2-1/2"	TMK-3	$95-$105
I/40/0	2" x 2-1/2"	TMK-4	$85-$95
I/40/0	2" x 2-1/2"	TMK-5	$80-$85
I/40/0	2" x 2-1/2"	TMK-6	$75-$80

Hum No.	Basic Size	Trademark	Current Value
I/40/0	2" x 2-1/2"	TMK-7	$70-$75
I/40/0	2" x 2-1/2"	TMK-8	$70
III/40/0	2" x 2-1/2"	TMK-1	$150-$200
III/40/0	2" x 2-1/2"	TMK-2	$100-$125
III/40/0	2" x 2-1/2"	TMK-3	$90-$100
III/40/0	2" x 2-1/2"	TMK-4	$80-$90
III/40/0	2" x 2-1/2"	TMK-5	$70-$80
III/40/0	2" x 2-1/2"	TMK-6	$60-$70
III/40/1	2-1/2" x 2-3/4"	TMK-1	$300-$350
III/40/1	2-1/2" x 2-3/4"	TMK-2	$250-$300
III/40/1	2-1/2" x 2-3/4"	TMK-3	$200-$250

Hum 41: Singing Lesson (Closed Number)

This figure had been listed as a closed number, but the existence of the piece is now substantiated. Details are not known, but the piece is said to be similar to Singing Lesson (Hum 63) without the base. There are no known examples, but samples in this category have turned up from time to time. Collector value is $5,000-$10,000.

Hum 42: Good Shepherd

Master sculptor Reinhold Unger is credited with the design of this figurine in 1935.

The 42 mold number has been found with the decimal point designator. There are two very rare variations: a blue gown rather than the normal brownish-red color and a white gown with blue stars. This is found on the 42/0 size in the Crown (TMK-1) and Full Bee (TMK-2) figures.

No longer produced in the 7-1/2" size, and the 6-1/4" size was temporarily withdrawn in January 1999.

Hum No.	Basic Size	Trademark	Current Value
42/0	6-1/4"	TMK-1	$750-$900
42/0	6-1/4"	TMK-2	$430-$600
42/0	6-1/4"	TMK-3	$375-$430
42/0	6-1/4"	TMK-4	$325-$375
42/0	6-1/4"	TMK-5	$300-$325
42/0	6-1/4"	TMK-6	$290-$300
42/0	6-1/4"	TMK-7	$280-$290
42/I	7-1/4" x 8"	TMK-3	$5,000-$6,000
42/I	7-1/2"	TMK-1	$7,000-$8,000
42/I	7-1/2"	TMK-2	$6,000-$7,000

Good Shepherd, Hum 42. Left: Incised Crown Mark (TMK-1) colored blue, 7-5/8". Right: 42/0, Full Bee (TMK-2) trademark, black "Germany," 6-1/2".

Hum 43: March Winds

Designed by master sculptor Reinhold Unger, this figurine is one of the original 46 released in 1935 and has been called "Urchin" in old company catalogs.

There appear to be two slightly different designs. In the earlier pieces, the boy looks more toward the rear than in the newer ones, but there are no significant variations to be found.

A smaller size was added during the TMK-7 period and that piece remains in production today.

Hum No.	Basic Size	Trademark	Current Value
43/5/0	2-3/4"	TMK-7	$55
43	5"	TMK-1	$450-$600
43	5"	TMK-2	$275-$375
43	5"	TMK-3	$250-$275
43	5"	TMK-4	$200-$250
43	5"	TMK-5	$190-$200
43	5"	TMK-6	$185-$190
43	4-3/4" x 5-1/2"	TMK-7	$180-$185
43	4-3/4" x 5-1/2"	TMK-8	$180

Photo courtesy Goebel of North America.

The last version of March Winds, Hum 43, appeared in TMK-7 and today is worth $180-$185.

March Winds, Hum 43. The left figure bears the Full Bee (TMK-2) trademark, is 5-1/2" and bears a black "Germany" beneath the base. The one on the right has a small Stylized Bee (TMK-3) trademark and is 4-7/8" tall.

Hum 44/A: Culprits and Hum 44/B: Out Of Danger (Table Lamps)

Both of these lamps, designed my master sculptor Arthur Moeller, were part of the original 46 designs released in 1935. Both are about 8-1/2" tall and were temporarily withdrawn from production at the end of 1989.

There are no significant variations that would affect the collector value of either one; only minor changes such as the location of the switch.

Hum No.	Basic Size	Trademark	Current Value
44	8-1/2" to 9-1/2"	TMK-1	$650-$750
44/A	8-1/2" to 9-1/2"	TMK-1	$500-$650
44/A	8-1/2" to 9-1/2"	TMK-2	$430-$480
44/A	8-1/2" to 9-1/2"	TMK-3	$400-$430
44/A	8-1/2"	TMK-4	$375-$400
44/A	8-1/2"	TMK-5	$350-$375
44/A	8-1/2"	TMK-6	$325-$350
44/B	8-1/2" to 9-1/2"	TMK-1	$500-$650
44/B	8-1/2" to 9-1/2	TMK-2	$430-$480
44/B	8-1/2" to 9-1/2	TMK-3	$400-$430

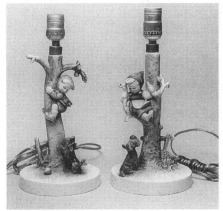

Left: Culprit table lamp, Hum 44/A. Double Full Bee mark (TMK-2) incised and stamped, black "Germany," W. Goebel, 9-1/4". Right: Out Of Danger table lamp, Hum 44/B. Full Bee mark (TMK-2), black "Germany," W. Goebel, 8-3/8".

Hum No.	Basic Size	Trademark	Current Value
44/B	8-1/2"	TMK-4	$375-$400
44/B	8-1/2"	TMK-5	$350-$375
44/B	8-1/2"	TMK-6	$325-$350

Hum 45: Madonna With Halo and Hum 46: Madonna Without Halo

These Madonnas, designed by master sculptor Reinhold Unger, were part of the original 46 figures that were released in 1935 at the Leipzig Fair. They are often confusing to collectors because of their similarity.

Apparently, they are also occasionally confused with each other at the factory. Sometimes, the mold number appears on the wrong piece, possibly explained in some cases by the fact that the two pieces are identical without the halo, which is an add-on piece during assembly. The fact that they are sometimes found with both mold numbers incised on one piece lends evidence to the theory that the body is from the same mold and the mold number is impressed after assembly, but before firing.

At least nine legitimate variations have been found. The chief differences are in size, color, and glaze treatment. They are found in color and white overglaze. The known color variations are beige, rose, light blue, royal blue, and ivory. They have also been found in terra cotta.

In 1982, both the 45/III and the 46/III were temporarily withdrawn from production, and in 1984, the 45/0 and 46/0 were also withdrawn temporarily. The 46/I was temporarily withdrawn in 1989, apparently leaving only the 45/I, Madonna With Halo, available to collectors.

While variations are rampant, only the appearance in terra cotta, which is valued at $2,000-$3,000, and one other has any significant effect on value. There is a variation where there are red-painted stars on the underside of the halo. This variation can as much as triple the value for its counterpart without the stars.

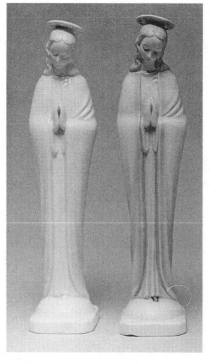

Madonna With Halo, Hum 45/0. Left: White overglaze, small Stylized Bee (TMK-3), 10-3/4". Right: Full Bee (TMK-2) trademark in an incised circle, red stars in the halo, 10-1/2". The halo has blue stars in the Last Bee (TMK-5) era.

Hum No.	Basic Size	Trademark	Value (White)	Value (Color)
45/0	10-1/2"	TMK-1	$125-$175	$200-$275
45/0	10-1/2"	TMK-2	$90-$125	$100-$175
45/0	10-1/2"	TMK-3	$45-$70	$85-$95
45/0	10-1/2"	TMK-4	$50-$55	$70-$85
45/0	10-1/2"	TMK-5	$45-$50	$65-$70
45/0	10-1/2"	TMK-6	$40-$45	$60-$65
45/I	11-1/2" to 13-1/4"	TMK-1	$150-$200	$300-$400
45/I	11-1/2" to 13-1/4"	TMK-2	$100-$150	$175-$225
45/I	11-1/2" to 13-1/4"	TMK-3	$90-$100	$170-$175
45/I	11-1/2" to 13-1/4"	TMK-4	$85-$95	$165-$170
45/I	11-1/2" to 13-1/4"	TMK-5	$80-$85	$160-$165
45/I	11-1/2" to 13-1/4"	TMK-6	$75-$80	$155-$160
45/I	11-1/2" to 13-1/4"	TMK-7	$75-$80	$150-$155
45/I	11-1/2" to 13-1/4"	TMK-8	$75	$150
45/III	16-1/4"	TMK-1	$250-$350	$400-$600
45/III	16-1/4"	TMK-2	$175-$225	$275-$375
45/III	16-1/4"	TMK-3	$140-$160	$175-$220
45/III	16-1/4"	TMK-4	$115-$140	$165-$175
45/III	16-1/4"	TMK-5	$110-$115	$155-$165
45/III	16-1/4"	TMK-6	$105-$110	$150-$155
46/0	10-1/4"	TMK-1	$125-$175	$200-$275
46/0	10-1/4"	TMK-2	$85-$125	$95-$175
46/0	10-1/4"	TMK-3	$55-$70	$85-$95

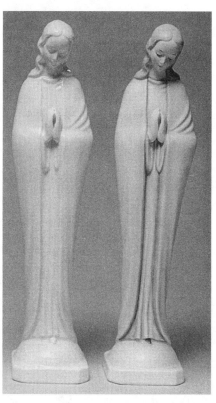

Madonna Without Halo, Hum 46/0. Left is white overglaze and right is painted. Both are small Stylized Bee (TMK-3) pieces measuring 10-1/2".

Hum No.	Basic Size	Trademark	Value (White)	Value (Color)
46/0	10-1/4"	TMK-4	$50-$55	$70-$85
46/0	10-1/4"	TMK-5	$45-$50	$65-$70
46/0	10-1/4"	TMK-6	$40-$45	$60-$65
46/I	11-1/4"	TMK-1	$300-$400	$300-$400
46/I	11-1/4"	TMK-2	$170-$225	$170-$225
46/I	11-1/4"	TMK-3	$160-$170	$160-$170
46/I	11-1/4"	TMK-4	$155-$160	$155-$160
46/I	11-1/4"	TMK-5	$145-$150	$145-$150
46/I	11-1/4"	TMK-6	$140-$145	$140-$145
46/III	16"	TMK-1	$250-$350	$400-$600
46/III	16"	TMK-2	$175-$225	$275-$375
46/III	16"	TMK-3	$140-$265	$175-$220
46/III	16"	TMK-4	$120-$140	$165-$175
46/III	16"	TMK-5	$115-$120	$160-$165
46/III	16"	TMK-6	$110-$115	$155-$160

Madonna With Halo, Hum 45/I, is still in production today, shown here in TMK-8.

Hum 47: Goose Girl

A very popular piece first modeled by master sculptor Arthur Moeller in 1936, this figurine is probably the most famous among collectors and non-collectors alike. Interestingly, for a model that dates back practically to day one and in three sizes, there are no variations significant enough to have an effect on collector value. The occurrence of the decimal designator might have a slight influence with some collectors, but not a great degree of significance.

There is, of course, the Goose Girl with a bowl attached. This piece is thought to be unique; a sample that somehow found its way into the collector market. There are two similar pieces with bowls attached: Congratulations (Hum 17) and Meditation (Hum 13).

Goose Girl bowl. This exceedingly rare piece was found in Germany in 1989. It measures 4-7/8" and has an incised Crown Mark. Upon examining it closely, it appears that the bowl was attached to the figurine before firing, lending legitimacy to the speculation that it was fashioned by Goebel. The bowl is a Double Crown Mark piece and has an incised mold number "1". Two other bowl pieces have shown up with a different style of bowl: Meditation (Hum 13) and Congratulations (Hum 17).

Goose Girl, Hum 47. Left: 47/0, Full Bee mark, black "Germany," 5-1/4". Center: 47/0, Stylized Bee mark, 4-3/4". Right: 47 3/0, Full Bee mark, black "Germany," 4-1/4".

One of today's Goose Girl figurine variations at 4-3/4" and numbered 47/0.

Hum No.	Basic Size	Trademark	Current Value
47/3/0	4"	TMK-1	$500-$650
47/3/0	4"	TMK-2	$300-$400
47/3/0	4"	TMK-3	$250-$300
47/3/0	4"	TMK-4	$225-$250
47/3/0	4"	TMK-5	$215-$225
47/3/0	4"	TMK-6	$205-$215
47/3/0	4" to 4-1/4"	TMK-7	$200-$205
47/3/0	4" to 4-1/4"	TMK-8	$200
47	5"	TMK-1	$800-$900
47/0	4-3/4"	TMK-1	$650-$800
47/0	4-3/4"	TMK-2	$400-$650
47/0	4-3/4"	TMK-3	$350-$400
47/0	4-3/4"	TMK-4	$300-$350
47/0	4-3/4"	TMK-5	$285-$300
47/0	4-3/4"	TMK-6	$280-$285
47/0	4-3/4"	TMK-7	$275-$280
47/0	4-3/4"	TMK-8	$275
47/II	7-1/2"	TMK-1	$1,000-$1,300
47/II	7-1/2"	TMK-2	$700-$900
47/II	7-1/2"	TMK-3	$600-$700
47/II	7-1/2"	TMK-4	$500-$600
47/II	7-1/2"	TMK-5	$420-$440
47/II	7-1/2"	TMK-6	$420-$420
47/II	7" to 7-1/2"	TMK-7	$400-$410

Hum 48: Madonna (Wall Plaque)

Master sculptor Reinhold Unger is credited with the design of this bas-relief plaque in 1936. It has been known to appear in a white overglaze in the 48/0 and the 48/II sizes in a bisque finish. The white overglaze pieces appear in the Crown Mark (TMK-1) and are very rare.

The 48/II can sometimes be found as 48/2. There are two variations of the 48/II in the Crown Mark (TMK-1).

The 48/II size was temporarily withdrawn on December 31, 1984, and the 48/0 size was temporarily withdrawn at the end of 1989.

Hum No.	Basic Size	Trademark	Current Value
48/0	3" x 4"	TMK-1	$325-$375
48/0	3" x 4"	TMK-2	$275-$225
48/0	3" x 4"	TMK-3	$115-$135
48/0	3" x 4"	TMK-4	$100-$115
48/0	3" x 4"	TMK-5	$90-$100
48/0	3" x 4"	TMK-6	$85-$90
48	4-3/4" x 6"	TMK-1	$650-$850
48/II	4-3/4" x 6"	TMK-1	$550-$800
48/II	4-3/4" x 6"	TMK-2	$375-$525
48/II	4-3/4" x 6"	TMK-3	$190-$250
48/II	4-3/4" x 5-3/4"	TMK-4	$165-$190
48/II	4-3/4" x 6"	TMK-5	$135-$145
48/II	4-3/4" x 6"	TMK-6	$130-$135
48/V	8-1/4" x 10-1/2"	TMK-1	$1,500-$2,000
48/V	8-1/4" x 10-1/2"	TMK-2	$1,250-$1,500
48/V	8-1/4" x 10-1/2"	TMK-3	$1,000-$1,250
48/II (white)	4-3/4" x 5-3/4"	TMK-3	$500-$600

Madonna wall plaque, Hum 48/2. Left: Stylized Bee mark, 4-5/8" x 5-3/4", white overglaze. Right: Full Bee mark, 4-5/8" x 5-5/8".

Hum 49: To Market

Master sculptor Arthur Moeller first designed this piece in 1936, when it was then called "Brother and Sister."

The 49/I size was out of current production for at least 20 years and then reinstated in the early 1980s. Goebel placed it on a temporarily withdrawn from production status on December 31, 1984, and it remains so today. Also temporarily withdrawn, effective January 1999, is the 49/0 size. The smallest size at 4" (49/3/0) is the only one still in production today.

The 49 mold number has occasionally been found with the decimal point size designator. Some 49/0 versions have surfaced with no bottle in the basket. The 49/3/0 size is routinely produced with no bottle in the basket.

Hum No.	Basic Size	Trademark	Current Value
49/3/0	4"	TMK-1	$500-$650
49/3/0	4"	TMK-2	$300-$375
49/3/0	4"	TMK-3	$250-$275
49/3/0	4"	TMK-4	$210-$230
49/3/0	4"	TMK-5	$200-$210
49/3/0	4"	TMK-6	$190-$200
40/3/0	4"	TMK-7	$185-$190

Hum No.	Basic Size	Trademark	Current Value
49/3/0	4"	TMK-8	$185
49/0	5-1/2"	TMK-1	$750-$1,000
49/0	5-1/2"	TMK-2	$450-$625
49/0	5-1/4"	TMK-3	$425-$450
49/0	5-1/2"	TMK-4	$375-$425
49/0	5-1/2"	TMK-5	$350-$375
49/0	5-1/2"	TMK-6	$335-4350
49/0	5-1/2"	TMK-7	$325-$335
49	6-1/4"	TMK-1	$1,400-$1,700
49	6-1/4"	TMK-2	$1,200-$1,400
49	6-1/4"	TMK-5	$600-$700
49/I	6-1/4"	TMK-1	$1,400-$1,700
49/I	6-1/4"	TMK-2	$1,200-$1,400
49/I	6-1/4"	TMK-3	$550-$700
49/I	6-1/4"	TMK-4	$500-$550
49/I	6-1/4"	TMK-5	$450-$475
49	6-1/4"	TMK-6	$425-$450

To Market, Hum 49. Left: 49./0., double Crown Mark, dough-nut base, 5-7/16". Right: 49/0, Last Bee, 5-3/8".

Today's variation of To Market, Hum 49/3/0, which is 4" high and bears TMK-8.

Hum 50: Volunteers

Once called "Playing Soldiers," this figurine was designed by master sculptor Reinhold Unger in 1936.

The 50/0 and 50/I sizes were out of production for some years and are difficult to find with the older trademarks. Both were reinstated in 1979. The 50/I was again withdrawn in December 1984 and the 50/0 version was temporarily withdrawn on June 15, 2002. The only variation still in production today, therefore, is 50/2/0.

The small Hum 50/2/0, Volunteers, was released with a special backstamp commemorating the allied victory in Operation Desert Storm. Limited to 10,000 pieces worldwide, it was to be sold only through military post and base exchanges at a retail price of $150-$175. This particular variation has already risen to a range of $275-$350 on the collector market.

In the wake of the terrorist attacks on the World Trade Center and Pentagon on September 11, 2001 and the resulting American military effort, Goebel alerted its M.I. Hummel Club chapters that it would make a commitment to donate appropriately themed figurines to local chapters to be used as raffle prizes. Any proceeds from such fund-raising events would then go to benefit the families of the victims. Seven figurines, including this one, were selected as appropriate due to their patriotic or firefighter/police/medical personnel themes.

In 2002, a special edition of Volunteers was introduced in recognition of the figurine's 50th year in production. It carried a unique diamond-shaped "50th Anniversary" backstamp and came with a certificate of authenticity and a diamond-shaped anniversary medallion with "50" on it.

Hum No.	Basic Size	Trademark	Current Value
50/2/0	5"	TMK-1	$410-$510
50/2/0	5"	TMK-2	$435-$535
50/2/0	5"	TMK-3	$355-$400
50/2/0	5"	TMK-4	$325-$350
50/2/0	5"	TMK-5	$275-$305
50/2/0	5"	TMK-6	$265-$275
50/2/0	4-3/4" to 5"	TMK-7	$240-$265
50/2/0	4-3/4" to 5"	TMK-8	$235
50/2/0 (50th anniversary)	5"	TMK-8	$265
50/0	5-1/2"	TMK-1	$855-$1,110
50/0	5-1/2"	TMK-2	$510-$660
50/0	5-1/2"	TMK-3	$455-$480

Hum No.	Basic Size	Trademark	Current Value
50/0	5-1/2" to 6"	TMK-4	$405-$455
50/0	5-1/2"	TMK-5	$365-$395
50/0	5-1/2"	TMK-6	$355-$365
50/0	5-1/2" to 6"	TMK-7	$350-$355
50/0	4-3/4" to 6"	TMK-8	$350
50	6-1/2"	TMK-1	$1,260-$1,560
50/I	6-1/2"	TMK-1	$1,210-$1,510
50/I	6-1/2"	TMK-2	$755-$955
50/I	6-1/2"	TMK-3	$605-$755
50/I	6-1/2" to 7"	TMK-4	$555-$605
50/I	6-1/2"	TMK-5	$480-$510
50/I	6-1/2"	TMK-6	$455-$480

Volunteers, Hum 50. Left: 50/0, incised Crown Mark, black "Germany," 5-7/8". Center: 50/0, Full Bee in an incised circle, black "Western Germany," and 6-1/16". Right: 50 2/0, TMK-6, 4-7/8", and white overglaze.

Photo showing the Desert Shield/Desert Storm backstamp on the base of the Volunteers figurine. The normal month and day date found with the backstamp is February 28. There is a rare version where it reads February 24. The number of these is not known, but a few of them have been found.

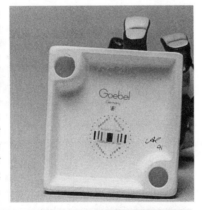

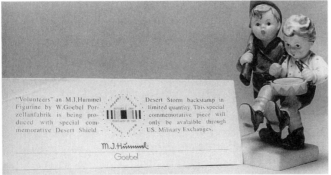

Volunteers, Hum 50, with mold number 50 2/0 and TMK-7. This is the Volunteers with the special Desert Shield/Desert Storm backstamp.

One present-day (TMK-8) variation of Volunteers exists as Hum 50/2/0, measures from 4-3/4" to 5", and is worth $235.

Hum 51: Village Boy

Placed in production in the early years, master sculptor Arthur Moeller first designed this figurine in 1936.

The 51/I was taken out of production sometime in the 1960s, and the early figures are considered rare. Out of production for some 20 years, the 51/I was placed back in production for a short time and was once again placed on temporarily withdrawn status, effective December 31, 1984. It remains so today. The 5" version (51/2/0) also was temporarily withdrawn from production, effective June 15, 2002.

In the mid-1990s, Goebel introduced a new, smaller size (51/5/0) as part of the six-piece "Pen Pals" series of personalized name card table decorations. However, that piece, too, has since been temporarily withdrawn from production.

There were many minor variations over the years, but the one most important to collectors occurs in the Crown Mark (TMK-1) 51/3/0 size. The boy wears a blue jacket and a yellow kerchief instead of the normal green jacket and red kerchief. When found, this variation is valued at about $1,500-$2,000.

Hum No.	Basic Size	Trademark	Current Value
51/5/0	2-3/4"	TMK-7	$55
51/3/0	4"	TMK-1	$350-$450
51/3/0	4"	TMK-2	$225-$300
51/3/0	4"	TMK-3	$175-$200
51/3/0	4"	TMK-4	$155-$175
51/3/0	4"	TMK-5	$150-$155
51/3/0	4"	TMK-6	$145-$150
51/3/0	4"	TMK-7	$140-$145
51/3/0	4"	TMK-8	$140
51/2/0	5"	TMK-1	$400-$525
51/2/0	5"	TMK-2	$250-$350
51/2/0	5"	TMK-3	$225-$250
51/2/0	5"	TMK-4	$200-$225
51/2/0	5"	TMK-5	$185-$200
51/2/0	5"	TMK-6	$180-$185
51/2/0	5"	TMK-7	$175-$180
51/2/0	5"	TMK-8	$175
51/0	6"	TMK-1	$700-$900
51/0	6"	TMK-2	$450-$550
51/0	6"	TMK-3	$375-$400
51/0	6"	TMK-4	$325-$375
51/0	6"	TMK-5	$300-$325
51/0	6"	TMK-6	$290-$300
51/0	6"	TMK-7	$280-$285
51	7-1/4"	TMK-1	$900-$1,150
51/I	7-1/4"	TMK-1	$800-$1,110
51/I	7-1/4"	TMK-2	$500-$600
51/I	7-1/4"	TMK-3	$400-$475
51/I	7-1/4"	TMK-4	$350-$400
51/I	7-1/4"	TMK-5	$325-$350
51/I	7-1/4"	TMK-6	$300-$325

At 4" and $140, the 51/3/0 variation of Village Boy is one of the versions in production today (TMK-8).

Photo courtesy Goebel of North America.

Village Boy, Hum 51, Left: 51./0., double Crown mark, doughnut base, 6-1/2". Right: 51/0, Last Bee, 6-3/8".

Hum 52: Going To Grandma's

A very early figurine in the line, this figurine was designed by master sculptor Reinhold Unger in 1936 and called "Little Mothers of the Family" in early literature.

All of the older pieces in both sizes are found in the square base. A redesign and a new oval base were part of the transition to the Last Bee (TMK-5) era. You can, therefore, find TMK-5 pieces with either base, but the older, square base is the most desirable.

The figure has been found with the decimal designator in the Crown Mark (TMK-1).

The 52/I size was temporarily withdrawn on December 31, 1984.

Hum No.	Basic Size	Trademark	Current Value
52/0	4-3/4"	TMK-1	$750-$1,000
52/0	4-3/4"	TMK-2	$450-$600
52/0	4-3/4"	TMK-3	$400-$450
52/0	4-3/4"	TMK-4	$325-$375
52/0	4-3/4"	TMK-5	$300-$325
(square base)			
52/0	4-3/4"	TMK-5	$250-$270
(oval base)			
52/0	4-3/4"	TMK-6	$290-$300
52/0	4-1/2" to 5"	TMK-7	$285-$290
52/0	4-1/2" to 5"	TMK-8	$285
52	6"	TMK-1	$1,300-$1,600
52	6-1/4"	TMK-2	$850-$1,000
52/I	6"	TMK-1	$1,250-$1,500
52/I	6" to 6-1/2"	TMK-5	$425-$525
(new oval)			
52/I	6"	TMK-2	$800-$950
52/I	6"	TMK-3	$650-$800
52/I	6"	TMK-5	$500-$800
(old rectangle)			
52/I	6"	TMK-6	$400-$425

Going To Grandma's, Hum 52. Left: Decimal designator in the mold number 52., incised Crown Mark (TMK-1), black "Made in Germany" stamped on and lacquered over, 6". Right: 52/I, Stylized Bee (TMK-3) mark in an incised circle, black "Western Germany," 6-1/4".

Going To Grandma's, Hum 52. Shows the appearance of the cone when it holds candies and the later model oval base.

Today's version (TMK-8) of Going To Grandma's, Hum 52/0, which is worth $285.

Hum 53: Joyful

This figurine, designed by master sculptor Reinhold Unger in 1936, was once known as "Banjo Betty."

There are major size variations. As the figure emerged from the Crown Mark (TMK-1) era and transitioned into the Full Bee (TMK-2) period, it began to grow larger. Both the normal sizes and the larger variations appeared during the Full Bee period and by the time the transition to the Stylized Bee (TMK-3) was finished, it was back to the normal 4" basic size. The oversize pieces consistently bring a higher price than the normal size pieces. They are valued at about 20%-25% more than the normal size.

A much rarer variation is the orange dress (instead of the normal blue) found on some very early Crown Mark (TMK-1) pieces. Collector value: $3,000-$3,500.

Similar to some of the other pieces, this piece was also produced in a sample with an attached bowl/pot, but was rejected by the Siessen Convent and never placed into production. If found, it is worth $5,000-$10,000.

This piece was temporarily withdrawn from production in January 1999.

Joyful, Hum 53. Left: Full Bee (TMK-2) mark in an incised circle, black "Germany," 3-3/4". Right: Carries TMK-5 and measures 3-3/4".

Hum No.	Basic Size	Trademark	Current Value
53	4"	TMK-1	$350-$450
53	4"	TMK-2	$225-$310
53	4"	TMK-3	$190-$225
53	4"	TMK-4	$170-$190
53	4"	TMK-5	$150-$170
53	4"	TMK-6	$145-$150
53	3-1/2"	TMK-7	$140-$145

Hum III/53: Joyful (Candy Box)

There are two styles of candy boxes: bowl-like and jar-like. The transition from the old bowls to the new jars took place in the Stylized Bee (TMK-3) period. There are, therefore, old and new styles to be found with the Stylized Bee trademark. The older style would, of course, be the more desirable to collectors.

This piece was temporarily withdrawn on December 31, 1989; however, in 1996, a music box variation of the piece became available in Europe only. The music boxes are numbered IV/53, bear TMK-7, and have a brown banjo.

Hum No.	Basic Size	Trademark	Current Value
III/53	6-1/4"	TMK-1	$750-$850
III/53	6-1/4"	TMK-2	$575-$650
III/53 (old style)	6-1/4"	TMK-3	$475-$550
III/53 (new style)	6-1/4"	TMK-3	$300-$350
III/53	6-1/4"	TMK-4	$250-$275
III/53	6-1/4"	TMK-5	$225-$250
III/53	6-1/4"	TMK-6	$200-$225
IV/53	5-3/4"	TMK-7	$175 (Europe only)

Joyful candy dish, Hum III/53. Old style bowl on left, new style on the right.

Hum 54: Silent Night (Candleholder)

This piece, which was designed by master sculptor Reinhold Unger in 1936, is almost identical to the Advent Group (Hum 31) candleholder, except that most of the Hum 31 figures have a black child on the left, and most of the Hum 54 figures have a white child on the left.

There have been at least three distinctly different molds.

The significant variation to be found, and the most valuable, is that of the black child. These can be found in the Crown Mark (TMK-1) and the Full Bee (TMK-2) trademarks only. They are valued at $7,500-$12,000. There is also an even more valuable piece with two black children in a Full Bee (TMK-2), which is worth $10,000-$15,000.

This piece was temporarily withdrawn in January 1999.

Hum No.	Basic Size	Trademark	Current Value
54	3-1/2" x 4-3/4"	TMK-1	$850-$1,110
54	3-1/2" x 4-3/4"	TMK-2	$550-$700
54	3-1/2" x 4-3/4"	TMK-3	$475-$500
54	3-1/2" x 4-3/4"	TMK-4	$425-$475
54	3-1/2" x 4-3/4"	TMK-5	$400-$425
54	3-1/2" x 4-3/4"	TMK-6	$375-$395
54 (with black child)	3-1/2" x 4-3/4"	TMK-1	$10,000-$12,000
54 (with black child)	3-1/2" x 4-3/4"	TMK-2	$7,500-$10,000
54 (two black children)	3-1/2" x 4-3/4"	TMK-2	$10,000-$15,000
54	3-1/2" x 4-3/4"	TMK-7	$360-$370

Silent Night, Hum 54. Left: Full Bee (TMK-2), black "Germany," 3-3/4". Center: Double Full Bee (TMK-2), incised and stamped; black "Germany," 3-3/4". Right: Last Bee (TMK-6), 3-1/2".

Hum 55: Saint George

This figure, which was designed by master sculptor Reinhold Unger in 1936, is substantially different in style from most others in the collection and is difficult to locate most of the time.

The following sizes have been encountered in various lists: 6-1/4", 6-5/8", and 6-3/4". Some of the early TMK-1 pieces will have a bright red painted saddle. This is the rarest variation and brings $2,500-$3,000. There are reports of the existence of a white overglaze version as well.

This piece was temporarily withdrawn from production in January 1999.

Hum No.	Basic Size	Trademark	Current Value
55 (red saddle)	6-3/4"	TMK-1	$2,500-$3,000
55	6-3/4"	TMK-1	$1,000-$1,300
55	6-3/4"	TMK-2	$600-$750
55	6-3/4"	TMK-3	$450-$525
55	6-3/4"	TMK-4	$400-$450
55	6-3/4"	TMK-5	$375-$400
55	6-3/4"	TMK-6	$360-$375
55	6-3/4"	TMK-7	$350-$360

Saint George, Hum 55. The mold number is incised with the decimal designator on this particular example thus: "55.". It has an incised Crown Mark and stamped Full Bee mark and measures 7".

Hum 56/A: Culprits and Hum 56/B: Out of Danger

First modeled by master sculptor Arthur Moeller in 1936, Culprits was released in the mid-1930s. Out of Danger, which was also designed by Moeller, was not introduced until the early 1950s though. There have been minor changes over the years, including the fact that both the boy and girl had open eyes on older pieces and now have eyes cast down toward the dogs, but none of the changes have had any influence on normal collector values.

Hum No.	Basic Size	Trademark	Current Value
56	6-1/4"	TMK-1	$860-$1,110
56	6-1/4"	TMK-2	$510-$670
56/A	6-1/4"	TMK-2	$510-$670
56/A	6-1/4"	TMK-3	$450-$500
56/A	6-1/4"	TMK-4	$380-$460
56/A	6-1/4"	TMK-5	$365-$375
56/A	6-1/4"	TMK-6	$350-$360
56/A	6-1/4"	TMK-7	$350-$360
56/A	6-1/4"	TMK-8	$350-$360
56/B	6-1/4"	TMK-2	$520-$610
56/B	6-1/4"	TMK-3	$450-$500
56/B	6-1/4"	TMK-4	$380-$460
56/B	6-1/4"	TMK-5	$365-$375
56/B	6-1/4"	TMK-6	$350-$360
56/B	6-1/4" to 6-3/4"	TMK-7	$350-$360
56/B	6-1/4" to 6-3/4"	TMK-8	$350-$360

Out of Danger, Hum 56/B. Left: Small Stylized Bee (TMK-3) piece measuring 6-1/4". Right: This figure has the TMK-6 mark and is 6-1/8" tall.

Culprits, Hum 56/A. Left: Stylized Bee mark, 6-3/8". Right: Last Bee, 6-3/4".

Photo courtesy Goebel of North America.

Culprits, Hum 56/A, is still in production today (TMK-8).

Photo courtesy Goebel of North America.

Today's version (TMK-8) of Out of Danger, Hum 56/B.

Hum 57: Chick Girl

There are many mold types and sizes of this figurine, which was first designed by master sculptor Reinhold Unger in 1936 and then redesigned in 1964 by master sculptor Gerhard Skrobek. In the past, it has been called both "Little Chicken Mother" and "The Little Chick Girl."

The chief mold variation shows different numbers of chicks on the base. For instance, the 57/0 has two chicks, and the larger, 57/I, has three. It also has been found with mold number and no size designator in the 4-1/4" size, "57."

Like some of the other pieces, a sample of Chick Girl with a bowl/pot was produced in 1936, but never placed into production. If found, this piece would be worth $5,000-$7,000.

Chick Girl, Hum 57. Left: Double Crown Mark (TMK-1), 4-1/8". Right: 57/I, Stylized Bee mark (TMK-3), 4-5/16".

Hum No.	Basic Size	Trademark	Current Value
57/2/0	3"	TMK-5	$145-$150
57/2/0	3"	TMK-6	$190-$200
57/2/0	3"	TMK-7	$180-$185
57/2/0	3"	TMK-8	$180-$185
57/0	3-1/2"	TMK-1	$510-$650
57/0	3-1/2"	TMK-2	$310-$375
57/0	3-1/2"	TMK-3	$250-$290
57/0	3-1/2"	TMK-4	$230-$260
57/0	3-1/2"	TMK-5	$210-$220
57/0	3-1/2"	TMK-6	$210-$220
57/0	3-1/2"	TMK-7	$195-$200

Hum No.	Basic Size	Trademark	Current Value
57/0	3-1/2"	TMK-8	$215
57	4-1/4"	TMK-1	$810-$1,050
57/I	4-1/4"	TMK-1	$750-$1,000
57	4-1/4"	TMK-2	$510-$655
57/I	4-1/4"	TMK-2	$450-$600
57/I	4-1/4"	TMK-3	$410-$460
57/I	4-1/4"	TMK-4	$355-$405
57/I	4-1/4"	TMK-5	$345-$355
57/I	4-1/4"	TMK-6	$330-$350
57/I	4-1/4"	TMK-7	$320-$330

Hum III/57: Chick Girl (Candy Box)

There are two styles of candy boxes: bowl-like and jar-like. The transition from the old bowls to the new jars took place in the Stylized Bee period, so both can be found with TMK-3. Naturally the old style is the more desirable.

This piece was temporarily withdrawn on December 31, 1989; however, in 1996, a music box variation of the piece became available in Europe only (just as occurred with Joyful, Hum III/53). The music boxes are numbered IV/57, bear TMK-7, and measure 6".

Chick Girl Candy Dish, Hum III/57. Stylized Bee mark (TMK-3). Old-style bowl.

Hum No.	Basic Size	Trademark	Current Value
III/57	5-1/4"	TMK-1	$760-$850
III/57	5-1/4"	TMK-2	$580-$650
III/57 (old)	5-1/4"	TMK-3	$475-$550
III/57 (new)	5-1/4"	TMK-3	$310-$350
III/57	5-1/4"	TMK-4	$260-$285
III/57	5-1/4"	TMK-5	$235-$260
III/57	5-1/4"	TMK-6	$210-$230
IV/57	6"	TMK-7	$175 (Europe only)

Hum 58: Playmates

Originally known as "Just Friends," this piece was designed by master sculptor Reinhold Unger in 1936. There are no variations in any trademark era that have any significant effect on value. A similar figure was used on bookend Hum 61/A and candy box Hum III/58.

Hum No.	Basic Size	Trademark	Current Value
58/2/0	3-1/2"	TMK-5	$145-$150
58/2/0	3-1/2"	TMK-6	$185-$195
58/2/0	3-1/2"	TMK-7	$180-$190
58/2/0	3-1/2"	TMK-8	$180-$190
58/0	4"	TMK-1	$510-$660
58/0	4"	TMK-2	$300-$375
58/0	4"	TMK-3	$260-$300
58/0	4"	TMK-4	$230-$260
58/0	4"	TMK-5	$210-$220
58/0	4"	TMK-6	$210-$220
58/0	4"	TMK-7	$195-$200
58/0	4"	TMK-8	$195
58	4-1/2"	TMK-1	$810-$1,060
58/I	4-1/2"	TMK-1	$750-$1,000
58	4-1/2"	TMK-2	$500-$600
58/I	4-1/2"	TMK-2	$460-$610
58/I	4-1/2"	TMK-3	$400-$450
58/I	4-1/2"	TMK-4	$350-$400
58/I	4-1/2"	TMK-5	$345-$355
58/I	4-1/2"	TMK-6	$320-$340
58/I	4-1/4"	TMK-7	$315-$325

Playmates, Hum 58/0. Left: Full Bee (TMK-2), black "Germany," 3-7/8". Right: Small Stylized Bee mark (TMK-3), 3-7/8".

Numbered 58/0 and measuring 4", Playmates is still in production today.

Photo courtesy Goebel of North America.

Hum III/58: Playmates (Candy Box)

There are two styles of candy boxes: bowl-like and jar-like. The transition from the old bowls to the new jars took place during the Stylized Bee (TMK-3) period, therefore each may be found with that trademark. The older style is, of course, more desirable to collectors.

This piece was temporarily withdrawn on December 31, 1989; however, in 1996, Danbury Mint issued a new "M.I. Hummel" collector box that was sold by mail-order only. It bears TMK-7.

Also in 1996, a music box variation of the piece became available in Europe only (just as occurred with Joyful, Hum III/53, and Chick Girl, Hum III/57). The music boxes are numbered IV/58, bear TMK-7, and have color graphics along the lower edge.

Hum No.	Basic Size	Trademark	Current Value
III/58	5-1/4"	TMK-1	$760-$790
III/58	5-1/4"	TMK-2	$580-$660
III/58 (old)	5-1/4"	TMK-3	$475-$550
III/58 (new)	5-1/4"	TMK-3	$310-$350
III/58	5-1/4"	TMK-4	$260-$285

Hum No.	Basic Size	Trademark	Current Value
III/58	5-1/4"	TMK-5	$230-$250
III/58	5-1/4"	TMK-6	$210-$225
III/58	5-1/2"	TMK-7	$210
IV/58	6-1/2"	TMK-7	$175 (Europe only)

Playmates Candy Dish, Hum III/58. Old-style bowl.

Hum 59: Skier

Master sculptor Reinhold Unger created this figurine in 1936.

Newer models have metal ski poles and older models have wooden poles. For a short time, this piece was made with plastic poles. The poles are replaceable and are not considered significant in the valuation of the piece in the case of wooden and metal poles. There is, however, some difficulty with the plastic ski poles found on most of the Stylized Bee (TMK-3) pieces. The small round discs at the bottom of the poles are molded integral with the pole. Some collectors and dealers feel that the intact plastic ski poles on the Stylized Bee pieces are a bit more valuable than those with wooden or metal replacements.

Hum No.	Basic Size	Trademark	Current Value
59.	5-1/4"	TMK-1	$710-$860
59	5-1/4"	TMK-1	$710-$860
59	5-1/4"	TMK-2	$425-$525
59	5-1/4"	TMK-3	$330-$350
59	5-1/4"	TMK-4	$280-$300
59	5-1/4"	TMK-5	$250-$270
59	5-1/4"	TMK-6	$245-$250
59	5" to 6"	TMK-7	$240-$250
59	5" to 6"	TMK-8	$235

Photo courtesy Goebel of North America.

Today's variation (TMK-8) of Skier, which is 5" to 6" and worth $235.

Skier, Hum 59. Left: Stylized Bee mark (TMK-3), wooden poles. Center: Last Bee (TMK-5), metal poles. Right: Last Bee, plastic poles. All measure 5-1/4".

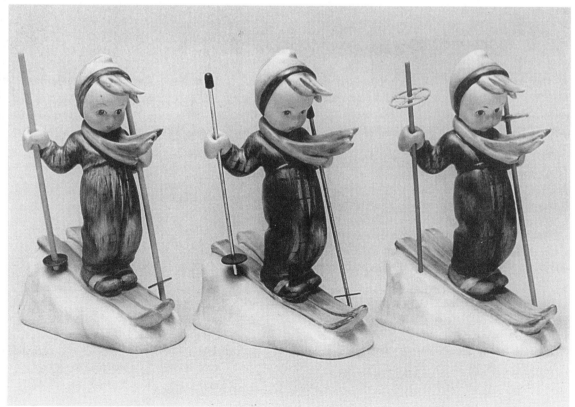

Hum 60/A and Hum 60/B: Farm Boy and Goose Girl (Bookends)

The overall height of the bookends is 6", while the figurines themselves measure 4-3/4". Notice the lack of bases on the figurines. Most often the trademark is found stamped on the wooden base and not on the figurines. Noted collector Robert Miller has confirmed, by removing the boy from a 60/A bookend, that some of the earliest production pieces are occasionally found with the mold number incised on the bottom of the feet. The mold number has also been observed on the back of the slippers on other early pieces.

There are no significant variations affecting value.

These bookends were temporarily withdrawn from production status in December 31, 1984.

Hum No.	Basic Size	Trademark	Current Value
60/A&B	6"	TMK-1	$960-$1,260
60/A&B	6"	TMK-2	$660-$960
60/A&B	6"	TMK-3	$425-$500
60/A&B	4-3/4"	TMK-4	$410-$435
60/A&B	6"	TMK-5	$410-$435
60/A&B	6"	TMK-6	$410-$435

Farm Boy (Hum 60A) and Goose Girl (Hum 60B) bookends. Left figure measures 3-3/8" and the other 4-7/8". Both bear the Stylized Bee mark (TMK-3).

Hum 61/A and Hum 61/B: Playmates and Chick Girl (Bookends)

Overall height of each bookend is 6", while the figures are 4". Note that the figures used do not have the usual base. The trademark is usually marked on the wood portion. The trademark and mold number may or may not appear on the bottom of the figures if removed from the base. Some bookend pieces are marked so, especially the earliest.

The bookends were temporarily withdrawn on December 31, 1984.

Hum No.	Basic Size	Trademark	Current Value
61/A&B	6"	TMK-1	$960-$1,260
61/A&B	6"	TMK-2	$650-$950
61/A&B	6"	TMK-3	$430-$500
61/A&B	4"	TMK-4	$430-$500
61/A&B	6"	TMK-5	$410-$425
61/A&B	6"	TMK-6	$410-$425

Playmates (Hum 61A) and Chick Girl (Hum 61B) bookends. Both have Stylized Bee marks (TMK-3). Left figure measures 4-1/4" and right measures 4".

Hum 62: Happy Pastime (Ashtray)

Master sculptor Arthur Moeller first designed this piece in 1936 and there have been no significant variations affecting value since. This piece, as all ashtrays, has been temporarily withdrawn from production with no published reinstatement date.

The figure used is similar to Hum 69, except that the bird is positioned on the edge of the tray rather than on the girl's leg as on the Hum 69.

The Happy Pastime ashtray figure turned up in 1993 without its ashtray. This is an anomaly and has no significant value. It is interesting, but is likely to be a unique accident. It apparently got packed and shipped out of the factory unnoticed.

Hum No.	Basic Size	Trademark	Current Value
62	3-1/2" x 6-1/4"	TMK-1	$410-$650
62	3-1/2" x 6-1/4"	TMK-2	$305-$355

Hum No.	Basic Size	Trademark	Current Value
62	3-1/2" x 6-1/4"	TMK-3	$230-$250
62	3-1/2" x 6-1/4"	TMK-4	$200-$225
62	3-1/2" x 6-1/4"	TMK-5	$185-$200
62	3-1/2" x 6-1/4"	TMK-6	$155-$180

Happy Pastime ashtray, Hum 62. Last Bee (TMK-5), 3-1/2".

Hum 63: Singing Lesson

First designed by master sculptor Arthur Moeller in 1937 and called "Duet" and "Critic," Singing Lesson has changed a little over the years but has no significant variations. Occasionally it has been found with the decimal designator (63.) on the Crown Mark (TMK-1). This is an indication that it is an early Crown piece, but it does not have a significant impact on value.

Hum No.	Basic Size	Trademark	Current Value
63	2-3/4"	TMK-1	$400-$500
63	2-3/4"	TMK-2	$260-$360
63	2-3/4"	TMK-3	$185-$200
63	2-3/4"	TMK-4	$165-$185
63	2-3/4"	TMK-5	$160-$165

Hum No.	Basic Size	Trademark	Current Value
63	2-3/4"	TMK-6	$160-$165
63	2-3/4"	TMK-7	$150-$155
63	2-3/4"	TMK-8	$150

Photo courtesy Goebel of North America.

Singing Lesson, Hum 63. Left: Mold number of 63., incised Crown Mark (TMK-1), U.S. Zone Germany, 3". Center: 63., double Crown Mark, Made in Germany, 2-3/4". Right: Last Bee (TMK-5), 3".

At $150, Singing Lesson, Hum 63, is in current production (TMK-8).

Hum III/63: Singing Lesson (Candy Box)

There are two styles of bowls. The transition from the old to the new took place in the Stylized Bee (TMK-3) period, therefore both are found with the Stylized Bee trademark. The old style with this mark is, of course, the more desirable to collectors.

In 1996, a music box variation of the piece became available in Europe only (just as occurred with Joyful, Hum III/53, Chick Girl, Hum III/57, and Playmates, Hum III/58). The music boxes are numbered IV/63, bear TMK-7, and have color graphics around the box.

Hum No.	Basic Size	Trademark	Current Value
III-63	5-1/4"	TMK-1	$750-$850
III-63	5-1/4"	TMK-2	$585-$650
III-63 (old)	5-1/4"	TMK-3	$480-$550
III-63 (new)	5-1/4"	TMK-3	$310-$360
III-63	5-1/4"	TMK-4	$250-$275
III-63	5-1/4"	TMK-5	$210-$235
III-63	5-1/4"	TMK-6	$210-$235
IV/63	4-3/4"	TMK-7	$175 (Europe only)

Singing Lesson candy dish, Hum III/63. Left: Last Bee (TMK-5). Right: Stylized Bee mark (TMK-5), old-style bowl.

Hum 64: Shepherd's Boy

Master sculptor Arthur Moeller first designed this figurine in 1937 and Gerhard Skrobek restyled it in the late-1970s with a new textured finish. It was originally called "The Good Shepherd," and although there seem to be a number of size variations to be found, there are no significant variations that could affect the normal pricing of the various trademarked figurines.

Shepherd's Boy, Hum 64. Full Bee mark, black "Germany," 6-1/8".

Hum No.	Basic Size	Trademark	Current Value
64	5-1/2"	TMK-1	$700-$850
64	5-1/2"	TMK-2	$410-$460
64	5-1/2"	TMK-3	$355-$405
64	5-1/2"	TMK-4	$310-$360
64	5-1/2"	TMK-5	$290-$300
64	5-1/2"	TMK-6	$285-$295
64	5-1/2"	TMK-7	$280-$285
64	5-1/2"	TMK-8	$280-$285

Shepherd's Boy, Hum 64. Left: Full Bee mark (TMK-2) with a registered trademark symbol associated, black "Germany," 5-3/4". Right: Last Bee (TMK-5), 5-1/2".

Shepherd's Boy is still in production today (TMK-8).

Photo courtesy Goebel of North America.

Hum 65: Farewell

Master sculptor Arthur Moeller designed this piece in 1937 and Gerhard Skrobek restyled it in 1964. Early company literature called this figurine "So Long" or "Good Bye."

The first models of this figurine, the 65/0 size, in a small 4" basic size, are very rare and highly sought by serious collectors. Apparently a very limited number were made. They are found in the Crown Mark (TMK-1) and the Full Bee (TMK-2) only.

The 4-3/4" basic size carried the 65/I mold number for a while, but in the late-1970s it became 65 only. This size is also sometimes found with the decimal designator on the early Crown Mark and Full Bee mark pieces.

Farewell, Hum 65. Left: Incised Crown Mark and a stamped Full Bee mark, black "Germany," 4-7/8". Right: Full Bee mark in an incised circle, black "Germany," 4-7/8".

An interesting variation occurred in TMK-6 era. It seems that a few of the baskets were attached wrong, resulting in a gap between the arm and the basket on the inside. The pieces with this variation are valued a bit above normal by some collectors. Mistakes such as this are not common, but do happen on occasion. For instance, sometimes a bottle is inadvertently left out of a basket during assembly. Most of the time, it is only an interesting oddity, but enough of the incorrect-basket Farewell models were made that it is an attractive figure to some collectors.

Farewell is a retired figurine. The mold was scheduled to be broken up on December 31, 1993. All that were produced during 1993 bear a special "Final Issue" backstamp and were accompanied by a small medallion proclaiming it as a "Final Issue."

Hum No.	Basic Size	Trademark	Current Value
65/0	4"	TMK-2	$6,000-$8,000
65/0	4"	TMK-3	$5,000-$6,000
65.	4-3/4"	TMK-1	$760-$1,000
65/I	4-3/4"	TMK-1	$760-$1,000
65.	4-3/4"	TMK-2	$455-$575
65/I	4-3/4"	TMK-2	$455-$575
65/I	4-3/4"	TMK-3	$410-$460
65/I	4-3/4"	TMK-4	$350-$400
65/I	4-1/2" to 4-7/8"	TMK-5	$330-$360
65	4-3/4"	TMK-5	$330-$360
65	4-3/4"	TMK-6	$310-$335
65	4-3/4"	TMK-7	$280-$310

Hum 66: Farm Boy

A figure similar to that used in bookend Hum 60/A, this piece was modeled by master sculptor Arthur Moeller in 1937 and has been called "Three Pals" and "Happy-Go-Lucky Fellow" in the past. Older versions have larger shoes. In fact, in the older version, the whole piece appears fatter overall. It is occasionally found with the decimal point size designator.

Hum No.	Basic Size	Trademark	Current Value
66	5-1/4"	TMK-1	$700-$900
66	5-1/4"	TMK-1	$700-$900
66	5-1/4"	TMK-2	$410-$550
66	5-1/4"	TMK-3	$350-$410
66	5-1/4"	TMK-4	$320-$360
66	5-1/4"	TMK-5	$290-$315
66	5-1/4"	TMK-6	$280-$290
66	5" to 5-3/4"	TMK-7	$275-$280
66	5" to 5-3/4"	TMK-8	$275

Farm Boy, Hum 66. Left: Decimal designator in mold number 66., double Crown Mark (TMK-1), doughnut base. "Made in Germany" stamped on base and lacquered over, 5-1/8". Right: Full Bee (TMK-2) in an incised circle, black "Germany," doughnut base, 6".

Hum 67: Doll Mother

Released in 1937 at the Leipzig Trade Fair, Doll Mother was designed by master sculptor Arthur Moeller and first known as "Little Doll Mother" and "Little Mother of Dolls."

A color variation has recently surfaced whereby the blanket is white with red cross stripes rather than the typical pink blanket with red stripes. This unique piece bears TMK-1 and is worth $750-$1,000.

In 1997, a special 60th Anniversary Doll Mother figurine was issued with special backstamp and round gold medallion reading: "HUM 67 Doll Mother 1937-1997" and "60th."

Hum No.	Basic Size	Trademark	Current Value
67.	4-3/4"	TMK-1	$650-$850
67	4-3/4"	TMK-1	$650-$850
67	4-3/4"	TMK-2	$410-$510
67	4-3/4"	TMK-3	$330-$350
67	4-3/4"	TMK-4	$280-$325
67	4-3/4"	TMK-5	$255-$280
67	4-3/4"	TMK-6	$250-$255
67	4-1/4" to 4-3/4"	TMK-7	$245-$250
67	4-1/4" to 4-3/4"	TMK-8	$245-$250

Doll Mother, Hum 67. Left: 67., Double Crown Mark, "Made in Germany," 4-3/8". Right: Full Bee mark, black "Germany," 4-3/4".

Photo courtesy Goebel of North America.

Doll Mother is still in production today (TMK-8).

Hum 68: Lost Sheep

Master sculptor Arthur Moeller modeled this piece in 1937, but it has been restyled by several modelers over the years.

Sizes found referenced in lists are as follows: 4-1/4", 4-1/2", 5-1/2", and 6-1/2". This figure is found most commonly with green pants. A reference to a figure with orange pants (6-1/2") was found, but the color variation considered rarest is the one with brown pants. The collector value for the brown pants variation is about 25% higher than the value for the normal green pants piece.

There are four or five different color variations involving the coat, pants, and shirt of the figure. Oversize pieces bring premium prices.

The decimal point designator has been found on some early Crown Mark (TMK-1) figures.

The 68/0 and 68/2/0 sizes were retired at the end of 1992. Each of them made in 1992 bear the special "Final Issue" backstamp and came with a special "Final Issue" medallion.

Lost Sheep, Hum 68. Left: Incised Full Bee (TMK-2) trademark and a doughnut base with a black "Germany" beneath, 6". Right: 68/0 mold number with the Last Bee (TMK-5) trademark. Measures 5-1/2".

Hum No.	Basic Size	Trademark	Current Value
68/2/0	4-1/2"	TMK-2	$250-$350
68/2/0	4-1/2"	TMK-3	$225-$250
68/2/0	4-1/2"	TMK-4	$195-$230
68/2/0	4-1/2"	TMK-5	$185-$195
68/2/0	4-1/2"	TMK-6	$175-$185
68/2/0	4-1/4" to 4-1/2"	TMK-7	$165-$175
68	5-1/2"	TMK-1	$610-$760
68	5-1/2"	TMK-1	$610-$760
68	5-1/2"	TMK-2	$400-$500
68/0	5-1/2"	TMK-2	$350-$450
68	5-1/2"	TMK-3	$355-$405

Hum No.	Basic Size	Trademark	Current Value
68/0	5-1/2"	TMK-3	$310-$360
68/0	5-1/2"	TMK-4	$280-$310
68/0	5-1/2"	TMK-5	$250-$275
68/0	5-1/2"	TMK-6	$230-$250
68/0	5-1/2"	TMK-7	$210-$235

Hum 69: Happy Pastime

This figurine, which was modeled by master sculptor Arthur Moeller, was in a group of pieces that was issued a short time after the initial 46 were released. It was called "Knitter" in early company literature.

There have been changes over the years, but nothing significant enough to influence the normal pricing in any trademark era.

Happy Pastime was retired on December 31, 1996. All figures produced in 1996 bear the "Final Issue" backstamp and came with a special gold commemorative tag.

Hum No.	Basic Size	Trademark	Current Value
69	3-1/4"	TMK-1	$500-$650
69	3-1/4"	TMK-2	$310-$410
69	3-1/4"	TMK-3	$250-$280
69	3-1/4"	TMK-4	$230-$250
69	3-1/4"	TMK-5	$210-$225
69	3-1/4"	TMK-6	$205-$215
69	3-1/4" to 3-1/2"	TMK-7	$195-$205

From left, Happy Pastime, Hum 69, with TMK-3 and TMK-6.

Hum III/69: Happy Pastime (Candy Box)

There are two styles of candy boxes: bowl-like and jar-like. The transition from the old bowls to the new jars took place during the Stylized Bee (TMK-3) period, so both the old and new can be found bearing that trademark.

This candy box was temporarily withdrawn in December 1989.

Hum No.	Basic Size	Trademark	Current Value
III/69	6"	TMK-1	$750-$850
III/69	6"	TMK-2	$580-$660
III/69 (old)	6"	TMK-3	$485-$560
III/69 (new)	6"	TMK-3	$300-$350
III/69	6"	TMK-4	$255-$280
III/69	6"	TMK-5	$225-$250
III/69	6"	TMK-6	$200-$225

Happy Pastime candy dish, Hum III/69, with Last Bee (TMK-5).

Hum 70: Holy Child

The collective effort of several modelers, this piece was released in 1937 and has also been called "Child Jesus."

The piece has been known to exist in the rare white overglaze finish, which was sold only in Belgium, and in much sought-after oversize pieces, generally valued at about 20% above the normal value listed.

There was a general restyling of the whole collection over the years, to the more textured finish of the clothing of today's figures.

This figurine was temporarily withdrawn from production in 1999.

Hum No.	Basic Size	Trademark	Current Value
70	6-3/4"	TMK-1	$750-$850
70	6-3/4"	TMK-2	$385-$500
70	6-3/4"	TMK-3	$350-$380
70	6-3/4"	TMK-4	$325-$350
70	6-3/4"	TMK-5	$300-$325
70	6-3/4"	TMK-6	$300-$310
70	6-3/4"	TMK-7	$280-$285

The Holy Child, Hum 70. Left: Full Bee (TMK-2), black "Germany," 7-3/8". Right: Last Bee (TMK-5), 6-7/8".

Hum 71: Stormy Weather

This figure, which was designed by master sculptor Reinhold Unger in 1937, has been known as "Under One Roof."

Some earlier models were produced with a split base underneath. The split base model with the Full Bee (TMK-2) mark shows that the split is laterally oriented. The new models also have the split base, but it is oriented longitudinally.

A Crown Mark (TMK-1) Stormy Weather has been found that differs from the norm. Among other things, the boy figure in the piece has no kerchief. It is most likely a prototype, inasmuch as it is not signed.

Other than the oddity described above, there were no significant variations over the years until the small 71/2/0 (5") was introduced. After a period of time, it became obvious that the method of painting the underside of the umbrella had changed. The first models exhibit the brush strokes of hand-painting, and the later ones had been airbrushed. Serious collectors seek out this variation. It is valued at about $500-$600.

The 71 mold number was changed to 71/I during TMK-6 period. The mold number can be found rendered either way on those pieces.

In 1997, a special variation of 71/2/0 was produced for the QVC television program and sold by mail-order at $279.50 plus shipping and handling. This variation featured a yellow umbrella with tan-colored highlights, a decal signature on the back of the umbrella, and a special "60th Anniversary" backstamp.

Hum No.	Basic Size	Trademark	Current Value
71/2/0	5"	TMK-6	$355-$365
71/2/0	4-1/2" to 5"	TMK-7	$350-$355
71/2/0	4-1/2" to 5"	TMK-8	$350-$355
71	6-1/4"	TMK-1	$1,100-$1,350
71	6-1/4"	TMK-2	$800-$960
71	6-1/4"	TMK-3	$650-$675
71	6-1/4"	TMK-4	$600-$650
71	6-1/4"	TMK-5	$550-$600
71	6-1/4"	TMK-6	$525-$550
71/I	6-1/4"	TMK-6	$525-$535
71/I	6" to 6-1/4"	TMK-7	$510-$520
71/I	6" to 6-1/4"	TMK-8	$510-$520

Stormy Weather, Hum 71. Left: Crown Mark, split base, 6". Right: Stylized Bee mark in an incised circle, black "Western Germany," split base, 6".

The smaller present-day variation of Stormy Weather, Hum 71/2/0.

Photo courtesy Goebel of North America.

Hum 72: Spring Cheer

Designed by master sculptor Reinhold Unger in 1937 and released soon after the initial issue of 46, this figurine was originally called "Spring Flowers." It is modeled from the Hummel art called Just for You, H 271. Another piece modeled from the same artwork—Forever Yours, Hum 793—became the renewal premium for M.I. Hummel Club members who renew for their 20th year of membership.

There have been some significant variations in Spring Cheer over its years of production. It was initially released in a yellow dress and with no flowers in the right hand. These can be found in the Crown Mark (TMK-1), the Full Bee (TMK-2), and the Stylized Bee (TMK-3). During the Stylized Bee (TMK-3), the figure was produced with a green dress and flowers in the right hand. Current pieces are configured in the latter way. However, some of the old (no flowers in right hand) models were left over, and these were painted with a green dress to match the new model. This is the rarest of the two green dress models and is worth $1,200-$1,500.

The company lists the figurine as temporarily withdrawn from production as of December 31, 1984.

Spring Cheer, Hum 72. Left: Full Bee (TMK-2), black "Germany," 5-1/2". Note there are no flowers in the right hand. The dress is yellow. Center: Stylized Bee (TMK-1) mark, no flowers in right hand, green dress, 5-1/4". All newer versions have flowers in the right hand as in the right figurine in the photo.

Hum No.	Basic Size	Trademark	Current Value
72	5"	TMK-1	$500-$650
72	5"	TMK-2	$335-$400
72	5"	TMK-3	$300-$325
72	5"	TMK-4	$250-$300
72	5"	TMK-5	$225-$250
72	5"	TMK-6	$200-$225

Hum 73: Little Helper

Master sculptor Reinhold Unger created this figurine in 1937 and it had been called "Diligent Betsy" and "The Little Sister" in early company literature.

There are no significant variations from any of the trademark eras affecting the normal values for this figurine. The TMK-8 piece, however, has been paired with the present-day rendition of Cheeky Fellow, Hum 554, to create the Treehouse Treats Collector's Set. See Hum 554 for photo of the set.

Little Helper, Hum 73. The older is on the right. It has an incised Full Bee trademark (TMK-2) and measures 4-3/8". The one on the left is a 4" Stylized Bee (TMK-3) piece.

Today's variation (TMK-8) of Little Helper, which is 4-1/4" to 4-1/2" and worth $140.

Photo courtesy Goebel of North America.

Hum No.	Basic Size	Trademark	Current Value
73	4-1/4"	TMK-1	$410-$500
73	4-1/4"	TMK-2	$250-$325
73	4-1/4"	TMK-3	$195-$200
73	4-1/4"	TMK-4	$160-$195
73	4-1/4"	TMK-5	$150-$155
73	4-1/4"	TMK-6	$150-$155
73	4-1/4" to 4-1/2"	TMK-7	$140-$145
73	4-1/4" to 4-1/2"	TMK-8	$140

Hum 74: Little Gardener

This figure, which was modeled by master sculptor Reinhold Unger in 1937, was found in several lists with the following sizes: 4", 4-1/4", and 4-1/2". Earlier versions are found on an oval base, and more recent or current pieces are on the round base.

The major variation encountered is a dark green dress rather than the present lighter-colored dress. Some of the earliest models have a very light green or yellowish dress.

Some other variations make it easy to spot the older pieces. On the Crown Mark (TMK-1) and Full Bee (TMK-2) figures, the flower at the base is tall and almost egg-shaped. On the Stylized Bee (TMK-3) figures, the flower is about one-half the height of the earlier flowers, and from the Last Bee (TMK-5) on, they are rather flattened in comparison. These variations, however, have no effect on the normal value of the piece for their respective trademarks. They represent normal changes through the years.

There is one variation that bears watching. In the spring of 1992, Goebel took this figurine out of normal production for two years, resuming normal production in 1994.

From the spring of 1992 until the end of the year, Little Gardener was used as a district managers' special promotional piece and each piece bears a special promotion backstamp. The only place they were available was at authorized M.I. Hummel dealers conducting district manager special promotions and in Canada at artists' promotions. Each of these pieces bears the appropriate backstamp identifying it as such. The figurines were available on a first-come, first-served basis.

Hum No.	Basic Size	Trademark	Current Value
74	4-1/4"	TMK-1	$400-$500
74	4-1/4"	TMK-2	$230-$300
74	4-1/4"	TMK-3	$175-$200
74	4-1/4"	TMK-4	$500-$750
74	4-1/4"	TMK-5	$155-$160
74	4-1/4"	TMK-6	$145-$155
74	4" to 4-1/2"	TMK-7	$145-$150
74	4" to 4-1/2"	TMK-8	$145-$150

Little Gardener, Hum 74. Left: 74., incised Crown Mark, split base, 4-3/8". Note the height of the flower. Right: TMK-6, 4-1/2".

Little Gardener, Hum 74. Last Bee (TMK-5), 4-1/4".

Little Gardener is still in production today, shown here in TMK-8.

Hum 75: White Angel (Holy Water Font)

Although this piece, which was created in 1937 by master sculptor Reinhold Unger, has also known as "Angelic Prayer" or "White Angel Font," it is not white, but painted with color. Terra cotta variations have also surfaced over the years and those are worth $1,000-$1,500.

This piece was temporarily withdrawn from production in January 1999.

Hum No.	Basic Size	Trademark	Current Value
75	1-3/4" x 3-1/2"	TMK-1	$225-$275
75	1-3/4" x 3-1/2"	TMK-2	$130-$150
75	1-3/4" x 3-1/2"	TMK-3	$75-$85
75	1-3/4" x 3-1/2"	TMK-4	$60-$70
75	1-3/4" x 3-1/2"	TMK-5	$50-$60
75	1-3/4" x 3-1/2"	TMK-6	$45-$50
75	3-1/4" to 4-1/2"	TMK-7	$45-$50

White Angel font, Hum 75. Stylized Bee mark, 4-3/8".

Hum 76/A and Hum 76/B: Doll Mother and Prayer Before Battle (Bookends)

Originally modeled by master sculptor Arthur Moeller, these bookends are unique. It is possible, but not likely, that they might be found in a collector's possession. There are no known examples in private hands, only those in factory archives.

Hum No.	Basic Size	Trademark	Current Value
76 A&B	-	TMK-1	$10,000-$15,000

Hum 77: Cross With Doves (Holy Water Font)

In past editions of this book, it was reported that there was only one example of this piece and it was in the factory archives. Created by master sculptor Reinhold Unger in 1937, it was thought that the piece never went into production as it was listed as a closed edition in October 1937. However, at least 10 now reside in private collections. The one in the accompanying photos is an incised Crown Mark (TMK-1) piece with the M.I. Hummel signature on the back. It has been reported in white. If sold, this font would likely bring $5,000-$10,000, in color or white.

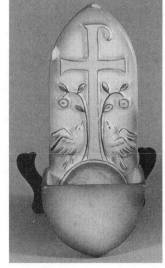

Cross With Doves font, Hum 77.

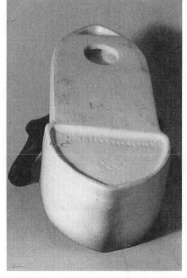

Backside of the Hum 77 font showing the Crown Mark and the M.I. Hummel incised signature.

The same piece after professional restoration.

Hum No.	Basic Size	Trademark	Current Value
77	1-3/4" x 6-1/4"	TMK-1	$5,000-$10,000

Known in the past as "In the Crib" and "Infant of Krumbad," this piece was first designed by master sculptor Erich Lautensack in 1937. It was then redesigned in 1965 by master sculptor Gerhard Skrobek.

This figurine can be found in seven different sizes and three finishes. All sizes, except one, have been either retired or temporarily withdrawn from production, with no stated reintroduction date.

The normal finish is a sepia-tone bisque. The figures were available painted in full color for a time, then withdrawn, reissued and finally discontinued. There was also a white overglaze finish reportedly produced for European market only. The color pieces are valued at two times the normal price listed for the size, and the white overglaze figures are valued at about two to three times the normal price, also depending on the size.

There are two pieces still available. One is the small 78/0, 2-1/4" size, which is difficult to get because this size was discontinued in the Stylized Bee (TMK-3) period. It has been redesigned and issued in the sepia-tone finish without the 78/0 incised mold number. It bears only TMK-6 or TMK-7 and is sold in the Siessen Convent only. It is unavailable elsewhere. The other one is also available only at the convent. It is the 4-1/2" Hum 78/II/1/2.

Hum No.	Basic Size	Trademark	Current Value
78/0	1-3/4"	TMK-2	$200-$300
78/0	1-3/4"	TMK-3	$150-$200
78/0	1-3/4"	TMK-6	$110
78/I	2-1/2"	TMK-3	$45-$55
78/I	2-1/2"	TMK-4	$35-$40
78/I	2-1/2"	TMK-5	$30-$35
78/I	2-1/2"	TMK-6	$30-$40
78/II	3-1/2"	TMK-3	$50-$60
78/II	3-1/2"	TMK-4	$45-$55
78/II	3-1/2"	TMK-5	$40-$50
78/II	3-1/2"	TMK-6	$35-$40
78/III	5-1/4"	TMK-1	$350-$400
78/III	5-1/4"	TMK-2	$250-$350
78/III	5-1/4"	TMK-3	$65-$75
78/III	5-1/4"	TMK-4	$55-$60
78/III	5-1/4"	TMK-5	$50-$60
78/III	5-1/4"	TMK-6	$45-$50
78/V	7-3/4"	TMK-3	$130-$150
78/V	7-3/4"	TMK-4	$100-$125
78/V	7-3/4"	TMK-5	$90-$100
78/V	7-3/4"	TMK-6	$80-$90
78/VI	10"	TMK-1	$600-$850
78/VI	10"	TMK-2	$425-$625
78/VI	10"	TMK-3	$200-$250
78/VI	10"	TMK-4	$200-$250
78/VI	10"	TMK-5	$155-$175
78/VI	10"	TMK-6	$155-$175
78/VIII	13-1/2"	TMK-1	$750-$1,000
78/VIII	13-1/2"	TMK-2	$500-$750
78/VIII	13-1/2"	TMK-3	$350-$400
78/VIII	13-1/2"	TMK-4	$350-$400
78/VIII	13-1/2"	TMK-5	$300-$325
78/VIII	13-1/2"	TMK-6	$300-$325
78/II/1/2*	4"	TMK-6	$100-$150
78/II/1/2*	4-1/2"	TMK-7	$75-$100
78/II/1/2*	4-1/2"	TMK-8	$75-$100

*One of the two only pieces in the collection to use this one-half designator. The other is Hum 21, Heavenly Angel.

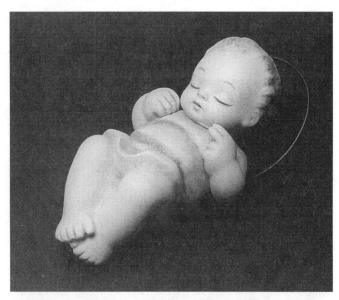

Blessed Child, Hum 78. This one bears the Full Bee trademark, measures 4-3/4" in length and has the original wire halo.

Hum 79: Globe Trotter

One of the pre-World War II releases, this figurine was originally designed by master sculptor Arthur Moeller in 1937. There are no significant variations that directly affect the value of the pieces under the various trademarks, but there are some interesting variations that can help you spot the earlier figures without examining the marks. The Crown Mark (TMK-1) and Full Bee (TMK-2) exhibit a double weave in the baskets (see accompanying photos). With a redesign in 1955, the weaving changed from double weave to single weave during the Stylized Bee (TMK-3) era, so you may find them in either configuration in that trademark. A few of the older marked figures will also sport a dark green hat instead of the normal reddish brown color.

Globe Trotter was permanently retired in 1991.

Hum No.	Basic Size	Trademark	Current Value
79	5"	TMK-1	$500-$750
79	5"	TMK-2	$375-$500
79 (old style)	5"	TMK-3	$310-$360
79	5"	TMK-4	$280-$300
79	5"	TMK-5	$250-$275
79	5"	TMK-6	$225-$250
79	5" to 5-1/4"	TMK-7	$200-$235

Globe Trotter, Hum 79. Left: Stamped Crown Mark (TMK-1), doughnut base, and 4-7/8". Right: Incised Full Bee (TMK-2), black "Germany," doughnut base, 5-1/4".

Globe Trotter, Hum 79. Rear shot showing the old style double weave basket.

Globe Trotter, Hum 79. Rear view showing the different basket weave patterns discussed in text. Older figure is on the left.

Globe Trotter, Hum 79. This photo shows the Final Issue Medallion and the new style single weave basket.

Hum 80: Little Scholar

Master sculptor Arthur Moeller designed this piece in 1937 and there have been no figures produced with variations that would affect their normal value. There is one variation, however, that may help you pick out the older pieces without examining the bases. The Crown Mark (TMK-1) and the Full Bee mark (TMK-2) pieces will have dark brown shoes instead of the lighter color of those produced later.

In 2002, a smaller 4-1/4" version of this figurine was introduced with model number Hum 80/2/0. It originally retailed for $175.

Hum No.	Basic Size	Trademark	Current Value
80	5-1/2"	TMK-1	$650-$800
80	5-1/2"	TMK-2	$380-$500
80	5-1/2"	TMK-3	$325-$350
80	5-1/2"	TMK-4	$280-$325
80	5-1/2"	TMK-5	$260-$280
80	5-1/2"	TMK-6	$225-$275
80	5-1/4" to 5-3/4"	TMK-7	$250-$275
80	5-1/4" to 5-3/4"	TMK-8	$250-$275
80/2/0	4-1/4"	TMK-8	$175

Little Scholar, Hum 80. Has the Full Bee (TMK-2) trademark, doughnut base, black "Germany," and is 5-5/8".

Little Scholar is still in production today, shown here in TMK-8.

Hum 81: School Girl

At one time called "Primer Girl" and "Little Scholar," this figurine was designed by master sculptor Arthur Moeller in 1937.

There are no variations affecting the value of any of the models of this piece. There are, however, some worth noting. The smallest of the figures, the 81/2/0, has flowers in the basket. All other sizes are devoid of flowers. The older figures have a black book bag and a pink blouse.

The figure has been found with the decimal point designator on the Crown Mark (TMK-1) larger 5-1/4" basic size.

Goebel issued a special edition of this figurine in the Hum 81/2/0 size in 1996 in commemoration of the 125th anniversary of the company. Each figure bears a special "125th Anniversary" backstamp. In addition, the inscription "International Collectible Exposition" is placed around the base.

The larger 81/0 variation was temporarily withdrawn from production in 1999.

School Girl, Hum 81. Note the flowers in the basket. Stylized Bee trademark, 4-1/2".

Today's rendition (TMK-8) of School Girl, Hum 81/2/0, which measures 4-1/4" to 4-3/4" and is worth $175.

Hum No.	Basic Size	Trademark	Current Value
81/2/0	4-1/4"	TMK-1	$450-$600
81/2/0	4-1/4"	TMK-2	$250-$350
81/2/0	4-1/4"	TMK-3	$230-$250
81/2/0	4-1/4"	TMK-4	$200-$225
81/2/0	4-1/4"	TMK-5	$185-$200
81/2/0	4-1/4"	TMK-6	$175-$185
81/2/0	4-1/4" to 4-3/4"	TMK-7	$175-$180
81/2/0	4-1/4" to 4/3/4"	TMK-8	$175
81.	5-1/4"	TMK-1	$600-$750
81/0	5-1/4"	TMK-1	$550-$700
81	5-1/4"	TMK-2	$350-$475
81/0	5-1/4"	TMK-2	$325-$450
81/0	5-1/4"	TMK-3	$300-$325
81/0	5-1/4"	TMK-4	$275-$300
81/0	5-1/4"	TMK-5	$250-$275
81/0	5-1/4"	TMK-6	$235-$250
81/0	4-3/4" to 5-1/4"	TMK-7	$225-$240

(60th Anniversary Decal 1998)

School Girl, Hum 81. Left: 81/0 Full Bee mark, black "Germany," doughnut base, 5-1/4". Right: 81/0, Last Bee, 4-7/8".

Hum 82: School Boy

Listed as "Little Scholar," "School Days," and "Primer Boy" in company literature throughout the years, this piece was originally crafted by master sculptor Arthur Moeller in 1938. Sizes found in various lists are 4", 4-3/4", 5-1/2", and 7-1/2". It is occasionally found having the decimal point size designator in the Crown Mark (TMK-1) pieces. There are no other significant variations.

The larger 82/II size was temporarily withdrawn from production in 1999.

School Boy, Hum 82/0. Left: Double Crown mark, doughnut base, 4-7/8". Center: Full Bee mark in an incised circle, black "Germany," 5". Right: Full Bee mark, black "Germany," doughnut base, 5-3/4".

Hum No.	Basic Size	Trademark	Current Value
82/2/0	4"	TMK-1	$450-$600
82/2/0	4"	TMK-2	$250-$350
82/2/0	4"	TMK-3	$225-$260
82/2/0	4"	TMK-4	$200-$225
82/2/0	4"	TMK-5	$185-$200
82/2/0	4"	TMK-6	$175-$180
82/2/0	4" to 4-1/2"	TMK-7	$175-$180
82/2/0	4" to 4-1/2"	TMK-8	$175
82.	5-1/2"	TMK-1	$625-$775
82/0	4-3/4" to 6"	TMK-1	$600-$750
82/0	5-1/2"	TMK-2	$350-$500
82/0	5-1/2"	TMK-3	$335-$360
82/0	5-1/2"	TMK-4	$275-$325
82/0	5-1/2"	TMK-5	$250-$275
82/0	5-1/2"	TMK-6	$240-$250
82/0	4-3/4" to 6"	TMK-7	$240-$250
82/0	4-3/4" to 6"	TMK-8	$240
82/II	7-1/2"	TMK-1	$1,200-$1,600
82/II	7-1/2"	TMK-2	$900-$1,100
82/II	7-1/2"	TMK-3	$600-$700
82/II	7-1/2"	TMK-5	$550-$625
82/II	7-1/2"	TMK-6	$525-$550
82/II	7-1/2"	TMK-7	$500-$515

One of two present-day (TMK-8) variations of School Boy; this one is 82/0 and measures 4-3/4" to 6".

Photo courtesy Goebel of North America.

Hum 83: Angel Serenade With Lamb

Another piece in the collection with a similar name (Angel Serenade) is part of the Nativity Set. They do not look alike, but the name may confuse you.

Originally called "Psalmist," this piece was designed by master sculptor Reinhold Unger in 1938.

There are no significant variations, only minor changes over the years. Until recently, these figures were apparently made in limited quantities (from the TMK-3 period to TMK-6 period), but now they seem to be readily available again.

Angel Serenade With Lamb, Hum 83. Full Bee mark in an incised circle, black "Germany," 5-3/4".

Hum No.	Basic Size	Trademark	Current Value
83	5"	TMK-1	$600-$750
83	5"	TMK-2	$510-$560
83	5"	TMK-3	$400-$500
83	5"	TMK-4	$300-$400
83	5"	TMK-5	$275-$300
83	5"	TMK-6	$265-$275
83	5-1/2" to 5-3/4"	TMK-7	$255-$265

(60th Anniversary Decal 1998)

The most recent variation (TMK-7) of Angel Serenade With Lamb, Hum 83.

Photo courtesy Goebel of North America.

Hum 84: Worship

In 1938, master sculptor Reinhold Unger originally crafted this piece, which was previously called "At the Wayside" and "Devotion." Sizes reported in various lists are 5", 6-3/4", and 14-1/2". The figure has been found with the decimal point size designator.

The 84/V size was temporarily withdrawn from production at the end of 1989 with no reinstatement date revealed.

Hum No.	Basic Size	Trademark	Current Value
84 (white)	5-1/4"	TMK-1	$1,000-$1,500
84	5-1/4"	TMK-1	$475-$625
84/0	5"	TMK-1	$450-$625
84/0	5"	TMK-2	$300-$375
84/0	5"	TMK-3	$255-$280
84/0	5"	TMK-4	$225-$260
84/0	5"	TMK-5	$200-$215
84/0	5"	TMK-6	$200-$210
84/0	5"	TMK-7	$195-$200
(60th Anniversary Decal 1998)			
84/0	5"	TMK-8	$195
84/V	13"	TMK-1	$2,000-$3,000
84/V	13"	TMK-2	$1,500-$2,000
84/V	13"	TMK-3	$1,230-$1,450
84/V	13"	TMK-4	$1,175-$1,225
84/V	13"	TMK-5	$1,150-$1,175
84/V	13"	TMK-6	$1,125-$1,150

Worship, Hum 84. Mold number is rendered as 84./5. and the figurine bears the large Stylized Bee mark (TMK-3). It measures 13-1/8".

Still in production today (TMK-8) is Worship, Hum 84/0, standing 5" tall.

Photo courtesy Goebel of North America.

Hum 85: Serenade

Introduced in the late-1930s and originally modeled by master sculptor Arthur Moeller, this figurine has undergone normal changes of style, colors, and finishes over the years, but none have had a significant impact on the collector value. It has been called "The Flutist" in some early company literature.

An interesting variation concerns the boy's fingers on the flute. You can find figures with some fingers extended (see color section for an example) while other versions have all fingers down. It seems, however, that there is no association with any particular mark or marks one way or the other.

The decimal designator can be found with the mold number on the older Crown Mark (TMK-1) pieces in both sizes.

There is a beautiful blue Hum 85 in the 7-1/2" size illustrated in the color section. It has no apparent markings. So far, this is the only one in a blue suit to be found. It seems peculiar that the normal Serenades were not rendered in blue, as that is the color M.I. Hummel used in the original artwork (H 342) on which the piece is modeled. There has also been a Serenade found with the incised mold number 85/0. This one is painted with an airbrush rather than the usual brush. Both of these are most likely samples that did not obtain the approval of the convent.

Recently, a 12-1/2" version of Serenade was introduced as part of the "Millennium Love" series, which also included Sweet Music (Hum 186/III), Little Fiddler (Hum 2/III), Band Leader (Hum 129/III), and Soloist (Hum 135/III). These oversized pieces (Hum 85/III) were in limited supply and had to be special-ordered through an authorized M.I. Hummel retailer.

The 85/4/0 and 85/II size variations have been temporarily withdrawn from production.

Hum No.	Basic Size	Trademark	Current Value
85/4/0	3-1/2"	TMK-5	$70-$85
85/4/0	3-1/2"	TMK-6	$125-$135
85/4/0	3-1/2"	TMK-7	$120-$125
85/0	4-3/4"	TMK-1	$400-$500
85/0	4-3/4"	TMK-2	$225-$300
85/0	4-3/4"	TMK-3	$200-$225
85/0	4-3/4"	TMK-4	$185-$200
85/0	4-3/4"	TMK-5	$175-$185
85/0	4-3/4"	TMK-6	$165-$170
85/0	4-3/4" to 5-1/4"	TMK-7	$165-$175
85/0	4-3/4" to 5-1/4"	TMK-8	$165
85.	7-1/2"	TMK-1	$1,250-$1,550
85/II	7-1/2"	TMK-1	$1,200-$1,500
85/II	7-1/2"	TMK-2	$750-$950
85	7-1/2"	TMK-2	$775-$975
85/II	7-1/2"	TMK-3	$650-$700
85/II	7-1/2"	TMK-4	$600-$650
85/II	7-1/2"	TMK-5	$550-$600
85/II	7-1/2"	TMK-6	$525-$550
85/II	7" to 7-1/2"	TMK-7	$500-$510
85/III	12-1/2"	TMK-8	$1,550

Serenade, Hum 85/II. Full Bee mark, black "Germany," doughnut base, 7-5/8".

TMK-8 version of Serenade, Hum 85/0, which is 4-3/4" to 5-1/4" and worth $165.

Hum 86: Happiness

Another late-1930s entry into the collection, this piece was first crafted by master sculptor Reinhold Unger in 1938. Although its name has changed from the original "Wandersong" and "Traveler's Song," there have been no other changes or variations significant enough to affect value. Sizes reported in various lists are 4-1/2", 4-1/4", 5", and 5-1/2".

Hum No.	Basic Size	Trademark	Current Value
86	4-3/4"	TMK-1	$400-$500
86	4-3/4"	TMK-2	$255-$355
86	4-3/4"	TMK-3	$200-$230
86	4-3/4"	TMK-4	$175-$200
86	4-3/4"	TMK-5	$170-$180
86	4-3/4"	TMK-6	$165-$175
86	4-1/2" to 5"	TMK-7	$160-$165
(60th Anniversary Decal 1998)			
86	4-1/2" to 5"	TMK-8	$160

Happiness, Hum 86. Left: Full Bee (TMK-2), black "Germany," 5-1/8". Right: Last Bee (TMK-5) mark, 5-1/2".

Today's variation (TMK-8) of Happiness, which is worth $160.

Photo courtesy Goebel of North America.

Hum 87: For Father

For Father is yet another late-1930s release, formerly called "Father's Joy" and originally designed by master sculptor Arthur Moeller in 1938.

The significant variations have to do with the beer stein and the color of the radishes. A few early Crown Mark (TMK-1) pieces have been found with the initials "HB" painted on the stein (see accompanying photograph). The radishes on these figures have a definite greenish cast. These pieces are rare and can be priced as high as $5,000.

The other important variation is found on Full Bee (TMK-2) and Stylized Bee (TMK-3) trademark figures, where the radishes are colored orange to more closely resemble carrots than radishes. The collector value for this variation is $2,500-$4,000.

In 1996, Goebel announced the "Personal Touch" figurines, one of which was For Father. Goebel will inscribe onto the figure a personalization of your choice. The other three original figures used for personalization in the "Personal Touch" line were Bird Duet (Hum 69), Latest News (Hum 184), and The Guardian (Hum 455).

For Father Hum 87. Left: Full Bee mark (TMK-2), doughnut base, black "Germany," red radishes, 5-11/16". Right: Stamped Full Bee mark (TMK-2) in an incised circle, black "Western Germany," doughnut base, brown radishes, 5-3/4".

For Father, Hum 87. Mold number is rendered with the decimal designator 87., double Crown Mark, doughnut base. Note the "HB" on the stein standing for Hofbrau House in Munich. This is a very scarce item. Also there is a very distinct green highlighting on the radishes not appearing on any other variations.

For Father, Hum 87, is still in production today (TMK-8).

In the summer of 2002, a smaller 4-1/4" variation of For Father was announced. Sculpted by master sculptor Helmut Fischer, the smaller piece carries model number 87/2/0, a "First Issue 2002" backstamp, and TMK-8.

Hum No.	Basic Size	Trademark	Current Value
87	5-1/2"	TMK-1	$650-$800
87	5-1/2"	TMK-2	$400-$530
87	5-1/2"	TMK-3	$325-$375

Hum No.	Basic Size	Trademark	Current Value
87	5-1/2"	TMK-4	$275-$330
87	5-1/2"	TMK-5	$265-$280
87	5-1/2"	TMK-6	$260-$270
87	5-1/2"	TMK-7	$255-$265
(60th Anniversary Decal 1998)			
87	5-1/2"	TMK-8	$255
87/2/0	4-1/4"	TMK-8	$190

Hum 88: Heavenly Protection

This figure, which was originally crafted by master sculptor Reinhold Unger, was first introduced in the late-1930s in the 9-1/4" size with a decimal designator (88.) or 88 (without the decimal) in the Crown Mark (TMK-1), the Full Bee (TMK-2), and the Stylized Bee (TMK-3) trademarks.

The transition from the 88 to the 88/II mold number took quite some time. It began in the Full Bee era and was completed in the Stylized Bee era, so you can find the mold number rendered either way with either of those two trademarks.

The large size has been found in white overglaze in the Crown and Full Bee marks.

There is a similar piece in the Goebel line that some theorize may have either inspired Heavenly Protection or was inspired by it. It is mold number HS 1 and is illustrated in Chapter 5. Also see Hum 108.

The larger 88/II size was temporarily withdrawn in 1994, reinstated for a short time, and once again withdrawn from production in 1999.

Heavenly Protection, Hum 88. Left: Full Bee (TMK-2) mark, base split in quarters beneath, black "Germany," 9-3/8". Right: 88/II, small Stylized Bee (TMK-3), doughnut base, 8-5/8".

Hum No.	Basic Size	Trademark	Current Value
88/I	6-3/4"	TMK-3	$650-$750
88/I	6-3/4"	TMK-4	$575-$660
88/I	6-3/4"	TMK-5	$550-$575
88/I	6-3/4"	TMK-6	$525-$535
88/I	6-1/4" to 6-3/4"	TMK-7	$510-$525
(60th Anniversary Decal 1998)			
88/I	6-1/4" to 6-3/4"	TMK-8	$510-$525
88. or 88	9-1/4"	TMK-1	$1,800-$2,400
88. or 88	9-1/4"	TMK-2	$1,300-$1,600
88. or 88	9-1/4"	TMK-3	$1,100-$1,200
88/II	9-1/4"	TMK-2	$1,000-$1,300
88/II	9-1/4"	TMK-3	$1,000-$1,100
88/II	9-1/4"	TMK-4	$900-$1,000
88/II	9-1/4"	TMK-5	$850-$925
88/II	9-1/4"	TMK-6	$525-$850
88/II	8-3/4" to 9"	TMK-7	$800-$825

Today's TMK-8 version of Heavenly Protection, Hum 88/I.

Hum 89: Little Cellist

Master sculptor Arthur Moeller originally designed this figurine in 1938 under the name "Musician." Other than the name change, there have been no major variations over the years that would have an impact on the collector value of this figurine.

There are some differences worth noting, however. The newer models have a base that has flattened corners (see accompanying photograph). The older models have squared-off corners. Also in the older models, the boy's head is up and his eyes are wide open, whereas on the new models the head is down and his eyes are cast down as if concentrating on his steps. The transition from old to new style was during the Stylized Bee (TMK-3) era, so the old and the new can be found with this mark, the older obviously being the more desirable to collectors.

The larger 89/II size was temporarily withdrawn from production in 1993.

Hum No.	Basic Size	Trademark	Current Value
89/I	6"	TMK-1	$650-$850
89/I	6"	TMK-2	$400-$530
89/I	6"	TMK-3	$325-$380
89/I	6"	TMK-4	$285-$325

Little Cellist, Hum 89. Left: 89/I, double Crown Mark (TMK-1), 4-6/16". Right: 89/I, small Stylized Bee (TMK-3) mark, 5-5/16". Note the difference in the eyes and the bases of the old versus the newer piece.

Little Cellist, Hum 89. Left: 89/II, Stylized Bee (TMK-3) stamped in an incised circle, 7-7/8", black "Western Germany." Right: 89/II, Last Bee (TMK-5) trademark, 7-1/2". Note the textured hat and clothing on the newer of the two pieces and the different bases.

Hum No.	Basic Size	Trademark	Current Value	Hum No.	Basic Size	Trademark	Current Value
89/I	6"	TMK-5	$265-$285	89/II	7-1/2" to 7-3/4"	TMK-1	$1,200-$1,500
89/I	6"	TMK-6	$260-$270	89/II	7-1/2" to 7-3/4"	TMK-2	$800-$1,000
89/I	5-1/4" to 6-1/4"	TMK-7	$255-$265	89/II	7-1/2" to 7-3/4"	TMK-3	$650-$750
(60th Anniversary Decal 1998)				89/II	7-1/2" to 7-3/4"	TMK-4	$600-$650
89/I	5-1/4" to 6-1/4"	TMK-8	$255-$265	89/II	7-1/2" to 7-3/4"	TMK-5	$500-$550
89.	8"	TMK-1	$1,400-$1,750	89/II	7-1/2" to 7-3/4"	TMK-6	$475-$500
89	8"	TMK-1	$1,250-$1,600	89/II	7-1/2" to 7-3/4"	TMK-7	$450-$475

Hum 90/A and Hum 90/B: Eventide and Adoration (Bookends)

Up until late-1984 it was thought that these pieces were never produced except in sample form and never were released on the market. The Adoration half of the set has been found, however. It is not likely that these bookends were ever put into production, but more than one was obviously made as at least two of the Adoration halves have made it into private collections.

Hum No.	Basic Size	Trademark	Current Value
90/A&B	-	-	$10,000-$15,000
90/B	4"	-	$5,000-$7,500

Adoration, Hum 90/B, half of the bookends. No apparent markings. Measures 3-3/4" (figure only).

Hum 91/A and 91/B: Angel at Prayer (Holy Water Font)

The angel facing left likely was made first since it exists in TMK-1 by itself and without an "A" designator. Thereafter, however, the fonts were released as a set with one facing left (91/A) and the other right (91/B).

The only notable variation in these figures is that the older ones have no halo and the newer models do. The transition from no halo to halo took place in the Stylized Bee (TMK-3) era, and both types of figures may be found in that trademark.

Hum No.	Basic Size	Trademark	Current Value
91/A&B	2" x 4-3/4"	TMK-2	$200-$260
91/A&B	2" x 4-3/4"	TMK-3	$130-$155
91/A&B	2" x 4-3/4"	TMK-3	$130-$155
91/A&B	2" x 4-3/4"	TMK-4	$115-$130
91/A&B	2" x 4-3/4"	TMK-5	$110-$120
91/A&B	2" x 4-3/4"	TMK-6	$105-$115
91/A&B	3-3/8" x 5"	TMK-7	$105-$110
91/A&B	3-3/8" x 5"	TMK-8	$105-$110

Hum No.	Basic Size	Trademark	Current Value
91	3-1/4" x 4-1/2"	TMK-1	$400-$500
91/A&B	2" x 4-3/4"	TMK-1	$400-$500

Angel at Prayer fonts, Hum 91/A and Hum 91/B. Left: 91B, Last Bee, and 5". Right: 91A, Stylized Bee mark, 4-7/8".

Today's rendition (TMK-8) of Angel at Prayer fonts, Hum 91/A and Hum 91/B.

Hum 92: Merry Wanderer (Wall Plaque)

Master sculptor Arthur Moeller originally designed this piece in 1938 and it has gone through several redesigns since.

There are two distinct sizes to be found in the Crown (TMK-1) and Full Bee (TMK-2) trademark pieces. The newer ones are all in the smaller size. There are also some differences with regard to the placement of the incised M.I. Hummel signature, but there are no variations having a significant impact on the collector value. Some of the older Crown Mark pieces have been found with the decimal designator.

The piece was temporarily withdrawn from production in 1989.

Merry Wanderer plaque, Hum 92. Last Bee, 4-3/4" x 5".

Hum No.	Basic Size	Trademark	Current Value
92	4-3/4" x 5-1/8"	TMK-1	$450- $575
92	4-3/4" x 5-1/8"	TMK-2	$280-$350
92	4-3/4" x 5-1/8"	TMK-3	$225-$275
92	4-3/4" x 5-1/8"	TMK-4	$175-$225
92	4-3/4" x 5-1/8"	TMK-5	$165-$175
92	4-3/4" x 5-1/8"	TMK-6	$150-$165

Hum 93: Little Fiddler (Wall Plaque)

Originally crafted by master sculptor Arthur Moeller in 1938, this plaque bears the Little Fiddler motif, which appears many times in the collection. The older models show less background detail.

The accompanying photograph shows both the old and the newer designs. The older one is quite rare and is valued at $3,000-$4,000.

Some pieces display a 1938 copyright date, while others do not. Additionally, some bear the "M.I. Hummel" signature on both front and back, while other have it on either just the front or just the back.

This plaque was temporarily withdrawn from production on December 31, 1989.

Little Fiddler plaque, Hum 93. Left: 93., double Crown Mark, 4-3/4" x 5-1/8". Right: Last Bee, 4-3/4" x 5-1/8".

Hum No.	Basic Size	Trademark	Current Value
93	4-3/4" x 5-1/8"	TMK-1	$450-$575
93	4-3/4" x 5-1/8"	TMK-2	$275-$360
93	4-3/4" x 5-1/8"	TMK-3	$225-$275
93	4-3/4" x 5-1/8"	TMK-4	$175-$230
93	4-3/4" x 5-1/8"	TMK-5	$165-$175
93	4-3/4" x 5-1/8"	TMK-6	$150-$165
93 (rare old style)		TMK-1	$3,000-$4,000

Hum 94: Surprise

Designed by a group of sculptors and first placed in the line in the late-1930s in two basic sizes, this figurine continues in production in only the smaller of those sizes today. It has been called "The Duet" and "Hansel and Gretel" in past company literature, as well as "What's Up?"

The 94/I size has been found erroneously marked 94/II. The error was apparently caught early, for only a very few have shown up.

Older examples of the 94/I size have been found without the "/I".

The smaller 94/3/0 size is less detailed than the larger 94/I size, which was temporarily withdrawn from production in 1999.

Hum No.	Basic Size	Trademark	Current Value
94/3/0	4-1/4"	TMK-1	$450-$550
94/3/0	4-1/4"	TMK-2	$275-$380
94/3/0	4-1/4"	TMK-3	$225-$250
94/3/0	4-1/4"	TMK-4	$200-$225
94/3/0	4-1/4"	TMK-5	$195-$210
94/3/0	4-1/4"	TMK-6	$185-$195
94/3/0	4" to 4-1/4"	TMK-7	$180-$190
94/3/0	4" to 4-1/4"	TMK-8	$180
94	5-1/2"	TMK-1	$800-$1,000
94	5-1/2"	TMK-2	$550-$700
94/I	5-1/2"	TMK-1	$750-$950
94/I	5-1/2"	TMK-2	$500-$650
94/I	5-1/2"	TMK-3	$425-$475
94/I	5-1/2"	TMK-4	$400-$425
94/I	5-1/2"	TMK-5	$350-$400
94/I	5-1/2"	TMK-6	$340-$355
94/I	5-1/4" to 5-1/2"	TMK-7	$325-$340

Surprise, Hum 94. Left: Crown Mark, "U.S.-ZONE Germany," 5-3/4". Right: 94/1, Stylized Bee mark, 5-1/2".

Photo courtesy Goebel of North America.

Still in production today in a 4-1/4" size is Surprise, Hum 94/3/0.

Hum 95: Brother

Previously known as "Our Hero" and "Hero of the Village" and designed collectively by a group of sculptors, this figurine can be found in many size and color variations. For example, the older mold style comes with a blue coat.

The earliest Crown Mark (TMK-1) pieces can be found with the decimal point designator, but there are no other variations of any great significance. It is the same boy used in Surprise (Hum 94).

The 1998 piece bears a special "60th Anniversary" decal and metal tag.

Hum No.	Basic Size	Trademark	Current Value
95	5-1/2"	TMK-1	$600-$800
95	5-1/2"	TMK-2	$350-$500
95	5-1/2"	TMK-3	$310-$325
95	5-1/2"	TMK-4	$280-$300
95	5-1/2"	TMK-5	$250-$275
95	5-1/2"	TMK-6	$245-$255
95	5-1/4" to 5-3/4"	TMK-7	$240-$250
(60th Anniversary Decal 1998)			
95	5-1/4" to 5-3/4"	TMK-8	$240

Today's TMK-8 version of Brother, Hum 95.

Brother, Hum 95. Left: 95., no apparent trademark, but probably a Crown era piece, doughnut base, 5-1/2". Center: TMK-3, 5-5/8". Right: TMK-6, 5-5/8".

Hum 96: Little Shopper

Introduced in the late-1930s and formerly known as "Errand Girl," "Gretel," and "Meg," this figurine has changed little over the years. Like some of the other pieces crafted in 1938, it was the collective work of a group of sculptors. It is the same girl used in Surprise (Hum 94).

Hum No.	Basic Size	Trademark	Current Value
96	4-3/4"	TMK-1	$430-$550
96	4-3/4"	TMK-2	$275-$350
96	4-3/4"	TMK-3	$215-$250
96	4-3/4"	TMK-4	$195-$215
96	4-3/4"	TMK-5	$180-$190
96	4-3/4"	TMK-6	$175-$185
96	4-1/2" to 5"	TMK-7	$170-$175
96	4-1/2" to 5"	TMK-8	$170-$175

Little Shopper, Hum 96. Small Stylized Bee (TMK-3), 4-1/2".

Little Shopper, Hum 96, is still in production today (TMK-8).

Hum 97: Trumpet Boy

Originally called "The Little Musician," this piece was designed by master sculptor Arthur Moeller in 1938.

In addition to many size variations, there is an especially notable color variation. The boy's coat is normally green, but some of the older models, particularly those produced during the post-war U.S. Occupation era, have a blue painted coat.

Trumpet Boy in the Crown Mark (TMK-1) is fairly rare, but most assuredly exists. The Crown Mark era piece will have "Design Patent No. 116, 464" inscribed beneath (see accompanying photo).

A query with a photograph to Goebel regarding this anomaly brought the following response: "The Trumpet Boy shown in the photo seems to be a very old figurine dating back to pre-war years. The bottom of the piece allows the assumption that production date may go back as far as the late-1930s (possibly cast from the first model). The stamp Design Patent No. 116.464 indicates that the piece was originally shipped to England. All merchandise shipped at that time to that country was liable to be marked with the respective design patent number . . .". The collector value for a Trumpet Boy so marked is $1,000-$1,500.

Hum No.	Basic Size	Trademark	Current Value
97	4-3/4"	TMK-1	$400-$525
97	4-3/4"	TMK-2	$250-$300
97	4-3/4"	TMK-3	$200-$230
97	4-3/4"	TMK-4	$185-$225
97	4-3/4"	TMK-5	$175-$185
97	4-3/4"	TMK-6	$165-$175
97	4-3/4"	TMK-7	$150-$160

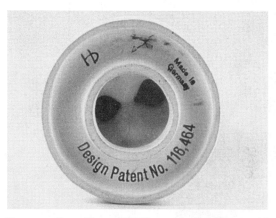

Trumpet Boy, Hum 97. Shows the unique mold number rendering discussed in the accompanying text.

Trumpet Boy, Hum 97. Stylized Bee (TMK-3), 4-1/2".

The most recent variation of Trumpet Boy, Hum 97, with TMK-7.

Hum 98: Sister

This figure, which was crafted by master sculptor Arthur Moeller in 1938, was introduced in the late-1930s in the 5-3/4" basic size with the incised number 98, and a smaller size was introduced during the Stylized Bee (TMK-3) trademark period with the incised 98/2/0. The piece was originally known as "The Shopper" and "The First Shopping" in early company literature, and this is the same girl used in To Market (Hum 49).

Some of the larger size pieces from the Crown Mark (TMK-1) era through the Stylized Bee (TMK-3) era are found with the 98 mold number with and without the decimal designator (see Hum 788/B).

A special "60th Anniversary" decal appeared on the 1998 piece created in the smaller 98/2/0 size.

The larger 98/0 size was temporarily withdrawn from production in 1999.

Hum No.	Basic Size	Trademark	Current Value
98/5/0	2-3/4"	TMK-7	$55
98/2/0	4-3/4"	TMK-3	$230-$250
98/2/0	4-3/4"	TMK-4	$190-$225
98/2/0	4-3/4"	TMK-5	$185-$195
98/2/0	4-3/4"	TMK-6	$180-$185
98/0	4-12" to 4-3/4"	TMK-7	$175-$180
(60th Anniversary decal 1998)			
98/0	4-1/2" to 4-3/4"	TMK-8	$175
98.	5-1/4"	TMK-1	$550-$700
98.	5-3/4"	TMK-2	$350-$450
98.	5-3/4"	TMK-3	$325-$350
98/0	5-3/4"	TMK-3	$300-$325
98/0	5-3/4"	TMK-4	$275-$300
98/0	5-3/4"	TMK-5	$250-$275
98/0	5-3/4"	TMK-6	$240-$255
98/0	5-1/4" to 5-1/2"	TMK-7	$230-$235

Sister, Hum 98. Left: Full Bee mark (TMK-2), black "Germany," doughnut base, 5-3/4". Right: 98/2/0, Last Bee (TMK-5), 1962 copyright date, 4-3/4".

Photo courtesy Goebel of North America.

Today's variation (TMK-8) of Sister, Hum 98/2/0, which is 4-1/2" to 4-3/4" tall and worth $175.

Hum 99: Eventide

Crafted by the collective efforts of a group of sculptors, this piece is almost identical to Wayside Devotion (Hum 28) but without the shrine.

There are three versions of this figurine to be found. Apparently when first released in the late-1930s the lambs were placed toward the left side of the base. For whatever reason, they were moved to the right side soon after and there they remained through the most recent production of the piece (TMK-7). This piece has also been found without the sheep. The collector value range for both the left-side sheep and the no sheep versions is $3,000-$3,500. There is also a rare white overglazed version valued at about the same amount.

This figurine was temporarily withdrawn from production in 1999.

Eventide, Hum 99. Stylized Bee mark (TMK3), 4-1/2".

Hum No.	Basic Size	Trademark	Current Value
99	4-3/4"	TMK-1	$950-$1,250
99	4-3/4"	TMK-2	$600-$750
99	4-3/4"	TMK-3	$500-$550
99	4-3/4"	TMK-4	$430-$500
99	4-3/4"	TMK-5	$395-$430
99	4-3/4"	TMK-6	$375-$395
99	4-1/4" x 5"	TMK-7	$360-$375
99 (rare version)		TMK-1	$3,000-$3,500

Hum 100: Shrine (Table Lamp)

In 1938, sculptor Erich Lautensack designed this extremely rare 7-1/2" table lamp containing a figure similar to Adoration (Hum 23). As far as can be determined, only three or four currently exist in collectors' hands. The lamps found so far bear the Crown (TMK-1) or the Full Bee (TMK-2) trademarks. There are two versions of the lamppost. The most common is the tree trunk post. The rarest is the fluted post.

Hum No.	Basic Size	Trademark	Current Value
100	7-1/2"	TMK-1	$8,000-$10,000
100	7-1/2"	TMK-2	$8,000-$10,000

Hum 101: To Market (Table Lamp)

This piece, which was designed by master sculptor Arthur Moeller in 1937, was quickly listed as a closed edition the same year. However, after a redesign by Moeller in 1952, a limited number were produced again in the early 1950s. This lamp is an adaptation of To Market (Hum 49).

There are two versions of this lamp with regard to the lamp stem or post. Of the few that have been found, most exhibit the "tree trunk" base, which was part of the 1950s redesign (see accompanying photograph). Rarer are the less elaborate fluted stem and plain stem examples. The "plain" description refers only to the paint finish; the CM fluted stem is painted white, whereas the plain version is painted light beige. The plain version is found in both the Crown and the Full Bee trademarks.

To Market table lamp, Hum 101. Rear view showing the regular and the tree trunk style lamp stem.

Hum No.	Basic Size	Trademark	Current Value
101 (plain)	6-1/2"	TMK-1	$8,000-$10,000
101 (plain)	6-1/2"	TMK-2	$6,000-$8,000
101 (tree trunk)	7-1/2"	TMK-1	$1,500-$2,000
101	7-1/2"	TMK-2	$750-$1,000
101	7-1/2"	TMK-3	$500-$750

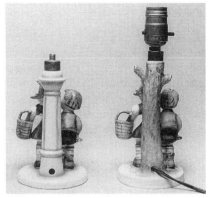

To Market table lamp, Hum 101. Left: Full Bee mark (TMK-2), 6-1/2". Right: Stylized Bee in an incised circle, 7-1/8".

Hum 102: Volunteers (Table Lamp)

Another Erich Lautensack design from 1937, there are only a few examples of this piece known to exist in private collections. It was listed as a closed edition in April 1937 and the few found so far all bear the Crown Mark (TMK-1) and have a plain white post.

Hum No.	Basic Size	Trademark	Current Value
102	7-1/2"	TMK-1	$8,000-$10,000

Volunteers table lamp, Hum 102, at 7-1/2" with TMK-1.

Photo courtesy Goebel of North America.

Hum 103: Farewell (Table Lamp)

Master sculptor Erich Lautensack designed this is an extremely rare piece in 1937 and it was listed as a closed edition the very same year. Very few are known to exist.

Hum No.	Basic Size	Trademark	Current Value
103	7-1/2"	TMK-1	$8,000-$10,000

Farewell table lamp, Hum 103, at 7-1/2" with TMK-1.

Photo courtesy Goebel of North America.

Hum 104: Eventide (Table Lamp)

Very few examples of this table lamp, which was crafted by master sculptor Reinhold Unger in 1938, are known to be in collectors' hands at present. It is similar to the figurine of the same name, Hum 99, except for the positioning of the lambs, which are centered in front of the children on the lamp base rather than off to the right as in the figurine.

Hum No.	Basic Size	Trademark	Current Value
104	7-1/2"	TMK-1	$8,000-$10,000

Hum 105: Adoration With Bird

First discovered about 1977, this piece was not previously thought to exist. It bears the mold number 105. This number was a "closed number," a number supposedly never used and never intended for use on an original Hummel piece. There have been at least 10 to 15 pieces found since the initial discovery. Because of its similarity to Hum 23, Adoration, it was probably designed by master sculptor Reinhold Unger, although there are no records to verify that assumption. The major variation in the figures that have been found is in the girl's pigtail, in which some are very detailed and others are not.

Hum No.	Basic Size	Trademark	Current Value
105	4-3/4"	TMK-1	$7,000-$8,000

Adoration With Bird, Hum 105. Double Crown Mark (TMK-1), split base, 4-13/16".

Hum 106: Merry Wanderer (Wall Plaque)

Limited examples have been found of this extremely rare plaque, which was designed by master sculptor Arthur Moeller in 1938 and apparently only made for a short time. Perhaps this is because the plaque is basically the same as Hum 92, Merry Wanderer plaque, except for the wooden frame. Of those that have been found, all have the Crown Mark (TMK-1).

Hum No.	Basic Size	Trademark	Current Value
106	6" x 6"	TMK-1	$3,000-$4,000

Merry Wanderer wall plaque, Hum 106, which was made only with TMK-1.

Photo courtesy Goebel of North America.

Hum 107: Little Fiddler (Wall Plaque)

Limited examples of this extremely rare plaque have been found, even though it is listed as a closed edition. Crafted by master sculptor Arthur Moeller in 1938, it was apparently only made for a short time. Perhaps this is because the plaque is basically the same as Hum 93, Little Fiddler plaque, except for the wooden frame. Those that have been found all have the Crown Mark (TMK-1).

Hum No.	Basic Size	Trademark	Current Value
107	6" x 6"	TMK-1	$3,000-$4,000

Little Fiddler wall plaque, Hum 107, another piece that was made only during the Crown Mark (TMK-1) period.

Photo courtesy Goebel of North America.

Hum 108: Angel With Two Children at Feet (Wall Plaque in Relief, Closed Number)

It is unlikely that any of these will ever find their way into collectors' hands since it is a closed number with only one reference in factory records in 1938. It was apparently designed by master sculptor Reinhold Unger the same year and is thought that it was not approved by Siessen Convent for regular production.

A 1950s Goebel catalog lists the plaque as described, but it is not listed as a Hummel design. The deduction is made because of the description similar to the name and the mold number designation of 108 listed in factory records.

Hum No.	Basic Size	Trademark	Current Value
108	-	TMK-1	$10,000-$15,000
Goebel HS01	10-1/4"	TMK-1	$3,000-$5,000
Goebel HS01	10-1/4"	TMK-1 & 2	$2,500-$4,500

Angel With Two Children at Feet, Hum 108, a beautiful wall plaque that was never distributed and exists in archive samples only (TMK-1).

Photo courtesy Goebel of North America.

Hum 109: Happy Traveler

This figurine, which was designed by master sculptor Arthur Moeller in 1938, was placed in production in the late-1930s in a 5" basic size. An 8" basic size was added in the Full Bee (TMK-2) era and then retired in 1982.

There has been a curious variation to surface in the 109/0 size. The normal colors for the figurine are brown for the hat and green for the jacket. The variation has a green hat and a blue jacket. It has no trademark and is the only one known. It may be unique.

The 109/0 size was temporarily withdrawn from production on June 15, 2002.

Hum No.	Basic Size	Trademark	Current Value
109/0	4-3/4" to 5"	TMK-2	$275-$350
109/0 or 109	4-3/4" to 5"	TMK-3	$225-$250
109/0 or 109	4-3/4" to 5"	TMK-4	$200-$225
109/0 or 109	4-3/4" to 5"	TMK-5	$185-$190
109/0	4-3/4" to 5"	TMK-6	$185-$190
109/0	4-3/4" to 5"	TMK-7	$175-$185
109/0	4-3/4" to 5"	TMK-8	$175
109/II	8"	TMK-1	$1,200-$1,500

Hum No.	Basic Size	Trademark	Current Value
109/II	8"	TMK-2	$800-$900
109/II	8"	TMK-3	$500-$550
109/II	8"	TMK-4	$450-$500
109/II	8"	TMK-5	$400-$425
109/II	8"	TMK-6	$380-$400

Happy Traveler, Hum 109/0. Left: Full Bee piece with black "Germany," doughnut base and the normal green color coat. Right: This is a doll face Hum 109/0 with a blue plaid coat. It has no apparent base markings. Both measure 5".

Happy Traveler, Hum 109. Left is mold number 109/0 with Full Bee (TMK-2) mark, a doughnut base, 5-1/8", black "Germany." Right has mold number 109, Last Bee (TMK-5) trademark and measures 4-3/4".

Photo courtesy Goebel of North America.

Happy Traveler, Hum 109/0, remains in production today (TMK-8) at 4-3/4" to 5" and $175.

Hum 110: Let's Sing

Master sculptor Reinhold Unger designed this piece, which was one of the group of new designs introduced in the late-1930s. Although there are many size variations, there have been no variations significant enough to have any impact on the normal pricing structure for the various pieces.

Hum No.	Basic Size	Trademark	Current Value
110	3-1/2"	TMK-1	$475-$600
110	3-1/2"	TMK-2	$330-$400
110/0	3-1/4"	TMK-1	$350-$500
110/0	3-1/4"	TMK-2	$225-$300
110/0	3-1/4"	TMK-3	$195-$225
110/0	3-1/4"	TMK-4	$165-$200
110/0	3-1/4"	TMK-5	$160-$170
110/0	3-1/4"	TMK-6	$155-$165
110/0	3" to 3-1/4"	TMK-7	$150-$155

Hum No.	Basic Size	Trademark	Current Value
110/0	3" to 3-1/4"	TMK-8	$150
110/I	3-7/8"	TMK-1	$310-$400
110/I	3-7/8"	TMK-2	$300-$380
110/I	3-7/8"	TMK-3	$250-$300
110/I	3-7/8"	TMK-4	$230-$250
110/I	3-7/8"	TMK-5	$210-$230
110/I	3-7/8"	TMK-6	$200-$210
110/I	3-1/4" to 4"	TMK-7	$200-$210
110/I	3-1/4" to 4"	TMK-8	$200

Photo courtesy Goebel of North America.

Let's Sing, Hum 110. Left: Bears no mold number, Full Bee (TMK-2) trademark, 3-1/2", black "Germany," "© W. Goebel." Center: Mold number 110/0, Three Line Mark (TMK-4), 1938 copyright date, 3". Right: Mold number 110/0, Last Bee (TMK-5), 3-1/4".

One of today's (TMK-8) variations of Let's Sing, Hum 110/I, which is 3" to 3-1/4" and worth $150.

Hum III/110: Let's Sing (Candy Box)

There are two styles of candy boxes: bowl-like and jar-like. The transition from the old bowls to the new jars took place during the Stylized Bee (TMK-3) period. Therefore both the old and the new can be found in the Stylized Bee mark.

This piece was temporarily removed from production in 1989.

Hum No.	Basic Size	Trademark	Current Value
III/110	6"	TMK-1	$750-$850
III/110	6"	TMK-2	$575-$650
III/110 (old)	6"	TMK-3	$480-$550
III/110 (new)	6"	TMK-3	$300-$350
III/110	6"	TMK-4	$250-$275
III/110	6"	TMK-5	$225-$250
III/110	6"	TMK-6	$200-$230

Let's Sing candy dish, Hum III/110, with TMK-5.

Hum 111: Wayside Harmony

This figure, which was crafted in 1938 by master sculptor Reinhold Unger, was introduced in the late-1930s. It was previously called "Just Sittin-Boy."

It has changed a bit over the years, but there are no variations that have any significant impact on the collector value. However, there does exist a curious variation where the bird is missing. This is an aberration wherein the bird was probably inadvertently left off during assembly. This sometimes happens to small parts and is not considered a rare variation.

This piece has been known to appear with Roman numeral size designators instead of the Arabic number indicated.

The Hum 111/I size was temporarily withdrawn from production on June 15, 2002.

Hum No.	Basic Size	Trademark	Current Value
111/3/0	3-3/4"	TMK-1	$400-$550
111/3/0	3-3/4"	TMK-2	$275-$350
111/3/0	3-3/4"	TMK-3	$225-$250
111/3/0	3-3/4"	TMK-4	$200-$225
111/3/0	3-3/4"	TMK-5	$185-$200
111/3/0	3-3/4"	TMK-6	$185-$190
111/3/0	3-3/4" to 4"	TMK-7	$175-$185
111/3/0	3-3/4" to 4"	TMK-8	$175
111.	5"	TMK-1	$700-$850
111/I	5"	TMK-1	$650-$800
111/I	5"	TMK-2	$450-$550
111/I	5"	TMK-3	$400-$450
111/I	5"	TMK-4	$350-$400
111/I	5"	TMK-5	$350-$360
111/I	5"	TMK-6	$340-$350
111/I	5" to 5-1/2"	TMK-7	$325-$335

Wayside Harmony, Hum 111. Left: 111/I, incised Full Bee mark, black "Germany," © W. Goebel, 5-1/2". Right: 111/I, Three Line Mark, incised 1938 copyright date, 5-1/8".

Today's variation (TMK-8) of Wayside Harmony, Hum 111/3/0, which is 3-3/4" to 4" and worth $175.

Hum 11/111: Wayside Harmony (Table Lamp)

This lamp, which is the same design as the figurine of the same name (Hum 111), was made for a short period of time in the 1950s. Perhaps to avoid confusion and/or to conform with the mold numbering system, the lamp was slightly redesigned and assigned a new number, Hum 224/I. Whatever the reason, there are a few of these II/111 Wayside Harmony lamps around. They occur in the Crown (TMK-1), Full Bee (TMK-2), and Stylized Bee (TMK-3). The figures are quite scarce, but for some reason are not worth as much as some of the other equally as rare pieces.

Hum No.	Basic Size	Trademark	Current Value
II/111	7-1/2"	TMK-1	$600-$800
II/111	7-1/2"	TMK-2	$450-$550
II/111	7-1/2"	TMK-3	$380-$525

Hum 112: Just Resting

Master sculptor Reinhold Unger designed this piece in 1938, when it was then called "Just Sittin-Girl."

There have been no variations significant enough to influence the normal pricing structure of this piece. However, one example has been found of a curious variation on the 112/I size; there is no basket present on the base. This was probably the result of an inadvertent omission while it was being assembled, and somehow, it slipped by the quality control inspectors. This happens occasionally with small pieces such as bottles in baskets and birds. It is not usually considered important but merely a curiosity.

The larger 112/I size was temporarily withdrawn from production in 1999.

Hum No.	Basic Size	Trademark	Current Value
112/3/0	3-3/4"	TMK-1	$400-$550
112/3/0	3-3/4"	TMK-2	$275-$350
112/3/0	3-3/4"	TMK-3	$230-$250
112/3/0	3-3/4"	TMK-4	$200-$230
112/3/0	3-3/4"	TMK-5	$185-$210
112/3/0	3-3/4"	TMK-6	$180-$185
112/3/0	3-3/4" to 4"	TMK-7	$175-$180
112/3/0	3-3/4" to 4"	TMK-8	$175
112	5"	TMK-1	$700-$850
112/I	5"	TMK-1	$650-$800
112/I	5"	TMK-2	$450-$550
112/I	5"	TMK-3	$400-$450
112/I	5"	TMK-4	$350-$405
112/I	5"	TMK-5	$345-$355
112/I	5"	TMK-6	$330-$350
112/I	4-3/4" to 5-1/2"	TMK-7	$325-$330

Just Resting, Hum 112/I. Left: Stamped and incised Full Bee (TMK-2) mark, black "Germany," W. Goebel, 5-1/8". Right: Three Line Mark (TMK-4), 1938 copyright date, 4-7/8".

Photo courtesy Goebel of North America.

Today's rendition (TMK-8) of Just Resting, Hum 112/3/0, which is 3-3/4" to 4" and is worth $175.

Hum II/112: Just Resting (Table Lamp)

This lamp, which is the same design as the figurine of the same name (Hum 112), was made for a short period of time in the 1950s. Perhaps to avoid confusion and/or conform the mold numbering system, the number was changed to 225/I with a concurrent slight redesign. Whatever the reason, there are a few of these II/112 Just Resting lamps around. They occur in the Crown (TMK-1), Full Bee (TMK-2), and Stylized Bee (TMK3). Although quite rare, for some reason these lamps, like the Wayside Harmony lamps (Hum II/111), are not worth as much as some of the equally hard to find pieces.

Hum No.	Basic Size	Trademark	Current Value
II/112	7-1/2"	TMK-1	$600-$800
II/112	7-1/2"	TMK-2	$450-$550
II/112	7-1/2"	TMK-3	$375-$525
112	7"	TMK-1&1	$5,000-$6,000

Hum 113: Heavenly Song (Candleholder)

This four-figure piece, which was crafted in 1938 by master sculptor Arthur Moeller, is a candleholder. It is quite similar to Hum 54, Silent Night, and was produced in extremely small numbers. Only a few are known to exist in private collections. The actual number is not known, but less than 50 would be a reasonable estimate. They do pop up from time to time and have been found in the Crown (TMK-1), Full Bee (TMK-2), Stylized Bee (TMK-3), and Last Bee (TMK-5), but it is extremely rare in any trademark. It has also been found in the faience style, but is extremely rare in that finish as well and would be worth $3,000-$5,000.

Goebel announced in 1981 that it was removing Heavenly Song from production permanently.

Hum No.	Basic Size	Trademark	Current Value
113	3-1/2" x 4-3/4"	TMK-1	$6,000-$10,000
113	3-1/2" x 4-3/4"	TMK-2	$4,500-$5,500
113	3-1/2" x 4-3/4"	TMK-3	$3,500-$4,500
113	3-1/2" x 4-3/4"	TMK-5	$3,000-$3,500

Heavenly Song candleholder, Hum 113. This is a rare porcelain-like figurine that may fall into the faience category. It is much like the left figurine in the previous photograph. The middle child's dress is dark green and the baby's gown is a very dark blue. This one has an incised Crown (TMK-1), but the incised M.I. Hummel signature is either too light to discern or absent.

Heavenly Song candleholder, Hum 113. Left: Double Crown Mark (TMK-1), 3-1/2". Note the shiny porcelain-like finish and atypical paint. Right: Large Stylized Bee (TMK-3) in an incised circle, black "Western Germany," 2-5/8".

Hum 114: Let's Sing (Ashtray)

This piece, which was crafted by master sculptor Reinhold Unger in 1938, is an ashtray with a figure very like Hum 110 at the edge of the dish. It is found with the figure on either the right or left side of the tray. Viewed from the front, the older ones have the figure on the right side. There are very few of this variation known. It was changed during the Full Bee (TMK-2) so it can be found with either the Crown or Full Bee trademark.

As is the case with all the ashtrays in the line, this piece is listed as temporarily withdrawn from production with no reinstatement date given.

Hum No.	Basic Size	Trademark	Current Value
114 (on right)	3-1/2" x 6-3/4"	TMK-1	$850-$1,000
114 (on right)	3-1/2" x 6-3/4"	TMK-2	$600-$850
114	3-1/2" x 6-3/4"	TMK-2	$250-$350
114	3-1/2" x 6-3/4"	TMK-3	$230-$255
114	3-1/2" x 6-3/4"	TMK-4	$175-$230
114	3-1/2" x 6-3/4"	TMK-5	$165-$175
114	3-1/2" x 6-3/4"	TMK-6	$150-$165

Let's Sing ashtray, Hum 114. Left: Last Bee (TMK-5), 3-5/8". Right: Full Bee (TMK-2), 3-1/2".

Hum 115: Girl With Nosegay, Hum 116: Girl With Fir Tree, and Hum 117: Boy With Horse (Advent Group Candleholders)

This group of three figurines has a Christmas theme, and each of the figures is provided with a candle receptacle. Master sculptor Reinhold Unger is credited with the design in 1938.

The original models were made with the "Mel" prefix followed by 1, 2, and 3 for 115, 116, and 117 respectively. These were prototypes, but many apparently got into the market (see the section on "Mel" pieces in Chapter 5). These pieces tend to sell for $300-$350 apiece.

All three pieces in the 3-1/2" size were temporarily withdrawn from production on June 15, 2002.

Hum No.	Basic Size	Trademark	Current Value
115	3-1/2"	TMK-1	$200-$255
115	3-1/2"	TMK-2	$115-$135
115	3-1/2"	TMK-3	$85-$95
115	3-1/2"	TMK-4	$80-$90
115	3-1/2"	TMK-5	$75-$80
115	3-1/2"	TMK-6	$70-$75
115	3-1/2"	TMK-7	$70-$75
115	3-1/2"	TMK-8	$70
116	3-1/2"	TMK-1	$200-$250
116	3-1/2"	TMK-2	$115-$140
116	3-1/2"	TMK-3	$85-$90
116	3-1/2"	TMK-4	$80-$90
116	3-1/2"	TMK-5	$75-$85
116	3-1/2"	TMK-6	$70-$75
116	3-1/2"	TMK-7	$70-$75
116	3-1/2"	TMK-8	$70
117	3-1/2"	TMK-1	$200-$250
117	3-1/2"	TMK-2	$115-$140
117	3-1/2"	TMK-3	$85-$90
117	3-1/2"	TMK-4	$80-$85
117	3-1/2"	TMK-5	$75-$80
117	3-1/2"	TMK-6	$70-$75
117	3-1/2"	TMK-7	$70-$75
117	3-1/2"	TMK-8	$70

Advent Group candleholders. Left: Hum 115, small Stylized Bee (TMK-3) mark, 3-1/2". Center: Hum 116, small Stylized Bee mark, 3-5/8". Right: Hum 117, small Stylized Bee, 3-1/2".

Girl With Nosegay, Hum 115, in TMK-8.

Photo courtesy Goebel of North America.

TMK-8 version of Girl With Fir Tree, Hum 116.

Photo courtesy Goebel of North America.

Today's variation (TMK-8) of Boy With Horse, Hum 117.

Photo courtesy Goebel of North America.

Hum 118: Little Thrifty

This figurine, originally designed by master sculptor Arthur Moeller in 1939 and introduced in the late-1930s, is also a coin bank. It is usually found with a key and lockable metal plug beneath the base, but these are sometimes lost over the years.

Although not terribly significant in terms of value, there is a difference in design between the older and the newer pieces. The most obvious is a less thick base on the new design. This design change took place during the Stylized Bee (TMK-3) trademark period after a redesign by master sculptor Rudolf Wittman in 1963, so the old and the new designs can be found with that mark, but there is no bearing on value.

Hum No.	Basic Size	Trademark	Current Value
118	5"	TMK-1	$500-$750
118	5"	TMK-2	$400-$450
118	5"	TMK-3	$225-$280
118	5"	TMK-4	$200-$210
118	5"	TMK-5	$200-$210
118	5"	TMK-6	$190-$195
118	5"	TMK-7	$185-$190
118	5"	TMK-8	$185-$190

Little Thrifty, Hum 118. The one on the left represents the older design. It measures 5-1/2", has the large Stylized Bee (TMK-3) trademark and bears a black "Germany" beneath the base. The one on the right has the Last Bee (TMK-5) trademark and is 5-1/8" in height. Note the variation in the bases.

The present-day rendition (TMK-8) of Little Thrifty, Hum 118.

Photo courtesy Goebel of North America.

Hum 119: Postman

Master sculptor Arthur Moeller crafted this piece in 1939, and it was introduced about 1940.

This figure has been released in several different sizes and distinct mold variations, but only one size was listed until 1989, when a smaller version (119/2/0) was released. With the release of the 119/2/0, the larger 119 became 119/0 beginning with TMK-6 pieces.

There are no variations significant enough to influence normal values for the Postman.

Postman, Hum 119. Left: TMK-3, 4-7/8". Right: 119 2/0, TMK-6, 1985 copyright date, 4-1/2".

Hum No.	Basic Size	Trademark	Current Value
119/2/0	4-1/2"	TMK-6	$175-$185
119/2/0	4-1/2"	TMK-7	$170-$175
119/2/0	4-1/2"	TMK-8	$170
119	5-1/4"	TMK-1	$600-$750
119	5-1/4"	TMK-2	$350-$450
119	4-3/4"	TMK-3	$300-$330
119	5-1/4"	TMK-4	$275$300
119	5-1/4"	TMK-5	$250-$275
119	5-1/4"	TMK-6	$250-$255
119/0	5-1/4"	TMK-6	$245-$250
119/0	5-1/2"	TMK-7	$240-$245
119/0	5-1/2"	TMK-8	$235

Today's 5-1/2" version of Postman, Hum 119/0.

Hum 120: Joyful and Let's Sing (Bookends)

No examples known of these double figure bookends on wooden base to be in private collections. Known from factory records only. It has been listed as a closed edition since 1939.

Hum No.	Basic Size	Trademark	Current Value
120	-	TMK-1	$10,000-$20,000

Hum 121: Wayside Harmony and Just Resting (Bookends)

Only half of this two-piece bookend duo on wooden base is known to be in a private collection. It has been listed as a closed edition since 1939. The figures on the wooden base are very similar to the Hum 111 and Hum 112, but have different incised mold numbers.

Hum No.	Basic Size	Trademark	Current Value
121/A	-	TMK-1	$5,000-$10,000
121/B	-	TMK-1	$5,000-$10,000

The Wayside Harmony bookend half of Hum 121. The other half, Just Resting, is not known to exist in any private collections.

Hum 122: Puppy Love and Serenade With Dog (Bookends)

No examples of this bookend ensemble on wooden bases are known to be in private collections. Listed as a closed edition in 1939, it exists in factory archives only.

Hum No.	Basic Size	Trademark	Current Value
122	-	TMK-1	$10,000-$20,000

Only the Puppy Love half of the bookend set, Hum 122.

Hum 123: Max and Moritz

Released about 1940 and first designed by master sculptor Arthur Moeller, this figurine was once known as "Good Friends."

An important variation has been found in a few Crown Mark (TMK-1) examples, where the figure has black hair rather than the lighter, blonde hair. In fact, these figures appear to be painted in darker colors overall. When found, these pieces are valued at about $1,500.

The same characters that make up this piece have been made into two new ones: Scamp (Hum 553) and Cheeky Fellow (Hum 554).

Hum No.	Basic Size	Trademark	Current Value
123	5-1/4"	TMK-1	$650-$800
123	5-1/4"	TMK-2	$400-$500
123	5-1/4"	TMK-3	$325-$375
123	5-1/4"	TMK-4	$300-$325
123	5-1/4"	TMK-5	$275-$295
123	5-1/4"	TMK-6	$265-$275
123	5" to 5-1/2"	TMK-7	$260-$270
123	5" to 5-1/2"	TMK-8	$260

Max and Moritz, Hum 123. The one on the right is the older, bearing the Full Bee Mark (TMK-2). It has a doughnut base and an incised 1939 copyright date, is 5-3/8" tall and has W. Goebel inscribed in script. The left figure has the Three Line Mark (TMK-4), measures 5" and has a doughnut base.

Max and Moritz, Hum 123, is still in production today (TMK-8).

Photo courtesy Goebel of North America.

Hum 124: Hello

First designed by master sculptor Arthur Moeller in 1939 and introduced around 1940, this figurine was once known as "The Boss" and "Der Chef." This figurine is the same one used in the perpetual calendar bearing the same name, Hum 788/A.

When first released, it had gray pants and coat and a pink vest. This changed to green pants, brown coat, and pink vest, and then finally to the brown coat and pants with white vest used on the pieces from sometime in the Stylized Bee (TMK-3) period to the present. The variation in shortest supply is the green pants version.

The figure has been found with the decimal designator in the Crown (TMK-1) and Full Bee (TMK-2).

The larger 124/I size has been temporarily removed from production.

Hello, Hum 124. Left: 124/0, Full Bee (TMK-2) in an incised circle, doughnut base, black "Germany" beneath the base, five buttons on vest (only four of which are painted), green pants, brown jacket, red hair, 6-1/4". Right: 124/I, TMK-5, doughnut base, five painted buttons, brown pants, purple jacket, brown hair, 6-3/8".

Hum No.	Basic Size	Trademark	Current Value
124	6-1/2"	TMK-1	$800-$1,000
124	6-1/2"	TMK-2	$450-$600
124/0	5-3/4" to 6-1/4"	TMK-2	$400-$450
124/0	5-3/4" to 6-1/4"	TMK-3	$350-$400
124/0	5-3/4" to 6-1/4"	TMK-4	$300-$350
124/0	5-3/4" to 6-1/4"	TMK-5	$265-$300
124/0	5-3/4" to 6-1/4"	TMK-6	$260-$265
124/0	5-3/4" to 6-1/4"	TMK-7	$260-$265
124/0	5-3/4" to 6-1/4"	TMK-8	$260
124/I	7"	TMK-1	$800-$1,000
124/I	7"	TMK-2	$450-$600
124/I	7"	TMK-3	$400-$450
124/I	7"	TMK-4	$350-$400
124/I	7"	TMK-5	$300-$350
124/I	7"	TMK-6	$275

Photo courtesy Goebel of North America.

The present-day rendition (TMK-8) of Hello, Hum 124/0, which is between 5-3/4" and 6-1/4" tall and is worth $260.

Hum 125: Vacation Time (Wall Plaque)

Originally called "Happy Holidays" and "On Holiday," this piece was the original design of master sculptor Arthur Moeller. It was redesigned in 1960, however, leaving two distinctly different designs. The transition from the old to the new took place in the Stylized Bee (TMK-3) period, so you can find the old and the new styles in that trademark. The newest style has now lost one fence picket for a count of five. The old has six.

This piece was temporarily withdrawn from production in 1989, released again in 1998 as part of the Vacation Time HummelScape package (TMK-7), and not produced again since.

Hum No.	Basic Size	Trademark	Current Value
125	4-3/8" x 5-1/4"	TMK-1	$600-$750
125	4-3/8" x 5-1/4"	TMK-2	$450-$550
125 (old)	4" x 4-3/4"	TMK-3	$375-$450
125 (new)	4" x 4-3/4"	TMK-3	$275-$350
125	4" x 4-3/4"	TMK-4	$260-$275
125	4" x 4-1/4"	TMK-5	$250-$260
125	4" x 4-1/4"	TMK-6	$240-$250
125	4" x 4-3/4"	TMK-7	$230-$240

Vacation Time plaque, Hum 125. Left: Full Bee, six pickets in the fence, 4-3/8" x 5-3/8". Right: Last Bee, five pickets in the fence, 4" x 4-7/8".

Hum 126: Retreat to Safety (Wall Plaque)

This plaque, which was first created by master sculptor Arthur Moeller in 1939, was in continuous production until 1989, when it was temporarily withdrawn from production. Although the colors differ, it is the same design as the figurine of the same name, Hum 201. There are no significant variations to affect collector values.

Retreat to Safety plaque, Hum 126.

Hum No.	Basic Size	Trademark	Current Value		Hum No.	Basic Size	Trademark	Current Value
126	4-3/4" x 4-3/4"	TMK-1	$550-$700		126	4-3/4" x 4-3/4"	TMK-4	$230-$280
126	4-3/4" x 4-3/4"	TMK-2	$400-$500		126	4-3/4" x 4-3/4"	TMK-5	$200-$210
126	4-3/4" x 4-3/4"	TMK-3	$275-$350		126	4-3/4" x 4-3/4"	TMK-6	$185-$190

Hum 127: Doctor

Doctor, which was the original work of master sculptor Arthur Moeller, joined the line about 1940. It was formerly known as "The Doll Doctor."

The sizes in various lists range from 4-3/4" to 5-1/4". The larger sizes are generally the older pieces.

On the Crown Mark (TMK-1) and Full Bee (TMK-2) figures, the doll's feet extend slightly beyond the edge of the base. They must have proven vulnerable to breakage because the feet were restyled so they no longer extended over the base.

Hum No.	Basic Size	Trademark	Current Value
127	4-3/4"	TMK-1	$450-$650
127	4-3/4"	TMK-2	$300-$350
127	4-3/4"	TMK-3	$230-$280
127	4-3/4"	TMK-4	$200-$230
127	4-3/4"	TMK-5	$200-$210
127	4-3/4"	TMK-6	$185-$190
127	4-3/4" to 5-1/4"	TMK-7	$180-$185
127	4-3/4" to 5"	TMK-8	$180

Doctor, Hum 127. Full Bee (TMK-2), black "Germany," doughnut base, 5-1/4".

Doctor is still in production today (TMK-8) and is worth $180.

Hum 128: Baker

Although this figure, which was first created by master sculptor Arthur Moeller in 1939, underwent changes over the years, none are important enough to influence the normal values of the pieces. Slight color variations do occur, and the older pieces (TMK-1) have open eyes.

Hum No.	Basic Size	Trademark	Current Value
128	4-3/4"	TMK-1	$600-$750
128	4-3/4"	TMK-2	$350-$430
128	4-3/4"	TMK-3	$300-$325
128	4-3/4"	TMK-4	$275-$300
128	4-3/4"	TMK-5	$250-$275
128	4-3/4"	TMK-6	$240-$245
128	4-3/4" to 5"	TMK-7	$235-$240
128	4-3/4" to 5"	TMK-8	$235

Baker, Hum 128. Left: Full Bee (TMK-2), black "Germany," doughnut base, 5-1/8". Center: Stylized Bee (TMK-3), 4-3/4". Right: TMK-6, 4-7/8".

Today's variation (TMK-8) of Baker, which is worth $235.

Hum 129: Band Leader

This piece, which was first referred to as "Leader," was originally designed by master sculptor Arthur Moeller in 1939. There have been no significant mold variations.

Band Leader, like several other figurines, makes up the Hummel orchestra.

A new, smaller size (Hum 129/4/0) without the music stand was introduced in 1987 as the fourth in a four-part series of small figurines intended to match four mini-plates in the same motifs.

In the summer of 2002, a 13-1/2" version of Band Leader was introduced as the fifth and final edition of the "Millennium Love" series, which also included Sweet Music (Hum 186/III), Soloist (Hum 135/III), Little Fiddler (Hum 2/III), and Serenade (Hum 85/III). These oversized pieces (Hum 129/III) were in limited supply and had to be special-ordered through an authorized M.I. Hummel retailer.

The smaller 129/4/0 size was temporarily withdrawn in 1997 and then listed as a closed edition in 1999.

Band Leader, Hum 129. Left: Full Bee in an incised circle, black "Germany," split base in quarters, 6". Right: Last Bee, 5-1/8".

Hum No.	Basic Size	Trademark	Current Value
129/4/0	3-1/2"	TMK-6	$130-$140
129/4/0	3-1/4"	TMK-7	$120-$125
129	5-1/4"	TMK-1	$600-$750
129	5-1/4"	TMK-2	$350-$450
129	5-1/4"	TMK-3	$300-$350
129	5-1/4"	TMK-4	$265-$290
129	5-1/4"	TMK-5	$245-$270
129/0	5-1/4"	TMK-6	$245-$250
129/0	5" to 5-1/4"	TMK-7	$240-$250
129/0	5" to 5-1/4"	TMK-8	$235
129/II (Special Edition)		TMK-7	$235 (Hong Kong only)
129/III	13-1/2"	TMK-8	$1,550

The TMK-7 variation of Band Leader, Hum 129 4/0, which was a 3-1/4" size that is not produced today.

Photo courtesy Goebel of North America.

Hum 130: Duet

First crafted by master sculptor Arthur Moeller in 1939 and originally called "The Songsters," this piece occurs in many size variations from 5" to 5-1/2".

Some older figures with the Crown Mark (TMK-1) have a very small lip on the front of the base, sort of a mini-version of the stepped or double base variation found on the Merry Wanderer. These lip base Duets also have incised musical notes on the sheet music and are more valuable than the regular pieces.

Another variation is the absence of the kerchief on the figure wearing the top hat. This is found on some Full Bee (TMK-2) and Stylized Bee (TMK-3) pieces. If found, they are valued at $3,000-$3,500.

This piece is another of the figurines that make up the Hummel orchestra. It is similar to the combined designs of Street Singer (Hum 131) and Soloist (Hum 135).

Duet was permanently retired in 1995, with the mold destroyed.

Duet, Hum 130. Left: 130., double incised Crown Marks (one of which is colored blue), 5-1/4". Right: Full Bee (TMK-2), black "Germany," 5-5/8".

Hum No.	Basic Size	Trademark	Current Value
130	5-1/4"	TMK-1	$800-$1,000
130	5-1/4"	TMK-2	$550-$650
130	5-1/4"	TMK-3	$400-$450
130	5-1/4"	TMK-4	$335-$400
130	5-1/4"	TMK-5	$330-$335

Hum No.	Basic Size	Trademark	Current Value
130	5-1/4"	TMK-6	$315-$330
130	5" to 5-1/2"	TMK-7	$300-$315
130 (without ties)		TMK-2 or 3	$2,000-$3,500
130 (with "lip" base)		TMK-1	$1,000-$1,500

Hum 131: Street Singer

This figure, which was designed by master sculptor Arthur Moeller in 1939 and formerly known as "Soloist," is another of the Hummel orchestra pieces.

Although there have been size and minor color variations over the years, there are no significant mold variations to be found.

Hum No.	Basic Size	Trademark	Current Value
131	5" to 5-1/2"	TMK-1	$550-$700
131	5" to 5-1/2"	TMK-2	$375-$450
131	5" to 5-1/2"	TMK-3	$300-$350
131	5" to 5-1/2"	TMK-4	$270-$300
131	5" to 5-1/2"	TMK-5	$245-$265
131	5" to 5-1/2"	TMK-6	$235-$245
131	5" to 5-1/2"	TMK-7	$230-$235
131	5" to 5-1/2"	TMK-8	$230

Street Singer, Hum 131. Left: Mold number 131., but no apparent trademark. An underlined "Originalnalmuster" is on the base as shown here, which means this was a master model. Right: Stylized Bee (TMK-3), 5".

Street Singer is still in production today (TMK-8) with a value of $230.

Hum 132: Star Gazer

Master sculptor Arthur Moeller originally crafted this piece in 1939, and it underwent a slight redesign in 1980 in with the textured finish was added and corners of the base were rounded.

A few of the older Crown Mark (TMK-1) pieces have a darker blue shirt, but the normal color on later pieces is a lighter blue or purple.

The straps on the boy's lederhosen are normally crossed in the back. If there are no straps, the value is increased, valued at about 20% above the normal value.

A special edition was released in 1996 for sale to the U.S. military troops stationed in Bosnia. The inscription read: "Looking for a Peaceful World." It is worth $250-$300.

This figurine was temporarily withdrawn from production on June 15, 2002.

Star Gazer, Hum 132. Left: Full Bee mark in an incised circle, black "Germany," 4-7/8". Right: Stylized Bee mark, split base, 4-7/8".

Star Gazer in present-day TMK-8.

Hum No.	Basic Size	Trademark	Current Value
132	4-3/4"	TMK-1	$600-$800
132	4-3/4"	TMK-2	$400-$500
132	4-3/4"	TMK-3	$330-$375
132	4-3/4"	TMK-4	$275-$325
132	4-3/4"	TMK-5	$260-$275
132	4-3/4"	TMK-6	$250-$260
132	4-3/4"	TMK-7	$245-$250
132	4-3/4" to 5"	TMK-8	$245

Hum 133: Mother's Helper

Created by master sculptor Arthur Moeller in 1939, this figurine has but one major variation to look for. Several Crown-era (TMK-1) pieces have surfaced with the stool reversed and only one leg of the stool showing when viewed from the rear. The norm has two legs visible from the rear. This unique variation is worth $750-$1,000.

This piece, with the presence of the cat, is similar to Helping Mother (Hum 325), which is a possible future edition.

Hum No.	Basic Size	Trademark	Current Value
133	5"	TMK-1	$550-$700
133	5"	TMK-2	$375-$450
133	5"	TMK-3	$300-$325
133	5"	TMK-4	$275-$300
133	5"	TMK-5	$250-$275
133	5"	TMK-6	$245-$250
133	4-3/4" to 5"	TMK-7	$240-$245
133	4-3/4" to 5"	TMK-8	$240

Mother's Helper, Hum 133. The original 1939 design is represented by the figure on the left. It bears the small Stylized Bee (TMK-3) trademark in an incised circle and measures 5". The right figure in the photo is a Last Bee (TMK-5) piece. It has a doughnut base and is 4-3/4" tall.

Today's rendition (TMK-8) of Mother's Helper, Hum 133.

Hum 134: Quartet (Wall Plaque)

Another of the circa 1940 releases, this plaque was designed by master sculptor Arthur Moeller in 1939.

The older pieces have the "M.I. Hummel" signature on the back, while the newer plaques have an incised front signature. Also of note on the older pieces is the existence of two holes for the cord to hang on the wall. The newer versions have a single, centered hole on the back. Despite these differences, there are no significant mold variations influencing the normal pricing structure.

This plaque was temporarily removed from production, as of 1990.

Quartet, plaque, Hum 134. Stylized Bee, 5-1/2" x 6-1/4".

Hum No.	Basic Size	Trademark	Current Value
134	5-1/2" x 6-1/4"	TMK-1	$800-$1,000
134	5-1/2" x 6-1/4"	TMK-2	$525-$625
134	5-1/2" x 6-1/4"	TMK-3	$380-$425
134	5-1/2" x 6-1/4"	TMK-4	$325-$375
134	5-1/2" x 6-1/4"	TMK-5	$260-$275
134	5-1/2" x 6-1/4"	TMK-6	$250-$265

Hum 135: Soloist

Created by master sculptor Arthur Moeller in 1940 and released in the early 1940s as "High Tenor," this piece has remained in continuous production since. It has no significant mold variations influencing price.

In 1986, a new smaller version, 135/4/0, was released as the third in a series of four small figurines and matching mini-plates. Because of the new size designator in the smaller model, the larger model is now incised with the mold number 135/0. This change occurred in TMK-6 era, only to be followed shortly thereafter by the temporary withdrawal of the smaller version (135/4/0) in 1997.

In 1996, an even smaller variation (135/5/0) was produced as part of the "Pen Pals" series of personalized name card table decorations. That size occurs in TMK-7 only and has not been produced since.

Soloist, Hum 135. 4-7/8", Stylized Bee (TMK-3) trademark, black "Western Germany."

The 3-1/2" size of Soloist, Hum 135/4/0, shown in TMK-7 here is not currently in production.

Soloist, Hum 135/0, in today's TMK-8.

Photo courtesy Goebel of North America.

Recently, a 13" version of Soloist was introduced as part of the "Millennium Love" series, which also included Sweet Music (Hum 186/III), Little Fiddler (Hum 2/III), Band Leader (Hum 129/III), and Serenade (Hum 85/III). These oversized pieces (Hum 85/III) were in limited supply and had to be special-ordered through an authorized M.I. Hummel retailer.

Hum No.	Basic Size	Trademark	Current Value
135/5/0	2-3/4"	TMK-7	$55
135/4/0	3-1/2"	TMK-6	$125-$145
135/4/0	3"	TMK-7	$120-$125

Hum No.	Basic Size	Trademark	Current Value
135	4-3/4"	TMK-1	$400-$500
135	4-3/4"	TMK-2	$300-$350
135	4-3/4"	TMK-3	$200-$230
135	4-3/4"	TMK-4	$185-$200
135	4-3/4"	TMK-5	$175-$185
135	4-3/4"	TMK-6	$175-$180
135/0	4-3/4"	TMK-6	$165-$175
135/0	4-3/4"	TMK-7	$165-$170
135/0	4-3/4"	TMK-8	$165
135/III	13"	TMK-8	$1,550

Hum 136: Friends

Crafted by master sculptor Reinhold Unger in 1940 and released about the same time in two sizes, this figurine was formerly known as "Good Friends" and "Friendship." Sizes found in various lists are 5", 10-3/4", and 11-1/2".

There have been at least two examples of this piece found that are made of a terra cotta. These are in the 10" size with incised Crown Mark (TMK-1). And another unique finish exists in dark chocolate brown in a 9-3/4" size. These are extremely rare pieces.

Also found in white overglaze in the Crown Mark (TMK-1), this very rare variation is valued at $4,000-$5,000.

The larger 136/V size was temporarily withdrawn from production in 1999.

Hum No.	Basic Size	Trademark	Current Value
136/I	5" to 5-3/8"	TMK-1	$800-$950
136/I	5" to 5-3/8"	TMK-2	$400-$500
136/I	5" to 5-3/8"	TMK-3	$325-$375
136/I	5" to 5-3/8"	TMK-4	$275-$330
136/I	5" to 5-3/8"	TMK-5	$250-$275
136/I	5" to 5-3/8"	TMK-6	$245-$255

Hum No.	Basic Size	Trademark	Current Value
136/I	5" to 5-3/8"	TMK-7	$240-$245
136/I	5" to 5-3/8"	TMK-8	$240
136	10-3/4"	TMK-1	$3,000-$4,000
136	10-3/4"	TMK-2	$2,000-$3,000
136 (terra cotta)	10"	TMK-1	$10,000-$15,000
136 (dark brown)	9-3/4"	TMK-1	$10,000-$15,000
136/V	10-3/4" to 11"	TMK-1	$3,000-$4,000
136/V	10-3/4" to 11"	TMK-2	$1,750-$2,500
136/V	10-3/4" to 11"	TMK-3	$1,600-$1,750
136/V	10-3/4" to 11"	TMK-4	$1,500-$1,600
136/V	10-3/4" to 11"	TMK-5	$1,450-$1,500
136/V	10-3/4" to 11"	TMK-6	$1,400-$1,450
136/V	10-3/4" to 11"	TMK-7	$1,350-$1,385

Friends, Hum 136. Left: 136., Crown Mark, white overglaze, 11-1/4". Center: 136., Crown Mark, terra cotta finish, 10-1/4". Right: 136., Crown Mark, "U.S. ZONE Germany," 10-3/4".

Photo courtesy Goebel of North America.

Today's version (TMK-8) of Friends, Hum 136/I, which measures 5" to 5-3/8" and is worth $240.

Hum 137/A and Hum 137/B: Child In Bed (Wall Plaques)

This set of plaques, which has been called "Baby Ring With Ladybug" and "Ladybug Plaque" in early company literature, was created by master sculptor Arthur Moeller in 1940. One child is looking to its right (137/A) and the other looking to its left (137/B). The mold number is found as 137/B until the Last Bee (TMK-5) era, when the B was dropped.

Until the mid-1980s, it was only speculated that there might have been a matching piece with the mold number 137/A. When one surfaced in Hungary and a few others followed, it was apparent that although they had indeed been produced, they are extremely rare.

A "Mel 14" variation has been found recently and although it has no "M.I. Hummel" signature, it does bear an incised "Mel 14" along with a Double Crown trademark.

Hum 137 was temporarily withdrawn from production in 1999.

Child In Bed plaque, Hum 137/B. Stylized Bee (TMK-3), 3".

Hum No.	Basic Size	Trademark	Current Value
137/B	3" x 3"	TMK-3	$110-$135
137/B	3" x 3"	TMK-4	$85-$110
137/B	3" x 3"	TMK-5	$80-$85
137	3" x 3"	TMK-5	$80-$90
137	3" x 3"	TMK-6	$70-$80
137	3" x 3"	TMK-7	$70-$75
MEL 14	3" x 3"	TMK-1	$2,000-$2,500

Hum No.	Basic Size	Trademark	Current Value
137/A	3" x 3"	TMK-1	$5,000-$7,000
137/B	3" x 3"	TMK-1	$350-$550
137/B	3" x 3"	TMK-2	$200-$225

Hum 138: Tiny Baby In Crib (Wall Plaque)

Although all factory records indicate that this piece was never released for sale to the consumer and only prototypes were produced, at least six are known to reside in private collections. Master sculptor Arthur Moeller created it in 1940.

These figures have also been found with the "Mel" designator as "Mel 15."

Photo courtesy Goebel of North America.

Tiny Baby In Crib wall plaque, Hum 138.

Hum No.	Basic Size	Trademark	Current Value
138	2-1/4" x 3"	TMK-1	$4,000-$5,000
138	2-1/4" x 3"	TMK-2	$3,000-$3,500
MEL 15	2-1/4" x 3"	TMK-1	$2,000-$2,500

Hum 139: Flitting Butterfly (Wall Plaque)

Flitting Butterfly plaque, Hum 139, with Full Bee (TMK-2) in an incised circle, 2-3/8" square.

Designed by master sculptor Arthur Moeller in 1940 and originally called "Butterfly Plaque," this figure has not undergone any significant mold variation that would affect the normal value for the various trademarked pieces.

A few pieces bearing "Mel 16" do exist from 1940 and are worth substantially more than the regular variations.

This figure was out of production for some time, thus the absence of a Three Line (TMK-4) example. It was reissued in a new mold design with the same number during the Last Bee (TMK-5) period and continued in production until 1999 when it was temporarily withdrawn.

Hum No.	Basic Size	Trademark	Current Value
139	2-1/2" x 2-1/2"	TMK-1	$350-$550
139	2-1/2" x 2-1/2"	TMK-2	$200-$250
139	2-1/2" x 2-1/2"	TMK-3	$100-$150
139	2-1/2" x 2-1/2"	TMK-5	$75-$80
139	2-1/2" x 2-1/2"	TMK-6	$75-$80
139	2-1/2" x 2-1/2"	TMK-7	$75-$80
MEL 16	2-1/2" x 2-1/2"	TMK-1	$2,000-$2,500

Hum 140: The Mail is Here (Wall Plaque)

This plaque, also once known as "Post Carriage" and "Mail Coach," predates the figurine by the same name and design (Hum 226). It was crafted by master sculptor Arthur Moeller in 1940 and introduced into the line the same year.

Although there are no significant mold variations, there is a finish variation of importance. Some of the early plaques were produced in white overglaze for the European market. These are found bearing the Crown Mark (TMK-1) and are valued at $1,000-$1,500.

There are minor variations noticeable in the doors and windows of the coach, as well as the handle of the horn, but none significantly affect values.

This plaque was temporarily withdrawn in 1989.

The Mail is Here plaque, Hum 140. Last Bee (TMK-5), 6-3/4" x 4-1/2".

Hum No.	Basic Size	Trademark	Current Value
140	4-1/2" x 6-3/4"	TMK-1	$1,000-$1,500
(white overglaze)			
140	4-1/2" x 6-1/4"	TMK-1	$650-$950
140	4-1/2" x 6-1/4"	TMK-2	$450-$550
140	4-1/2" x 6-1/4"	TMK-3	$325-$350
140	4-1/2" x 6-1/4"	TMK-4	$300-$330
140	4-1/2" x 6-1/4"	TMK-5	$275-$300
140	4-1/2" x 6-1/4"	TMK-6	$250-$275

Hum 141: Apple Tree Girl

This figurine, which was designed by master sculptor Arthur Moeller in 1940, has also been known as "Spring" and "Springtime." The following sizes are found in various lists: 4", 4-1/4", 6", 6-3/4", 10", 10-1/4", and 32".

In one list, references were made to a "rare old base" and a "brown base." These are apparently references to the "tree trunk base" variation. This variation will bring about 30% more than the value given in the chart below.

The smallest size (141/3/0) has no bird perched on the branch, in contrast to all the larger sizes. (Although there has been at least one, a 141/I, reported to have no bird; perhaps a factory worker's inadvertent omission.)

The jumbo 141/X size was temporarily withdrawn from production in 1990.

Hum No.	Basic Size	Trademark	Current Value
141/3/0	4" to 4-1/4"	TMK-1	$400-$500
141/3/0	4" to 4-1/4"	TMK-2	$300-$350
141/3/0	4" to 4-1/4"	TMK-3	$225-$250
141/3/0	4" to 4-1/4"	TMK-4	$200-$230
141/3/0	4" to 4-1/4"	TMK-5	$185-$195
141/3/0	4" to 4-1/4"	TMK-6	$175-$185

Apple Tree Girl, Hum 141. Left: 141 3/0, Full Bee (TMK-2), black "Germany," painted brown base, 4-5/16". Right: 141/3/0, Full Bee mark, black "Germany," 4-1/4".

Shown here is the 141/3/0 variation of Apple Tree Girl, which is the smallest of today's current line of this figurine at about 4" and is worth $170. Other sizes still in production today (TMK-8) include: 10-1/4" (142/V); and 6-7/8" (142/I).

Photo courtesy Goebel of North America.

Hum No.	Basic Size	Trademark	Current Value
141/3/0	4" to 4-1/4"	TMK-7	$175-$180
141/3/0	4" to 4-1/4"	TMK-8	$170
141	6" to 6-3/4"	TMK-1	$800-$900
141	6" to 6-3/4"	TMK-2	$600-$700
141/I	6" to 6-3/4"	TMK-1	$700-$800
141/I	6" to 6-3/4"	TMK-2	$525-$625
141/I	6" to 6-3/4"	TMK-3	$425-$450
141/I	6" to 6-3/4"	TMK-4	$365-$425
141/I	6" to 6-3/4"	TMK-5	$350-$365
141/I	6" to 6-3/4"	TMK-6	$340-$350
141/I	6" to 6-3/4"	TMK-7	$330-$345

Hum No.	Basic Size	Trademark	Current Value
141/I	6" to 6-3/4"	TMK-8	$330
141/V	10-1/4"	TMK-4	$1,500-$1,700
141/V	10-1/4"	TMK-5	$1,450-$1,500
141/V	10-1/4"	TMK-6	$1,425-$1,450
141/V	10-1/4"	TMK-7	$1,400-$1,425
141/V	10-1/4"	TMK-8	$1,400
141/X*	32"	TMK-5	$15,000-$25,000
141/X*	32"	TMK-6	$25,000

*There are a few of these "Jumbo" figures in collectors' hands. They are generally used as promotional figures in showrooms and shops. Rarely do they bring full retail price.

Hum 142: Apple Tree Boy

Apple Tree Girl's companion piece, this figure has also been known as "Fall" and "Autumn." Just as with the girl, it too was crafted by master sculptor Arthur Moeller in 1940 and has been changed many times over the years. Sizes found in various lists are as follows: 3-3/4", 4", 4-1/2", 6", 6-7/8", 10", 10-1/4", 30", and 32".

In one list references were made to a "rare old base" and a "brown base." These are apparently references to the "tree trunk base" variation. This variation will bring about 30% more than the figure in the value chart here.

The smallest size (142/3/0) has no bird perched on the branch, in contrast to all the larger sizes.

Hum No.	Basic Size	Trademark	Current Value
142/3/0	4" to 4-1/4"	TMK-1	$400-$500
142/3/0	4" to 4-1/4"	TMK-2	$300-$350
142/3/0	4" to 4-1/4"	TMK-3	$225-$250
142/3/0	4" to 4-1/4"	TMK-4	$200-$230
142/3/0	4" to 4-1/4"	TMK-5	$185-$195
142/3/0	4" to 4-1/4"	TMK-6	$175-$185
142/3/0	4" to 4-1/4"	TMK-7	$170-$175
142/3/0	4" to 4-1/4"	TMK-8	$170
142	6" to 6-7/8"	TMK-1	$800-$900
142	6" to 6-7/8"	TMK-2	$600-$700
142/I	6" to 6-7/8"	TMK-1	$700-$800
142/I	6" to 6-7/8"	TMK-2	$525-$625
142/I	6" to 6-7/8"	TMK-3	$425-$450

Apple Tree Boy, Hum 142. Left: 142 3/0, double Full Bee mark (incised and stamped), black "Germany," old style rounded, brown color base, 4". Right: 142 3/0, Stylized Bee mark in an incised circle, newer style base, 3-15/16".

Shown here is the 142/3/0 variation of Apple Tree Boy, which is the smallest of today's current line of this figurine at about 4" and is worth $170. Other sizes still in production today (TMK-8) include: 30" to 32" (142/X), 10-1/4" (142/V), and 6-7/8" (142/I).

Photo courtesy Goebel of North America.

Hum No.	Basic Size	Trademark	Current Value
142/I	6" to 6-7/8"	TMK-4	$360-$430
142/I	6" to 6-7/8"	TMK-5	$350-$365
142/I	6" to 6-7/8"	TMK-6	$340-$350
142/I	6" to 6-7/8"	TMK-7	$330-$345
142/I	6" to 6-7/8"	TMK-8	$330
142/V	10-1/4"	TMK-3	$1,750-$2,000
142/V	10-1/4"	TMK-4	$1,500-$1,700
142/V	10-1/4"	TMK-5	$1,450-$1,500
142/V	10-1/4"	TMK-6	$1,425-$1,450
142/V	10-1/4"	TMK-7	$1,400-$1,425

Hum No.	Basic Size	Trademark	Current Value
142/V	10-1/4"	TMK-8	$1,400
142/X*	30"	TMK-2	$26,000-$30,000
142/X*	30"	TMK-3	$17,000-$26,000
142/X*	30"	TMK-4	$16,000-$25,000
142/X*	30" to 32"	TMK-5	$15,000-$25,000
142/X*	30" to 32"	TMK-6	$15,000-$25,000
142/X*	30" to 32"	TMK-7	$15,000-$25,000
142/X*	30" to 32"	TMK-8	$25,000

*There are a few of these "Jumbo" figures in collectors' hands. They are generally used as promotional figures in showrooms and shops. Rarely do they bring full retail price.

Hum 143: Boots

Created by master sculptor Arthur Moeller in 1940 and originally called "Shoemaker," this figure was first released around 1940 in the larger size and followed a short time later by the smaller size variation. Although many size variations have been found, none is significant in terms of affecting value.

Goebel retired both sizes of Boots in 1998, never to produce this figurine again.

Hum No.	Basic Size	Trademark	Current Value
143/0	5" to 5-1/2"	TMK-1	$550-$700
143/0	5" to 5-1/2"	TMK-2	$375-$450
143/0	5" to 5-1/2"	TMK-3	$300-$325
143/0	5" to 5-1/2"	TMK-4	$275-$300
143/0	5" to 5-1/2"	TMK-5	$250-$275

Hum No.	Basic Size	Trademark	Current Value
143/0	5" to 5-1/2"	TMK-6	$235-$245
143/0	5" to 5-1/2"	TMK-7	$225-$235
143/I	6-1/2" to 6-3/4"	TMK-1	$850-$1,000
143/I	6-1/2" to 6-3/4"	TMK-2	$600-$700
143/I	6-1/2" to 6-3/4"	TMK-3	$450-$525
143/I	6-1/2" to 6-3/4"	TMK-4	$425-$450
143/I	6-1/2" to 6-3/4"	TMK-5	$390-$425
143/I	6-1/2" to 6-3/4"	TMK-6	$375-$395
143/I	6-1/2" to 6-3/4"	TMK-7	$365-$375
143	6-3/4"	TMK-1	$900-$1,050
143	6-3/4"	TMK-2	$650-$750

The most recent variation of Boots, Hum 143/1, was produced in TMK-7. Since then, the figurine has been retired and today is worth at least $365.

Photo courtesy Goebel of North America.

Boots, Hum 143. Left: Full Bee mark, black "Germany," doughnut base 6-13/16". Right: 143/1, Stylized Bee mark, doughnut base, 6-3/4".

Hum 144: Angelic Song

Formerly known as "Angels" and "Holy Communion," this piece was created in 1941 by master sculptor Reinhold Unger. There are no significant variations of Angelic Song affecting the normal value of the pieces.

Hum No.	Basic Size	Trademark	Current Value
144	4"	TMK-1	$400-$525
144	4"	TMK-2	$275-$325
144	4"	TMK-3	$225-$250
144	4"	TMK-4	$200-$225
144	4"	TMK-5	$185-$200
144	4"	TMK-6	$180-$185
144	4"	TMK-7	$175-$180
144	4"	TMK-8	$175

Angelic Song, Hum 144. Left: Last Bee (TMK-5), 4-1/8". Below: Current TMK-8 piece.

Photo courtesy Goebel of North America.

Hum 145: Little Guardian

Created by master sculptor Reinhold Unger in 1941, this figurine is still in production today. There are no variations significant enough to impact collector values, although the older pieces are just slightly bigger than the newer ones.

Hum No.	Basic Size	Trademark	Current Value
145	3-3/4" to 4"	TMK-1	$400-$530
145	3-3/4" to 4"	TMK-2	$275-$325
145	3-3/4" to 4"	TMK-3	$225-$250
145	3-3/4" to 4"	TMK-4	$200-$225
145	3-3/4" to 4"	TMK-5	$185-$200
145	3-3/4" to 4"	TMK-6	$180-$185
145	3-3/4" to 4"	TMK-7	$175-$180
145	3-3/4" to 4"	TMK-8	$175

Photo courtesy Goebel of North America.

Two variations of Little Guardian, Hum 145. The one at far left measures 3-5/8" and has TMK-5; the other is today's TMK-8 version of the figurine.

Hum 146: Angel Duet (Holy Water Font)

Originally designed by master sculptor Reinhold Unger in 1941, this piece has undergone several redesigns throughout the years. There have been many variations with regard to the shapes and positions of the heads and wings of angels, but none significant.

This font was temporarily withdrawn from production in 1999.

Hum No.	Basic Size	Trademark	Current Value
146	3-1/2" x 4-3/4"	TMK-1	$175-$225
146	3-1/2" x 4-3/4"	TMK-2	$125-$150
146	3-1/2" x 4-3/4"	TMK-3	$80-$100
146	3-1/2" x 4-3/4"	TMK-4	$75-$80
146	3-1/2" x 4-3/4"	TMK-5	$70-$75
146	3-1/2" x 4-3/4"	TMK-6	$65-$75
146	3-1/2" x 4-3/4"	TMK-7	$60-$70

Angel Duet font, Hum 146. Stylized Bee mark, 4-5/8".

Hum 147: Angel Shrine (Holy Water Font)

This figure, which was designed by master sculptor Reinhold Unger in 1941 and previously known as "Angel Devotion," has been in continuous production since its release in the early 1940s. There are no important mold or finish variations affecting its value, although some of the older pieces are slightly larger and the back of the font and water bowls have changed a bit over the years.

Hum No.	Basic Size	Trademark	Current Value
147	3-1/8" x 5-1/4"	TMK-1	$225-$275
147	3-1/8" x 5-1/4"	TMK-2	$125-$175
147	3" x 5"	TMK-3	$80-$100
147	3" x 5"	TMK-4	$75-$80
147	3" x 5"	TMK-5	$75-$80
147	3" x 5"	TMK-6	$65-$70
147	3" x 5"	TMK-7	$62-$65
147	3" x 5"	TMK-8	$62

Photo courtesy Goebel of North America.

Angel Shrine font, Hum 147. Left: Stylized Bee (TMK-3) at 5-1/4". Right: Current-production TMK-8 piece at 5".

Hum 148: Unknown (Closed Number)

Listed as a closed number since 1941, records indicate that this piece could be a Farm Boy (Hum 66) with no base. No examples have ever been found. You can remove the figure from the bookend Hum 60/A and have the same figure, but the mold number will not be present.

Hum 149: Unknown (Closed Number)

Records indicate that this piece, listed as a closed number since 1941, could be a Goose Girl (Hum 47) with no base. No known examples in collectors' hands. You can remove the figure from the bookend Hum 60/B and have the same piece, but the mold number will not be present.

Hum 150: Happy Days

This piece, which was the collective effort of a group of sculptors and once called "Happy Little Troubadours," is referenced in numerous size variations throughout the years. It has been found with the decimal point designator. There are no mold or finish variations significant enough to influence values.

Both the 150/0 and 150/I sizes were temporarily withdrawn from production in 1999.

Hum No.	Basic Size	Trademark	Current Value
150/2/0	4-1/4"	TMK-2	$325-$400
150/2/0	4-1/4"	TMK-3	$250-$275
150/2/0	4-1/4"	TMK-4	$225-$250
150/2/0	4-1/4"	TMK-5	$215-$225
150/2/0	4-1/4"	TMK-6	$210-$215
150/2/0	4-1/4"	TMK-7	$200-$210
150/2/0	4-1/4"	TMK-8	$200
150/0	5-1/4"	TMK-2	$525-$625
150/0	5-1/4"	TMK-3	$425-$475
150/0	5-1/4"	TMK-4	$400-$425

Happy Days, Hum 150. Left: 150/0. Full Bee (TMK-2) mark, black "Germany," split base, 5-1/4". Right: 150/0, Last Bee (TMK-5) mark, 5-1/8".

Hum No.	Basic Size	Trademark	Current Value
150/0	5-1/4"	TMK-5	$365-$390
150/0	5" to 5-1/2"	TMK-6	$340-$360
150/0	5" to 5-1/2"	TMK-7	$340-$345
150	6"	TMK-1	$1,300-$1,600
150	6"	TMK-2	$900-$1,000
150/I	6"	TMK-1	$1,250-$1,550
150/I	6"	TMK-2	$850-$950
150/I	6"	TMK-3	$675-$775
150/I	6"	TMK-5	$550-$600
150/I	6"	TMK-6	$525-$550
150/I	6-1/4" to 6-1/2"	TMK-7	$550-$600

Today's variation (TMK-8) of Happy Days, Hum 150/2/0, which measures 4-1/4" and is worth $200.

Hum 151: Madonna Holding Child

Sometimes called the "Blue Cloak Madonna" or "Madonna with the Blue Cloak" because of the most commonly found painted finish, this figure has appeared in other finishes. The rarest three finishes are those with the rich dark brown cloak, the dark blue cloak, and the ivory cloak.

From left: 12-1/2" brown cloak piece with decimal designator "151.", incised Crown Mark (TMK-1), stamped Full Bee (TMK-2), and black "Germany": 12-7/8" white overglaze variation with Double Full Bee (TMK-2), incised and stamped; and 12-3/4" blue cloak with Full Bee (TMK-2).

Always occurring in the Crown Mark (TMK-1), these are valued at $9,000-$12,000 depending on condition.

Sizes ranging from 12" to 14" have been referenced, and the figure has appeared with the Crown, Full Bee (TMK-2), and Stylized Bee (TMK-3) marks.

This figurine was temporarily withdrawn from production in 1989. It was back in production in a blue and white overglaze as per the 1993 Goebel price listing, but in 1995 was listed once again as temporarily withdrawn from production.

Hum No.	Basic Size	Color	TMK	Current Value
151	12-1/2"	blue	TMK-1	$2,000-$3,000
151	12-1/2"	blue	TMK-2	$2,000-$2,500
151	12-1/2"	blue	TMK-5	$925-$950
151	12-1/2"	blue	TMK-6	$900-$925
151	12-1/2"	white	TMK-1	$1,500-$2,500
151	12-1/2"	white	TMK-2	$1,000-$2,000
151	12-1/2"	white	TMK-5	$425-$450
151	12-1/2"	white	TMK-6	$400-$425
151	12-1/2"	brown	TMK-1	$9,000-$12,000
151	12-1/2"	ivory	TMK-1	$9,000-$12,000
151	12-1/2"	dark blue	TMK-1	$9,000-$12,000

Hum 152/A: Umbrella Boy

Created by master sculptor Arthur Moeller in 1942 and introduced in one size in the early 1940s, the earliest Crown Mark (TMK-1) examples were produced with the incised mold number 152. Early literature calls the piece both "In Safety" and "Boy Under Umbrella."

A second, smaller size was introduced in the Full Bee (TMK-2) period. There are no mold or finish variations that influence value.

The newest edition of this piece, Hum 152/A/2/0, was released in a "downsized edition" of 3-1/2" in 2002.

Left: Umbrella Boy, Hum 152/0/A, Three Line Mark (TMK-4), incised 1957 copyright date, 4-5/8" Right: Umbrella Girl, Hum 152/0/B, Three Line Mark, incised 1957 copyright date, 4-3/4".

Umbrella Boy in 8" size (152/II/A), which is a current-production TMK-8 piece.

Hum No.	Basic Size	Trademark	Current Value
152/A/2/0	3-1/2"	TMK-8	$300
152/0/A	5"	TMK-2	$1,100-$1,600
152/0/A	5"	TMK-3	$850-$1,000
152/0/A	5"	TMK-4	$750-$850
152/0/A	5"	TMK-5	$725-$750
152/0/A	5"	TMK-6	$700-$725
152/0/A	4-3/4"	TMK-7	$675-$700
152/0/A	4-3/4"	TMK-8	$675-$700
152	8"	TMK-1	$4,000-$7,000
152	8"	TMK-2	$2,400-$2,900
152/A	8"	TMK-2	$2,200-$2,700
152/A	8"	TMK-3	$1,800-$2,000
152/A	8"	TMK-4	$1,725-$1,800
152/II/A	8"	TMK-4	$1,725-$1,800
152/II/A	8"	TMK-5	$1,700-$1,725
152/II/A	8"	TMK-6	$1,675-$1,700
152/II/A	8"	TMK-7	$1,650-$1,675
152/II/A	8"	TMK-8	$1,650-$1,675

Hum 152/B: Umbrella Girl

Obviously created by master sculptor Arthur Moeller to match the Umbrella Boy, one wonders why this figure was introduced at the end of the 1940s, several years after Umbrella Boy.

In any case, it may be found in two sizes, the smaller appearing in the Full Bee (TMK-2) period. Also known early on as "In Safety" and "Girl Under Umbrella." There are no significant variations influencing values.

The newest edition of this piece, Hum 152/B/2/0, was released in a "downsized edition" of 3-1/2" in 2002.

Hum No.	Basic Size	Trademark	Current Value
152/II/B	8"	TMK-5	$1,700-$1,725
152/II/B	8"	TMK-6	$1,675-$1,700
152/II/B	8"	TMK-7	$1,650-$1,675
152/II/B	8"	TMK-8	$1,650-$1,675

Hum No.	Basic Size	Trademark	Current Value
152/B/2/0	3-1/2"	TMK-8	$300
152/0/B	4-3/4"	TMK-2	$1,100-$1,600
152/0/B	4-3/4"	TMK-3	$850-$1,000
152/0/B	4-3/4"	TMK-4	$750-$850
152/0/B	4-3/4"	TMK-5	$725-$750
152/0/B	4-3/4"	TMK-6	$700-$725
152/0/B	4-3/4"	TMK-7	$675-$700
152/0/B	4-3/4"	TMK-8	$675-$700
152/B	8"	TMK-1	$4,000-$7,000
152/B	8"	TMK-2	$2,200-$2,700
152/B	8"	TMK-3	$1,800-$2,000
152/B	8"	TMK-4	$1,725-$1,800
152/II/B	8"	TMK-4	$1,725-$1,800

Umbrella Girl in the 8" size (152/II/B), which is still in production today (TMK-8).

Hum 153: Auf Wiedersehen

This figure, whose name means "goodbye" in English, was first released in the 1950s in the 7" basic size. It was designed by master sculptor Arthur Moeller in 1943 and was originally called "Good Bye." A smaller size was introduced during the Full Bee (TMK-2) era. Both sizes have been restyled in recent years.

In a rare version of this double figure piece, the little boy wears a Tyrolean cap. This variation is found only in the 153/0 size. In most examples of these pieces, he wears no hat but is waving a handkerchief, as is the girl. The rare version is valued at about $3,000-$4,000. The 153/I size is listed as reinstated. (See color section.)

In 1993, Goebel issued a special edition of this figurine along with a replica of the Berlin Airlift Memorial at Templehof Airport in Berlin, Germany. This was to commemorate the Berlin Airlift at the end of World War II. Both pieces bear a special backstamp containing the flags of Germany, France, England, and the United States. The edition was limited to 25,000. The original issue was priced at $330 and is still valued at about the same.

Both sizes of this piece were permanently retired in December 2000 and will not be made again. Pieces made that year have "Final Issue 2000" backstamps and all gold "Final Issue" medallions in addition to TMK-8. The larger 153/I size was retired on QVC exclusively and came with a HummelScape in a limited edition of 6,500 pieces.

Auf Wiedersehen, Hum 153. Left: 153/0, Full Bee mark, black "Germany," 5-1/4". Right: 153/0, Stylized Bee, 5-3/8".

Bases of the memorial replica and Hum 153/0 respectively, showing the special markings.

Special edition of Auf Wiedersehen on wood base with the porcelain Airlift Memorial replica piece. Both have a special backstamp and the edition is limited to 25,000. Wall: 7-1/2". Figurine: Hum 153/0, 5-1/2".

Current rendition (TMK-8) of Auf Wiedersehen, Hum 153/0, which is worth $285.

Photo courtesy Goebel of North America.

Hum No.	Basic Size	Trademark	Current Value	Hum No.	Basic Size	Trademark	Current Value
153/0	5-1/2" to 6"	TMK-2	$425-$525	153	6-3/4" to 7"	TMK-2	$650-$750
153/0	5-1/2" to 6"	TMK-3	$350-$400	153/I	6-3/4" to 7"	TMK-1	$750-$1,050
153/0	5-1/2" to 6"	TMK-4	$320-$350	153/I	6-3/4" to 7"	TMK-2	$600-$700
153/0	5-1/2" to 6"	TMK-5	$300-$320	153/I	6-3/4" to 7"	TMK-3	$475-$525
153/0	5-1/2" to 6"	TMK-6	$280-$300	153/I	6-3/4" to 7"	TMK-4	$425-$475
153/0	5-1/2" to 6"	TMK-7	$285-$295	153/I	6-3/4" to 7"	TMK-5	$360-$390
153/0	5-1/2" to 6"	TMK-8	$285	153/I	6-3/4" to 7"	TMK-6	$340-$360
153/0 (hat)	5-1/4"	TMK-2	$3,000-$4,000	153/I	6-3/4" to 7"	TMK-7	$330-$340
153	6-3/4" to 7"	TMK-1	$900-$1,200	153/I	6-3/4" to 7"	TMK-8	$330-$340

Hum 154: Waiter

First crafted by master sculptor Arthur Moeller in 1943 and known as "Chef of Service" and "Little Waiter," this figurine has appeared with several different labels on the wine bottle. All are now produced with a "Rhine Wine" label. The variation in which the label on the bottle reads "Whiskey" is from the Full Bee (TMK-2) era and is valued at $1,600-$2,100.

Earlier versions of the piece have much darker pants than those in current production. The first figurines have a gray coat and gray striped trousers. In the 1950s, the coat became blue and the pants tan striped.

The larger 154/I size was temporarily withdrawn from production in 1999.

Hum No.	Basic Size	Trademark	Current Value
154/0	6" to 6-1/4"	TMK-1	$600-$800
154/0	6" to 6-1/4"	TMK-2	$375-$475
154/0	6" to 6-1/4"	TMK-3	$325-$350
154/0	6" to 6-1/4"	TMK-4	$300-$325

Hum No.	Basic Size	Trademark	Current Value
154/0	6" to 6-1/4"	TMK-5	$260-$280
154/0	6" to 6-1/4"	TMK-6	$255-$260
154/0	6" to 6-1/4"	TMK-7	$250-$255
154/0	6" to 6-1/4"	TMK-8	$250
154/I	6-1/2" to 7"	TMK-1	$750-$1,000
154/I	6-1/2" to 7"	TMK-2	$500-$600
154/I	6-1/2" to 7"	TMK-3	$450-$500
154/I	6-1/2" to 7"	TMK-4	$375-$450
154/I	6-1/2" to 7"	TMK-5	$350-$375
154/I	6-1/2" to 7"	TMK-6	$340-$350
154/I	6-1/2" to 7"	TMK-7	$325-$335
154	6-1/2"	TMK-1	$850-$1,150
154	6-1/2"	TMK-2	$550-$700
154/0	6-1/4"	TMK-2	$1,600-$2,100
(whiskey variation)			

Waiter, Hum 154. Left to right (A through D): A. 154., Crown mark, doughnut base, "U.S. ZONE Germany," 6-1/2". B. 154., Crown mark, doughnut base, black "Germany," 6-1/2". C. 154/0, Full bee mark, Donut base, Black "Germany," 6-1/8". D. 154/1 Stylized Bee mark, doughnut base, 6-13/16".

Today's rendition (TMK-8) of Waiter, Hum 154/0, which is worth $250.

Hum 155: Madonna Holding Child (Closed Number)

Records indicate this figure may be a Madonna holding child. Crafted by master sculptor Reinhold Unger, it has been a closed number since 1943. The photograph shown here is of the Madonna plaque. It is large, measuring 13" high. It has the incised "M.I. Hummel" signature and mold number, a Crown Mark (TMK-1) and "W. Goebel" on the back. Because it is unique and there is no trade data, no realistic collector value can be determined.

Hum 156: Unknown (Closed Number)

Records indicate this piece, which was created by master sculptor Arthur Moeller in 1943 and listed as a closed number ever since, may be a wall plaque of a mother and child. No known examples.

Madonna Holding Child, Hum 155, plaque. 13" high incised Hummel signature, mold number, Crown trademark and W. Goebel.

Hum 157 through Hum 162: "Town Children" (Closed Numbers)

These are 1940s sample figurines where the children are dressed much more formally than in typical figurines. Master sculptor Arthur Moeller crafted the first three numbers in 1943, and the last three were crafted by master sculptor Reinhold Unger the same year. There are sample models of some of them in the Goebel archives and they are atypical of M.I. Hummel figurines. They do not wear the traditional costumes, but rather appear to be dressed in more modern clothes.

Sister Maria Innocentia is known to have asked on at least one occasion, "How shall I draw for the Americans?" One can speculate that these pieces, never approved by the convent, were an attempt to produce a few for the American market.

Until recently these numbers have been listed as unknown. Records indicate that the figurines were modeled and considered for production but never released. None are known outside the archives. (See photo accompanying, Hum 157 and Hum 158.) The descriptions are as follows: standing boy with flower basket behind back (Hum 157); standing girl holding dog and with suitcase at her feet (Hum 158); standing girl cradling flowers in her arms (Hum 159); standing girl in tiered dress holding flower bouquet (Hum 160); standing girl with hands in pockets (Hum 161); and standing girl holding a handbag (Hum 162).

Referred to as "Town Children," this boy and girl were never named or produced. As you'll recognize immediately, the subjects are slimmer and more citified than the rural look that is typical of M.I. Hummel children. These samples were sculpted in 1943.

Hum 163: Whitsuntide

This figure, which was originally named "Christmas" and is sometimes known as "Happy New Year," was created by master sculptor Arthur Moeller in 1946. It is one of the early releases and was removed from production about 1960, then reinstated in 1977, and temporarily withdrawn in 1999. The older pieces are very scarce and highly sought by collectors.

In older versions, the angel appears holding a red or a yellow candle and is without the candle in newer models.

Hum No.	Basic Size	Trademark	Current Value
163	7-1/4"	TMK-1	$1,000-$1,200
163	7-1/4"	TMK-2	$850-$1,000
163	7-1/4"	TMK-3	$650-$800
163	7-1/4"	TMK-5	$350-$390
163	7-1/4"	TMK-6	$340-$350
163	6-1/2" to 7"	TMK-7	$330-$345

Whitsuntide, Hum 163. Left: Incised Crown Mark, red candle in angel's hand. Right: Last Bee trademark (TMK-5), no candle. Both measure 6-3/4".

Whitsuntide, Hum 163. Full Bee mark in an incised circle, black "Western Germany," split base (in quarters), 7".

Hum 164: Worship (Holy Water Font)

Master sculptor Reinhold Unger crafted this font in 1946. From its introduction to the line in the mid-1940s to current production models, there have been no significant variations that have any impact on value.

Hum No.	Basic Size	Trademark	Current Value
164	3-1/4" x 5"	TMK-1	$250-$300
164	3-1/4" x 5"	TMK-2	$150-$200
164	3-1/4" x 5"	TMK-3	$95-$115
164	3-1/4" x 5"	TMK-4	$75-$95
164	3-1/4" x 5"	TMK-6	$65-$70
164	3-1/4" x 5"	TMK-7	$62-$65
164	3-1/4" x 5"	TMK-8	$62

Worship font, Hum 164, Crown Mark, black "Germany," 4-13/16". Right: Stylized Bee mark, 4-7/8".

Photo courtesy Goebel of North America.

Worship, Hum 164, is still in production today (TMK-8).

Hum 165: Swaying Lullaby (Wall Plaque)

Created by master sculptor Arthur Moeller in 1946 and once called "Child in a Hammock," this plaque was apparently made in limited quantities and then at some point was removed from production. It does occur in all trademarks, however, and was reinstated in 1978, only to be withdrawn from production again in 1989.

In 1999, it was reissued in TMK-7 along with a Sweet Dreams HummelScape.

The translation of the inscription on the front of this piece is: "Dreaming of better times."

Swaying Lullaby plaque, Hum 165. Full Bee mark, 4-1/2" x 5-1/4".

Hum No.	Basic Size	Trademark	Current Value
165	4-1/2" x 5-1/4"	TMK-1	$800-$1,100
165	4-1/2" x 5-1/4"	TMK-2	$550-$800
165	4-1/2" x 5-1/4"	TMK-3	$375-$525
165	4-1/2" x 5-1/4"	TMK-5	$225-$250
165	4-1/2" x 5-1/4"	TMK-6	$200-$225
165	4-1/2" x 5-1/4"	TMK-7	$325

(with HummelScape)

Hum 166: Boy With Bird (Ashtray)

Originally designed by master sculptor Arthur Moeller in 1946 and introduced into the collection in the mid-1940s, this figure was in continuous production until 1989, when it was listed as temporarily withdrawn. There are no significant mold or finish variations.

Hum No.	Basic Size	Trademark	Current Value
166	3-1/4" x 6-1/4"	TMK-1	$450-$650
166	3-1/4" x 6-1/4"	TMK-2	$275-$325
166	3-1/4" x 6-1/4"	TMK-3	$195-$210
166	3-1/4" x 6-1/4"	TMK-4	$165-$195
166	3-1/4" x 6-1/4"	TMK-5	$150-$160
166	3-1/4" x 6-1/4"	TMK-6	$145-$150

Boy With Bird ashtray, Hum 166. Last Bee (TMK-5), 3-1/4" x 6".

Hum 167: Angel With Bird (Holy Water Font)

Sometimes called "Angel Sitting" or "Angel-Bird," this font was crafted by master sculptor Reinhold Unger and first produced in the mid-1940s. There have been changes over the years but none that have any effect on the normal values. It is still in production today.

Angel With Bird font, Hum 167, in today's TMK-8.

Hum No.	Basic Size	Trademark	Current Value
167	3-1/4" x 4-1/4"	TMK-1	$250-$300
167	3-1/4" x 4-1/4"	TMK-2	$150-$200
167	3-1/4" x 4-1/4"	TMK-3	$90-$115
167	3-1/4" x 4-1/4"	TMK-4	$75-$90
167	3-1/4" x 4-1/4"	TMK-5	$70-$75
167	3-1/4" x 4-1/4"	TMK-6	$65-$75
167	3-1/4" x 4-1/8"	TMK-7	$62-$65
167	3-1/4" x 4-1/8"	TMK-8	$62-$65

Hum 168: Standing Boy (Wall Plaque)

Crafted by master sculptor Arthur Moeller in 1948, this piece must have been produced in limited numbers for the first 20 years because examples in the first three trademarks have never been available in any but small quantities.

It was taken out of production in the Stylized Bee (TMK-3) period, reinstated in 1978 and taken out of production yet again in 1989.

In 1979, this plaque served as the inspiration for a new figurine crafted in its likeness: Valentine Joy (Hum 399).

Standing Boy plaque, Hum 168. Full Bee mark in an incised circle, 4" x 5-1/2".

Hum No.	Basic Size	Trademark	Current Value
168	4-1/8" x 5-1/2"	TMK-1	$800-$1,100
168	4-1/8" x 5-1/2"	TMK-2	$550-$800
168	4-1/8" x 5-1/2"	TMK-3	$375-$525
168	4-1/8" x 5-1/2"	TMK-5	$225-$250
168	4-1/8" x 5-1/2"	TMK-6	$200-$225

Hum 169: Bird Duet

There are many variations in this figure, which was designed by master sculptor Arthur Moeller in 1945, but none that have any impact on the normal values of the pieces. It was introduced in the 1940s and has been in continuous production since.

Goebel announced the production of "Personal Touch" figurines in 1996. At that time, four figurines in the line lent themselves well to this application of personalization: Bird Duet was one of these. The other three were Latest News (Hum 184), The Guardian (Hum 455), and For Father (Hum 87).

This piece is also sold as a gift set with the Celestial Harmony HummelScape.

Hum No.	Basic Size	Trademark	Current Value
169	4"	TMK-1	$425-$550
169	4"	TMK-2	$250-$325
169	4"	TMK-3	$215-$230
169	4"	TMK-4	$195-$210
169	4"	TMK-5	$185-$195
169	4"	TMK-6	$180-$185
169	4"	TMK-7	$175-$180
169	4"	TMK-8	$17

Bird Duet, Hum 169. Left: Crown Mark, 4". Right: Last Bee, 4".

Photo courtesy Goebel of North America.

Today's rendition (TMK-8) of Bird Duet, Hum 169.

Hum 170: School Boys

Originally crafted by master sculptor Reinhold Unger in 1943 and released in only one size in the 1940s, this figurine was introduced in a new smaller size in the Stylized Bee (TMK-3) period. The larger size, 180/III, was permanently retired by Goebel in 1982. It is now considered a closed edition.

Once called "Difficult Problems," there are no variations important enough to affect values.

The middle boy was the inspiration for the Authorized Retailer Plaque (Hum 460), which was released in 1986 in eight different languages.

Hum No.	Basic Size	Trademark	Current Value
170/I	7-1/2"	TMK-3	$1,650-$1,750
170/I	7-1/2"	TMK-4	$1,550-$1,600
170/I	7-1/2"	TMK-5	$1,500-$1,550
170/I	7-1/2"	TMK-6	$1,450-$1,500
170/I	7-1/2"	TMK-7	$1,400-$1,450
170/I	7-1/2"	TMK-8	$1,400
170	10"	TMK-1	$4,000-$5,000
170	10"	TMK-2	$3,000-$4,000
170	10"	TMK-3	$2,200-$2,300
170/III	10"	TMK-3	$2,200-$2,300
170/III	10"	TMK-4	$2,100-$2,200
170/III	10"	TMK-5	$2,000-$2,100
170/III	10"	TMK-6	$1,900-$2,000

School Boys, Hum 170/I. Last Bee trademark, 1961 copyright date, and 7-3/4".

Today's variation (TMK-8) of School Boys, Hum 170/I, which is 7-1/2" and worth $1,400.

Hum 171: Little Sweeper

First designed by master sculptor Reinhold Unger in 1944 and released in the mid-1940s in one size, 171. A smaller size, 171/4/0, was introduced in 1988 as part of a four-piece series with matching mini-plates called "Little Homemakers" series. As a result of this new mold number, the old 171 mold number was changed to 171/0. There are no variations significant enough to have an impact on collector values.

The smaller 171/4/0 size was temporarily withdrawn in 1997.

Hum No.	Basic Size	Trademark	Current Value
171/4/0	3"	TMK-6	$125-$140
171/4/0	3"	TMK-7	$115-$120
171	4-1/2"	TMK-1	$400-$500
171	4-1/2"	TMK-2	$250-$300
171	4-1/2"	TMK-3	$230-$240
171	4-1/2"	TMK-4	$195-$230
171	4-1/2"	TMK-5	$190-$195
171	4-1/2"	TMK-6	$185-$190
171/0	4-1/2"	TMK-6	$180-$185
171/0	4-1/2"	TMK-7	$175-$180
171/0	4-1/2"	TMK-8	$180

Little Sweeper, Hum 171/0, remains in the line today (TMK-8) at 4-1/2" and $180.

Photo courtesy Goebel of North America.

Little Sweeper, Hum 171. Left: Full Bee (TMK-2), 4-3/4", black "Germany." Right: Last Bee (TMK-5), 4-1/4".

Hum 172: Festival Harmony (Angel With Mandolin)

Master sculptor Reinhold Unger is responsible for this 1947 design in the larger size only with incised "172."

The major variations of this figure are found in the Crown (TMK-1) and Full Bee (TMK-2) marks. The earliest TMK-1 and some TMK-2 (very rare) have flowers extending from the base well up onto the gown, and the bird is perched on top of the flowers (rather than on the mandolin as in later models). This variation of the piece is valued at $2,500-$3,500, depending on condition as trademark.

The majority of the Full Bee pieces show the flowers just barely extending up over the bottom edge of the gown and the bird situated on the mandolin. The above variations invariably are found on pieces marked with the plain incised mold number 172.

There is one example in existence where the bird is perched on the arm, rather than on the mandolin. This was probably an error in assembly that somehow made it past the quality control inspection. There are several instances

Festival Harmony, Hum 172. Left to right (A through D): A. Incised Crown Mark (TMK-1) and a stamped Full Bee (TMK-2). Doughnut base, 10-3/4", stamped with "© W. Goebel" beneath the base. B. Same as the previous except for a different bird and a black "Germany." C. Full Bee piece exhibiting the same characteristics listed for the previous figure except for the now very small flowers and the bird moved to the mandolin. The bird is colored brown. D. This one has a small Stylized Bee. Note the textured gown and the altered flowers. The bird is now colored blue. It measures 10-1/8".

of this type of error among other figures with small pieces (such as bottles in baskets), and it usually does not influence value.

The 172/II size was temporarily withdrawn from production on December 31, 1984, and the 172/0 and 172/4/0 sizes were withdrawn in 1999.

Hum No.	Basic Size	Trademark	Current Value
172/4/0	3-1/8"	TMK-7	$120-$125
172/0	8"	TMK-3	$500-$650
172/0	8"	TMK-4	$400-$475
172/0	8"	TMK-5	$380-$400
172/0	8"	TMK-6	$360-$380
172/0	8"	TMK-7	$350-$360

Hum No.	Basic Size	Trademark	Current Value
172 (bird on flowers)	10-3/4"	TMK-1	$3,000-$3,500
172 (bird on flowers)	10-3/4"	TMK-2	$2,500-$3,000
172 (bird on mandolin)	10-3/4"	TMK-2	$1,250-$1,500
172 (bird on mandolin)	10-3/4"	TMK-3	$1,000-$1,250
172/II	10-3/4"	TMK-3	$650-$800
172/II	10-3/4"	TMK-4	$550-$600
172/II	10-3/4"	TMK-5	$475-$500
172/II	10-3/4"	TMK-6	$450-$475

Hum 173: Festival Harmony (Angel With Flute)

Master sculptor Reinhold Unger is credited with this 1947 design in the larger size only with incised "173." It has been restyled several times throughout the years.

The major variations of this figure are to be found with the Crown (TMK-1) and Full Bee (TMK-2) marks. The Crown and some (very rare) Full Bee pieces have the flowers extending from the base well up onto the gown front. This variation of the piece is valued at $3,000-$3,500. Most of the Full Bee pieces have the flowers barely extending from the base up over the bottom edge of the gown. These variations are always found on the pieces marked with the plain incised 173 with no size designator.

The Hum 173 Crown and Full Bee trademarked figures seem to be in shorter supply than those same pieces in the 172 mold number. Probably they were not sold in the same quantities because of the flutes' vulnerability to breakage.

The 173/II size was temporarily withdrawn from production effective December 31, 1984, and the other two sizes were withdrawn in 1999.

Hum No.	Basic Size	Trademark	Current Value
173/4/0	3-1/8"	TMK-7	$120-$130
173/0	8"	TMK-3	$500-$650
173/0	8"	TMK-4	$400-$475
173/0	8"	TMK-5	$380-$400
173/0	8"	TMK-6	$360-$380
173/0	8"	TMK-7	$360-$385
173 (high flowers)	11"	TMK-1	$3,000-$3,500
173 (high flowers)	11"	TMK-2	$2,500-$3,000
173 (medium flowers)	11"	TMK-2	$1,250-$1,500
173 (low flowers)	11"	TMK-3	$1,000-$1,250
173/II	11"	TMK-3	$650-$800
173/II	11"	TMK-4	$550-$600
173/II	11"	TMK-5	$475-$500
173/II	11"	TMK-6	$450-$475

Festival Harmony, Hum 173. Left to right (A through D): A. Bears the mold number with decimal size designator, 172., an incised Crown Mark (TMK-1) and stamped Full Bee (TMK-2). It measures 1-1/4", has a doughnut base, and a black "Germany." B. Exhibits the same characteristics as the previous one except it measures 11". C. The mold number on this one is a plain 173. It has a Full Bee trademark, doughnut base, measures 11" and has a black "Germany." Note the bird is much smaller and the very small flowers. D. This mold number is 173/II; it bears TMK-6 and measures 10-7/8". Note the absence of flowers and the textured gown.

Hum 174: She Loves Me, She Loves Me Not

The work of master sculptor Arthur Moeller in 1945, this piece was released in the 1940s and has been in continuous production in one size since then.

The earliest models were produced with eyes open and a very small feather in the hat. A flower was added to the left fence post and the feather grew larger on the Full Bee (TMK-2) pieces, although some are found in the older style.

The third change was manifest by the time the Three Line Mark (TMK-4) was in use, where the fence post flower is missing and the boy's eyes are downcast. There are transition pieces for each of these changes, so you may encounter the changes associated with more than one trademark.

The current production pieces have the eyes cast downward.

Hum No.	Basic Size	Trademark	Current Value
174	4-1/4"	TMK-1	$550-$700
174	4-1/4"	TMK-2	$350-$450
174	4-1/4"	TMK-3	$290-$300
174	4-1/4"	TMK-4	$260-$290
174	4-1/4"	TMK-5	$250-$260
174	4-1/4"	TMK-6	$245-$250
174	4-1/4"	TMK-7	$240-$250
174	4-1/4"	TMK-8	$250

She Loves Me, She Loves Me Not, Hum 174. Left: Full Bee mark in an incised circle, black "Western Germany," 4-3/8". Center: Three Line Mark, incised 1955 copyright date, and 4-3/8". Right: Stylized Bee mark, 4-1/4".

Photo courtesy Goebel of North America.

Still in production today (TMK-8), She Loves Me, She Loves Me Not has remained the same size, and thus the same mold number, over the years.

Hum 175: Mother's Darling

First known as "Happy Harriet," this figurine was designed by master sculptor Arthur Moeller in 1945 with several revisions since.

Mother's Darling, Hum 175. The left figure is older, with an incised Crown Mark (TMK-1) and a black Full Bee (TMK-2) trademark. The one on the right has the Stylized Bee (TMK-3) trademark. They both measure 5-1/2".

The most significant variation of this figure is found in the color of the bags. The older versions have bags colored light pink and yellow-green. The newer ones are blue and red. These variations are insignificant except they allow the collector to spot older pieces without examining the bases. Differences in value are based on earlier trademarks, rather than color variation.

This figurine was permanently retired in 1997. During that year, all those produced carried the "Final Issue 1997" backstamp and came with small gold "Final Issue" medallion.

Hum No.	Basic Size	Trademark	Current Value
175 (pink and green)	5-1/2"	TMK-1	$600-$800
175 (pink and green)	5-1/2"	TMK-2	$400-$525
175 (both ways)	5-1/2"	TMK-3	$325-$375
175	5-1/2"	TMK-4	$285-$325
175	5-1/2"	TMK-5	$260-$285
175	5-1/2"	TMK-6	$250-$260
175	5-1/2"	TMK-7	$240-$250

Hum 176: Happy Birthday

Created by master sculptor Arthur Moeller in only one size in 1945, the 176/0 has been written "176" (without using the "/0" designator) in the Crown (TMK-1) and Full Bee (TMK-2) marks. It utilizes the decimal point designator ("176.") in the Crown and Full Bee marks as well.

The smaller 176/0 size was introduced in the 1950s and the other piece was renumbered as 176/I.

There are no mold or finish variations that influence current value.

The larger 176/I size was temporarily withdrawn from production in 1999.

Hum No.	Basic Size	Trademark	Current Value
176/0	5"	TMK-2	$400-$500
176/0	5"	TMK-3	$325-$375
176/0	5"	TMK-4	$280-$325
176/0	5"	TMK-5	$275-$285
176/0	5"	TMK-6	$265-$275
176/0	5"	TMK-7	$260-$265
176/0	5"	TMK-8	$260
176	5-1/2"	TMK-1	$850-$1,150
176	5-1/2"	TMK-2	$600-$750
176/I	5-1/2"	TMK-1	$800-$1,000
176/I	5-1/2"	TMK-2	$550-$700
176/I	5-1/2"	TMK-3	$450-$525
176/I	5-1/2"	TMK-4	$390-$450
176/I	5-1/2"	TMK-5	$360-$390
176/I	5-1/2"	TMK-6	$345-$360
176/I	5-1/2"	TMK-7	$330-$345

Happy Birthday, Hum 176. Left: Decimal designator in the mold number 176., incised Crown Mark (TMK-1), black "Germany," 5-5/8". Right: Decimal designator in the mold number 176., incised Crown Mark (TMK-1) and Full Bee (TMK-2), doughnut base, black "Germany," 5-1/2".

The TMK-8 rendition of Happy Birthday, Hum 176/0, which is 5" and valued at $260.

Photo courtesy Goebel of North America.

Hum 177: School Girls

First designed by master sculptor Reinhold Unger in 1946 and produced in the 1940s, this figurine remains in the line today in a smaller size. It was originally known as "Master Piece."

No mold or finish variations have an influence on value, outside the normal evolutionary changes on the various trademarked figures. There are similarities between this piece and Stitch in Time (Hum 255) and Knitting Lesson (Hum 256).

The smaller 177/I size was first issued in the 1960s with an incised 1961 copyright date.

The 177/III was permanently retired in 1982. It is now a closed edition, never to be produced again.

School Girls, Hum 177/I. Last Bee trademark, 1961 copyright date, and 7-1/2".

Hum No.	Basic Size	Trademark	Current Value
177/I	7-1/2"	TMK-3	$1,650-$1,750
177/I	7-1/2"	TMK-4	$1,550-$1,600
177/I	7-1/2"	TMK-5	$1,500-$1,550
177/I	7-1/2"	TMK-6	$1,450-$1,500
177/I	7-1/2"	TMK-7	$1,400-$1,450
177/I	7-1/2"	TMK-8	$1,400
177	9-1/2"	TMK-1	$4,000-$5,000
177	9-1/2"	TMK-2	$3,000-$4,000
177	9-1/2"	TMK-3	$2,200-$2,300
177/III	9-1/2"	TMK-3	$2,200-$2,300
177/III	9-1/2"	TMK-4	$2,100-$2,200
177/III	9-1/2"	TMK-5	$2,000-$2,100
177/III	9-1/2"	TMK-6	$1,900-$2,000

The TMK-8 rendition of Happy Birthday, Hum 176/0, which is 5" and valued at $260.

Hum 178: The Photographer

This figure was created by master sculptor Reinhold Unger in 1948 in only one size and is still produced in the same size today. Color and mold variations do exist, but outside of the value differences due to trademark changes, the variations have no influence on the value of the pieces.

Hum No.	Basic Size	Trademark	Current Value
178	4-3/4"	TMK-1	$750-$1,100
178	4-3/4"	TMK-2	$500-$650
178	4-3/4"	TMK-3	$430-$480
178	4-3/4"	TMK-4	$370-$430
178	4-3/4"	TMK-5	$345-$370
178	4-3/4"	TMK-6	$340-$345
178	4-3/4"	TMK-7	$335-$345
178	4-3/4"	TMK-8	$335

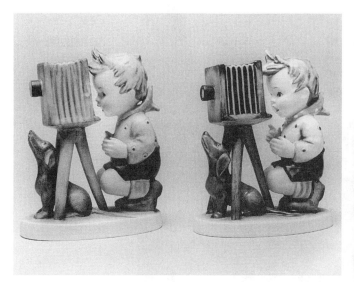

The Photographer, Hum 178. Left: Three Line Mark (TMK-4), incised copyright symbol ©, 1948 copyright date, 4-3/4". Right: TMK-6, 1948 copyright date, 4-5/8".

The Photographer, Hum 178, is still in production today (TMK-8).

Hum 179: Coquettes

The design of master sculptor Arthur Moeller in 1948, older versions of this figure have a blue dress and yellow flowers on the back of the fence posts. The girls are a bit chubbier, and the hairstyle of the girl with the red kerchief is swept back.

First released around 1950, this figure was not produced with any mold or finish variations that significantly impact its price. It was temporarily withdrawn from production in 1999.

Coquettes, Hum 179. Stylized Bee (TMK-3), 5".

Hum No.	Basic Size	Trademark	Current Value
179	5-1/4"	TMK-1	$800-$1,100
179	5-1/4"	TMK-2	$500-$650
179	5-1/4"	TMK-3	$450-$500
179	5-1/4"	TMK-4	$375-$450
179	5-1/4"	TMK-5	$350-$375
179	5-1/4"	TMK-6	$335-$350
179	5-1/4"	TMK-7	$325-$340

Hum 180: Tuneful Goodnight (Wall Plaque)

Master sculptor Arthur Moeller designed this piece in 1946, when it was known as "Happy Bugler" plaque. This plaque is rare in the older marks. It was redesigned toward the end of the Last Bee (TMK-5) era. The newer design has the bugle in a more forward position, making it very vulnerable to breakage.

Some of the early Crown (TMK-1) pieces are made of porcelain, rather than the usual ceramic material.

This piece was temporarily withdrawn in 1989.

Hum No.	Basic Size	Trademark	Current Value
180 (porcelain)	4-1/2" x 4-1/4"	TMK-1	$900-$1,200
180	5" x 4-3/4"	TMK-1	$600-$800
180	5" x 4-3/4"	TMK-2	$400-$550
180	5" x 4-3/4"	TMK-3	$350-$400
180	5" x 4-3/4"	TMK-4	$300-$350
180	5" x 4-3/4"	TMK-5	$225-$245
180	5" x 4-3/4"	TMK-6	$200-$225

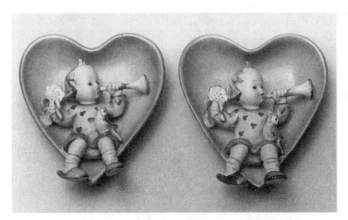

Tuneful Good Night plaque, Hum 180. Left: Incised Crown Mark, 4-3/4" x 5". Right: Stylized Bee in an incised circle, black "West Germany," 4-3/4" x 5".

Tuneful Goodnight, Hum 180, shown here as part of a Collector's Set.

Photo courtesy Goebel of North America.

Hum 181: Old Man Reading Newspaper (Closed Number)

Sometimes referred to as "Old People" or "The Mamas and the Papas," this figure and Hum 189 through Hum 191 and Hum 202, are the only known M.I. Hummel figurines to feature old people as the subjects. Designed by master sculptor Arthur Moeller in 1948, they are more like caricatures than realistic renderings.

An American collector discovered the first four in Europe. The fifth piece, a table lamp (Hum 202), turned up later. These discoveries filled in gaps in the mold number sequence previously designated closed numbers, the term Goebel applies to pieces never placed in production.

At least three complete sets of the five pieces are positively known to exist: one set in the company archives and two others in private collections. There have been other single pieces found, and there are reports of three or more sets in the U.S. There is little doubt that some others do exist, either singly or in sets, but the number is likely to be extremely small. They were made in samples only and apparently rejected by the Siessen Convent as atypical of Hummel art.

Hum No.	Basic Size	Trademark	Current Value
181	6-3/4"	-	$15,000-$20,000

The Mamas and Papas. Left: Hum 181, Old Man Reading Newspaper, 6-3/8". Right: Hum 189, Old Woman Knitting, and 6-13/16".

Hum 182: Good Friends

Created by master sculptor Arthur Moeller in 1946 and released around the late-1940s, Good Friends remains in production today. It was first known as "Friends."

Produced in one size only, there are no variations influencing the regular collector value for the various trademarked pieces.

Hum No.	Basic Size	Trademark	Current Value
182	4"	TMK-1	$550-$750
182	4"	TMK-2	$350-$475
182	4"	TMK-3	$300-$325
182	4"	TMK-4	$265-$300
182	4"	TMK-5	$250-$265
182	4"	TMK-6	$240-$250
182	4"	TMK-7	$235-$240
182	4"	TMK-8	$235

Good Friends, Hum 182. Left: Stylized Bee (TMK-3), doughnut base, 4". Right: TMK-6, 4-1/4".

Today's variation (TMK-8) of Good Friends, Hum 182, which is worth $235-$240.

Photo courtesy Goebel of North America.

Hum 183: Forest Shrine

This figure, which was the work of master sculptor Reinhold Unger in 1946, was released some time around the late-1940s. Apparently the figures, once called "Doe at Shrine," were produced in limited quantities because those with early trademarks are in short supply. They were removed from production some time around the end of the Stylized Bee (TMK-3) period, but put back in 1977. This is probably the reason they are not found bearing the Three Line Mark (TMK-4).

This piece was temporarily withdrawn from production in January 1999.

Hum No.	Basic Size	Trademark	Current Value
183	7" x 9"	TMK-1	$1,500-$1,900
183	7" x 9"	TMK-2	$1,000-$1,300
183	7" x 9"	TMK-3	$700-$950
183	7" x 9"	TMK-5	$650-$700
183	7" x 9"	TMK-6	$625-$650
183	7" x 9"	TMK-7	$595-$600

Forest Shrine, Hum 183. Left: Decimal designator with mold number, 183., incised Crown mark (TMK-1) and stamped Full Bee (TMK-2) mark, black "Germany," split base, 9". Right: TMK-6, 9".

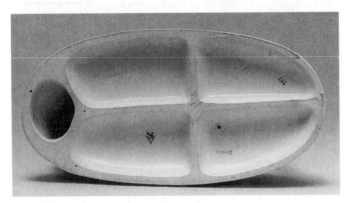

Forest Shrine, Hum 183, showing the base split in quarters.

Hum 184: Latest News

First produced by master sculptor Arthur Moeller in 1946, the older pieces have square bases and wide-open eyes. The figure was remodeled in the 1960s and given a round base and lowered eyes so the boy appears more like he is reading his paper.

Early Crown Mark (TMK-1) pieces can be found made of porcelain, rather than the typical ceramic material. These are rare and therefore worth more than the other Crown examples.

The figures are found with a variety of newspaper names. For a time the figures were produced with any name requested by merchants (i.e. their hometown newspapers). Later models bear the newspaper names: "Das Allerneuste," "Latest News," and "Munchener Presse." As of 1985, the only newspaper name used was "Latest News." These three titles are the most common. Some of the rarer titles can range in value from $750 to $1,500. Be careful in cleaning these items; if you rub too hard or use harsh cleaners, you may rub off the titles. The figures were also produced for a time with no titles.

In 1996, Goebel began producing a special limited edition of Latest News. This design used the U.S. Armed Forces

Latest News, Hum 184. Left to right (A through D): A. Daily Mail. Has the decimal designator in the mold number 184., Crown Mark (TMK-1), U.S. ZONE Germany in a rectangular box beneath. B. Bermuda News, 1909-1959. C. Latest News. Stylized Bee (TMK-3) mark in an incised circle, black "Western Germany." D. "LB Goebel - NACH." Last Bee (TMK-5) trademark. Note the round base. All four measure 5-1/8".

newspaper masthead Stars and Stripes on the front page and a drawing of the famous Checkpoint Charlie of the Berlin Wall on the back page. The edition is limited to 20,000.

Another special edition produced in 1996 is entitled The Chancellor's Visit. A special backstamp identifies it as such. This figure was accompanied by a wooden base with a brass plate reading: "In commemoration of Chancellor Dr. Helmut Kohl's historic meeting with President Bill Clinton, Milwaukee, Wisconsin, May 23, 1996." The newspaper is imprinted with the Milwaukee Journal-Sentinel masthead and the headline reads: "Clinton and Chancellor Helmut Kohl Meet in Milwaukee Today." An undisclosed number (probably very few) of these figures were produced in a limited edition for Mader's Tower Gallery.

Goebel announced the production of Personal Touch figurines in 1996. At that time, four figurines in the line lent themselves well to this application: Latest News was one of these. The other three were: Bird Duet (Hum 169), The Guardian (Hum 455), and For Father (Hum 87).

Hum No.	Basic Size	Trademark	Current Value
184 (porcelain)	4-1/4" to 4-1/2"	TMK-1	$1,500-$2,000
184	5" to 5-1/4"	TMK-1	$800-$1,100
184	5" to 5-1/4"	TMK-2	$550-$700
184	5" to 5-1/4"	TMK-3	$425-$500
184	5" to 5-1/4"	TMK-4	$380-$425
184	5" to 5-1/4"	TMK-5	$360-$380
184	5"	TMK-6	$350-$360
184	5"	TMK-7	$340-$350
184	5"	TMK-8	$340-$350

As part of the "Personal Touch" figurine series, Latest News, Hum 184, is able to be personalized perhaps with a couple's last name and their wedding date as shown here.

Photo courtesy Goebel of North America.

Photo courtesy Goebel of North America.

Latest News, Hum 184, is still in production today (TMK-8) at 5" and $340-$350.

Hum 185: Accordion Boy

First styled by master sculptor Reinhold Unger in 1947, this piece remained in continuous production until 1994. Once called "On the Alpine Pasture," there have been no significant variations in the mold or the finish that would affect value. Minor color variations do exist, however, in the accordion.

This piece is one of several figurines that comprise the Hummel orchestra.

Goebel permanently retired Accordion Boy in 1994. It will never be produced again. Figures made in the final year of production bear the "Final Issue 1994" backstamp and came with the small gold "Final Issue" commemorative tag.

Accordion Boy, Hum 185. Left: 185., Incised Full Bee mark, black "Germany," doughnut base, 5-1/2". Right: Stylized Bee mark, 5-3/8".

Hum No.	Basic Size	Trademark	Current Value
185	5-1/4"	TMK-1	$550-$750
185	5-1/4"	TMK-2	$375-$450
185	5-1/4"	TMK-3	$300-$325
185	5-1/4"	TMK-4	$275-$300

Hum No.	Basic Size	Trademark	Current Value
185	5-1/4"	TMK-5	$245-$275
185	5-1/4"	TMK-6	$225-$250
185	5-1/4"	TMK-7	$200-$225

Hum 186: Sweet Music

This piece was the original work of master sculptor Reinhold Unger in 1947. It was once known as "Playing to the Dance."

The most significant variation of Sweet Music is the striped slippers shown on the figure in the accompanying photo. It is found on the Crown Mark (TMK-1) figures and will bring $1,000-$1,500, depending upon condition. The plain painted slippers are also found on Crown Mark era figures.

It is one of several figurines that make up the Hummel orchestra.

Recently, a 12-1/2" version of Sweet Music was introduced as part of the "Millennium Love" series, which also included Serenade (Hum 85/III), Little Fiddler (Hum 2/III), Band Leader (Hum 129/III), and Soloist (Hum 135/III). These oversized pieces (Hum 85/III) were in limited supply and had to be special-ordered through an authorized M.I. Hummel retailer.

Hum No.	Basic Size	Trademark	Current Value
186 (striped slippers)	5" to 5-1/2"	TMK-1	$1,000-$1,500
186	5-1/4"	TMK-1	$550-$750
186	5-1/4"	TMK-2	$375-$450
186	5-1/4"	TMK-3	$300-$325
186	5-1/4"	TMK-4	$275-$300
186	5-1/4"	TMK-5	$250-$275
186	5-1/4"	TMK-6	$240-$245
186	5"	TMK-7	$235-$245
186	5"	TMK-8	$235-$245
186/III	13-1/2"	TMK-8	$1,550

Sweet Music, Hum 186. Left: Full Bee mark, black "Germany," 5-1/4". Right: Stylized Bee mark, black "Western Germany," 5".

Photo courtesy Goebel of North America.

Today's variation (TMK-8) of Sweet Music, Hum 186.

Hum 187: Dealer Plaques and Display Plaques

Originally crafted by master sculptor Reinhold Unger in 1947, the 187 mold number was used on all dealer plaques until 1986, when it was taken out of production (see Hum 460).

The older pieces have the traditional bumblebee perched on top. The piece was redesigned in 1972 to have a raised round area known as the "moon top" in place of the traditional bumblebee and was imprinted with the Stylized Bee (TMK-3). The plaques in TMK-7 do not have this round medallion-like area. Some plaques have been found with the mold numbers 187/A and 187/C.

The accompanying picture is of a special edition of the display plaque made available for a short time to local chapter members of what was then the Goebel Collectors' Club. As you can see, they were personalized with chapter and member name.

A number of the 187-mold plaques in existence in Europe were made specifically for individual stores and displayed the store name, in addition to the traditional wordings.

A suggested retail price list from a few years ago indicates the availability of a "Display Plaque Retailer" and a "Display Plaque Collector." The list suggested that each bore the 187 mold number. Neither is offered anymore.

Please see the description of the Goebel Employee Service Plaque in Chapter Five.

Hum No.	Basic Size	Trademark	Current Value
187	5-1/2" x 4"	TMK-1	$1,250-$1,600
187	5-1/2" x 4"	TMK-2	$750-$900
187	5-1/2" x 4"	TMK-3	$500-$600
187	5-1/2" x 4"	TMK-4	$450-$500
187	5-1/2" x 4"	TMK-5	$175-$225
187/A	5-1/2" x 4"	TMK-5	$175-$225
187/A	5-1/2" x 4"	TMK-6	$150-$175
187/A	5-1/2" x 4"	TMK-6	$115-$120
187/A	5-1/2" x 4"	TMK-7	$110-$115

Display Plaque, Hum 187, with FullBee (TMK-2) and "© W. Goebel".

A specially customized Hum 187 Dealer plaque. Goebel has been known to do this for dealers from time to time.

Display Plaque, Hum 187. A special edition commemorating 100 years of service by the Army and Air Force Exchange Service (AAFES).

Display Plaques. Left to right (A through D): A. Hum 187, but there is no apparent mold number or trademark. Measures 3-3/4". B. Hum 187, Full Bee mark, 3-3/4". "SCHMID BROS. Inc. BOSTON" painted on the satchel. The rare variation is in bas-relief, molded in. C. Hum 211, Full Bee, white overglaze, 3-7/8". D. Hum 213, Spanish language, Full Beemark, "(R)," 4".

Hum 188: Celestial Musician

Until 1983, this piece was made only in the 7" size, with a mold number of 188. Beginning in 1983, a smaller size was produced. The smaller size is 5-1/2" and bears the mold number 188/0. At the same time, the mold number of the 188 was changed to 188/I on the TMK-7 pieces to reflect the difference.

This figure, which was first designed by master sculptor Reinhold Unger in 1948, has reportedly surfaced in white overglaze. Other than that, there have been no significant variations that would influence normal values for the various trademarked pieces.

The 188/I size was temporarily withdrawn from production in 1999 and the 188/4/0 size was temporarily withdrawn on June 15, 2002.

Hum No.	Basic Size	Trademark	Current Value
188/4/0	3-1/8"	TMK-7	$124-$130
188/4/0	3-1/8"	TMK-8	$124
188/0	5"	TMK-6	$260-$270
188/0	5"	TMK-7	$255-$260
188/0	5"	TMK-8	$255
188	7"	TMK-1	$1,500-$2,000
188	7"	TMK-2	$850-$1,100
188	7"	TMK-3	$425-$475
188	7"	TMK-4	$375-$425
188	7"	TMK-5	$330-$350
188	7"	TMK-6	$320-$330
188/I	7"	TMK-6	$310-$320
188/I	7"	TMK-7	$300-$310

Celestial Musician, Hum 188. Left: Three Line Mark, incised 1948 copyright date, and 6-3/4". Right: TMK-6, incised 1948 copyright date, and 7".

A recent version of Celestial Musician, in 3-1/8" size with mold number 188/4/0 and TMK-8. This piece was temporarily withdrawn from production in June 2002.

Current-production example (TMK-8) of Celestial Musician, Hum 188/0.

Hum 189: Old Woman Knitting (Closed Number)

(See description under Hum 181.)

Hum No.	Basic Size	Current Value
189	6-3/4"	$15,000-$20,000

Hum 190: Old Woman Walking to Market (Closed Number)

(See description under Hum 181.)

Hum No.	Basic Size	Current Value
190	6-3/4"	$15,000-$20,000

Hum 191: Old Man Walking to Market (Closed Number)

(See description under Hum 181.)

Hum No.	Basic Size	Current Value
191	6-3/4"	$15,000-$20,000

Hum 192: Candlelight (Candleholder)

There are two distinct versions of this piece, which was first designed by master sculptor Reinhold Unger in 1948 and originally called "Carrier of Light." The chief difference is found in the candle receptacle. This variation is found on the Crown Mark (TMK-1) and Full Bee (TMK-2) figurines. The transition from this older style to the newer one where the candle socket is held in the hand (no extension) took place in the Stylized Bee (TMK-3) era, so you may also find the old design so marked.

This candleholder was temporarily withdrawn from production in 1999.

Hum No.	Basic Size	Trademark	Current Value
192	6-1/4"	TMK-1	$1,350-$1,800
192	6-3/4"	TMK-2	$800-$1,000
192	6-3/4"	TMK-3	$600-$700
(long candle)			
192	6-3/4"	TMK-3	$350-$375
(short candle)			
192	6-3/4"	TMK-4	$315-$350
192	6-3/4"	TMK-5	$290-$315
192	6-3/4"	TMK-6	$275-$290
192	6-3/4"	TMK-7	$270-$275

Candlelight, Hum 192. Left: Incised Full Bee mark (TMK-2). "© W. Goebel," black "Germany," doughnut base, 6-3/4". Right: Last Bee (TMK-5), incised 1948 copyright date, 6-3/4".

Hum 193: Angel Duet (Candleholder)

This candleholder, which was the original work of master sculptor Reinhold Unger in 1948, is essentially the same design as Hum 261 except that the 261 is not a candleholder.

This piece has been produced in two variations, noticeable in the rear view of the figure. One shows the angel not holding the songbook and with an arm around the waist of the other. In the other design, one angel has a hand on the shoulder of the other angel. Both versions are found in Crown Mark (TMK-1) and Full Bee (TMK-2). The transition to the new arm-around-waist figure took place during the Full Bee period.

This piece has been found in white overglaze. It is extremely rare and would be worth $3,000-$4,000 if found.

This candleholder was temporarily withdrawn from production in 1999.

Angel Duet candleholder, Hum 193. TMK-6, 5".

Hum No.	Basic Size	Trademark	Current Value
193	5"	TMK-1	$1,350-$1,800
193	5"	TMK-2	$600-$700
193	5"	TMK-3	$325-$400
193	5"	TMK-4	$290-$325
193	5"	TMK-5	$265-$290
193	5"	TMK-6	$255-$265
193	5"	TMK-7	$250-$255

Hum 194: Watchful Angel

Once called "Angelic Care" and "Guardian Angel," this figurine was designed by master sculptor Reinhold Unger in 1948 and entered the line shortly thereafter. There are no significant mold or finish variations reported. Most pieces have an incised 1948 copyright date.

Hum No.	Basic Size	Trademark	Current Value
194	6-1/2"	TMK-1	$1,600-$2,100
194	6-1/2"	TMK-2	$650-$800
194	6-1/2"	TMK-3	$475-$575
194	6-1/2"	TMK-4	$400-$475
194	6-1/2"	TMK-5	$370-$400
194	6-1/2"	TMK-6	$365-$370
194	6-1/2"	TMK-7	$360-$365
194	6-1/2"	TMK-8	$360

Watchful Angel, Hum 194, with TMK-4 and incised 1948 copyright date.

Hum 195: Barnyard Hero

Introduced into the line in 1948 and the work of master sculptor Reinhold Unger, this figure has undergone some major mold changes over the years, but most were associated with a trademark change or a change in the finish of the entire collection. None has had a significant influence on collector values.

The smaller 195/2/0 size was introduced in the 1950s and remains in production today. The larger 195/I size, however, was temporarily withdrawn from production in 1999.

Hum No.	Basic Size	Trademark	Current Value
195/2/0	3-3/4" to 4"	TMK-2	$350-$425
195/2/0	3-3/4" to 4"	TMK-3	$275-$300
195/2/0	3-3/4" to 4"	TMK-4	$225-$275
195/2/0	3-3/4" to 4"	TMK-5	$200-$220
195/2/0	3-3/4" to 4"	TMK-6	$195-$200

Hum No.	Basic Size	Trademark	Current Value
195/2/0	3-3/4" to 4"	TMK-7	$190-$195
195/2/0	3-3/4" to 4"	TMK-8	$190
195	5-3/4" to 6"	TMK-1	$1,000-$1,200
195	5-3/4" to 6"	TMK-2	$650-$750
195/I	5-1/2"	TMK-2	$600-$700
195/I	5-1/2"	TMK-3	$475-$525
195/I	5-1/2"	TMK-4	$420-$475
195/I	5-1/2"	TMK-5	$375-$420
195/I	5-1/2"	TMK-6	$360-$375
195/I	5-1/2"	TMK-7	$350-$360

Barnyard Hero, Hum 195. Left: Incised Crown mark and a stamped Full Bee mark, split base, black "Germany," blue "© W. Goebel," 5-3/4". Right: 195/I, Three Line Mark, incised 1948 copyright date, 5-3/4".

Today's Barnyard Hero variation with 195/2/0 and TMK-8.

Photo courtesy Goebel of North America.

Hum 196: Telling Her Secret

This figurine, which was designed by master sculptor Reinhold Unger in 1948, was introduced shortly thereafter in a 6-3/4" basic size only. Its original name was "The Secret" and the girl on the right is the same as that in Which Hand? (Hum 258).

During the Full Bee (TMK-2) period, a second, smaller size (196/0) was introduced. With this new size came a change of the mold number for the larger one, from 196 to 196/I. The Full Bee (TMK-2) can be found with either mold number.

The larger 196/I size was temporarily withdrawn in 1984, but the smaller variation remains in the line today.

Hum No.	Basic Size	Trademark	Current Value
196/0	5-1/4"	TMK-2	$600-$725
196/0	5-1/4"	TMK-3	$450-$500
196/0	5-1/4"	TMK-4	$390-$450
196/0	5-1/4"	TMK-5	$360-$390
196/0	5-1/4"	TMK-6	$355-$360
196/0	5-1/4"	TMK-7	$350-$355
196/0	5-1/4"	TMK-8	$350
196	6-3/4"	TMK-1	$1,200-$1,500
196	6-3/4"	TMK-2	$800-$1,000

Hum No.	Basic Size	Trademark	Current Value
196/I	6-3/4"	TMK-2	$750-$950
196/I	6-3/4"	TMK-3	$500-$550
196/I	6-3/4"	TMK-4	$450-$500
196/I	6-3/4"	TMK-5	$425-$450
196/I	6-3/4"	TMK-6	$400-$425

Photo courtesy Goebel of North America.

The most recent variation of Telling Her Secret, which bears mold number 196/0 and TMK-8.

Telling Her Secret, Hum 196. Left: 196/I, Full Bee mark in an incised circle, incised 1948 copyright date, black "Western Germany," 6-1/2". Right: 196/0, TMK-6, incised 1948 copyright date, 5-1/2". White overglaze.

Hum 197: Be Patient

Stopped here. There are no important mold or finish variations to be found on this late-1940s release, which was first crafted by master sculptor Reinhold Unger in 1948 and previously called "Mother of Ducks." There is, however, a mold number variation that is significant. The figure was first produced in only one size with an incised mold number of 197. When a smaller size, 197/2/0, was produced in the Stylized Bee (TMK-3) period, the mold number on the larger one was changed to 197/I.

Attendees of the 1994 Disneyana Convention were given the opportunity to purchase a limited-edition set of figurines on a wooden base. A regular-production Be Patient (Hum 197/2/0) bearing TMK-7 was paired with a Minnie Mouse figurine posed the same way. Minnie bears the incised mold number 17324, a limited-edition indicator, and TMK-7. The issue price for the set was $395. It can now bring around $600-$750.

The larger 197/I size of Be Patient was temporarily withdrawn from production in 1999, but the smaller variation remains in production today.

Hum No.	Basic Size	Trademark	Current Value
197/2/0	4-1/4"	TMK-2	$400-$500
197/2/0	4-1/4"	TMK-3	$300-$350
197/2/0	4-1/4"	TMK-4	$260-$300
197/2/0	4-1/4"	TMK-5	$240-$260
197/2/0	4-1/4"	TMK-6	$235-$240

Hum No.	Basic Size	Trademark	Current Value
197/2/0	4-1/4"	TMK-7	$230-$235
197/2/0	4-1/4"	TMK-8	$235
197	6-1/4"	TMK-1	$800-$1,000
197	6-1/4"	TMK-2	$550-$700
197/I	6-1/4"	TMK-2	$500-$650
197/I	6-1/4"	TMK-3	$425-$475
197/I	6-1/4"	TMK-4	$360-$425
197/I	6-1/4"	TMK-5	$350-$360
197/I	6-1/4"	TMK-6	$340-$350
197/I	6-1/4"	TMK-7	$330-$340

Photo courtesy Goebel of North America.

Current-production (TMK-8) example of Be Patient, Hum 197.

Be Patient, Hum 197. Left: Full Bee (TMK-2), "© W. Goebel," black "Germany," and 6-1/2". Right: 197/I, Last Bee, incised 1948 copyright date, and 6".

Hum 198: Home From Market

There are no important mold or finish variations to be found on this late-1940s release, which was the design of master sculptor Arthur Moeller in 1948. There is, however, a mold number variation that is significant. The figure was first produced in only one size with the incised mold number 198. When a smaller size, 198/2/0, was issued in the Stylized Bee (TMK-3) period, the mold number of the larger figure changed to 198/I.

The larger 198//I size was temporarily withdrawn from production in 1999, but the smaller variation is still available today.

Hum No.	Basic Size	Trademark	Current Value
198	4-1/2"	TMK-2	$325-$375
198/2/0	4-3/4"	TMK-2	$300-$350
198/2/0	4-3/4"	TMK-3	$225-$250
198/2/0	4-3/4"	TMK-4	$200-$225
198/2/0	4-3/4"	TMK-5	$190-$200
198/2/0	4-3/4"	TMK-6	$185-$190

Hum No.	Basic Size	Trademark	Current Value
198/2/0	4-3/4"	TMK-7	$180-$185
198/2/0	4-3/4"	TMK-8	$180
198	5-3/4"	TMK-1	$650-$800
198	5-3/4"	TMK-2	$450-$550
198/I	5-3/4"	TMK-2	$400-$500
198/I	5-3/4"	TMK-3	$325-$375
198/I	5-3/4"	TMK-4	$275-$325
198/I	5-3/4"	TMK-5	$260-$275
198/I	5-3/4"	TMK-6	$250-$260
198/I	5-3/4"	TMK-7	$240-$245

Home From Market, Hum 198. Left: Full Bee mark in an incised circle, 1948 copyright date, black "Germany," © by W. Goebel, 5-7/8". Right: 198/I, Three Line Mark (TMK-4), 1948 copyright date, doughnut base, 5-1/2".

Home From Market, Hum 198, with a red line on the base. This indicates that this particular piece was a master model. Note the archive medallion wired and sealed around the legs.

Photo courtesy Goebel of North America.

Today's 4-3/4" version of Home From Market with mold number 198/2/0 and TMK-8.

Hum 199: Feeding Time

Crafted by master sculptor Arthur Moeller in 1948, there are no major mold or finish variations outside the normal evolution of this figurine. There is, however, a mold number variation that is important. This piece was first produced in the late-1940s in only one size with the incised mold number 199. It was also sometimes found as "199." with the decimal designator. When a new smaller size, 199/0, was introduced during the Stylized Bee (TMK-3) era, the number on the larger size was changed to 199/I.

The older pieces have blonde hair and the newer ones dark hair. The facial features are slightly different on the newer pieces as well.

The larger 199/I size was temporarily withdrawn from production in 1999, but the smaller variation continues in the line today.

Hum No.	Basic Size	Trademark	Current Value	Hum No.	Basic Size	Trademark	Current Value
199/0	4-1/4"	TMK-2	$400-$75	199	5-3/4"	TMK-2	$525-$625
199/0	4-1/4"	TMK-3	$300-$350	199/I	5-3/4"	TMK-2	$475-$575
199/0	4-1/4"	TMK-4	$265-$300	199/I	5-3/4"	TMK-3	$425-$475
199/0	4-1/4"	TMK-5	$245-$265	199/I	5-3/4"	TMK-4	$375-$425
199/0	4-1/4"	TMK-6	$240-$245	199/I	5-3/4"	TMK-5	$340-$375
199/0	4-1/4"	TMK-7	$235-$240	199/I	5-3/4"	TMK-6	$325-$340
199/0	4-1/4"	TMK-8	$235	199/I	5-3/4"	TMK-7	$315-$325
199	5-3/4"	TMK-1	$800-$1,000				

Feeding Time with the most recent mold number (199/0), TMK-8, and 4-1/4" basic size.

Feeding Time, Hum 199. Left: Full Bee mark, black "Germany," "© W. Goebel," doughnut base, 5-1/2". Right: 199/1. Full Bee in an incised circle, black "Germany," "© W. Goebel," incised 1948 copyright date, doughnut base, and 5-1/2".

Hum 200: Little Goat Herder

There are no important mold or color variations outside those occurring during the normal evolution of the figurine, which was the original design of master sculptor Arthur Moeller in 1948. There is, however, a mold number variation that is significant. This figure was first produced in only one size, with the incised mold number 200. It also sometimes appeared as "200." with the decimal designator. When a new smaller basic size of 4-3/4" was introduced in the Stylized Bee (TMK-3) era, the mold number on the larger size was changed to 200/I.

Some of the Full Bee (TMK-2) pieces in the smaller size have been found with the "M.I." initials directly above the "Hummel," rather than next to it as is traditional.

Hum No.	Basic Size	Trademark	Current Value
200/0	4-3/4"	TMK-2	$400-$500
200/0	4-3/4"	TMK-3	$300-$325
200/0	4-3/4"	TMK-4	$270-$300
200/0	4-3/4"	TMK-5	$245-$270
200/0	4-3/4"	TMK-6	$240-$245
200/0	4-3/4"	TMK-7	$235-$240
200/0	4-3/4"	TMK-8	$235

Little Goat Herder, Hum 200. Both of these are the same basic size, according to their mold numbers, though they differ in actual measurement. The larger one on the left is the 200/1 measuring 5-3/4", has a Full Bee (TMK-2) trademark in an incised circle, a "© by W. Goebel," a black "Germany" and a 1948 copyright date. The one on the right is the 200/I measuring 5-1/4", has a Three Line Mark (TMK-4) piece and also has an incised 1948 copyright date.

Hum No.	Basic Size	Trademark	Current Value
200	5-1/2"	TMK-1	$650-$850
200	5-1/2"	TMK-2	$500-$600
200/I	5-1/2"	TMK-2	$450-$550
200/I	5-1/2"	TMK-3	$350-$400
200/I	5-1/2"	TMK-4	$300-$350
200/I	5-1/2"	TMK-5	$280-$300
200/I	5-1/2"	TMK-6	$275-$280
200/I	5-1/2"	TMK-7	$270-$275
200/I	5-1/2"	TMK-8	$270

The present-day 5-1/2" variation of Little Goat Herder, Hum 200/I, which carries TMK-8.

Hum 201: Retreat to Safety

Designed by master sculptor Reinhold Unger in 1948 and once called "Afraid," there are no important mold or finish variations outside those occurring during the normal evolution of this figure. There is, however, a significant mold number variation. The figure was first produced in one size only with the incised mold number 201. It also sometimes appeared with the decimal point designator. When a new smaller size of 4" was introduced, the mold number on the 5-1/2" size was changed to 201/I.

The larger 201/I size was temporarily withdrawn from production in 1999.

Hum No.	Basic Size	Trademark	Current Value
201/2/0	4"	TMK-2	$350-$425
201/2/0	4"	TMK-3	$275-$300
201/2/0	4"	TMK-4	$225-$275

Hum No.	Basic Size	Trademark	Current Value
201/2/0	4"	TMK-5	$200-$220
201/2/0	4"	TMK-6	$195-$200
201/2/0	4"	TMK-7	$190-$195
201/2/0	4"	TMK-8	$190
201	5-1/2"	TMK-1	$1,000-$1,200
201	5-1/2"	TMK-2	$650-$750
201/I	5-1/2"	TMK-2	$600-$700
201/I	5-1/2"	TMK-3	$475-$525
201/I	5-1/2"	TMK-4	$420-$475
201/I	5-1/2"	TMK-5	$375-$420
201/I	5-1/2"	TMK-6	$360-$375
201/I	5-1/2"	TMK-7	$350-$360

Retreat to Safety, Hum 201. Left: Full Bee (TMK-2) with a "(R)" associated, "© W. Goebel," black "Germany," split base. Right: 201/I, Three Line Mark (TMK-4), incised 1948 copyright date.

A more recent variation of Retreat to Safety, Hum 201/2/0.

Hum 202: Old Man Reading Newspaper (Table Lamp, Closed Number)

Same figure as Hum 181, except on a lamp. It was made as a sample only by master sculptor Arthur Moeller in 1948 after the Siessen Convent rejected it for production.

It was listed as a closed number that same year. See further description under Hum 181.

Hum No.	Basic Size	Current Value
202	8-1/4"	$15,000-$20,000

Hum 203: Signs of Spring (Closed Edition)

Crafted by master sculptor Arthur Moeller and released about 1950, there is a significant mold variation in the 4" basic size, 203/2/0. This size, which was first called "Scandal," was introduced in the Full Bee (TMK-2) period, when the figure had both feet on the ground and was wearing shoes. At some point during this period, it was remodeled so that her right foot was raised above the ground and the foot had no shoe. The first variation with the two shoes is scarcer.

Another mold variation is worthy of note. One version of this figure has four fence pickets instead of the usual three, and there are more flowers present. The mold number of the example in the photo appears to have been scratched into the figure by hand before firing. This is probably a prototype, for no more have surfaced.

There is also a variation in mold numbering. This figure was first released in the 201 mold number in only the 5" size. When the smaller 4" size, 203/2/0, was released in the Full Bee era, the mold number of the larger size was changed to 203/I. The earlier "203" is also occasionally found with the decimal designator.

Both sizes of Signs of Spring were permanently retired in 1990.

Hum No.	Basic Size	Trademark	Current Value
203/2/0 (with two shoes)	4"	TMK-2	$1,200-$1,500
203/2/0	4"	TMK-2	$425-$500
203/2/0	4"	TMK-3	$350-$400
203/2/0	4"	TMK-4	$275-$350
203/2/0	4"	TMK-5	$250-$275

Hum No.	Basic Size	Trademark	Current Value
203/2/0	4"	TMK-6	$225-$275
203	5"	TMK-1	$750-$1,000
203	5"	TMK-2	$550-$650
203/I	5"	TMK-2	$500-$600
203/I	5"	TMK-3	$400-$450
203/I	5"	TMK-4	$350-$400
203/I	5"	TMK-5	$300-$325
203/I	5"	TMK-6	$275-$300

Signs of Spring, Hum 203/I. Three Line Mark (TMK-4), 1948 copyright date, 5".

Signs of Spring, Hum 203. This is a very rare and unusual variation. Note the fourth fence post and additional flowers.

Base of the four-picket variation showing the unusual split base. Stamped Full Bee, "© W. Goebel, and "black" Germany." The mold number appears to have been rendered

Hum 204: Weary Wanderer

This figurine, which was first known as "Tired Little Traveler," was designed by master sculptor Reinhold Unger in 1949. Most pieces bear an incised 1949 copyright date.

There is a major variation associated with this figurine. The normal figurine has eyes painted with no color. The variation has blue eyes. There are only a handful of blue-eyed pieces presently known to be in collectors' hands. These are valued at about $2,000-$3,000 each.

Hum 204 was temporarily withdrawn from production in 1999.

Hum No.	Basic Size	Trademark	Current Value
204	6"	TMK-1	$700-$900
204	6"	TMK-2	$500-$600
204	6"	TMK-3	$375-$425
204	6"	TMK-4	$325-$375
204	6"	TMK-5	$300-$325
204	6"	TMK-6	$295-$300
204	6"	TMK-7	$280-$290

Weary Wanderer, Hum 204. Left: Incised Full Bee (TMK-2) mark, black "Germany," © W. Goebel, 5-7/8". Right: Stamped Full Bee (TMK-2), black "Germany," © W. Goebel, 5-3/4".

Hum 205: German Language Dealer Plaque or Display Plaque

There are several merchant display plaques used by dealers. Master sculptor Reinhold Unger first designed each in 1949 and has a large bumblebee perched atop the plaque and a Merry Wanderer figure attached to the right side. All are 5-1/2" x 4-1/2" in basic size. Although listed as a closed edition in 1949, some plaques do carry the Stylized Bee (TMK-3), which means they were produced after 1949. See other dealer plaques: Hum 187, 208, 209, 210, 211, and 213.

Hum No.	Basic Size	Trademark	Current Value
205	5-1/2" x 4-1/2"	TMK-1	$1,400-$1,700
205	5-1/2" x 4-1/2"	TMK-2	$1,000-$1,200
205	5-1/2" x 4-1/2"	TMK-3	$850-$1,000

German Language Dealer Plaque, Hum 205.

Hum 206: Angel Cloud (Holy Water Font)

Angel Cloud font, Hum 206, in Three Line Mark (TMK-4) with incised 1949 copyright date.

Master sculptor Reinhold Unger is responsible for the design of this piece, which was released in the early 1950s and has been redesigned several times. The newer pieces carry an incised 1949 copyright date.

It has been in and out of production since the beginning but apparently in very limited quantities each time. The older trademarks have always been in short supply.

This piece was once again temporarily withdrawn in 1999.

Hum No.	Basic Size	Trademark	Current Value
206	2-1/4" x 4-3/4"	TMK-1	$350-$500
206	2-1/4" x 4-3/4"	TMK-2	$250-$350
206	2-1/4" x 4-3/4"	TMK-3	$200-$250
206	2-1/4" x 4-3/4"	TMK4	$70-$90
206	2-1/4" x 4-3/4"	TMK-5	$65-$70
206	2-1/4" x 4-3/4"	TMK-6	$62-$65
206	2-1/4" x 4-3/4"	TMK-7	$60-$62

Hum 207: Heavenly Angel (Holy Water Font)

Modeled by master sculptor Reinhold Unger in 1949 and first released in the early 1950s, this piece has the distinction of the highest mold number in the collection that can be found with the Crown Mark (TMK-1). There are a number of variations to be found, but none have any significant impact on collector value. This piece was the inspiration for the first Annual Plate (Hum 264), which was produced in 1971.

Heavenly Angel Holy Water font, Hum 207, shown here in Three Line Mark (TMK-4) with incised 1949 copyright date.

The Heavenly Angel Holy Water font in present-day trademark, TMK-8.

Photo courtesy Goebel of North America.

Hum No.	Basic Size	Trademark	Current Value
207	2" x 4-3/4"	TMK-1	$350-$500
207	2" x 4-3/4"	TMK-2	$150-$175
207	2" x 4-3/4"	TMK-3	$100-$125
207	2" x 4-3/4"	TMK-4	$75-$90
207	2" x 4-3/4"	TMK-5	$70-$75
207	2" x 4-3/4"	TMK-6	$65-$70
207	2" x 4-3/4"	TMK-7	$62-$65
207	2" x 4-3/4"	TMK-8	$62

Hum 208: French Language Dealer Plaque

There are several merchant display plaques used by dealers. Each has a large bumblebee perched atop the plaque and a Merry Wanderer figure attached to the right side. All except the Spanish variation are 5-1/2" x 4-1/2" in basic size. See other dealer plaques: Hum 187, 205, 209, 210, 211, and 213.

Hum 208, French Language Dealer Plaque, with Full Bee (TMK-2).

Hum No.	Basic Size	Trademark	Current Value
208	5-1/2" x 4-1/2"	TMK-2	$4,000-$6,000
208	5-1/2" x 4-1/2"	TMK-3	$3,000-$4,000

Hum 209: Swedish Language Dealer Plaque

There are several merchant display plaques used by dealers. Each has a large bumblebee perched atop the plaque and a Merry Wanderer figure attached to the right side. All except the Spanish variation are 5-1/2" x 4-1/2" in basic size. Two distinctly different lettering designs have been found. See other dealer plaques: Hum 187, 205, 208, 210, 211, and 213.

Hum 209, Swedish Language Dealer Plaque, with Full Bee (TMK-2).

Hum No.	Basic Size	Trademark	Current Value
209	5-1/2" x 4-1/2"	TMK-2	$4,000-$6,000

Hum 210: English Language Dealer Plaque

There are several merchant display plaques used by dealers. Each has a large bumblebee perched atop the plaque and a Merry Wanderer figure attached to the right side. All except the Spanish variation are 5-1/2" x 4-1/2" in basic size. Hum 210, the English language plaque, is a Schmid Brothers display plaque made specifically for this distributor. "Schmid Bros., Boston" is found molded in bas-relief on the suitcase. There are only four pieces known to exist. See other dealer plaques: Hum 187, 205, 208, 209, 211, and 213.

Hum No.	Basic Size	Trademark	Current Value
208	5-1/2" x 4-1/2"	TMK-2	$20,000-$25,000

Hum 211: English Language Dealer Plaque

There are several merchant display plaques used by dealers. Each has a large bumblebee perched atop the plaque and a Merry Wanderer figure attached to the right side. All except the Spanish variation are 5-1/2" x 4-1/2" in basic size. Hum 211, the English language plaque, is even more rare than the other English plaque (Hum 210). There are only two known examples of Hum 211 in collectors' hands. One is in white overglaze with no color and the other is in full color. The full-color example is the only dealer plaque to use the word "Oeslau" as the location of Goebel in Bavaria. The name has since been changed to Rodental, but this is not found on any plaques. See other dealer plaques: Hum 187, 205, 208, 209, 210, and 213.

Hum No.	Basic Size	Trademark	Current Value
211	5-1/2" x 4-1/2"	TMK-2	$20,000-$25,000

Hum 212: Orchestra (Closed Number)

This was previously suspected to be another dealer plaque. Then, it was thought that this number was intended to be utilized with the letters A through F as mold numbers for a set of musician pieces called Orchestra. It is now known that this mold number was used for a short time merely as an inventory designation for the Band Leader (Hum 129) and several of the musical figurines. The number was not incised on the figures.

Hum 213: Spanish Language Dealer Plaque

There are several merchant display plaques used by dealers. Each has a large bumblebee perched atop the plaque and a Merry Wanderer figure attached to the right side. Hum 213, the Spanish language plaque, is slightly bigger than the other dealer plaques at 5-3/4" x 4-1/2". See other dealer plaques: Hum 187, 205, 208, 209, 210, and 211.

Hum No.	Basic Size	Trademark	Current Value
213	5-3/4" x 4-1/2"	TMK-2	$8,000-$10,000

Hum 214: Nativity Set

In the early Hum 214 sets, which were first designed by master sculptor Reinhold Unger in 1951, the Madonna and Infant Jesus were molded as one piece. The later figures are found as two separate pieces. The one-piece variations are closed editions.

Hum 366 (Flying Angel) is frequently used with this set. One old model camel and two more recently issued camels are also frequently used with the set, but these are not Hummel pieces.

The Hum 214 Nativity Set, featuring figures A through O as well as the flying angel.

Collectors may note the omission of 214/I in the listing below. It has long been assumed that the mold number was never used because of the possible confusion that might result from the similarity of the "I" and the "1" when incised as a mold number. The existence of a Hum 214/I has now been substantiated. The piece found is in white overglaze and is of two connected geese similar to the geese in the Goose Girl figure. It has the incised M.I. Hummel signature.

Because there are so many pieces under this listing, the following guide will first help you with the names matched to the Hum numbers for each figurine. The pricing list then follows that identifying list.

- 214/A and 214/A/I: Virgin Mary and Infant Jesus (one-piece variation)
- 214/A and 214/A/I: Virgin Mary
- 214/A (or 214 A/K) and 214/A/K/I: Infant Jesus
- 214/B and 214/B/I: Joseph
- 214/C and 214/C/I: Angel, standing (Good Night Angel)
- 214/D and 214/D/I: Angel, kneeling (Angel Serenade)
- 214/E and 214/E/I: We Congratulate
- 214/F and 214/F/I: Shepherd, standing with sheep
- 214/G and 214/G/I: Shepherd, kneeling
- 214/H and 214/H/I: Shepherd Boy, kneeling with flute (Little Tooter)
- 214/J and 214/J/I: Donkey

- 214/K and 214/K/I: Ox/cow
- 214/L and 214/L/I: Moorish king, standing
- 214/M and 214/M/I: King, kneeling on one knee
- 214/N and 214/N/I: King, kneeling with box
- 214/O and 214/O/I: Lamb

- 366 and 366/1: Flying Angel

There are also two wooden stables without Hum numbers to go with both the 12- to 16-piece sets and the three-piece sets. Current retail value on the larger stable is $115, and the smaller stable retails for $50.

Hum No.	Basic Size	Trademark	Current Value (color)	Current Value (white)
214/A	6-1/2" (one piece)	TMK-2	$2,000-$2,500	$2,500-$3,000
214/A	6-1/4" to 6-1/2"	TMK-2	$300-$400	$400-$500
214/A	6-1/4" to 6-1/2"	TMK-3	$250-$285	$325-$400
214/A	6-1/4" to 6-1/2"	TMK-4	$225-$250	$250-$325
214/A	6-1/4" to 6-1/2"	TMK-5	$210-$225	$200-$225
214/A	6-1/4" to 6-1/2"	TMK-6	$205-$210	$200-$225
214/A/I	6-1/4" to 6-1/2"	TMK-7	$200-$205	N/A
214/A/M/I	6-1/4" to 6-1/2"	TMK-8	$200	N/A
214/A	1-1/2" x 3-1/2"	TMK-2	$110-$135	$215-$260
214/A	1-1/2" x 3-1/2"	TMK-3	$95-$100	$160-$215
214/A	1-1/2" x 3-1/2"	TMK-4	$90-$95	$85-$110
214/A	1-1/2" x 3-1/2"	TMK-5	$85-$90	$60-$75
214/A/K	1-1/2" x 3-1/2"	TMK-6	$80-$85	$60-$75
214/A/K/I	1-1/2" x 3-1/2"	TMK-7	$75-$80	N/A
214/A/K/I	1-1/2" x 3-1/2"	TMK-8	$75	N/A
214/B	7-1/2"	TMK-2	$300-$400	$350-$425
214/B	7-1/2"	TMK-3	$250-$285	$275-$350
214/B	7-1/2"	TMK-4	$225-$250	$225-$275
214/B	7-1/2"	TMK-5	$210-$225	$175-$200
214/B	7-1/2"	TMK-6	$205-$210	$150-$175
214/B/I	7-1/2"	TMK-7	$200-$205	N/A
214/B/I	7-1/2"	TMK-8	$200	N/A
214/C	3-1/2"	TMK-2	$160-$200	$370-$420
214/C	3-1/2"	TMK-3	$125-$150	$320-$370
214/C	3-1/2"	TMK-4	$115-$125	$270-$320
214/C	3-1/2"	TMK-5	$110-$115	N/A
214/C	3-1/2"	TMK-6	$105-$110	N/A
214/C/I	3-1/2"	TMK-7	$100-$105	N/A
214/C/I	3-1/2"	TMK-8	$100	N/A
214/C/I	3-1/2"	TMK-8	$110	N/A
(50th anniversary)				
214/D	3"	TMK-2	$160-$200	$245-$295
214/D	3"	TMK-3	$125-$145	$220-$245
214/D	3"	TMK-4	$115-$125	$170-$220
214/D	3"	TMK-5	$110-$115	N/A
214/D	3"	TMK-6	$105-$110	N/A
214/D/I	3"	TMK-7	$100-$105	N/A
214/D/I	3"	TMK-8	$100	N/A
214/D/I	3"	TMK-8	$110	N/A
(50th anniversary)				
214/E	3-3/4"	TMK-2	$325-$390	$400-$475
214/E	3-3/4"	TMK-3	$250-$285	$325-$400
214/E	3-3/4"	TMK-4	$215-$250	$275-$325
214/E	3-3/4"	TMK-5	$195-$205	N/A
214/E	3-3/4"	TMK-6	$190-$195	N/A
214/E/I	3-3/4"	TMK-7	$185-$190	N/A

Hum No.	Basic Size	Trademark	Current Value (color)	Current Value (white)
214/E/I	3-3/4"	TMK-8	$185	N/A
214/E/I	3-1/2"	TMK-8	$195	N/A
(50th anniversary)				
214/F	7"	TMK-2	$345-$420	$375-$475
214/F	7"	TMK-3	$255-$290	$325-$400
214/F	7"	TMK-4	$220-$255	$275-$325
214/F	7"	TMK-5	$195-$210	N/A
214/F	7"	TMK-6	$190-$195	N/A
214/F/I	7"	TMK-7	$185-$190	N/A
214/F/I	7"	TMK-8	$185	N/A
214/G	5"	TMK-2	$260-$310	$275-$325
214/G	5"	TMK-3	$205-$265	$225-$275
214/G	5"	TMK-4	$175-$200	$175-$225
214/G	5"	TMK-5	$165-$175	N/A
214/G	5"	TMK-6	$160-$165	N/A
214/G/I	5"	TMK-7	$155-$160	N/A
214/G/I	5"	TMK-8	$155	N/A
214/H	3-3/4" to 4"	TMK-2	$235-$280	$275-$325
214/H	3-3/4" to 4"	TMK-3	$185-$210	$225-$275
214/H	3-3/4" to 4"	TMK-4	$165-$185	$175-$225
214/H	3-3/4" to 4"	TMK-5	$160-$165	N/A
214/H	3-3/4" to 4"	TMK-6	$155-$160	N/A
214/H/I	3-3/4" to 4"	TMK-7	$150-$155	N/A
214/H/I	3-3/4" to 4"	TMK-8	$150	N/A
214/J	5"	TMK-2	$135-$165	$185-$260
214/J	5"	TMK-3	$105-$120	$160-$185
214/J	5"	TMK-4	$100-$105	$135-$160
214/J	5"	TMK-5	$95-$100	N/A
214/J	5"	TMK-6	$90-$95	N/A
214/J/I	5"	TMK-7	$85-$90	N/A
214/J/I	5"	TMK-8	$85	N/A
214/K	3-1/2" to 6-1/4"	TMK-2	$135-$165	$185-$260
214/K	3-1/2" to 6-1/4"	TMK-3	$105-$120	$160-$185
214/K	3-1/2" to 6-1/4"	TMK-4	$100-$105	$135-$160
214/K	3-1/2" to 6-1/4"	TMK-5	$95-$100	N/A
214/K	3-1/2" to 6-1/4"	TMK-6	$90-$95	N/A
214/K/I	3-1/2" to 6-1/4"	TMK-7	$85-$90	N/A
214/K/I	3-1/2" to 6-1/4"	TMK-8	$85	N/A
214/L	8" to 8-1/4"	TMK-2	$345-$420	$380-$480
214/L	8" to 8-1/4"	TMK-3	$275-$315	$280-$380
214/L	8" to 8-1/4"	TMK-4	$235-$275	$225-$275
214/L	8" to 8-1/4"	TMK-5	$220-$225	N/A
214/L	8" to 8-1/4"	TMK-6	$215-$220	N/A
214/L/I	8" to 8-1/4"	TMK-7	$210-$215	N/A
214/L/I	8" to 8-1/4"	TMK-8	$210	N/A
214/M	5-1/2"	TMK-2	$320-$420	$380-$480
214/M	5-1/2"	TMK-3	$270-$305	$280-$380
214/M	5-1/2"	TMK-4	$230-$270	$225-$275
214/M	5-1/2"	TMK-5	$215-$220	N/A
214/M	5-1/2"	TMK-6	$210-$215	N/A
214/M/I	5-1/2"	TMK-7	$205-$210	N/A

Hum No.	Basic Size	Trademark	Current Value (color)	Current Value (white)
214/M/I	5-1/2"	TMK-8	$205	N/A
214/N	5-1/2"	TMK-2	$320-$390	$380-$480
214/N	5-1/2"	TMK-3	$250-$285	$280-$380
214/N	5-1/2"	TMK-4	$215-$250	$225-$275
214/N	5-1/2"	TMK-5	$200-$205	N/A
214/N	5-1/2"	TMK-6	$195-$200	N/A
214/N/I	5-1/2"	TMK-7	$190-$195	N/A
214/N/I	5-1/2"	TMK-8	$190	N/A
214/O	1-3/4" x 2-1/2"	TMK-2	$45-$55	$110-$135
214/O	1-3/4" x 2-1/2"	TMK-3	$40-$45	$85-$110
214/O	1-3/4" x 2-1/2"	TMK-4	$35-$40	$60-$75
214/O	1-3/4" x 2-1/2"	TMK-5	$32-$35	N/A
214/O	1-3/4" x 2-1/2"	TMK-6	$28-$32	N/A
214/O/I	1-3/4" x 2-1/2"	TMK-7	$25-$30	N/A
214/O/I	1-3/4" x 2-1/2"	TMK-8	$25	N/A
366	3-1/2"	TMK-4	$220-$270	$230-$280
366	3-1/2"	TMK-5	$165-$170	$155-$180
366	3-1/2"	TMK-6	$160-$165	$155-$180
366/I	3-1/2"	TMK-7	$155-$160	N/A
366/I	3-1/2"	TMK-8	$155	N/A

In 1988, Goebel introduced a smaller, third size of the Nativity Set. These are offered as three- or four-piece sets in the initial years of the offer and as separate pieces subsequently. Here is the pricing for those pieces:

Hum No.	Size	Figure	Trademark	Current Value
214/A/M/0	5-1/4"	Madonna	TMK-6	$165-$170
214/A/M/0	5-1/4"	Madonna	TMK-7	$160-$165
214/A/M/0	5-1/4"	Madonna	TMK-8	$160
214/A/K/0	2-7/8"	Infant Jesus	TMK-6	$60-$65
214/A/K/0	2-7/8"	Infant Jesus	TMK-7	$55-$60
214/A/K/0	2-7/8"	Infant Jesus	TMK-8	$55
214/B/0	6-1/8"	Joseph	TMK-6	$165-$170
214/B/0	6-1/8"	Joseph	TMK-7	$160-$165
214/B/0	6-1/8"	Joseph	TMK-8	$160
214/D/0	2-7/8"	Angel Serenade	TMK-7/8	$95
214/J/0	3-7/8"	Donkey	TMK-6	$65-$70
214/J/0	3-7/8"	Donkey	TMK-7	$60-$65
214/J/0	3-7/8"	Donkey	TMK-8	$60
214/K/0	2-3/4"	Ox	TMK-6	$65-$70
214/K/0	2-3/4"	Ox	TMK-7	$60-$65
214/K/0	2-3/4"	Ox	TMK-8	$60
214/O/0	1-1/2"	Lamb	TMK-6	$30-$35
214/O/0	1-1/2"	Lamb	TMK-7	$25-$30
214/O/0	1-1/2"	Lamb	TMK-8	$25
214/L/0	6-1/4"	King (Standing)	TMK-6	$185-$190
214/L/0	6-1/4"	King (Standing)	TMK-7	$180-185
214/L/0	6-1/4"	King (Standing)	TMK-8	$180
214/M/0	4-1/4"	King (On one knee)	TMK-6	$175-$180
214/M/0	4-1/4"	King (On one knee)	TMK-7	$170-$175
214/M/0	4-1/4"	King (On one knee)	TMK-8	$170
214/N/0	4-1/2"	King (On both knees)	TMK-6	$170-$175
214/N/0	4-1/2"	King (On both knees)	TMK-7	$165-$170

Hum No.	Size	Figure	Trademark	Current Value
214/N/0	4-1/2"	King (On both knees)	TMK-8	$165
214/F/0	5-3/4"	Shepherd (Standing)	TMK-6	$185-$190
214/F/0	5-3/4"	Shepherd (Standing)	TMK-7	$180-$185
214/F/0	5-3/4"	Shepherd (Standing)	TMK-8	$180
214/G/0	4"	Shepherd Boy	TMK-6	$150-$155
214/G/0	4"	Shepherd Boy	TMK-7	$145-$150
214/G/0	4"	Shepherd Boy	TMK-8	$145
214/H/0	3-1/4"	Little Tooter	TMK-6	$125-$130
214/H/0	3-1/4"	Little Tooter	TMK-7	$120-$125
214/H/0	3-1/4"	Little Tooter	TMK-8	$120
366/0	2-3/4"	Flying Angel	TMK-6	$135-$140
366/0	2-3/4"	Flying Angel	TMK-7	$130-$135
366/0	2-3/4"	Flying Angel	TMK-8	$130

Hum 215: Unknown (Closed Number)

Not likely to be found. Records indicate it could possibly be a standing Jesus child holding a lamb in his arms.

Hum 216: Unknown (Closed Number)

Not likely to be found. No known examples anywhere, if it exists. Records indicate it might be a Joyful (Hum 53) ashtray.

Hum 217: Boy With Toothache

This figurine, which was first crafted by master sculptor Arthur Moeller in 1951 and previously called "At the Dentist" and "Toothache," was released in the 1950s. It has no significant mold or finish variations affecting the normal values.

Older models of the figure will have the "WG" after the M.I. Hummel incised signature. This mark is illustrated and discussed in the trademark section at the front of the book. Newer models carry the 1951 incised copyright date.

In 2002, a special edition of Boy With Toothache was introduced in recognition of the figurine's 50th year in production. It carried a unique diamond-shaped "50th Anniversary" backstamp and came with a certificate of authenticity and a diamond-shaped anniversary medallion with "50" on it.

Boy With Toothache (Hum 217) shown here in the Three Line Mark (TMK-4) variation.

The same figurine, Boy With Toothache, only this time shown in the most recent trademark (TMK-8).

Photo courtesy Goebel of North America.

Hum No.	Basic Size	Trademark	Current Value
217	5-1/2"	TMK-2	$425-$525
217	5-1/2"	TMK-3	$320-$370
217	5-1/2"	TMK-4	$270-$320
217	5-1/2"	TMK-5	$250-$270
217	5-1/2"	TMK-6	$245-$250
217	5-1/2"	TMK-7	$240-$245
217	5-1/2"	TMK-8	$240
217 (50th anniversary)	5-1/2"	TMK-8	$250

Hum 218: Birthday Serenade

Master sculptor Reinhold Unger designed this piece in 1952. The most significant variation found of this figure is the "reverse mold variation." In the older versions of this double-figure piece, the girl plays the concertina and the boy plays the flute. In the newer models the instruments are the other way around.

The older, Full Bee (TMK-2) pieces with the reverse mold were changed beginning in the next trademark period, the Stylized Bee (TMK-3), so you can find the old design in that mark as well. There must have been many of the old design left in stock, for you can even find them bearing the Three Line Mark (TMK-4). Note that the boy lost his kerchief when he was given the concertina or accordion.

The larger 218/0 size was temporarily withdrawn from production in 1999.

Hum No.	Basic Size	Trademark	Current Value
218/2/0	4-1/4"	TMK-2	$610-$650
218/2/0 (old style)	4-1/4"	TMK-3	$550-$610
218/2/0 (new style)	4-1/4"	TMK-3	$260-$300
218/2/0 (old style)	4-1/4"	TMK-4	$450-$550
218/2/0 (new style)	4-1/4"	TMK-4	$230-$260
218/2/0	4-1/4"	TMK-5	$215-$230
218/2/0	4-1/4"	TMK-6	$210-$215
218/2/0	4-1/4"	TMK-7	$205-$210
218/2/0	4-1/4"	TMK-8	$200
218/0	5-1/4"	TMK-2	$880-$980
218/0 (old style)	5-1/4"	TMK-3	$780-$880
218/0 (new style)	5-1/4"	TMK-3	$450-$500
218/0 (old style)	5-1/4"	TMK-4	$730-$830
218/0 (new style)	5-1/4"	TMK-4	$375-$450
218/0	5-1/4"	TMK-5	$350-$375
218/0	5-1/4"	TMK-6	$340-$350
218	5-1/4"	TMK-2	$900-$1,000
218/I*	5-1/4"	TMK-2	$1,000-$1,500

*218/I is a possible factory error.

Reversed instruments variations of Birthday Serenade, Hum 218. At left is the Full Bee (TMK-2) variation and the one on the right is 218/0 in the Last Bee (TMK-5) era.

Photo courtesy Goebel of North America.

Birthday Serenade in yet another variation as 218/2/0 in TMK-8.

Hum 219/2/0: Little Velma

This figure, which has been known as "Girl With Frog" and was first crafted in 1952 by master sculptor Reinhold Unger, bears a number with the "closed number" designation, supposedly meaning a number that never has been and never will be used to designate a Hummel figurine. It is a girl sitting on a fence, looking down at a frog on the ground. The factory never officially released it, although it has turned up due to a no-longer practical policy of distributing pre-production samples. It was never placed in production due to its similarity to Hum 195 and Hum 201.

The owner of the first example of this figure to be uncovered has named it Little Velma. It was designed in 1952. At least 15 to 20 examples have been found to date, only in the Full Bee (TMK-2).

Little Velma, Hum 219/2/0, at approximately 4" and carrying the Full Bee (TMK-2) and registered trademark symbol, "© W. Goebel."

Hum No.	Basic Size	Trademark	Current Value
219/2/0	4"	TMK-2	$4,000-$6,000

Hum 220: We Congratulate

IA very similar figure to Hum 214/E (Nativity Set piece), except this figure is on a base and 214/E is not, and the girl has no wreath of flowers in her hair. A lederhosen strap was also added to the boy.

This piece, which was first designed by master sculptor Arthur Moeller in 1952, was introduced in the 1950s and has been produced with one variation of some significance. At first, the piece was produced with a 220/2/0 designator. It was soon dropped, leaving only the mold number 220 incised on the base.

Hum No.	Basic Size	Trademark	Current Value
220/2/0	4"	TMK-2	$475-$575
220	4"	TMK-2	$325-$400
220	4"	TMK-3	$245-$275
220	4"	TMK-4	$215-$245
220	4"	TMK-5	$205-$215
220	4"	TMK-6	$200-$205
220	4"	TMK-7	$195-$200
220	4"	TMK-8	$195

We Congratulate, Hum 220, shown here in Three Line Mark (TMK-4).

The most recent variation of We Congratulate, with TMK-8.

Hum 221: Happy Pastime (Candy Box, Closed Number)

Previously listed as unknown, it is now known that this is a pre-production sample made by master sculptor Arthur Moeller in 1952 and never released. It is essentially Hum 69 (Happy Pastime) affixed to the top of a round candy jar that is decorated with flowers. It is valued at $5,000-$10,000.

Happy Pastime candy box, Hum 221, exists only in sample form.

Hum 222: Madonna (Wall Plaque)

An extremely rare piece, which was first designed by master sculptor Reinhold Unger in 1952, it has been out of current production for some time. Similar in design to Madonna Plaque (Hum 48), this plaque is unique in that a metal frame surrounds it. This piece has been found with several different designs of wire frame around it. Most were originally made with a felt backing. Each may be found with any design of the wire frame or no frame at all.

Madonna wall plaque, Hum 222. No apparent mark other than mold number. Measures 4" x 5". The wire frame is detachable.

Hum No.	Basic Size	Trademark	Current Value
222	4" x 5"	TMK-2	$750-$1,250
222	4" x 5"	TMK-3	$750-$1,000

Hum 223: To Market (Table Lamp)

First crafted by master sculptor Arthur Moeller in 1937 as Hum 101 and later restyled and introduced in the 1950s, this lamp was temporarily withdrawn from production in 1989. There are no mold or finish variations significant enough to affect normal values. See the Hum 101 entry for a description of a lamp of similar design. You'll note that the pricing here goes through present-day TMK-8; that is because although withdrawn from production in the U.S. market, the lamp is still available in Europe.

To Market table lamp, Hum 223. Stylized Bee mark (TMK-3), 8-3/4", without the light fixture.

Hum No.	Basic Size	Trademark	Current Value
223	9-1/2"	TMK-2	$700-$850
223	9-1/2"	TMK-3	$650-$700
223	9-1/2"	TMK-4	$575-$650
223	9-1/2"	TMK-5	$550-$575
223	9-1/2"	TMK-6	$525-$550
223	9-1/2"	TMK-7	$500-$510
223	9-1/2"	TMK-8	$495

Hum 224: Wayside Harmony (Table Lamp)

Wayside Harmony table lamp, Hum 224/II, with TMK-6.

First introduced as a redesign of the Hum 111 lamp in the 1950s, this lamp, which was the work of master sculptor Reinhold Unger in 1952, was produced in two sizes. Both were temporarily withdrawn from production in 1989. There are no finish or mold variations that have an impact on normal values.

You'll note that the pricing here goes through present-day TMK-8; that is because although withdrawn from production in the U.S. market, the lamp is still available in Europe.

Hum No.	Basic Size	Trademark	Current Value
224/I	7-1/2"	TMK-2	$550-$600
224/I	7-1/2"	TMK-3	$450-$475
224/I	7-1/2"	TMK-4	$425-$450
224/I	7-1/2"	TMK-5	$400-$425
224/I	7-1/2"	TMK-6	$350-$400
224/I	7-1/2"	TMK-7	$350-$400
224/I	7-1/2"	TMK-8	$350
224	9-1/2"	TMK-2	$650-$800
224	9-1/2"	TMK-3	$510-$610
224/II	9-1/2"	TMK-2	$650-$800
224/II	9-1/2"	TMK-3	$500-$600
224/II	9-1/2"	TMK-4	$475-$500
224/II	9-1/2"	TMK-5	$450-$475
224/II	9-1/2"	TMK-6	$400-$450
224/II	9-1/2"	TMK-7	$400-$450
224/II	9-1/2"	TMK-8	$400

Hum 225: Just Resting (Table Lamp)

First crafted by master sculptor Reinhold Unger in 1952 and released in the 1950s as a redesign of the Hum 112, it was listed as temporarily withdrawn from production by Goebel in 1989. However, like Hum 224 and 225, pricing here continues through TMK-8 since the piece is available in the European market.

Hum No.	Basic Size	Trademark	Current Value
225/I	7-1/2"	TMK-2	$550-$600
225/I	7-1/2"	TMK-3	$450-$475
225/I	7-1/2"	TMK-4	$425-$450
225/I	7-1/2"	TMK-5	$400-$425
225/I	7-1/2"	TMK-6	$350-$400
225/I	7-1/2"	TMK-7	$350-$400
225/I	7-1/2"	TMK-8	$350
225	7-1/2"	TMK-2	$650-$800
225	7-1/2"	TMK-3	$500-$600
225/II	9-1/2"	TMK-2	$650-$800
225/II	9-1/2"	TMK-3	$500-$600
225/II	9-1/2"	TMK-4	$475-$500
225/II	9-1/2"	TMK-5	$450-$470
225/II	9-1/2"	TMK-6	$400-$450
225/II	9-1/2"	TMK-7	$400-$450
225/II	9-1/2"	TMK-8	$400

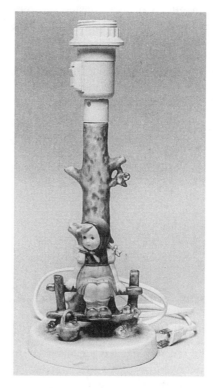

Just Resting table lamp, Hum 225/II, shown in TMK-6.

Hum 226: The Mail is Here

First crafted by master sculptor Arthur Moeller in 1952 and introduced into the line in the 1950s, it was known as "Mail Coach." This name is still favored by many collectors. Incidentally, this figure was preceded by a wall plaque utilizing the same motif (Hum 140).

The piece generally carries an incised 1952 copyright date and some older pieces have a very light "M.I. Hummel" signature, while others have the signature painted on due to the light impression.

There are no major variations affecting normal values. The figure remains in production today.

Hum No.	Basic Size	Trademark	Current Value
226	4-1/4" x 6-1/4"	TMK-2	$1,100-$1,350
226	4-1/4" x 6-1/4"	TMK-3	$850-$1,000
226	4-1/4" x 6-1/4"	TMK-4	$700-$800
226	4-1/4" x 6-1/4"	TMK-5	$650-$700
226	4-1/4" x 6-1/4"	TMK-6	$625-$650
226	4-1/4" x 6-1/4"	TMK-7	$615-$625
226	4-1/4" x 6-1/4"	TMK-8	$610

The Mail is Here, Hum 226. This example is an older piece with a Full Bee (TMK-2) trademark in an incised circle. It also has a "by W. Goebel," a black "West Germany" and measures 4-1/4" x 6-1/2".

Today's TMK-8 version of Hum 226, The Mail is Here.

Photo courtesy Goebel of North America.

Hum 227: She Loves Me, She Loves Me Not (Table Lamp)

This piece, which was the work of master sculptor Arthur Moeller in 1953, is a 7-1/2" lamp base utilizing Hum 174 as part of the design. Older pieces depict the figure much larger and the boy's eyes open.

Goebel listed it as temporarily withdrawn from production in 1989.

Hum No.	Basic Size	Trademark	Current Value
227	7-1/2"	TMK-2	$650-$850
227	7-1/2"	TMK-3	$475-$525
227	7-1/2"	TMK-4	$425-$475
227	7-1/2"	TMK-5	$400-$425
227	7-1/2"	TMK-6	$375-$400

She Loves Me, She Loves Me Not table lamp, Hum 227, which was produced through TMK-6.

Hum 228: Good Friends (Table Lamp)

This piece, another crafted by master sculptor Arthur Moeller in 1953, is a 7-1/2" lamp base utilizing Hum 182 as part of the design. The older pieces have a much larger figure, even though the overall size remained 7-1/2".

Goebel listed it as temporarily withdrawn from production in 1989.

Hum No.	Basic Size	Trademark	Current Value
228	7-1/2"	TMK-2	$650-$850
228	7-1/2"	TMK-3	$475-$525
228	7-1/2"	TMK-4	$425-$475
228	7-1/2"	TMK-5	$400-$425
228	7-1/2"	TMK-6	$375-$400

Good Friends table lamp, Hum 228, which has not been in production since the TMK-6 era.

Hum 229: Apple Tree Girl (Table Lamp)

This 7-1/2" table lamp, which was designed by master sculptor Arthur Moeller in 1953, utilized Hum 141 as part of the design. It was previously known as "Spring" and "Springtime," and the older pieces have a much larger figure, even though the overall size remained 7-1/2".

It was listed as temporarily out of production in 1989.

Hum No.	Basic Size	Trademark	Current Value
229	7-1/2"	TMK-2	$900-$1,000
229	7-1/2"	TMK-3	$475-$525
229	7-1/2"	TMK-4	$425-$475
229	7-1/2"	TMK-5	$400-$425
229	7-1/2"	TMK-6	$375-$400

Apple Tree Girl table lamp, Hum 229.

Hum 230: Apple Tree Boy (Table Lamp)

This 7-1/2" lamp base, which was designed by master sculptor Arthur Moeller in 1953, utilized Hum 142 as part of the design. It was previously known as "Autumn" and "Fall," and the older pieces have a much larger figure, even though the overall size remained 7-1/2".

This piece was listed as temporarily withdrawn from production in 1989.

Hum No.	Basic Size	Trademark	Current Value
230	7-1/2"	TMK-2	$900-$1,000
230	7-1/2"	TMK-3	$475-$525
230	7-1/2"	TMK-4	$425-$475
230	7-1/2"	TMK-5	$400-$425
230	7-1/2"	TMK-6	$375-$400

Photo courtesy Goebel of North America.

Apple Tree Boy table lamp, Hum 230.

Hum 231: Birthday Serenade (Table Lamp)

This particular lamp, which was first designed by master sculptor Reinhold Unger, was out of production for many years. It utilizes the Hum 218 (Birthday Serenade) as its design. The old model is found in the Full Bee (TMK-2) and reflects the same old mold design (girl with accordion and boy with flute). These old mold design lamps measure about 9-3/4" tall and are fairly scarce.

In 1976, Hum 231 was reissued after master sculptor Rudolf Wittman redesigned it with the instruments reversed. Now the girl plays the flute, and the boy plays the accordion. The newer pieces are found with the TMK-5 and TMK-6. (See Hum 234.)

Goebel listed this lamp as temporarily withdrawn from production as of December 31, 1989.

Hum No.	Basic Size	Trademark	Current Value
231	9-3/4"	TMK-2	$2,000-$3,000
231	9-3/4"	TMK-5	$550-$600
231	9-3/4"	TMK-6	$525-$550

Birthday Serenade table lamp, Hum 231, shown here in TMK-6.

Hum 232: Happy Days (Table Lamp)

The Happy Days table lamp was first designed by master sculptor Reinhold Unger in 1954 and placed into production in the 1950s. Essentially the same design as Hum 232 (only larger), it was apparently made in limited numbers in the early days because those with the Full Bee (TMK-2) trademark have always been in short supply.

After a redesign in 1976, the figures were available in TMK-5 and TMK-6, but the factory listed them as temporarily withdrawn from production in late-1989.

Hum No.	Basic Size	Trademark	Current Value
232	9-3/4"	TMK-2	$1,200-$1,700
232	9-3/4"	TMK-5	$525-$550
232	9-3/4"	TMK-6	$500-$525

Hum 233: Unknown (Closed Number)

This figure is unlikely to be found. There is evidence to suggest that this is a preliminary design for Bird Watcher (Hum 300). No known examples anywhere.

Hum 234: Birthday Serenade (Table Lamp)

This lamp, like the larger Hum 231 table lamp of the same name, was first designed by master sculptor Reinhold Unger and apparently also removed from production or limited in production for a time after its initial release. Unlike the Hum 231 lamp, however, it can be found in all trademarks through TMK-6 beginning with the Full Bee (TMK-2).

It was redesigned by master sculptor Rudolf Wittman in the late-1970s with the instruments reversed, just as the Hum 231 lamp was. It can be found in the old or new styles in the Full Bee.

It was temporarily withdrawn from production in 1989.

Hum No.	Basic Size	Trademark	Current Value
234	7-3/4"	TMK-2	$1,600-$2,100
234	7-3/4"	TMK-3	$1,100-$1,600
234	7-3/4"	TMK-4	$500-$1,000
234	7-3/4"	TMK-5	$450-$500
234	7-3/4"	TMK-6	$425-$450

Hum 235: Happy Days (Table Lamp)

This is a smaller size (7-3/4") of the Hum 232 lamp. It too was first crafted by master sculptor Reinhold Unger in 1954 and placed in production in the 1950s, only to be removed shortly thereafter.

It was reissued in a new design in the late-1970s—as was the larger lamp—only to be withdrawn from production again in 1989. Unlike the larger lamp, however, this one can be found in all trademarks starting with TMK-2 through TMK-6.

Happy Days table lamp, Hum 235, in TMK-6 with 1954 copyright date and measuring 7-3/4".

Hum No.	Basic Size	Trademark	Current Value
235	7-3/4"	TMK-2	$910-$1,110
235	7-3/4"	TMK-3	$625-$850
235	7-3/4"	TMK-4	$525-$625
235	7-3/4"	TMK-5	$475-$500
235	7-3/4"	TMK-6	$450-$475

Hum 236/A and Hum 236/B: No Name (Closed Number)

Only one example of each of these is known to exist at this time. They were first designed by master sculptor Arthur Moeller in 1954, but for whatever reason, not approved by the Siessen Convent for production.

The figures are two angels, one at the base of a tree and the other seated on a tree limb. Hum 236/A has one angel playing a harp at the base of a tree and the other seated on a tree limb above singing. The Hum 236/B has the tree angel blowing a horn and the seated angel playing a lute. No known examples exist outside the factory archives.

Hum No.	Basic Size	Trademark	Current Value
236/A	6-1/2"	TMK-2	$10,000-$15,000
236/B	6-1/2"	TMK-2	$10,000-$15,000

Hum 237: Star Gazer (Wall Plaque, Closed Number)

This piece is a plaque using the Star Gazer figurine in white overglaze as its design. It is a 1954 design that was again rejected by the Siessen Convent. Only one is known to exist in a private collection.

Hum No.	Basic Size	Trademark	Current Value
237	4-3/4" x 5"	TMK-2	$10,000-$15,000

Hum 238/A: Angel With Lute, Hum 238/B: Angel With Accordion, Hum 238/C: Angel With Trumpet (Angel Trio Set)

These three pieces, which were designed by master sculptor Gerhard Skrobek in 1967, are usually sold as a set and referred to as the "Angel Trio." In current production, they can be found in all trademarks since the Three Line Mark (TMK-4). On rare occasions, they can also be found in TMK-3; those pieces are worth $100-$125.

Each is 2" to 2-1/2" high and carries an incised 1967 copyright date.

They are essentially the same set as the Angel Trio (Hum 38, 39 and 40), but the three Hum 238 pieces are not candleholders.

Angel Trio set. Left: Angel with Lute, Hum 238/A, paper sticker with the Last Bee, incised 1967 copyright date, 2-3/8". Center: Angel with Accordion, Hum 238/B, paper sticker with the Last Bee. Incised 1967 copyright date, 2-3/8". Right: Angel with Horn, Hum 238/C, paper sticker with the Last Bee, 2-3/8".

Hum No.	Basic Size	Trademark	Current Value
238/A	2" to 2-1/2"	TMK-4	$100-$125
238/A	2" to 2-1/2"	TMK-5	$85-$100
238/A	2" to 2-1/2"	TMK-6	$75-$85
238/A	2" to 2-1/2"	TMK-7	$70-$75
238/A	2" to 2-1/2"	TMK-8	$70
238/B	2" to 2-1/2"	TMK-4	$100-$125
238/B	2" to 2-1/2"	TMK-5	$85-$100
238/B	2" to 2-1/2"	TMK-6	$75-$85
238/B	2" to 2-1/2"	TMK-7	$70-$75
238/B	2" to 2-1/2"	TMK-8	$70
238/C	2" to 2-1/2"	TMK-4	$100-$125

Hum No.	Basic Size	Trademark	Current Value
238/C	2" to 2-1/2"	TMK-5	$85-$100
238/C	2" to 2-1/2"	TMK-6	$75-$85
238/C	2" to 2-1/2"	TMK-7	$70-$7
238/C	2" to 2-1/2"	TMK-8	$70

Photo courtesy Goebel of North America.

Today's TMK-8 version of Angel Trio, from left: Angel With Lute, Angel With Accordion, and Angel With Horn.

Hum 239/A: Girl With Nosegay, Hum 239/B: Girl With Doll, Hum 239/C: Boy With Horse, and Hum 239/D: Girl With Fir Tree

The first three figures (Hum 239/A, 239/B, and 239/C) have traditionally been sold as a set and were known as "Children Trio" ever since they were placed into production in the 1960s. They are essentially the same as the Hum 115, Hum 116, and Hum 117, except that the three Hum 239 pieces have no receptacle for holding a candle. In 1997, the trio was expanded with a fourth figure, Girl With Fir Tree (Hum 239/D).

Also in 1997, a set of four ornaments was introduced. The ornaments are the same as the Hum 239 figurines, except they have brass ring hangers on top instead of bases on the bottom. They are designated with a "/0" after the regular Hum number. A variation of the ornaments is sold in Europe, does not include the brass hanging ring or the base, and is differentiated by a "/X" after the regular Hum number rather than the "/0."

Hum No.	Basic Size	Trademark	Current Value
239/A	3-1/2"	TMK-3	$150-$200
239/A	3-1/2"	TMK-4	$85-$100
239/A	3-1/2"	TMK-5	$80-$85
239/A	3-1/2"	TMK-6	$75-$80
239/A	3-1/2"	TMK-7	$70-$75
239/A	3-1/2"	TMK-8	$70
239/A/0	3"	TMK-7 and 8	$70
239/A/X	3"	TMK-7 and 8	$70
239/B	3-1/2"	TMK-3	$150-$200
239/B	3-1/2"	TMK-4	$85-$100
239/B	3-1/2"	TMK-5	$80-$85
239/B	3-1/2"	TMK-6	$75-$80

Set of four children, from top left: Girl With Nosegay (Hum 239/A), Girl With Doll (Hum 239/B), Boy With Horse (Hum 239/C), and Girl With Fir Tree (Hum 239/D).

In 1997, four ornaments in the same motifs as the figurines were released in a 3" size. Shown here in TMK-8 are, from top left: Girl With Nosegay (Hum 239/A/0), Girl With Doll (Hum 239/B/0), Boy With Horse (Hum 239/C/0), and Girl With Fir Tree (Hum 239/D/0).

Hum No.	Basic Size	Trademark	Current Value	Hum No.	Basic Size	Trademark	Current Value
239/B	3-1/2"	TMK-7	$70-$75	239/C	3-1/2"	TMK-7	$70-$75
239/B	3-1/2"	TMK-8	$70	239/C	3-1/2"	TMK-8	$70
239/B/0	3"	TMK-7 and 8	$70	239/C/0	3"	TMK-7 and 8	$70
239/B/X	3"	TMK-7 and 8	$70	239/C/X	3"	TMK-7 and 8	$70
239/C	3-1/2"	TMK-3	$150-$200	239/D	3-1/2"	TMK-7	$70-$75
239/C	3-1/2"	TMK-4	$85-$100	239/D	3-1/2"	TMK-8	$70
239/C	3-1/2"	TMK-5	$80-$85	239/D/0	3"	TMK-7 and 8	$70
239/C	3-1/2"	TMK-6	$75-$80	239/D/X	3"	TMK-7 and 8	$70

Hum 240: Little Drummer

Placed into production in the 1950s, this figurine was the original work of master sculptor Reinhold Unger in 1955. It is usually found with an incised copyright date of 1955. There are no variations significant enough to affect normal values for this piece.

Attendees at the 1993 Disneyana Convention were given the opportunity to purchase a pair of figurines on a wooden base. The figurines were a normal production model of the Little Drummer (Hum 240), and a matching Donald Duck figurine in the same pose. The Donald Duck drummer is marked with an incised mold number of 17323, TMK-7, and a limited edition notation. The edition was limited to 1,500. They were originally sold for $300 and are now valued at $500-$750.

Hum No.	Basic Size	Trademark	Current Value
240	4-1/4"	TMK-2	$310-$375
240	4-1/4"	TMK-3	$245-$260
240	4-1/4"	TMK-4	$200-$245
240	4-1/4"	TMK-5	$190-$200
240	4-1/4"	TMK-6	$185-$190
240	4-1/4"	TMK-7	$180-$185
240	4-1/4"	TMK-8	$175

Little Drummer, Hum 240. This piece bears the Last Bee (TMK-5) mark, measures 4-1/2" tall and has an incised 1955 copyright date.

Photo courtesy Goebel of North America.

Little Drummer in present-day TMK-8.

Hum 241: Joyous News, Angel With Lute (Holy Water Font, Closed Number)

The mold number 241 for this font, which was first designed by master sculptor Reinhold Unger in 1955, was used by mistake on the next piece listed (Angel Lights). This font design was produced only in sample form and never put into regular production. There is only a handful known to exist outside the factory archives, one of which is part of the Don Stephens Collection in Rosemont, Illinois.

Hum No.	Basic Size	Trademark	Current Value
241	3" x 4-1/2"	TMK-2	$1,500-$2,000

Angel With Lute font, Hum 241.

Hum 241: Angel Lights (Candleholder)

The work of master sculptor Gerhard Skrobek in 1976, this piece was first released in 1978 as "Angel Bridge." It is in the form of an arch placed on a plate. A figure sits attached to the top of the arch, with candle receptacles down each side of the arch. It is not attached to the plate base.

It has been suspended from production since January 1, 1990.

Hum No.	Basic Size	Trademark	Current Value
241	10-1/3" x 8-1/3"	TMK-5	$400-$500
241	10-1/3" x 8-1/3"	TMK-6	$300-$350

Angel Lights candleholder, Hum 241, with TMK-5 and incised 1977 copyright date.

Hum 242: Angel Joyous News With Trumpet (Holy Water Font, Closed Number)

This font, which was the design of master sculptor Reinhold Unger in 1955, was produced as a sample only and never put into production. Although once predicted that this piece would not likely find its way into private collections, a handful of pieces have since made their way into the collections of several individuals.

Hum No.	Basic Size	Trademark	Current Value
242	3" x 4-1/2"	TMK-2	$1,500-$2,000

Angel Joyous News With Trumpet font, Hum 242, which exists in TMK-2 samples only.

Photo courtesy Goebel of North America.

Hum 243: Madonna and Child (Holy Water Font)

Even though this piece, which was designed by master sculptor Reinhold Unger in 1955, was apparently not released until the 1960s, it can be found in all trademarks starting with the Full Bee (TMK-2). There are no significant variations affecting normal values for this figure.

Madonna and Child font, Hum 243, with TMK-4 at left and TMK-8 below.

Photo courtesy Goebel of North America.

Hum No.	Basic Size	Trademark	Current Value
243	3-1/4" x 4"	TMK-2	$250-$300
243	3-1/4" x 4"	TMK-3	$105-$130
243	3-1/4" x 4"	TMK-4	$80-$105
243	3-1/4" x 4"	TMK-5	$75-$80
243	3-1/4" x 4"	TMK-6	$70-$75
243	3-1/4" x 4"	TMK-7	$65-$70
243	3-1/4" x 4"	TMK-8	$65

Hum 244: Open Number

Hum 245: Open Number

Hum 246: Holy Family (Holy Water Font)

This font, which was originally designed by master sculptor Theo Menzenbach in 1955, was released into the line in the mid-1950s. It is usually found with the incised copyright date of 1955. There are no significant mold or finish variations affecting normal values.

Holy Family font, Hum 246, shown here with the Full Bee (TMK-2), incised 1955 copyright date, and black "Western Germany."

Hum No.	Basic Size	Trademark	Current Value
246	3" x 4"	TMK-2	$250-$300
246	3" x 4"	TMK-3	$105-$155
246	3" x 4"	TMK-4	$80-$105
246	3" x 4"	TMK-5	$75-$80
246	3" x 4"	TMK-6	$70-$75
246	3" x 4"	TMK-7	$65-$70
246	3" x 4"	TMK-8	$65

Hum 247: Standing Madonna With Child (Closed Number)

This beautiful piece was the work of master sculptor Reinhold Unger, designed in 1965 but apparently rejected by the Siessen Convent. It exists in sample form only in the factory archives.

Two rare samples of Standing Madonna With Child, Hum 247.

Photo courtesy M.I. Hummel Club.

Hum No.	Basic Size	Current Value
247	11-1/2"	$10,000-$15,000
247	13"	$10,000-$15,000

Hum 248: Guardian Angel (Holy Water Font)

This piece is a redesigned version of Hum 29, which is no longer in production. When placed in the collection as designed by master sculptor Gerhard Skrobek in 1958, it was a 2-3/8" x 5-3/8" and carried mold number is 248/0. A larger 2-3/4" x 6-1/4" piece was also designed (248/I) but never put into regular production.

This font was temporarily withdrawn from production in 1999.

Hum No.	Basic Size	Trademark	Current Value
248/I	2-3/4" x 6-1/4"	TMK-3	$1,000-$1,500
248/0	2-3/8" x 5-3/8"	TMK-3	$205-$255
248/0	2-3/8" x 5-3/8"	TMK-4	$80-$105
248/0	2-1/4" x 5-1/2"	TMK-5	$75-$80
248/0	2-1/4" x 5-1/2"	TMK-6	$70-$75
248/0	2-1/4" x 5-1/2"	TMK-7	$65-$70

Guardian Angel font, Hum 248.

Hum 249: Madonna and Child (Plaque in Relief, Closed Number)

Molded as a sample only, this plaque was never put into the line. It is essentially the same design as the Hum 48 Madonna Plaque with the background cut away. No known examples outside the Goebel archives.

Hum No.	Basic Size	Current Value
249	6-3/4" x 8-3/4"	$10,000-$15,000

Hum 250/A: Little Goat Herder and
Hum 250/B: Feeding Time (Bookends)

These bookends were the collective efforts of several designers and were placed in the line in 1964. If the figurines are removed from the wooden bookend bases, they are indistinguishable from the regular pieces (Hum 199 and Hum 200).

These figures were temporarily withdrawn from production at the end of 1989.

They are priced here as a set.

Hum No.	Basic Size	Trademark	Current Value
250/A &B	5-1/2"	TMK-2	$550-$750
250/A &B	5-1/2"	TMK-3	$375-$425
250/A &B	5-1/2"	TMK-5	$325-$350
250/A &B	5-1/2"	TMK-6	$300-$325

Little Goat Herder (Hum 250A) and Feeding Time (Hum 250B) bookends, shown here in TMK-6.

Hum 251/A: Good Friends and Hum 251/B: She Loves Me, She Loves Me Not (Bookends)

These bookends were the collective efforts of several designers and were placed into the line in 1964. If the figurines are removed from the wooden bookend bases, they are indistinguishable from the regular production figurines (Hum 174 and Hum 182).

Goebel listed these pieces as temporarily withdrawn from production in 1989.

They are priced here as a set.

Hum No.	Basic Size	Trademark	Current Value
251/A & B	5-1/2"	TMK-2	$550-$750
251/A & B	5-1/2"	TMK-3	$375-$425
251/A & B	5-1/2"	TMK-5	$325-$350
251/A & B	5-1/2"	TMK-6	$300-$325

Good Friends (Hum 251/A) and She Loves Me, She Loves Me Not (Hum 251B) bookends, shown here bearing the Stylized Bee (TMK-3).

Hum 252/A: Apple Tree Boy and Hum 252/B: Apple Tree Girl (Bookends)

Another collective designing effort, these bookends were placed in the collection in 1964. If the figures are removed from the bookends they are indistinguishable from the regular figurines (Hum 141 and Hum 142).

The bookends were temporarily withdrawn from production at the end of 1989.

They are priced here as a set.

Hum No.	Basic Size	Trademark	Current Value
252/A & B	5-1/2"	TMK-3	$375-$425
252/A & B	5-1/2"	TMK-5	$325-$350
252/A & B	5-1/2"	TMK-6	$300-$325

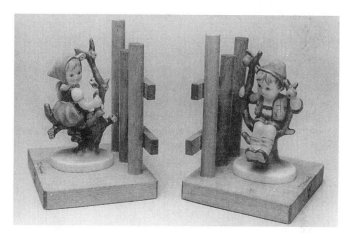

Apple Tree Girl and Apple Tree Boy bookends, Hum 252/A and Hum 252/B, displayed here with the Stylized Bee mark (TMK-3).

Hum 253: Unknown (Closed Number)

Goebel records indicate that this piece was a design much like the girl in Hum 52 (Going to Grandma's). There is no evidence that it was ever produced, and there are no known examples in the archives or anywhere else.

Hum 254: Unknown (Closed Number)

Goebel records indicate that this piece was a design much like the girl figure in Hum 150 (Happy Days). There is no evidence that it was ever produced, and there are no examples in the archives or anywhere else.

Hum 255: A Stitch In Time

First released in 1964 as a result of the combined efforts of several designers, this piece is similar to one of the girls depicted in Knitting Lesson (Hum 256) and School Girls (Hum 177). It has a 1963 incised copyright date. There are no significant variations that might affect normal values.

In 1990 a smaller size, 3", was added as part of a four-figurine series matching miniature plates in the same series. When this figure was introduced, the mold number for the larger size was changed to 255/I.

The 3" variation (255/4/0) was temporarily withdrawn in December 1997, followed by withdrawal of the larger size (255/I) in January 1999.

Hum No.	Basic Size	Trademark	Current Value
255/4/0	3"	TMK-6	$125-$140
255/4/0	3"	TMK-7	$115-$125
255	6-3/4"	TMK-3	$550-$800
255	6-3/4"	TMK-4	$375-$425
255	6-3/4"	TMK-5	$350-$375
255	6-3/4"	TMK-6	$340-$350
255/I	6-3/4"	TMK-7	$325-$335

Three Line (TMK-4), version of A Stitch In Time, Hum 255, with incised 1963 copyright date, doughnut base, and measuring 6-3/4".

Hum 256: Knitting Lesson

Introduced in 1964 with an incised 1963 copyright date, Knitting Lesson has no significant variations that might affect normal values. It is similar to the girls used in School Girls (Hum 177).

This figurine was temporarily withdrawn from production in 1999.

Hum No.	Basic Size	Trademark	Current Value
256	7-1/2"	TMK-3	$875-$1,150
256	7-1/2"	TMK-4	$625-$750
256	7-1/2"	TMK-5	$550-$575
256	7-1/2"	TMK-6	$540-$550
256	7-1/2"	TMK-7	$525-$535

Knitting Lesson, Hum 256. TMK-6, 1967 copyright date, 7-3/8".

Hum 257: For Mother

The collective work of several sculptors, this piece was introduced in the U.S. in 1964 and carries a 1963 incised copyright date. There are no significant mold or finish variations.

A new smaller-size figurine was released as a part of a four-piece series with matching mini-plates in 1985. When this was done the mold number for the larger size was changed to 257/0.

The 257/0 variation was temporarily withdrawn from production on June 15, 2002.

For Mother, Hum 257. Left: TMK-6, 1963 copyright date, 5-1/8". Right: 257/2/0, TMK-6, 1984 copyright date, 4".

Hum No.	Basic Size	Trademark	Current Value	Hum No.	Basic Size	Trademark	Current Value
257/5/0	2-3/4"	TMK-7	$55	257	5-1/4"	TMK-4	$270-$300
257/2/0	4"	TMK-6	$155-$160	257	5-1/4"	TMK-5	$255-$270
257/2/0	4"	TMK-7	$150-$155	257/0	5-1/4"	TMK-6	$250-$255
257/2/0	4"	TMK-8	$150	257/0	5-1/4"	TMK-7	$245-$250
257	5-1/4"	TMK-3	$625-$825	257/0	5-1/4"	TMK-8	$240

Hum 258: Which Hand?

Designed by a team of sculptors and first released in the U.S. in 1964, this piece has an incised copyright date of 1963. The girl is similar in design to Telling Her Secret (Hum 196). There are no mold or finish variation that would affect normal values.

Hum No.	Basic Size	Trademark	Current Value
258	5-1/4"	TMK-3	$625-$825
258	5-1/4"	TMK-4	$270-$300
258	5-1/4"	TMK-5	$250-$270
258	5-1/4"	TMK-6	$245-$250
258	5-1/4"	TMK-7	$240-$245
258	5-1/4"	TMK-8	$240

Photo courtesy Goebel of North America.

Which Hand?, Hum 258, with TMK-6 and incised 1963 copyright date.

Today's rendition (TMK-8) of Which Hand?, Hum 258.

Hum 259: Girl With Accordion (Closed Number)

This piece, which was the collective work of several designers in 1962, is almost exactly the same design as that of the girl with concertina or accordion in the Hum 218 (Birthday Serenade). It was produced in sample form only and never placed into production. Only one is known to reside in a private collection.

Hum No.	Basic Size	Current Value
259	4"	$10,000-$15,000

Hum 260: Nativity Set (Large)

The work of master sculptor Gerhard Skrobek in 1968, there was only sketchy information concerning complete nativity sets in this size and little more about the individual pieces in any of the many price lists studied. Below is a listing of each piece in the Hum 260 Nativity Set.

The set has been temporarily withdrawn from production since December 1989.

Photo courtesy Goebel of North America.

Large Nativity Set, Hum 260, shown here with all 16 pieces and the stable. This version is the latest, TMK-6.

Hum No.	Basic Size	Figure	Trademark	Value
260	16-piece set	all 16 (including stable)	TMK-4	$6,050-$6,310
260	16-piece set	all 16 (including stable)	TMK-5	$5,890-$6,050
260	16-piece set	all 16 (including stable)	TMK-6	$5,750-$5,890
260/A	9-3/4"	Madonna	TMK-4	$625-$650
260/A	9-3/4"	Madonna	TMK-5	$600-$625
260/A	9-3/4"	Madonna	TMK-6	$575-$600
260/B	11-3/4"	Joseph	TMK-4	$625-$650
260/B	11-3/4"	Joseph	TMK-5	$600-$625
260/B	11-3/4"	Joseph	TMK-6	$575-$600
260/C	5-3/4"	Infant Jesus	TMK-4	$140-$150
260/C	5-3/4"	Infant Jesus	TMK-5	$135-$140
260/C	5-3/4"	Infant Jesus	TMK-6	$130-$135
260/D	5-1/4"	Goodnight (Angel Standing)	TMK-4	$175-$185
260/D	5-1/4"	Goodnight (Angel Standing)	TMK-5	$170-$175
260/D	5-1/4"	Goodnight (Angel Standing)	TMK-6	$165-$170
260/E	4-1/4"	Angel Serenade (Kneeling)	TMK-4	$170-$175
260/E	4-1/4"	Angel Serenade (Kneeling)	TMK-5	$165-$170
260/E	4-1/4"	Angel Serenade (Kneeling)	TMK-6	$160-$165
260/F	6-1/4"	We Congratulate	TMK-4	$440-$460
260/F	6-1/4"	We Congratulate	TMK-5	$430-$440
260/F	6-1/4"	We Congratulate	TMK-6	$420-$430
260/G	11-3/4"	Shepherd (Standing)	TMK-4	$625-$650
260/G	11-3/4"	Shepherd (Standing)	TMK-5	$605-$625
260/G	11-3/4"	Shepherd (Standing)	TMK-6	$595-$606
260/H	3-3/4"	Sheep and Lamb	TMK-4	$125-$130
260/H	3-3/4"	Sheep and Lamb	TMK-5	$120-$125
260/H	3-3/4"	heep and Lamb	TMK-6	$115-$120
260/J	7"	Shepherd Boy (Kneeling)	TMK-4	$360-$375
260/J	7"	Shepherd Boy (Kneeling)	TMK-5	$350-$360
260/J	7"	Shepherd Boy (Kneeling)	TMK-6	$340-$350
260/K	5-1/8"	Little Tooter	TMK-4	$210-$225
260/K	5-1/8"	Little Tooter	TMK-5	$205-$210
260/K	5-1/8"	Little Tooter	TMK-6	$200-$205
260/L	7-1/2"	Donkey	TMK-4	$170-$175
260/L	7-1/2"	Donkey	TMK-5	$165-$170
260/L	7-1/2"	Donkey	TMK-6	$160-$165
260/M	6" x 11"	Cow (Lying)	TMK-4	$185-$195
260/M	6" x 11"	Cow (Lying)	TMK-5	$180-$185
260/M	6" x 11"	Cow (Lying)	TMK-6	$175-$180
260/N	12-3/4"	Moor King (Standing)	TMK-4	$590-$615
260/N	12-3/4"	Moor King (Standing)	TMK-5	$585-$590
260/N	12-3/4"	Moor King (Standing)	TMK-6	$580-$585
260/O	12"	King (Standing)	TMK-4	$590-$615
260/O	12"	King (Standing)	TMK-5	$585-$590
260/O	12"	King (Standing)	TMK-6	$580-$585
260/P	9"	King (Kneeling)	TMK-4	$565-$575
260/P	9"	King (Kneeling)	TMK-5	$555-$565
260/P	9"	King (Kneeling)	TMK-6	$550-$555
260/R	3-1/4" x 4"	Sheep (Lying)	TMK-4	$80-$85
260/R	3-1/4" x 4"	Sheep (Lying)	TMK-5	$75-$80
260/R	3-1/4" x 4"	Sheep (Lying)	TMK-6	$70-$75
260/S		Stable	N/A	$450

Hum 261: Angel Duet

This figure, which was the design of master sculptor Gerhard Skrobek in 1968, is essentially the same design as Hum 193, the candleholder of the same name, but this piece does not have a provision for a candle. It was apparently produced in very limited quantities, for it is somewhat difficult to find bearing the older, Three-Line Mark (TMK-4).

There are no major variations affecting value. Each piece carries an incised 1968 copyright date and there is no reverse mold variation as in the Hum 193 candleholder.

Hum No.	Basic Size	Trademark	Current Value
261	5-1/2"	TMK-4	$655-$855
261	5-1/2"	TMK-5	$270-$295
261	5-1/2"	TMK-6	$265-$270
261	5-1/2"	TMK-7	$260-$265
261	5-1/2"	TMK-8	$260

Angel Duet, Hum 261: This one is from the Last Bee (TMK-5) period and carries an incised 1968 copyright date.

Photo courtesy Goebel of North America.

Angel Duet, Hum 261, in today's TMK-8.

Hum 262: Heavenly Lullaby

First designed by master sculptor Gerhard Skrobek in 1968, this figure had undergone no significant mold variations. It bears an incised copyright date of 1968.

This figure is the same design as Hum 24/I (Lullaby) but does not have a provision for a candle. It was apparently produced in very limited quantities, for it is very difficult to locate in older trademarks.

This piece was temporarily withdrawn from production in 1999.

Hum No.	Basic Size	Trademark	Current Value
262	3-1/2" x 5"	TMK-4	$655-$855
262	3-1/2" x 5"	TMK-5	$235-$255
262	3-1/2" x 5"	TMK-6	$225-$235
262	3-1/2" x 5"	TMK-7	$215-$220

Heavenly Lullaby, Hum 262, shown here in TMK-5 and carrying an incised 1968 copyright date.

Hum 263: Merry Wanderer (Plaque in Relief)

A very rare plaque of the familiar Merry Wanderer motif, this piece was created by master sculptor Gerhard Skrobek in 1968. There is only one known to be outside the factory collection and in a private collection. As far as can be determined there are no more on the collector market. It is known to bear the Three Line Mark (TMK-4).

It appears to have been made from a regular Merry Wanderer mold with the base cut off and the backside flattened.

Hum No.	Basic Size	Trademark	Current Value
263	4" x 5-3/8"	TMK-4	$10,000-$15,000

Merry Wanderer plaque in relief, Hum 263, shown from the front and back.

Hum 264-279, 283-291: Annual Plates

In 1971, the factory produced its first annual plate. This plate utilized the Heavenly Angel (Hum 21) design and was released to the Goebel factory workers to commemorate the 100th anniversary of the W. Goebel firm. The plate was subsequently produced for regular sales without the factory worker inscription. It was received so well in the United States, it was decided that a similar plate would be released annually from then on. The 1971 plate was not released to European dealers.

Since 1971, Goebel has released one new design per year through 1991, each bearing a traditional Hummel figurine motif. The 1991 plate, Come Back Soon (Hum 291), marked the final issue in the 25-year series. The plates and their current market value are listed on the following pages.

There are three versions of this plate. The first is the "normal version." The second differs from the first only in that it has no holes for hanging. It was exported to England where tariff laws in 1971 placed a higher duty on the plate if it had holes than if not. The law states that holes make it a decorative object, subject to a higher duty rate. The third variation is the special original edition produced only for the Goebel factory workers. There is an inscription on the backside of the

1971-1973 Annual Plates: Hum 264, 265, and 266.

1974-1976 Annual Plates: Hum 267, 268, and 269.

1977-1979 Annual Plates: Hum 270, 271, and 272.

1980-1982 Annual Plates: Hum 273, 274, and 275.

1983-1985 Annual Plates: Hum 276, 277, and 278.

1986-1988 Annual Plates: Hum 279, 283, and 284.

1989-1990 Annual Plates: Hum 287, and 288.

1991-1992 Annual Plates: Hum 288, and 286.

1993 Annual Plate: Doll Bath, Hum 289.

The Final Edition of the 7-1/2" Annual Plates series: 1995's Come Back Soon, Hum 291.

1994 Annual Plate: Doctor, Hum 290.

Annual Plates in white overglaze, from left: Happy Pastime (Hum 271) with TMK-5 and 1972 copyright date and Singing Lesson (Hum 272) also with TMK-5 and an incised 1972 copyright date.

lower rim. It reads in German as follows: "Gewidmet Aller Mitarbeitern Im Jubilaumsjahr. Wirdanken ihnen fur ihre mitarbeit." Roughly translated, this means "thanks to the workers for their fine service." This last plate is the least common of the three, hence the most sought-after.

There are three known versions of the 1972 Goebel annual plate. The first is the "normal" one with the regular backstamp and the current Goebel trademark. The second has the same backstamp but bears the Three-Line Mark instead of the current mark. The third is exactly the same as the second but does not bear the inscription "Hand Painted," and the "2nd" is omitted from the identification of the plate as an annual plate.

Hum	Size	Plate Design	Trademark	Year	Current Value
264	7-1/2"	Heavenly Angel	TMK-4	1971	$500-$750
264	7-1/2"	Heavenly Angel*	TMK-4	1971	$1,200-$1,500
265	7-1/2"	Hear Ye, Hear Ye	TMK-4	1972	$50-$75
265	7-1/2"	Hear Ye, Hear Ye**	TMK-5	1972	$50-$75
266	7-1/2"	Globe Trotter	TMK-5	1973	$120-$200
267	7-1/2"	Goose Girl	TMK-5	1974	$50-$75
268	7-1/2"	Ride Into Christmas***	TMK-5	1975	$50-$75
269	7-1/2"	Apple Tree Girl****	TMK-5	1976	$50-$75
270	7-1/2"	Apple Tree Boy*****	TMK-5	1977	$5,000
270	7-1/2"	Apple Tree Boy	TMK-5	1977	$50-$75
271	7-1/2"	Happy Pastime	TMK-5	1978	$50-$75
272	7-1/2"	Singing Lesson	TMK-5	1979	$40-$60
273	7-1/2"	School Girl	TMK-6	1980	$40-$60
274	7-1/2"	Umbrella Boy	TMK-6	1981	$50-$75
275	7-1/2"	Umbrella Girl	TMK-6	1982	$125-$150
276	7-1/2"	Postman	TMK-6	1983	$200-$250
277	7-1/2"	Little Helper	TMK-6	1984	$50-$75
278	7-1/2"	Chick Girl	TMK-6	1985	$50-$75
279	7-1/2"	Playmates	TMK-6	1986	$125-$200
283	7-1/2"	Feeding Time	TMK-6	1987	$250-$300
284	7-1/2"	Little Goat Herder	TMK-6	1988	$125-$150
285	7-1/2"	Farm Boy	TMK-6	1989	$100-$125
286	7-1/2"	Shepherd's Boy	TMK-6	1990	$150-$200
287	7-1/2"	Just Resting	TMK-6	1991	$150-$200
287	7-1/2"	Just Resting	TMK-7	1991	$150-$200
288	7-1/2"	Wayside Harmony	TMK-7	1992	$150-$200
289	7-1/2"	Doll Bath	TMK-7	1993	$150-$200
290	7-1/2"	Doctor	TMK-7	1994	$150-$200
291	7-1/2"	Come Back Soon	TMK-7	1995	$175-$200

* In 1971, Goebel presented each of its employees a copy of the 1971 annual plate design, only with a special inscription on the back.

** Made at the same time as the Last Bee marked plate and represents a transition. Not appreciably more valuable.

*** Late in 1983 an annual plate was found in Germany. It was a 1975 Annual Plate but instead of the Ride Into Christmas motif it was a Little Fiddler. No doubt that this was a prototype plate considered for 1975, but obviously not selected. How it managed to find its way out of the factory is anybody's guess. It may have been the only one.

**** Somehow a number of the 1976 Annual Plates were inadvertently given the incorrect backstamp "Wildlife Third Edition, Barn Owl" and they were released. How many got out is anybody's guess. It has no value significance.

*****Early sample.

Hum 280, 218, 282: Anniversary Plates

These three anniversary plates are all larger (10") than the annual plates. Hum 280 utilizes the Stormy Weather (Hum 71) design. Hum 281 only uses one figure from the Spring Dance (Hum 353) figurine and the second girl from the Ring Around the Rosie figurine (Hum 348); it was incorrectly labeled Spring Dance on the back. Hum 282 uses the design from the figurine Auf Wiedersehen (Hum 153).

Anniversary Plates. Left to right: Stormy Weather, 1975, Hum 280; Spring Dance 1980, Hum 281; Auf Wiedersehen 1986, Hum 282

Hum	Size	Plate Design	Trademark	Year	Current Value
280	10"	Stormy Weather	TMK-5	1975	$100-$150
281	10"	Ring Around the Rosie	TMK-6	1980	$100-$150
282	10"	Auf Wiedersehen	TMK-6	1985	$150-$200

Hum 292, 293, 294, 295: Friends Forever (Plate Series)

This is a four-plate series designed by master sculptor Gerhard Skrobek in 1991 and introduced in 1992. At 7" diameter, the plates are smaller than the annual plates and have a decorative border.

Hum No.	Design	Trademark	Year	Current Value
292	Meditation	TMK-7	1992	$100-$150
293	For Father	TMK-7	1993	$100-$150
294	Sweet Greetings	TMK-7	1994	$100-$150
295	Surprise	TMK-7	1995	$100-$150

All four plates in the Friends Forever series, from left: Meditation, Hum 292 (1992); For Father, Hum 293 (1993); Sweet Greetings, Hum 294 (1994); and Surprise, Hum 295 (1995).

Hum 296, 297, 298, 299: Four Seasons (Plate Series)

This plate series, which is the work of master sculptor Helmut Fischer, began in 1996. The plates measure 7-1/2" in diameter and contrary to the norm, the plate design elements are three-dimensional: less than figural and more than bas-relief. The first in the series was issued at $195. It bears a 1996 copyright date and a "First Issue" backstamp.

Hum No.	Design	Trademark	Year	Current Value
296	Winter Melody	TMK-7	1996	$195-$200
297	Springtime Serenade	TMK-7	1997	$195-$200
298	Summertime Stroll	TMK-7	1998	$195-$200
299	Autumn Glory	TMK-7	1999	$195-$200

All four plates in the Four Seasons series, from left: Winter Melody, Hum 296 (1996); Springtime Serenade, Hum 297 (1997); Summertime Stroll, Hum 298 (1998); and Autumn Glory, Hum 299 (1999).

Hum 300: Bird Watcher

First known as "Tenderness," this figure was released in 1979. It was originally modeled by master sculptor Gerhard Skrobek (the first piece he ever modeled) in the Full Bee (TMK-2) period. Samples in that trademark have an incised copyright date of 1954 and are more valuable than the others. Early samples were, however, also made in TMK-3 and TMK-4, so these are quite valuable as well.

Far more easy to locate are the regular production pieces bearing the 1956 copyright date. They start with the Last Bee (TMK-5) and have been in continuous production since.

Hum No.	Basic Size	Trademark	Current Value
300	5"	TMK-2	$4,000-$5,000
300	5"	TMK-3	$2,000-$2,500
300	5"	TMK-4	$1,500-$2,000
300	5"	TMK-5	$265-$285
300	5"	TMK-6	$255-$265
300	5"	TMK-7	$250-$255
300	5"	TMK-8	$250

Bird Watcher, Hum 300. TMK-6, incised 1956 copyright date, 5".

Bird Watcher, Hum 300, in today's TMK-8.

Photo courtesy Goebel of North America.

Hum 301: Christmas Angel

A new release in 1989 and originally called "Delivery Angel," this piece was originally designed by master sculptor Theo Menzenbach in 1957, during the Stylized Bee (TMK-3) period. It was made in prototype with that trademark and given an incised copyright date of 1957. These early samples are far more valuable than those made after the redesign.

With the redesign by master sculptor Gerhard Skrobek in the late-1980s, the figure was made slightly smaller than the sample and released with TMK-6 and the same 1957 copyright date. This piece remains in production today.

Christmas Angel, Hum 301. TMK-6, incised 1957 copyright date, 4-3/4".

Hum No.	Basic Size	Trademark	Current Value
301	6-1/4"	TMK-3	$4,000-$5,000
301	6-1/4"	TMK-6	$300-$305
301	6-1/4"	TMK-7	$295-$300
301	6-1/4"	TMK-8	$290

Today's TMK-8 version of Christmas Angel, Hum 301.

Photo courtesy Goebel of North America.

Hum 302: Concentration (Possible Future Edition)

This figure was first designed by master sculptor Arthur Moeller in 1955 and made in sample form in the Full Bee (TMK-2) era, but regular production has not yet begun. It was originally known as "Knit One, Purl Two" and the girl is similar to Stitch in Time (Hum 255). The example in the accompanying photograph has the Full Bee (TMK-2) and a 1956 copyright date.

Hum No.	Basic Size	Trademark	Current Value
302	5"	TMK-2	$4,000-$5,000

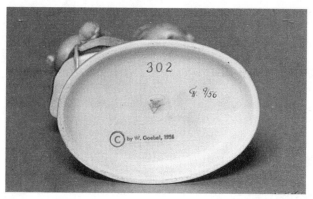

Base of the Concentration figurine showing the Full Bee (TMK-2) trademark in an incised circle. This piece is worth $4,000-$5,000.

Concentration, Hum 302, shown here in a rare sample since the piece has yet to be placed into regular production.

Hum 303: Arithmetic Lesson (Possible Future Edition)

First designed by master sculptor Arthur Moeller in 1955 and made in sample form in the Full Bee (TMK-2) era, this figure appears to be a combination of one boy and one girl from Hum 170 (School Boys) and Hum 177 (School Girls). The boy in this figure, which was originally known as "School Lesson," is also much like the boy in the Dealer Plaque (Hum 460). Note the line around the base in the accompanying photograph: a red line like that indicates that this is a sample figurine.

Hum No.	Basic Size	Trademark	Current Value
303	5-1/4"	TMK-2	$4,000-$5,000

Another rare sample shown here: Arithmetic Lesson, Hum 303, which is currently listed as a possible future edition.

Hum 304: The Artist

This figurine, which was the original work of master sculptor Karl Wagner in 1955, was placed in regular production about 1970 after it was restyled by master sculptor Gerhard Skrobek. There is reason to believe it may have been made in extremely limited quantities in the Full Bee (TMK-2) era and somewhat limited in the Stylized Bee (TMK-3) era. The figure in the accompanying photograph bears that mark and a 1955 incised copyright date.

Hum No.	Basic Size	Trademark	Current Value
304	5-1/4"	TMK-2	$4,000-$5,000
304	5-1/4"	TMK-3	$2,000-$3,000
304	5-1/4"	TMK-4	$1,000-$1,200

The Artist, Hum 304. Left: TMK-6, incised 1955 copyright date. Right: Inked-in incised mold number indicating that this is a master model. It bears a stamped Full Bee trademark and "by W. Goebel, 1955." Note the paint drip on the base. This feature has never made it to the production piece.

Hum No.	Basic Size	Trademark	Current Value
304	5-1/4"	TMK-5	$305-$335
304	5-1/4"	TMK-6	$295-$305
304	5-1/4"	TMK-7	$290-$295
304	5-1/4"	TMK-8	$290

The Artist, Hum 304, Three Line Mark, incised 1955 copyright date, 5-1/4".

The Artist, Hum 304, remains in production today and is shown here in TMK-8.

Base of The Artist, showing the inked-in incised mold number indicating that this a figurine from the Mother Mold, a master model.

Hum 305: The Builder

The first sample of this figure, which was created by master sculptor Gerhard Skrobek in 1955, was made in the Full Bee (TMK-2) period and bears that trademark. These early samples are substantially more valuable than the figures made since.

This figurine was originally introduced into the line in 1963, and there are no significant mold or finish variations affecting the normal values, but a Full Bee trademarked piece is rare.

It was temporarily withdrawn from production on June 15, 2002.

Hum No.	Basic Size	Trademark	Current Value
305	5-1/2"	TMK-2	$4,000-$5,000
305	5-1/2"	TMK-3	$1,000-$1,500
305	5-1/2"	TMK-4	$330-$375
305	5-1/2"	TMK-5	$305-$330
305	5-1/2"	TMK-6	$295-$305
305	5-1/2"	TMK-7	$290-$295
305	5-1/2"	TMK-8	$290

The Builder, Hum 305, Three Line Mark, incised 1955 copyright date, 5-3/8".

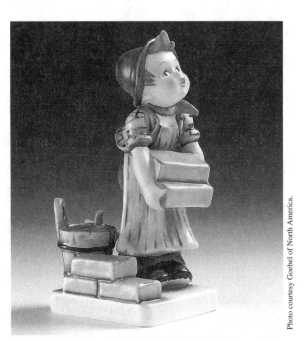

Today's rendition (TMK-8) of The Builder, Hum 305.

Hum 306: Little Bookkeeper

The first example of this figure, which was created by master sculptor Arthur Moeller in 1955, was made in the Full Bee (TMK-2) era and those prototypes bear that trademark. These early samples are substantially more valuable than the figures made since.

There are no significant mold or finish variations affecting normal values, but a Full Bee trademarked example is rare.

Temporarily withdrawn from production on June 15, 2002.

Hum No.	Basic Size	Trademark	Current Value
306	4-3/4"	TMK-2	$4,000-$5,000
306	4-3/4"	TMK-3	$1,000-$1,500
306	4-3/4"	TMK-4	$375-$450
306	4-3/4"	TMK-5	$350-$375
306	4-3/4"	TMK-6	$345-$350
306	4-3/4"	TMK-7	$340-$345
306	4-3/4"	TMK-8	$355

TMK-8 variation of Little Bookkeeper, Hum 306.

Photo courtesy Goebel of North America.

Little Bookkeeper, Hum 306. Left: Three Line Mark (TMK-4), 1955 copyright date. Right: Last Bee (TMK-5) trademark, 1955 copyright date. Both measure 4-1/2". Shows head position variation.

Hum 307: Good Hunting

This figure, which was the result of combined efforts by master sculptor Reinhold Unger and Helmut Wehlte in 1955, was first introduced in 1962, in the Full Bee (TMK-2) era. These early samples are substantially more valuable than the figures made since.

Figures with the Stylized Bee (TMK-3) trademark and later are the most common.

In older versions of this piece, the boy holds the binoculars significantly lower than they are held in the figure made today, but this and any other mold and finish variations have no effect on normal values. The variations merely reflect the normal changes in the evolution of the figurine.

Hum No.	Basic Size	Trademark	Current Value
307	5-1/4"	TMK-2	$4,000-$5,000
307	5-1/4"	TMK-3	$1,000-$1,500
307	5-1/4"	TMK-4	$375-$425
307	5-1/4"	TMK-5	$295-$325
307	5-1/4"	TMK-6	$290-$295
307	5-1/4"	TMK-7	$285-$290
307	5-1/4"	TMK-8	$300

Today's version (TMK-8) of Good Hunting, Hum 307.

Photo courtesy Goebel of North America.

Good Hunting, Hum 307. Left: Three Line Mark (TMK-4), 1955 copyright date, 5". Right: TMK-6 mark, 1955 copyright date, 5-1/8".

Hum 308: Little Tailor

This figure, which was first designed by master sculptor Horst Ashermann in 1955, was first produced in the Full Bee (TMK-2) era, but not placed in the line until 1972. There are a few of the Full Bee and Stylized Bee (TMK-3) pieces around, but they are rare.

There was a major mold redesign in the Last Bee (TMK-5) era and the old and new figures may be found in that trademark, although the old style is difficult to find. Early pieces carry the incised 1955 copyright date, while the newer styles have a 1972 incised copyright date.

See the accompanying photograph for the differences between the two styles.

Hum No.	Basic Size	Trademark	Current Value
308	5-1/2"	TMK-2	$4,000-$5,000
308	5-1/2"	TMK-3	$2,000-$3,000
308	5-1/2"	TMK-4	$1,000-$1,500
308 (old style)	5-1/2"	TMK-5	$750-$900
308 (new style)	5-1/2"	TMK-5	$300-$335
308	5-1/2"	TMK-6	$290-$300
308	5-1/2"	TMK-7	$285-$290
308	5-1/2"	TMK-8	$305

Photo courtesy Goebel of North America.

Little Tailor, Hum 308. This photo shows the difference between the old style (left) with an incised 1955 copyright date and the new (right), 1972 copyright date. The left measures 5-1/4" and the right, 5-5/8". Both bear the Last Bee trademark (TMK-5).

Little Tailor, Hum 308, is still in production today, shown here in TMK-8.

Hum 309: With Loving Greetings

When first released in 1983, the suggested retail price for this piece was $80, but an early sample piece, which was the work of master sculptor Karl Wagner in 1955, was made during the Full Bee (TMK-2) era. These pieces are substantially more valuable than any made since.

Take a look at the left-hand figure in the accompanying photograph for an example of this sample. When you compare it to the other two, you will see that the sample piece is more complex. This is a good illustration of how a figure can evolve from sample to production. Obviously, the paintbrush under the boy's arm was judged too vulnerable to breakage and was removed from the production model. Samples can also be found in TMK-3, TMK-4, and TMK-5.

When first introduced into the line in 1983, the inkwell was colored blue, and the writing on the tablet turquoise. In late-1987, the color of the inkwell was changed to

With Loving Greetings, Hum 309. Left: Full Bee in an incised circle, "by W. Goebel," 1955 copyright date, 3-1/2". This is the blue ink well with stopper variation. Note brush under left arm. Center: TMK-6, 1955 copyright date, 3-1/2". Blue inkwell. The brush is now missing. Right: TMK-6, 1955 copyright date, 3-1/2". Purplish brown inkwell.

brown and the color of the writing to blue. This change was made during TMK-6 period and can be found with the old or the new color in that trademark.

Hum No.	Basic Size	Trademark	Current Value
309	3-1/2"	TMK-2	$4,000-$5,000
309	3-1/2"	TMK-3	$3,000-$4,000
309	3-1/2"	TMK-4	$2,000-$3,000

Hum No.	Basic Size	Trademark	Current Value
309	3-1/2"	TMK-5	$1,000-$2,000
309 (blue pot)	3-1/2"	TMK-6	$250-$300
309 (brown)	3-1/2"	TMK-6	$230-$240
309	3-1/2"	TMK-7	$220-$225

Hum 310: Searching Angel (Wall Plaque)

This piece, which has been called "Angelic Concern," was first fashioned by master sculptor Gerhard Skrobek in 1955 during the Full Bee (TMK-2) period, but was not released for sale until 1979. This early sample is very rare, but it has been found. Other samples were also made during the Stylized Bee (TMK-3) and Three Line (TMK-4) periods. Pieces carry an incised 1955 copyright date.

This plaque was temporarily withdrawn from production in January 1999.

Hum No.	Basic Size	Trademark	Current Value
310	4" x 2-1/2"	TMK-2	$2,000-$3,000
310	4" x 2-1/2"	TMK-3	$1,200-$1,700
310	4" x 2-1/2"	TMK-4	$1,000-$1,500
310	4" x 2-1/2"	TMK-5	$300-$500
310	4" x 2-1/2"	TMK-6	$135-$140
310	4" x 2-1/2"	TMK-7	$135-$140

Searching Angel plaque, Hum 310. Left: Full Bee mark in an incised circle, incised 1955 copyright date, 3-3/8" x 4-1/4". Right: Last Bee, incised 1955 copyright date, 4-1/4" x 4-1/8".

Photo courtesy Goebel of North America.

The most recent variation (TMK-7) of Searching Angel, Hum 310.

Hum 311: Kiss Me

Kiss Me was first designed by master sculptor Reinhold Unger in 1955 and made in the Full Bee (TMK-2) era, but it was not released for sale until 1961, during the Stylized Bee (TMK-3) period. A few of these Full Bee pieces have made their way into the collectors' market. They are very rare and therefore substantially more valuable than pieces made since.

The mold was reworked later so that the doll the girl was holding did not appear to be a child. The figures can, therefore, be found either way in both the Stylized Bee (TMK-3) and Three Line (TMK-4) periods.

Hum No.	Basic Size	Trademark	Current Value
311	6"	TMK-2	$4,000-$5,000
311 (old style)	6"	TMK-3	$800-$1,100
311 (new style)	6"	TMK-3	$450-$500

Kiss Me, Hum 311. Left: Three Line Mark (TMK-4), 1955 copyright date, 6-1/8". Right: TMK-6, 6-1/4".

Hum No.	Basic Size	Trademark	Current Value
311 (old)	6"	TMK-4	$650-$950
311 (new)	6"	TMK-4	$375-$450
311	6"	TMK-5	$350-$375
311	6"	TMK-6	$340-$350
311	6"	TMK-7	$335-$340
311	6"	TMK-8	$355

TMK-8 variation of Kiss Me, Hum 311.

Hum 312: Honey Lover

IThis piece, which was created by master sculptor Helmut Wehlte in 1955, was first found illustrated as a possible future edition (PFE) in the Golden Anniversary Album when the book was released in 1984. At that point in time, a few had somehow already made their way into collectors' hands.

The figure is now officially on the market, having been released as a special M.I. Hummel Club exclusive in 1991. Released at $190, it is available to members after the 15th anniversary of their club membership.

Hum No.	Basic Size	Trademark	Current Value
312	3-3/4"	TMK-2	$4,000-$5,000
312/I	3-3/4"	TMK-6	$400-$500
312/I	3-3/4"	TMK-7	$235-$240
312/I	3-3/4"	TMK-8	$235

Honey Lover, Hum 312. Left: This 3-7/8" figure has a Full Bee mark and a hand-lettered mold number along with the frequently found normal "by W. Goebel". Additionally there is a painted red "Z," indicating that this particular piece is a prototype. Right: Also a Full Bee marked piece, this 4" figure bears a 1955 incised copyright date copyright date.

Honey Lover, Hum 312/I, with TMK-7 and incised 1955 copyright date. This issue is available exclusively to members of the M.I. Hummel Club who have attained 15 years of membership.

Underside of the base of Hum 312/I Honey Lover, showing the special club backstamp.

Hum 313: Sunny Morning

This piece, which was designed by master sculptor Arthur Moeller in 1955 and originally called "Slumber Serenade," was listed as a possible future edition in the last edition of this book, but has since been put into production as a new release for 2003 with mold number 313/0. Those issued in 2003 will carry the "First Issue 2003" backstamp, as well as TMK-8.

Early samples were made in the mid-1950s carrying the Full Bee (TMK-2). Somehow, at least three prototype pieces have made it into the collectors' market.

Hum No.	Basic Size	Trademark	Current Value
313	3-3/4"	TMK-2	$4,000-$5,000
313/0	4-1/4"	TMK-8	$300

Photo courtesy Goebel of North America.

Sunny Morning, Hum 313/0, shown here as the TMK-8 variation, which was released new for 2003.

Hum 314: Confidentially

Even though this figure was first introduced into the line in 1972, the Last Bee (TMK-5) period, it can also be found as early samples in the Full Bee (TMK-2), Stylized Bee (TMK-3), and the Three Line (TMK-4) eras.

It was the original design of master sculptor Horst Ashermann in 1955, but master sculptor Gerhard Skrobek redesigned the figure shortly after releasing it. The new and old styles, which include changes in the stand, the addition of a tie on the boy, and a change in the finish texture, are evident in the accompanying photograph. The old and new styles can be found with the Last Bee (TMK-5).

This piece was temporarily withdrawn from production in 1999.

Hum No.	Basic Size	Trademark	Current Value
314	5-1/2"	TMK-2	$4,000-$5,000
314	5-1/2"	TMK-3	$2,000-$3,000
314	5-1/2"	TMK-4	$1,000-$2,000
314 (old style)	5-1/2"	TMK-5	$800-$950
314 (new style)	5-1/2"	TMK-5	$350-$390
314	5-1/2"	TMK-6	$340-$350
314	5-1/2"	TMK-7	$325-$345

Confidentially, Hum 314. Left: Last Bee (TMK-5), incised 1955 copyright date, 5-3/8". Right: Last Bee (TMK-5), incised 1972 copyright date, 5-7/8".

Hum 315: Mountaineer

Modeled by master sculptor Gerhard Skrobek in 1955 and released in 1964 (TMK-3 period) at the World's Fair in New York City, this figure is also found, albeit rarely, as an early sample with the Full Bee (TMK-2) trademark.

There are no mold or finish variations that would have any effect on the normal values, although older pieces are slightly smaller and have a green stick rather than the dark gray stick of the newer pieces.

Mountaineer, Hum 315. This example is 5" in height, has the Three Line Mark (TMK-4), and bears an incised 1955 copyright date.

The M.I.Hummel Collection 211

Hum No.	Basic Size	Trademark	Current Value
315	5-1/4"	TMK-2	$4,000-$5,000
315	5-1/4"	TMK-3	$750-$1,000
315	5-1/4"	TMK-4	$285-$400
315	5-1/4"	TMK-5	$265-$285
315	5-1/4"	TMK-6	$260-$265
315	5-1/4"	TMK-7	$255-$260
315	5-1/4"	TMK-8	$270

Today's rendition (TMK-8) of Mountaineer, Hum 315.

Hum 316: Relaxation

This piece, which was once called "Nightly Ritual," was designed and produced in prototype by master sculptor Karl Wagner in 1955, in the Full Bee (TMK-2) period.

Listed as a possible future edition in the last edition of this book, the piece has since been put into production as a M.I. Hummel Club 25-year membership exclusive. The inscription on the bottom reads: "EXCLUSIVE EDITION Twenty-Five Year Membership M.I. HUMMEL CLUB" and carries the special club backstamp.

Hum No.	Basic Size	Trademark	Current Value
316	4"	TMK-2	$4,000-$5,000
316	4"	TMK-8	$300

This exclusive edition of Relaxation, Hum 316, is available only to M.I. Hummel Club members who have reached 25 years of membership.

Hum 317: Not For You

Even though this figurine, which was created by master sculptor Arthur Moeller in 1955, was not released for sale until 1961 during the Stylized Bee (TMK-3) period, it is occasionally found as an early sample bearing the Full Bee (TMK-2) trademark.

There are no mold or finish variations that affect the normal values for the figures with the various trademarks.

Hum No.	Basic Size	Trademark	Current Value
317	5-1/2"	TMK-2	$4,000-$5,000
317	5-1/2"	TMK-3	$750-$1,000
317	5-1/2"	TMK-4	$335-$435
317	5-1/2"	TMK-5	$290-$325
317	5-1/2"	TMK-6	$285-$290
317	5-1/2"	TMK-7	$280-$285
317	5-1/2"	TMK-8	$300

Not For You, Hum 317. Has an incised copyright date copyright date of 1955. It is 5-5/8" tall and bears the TMK-6 trademark.

Hum 318: Art Critic

This figure was first designed by master sculptor Horst Ashermann in 1955 and produced in prototype during the Full Bee (TMK-2) era, but was not released until 1991. At least two of these figures, marked with the Full Bee trademark, have found their way into the collectors' market. These early prototypes are worth substantially more than anything released since.

These figurines carry a 1955 incised copyright date and "First Issue 1991" backstamp in the first year of production. There are no significant mold or finish variations affecting the normal values.

The piece was temporarily withdrawn from production in 1999.

Hum No.	Basic Size	Trademark	Current Value
318	5-3/4"	TMK-2	$4,000-$5,000
318	5-3/4"	TMK-6	$335-$345
318	5-3/4"	TMK-7	$320-$330

Art Critic, Hum 318. Left: TMK-6, incised 1955 copyright date, 5-1/4", and "First Issue" backstamp dated 1991. Right: TMK-7 demonstration piece with only flesh tones and brown base color on the coat painted, "First Issue" backstamp, and incised 1955 copyright date.

Hum No.	Basic Size	Trademark	Current Value
319	5-1/4"	TMK-2	$4,000-$5,000
319	5-1/4"	TMK-3	$750-$1,000
319	5-1/4"	TMK-4	$375-$435
319	5-1/4"	TMK-5	$350-$375
319	5-1/4"	TMK-6	$345-$350
319	5-1/4"	TMK-7	$340-$345
319	5-1/4"	TMK-8	$355

Hum 319: Doll Bath

This figure was first designed by master sculptor Gerhard Skrobek in 1956 and produced in early sample form during the Full Bee (TMK-2) period, but was not released until 1962, during the Stylized Bee (TMK-3) period. There are some pieces out there with the Full Bee trademark, and these early samples are worth substantially more than the later releases.

In the 1970s, the entire collection underwent a change from the old smooth surface finish to a textured finish. Unlike many of the other figures in the collection, this one made a clean break from the old style finish (found only in the TMK-4 pieces) to the new textured finish (found on the TMK-5 pieces and all thereafter).

Doll Bath, Hum 319: This is the TMK-6 version.

Doll Bath, Hum 319. Both figures bear the Three Line Mark (TMK-4). The one on the left has an incised 1956 copyright date and the other has an copyright date of 197?. It was impossible to discern the fourth digit.

Hum 320: The Professor

First produced in prototype by master sculptor Gerhard Skrobek in 1955 during the Full Bee (TMK-2) era, this figure was not released until 1991.

The new pieces bear the mold number 320/0, but the Full Bee pieces have the mold number 320 with no size designator. These sample pieces are considerably larger than the production pieces and are worth considerably more than those released into production.

There are no significant variations affecting the normal collector values.

The 320/0 size was temporarily withdrawn from production on June 15, 2002.

Hum No.	Basic Size	Trademark	Current Value
320	5-3/4"	TMK-2	$4,000-$5,000
320/0	4-3/4"	TMK-7	$245-$255
320/0	4-3/4"	TMK-8	$258

The Professor, Hum 320/0, in TMK-7 with incised 1989 copyright date, and "First Issue" backstamp dated 1992.

The Professor, Hum 320. This is a master model. Note the red line around the base.

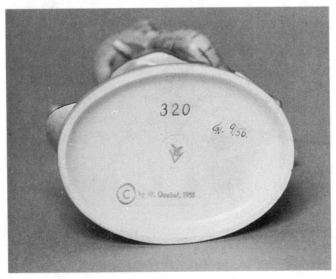

The Professor, Hum 320. The base of the Hum 320 master model. Note the inked incised mold number. This is routinely done on pieces made from the mother or master mold.

Hum 321: Wash Day

In the first sample figurines, made in the 1955 by master sculptor Reinhold Unger and Helmut Wehlte, the laundry being held up was much longer and attached to the rest of the laundry down in the basket. This was during the Full Bee (TMK-2) period. It is possible, though unlikely, that you will find this figure. These early samples are marked with the Full Bee (TMK-2) trademark and are significantly more valuable than the later variations.

In 1989, a new smaller version of this piece was issued as a part of a four-piece series with matching mini-plates. These versions do not have the laundry basket. They have an incised mold number of 321/4/0. When this mold was issued, Goebel changed the number on the larger piece to 321/I. You may find it either way on those figures with TMK-6 trademark.

The smaller 321/4/0 size was temporarily withdrawn from production in 1997.

Hum No.	Basic Size	Trademark	Current Value
321/4/0	3"	TMK-6	$125-$140
321/4/0	3"	TMK-7	$120-$125
321	5-3/4"	TMK-2	$4,000-$5,000
321	5-3/4"	TMK-3	$750-$1,000
321	5-3/4"	TMK-4	$400-$450
321	5-3/4"	TMK-5	$365-$395
321	5-3/4"	TMK-6	$360-$365
321/I	5-3/4"	TMK-6	$355-$360
321/I	5-3/4"	TMK-7	$350-$355
321/I	5-3/4"	TMK-8	$365

Photo courtesy Goebel of North America.

Photo courtesy Goebel of North America.

Three variations of Wash Day, Hum 321, from left: TMK-4 with incised 1957 copyright date and measuring 5-3/4"; TMK-7 with 321/4/0 mold number, no wash basket, and measuring 3"; and today's TMK-8 with mold number 321/I and measuring 5-3/4".

Hum 322: Little Pharmacist

This figurine was first designed by master sculptor Karl Wagner in 1955 and those early samples bear the Full Bee (TMK-2) trademark and are worth considerably more than regular production pieces.

There are several variations in the labeling of the medicine bottle at the figure's feet. The version written in German (see photo) was temporarily withdrawn from production as of December 31, 1984. One of the most difficult pieces to find is the version with "Castor Oil" on the bottle in Spanish ("Castor bil"). When found, it is on the Three Line Mark (TMK-4) pieces and is worth considerably more than the other variations at $2,000-$3,000.

In 1988 Little Pharmacist was redesigned, and all subsequent production of the figure reflects the following changes. The base was made shallower with rounded corners, which made the figure shorter than its former 6" size (now 5-3/4"). The coat is now curved in front at the bottom line. A breast pocket was added, the strap (in back) was made wider and a second button was added. The figure's bow tie was straightened and the eyeglass stems made to disappear into his hair.

Somehow in 1990 an unknown (but probably very small) number of these figures were produced with the bottle label in German ("Rizinusol") and the prescription in English ("Recipe"). A TMK-6 Little Pharmacist with these words have a collector value of $1,000-$1,500.

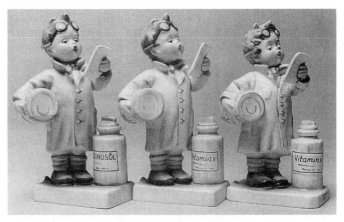

Little Pharmacist, Hum 322, shown here in three variations, from left: TMK-5, 1955 copyright date, and the word "Rezept" found on the prescription pad in his left hand; TMK-6, 1955 copyright date, and the word "RECIPE" on the pad; and TMK-6 with everything the same as the center figure, except that the hairstyle is different.

Today's rendition (TMK-8) of Little Pharmacist, Hum 322.

Photo courtesy Goebel of North America.

Hum No.	Basic Size	Trademark	Current Value
322	6"	TMK-2	$4,000-$5,000
322	6"	TMK-3	$750-$1,000
322	6"	TMK-4	$325-$335
322 (Spanish)	6"	TMK-4	$2,000-$3,000
322	6"	TMK-5	$295-$325
322	6"	TMK-6	$290-$295
322	6"	TMK-7	$285-$290
322	6"	TMK-8	$300

Hum 323: Merry Christmas (Wall Plaque)

Merry Christmas plaque, Hum 323, shown here in TMK-5.

Designed and made in sample form by master sculptor Gerhard Skrobek in 1955, during the Full Bee (TMK-2) period, this plaque was not offered for sale until 1979. The TMK-2 samples are worth significantly more than figures made since.

Samples were also made during the Stylized Bee (TMK-3) and Three Line (TMK-4) periods, and those too are worth more than the versions eventually released to the public during the Last Bee (TMK-5) era.

This plaque was temporarily withdrawn from production in January 1999.

Hum No.	Basic Size	Trademark	Current Value
323	4" x 5-1/4"	TMK-2	$2,000-$3,000
323	4" x 5-1/4"	TMK-2	$1,200-$1,700
323	4" x 5-1/4"	TMK-2	$1,000-$1,500
323	4" x 5-1/4"	TMK-5	$300-$500
323	4" x 5-1/4"	TMK-6	$145-$150
323	4" x 5-1/4"	TMK-7	$140-$145

Hum 324: At the Fence (Possible Future Edition)

This figure was designed by master sculptor Arthur Moeller in 1955 and produced in sample form in the 1950s, but has not yet been put into regular production and offered for sale. The one in the picture is marked with the Full Bee (TMK-2), as you can see. Somehow it managed to make it into the collectors' market. Notice the line painted around the base; this denotes a painter's sample, a model that the Goebel painters try to duplicate when producing the figurines.

Hum No.	Basic Size	Trademark	Current Value
324	4-3/4"	TMK-2	$4,000-$5,000

A rare sample of the possible future edition At the Fence, Hum 324, shown upright and tipped on its side to display the base markings.

Hum 325: Helping Mother (Possible Future Edition)

Originally designed by master sculptor Arthur Moeller in 1955 and produced in prototype during the Full Bee (TMK-2) trademark era of the 1950s, this figure exists in at least two private collections with the Full Bee trademark.

Hum No.	Basic Size	Trademark	Current Value
325	5"	TMK-2	$4,000-$5,000

Helping Mother, Hum 325, shown here as a rare sample, which is worth $4,000-$5,000.

Hum 326: Being Punished (Possible Future Edition)

The original design and prototype figure by master sculptor Gerhard Skrobek was made in 1957. Those figures, which were originally called "Naughty Boy," have an incised 1955 copyright date and bear the Full Bee (TMK-2) trademark.

Although the piece has not yet been released, more than one has made its way into the collector market. There may also be early samples with the Stylized Bee (TMK-3) trademark, but those reports have not been substantiated.

Being Punished, Hum 326, in sample form only since it is a possible future edition waiting to be put into regular production.

Hum No.	Basic Size	Trademark	Current Value
326	4" x 5"	TMK-2	$4,000-$5,000

Hum 327: The Run-a-way

Originally designed by master sculptor Helmut Wehlte in 1955, this figure was not released until 1972. Samples were produced with the Full Bee (TMK-2) and Stylized Bee (TMK-3) trademarks. The early samples are worth substantially more than figures made since, with the Full Bee variations the most desirable.

There exist at least two variations of Hum 327, due to a redesign by master sculptor Gerhard Skrobek in 1972. They have both been found with the Last Bee (TMK-5) trademark, although each bears a different copyright date. The older design (1955 copyright date) has flowers in the basket, gray jacket, gray hair, and the crook on the cane is turned more sideways. The newer design (1972 copyright date) has no flowers, a green hat, blue jacket, and the cane is situated with the crook pointing up.

Hum No.	Basic Size	Trademark	Current Value
327	5-1/4"	TMK-2	$4,000-$5,000
327	5-1/4"	TMK-3	$2,000-$3,000
327	5-1/4"	TMK-4	$1,100-$1,300
327 (old style)	5-1/4"	TMK-5	$900-$1,000
327 (new style)	5-1/4" 5	TMK-5	$300-$33
327	5-1/4"	TMK-6	$295-$300
327	5-1/4"	TMK-7	$290-$295
327	5-1/4"	TMK-8	$290

A present-day variation (TMK-8) of The Run-a-way, Hum 327.

Photo courtesy Goebel of North America.

The Run-a-way, Hum 327. Left: Last Bee (TMK-5), incised 1955 copyright date, 5-1/8". Right: Last Bee TMK-5), incised 1972 copyright date, 5-1/2".

Hum 328: Carnival

The original design was the work of master sculptors Reinhold Unger and Helmut Wehlte in 1955 and samples of this figure were made in the mid-1950s. Those sample pieces have a copyright date of 1955 and bear the Full Bee (TMK-2).

When the piece was put into regular production and offered for sale in the 1960s, it had the Three Line Mark (TMK-4), but a few have been found bearing the Stylized Bee (TMK-3) as well.

There are no major mold or finish variations affecting the normal values, although older pieces are slightly larger and do depict the object under the boy's arm as a noise-maker or "slapstick."

This piece was temporarily withdrawn from production in 1999.

Carnival, Hum 328, with Three Line Mark (TMK-4) and incised 1957 copyright date.

Hum No.	Basic Size	Trademark	Current Value
328	6"	TMK-2	$4,000-$5,000
328	6"	TMK-3	$750-$1,000
328	6"	TMK-4	$285-$330
328	6"	TMK-5	$265-$285
328	6"	TMK-6	$255-$265
328	6"	TMK-7	$245-$255

Photo courtesy Goebel of North America.

TMK-7 variation of Carnival, Hum 328.

Hum 329: Off to School (Possible Future Edition)

This figure, which was first known as "Kindergarten Romance," was originally designed by master sculptor Arthur Moeller in 1955 and samples were made during the Full Bee (TMK-2) and Stylized Bee (TMK-3) periods. It consists of a boy and girl walking along. The girl has a book satchel in the crook of her left arm. The boy figure is substantially similar to Hum 82 (School Boy).

Hum No.	Basic Size	Trademark	Current Value
329	5"	TMK-2	$4,000-$5,000
329	5"	TMK-3	$3,000-$4,000

Hum 330: Baking Day

This figure was first made in sample form by master sculptor Gerhard Skrobek in 1955. These early examples bear the 1955 copyright date, as do the pieces made since. The figure was not released until 1985, during TMK-6 period, but samples were produced in every trademark leading up to the release. Such samples are worth substantially more than the figures released thereafter.

Once called "Kneading Dough," there are no significant mold or finish variations affecting normal values.

The piece was temporarily withdrawn from production in January 1999.

Baking Day, Hum 330. TMK-6, incised 1955 copyright date, 5-1/4".

Hum No.	Basic Size	Trademark	Current Value
330	5-1/4"	TMK-2	$4,000-$5,000
330	5-1/4"	TMK-3	$2,500-$3,000
330	5-1/4"	TMK-4	$2,000-$2,500
330	5-1/4"	TMK-5	$1,500-$2,000
330	5-1/4"	TMK-6	$340-$350
330	5-1/4"	TMK-7	$330

Hum 331: Crossroads

Master sculptor Arthur Moeller first made this piece in 1955, with early samples bearing both the Full Bee (TMK-2) and Stylized Bee (TMK-3) trademarks.

It has been reported that there is a variation regarding the position of the trombone. It is not terribly obvious in the photo here, but if you look closely, you can see the end of the horn protruding above the boy's head. The reported variation is that the horn is reversed so that it points down instead of up as in the one pictured here. It is the result of a mistake in the assembly of the parts of the factory and is likely to be the only one in existence.

In 1990, Goebel issued a special edition of Crossroads to commemorate the demise of the Berlin Wall. Limited to 20,000 worldwide, it is the same figure except the "HALT" sign on the post is placed at the base of the post as if it had fallen or been torn down. Production of this edition took place during the transition from TMK-6 to TMK-7. Interestingly, it has been reported that only about 3,500 of the 20,000 were given the TMK-7.

The third variation is another edition created for the U.S. military forces. As with the special "Desert Storm" edition of Hum 50 (Volunteers), this one was sold through military base exchange stores only. This Desert Storm edition was a three-piece set. The figure is the regular production model with the sign on the post, but it has an American and German flag beneath the glaze under the base. A second piece is a representation of a piece of the wall with "Berlin Wall" on it in bas-relief. It also has the flags underneath along with the inscription "With esteem and grateful appreciation to the United States Military Forces for the preservation of peace and freedom." That same inscription is found on a brass plate on the front of the third piece, a wooden display base. The Berlin Wall piece is limited to 20,000 worldwide and sequentially hand-numbered beneath the base in the traditional manner of marking limited editions. The initial release price in 1992 was $265 for the set. It is valued at about $700 today.

Hum No.	Basic Size	Trademark	Current Value
331	6-3/4"	TMK-2	$4,000-$5,000
331	6-3/4"	TMK-3	$2,000-$3,000
331	6-3/4"	TMK-4	$775-$1,000
331	6-3/4"	TMK-5	$500-$545
331 (original)	6-3/4"	TMK-6	$485-$500
331 (commemorative)	6-3/4"	TMK-6	$750-$900
331 (commemorative)	6-3/4"	TMK-7	$950-$1,200
331 (original)	6-3/4"	TMK-7	$475-$485
331 (Desert Storm)	6-3/4"	TMK-7	$500-$775
331	6-3/4"	TMK-8	$475

The most recent version (TMK-7) of Crossroads, Hum 331, is shown here. As you can see, the "HALT" sign is back on the pole.

Photo courtesy Goebel of North America.

Crossroads, Hum 331. Left: Last Bee (TMK-5), incised 1955 copyright date, 6-3/8". Right: TMK-6, incised 1955 copyright date, 6-5/8". Special backstamp reading "M.I. Hummel 1990 a Celebration of Freedom." Note the "HALT" sign is on the ground.

Hum 332: Soldier Boy

Originally designed by master sculptor Gerhard Skrobek in 1955 and produced in prototype in the 1950s, this figure was not released for sale to the general public until 1963. The early samples, bearing the Full Bee (TMK-2) and a 1955 incised copyright date, are worth substantially more than the pieces released since.

Pieces later than TMK-2 have a 1957 incised copyright date.

There is a variation on the color of the cap medallion. It is painted red on older pieces and blue on the newer ones. The transition from red to blue took place in the Three Line Mark (TMK-4) period and can be found both ways bearing that trademark.

Goebel released a special limited edition in 1994 consisting of the figurine, a small porcelain replica of the shack at Checkpoint Charlie of Berlin Wall fame and a wooden base with a sign and brass ID plate (see accompanying photograph). The edition was limited to 20,000 and the pieces each bear a special backstamp identifying them appropriately. The release price was $330 and is still valued at about the same today.

This figurine was temporarily withdrawn from production in 1999.

Hum No.	Basic Size	Trademark	Current Value
332	6"	TMK-2	$4,000-$5,000
332	6"	TMK-3	$1,000-$1,500
332 (red)	6"	TMK-4	$250-$650
332 (blue)	6"	TMK-4	$210-225
332	6"	TMK-5	$275-$300
332	6"	TMK-6	$265-$275
332	6"	TMK-7	$250-$265

The special edition Checkpoint Charlie Soldier Boy display.

Soldier Boy, Hum 332. Left: Three Line Mark (TMK-4), 1957 copyright date, red cap medallion, 5-3/4". Right: All is now the same except this one has a blue-cap medallion.

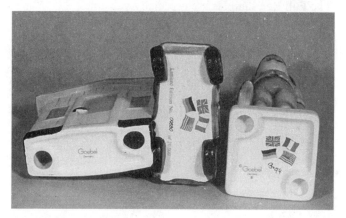

The bases of the Soldier Boy and Checkpoint Charlie Shack showing the special markings.

Hum 333: Blessed Event

This figure was designed by master sculptor Arthur Moeller in 1955 and produced as samples in the 1950s, but not released until 1964 (TMK-4 era) at the World's Fair in New York City. The samples in both the Full Bee (TMK-2) and Stylized Bee (TMK-3) eras are worth substantially more than the pieces released since.

No significant variations have been reported, although pieces can be found with 1955, 1956, or 1957 incised copyright dates.

Hum No.	Basic Size	Trademark	Current Value
333	5-1/2"	TMK-2	$4,000-$5,000
333	5-1/2"	TMK-3	$750-$1,000
333	5-1/2"	TMK-4	$425-$600
333	5-1/2"	TMK-5	$395-$425
333	5-1/2"	TMK-6	$390-$400
333	5-1/2"	TMK-7	$385-$390
333	5-1/2"	TMK-8	$400

Blessed Event, Hum 333. Three Line Mark, doughnut base, 5-1/4".

Photo courtesy Goebel of North America.

Today's variation (TMK-8) of Blessed Event, Hum 333.

Hum 334: Homeward Bound

This figurine was first made in sample form in the mid-1950s by master sculptor Arthur Moeller, but it was not released until 1971. Samples are known to exist in both the Full Bee (TMK-2) and Stylized Bee (TMK-3) trademarks. The Full Bee samples are especially valuable.

Older models of this design have a support molded in beneath the goat. The newer versions do not have this support. Examples of both styles exist in both the Three Line (TMK-4) and Last Bee (TMK-5) periods.

The piece was temporarily withdrawn from production in January 1999.

Hum No.	Basic Size	Trademark	Current Value
334	5"	TMK-6	$385-$395
334	5"	TMK-7	$365-$375

Hum No.	Basic Size	Trademark	Current Value
334	5"	TMK-2	$4,000-$5,000
334	5"	TMK-3	$1,000-$1,500
334 (old style)	5"	TMK-4	$700-$850
334 (new style)	5"	TMK-4	$460-$500
334 (old)	5"	TMK-5	$475-$500
334 (new)	5"	TMK-5	$395-$430

Homeward Bound, Hum 334. Left: Last Bee (TMK-6) mark, 1975 copyright date, split base, 5-1/2". Right: Last Bee (TMK-6), 1955 copyright date, doughnut base.

Hum 335: Lucky Boy

Designed in 1956 by master sculptor Arthur Moeller and produced in sample form (called "Fair Prizes") in both the Full Bee (TMK-2) and Stylized Bee (TMK-3) periods, this figurine was released in 1995. One example in the accompanying photographs has a red line painted around the base, used by the factory to denote a figure that is used as a sample model for the factory artists.

Lucky Boy was released in special limited edition in a 4-1/2" size (Hum 335/0). It was part of Goebel's 1995 celebration of 60 years of Hummel figurines; 250 U.S. dealers participated in Goebel's M.I. Hummel 60th Anniversary Open House. The figurine was limited to 25,000 worldwide with 15,000 of them bearing a special 60th anniversary backstamp. Collectors could only purchase figurines from participating dealers during the year. The other 10,000 pieces were made available in 1996 with the Goebel 125th anniversary backstamp. None will ever again be produced in this size. The release price was $190.

Hum No.	Basic Size	Trademark	Current Value
335	5"	TMK-2	$4,000-$5,000
335	5"	TMK-3	$3,000-$4,000
335/0	4-1/2"	TMK-7	$190-$200

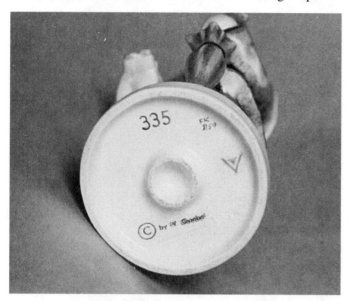

Base showing the Stylized Bee (TMK-3) trademark.

Lucky Boy, Hum 335/0. The special limited edition. It measures 2-1/2", bears an incised copyright date of 1989 and the 60th anniversary backstamp.

Factory sample of Lucky Boy, Hum 335. It has a 1956 copyright date and measures 5-3/8".

Hum 336: Close Harmony

This figure was crafted by master sculptor Gerhard Skrobek in 1956 and first produced in sample form in the Full Bee (TMK-2) era, but not released until the early 1960s. The early samples are worth substantially more than the pieces released since.

Inexplicably, this piece can be found with any one of three copyright dates: 1955, 1956, or 1957. There is a 1962 copyright date that is explained by a redesign in that year. Even more peculiar is that those in production currently are yet another redesign, but they bear the 1955 copyright date. This strange circumstance makes the pieces with the later copyright date of 1962 more valuable than those with the 1955 copyright date that are currently in production. This is the only figure in the collection that can be found with four different copyright dates.

This figure was temporarily withdrawn from production on June 15, 2002.

Close Harmony, Hum 336. Left: Three Line Mark (TMK-4), incised 1957 copyright date, doughnut base, and 5-3/8". Right: Three Line Mark (TMK-4), incised 1955 copyright date, and 5-1/4".

Hum No.	Basic Size	Trademark	Current Value
336	5-1/2"	TMK-2	$4,000-$5,000
336	5-1/2"	TMK-3	$1,000-$1,500
336	5-1/2"	TMK-4	$395-$525
336	5-1/2"	TMK-5	$365-$395
336	5-1/2"	TMK-6	$360-$365
336	5-1/2"	TMK-7	$355-$360
336	5-1/2"	TMK-8	$375

TMK-8 rendition of Close Harmony, Hum 336, which was temporarily withdrawn in June 2002.

Hum 337: Cinderella

Produced first in the Full Bee (TMK-2) era as samples by master sculptor Arthur Moeller and with more samples produced during the Stylized Bee (TMK-3), this figure was not placed in the collection until 1972. The early samples will bring premium prices.

Early pieces have either a 1958 or 1960 copyright date. Restyled in 1972 by master sculptor Gerhard Skrobek, the redesigned version carries a 1972 copyright date.

In the first versions of this figure, the eyes are open. Newer figures have the eyes closed. These variations represent two entirely different molds. Both versions have appeared bearing the Last Bee trademark (TMK-5).

Hum No.	Basic Size	Trademark	Current Value
337	5-1/2"	TMK-2	$4,000-$5,000
337	5-1/2"	TMK-3	$3,000-$4,000
337	5-1/2"	TMK-4	$1,500-$1,700
337 (old style)	5-1/2"	TMK-5	$1,200-$1,500
337 (new style)	5-1/2"	TMK-5	$350-$375
337	5-1/2"	TMK-6	$345-$350
337	5-1/2"	TMK-6	$340-$345
337	5-1/2"	TMK-6	$355

Cinderella, Hum 337. Left: Full Bee mark in an incised circle, "by W. Goebel," 4-5/8". Note the fourth bird (on the left shoulder). From the collection of Katherine Stephens. Right: Last Bee, incised 1957 copyright date, 4-1/2".

The most recent variation (TMK-7) of Cinderella, Hum 337.

Hum 338: Birthday Cake (Candleholder)

Birthday Cake, which was the work of master sculptor Gerhard Skrobek in 1956 and was originally called "A Birthday Wish," was added to the line in 1989. It measures 3-3/4" and has a receptacle for a candle as you can see in the accompanying photo. It has an incised copyright date of 1956.

There are two versions to be found. The differences are with regard to the texture of the top of the cake surface. About the first 2,000 pieces were produced with a smooth texture. This was changed to a rough texture ostensibly to correspond to the style of today.

It does exist in the Full Bee (TMK-2) prototype and has also turned up in the Stylized Bee (TMK-3).

This piece was temporarily withdrawn from production in January 1999.

Birthday Cake candleholder, Hum 338. TMK-6, incised 1957 copyright date, 3-9/16".

Hum No.	Basic Size	Trademark	Current Value
338	3-3/4"	TMK-2	$4,000-$5,000
338	3-3/4"	TMK-3	$3,000-$4,000
338	3-3/4"	TMK-6	$170-$175
338	3-3/4"	TMK-7	$165-$170

Hum 339: Behave!

In 1956, master sculptor Helmut Wehlte created this piece, which was first known as "Walking Her Dog."

The figurine was released in 1996 as a M.I. Hummel Club exclusive for the club. It has a special club backstamp in commemoration of 20 years of membership; issued only by those eligible returning a redemption card. It measures 5-1/2". The release price was $350. Notice the considerable difference between the sample piece and the regular production figurine.

Hum No.	Basic Size	Trademark	Current Value
339	5-1/2"	TMK-2	$5,000-$10,000
339	5-1/2"	TMK-3	$4,000-$5,000
339	5-1/2"	TMK-7	$450-$500
339	5-1/2"	TMK-8	$360
(with card)			

A TMK-7 version of Behave!, shown again both upright and on its side to expose the base marks.

Today's rendition (TMK-8) of Behave!, Hum 339.

Factory "sample" of Behave!, Hum 339, shown upright and turned on its side to show the base markings, which include a 1956 copyright date and Stylized Bee (TMK-3). The collector value is $4,000-$5,000.

Hum 340: Letter to Santa Claus

The first sample models, which were designed by master sculptor Helmut Wehlte in 1956, were an inch smaller (6-1/4") and had a tree trunk instead of a milled lumber post for the mailbox. The lumber post was the final design approved for production. Early samples exist in the Full Bee (TMK-2) both with the tree trunk post as well as the lumber post. Samples can also be found with the Stylized Bee (TMK-3). As always, the samples are worth substantially more than the figures released since.

The piece was first released in 1971 at $30. It was restyled with a new textured finish. This was a general change throughout the collection in the TMK-5 period and can be found either way bearing that trademark. The old pieces sport gray-green pants and the newer ones have red-orange pants.

Hum No.	Basic Size	Trademark	Current Value
340	6-1/4"	TMK-2	$15,000-$20,000
(tree trunk post)			
340	7-1/4"	TMK-2	$4,000-$5,000
(lumber post)			
340	7-1/4"	TMK-3	$3,000-$4,000
340	7-1/4"	TMK-4	$750-$1,000
340	7-1/4"	TMK-5	$400-$430
340	7-1/4"	TMK-6	$390-$395
340	7-1/4"	TMK-7	$385-$390
340	7-1/4"	TMK-8	$400

Photo courtesy Goebel of North America.

Letter to Santa, Hum 340, remains in production today, which is shown here (TMK-8).

Letter to Santa, Hum 340. This particular figurine measures 7-1/4", has an incised 1957 copyright date and bears the Three Line Mark (TMK-4).

Hum 341: Birthday Present

This piece, in 5" sample form bearing the Full Bee (TMK-2), Stylized Bee (TMK-3), and Three Line (TMK-4) trademarks, was found on the collectors' market long before its release in 1994. These early sample models, which were designed by master sculptor Gerhard Skrobek in 1956, are worth substantially more than the figures released since.

The production figurine is smaller at 3-3/4" and bears the "First Issue" and "SPECIAL EVENT" backstamps, as it was part of a district manager promotion during 1994. It was available in this configuration during that year only. The release price was $140.

This piece continues in general production today.

Birthday Present, Hum 341. The figure on the left is an early factory sample model measuring 5-1/4" and bearing the Stylized Bee (TMK-3) trademark. The one on the right is the smaller (4") current production piece. The copyright date is 1989.

The more recent smaller variation (3-3/4") of Birthday Present, Hum 341/3/0.

Photo courtesy Goebel of North America.

Hum No.	Basic Size	Trademark	Current Value
341	5" to 5-1/3"	TMK-2	$4,000-$5,000
341	5" to 5-1/3"	TMK-3	$3,000-$4,000
341	5" to 5-1/3"	TMK-4	$2,000-$3,000
341/3/0	3-3/4"	TMK-7	$175-$180
341/3/0	3-3/4"	TMK-8	$180

Hum 342: Mischief Maker

The work of master sculptor Arthur Moeller in 1956, this figurine exists in sample form with either the Full Bee (TMK-2) and Stylized Bee (TMK-3) trademarks.

This figure was not released for sale until 1972 at $26.50. There are no significant variations affecting normal values.

It was temporarily withdrawn from production in January 1999.

Hum No.	Basic Size	Trademark	Current Value
342	5"	TMK-2	$4,000-$5,000
342	5"	TMK-3	$2,000-$3,000
342	5"	TMK-4	$750-$1,000
342	5"	TMK-5	$350-$370
342	5"	TMK-6	$330-$350
342	5"	TMK-7	$315-$325

Mischief Maker, Hum 342. Has an incised copyright date of 1960, is 5" tall, and bears TMK-6.

Hum 343: Christmas Song

Christmas Song, Hum 343. TMK-6, 1957 copyright date, 6-3/8".

Originally known as "Singing Angel" in early company records, this is one of the six new designs released by Goebel in 1981. The work of master sculptor Gerhard Skrobek in 1956, there are early samples bearing the Full Bee (TMK-2), Stylized Bee (TMK-3), and Three Line (TMK-4) trademarks. As always, these are worth substantially more than the figures released since.

Photo courtesy Goebel of North America.

The 3-1/2" version of Christmas Song, Hum 343/4/0, shown here in TMK-8.

Photo courtesy Goebel of North America.

Today's larger variation of Christmas Song, Hum 343/I, which is 6-1/4".

A smaller 3-1/2" version (Hum 343/4/0) was released in 1996 as part of Goebel's 125th Anniversary. Those pieces carry an incised 1991 copyright date, TMK-7, and a combination "First Issue 1996" and "125th Anniversary Goebel" backstamp.

Both sizes remain in the line today.

Hum No.	Basic Size	Trademark	Current Value
343/4/0	3-1/2"	TMK-7	$115-$120
343/4/0	3-1/2"	TMK-8	$135

Hum No.	Basic Size	Trademark	Current Value
343	6-1/4"	TMK-2	$4,000-$5,000
343	6-1/4"	TMK-3	$2,000-$3,000
343	6-1/4"	TMK-4	$1,000-$2,000
343	6-1/4"	TMK-5	$750-$1,000
343	6-1/4"	TMK-6	$260-$265
343	6-1/4"	TMK-7	$255-$260
343/I	6-1/4"	TMK-8	$270

Hum 344: Feathered Friends

First designed by master sculptor Gerhard Skrobek and made in sample form in the mid-1950s, this piece was not released until 1972. Figurines have been found on the collectors' market, however, that bear earlier marks: Full Bee (TMK-2) and Stylized Bee (TMK-3). These are considered early samples and are worth substantially more than the figures released since.

There are no major mold or finish variations to be found that affect normal collector values.

This piece remains in production today.

Hum No.	Basic Size	Trademark	Current Value
344	4-3/4"	TMK-2	$4,000-$5,000
344	4-3/4"	TMK-3	$2,000-$3,000
344	4-3/4"	TMK-4	$750-$1,000
344	4-3/4"	TMK-5	$350-$370
344	4-3/4"	TMK-6	$340-$350
344	4-3/4"	TMK-7	$330-$340
344	4-3/4"	TMK-8	$350

Feathered Friends, Hum 344. TMK-6 mark, 1956 copyright date, 4-1/2".

TMK-8 variation of Feathered Friends, Hum 344.

Photo courtesy Goebel of North America.

Hum 345: A Fair Measure

This figure, the work of master sculptor Helmut Wehlte, was first made as samples in the mid-1950s, but it was not released until 1962. Early samples bear the Full Bee (TMK-2) and Stylized Bee (TMK-3) and are worth substantially more than the figures produced since.

At least two variations of this figure exist. The older design (1956 copyright date) shows the boy with

A Fair Measure, Hum 345. Left: Last Bee, incised 1956 copyright date, doughnut base, 5-3/8". Center: Last Bee, incised 1972 copyright date, split base, 5-5/8". Right: TMK-6, incised 1972 copyright date, split base. 5-5/8".

his eyes wide open. In the newer design (1972 copyright date) the boy is looking down so that it appears that he is looking at his work. See the accompanying photograph. This transition from eyes up to eyes down took place during the Last Bee (TMK-5) and can be found both ways with that trademark.

This figurine was temporarily withdrawn from production in January 1999.

Hum No.	Basic Size	Trademark	Current Value
345	4-3/4"	TMK-2	$4,000-$5,000
345	4-3/4"	TMK-3	$2,000-$3,000
345	4-3/4"	TMK-4	$1,000-$1,200
345 (old style)	4-3/4"	TMK-5	$800-$1,000
345 (new style)	4-3/4"	TMK-5	$350-$390
345	4-3/4"	TMK-6	$340-$350
345	4-3/4"	TMK-7	$325-$335

Hum 346: Smart Little Sister

The creation of master sculptor Gerhard Skrobek in 1956, samples of Smart Little Sister were first made in the 1950s, but not released for sale until 1962. It is nevertheless found with the earlier Full Bee (TMK-2) trademark, albeit rarely. The Stylized Bee (TMK-3) figures are not so rare; they seem to be available in a somewhat limited quantity.

There are no significant variations affecting normal values.

Hum No.	Basic Size	Trademark	Current Value
346	4-3/4"	TMK-2	$4,000-$5,000
346	4-3/4"	TMK-3	$1,000-$1,500
346	4-3/4"	TMK-4	$330-$360
346	4-3/4"	TMK-5	$300-$330
346	4-3/4"	TMK-6	$290-$300
346	4-3/4"	TMK-7	$285-$290
346	4-3/4"	TMK-8	$300

Today's version (TMK-8) of Smart Little Sister, Hum 346.

The Smart Little Sister, Hum 346. Left: Three Line Mark (TMK-4) and incised 1956 copyright date. Right: Last Bee (TMK-5) and incised 1956 copyright date. Both measure 4-3/8".

Photo courtesy Goebel of North America.

Hum 347: Adventure Bound

Also known as "Seven Swabians," this large, complicated multi-figure piece was crafted by Theo R. Menzenbach and first made as a sample in the mid-1950s but was not released for sale until 1971. It has been made continuously since, but it is produced in limited numbers because it is a difficult and time-consuming piece to make. They carry a 1971 incised copyright date.

There are at least three Full Bee (TMK-2) trademarked pieces known to be in private collections. These early samples are worth substantially more than pieces made since.

No significant variations affect normal collector value.

Adventure Bound, Hum 347. Three Line Mark (TMK-4), incised 1957 copyright date, and 8" long x 7" high.

Hum No.	Basic Size	Trademark	Current Value
347	7-1/4" x 8"	TMK-2	$10,000-$15,000
347	7-1/4" x 8"	TMK-4	$4,500-$5,500
347	7-1/4" x 8"	TMK-5	$4,000-$4,200
347	7-1/4" x 8"	TMK-6	$4,000-$4,100
347	7-1/4" x 8"	TMK-7	$3,975-$4,000
347	7-1/4" x 8"	TMK-8	$4,350

Adventure Bound, Hum 347, in today's TMK-8.

Hum 348: Ring Around the Rosie

This figure was first modeled in 1957 by master sculptor Gerhard Skrobek, but was not released until 1960 for the 25th anniversary of M.I. Hummel figurines. Sizes found in various price lists range from 6-3/4" to 7". The older ones tend to be the larger ones. They all bear a 1957 copyright date.

There are no significant variations affecting normal values.

Hum No.	Basic Size	Trademark	Current Value
348	6-3/4" to 7"	TMK-2	$10,000-$15,000
348	6-3/4" to 7"	TMK-3	$4,000-$5,000
348	6-3/4"	TMK-4	$3,500-$4,000
348	6-3/4"	TMK-5	$3,100-$3,200
348	6-3/4"	TMK-6	$3,000-$3,100
348	6-3/4"	TMK-7	$2,875-$3,000
348	6-3/4"	TMK-8	$3,200

Ring Around the Rosie, Hum 348 with Full Bee mark (TMK-2), in an incised circle and "© by W. Goebel, Oeslau 1957." There is a painted red "X" beneath the base, making it probable that this particular piece is a prototype.

Today's rendition (TMK-8) of Ring Around the Rosie, Hum 348.

Hum 349: Florist

This figurine, which was originally known as "Flower Lover" and crafted by master sculptor Gerhard Skrobek in 1957, was listed as a possible future edition in the previous edition of this book but has since been put into regular production as a new release for 2003. Those issued in 2003 will carry the "First Issue 2003" backstamp, as well as TMK-8. This figurine is the fourth edition in the matching plate and figurine series. The plate (Hum 924) carries the same name and is the Annual Plate for 2003.

Early samples do exist in earlier trademarks, but only one example is known to be in a private collection.

Hum No.	Basic Size	Trademark	Current Value
349	6-3/4" to 7-1/2"	TMK-2	$4,000-$5,000
349	6-3/4" to 7-1/2"	TMK-3	$3,000-$4,000
349	6-3/4" to 7-1/2"	TMK-4	$2,000-$3,000
349/0	5-1/4"	TMK-8	$300

The Florist, Hum 349/0, fourth edition in the matching plate and figurine series, 5-1/4" high.

Hum 350: On Holiday

First known as "Holiday Shopper" and made in the Stylized Bee (TMK-3) period, this figurine was a new release in 1981. Apparently a few samples, which were the work of master sculptor Gerhard Skrobek in 1964, were made in the Stylized Bee (TMK-3) and the Three Line (TMK-4) trademarks, for there have been a few uncovered. The remainder are found in TMK-5 or later trademarks.

In 2002, On Holiday was added to Goebel's special "Work in Progress" series of Collector's Sets. The series featured the figurine in three stages: one whiteware, one partially painted, and one complete. The set includes an authentic brush used by a Goebel painter and wooden display base. This was a limited edition of 500 sequentially numbered pieces available through QVC only. Hear Ye! Hear Ye! (Hum 15/0) was offered in the same type of progression set earlier in the year.

No significant mold or finish variations affect normal collector values.

Hum No.	Basic Size	Trademark	Current Value
350	5-1/2"	TMK-3	$4,000-$5,000
350	4-1/4"	TMK-4	$2,000-$3,000
350	4-1/4"	TMK-5	$1,500-$2,000
350	4-1/4"	TMK-6	$185-$190
350	4-1/4"	TMK-7	$180-$185
350	4-1/4"	TMK-8	$185

On Holiday, Hum 350. TMK-6. 1965 copyright date, 4-1/4".

Photo courtesy Goebel of North America.

Current-use TMK-8 variation of On Holiday, Hum 350.

Hum 351: The Botanist

First known as "Remembering" on early company literature, this piece is the 1965 design of master sculptor Gerhard Skrobek. It was not released, however, until 1982.

There is a very rare example of The Botanist known to exist with the Three Line Mark (TMK-4) and a 1965 copyright date. This is apparently an early sample. Another sample recently found with a 1965 copyright date has TMK-5 on it. All the newer pieces bear the 1972 copyright date.

The Botanist, Hum 351. TMK-6, incised 1972 copyright date, 4-5/8".

Hum No.	Basic Size	Trademark	Current Value
351	4"	TMK-4	$2,000-$3,000
351	4"	TMK-5	$1,500-$2,000
351	4"	TMK-6	$215-$225
351	4"	TMK-7	$210-$215
351	4"	TMK-8	$215

Today's TMK-8 version of The Botanist, Hum 351.

Hum 352: Sweet Greetings

Sweet Greetings was among the six new designs to be released in 1981, but it was modeled much earlier—in 1964—by master sculptor Gerhard Skrobek. Its original name was "Musical Morning."

Like a few other new releases of the time, it was apparently produced in limited numbers as samples in the Three Line Mark (TMK-4) era, for at least one figure is known to exist bearing that mark. Both the sample piece and the new release have a copyright date of 1965, although the sample is larger at 6-1/4".

Hum No.	Basic Size	Trademark	Current Value
352	6-1/4"	TMK-4	$4,000-$5,000
352	4-1/4"	TMK-5	$1,500-$2,000
352	4-1/4"	TMK-6	$215-$225
352	4-1/4"	TMK-7	$210-$215
352	4-1/4"	TMK-8	$215

Sweet Greetings, Hum 352, in present-day TMK-8.

Sweet Greetings, Hum 352. TMK-6, 1964 copyright date, 4-1/4".

Hum 353: Spring Dance

This figure, the work of several sculptors combined, first appeared in 1964. Early samples with the Stylized Bee Mark (TMK-3) do exist in both the 4-3/4" and 6-1/2" sizes. These samples are rare and are worth substantially more than the pieces released since.

The smaller size, 353/0, was released in 1978. The 353/0 with a Three Line Mark (TMK-4) is quite rare.

The larger size, 353/I, was temporarily withdrawn from production in 1982.

Spring Dance, Hum 353. Left: 353/0, Last Bee (TMK-5) 1963 copyright date, 5-3/8". Right: 353/1. Three Line Mark (TMK-4), 1963 copyright date, 6-3/4".

There are no significant variations that affect normal collector value.

Hum No.	Basic Size	Trademark	Current Value
353/0	4-3/4"	TMK-3	$3,000-$5,000
353/0	4-3/4"	TMK-4	$2,000-$3,000
353/0	4-3/4"	TMK-5	$390-$420
353/0	4-3/4"	TMK-6	$380-$390
353/0	4-3/4"	TMK-7	$375-$380
353/0	4-3/4"	TMK-8	$395
353/I	6-1/2"	TMK-3	$1,000-$2,000
353/I	6-1/2"	TMK-4	$650-$750
353/I	6-1/2"	TMK-5	$575-$600
353/I	6-1/2"	TMK-6	$550-$575
353	6-1/2"	TMK-3	$3,000-$5,000

Photo courtesy Goebel of North America.

Today's version (TMK-8) of Spring Dance, Hum 353/0, which is 4-3/4".

Hum 354/A: Angel With Lantern, Hum 354/B: Angel With Trumpet, and Hum 354/C: Angel With Bird (Holy Water Fonts, Closed Numbers)

These fonts have closed number designations. Three fonts exist in the Goebel archives as factory samples only. Apparently they were never produced in quantity due to Siessen Convent not approving the designs.

Hum 355: Autumn Harvest

Created by master sculptor Gerhard Skrobek in 1963 and first produced as a sample in the Stylized Bee (TMK-3) era, this figurine was not released for sale in any quantity until 1972. The earliest production pieces bear the Three Line Mark (TMK-4), but they are apparently in fairly short supply.

The figures have an incised copyright date of 1971.

There are no significant variations affecting normal collector values; however, the piece was permanently retired on December 31, 2002. Those figurines made in 2002 bear a "Final Issue 2002" backstamp and came with "Final Issue" medallion.

Autumn Harvest, Hum 355. Left: TMK-4, incised 1964 copyright date, and 4-7/8". Right: TMK-6, incised 1964 copyright date, and 5".

Hum No.	Basic Size	Trademark	Current Value
355	5"	TMK-3	$2,000-$3,000
355	5"	TMK-4	$1,000-$1,500
355	5"	TMK-5	$250-$275
355	5"	TMK-6	$245-$250
355	5"	TMK-7	$240-$245
355	5"	TMK-8	$250

Autumn Harvest, Hum 355, in today's TMK-8.

Hum 356: Gay Adventure

This figure, the design of master sculptor Gerhard Skrobek, was first produced as a sample in 1963 and was known as "Joyful Adventure" at the time. Early samples bear the Stylized Bee (TMK-3).

It was released for sale in 1972, bearing a 1971 incised copyright date.

There are no significant variations affecting normal collector values.

Temporarily withdrawn from production on June 15, 2002.

Hum No.	Basic Size	Trademark	Current Value
356	4-3/4"	TMK-3	$2,000-$3,000
356	4-3/4"	TMK-4	$1,000-$1,500
356	4-3/4"	TMK-5	$245-$265
356	4-3/4"	TMK-6	$240-$245
356	4-3/4"	TMK-7	$235-$240
356	4-3/4"	TMK-8	$245

Present-day version (TMK-8) of Gay Adventure, Hum 356.

Gay Adventure, Hum 356. Last Bee (TMK-5), 1971 copyright date, 4-3/4".

Hum 357: Guiding Angel, Hum 358: Shining Light, and Hum 359: Tuneful Angel

Originally crafted in 1958 by master sculptor Reinhold Unger with a 1960 copyright date, these angel pieces were not released until 1972. Issue price that year was $11 each.

They are sometimes sold as a set, although priced here individually.

There are no significant variations affecting normal values.

Hum No.	Basic Size	Trademark	Current Value
357	2-3/4"	TMK-4	$175-$225
357	2-3/4"	TMK-5	$115-$125
357	2-3/4"	TMK-6	$110-$115
357	2-3/4"	TMK-7	$105-$110
357	2-3/4"	TMK-8	$110
358	2-3/4"	TMK-4	$175-$225
358	2-3/4"	TMK-5	$115-$125
358	2-3/4"	TMK-6	$110-$115
358	2-3/4"	TMK-7	$105-$110
358	2-3/4"	TMK-8	$110
359	2-3/4"	TMK-4	$175-$225
359	2-3/4"	TMK-5	$115-$125
359	2-3/4"	TMK-6	$110-$115
359	2-3/4"	TMK-7	$105-$110
359	2-3/4"	TMK-8	$110

Guiding Angel, Hum 357, with TMK-6, 1960 copyright date, and measuring 2-7/8". Shining Light, Hum 358, with TMK-6, 1960 copyright date, and measuring 2-3/4". Tuneful Angel, Hum 359, with TMK-6, 1960 copyright date, and measuring 2-5/8".

Photo courtesy Goebel of North America.

From left, today's version (TMK-8) of Guiding Angel, Hum 357; Shining Light, Hum 358; and Tuneful Angel, Hum 359.

Hum 360/A: Boy, Hum 360/B: Girl, and Hum 360/C: Boy and Girl (Wall Vases)

Stylized Bee trademarked wall vases are considered rare. They were first produced in 1959, the work of master sculptor Gerhard Skrobek. For whatever reason, they were discontinued about 1960. All three pieces were then restyled and reissued in 1979 with TMK-5 and continued in production in TMK-6. They were temporarily withdrawn from production once again on December 31, 1989.

Of the three, the Boy and Girl (Hum 360/A) seems to be the most easily found. All three appear with the earliest and rarest Stylized Bee (TMK-3) trademark. Their basic size is 4-1/2" x 6".

Hum No.	Basic Size	Trademark	Current Value
360/A	4-1/2" x 6"	TMK-3	$525-$675
360/A	4-1/2" x 6"	TMK-5	$175-$185
360/A	4-1/2" x 6"	TMK-6	$165-$175
360/B	4-1/2" x 6"	TMK-3	$500-$650
360/B	4-1/2" x 6"	TMK-5	$150-$160
360/B	4-1/2" x 6"	TMK-6	$140-$150
360/C	4-1/2" x 6"	TMK-3	$500-$650
360/C	4-1/2" x 6"	TMK-5	$150-$160
360/C	4-1/2" x 6"	TMK-6	$140-$150

Wall vases, Hum 360/C, Hum 360/B, Hum 360/A. All three bear an incised Stylized Bee trademark (TMK-3), "by W. Goebel," black "Western Germany," incised 1958 copyright date and measure 5-3/4".

Hum 361: Favorite Pet

First made in prototype by master sculptor Theo R. Menzenbach in 1959, this figure was released for sale at the World's Fair in New York City in 1964. Early samples do exist with the Full Bee Mark (TMK-2) and are worth significantly more than the figures released since. All pieces carry a 1960 incised copyright date.

There are no significant variations affecting normal collector values.

Hum No.	Basic Size	Trademark	Current Value
361	4-1/2"	TMK-2	$4,000-$5,000
361	4-1/2"	TMK-3	$1,200-$1,700

Hum No.	Basic Size	Trademark	Current Value
361	4-1/2"	TMK-4	$375-$450
361	4-1/2"	TMK-5	$350-$375
361	4-1/2"	TMK-6	$345-$350
361	4-1/2"	TMK-7	$340-$345
361	4-1/2"	TMK-8	$340

Today's rendition (TMK-8) of Favorite Pet, Hum 361.

Favorite Pet, Hum 361. Three Line Mark (TMK-4), 1960 copyright date, doughnut base, and 4-1/4".

Photo courtesy Goebel of North America.

Hum 362: I Forgot (Possible Future Edition)

Made in sample form by master sculptor Theo R. Menzenbach in 1959 and originally listed as "Thoughtful," this figure has not yet been released for sale. It bears the Last Bee (TMK-5) trademark and a copyright date of 1959.

Early samples do exist in the factory archives in the Full Bee (TMK-2), Stylized Bee (TMK-3), and Three Line (TMK-4) trademarks.

Hum No.	Basic Size	Trademark	Current Value
362	4-1/4"	TMK-2	$4,000-$5,000
362	4-1/4"	TMK-3	$3,000-$4,000
362	4-1/4"	TMK-4	$2,000-$3,000
362	4-1/4"	TMK-5	$1,000-$2,000

I Forgot, Hum 362, shown here in sample form upright and turned on its side to expose the base markings.

Hum 363: Big Housecleaning

The original sample models of this figure, created by master sculptor Gerhard Skrobek in 1959, were made during the Full Bee (TMK-2) era. Released in 1972 at $28.50 apiece, these figurines bear an incised 1960 copyright date.

There are no significant variations affecting normal value for the figures.

Temporarily withdrawn from production in January 1999.

Hum No.	Basic Size	Trademark	Current Value
363	4"	TMK-2	$4,000-$5,000
363	4"	TMK-3	$2,000-$3,000
363	4"	TMK-4	$1,000-$1,500
363	4"	TMK-5	$350-$375
363	4"	TMK-6	$340-$350
363	4"	TMK-7	$320-$330

Big Housecleaning, Hum 363. TMK-6, incised 1980 copyright date, 4".

Hum 364: Supreme Protection

This piece, the fine craftsmanship of master sculptor Gerhard Skrobek in 1963, is a 9" full-color Madonna and child and is the first limited-edition figurine ever offered to the general public by Goebel. Released in 1984, it had been scheduled to be produced during that year only, in commemoration and celebration of what would have been Sister M.I. Hummel's 75th birthday. The figure has a special backstamp written in gold lettering identifying it as such: "M.I. Hummel—IN CELEBRATION OF THE 75th ANNIVERSARY OF THE BIRTH OF SISTER M.I. HUMMEL."

As the first figures became available, it was discovered that some 3,000 to 3,500 of them were released with a mistake in the stamp. The M.I. Hummel came out as "M.J. Hummel." The factory tried at first to correct the mistake by modifying the "J" in the decal to appear as an "I." However, they attempted to change it by cutting the decal and unfortu-

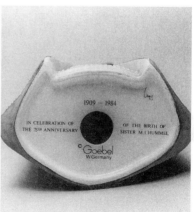

Supreme Protection, Hum 364. TMK-6 mark, 1964 copyright date, 9-1/8". Base photo showing the special inscription.

nately the modification didn't come off too well; the result demonstrated their attempt quite obviously. As a consequence there are three backstamp versions to be found: the correct backstamp, the poorly modified backstamp, and the "M.J. Hummel" incorrect backstamp. This particular backstamp variation is apparently in strong demand.

These Hum 364 figures have been found bearing the Three Line (TMK-4) and Last Bee (TMK-5) trademarks, but these are rare. They were probably sample pieces never meant to be sold.

Hum No.	Basic Size	Trademark	Current Value
364	9"	TMK-4	$3,000-$4,000
364	9"	TMK-5	$2,000-$3,000
364	9"	TMK-6	$350-$400
(regular signature)			
364	9"	TMK-6	$400-$600
(M.J. variation)			
364	9"	TMK-6	$600-$850
(M.J. altered version)			

Hum 365: Hummele

Listed as a possible future edition in the last edition of this book, this figurine has now been produced as a special exclusive edition to M.I. Hummel Club members only to commemorate the company's 90th anniversary in 1999. It was made for that year only and retired on May 31, 2000. It is the first club figurine to bear the newest backstamp (TMK-8).

This cute little cherub was first made in prototype by master sculptor Gerhard Skrobek in 1963 and has been listed in company records as both "The Wee Angel" and "Littlest Angel." The one in the accompanying photo bears the Three Line (TMK-4) trademark, an early sample that has blue eyes.

Hum No.	Basic Size	Trademark	Current Value
365	2-3/4"	TMK-4	$2,000-$3,000
365	2-3/4"	TMK-8	$150

Formerly called "The Littlest Angel," this particular example of Hum 365 bears the Three Line Mark and measures 2-3/4".

Exclusive edition of Hummele, Hum 365, in TMK-8.

Hummele, Hum 365, displayed here with a HummelScape.

Hum 366: Flying Angel

This figure, which was created by master sculptor Gerhard Skrobek in 1963, is commonly used with the nativity sets and has been produced in painted versions as well as white overglaze. The white ones are rare and valued at $300-$350.

The larger variation was first released in the Three Line (TMK-4) period and has remained in production throughout the years. It was renumbered as 366/I in TMK-8. The new smaller version (366/0) was introduced in 1989.

There are no significant variations affecting normal values.

Hum No.	Basic Size	Trademark	Current Value
366/0	3"	TMK-6	$130-$135
366/0	3"	TMK-7	$125-$130
366/0	3"	TMK-8	$133
366	3-1/2"	TMK-4	$225-$275
366	3-1/2"	TMK-5	$165-$170
366	3-1/2"	TMK-6	$160-$165
366	3-1/2"	TMK-7	$155-$160
366/I	3-1/2"	TMK-8	$160

Flying Angel, Hum 366, at 3-1/2" in TMK-6.

The smaller version of Flying Angel, Hum 366/0, at 2-3/4" in current-use TMK-8.

Photo courtesy Goebel of North America.

Hum 367: Busy Student

The combined efforts of several sculptors, this figurine was released in 1964 and has been continuously available since then. It has an incised 1963 copyright date and is similar to the girl in Smart Little Sister (Hum 346).

There are no significant variations in color, size, or design that affect normal values.

Hum No.	Basic Size	Trademark	Current Value
367	4-1/4"	TMK-3	$850-$1,000
367	4-1/4"	TMK-4	$225-$275
367	4-1/4"	TMK-5	$205-$220
367	4-1/4"	TMK-6	$200-$205
367	4-1/4"	TMK-7	$195-$200
367	4-1/4"	TMK-8	$200

Busy Student, Hum 367. Three Line Mark (TMK-4), incised 1963 copyright date, 4-1/4".

TMK-8 variation of Busy Student, Hum 367.

Photo courtesy Goebel of North America.

Hum 368: Lute Song (Possible Future Edition)

This figurine, which was designed by master sculptor Gerhard Skrobek in 1964 and first known as "Lute Player," is a standing girl playing the lute. This design is substantially similar to the girl in Close Harmony (Hum 336).

An early sample with the Three Line Mark (TMK-4) is known to exist, but it has yet to be put into regular production.

Hum No.	Basic Size	Trademark	Current Value
368	5"	TMK-4	$2,000-$3,000

Hum 369: Follow the Leader

This figurine was first made in prototype by master sculptor Gerhard Skrobek in 1964, but not released for sale until 1972 at $110. It carries a 1964 incised copyright date.

Early samples bearing the Stylized Bee (TMK-3) exist and are worth substantially more than figures released since.

There are no significant variations to affect the normal values.

Hum No.	Basic Size	Trademark	Current Value
369	7"	TMK-3	$4,000-$5,000
369	7"	TMK-4	$1,700-$2,225
369	7"	TMK-5	$1,400-$1,550
369	7"	TMK-6	$1,375-$1,400
369	7"	TMK-7	$1,350-$1,375
369	7"	TMK-8	$1,350

Today's rendition (TMK-8) of Follow the Leader, Hum 369.

Photo courtesy Goebel of North America.

Follow the Leader, Hum 369. TMK-6, 1964 copyright date, 7".

Hum 370: Companions (Possible Future Edition)

This design, the work of master sculptor Gerhard Skrobek in 1964, is much like To Market (Hum 49), except that the girl has been replaced with a boy that is remarkably like the boy of Hum 51 (Village Boy). It has been listed as "Brotherly Love" in old company literature.

This piece has been found as samples in the Stylized Bee (TMK-3), Three Line (TMK-4), and Last Bee (TMK-5) eras, but has yet to be put into regular production.

Hum No.	Basic Size	Trademark	Current Value
370	5"	TMK-3	$4,000-$5,000
370	5"	TMK-4	$3,000-$4,000
370	5"	TMK-5	$2,000-$3,000

Hum 371: Daddy's Girls

Daddy's Girls, which was crafted by master sculptor Gerhard Skrobek in 1964, was a new addition to the line in 1989 at $130. It has an incised copyright date of 1964 on the underside of the base. It was first known as "Sisterly Love."

Because it was first made as a sample in the Three Line (TMK-4) and Last Bee (TMK-5) periods, early samples do exist with those trademarks.

Hum No.	Basic Size	Trademark	Current Value
371	4-3/4"	TMK-4	$3,000-$4,000
371	4-3/4"	TMK-5	$2,000-$3,000
371	4-3/4"	TMK-6	$270-$280
371	4-3/4"	TMK-7	$265-$270
371	4-3/4"	TMK-8	$275

Daddy's Girls, Hum 371. TMK-6, incised 1964 copyright date, 4-3/4".

Daddy's Girls, Hum 371, in present-day TMK-8.

Photo courtesy Goebel of North America.

Hum 372: Blessed Mother (Possible Future Edition)

This figure, which is credited to master sculptor Gerhard Skrobek in 1964, is a standing Madonna and child. It was once known as "Virgin Mother and Child."

An early sample is known to exist in the Three Line Mark (TMK-4), but the figure has yet to be placed into regular production.

Hum No.	Basic Size	Trademark	Current Value
372	10-1/4"	TMK-4	$3,000-$4,000

Hum 373: Just Fishing

This figure, which was designed in 1964 by master sculptor Gerhard Skrobek, was released in early 1985 at a suggested retail price of $85. Once called "The Fisherman," it measures 4-1/4" x 4-1/2" and carries a 1965 incised copyright date.

Early Goebel promotional materials referred to this piece as an ashtray. This was in error, and probably due to the tray-like base representing the pond.

Early samples exist with the Three Line Mark (TMK-4) and are worth substantially more than the figures released since.

Just Fishing was temporarily withdrawn from production in January 1999.

Just Fishing, Hum 373. TMK-6 mark, 1965 copyright date, measures 4-1/8" with the pole.

Hum No.	Basic Size	Trademark	Current Value
373	4-1/4" x 4-1/2"	TMK-4	$3,000-$4,000
373	4-1/4" x 4-1/2"	TMK-5	$1,000-$1,500
373	4-1/4" x 4-1/2"	TMK-6	$270-$280
373	4-1/4" x 4-1/2"	TMK-7	$265-$270

Just Fishing, Hum 373. TMK-6 mark, 1965 copyright date, measures 4-1/8" with the pole.

Hum 374: Lost Stocking

Made as a sample by master sculptor Gerhard Skrobek in 1965, this figurine was not released for sale until 1972 in the Three Line (TMK-4) trademark period. The suggested retail price at release was $17.50.

Early samples bearing the Stylized Bee (TMK-3) do exist and are worth substantially more than the figures released since.

No significant variations affect normal values.

Temporarily withdrawn from production on June 15, 2002.

Hum No.	Basic Size	Trademark	Current Value
374	4-1/2"	TMK-3	$3,000-$4,000
374	4-1/2"	TMK-4	$1,000-$1,500
374	4-1/2"	TMK-5	$190-$200
374	4-1/2"	TMK-6	$185-$190
374	4-1/2"	TMK-7	$180-$185
374	4-1/2"	TMK-8	$185

Lost Stocking, Hum 374. This piece bears the Last Bee (TMK-5) trademark, measures 4-1/2" and has an incised copyright date of 1965.

The most recent variation (TMK-8) of Lost Stocking, Hum 374, which was temporarily withdrawn in June 2002.

Hum 375: Morning Stroll

First produced in sample form by master sculptor Gerhard Skrobek in 1964 with the Three Line Mark (TMK-4), this figurine was released in 1994. It measures 3-3/4" (a full inch smaller than the pre-production sample, which had been known as "Walking the Baby"). Those produced in 1994 bear a "First Issue" backstamp. The production piece is known as Hum 375/3/0.

Hum No.	Basic Size	Trademark	Current Value
375	4-3/4"	TMK-4	$3,000-$4,000
375/3/0	3-3/4"	TMK-7	$210-$215
375/3/0	3-3/4"	TMK-8	$215

Morning Stroll, Hum 375. This is an early factory sample piece. The base of the sample Morning Stroll showing the Three Line Mark (TMK-4).

Today's variation (TMK-8) of Morning Stroll, Hum 375/3/0.

Photo courtesy Goebel of North America.

Hum 376: Little Nurse

This piece, which was the original design of master sculptor Gerhard Skrobek in 1965, was one of the two designs released in 1982.

Although most of them are found with TMK-6, it is known that at least one exists bearing TMK-5 with a 1965 copyright date. TMK-6 or later trademarked pieces have a 1972 copyright date.

Early samples, which were originally called "First Aid," are also known to carry the Three Line Mark (TMK-4).

In the wake of the terrorist attacks on the World Trade Center and Pentagon on September 11, 2001 and the resulting American military effort, Goebel alerted its M.I. Hummel Club chapters that it would make a commitment to donate appropriately themed figurines to local chapters to be used as raffle prizes. Any proceeds from such fundraising events would then go to benefit the families of the victims. Seven figurines, including this one, were selected as appropriate due to their patriotic or firefighter/police/medical personnel themes.

Little Nurse, Hum 376. Bears the TMK-6, is 4-1/8" tall and has an incised 1972 copyright date.

Hum No.	Basic Size	Trademark	Current Value
376	4"	TMK-4	$3,000-$4,000
376	4"	TMK-5	$2,000-$3,000
376	4"	TMK-6	$295-$300
376	4"	TMK-7	$290-$295
376	4"	TMK-8	$295

TMK-8 variation of Little Nurse, Hum 376.

Hum 377: Bashful

This figure was first made in sample form by master sculptor Gerhard Skrobek in 1966 with the Three Line Mark (TMK-4) and can be found in samples bearing TMK-4 as well as production models with the same mark. Both the samples and the production models in that mark are fairly scarce. Later marks are more easily found.

There are no significant variations that affect normal values. The older pieces generally have a 1966 copyright date and sometimes a 1971 copyright date, but the new production figurines do not have an incised copyright date at all.

Hum No.	Basic Size	Trademark	Current Value
377 (sample)	4-3/4"	TMK-4	$3,000-$4,000
377	4-3/4"	TMK-4	$1,000-$1,500
377	4-3/4"	TMK-5	$250-$275
377	4-3/4"	TMK-6	$245-$250
377	4-3/4"	TMK-7	$240-$245
377	4-3/4"	TMK-8	$250

Today's version (TMK-8) of Bashful, Hum 377.

Bashful, Hum 377, with TMK-5, incised 1966 copyright date, and measuring 4-5/8".

Hum 378: Easter Greetings

The early sample models of Easter Greetings were made by master sculptor Gerhard Skrobek in 1966 during the Three Line Mark (TMK-4) period of production and can be found in samples bearing TMK-4 as well as production models with the same mark. Both the early samples and the regular production figurines bearing this mark are scarce. They have an incised copyright date of 1966 or 1971.

There are no significant mold or finish variations affecting normal collector values.

The figure was temporarily withdrawn from production in January 1999.

Hum No.	Basic Size	Trademark	Current Value
378 (sample)	5-1/2"	TMK-4	$3,000-$4,000
378	5-1/2"	TMK-4	$1,000-$1,500
378	5-1/2"	TMK-5	$250-$275
378	5-1/2"	TMK-6	$245-$250
378	5-1/2"	TMK-7	$230-$240

Easter Greetings, Hum 378. Left: TMK-5 piece with incised 1971 copyright date and measuring 5". Right: The most recent variation (TMK-7), which is worth $230-$240.

Hum 379: Don't Be Shy (Possible Future Edition)

This figure, the design of master sculptor Gerhard Skrobek in 1966, is a little girl with a kerchief on her head. She is feeding a bird perched on a fence post. Originally called "One For Me, One For You," early samples exist in the Stylized Bee (TMK-3) and Three Line (TMK-4) periods, but the piece has yet to be released into regular production.

Hum No.	Basic Size	Trademark	Current Value
379	4-1/4"	TMK-3	$4,000-$5,000
379	4-1/4"	TMK-4	$3,000-$4,000

Hum 380: Daisies Don't Tell

This is the Goebel Collectors' Club Special Edition figure offered exclusively to club members in 1981. As with all the others, it could be purchased by current members with redemption cards for $80 in the U.S. and $95 in Canada. As of May 31, 1985, it was no longer available, except at substantial prices on the secondary market.

The work of master sculptor Gerhard Skrobek in 1966, it was originally called "Does He?" The copyright date is 1972. There is at least one early sample known to exist bearing the Three Line Mark (TMK-4) and one copyright date of 1966. This latter piece is exceedingly rare.

Daisies Don't Tell, Hum 380. TMK-6, incised 1972 copyright date, 5".

Hum No.	Basic Size	Trademark	Current Value
380	5"	TMK-4	$3,000-$4,000
380	5"	TMK-5	$1,000-$2,000
380	5"	TMK-6	$275-$300

Hum 381: Flower Vendor

Master sculptor Gerhard Skrobek designed this piece in 1966, but it was not released until 1972 at the end of the Stylized Bee (TMK-3) and Three Line Mark (TMK-4) era. It can only be found in the latter (which are considered early samples and are fairly scarce). It has a 1971 incised copyright date and has been found in rare occurrence with a 1967 copyright date.

There are no significant variations affecting values.

Hum No.	Basic Size	Trademark	Current Value
381	5-1/2"	TMK-4	$3,000-$4,000
381	5-1/2"	TMK-5	$305-$330
381	5-1/2"	TMK-6	$300-$305
381	5-1/2"	TMK-7	$295-$300
381	5-1/2"	TMK-8	$305

Flower Vendor, Hum 381, shown here in the current-use TMK-8.

Flower Vendor, Hum 381. Left: 5-1/8" piece with TMK-5 and 1971 copyright date. Right: Demonstration piece with only flesh tones painted in.

Photo courtesy Goebel of North America.

Hum 382: Visiting an Invalid

This figurine, the creation of master sculptor Gerhard Skrobek in 1966, was released first in 1972 during the Three Line (TMK-4) era but is scarce and hard to find with that trademark.

There are no significant variations in color, size, or design.

It was temporarily withdrawn from production in January 1999.

Hum No.	Basic Size	Trademark	Current Value
382	4-15/16"	TMK-4	$1,000-$1,500
382	4-15/16"	TMK-5	$250-$275
382	4-15/16"	TMK-6	$240-$250
382	4-15/16"	TMK-7	$225-$230

Visiting an Invalid, Hum 382, with TMK-5, incised 1971 copyright date, and measuring 4-7/8".

Hum 383: Going Home

Crafted by master sculptor Gerhard Skrobek in 1966, this new piece for 1985 was released at a suggested retail price of $125. The first examples, initially known as "Fancy Free," were apparently made in the prototype phase in the Three Line Mark (TMK-4) period.

There are no significant variations that influence collector values, but the piece has been made into two separate figurines: Grandma's Girl (Hum 561) and Grandpa's Boy (Hum 562).

Hum No.	Basic Size	Trademark	Current Value
383	5"	TMK-4	$3,000-$4,000
383	5"	TMK-5	$2,000-$3,000
383	5"	TMK-6	$390-$400
383	5"	TMK-7	$385-$390
383	5"	TMK-8	$395

Going Home, Hum 383, in TMK-6 with 1972 copyright date and doughnut base.

Today's variation (TMK-8) of Going Home, Hum 383.

Photo courtesy Goebel of North America.

Hum 384: Easter Time

Occasionally called "Easter Playmates," this figure was first produced in sample form by master sculptor Gerhard Skrobek in 1967 during the Three Line Mark (TMK-4). It was first released for sale in 1972, at the very end of that period, so the figures are fairly scarce in that trademark. It bears an incised 1971 copyright date.

There are no significant variations that affect collector value.

Hum No.	Basic Size	Trademark	Current Value
384	3-15/16"	TMK-4	$1,000-$1,500
384	3-15/16"	TMK-5	$300-$330
384	3-15/16"	TMK-6	$295-$300
384	3-15/16"	TMK-7	$290-$295
384	3-15/16"	TMK-8	$300

Easter Time, Hum 384, in TMK-5 with incised 1971 copyright date.

Present-day version (TMK-8) of Easter Time, Hum 384.

Photo courtesy Goebel of North America.

Hum 385: Chicken-Licken

This figurine, first designed by master sculptor Gerhard Skrobek in 1967, was one of the 24 pieces first released in 1972 with the Three Line Mark (TMK-4). It has a copyright date of 1971 and has been in production ever since. The original release price was $28.50.

In 1990, Goebel released a smaller size, 3-1/4", with the incised mold number 385/4/0. The recommended retail price at release time was $85. That variation was temporarily withdrawn from production in 1997 and has since been made a closed edition.

There are no significant variations affecting collector value.

Hum No.	Basic Size	Trademark	Current Value
385/4/0	3-1/4"	TMK-6	$125-$140
385/4/0	3-1/4"	TMK-7	$120-$125
385	4-3/4"	TMK-4	$1,000-$1,500
385	4-3/4"	TMK-5	$350-$375
385	4-3/4"	TMK-6	$345-$350
385	4-3/4"	TMK-7	$335-$345
385	4-3/4"	TMK-8	$350

Chicken-Licken, Hum 385, with TMK-5 and, incised 1971 copyright date.

Chicken-Licken, Hum 385, in today's TMK-8.

Photo courtesy Goebel of North America.

Hum 386: On Secret Path

The original design of master sculptor Gerhard Skrobek in 1967, this is one of the 24 pieces first released in 1972 in the Three Line (TMK-4) trademark. It has a 1971 copyright and originally sold for $26.50.

There are no significant variations affecting the collector value.

It was temporarily withdrawn from production on June 15, 2002.

Hum No.	Basic Size	Trademark	Current Value
386	5-1/4"	TMK-4	$1,000-$1,500
386	5-1/4"	TMK-5	$300-$330
386	5-1/4"	TMK-6	$295-$300
386	5-1/4"	TMK-7	$290-$295
386	5-1/4"	TMK-8	$300

Photo courtesy Goebel of North America.

On Secret Path, Hum 386. Left: TMK-5 piece with 1971 copyright date and measuring 5-1/4". Right: The most recent variation (TMK-8), which was temporatily withdrawn from production in June 2002.

Hum 387: Valentine Gift

This rather special figure, which was the original design of master sculptor Gerhard Skrobek in 1967, was the first special edition figurine available only to members of the Goebel Collectors Club (now the M.I. Hummel Club), an organization sponsored by, and a division of, the Goebel firm. The figure was originally released in 1977 at $45 with a redemption card obtained through membership in the club. The size is 5-3/4" and inscription on blue decal read: "EXCLUSIVE SPECIAL EDITION No. 1 FOR MEMBERS OF THE GOEBEL COLLECTORS' CLUB." The most commonly found piece bears TMK-5.

Older pieces (TMK-4) are significantly more valuable, especially those with a bird sitting on top of the heart, which is inscribed with "i hab di gern" (translation: "I love you very much"). A few TMK-4 pieces without the inscription have surfaced over the years and sell for the same as the TMK-4 pieces without the bird ($2,000-$3,000).

As of May 31, 1984, the piece was no longer available except on the secondary market.

Valentine Gift, Hum 387, with matching M.I. Hummel Club exclusive miniature as a pendant. Figurine carries TMK-5, incised 1972 copyright date, and is a M.I. Hummel Club exclusive.

Hum No.	Basic Size	Trademark	Current Value
387 (with bird)	5-3/4"	TMK-4	$5,000-$7,500
387	5-3/4"	TMK-4	$2,000-$3,000
387	5-3/4"	TMK-5	$475-$600

Hum 388: Little Band (Candleholder)

The original design of master sculptor Gerhard Skrobek in 1967, this is a three-figure piece utilizing Hum 389, 390, and 391 on one base. It contains a candle receptacle. It was released in the Three Line (TMK-4) period and bears a 1968 incised copyright date.

This piece was temporarily withdrawn from production on December 31, 1990.

Little Band candleholder, Hum 388.

Hum No.	Basic Size	Trademark	Current Value
368	3" x 4-3/4"	TMK-4	$350-$450
368	3" x 4-3/4"	TMK-5	$300-$350
368	3" x 4-3/4"	TMK-6	$250-$300

Hum 388/M: Little Band (Candleholder and Music Box)

This is the same piece as Hum 388, but it is mounted on a wooden base with a music box inside. When the music box plays, the Little Band figure rotates. No significant variations affect collector values, but there are variations known in the type of music box as well as the tune played.

Goebel placed this figure on a list of pieces taken out of production temporarily on December 31, 1990.

Little Band music box and candleholder, Hum 388/M.

Hum No.	Basic Size	Trademark	Current Value
388/M	4-3/4" x 5"	TMK-4	$475-$500
388/M	4-3/4" x 5"	TMK-5	$450-$475
388/M	4-3/4" x 5"	TMK-6	$400-$425

Hum 389: Girl With Sheet Music, Hum 390: Boy With Accordion, and Hum 391: Girl With Trumpet (Little Band)

These three pieces, which were designed by master sculptor Gerhard Skrobek in 1968, are the same figures used on Hum 388, 388/M, 392, and 392/M. They each carry an incised 1968 copyright date.

No significant variations affect collector values for the various trademarked pieces.

Hum 391, Girl With Trumpet, was temporarily withdrawn from production on June 15, 2002.

Children Trio: Girl With Sheet Music, Hum 389, in TMK-5; Boy With Accordion, Hum 390, in TMK-4; and Girl With Trumpet, Hum 391, in TMK-5.

Hum No.	Basic Size	Trademark	Current Value
389	2-1/2"	TMK-4	$175-$225
389	2-1/2"	TMK-5	$115-$125
389	2-1/2"	TMK-6	$110-$115
389	2-1/2"	TMK-7	$105-$110
389	2-1/2"	TMK-8	$110
390	2-1/2"	TMK-4	$175-$225
390	2-1/2"	TMK-5	$115-$125
390	2-1/2"	TMK-6	$110-$115
390	2-1/2"	TMK-7	$100-$105
390	2-1/2"	TMK-8	$100

Hum No.	Basic Size	Trademark	Current Value
391	2-1/2"	TMK-4	$175-$225
391	2-1/2"	TMK-5	$115-$125
391	2-1/2"	TMK-6	$110-$115
391	2-1/2"	TMK-7	$105-$110
391	2-1/2"	TMK-8	$110

Photo courtesy Goebel of North America.

The TMK-8 version of the three pieces that make up the Children Trio, left to right: Girl With Sheet Music, Hum 389; Boy With Accordion, Hum 390; and Girl With Trumpet, Hum 391.

Hum 392: Little Band

This piece, which was modeled by master sculptor Gerhard Skrobek in 1968, is the same as Hum 388 except that it has no provision for a candle. It has a 1968 incised copyright date. There are no significant variations affecting collector value.

Little Band is listed as temporarily withdrawn from current production status.

Hum No.	Basic Size	Trademark	Current Value
392	4-3/4" x 3"	TMK-4	$350-$450
392	4-3/4" x 3"	TMK-5	$300-$350
392	4-3/4" x 3"	TMK-6	$275-$300

Little Band, Hum 392, this time without a candleholder as in Hum 388 and 388/M.

Hum 392/M: Little Band (Music Box)

This piece is the same piece as Hum 392, but it is placed atop a base with a music box inside. When the music plays the piece revolves.

There are no significant mold or finish variations affecting values; however, there are variations in the type of music box as well as the tunes played.

This music box was temporarily withdrawn from production in 1990.

Hum No.	Basic Size	Trademark	Current Value
392/M	4-1/4" x 5"	TMK-4	$475-$500
392/M	4-1/4" x 5"	TMK-5	$450-$475
392/M	4-1/4" x 5"	TMK-6	$400-$425

Little Band music box, Hum 392/M, shown here with TMK-4, 1968 copyright date, and two of three base styles.

Hum 393: Dove (Holy Water Font, Possible Future Edition)

The design of this font, which was created by master sculptor Gerhard Skrobek in 1968, includes a flying dove and a banner with the inscription: "+KOMM+HEILIGER+GUEST+." This translates into English as: "Come Holy Spirit."

Only one known example exists outside Goebel archives. It is an early sample that bears the Three Line Mark (TMK-4).

Hum No.	Basic Size	Trademark	Current Value
393	2-3/4" x 4-1/4"	TMK-4	$2,000-$3,000

Hum 394: Timid Little Sister

This two-figure piece, which was first designed by master sculptor Gerhard Skrobek in 1972, was a new design released with five others in 1981. When released, the price was $190.

An early sample has been found with the Last Bee trademark (TMK-5) and is worth considerably more than those made since. Both the older pieces and the commonly found, more recent pieces bear the 1972 copyright date.

There are no significant variations that affect collector value, although on occasion, the girl can be found with eyelashes.

Timid Little Sister, Hum 394, shown here with TMK-6, 1972 copyright date, and a base split laterally beneath.

Hum No.	Basic Size	Trademark	Current Value
394	7"	TMK-5	$3,000-$4,000
394	7"	TMK-6	$515-$525
394	7"	TMK-7	$500-$515
394	7"	TMK-8	$530

Today's TMK-8 version of Timid Little Sister, Hum 394.

Hum 395: Shepherd Boy

This 6-3/4" figurine was first made as a sample by master sculptor Gerhard Skrobek in 1971 and later released in 1996 in a smaller 4-7/8" size with mold number 395/0. The first year's figures will be marked with a combination "First Issue 1996" and "125th Anniversary Goebel" backstamp, TMK-7, and an incised 1972 copyright date.

An early sample, once called "Young Shepherd," has been found bearing the Last Bee (TMK-5) with a 1989 copyright date. It is worth significantly more than those figures released since.

Shepherd Boy was temporarily withdrawn from production on June 15, 2002.

Hum No.	Basic Size	Trademark	Current Value
395	6-3/4"	TMK-5	$3,000-$4,000
395/0	4-7/8"	TMK-7	$310-$315
395/0	4-7/8"	TMK-8	$280

Shepherd Boy, Hum 395, with TMK-7.

The most recent variation (TMK-8) of Shepherd Boy, Hum 395/0, which was temporarily withdrawn from production in June 2002.

Hum 396: Ride Into Christmas

This figurine, which was first designed by master sculptor Gerhard Skrobek in 1970 and released in 1972, remains quite popular and is in great demand by collectors. In fact, in the summer 2002 edition of the M.I. Hummel Club's Insights newsletter, it is noted that Skrobek considered this piece his favorite design of the hundreds he modeled during his many years at Goebel.

Goebel released a smaller version in 1982. The release of the smaller piece necessitated a change in the mold number of the larger one from 396 to 396/I.

The larger size bears a copyright date of 1971 and the smaller has a 1981 copyright date. There are no significant production variations that affect collector values for these pieces, although it should be noted that the same design was used on the 1975 Annual Plate (Hum 268).

Hum No.	Basic Size	Trademark	Current Value
396/2/0	4-1/4"	TMK-6	$275-$285
396/2/0	4-1/4"	TMK-7	$265-$270
396/2/0	4-1/4"	TMK-8	$290
396	5-3/4"	TMK-4	$2,000-$2,500
396	5-3/4"	TMK-5	$550-$575
396	5-3/4"	TMK-6	$525-$550
396/I	5-3/4"	TMK-6	$500-$525
396/I	5-3/4"	TMK-7	$495-$500
396/I	5-3/4"	TMK-8	$530
396/III	8-5/8"	TMK-7	PFE

Ride Into Christmas, Hum 396/I, the TMK-6 version shown with 1971 copyright date.

Photo courtesy Goebel of North America.

This version of Ride Into Christmas, Hum 396, is a demonstration piece with only the flesh tones painted on the face. It carries TMK-6 and an incised 1971 copyright date. It is worth $1,000-$1,500.

Ride Into Christmas is produced today (TMK-8) in two sizes: 5-3/4" (396/I, shown here) and 4-1/4" (396/2/0). The display shown here is the Gift Set, which includes Christmas Frolic Scape and retails for $495.

Hum 397: The Poet

The Poet, which master sculptor Gerhard Skrobek first crafted in 1973, was released in 1994 in a 6" size. Those produced in 1994 bear the "First Issue" backstamp, are marked Hum 397/I, and were temporarily withdrawn from production on June 15, 2002.

The figure was first made in sample form with the Three Line Mark (TMK-4), which are worth substantially more than any figures made since.

A smaller size (4") was issued in 1998 as a M.I. Hummel Club Exclusive (397/3/0). It was called "Poet at the Podium" and was crafted by master sculptor Helmut Fischer in 1988. Like other club figurines, it came with a redemption card. It was retired in May 2000.

Hum No.	Basic Size	Trademark	Current Value
397	6"	TMK-4	$3,000-$4,000
397/3/0	4"	TMK-7	$150-$175
397/I	6"	TMK-7	$250-$260

The Poet, Hum 397/3/0, shown here in the smaller, 4" size (TMK-7), along with desk piece.

Photo courtesy Goebel of North America.

The Poet, Hum 397/I, in TMK-7.

Hum 398: Spring Bouquet (Possible Future Edition)

This figurine, which was designed by master sculptor Gerhard Skrobek in 1973, is a girl picking flowers. She holds a bouquet in her left arm. Early samples have been found with the Last Bee (TMK-5), but the figure has yet to be put into regular production.

Hum No.	Basic Size	Trademark	Current Value
398	6-1/4"	TMK-5	$3,000-$4,000

Hum 399: Valentine Joy

This figurine, which was designed by master sculptor Gerhard Skrobek, is the fourth special edition offered exclusively to the members of the Goebel Collectors' Club (now the M.I. Hummel Club). Issued in 1980-81, the figures bear a 1979 copyright date and were available for $95 with the club redemption card. Each carries a special inscription on a blue decal that read: "EXCLUSIVE SPECIAL EDITION No. 4 FOR MEMBERS OF THE GOEBEL COLLECTORS' CLUB."

The wording on the heart translates to "I like you."

Although it is known that there are existing early samples with TMK-5 that are somewhat larger with a rounded base and bird at the boy's feet, the piece is normally found with TMK-6. The early samples carry a 1973 incised copyright date.

Hum No.	Basic Size	Trademark	Current Value
399	6-1/4"	TMK-5	$5,000-$7,500
399	5-3/4"	TMK-6	$250-$300

Valentine Joy, Hum 399, shown here at left with TMK-6, incised 1973 copyright date, split base, and at 6-1/4", while the one at the right is also TMK-6, but with a 1979 incised copyright date and height of 5-3/4". Note how the one at left has grass and a bird on its base.

Hum 400: Well Done! (Possible Future Edition)

This is a figure of two standing boys, which was originally crafted by master sculptor Gerhard Skrobek in 1973. The boy wearing shorts pats the shoulder of the other, who wears long pants.

Early samples are known to exist with TMK-5, but the piece has yet to be put into regular production.

Hum No.	Basic Size	Trademark	Current Value
400	6-1/4"	TMK-5	$3,000-$4,000

Hum 401: Forty Winks (Possible Future Edition)

Another Gerhard Skrobek design from 1973, this girl is seated with a small boy next to her. He is asleep with his head on her right shoulder. Early samples are known to exist with in TMK-5.

Hum No.	Basic Size	Trademark	Current Value
401	5-1/4"	TMK-5	$3,000-$4,000

Hum 402: True Friendship

Listed in the last edition of this book as a possible future edition, this figurine has since been placed into production. Master sculptor Gerhard Skrobek original designed the piece in 1973. It was first released in 2002, but early samples are known to exist with the Last Bee Mark (TMK-5).

Hum No.	Basic Size	Trademark	Current Value
402	4-3/4"	TMK-5	$3,000-$4,000
402	5-1/4"	TMK-8	$365

True Friendship, Hum 402, was released in 2002 at $365.

Photo courtesy Goebel of North America.

Hum 403: An Apple a Day

An Apple a Day, Hum 403, shown in TMK-6 with incised 1974 copyright date.

An Apple a Day, which was designed by master sculptor Gerhard Skrobek in 1973, was released in 1989. It carrires an incised 1974 copyright date. The price at the time of release was $195.

The fact that the design was copyrighted in the TMK-5 era makes it possible that the figure exists, at least as a sample, with that trademark. There are, however, no known examples of such sample pieces in private collections.

There are no significant variations that affect collector value.

Hum No.	Basic Size	Trademark	Current Value
403	6-1/2"	TMK-5	$3,000-$4,000
403	6-1/2"	TMK-6	$340-$350
403	6-1/2"	TMK-7	$330-$340
403	6-1/2"	TMK-8	$350

Today's variation (TMK-8) of An Apple a Day, Hum 403.

Photo courtesy Goebel of North America.

Hum 404: Sad Song (Possible Future Edition)

This figure, which is the 1973 design of master sculptor Gerhard Skrobek, is a standing boy singing. He looks as if he is about to cry and holds the sheet music behind his back with his right hand. Early samples are known to exist with TMK-5, but the piece has yet to be placed into regular production.

Hum No.	Basic Size	Trademark	Current Value
404	6-1/4"	TMK-5	$3,000-$4,000

Hum 405: Sing With Me

This piece, which was designed by master sculptor Gerhard Skrobek in 1973, was first released in 1985, although an early sample is known to exist in TMK-6. A copyright date of either 1973 or 1974 is found incised on the underside of the base. There are no significant variations that affect collector value.

Sing With Me was temporarily withdrawn from production in January 1999.

Hum No.	Basic Size	Trademark	Current Value
405	5"	TMK-5	$3,000-$4,000
405	5"	TMK-6	$375-$385
405	5"	TMK-7	$350-$360

Sing With Me, Hum 405, in TMK-6 with 1974 incised copyright date.

Hum 406: Pleasant Journey

Released in 1987, this piece, like the Chapel Time clock, is limited to those produced in 1987. The figure, which was crafted by master sculptor Gerhard Skrobek in 1974, is considered a closed edition. The original release price was $500.

Early samples in the Goebel archives bear TMK-5. The production figure, however, is found only with TMK-6. It was the second figurine in the Century Collection and carries a 1976 incised copyright date, the name "PLEASANT JOURNEY," and a blue decal with the following inscription: "M.I. HUMMEL CENTURY COLLECTION 1987 XX."

There are no variations affecting the figure's value.

Hum No.	Basic Size	Trademark	Current Value
406	7-1/8" x 6-1/2"	TMK-5	$5,000-$6,000
406	7-1/8" x 6-1/2"	TMK-6	$2,750-$3,000

The TMK-6 version of Pleasant Journey, Hum 406, with incised 1976 copyright date; a part of the Century Collection, 1987.

Hum 407: Flute Song (Possible Future Edition)

Master sculptor Gerhard Skrobek designed this figure of a seated boy playing the flute for the lamp standing in front of him in 1974. The boy is seated on what appears to be a stump. Early samples bear TMK-5, but the figurine has yet to be placed into regular production.

Hum No.	Basic Size	Trademark	Current Value
407	6"	TMK-5	$3,000-$4,000

Hum 408: Smiling Through

This is another redemption piece available only to members of the Goebel Collectors' Club (now the M.I. Hummel Club). It was released in 1985 at $125 to those with a redemption card. The mold number incised on the bottom of this figurine is actually 408/0. The reason for this is that a larger model was modeled by master sculptor Gerhard Skrobek in 1976, but never released. It was made as a sample only and resides in the factory archives now. This larger version was 5-1/2", while the one released to club members is only 4-3/4".

As of May 31, 1987, these figurines were available only on the secondary market and are found only in TMK-6. They carry a 1983 incised copyright date and blue decal with special inscription: "EXCLUSIVE SPECIAL EDITION No. 9 FOR MEMBERS OF THE GOEBEL COLLECTORS' CLUB."

There are no significant variations that affect value.

Hum No.	Basic Size	Trademark	Current Value
408	5-1/2"	TMK-5	$4,000-$5,000
408/0	4-3/4"	TMK-6	$350-$375

Smiling Through, Hum 408/0, in TMK-6 and carrying 1983 incised copyright date.

Hum 409: Coffee Break

This is another special edition piece, which was introduced in 1984, available exclusively to members of the Goebel Collectors' Club (now the M.I. Hummel Club). It was available to members with a redemption card until May 31, 1986. The issue price for Coffee Break was $90.

It is now available only on the secondary market and only in TMK-6; however, early samples made by master sculptor Gerhard Skrobek from an original Sister M.I. Hummel drawing do exist with TMK-5. The regular production pieces carry an incised 1976 copyright date, along with blue decal with special inscription: "EXCLUSIVE SPECIAL EDITION No. 8 FOR MEMBERS OF THE GOEBEL COLLECTORS' CLUB."

Hum No.	Basic Size	Trademark	Current Value
409	4"	TMK-5	$3,000-$4,000
409	4"	TMK-6	$300-$325

Coffee Break, Hum 409, with TMK-6 and incised 1976 copyright date.

Hum 410: Little Architect

New for 1993, this figure, which was crafted by master sculptor Gerhard Skrobek in 1978 and formerly known as "Truant," bears the mold number 410/I. It carries an incised 1978 copyright date and first-year pieces carry the "First Issue 1993" decal.

Early samples are known to exist with TMK-5, but the regular production pieces began with TMK-7. This piece remains in production today.

Hum No.	Basic Size	Trademark	Current Value
410	6"	TMK-5	$3,000-$4,000
410/I	6"	TMK-7	$345-$350
410/I	6"	TMK-8	$365

Today's variation (TMK-8) of Little Architect, Hum 410.

Photo courtesy Goebel of North America.

Hum 411: Do I Dare? (Possible Future Edition)

This figure, which was crafted by master sculptor Gerhard Skrobek in 1978, is a standing girl holding a flower in her left hand and a basket in the crook of her right arm.

Early samples do exist with TMK-5, but the piece has yet to be placed into regular production.

Hum No.	Basic Size	Trademark	Current Value
411	6"	TMK-5	$3,000-$4,000

Hum 412: Bath Time

The design of master sculptor Gerhard Skrobek in 1978, this figurine was released for sale in 1990 during TMK-6 era, but early samples do exist with TMK-5. It bears a 1978 incised copyright date and was $300 when issued. There are no significant variations that affect the collector value.

Bath Time was temporarily withdrawn from production on June 15, 2002.

Hum No.	Basic Size	Trademark	Current Value
412	6-1/4"	TMK-5	$3,000-$4,000
412	6-1/4"	TMK-6	$520-$530
412	6-1/4"	TMK-7	$505-$515
412	6-1/4"	TMK-8	$535

The TMK-6 variation of Bath Time, Hum 412, which bears a 1978 copyright date.

Hum 413: Whistler's Duet

This figurine, which master sculptor Gerhard Skrobek crafted in 1979, was released in late-1991. Early samples do however exist with TMK-5. It carries an incised 1979 copyright date and was $235 when released. No significant variations affect the collector value.

This piece was temporarily withdrawn from production on June 15, 2002.

Hum No.	Basic Size	Trademark	Current Value
413	4" to 4-1/2"	TMK-5	$3,000-$4,000
413	4" to 4-1/2"	TMK-6	$500-$1,000
413	4" to 4-1/2"	TMK-7	$320-$330

Hummel Mark (TMK-7) version of Whistler's Duet, Hum 413, with 1979 incised copyright date and "First Issue" backstamp dated 1992.

Hum 414: In Tune

One of six new designs released in 1981, this figurine was modeled by master sculptor Gerhard Skrobek in 1979. Early samples exist bearing TMK-5. Its basic size is 4", it carries a 1979 incised copyright date, and it is a matching figurine to the 1981 Annual Bell with the same name (Hum 703). Later, in 1997, the Springtime Serenade plate (Hum 297) also carried the same motif. There are no significant variations that affect the collector value.

The figure was temporarily withdrawn from production in January 1999.

Hum No.	Basic Size	Trademark	Current Value
414	4"	TMK-5	$3,000-$4,000
414	4"	TMK-6	$330-$340
414	4"	TMK-7	$315-$325

In Tune, Hum 414, in TMK-6 with 1979 copyright date.

Hum 415: Thoughtful

This figurine, which was the original work of master sculptor Gerhard Skrobek in 1979, is another of the new designs released by Goebel in 1981. It is a matching piece to the 1980 Annual Bell with the same name (Hum 702). The figurine has a 1980 incised copyright date and was $105 the year it was issued.

In 1996, Goebel issued a special edition of 2,000 Thoughtful figurines in conjunction with the release of master sculptor Gerhard Skrobek's new book *Hummels and Me, Life Stories*. The title pages on the special edition figurines' books are the same as Skrobek's book, the figurines were signed by Skrobek, and they bear the 125th anniversary backstamp. Collectors who bought that particular figurine in that year received the book for no extra charge.

Thoughtful, Hum 415, with TMK-6 and incised 1980 copyright date.

The present-day version (TMK-8) of Thoughtful, Hum 415.

Photo courtesy Goebel of North America.

Hum No.	Basic Size	Trademark	Current Value
415	4-1/2"	TMK-6	$275-$285
415	4-1/2"	TMK-7	$265-$300
(special edition)			
415	4-1/2"	TMK-7	$255-$260
415	4-1/2"	TMK-8	$270

Hum 416: Jubilee

Beginning in January of 1985, this very special figurine was made available to collectors. Production was limited to the number sold during 1985. The figure, which was crafted by master sculptor Gerhard Skrobek in 1979, has a special backstamp reading: "50 YEARS M.I. HUMMEL FIGURINES, 1935-1985." Right below the backstamp is the slogan, "The Love Lives On." This piece was made in celebration of the golden anniversary of Hummel figurines. The factory recommended retail price was $200.

At least two of these figures are found with "75" instead of "50" on the golden anniversary figure. The speculation is that this piece was originally designed to celebrate the 75th anniversary of perhaps M.I. Hummel's birthday.

Whatever the reason, the figures exist and their value would be in the mid- to high five-figure range.

Another unusual variation is one where the circle around the "50" is a shiny gold gift. This particular piece, one of only two known to be in private collections, bears TMK-5. Apparently Goebel had an idea for the golden anniversary, but the gilt didn't come out to the company's satisfaction after being fired, and it scrapped the idea. These figures are unique, and there is no way to realistically assign a value to them.

The normal Jubilees are found only with TMK-6 and an incised 1980 copyright date.

Hum No.	Basic Size	Trademark	Current Value
416	6-1/4"	TMK-6	$500-$600

Jubilee, Hum 416: Left example has TMK-6 and 1980 copyright date, while the one on the right is the variation with the gold gilt "50" as discussed in the acommanying text.

The special inscription backstamp beneath the base of Jubilee, Hum 416.

Hum 417: Where Did You Get That? (Possible Future Edition)

Crafted by master sculptor Gerhard Skrobek in 1982, this is a figure of a standing boy and girl. The boy holds his hat in both hands. It has three apples in it. The girl dangles her doll in her left hand. It is 5-1/4", carries a 1982 incised copyright date, and although it has never been put into regular production as it is, the two figurines that make up the piece do exist separately as Gift From a Friend (Hum 485) and I Wonder (Hum 486).

Hum 418: What's New?

Added to the line in 1990, What's New? was first modeled in 1980 by master sculptor Gerhard Skrobek. It has an incised 1980 copyright date and had a suggested retail price of $200 when released.

The M.I. Hummel Club announced a new edition of What's New? to honor the club's 20th anniversary. It is an exclusive members-only edition for the club year 1996-97. The newspaper the girl reads has the M.I. Hummel Club newsletter masthead (Insights: North American Edition) with an American or Canadian flag and the club dates. The inside also pictures the club's exclusive anniversary piece, Celebrate With Song, in full color. It was released to club members at $310.

Hum No.	Basic Size	Trademark	Current Value
418	5-1/4"	TMK-6	$340-$350
418	5-1/4"	TMK-7	$340-$350
(special edition)			
418	5-1/4"	TMK-7	$330-$340
418	5-1/4"	TMK-8	$350

Hum 418, What's New?, with TMK-6 and 1981 copyright date.

Today's rendition (TMK-8) of What's New?, Hum 418.

Hum 419: Good Luck (Possible Future Edition)

In this 6-1/4" figure, a standing boy has his left hand in his pocket, while he holds an umbrella under his right arm. Crafted in 1981 by master sculptor Gerhard Skrobek, it is a possible future edition only at this time.

Hum 420: Is It Raining?

This figurine, the design of master sculptor Gerhard Skrobek in 1981, was added to the line in 1989. The one in the accompanying photo measures 6" tall. It has a copyright date of 1981 and its retail price at release was $175. There are no significant variations to affect the collector value.

Hum No.	Basic Size	Trademark	Current Value
420	6"	TMK-6	$330-$340
420	6"	TMK-7	$325-$330
420	6"	TMK-8	$340

TMK-6 variation of Is It Raining?, Hum 420, which has a 1981 copyright date.

Hum 421: It's Cold

This is the sixth in a series of special offers made exclusively to members of the Goebel Collectors' Club (now the M.I. Hummel Club). It is available only from them initially, requiring a special redemption card issued to members. Each of these special editions has shown themselves to be good candidates for fairly rapid appreciation in collector value.

This figurine, the work of master sculptor Gerhard Skrobek following an original drawing by Sister M.I. Hummel, bears a 1981 incised copyright date and was sold with redemption card for $80. It is found only bearing TMK-6 and carries on blue decal the special inscription: "EXCLUSIVE SPECIAL EDITION No. 6 FOR MEMBERS OF THE GOEBEL COLLECTORS' CLUB."

There are no significant variations that affect the collector value of this figurine.

Hum No.	Basic Size	Trademark	Current Value
421	5" to 5-1/4"	TMK-6	$350-$400

It's Cold, Hum 421, in TMK-6 with incised 1981 copyright date.

Hum 422: What Now?

This piece, which was designed by master sculptor Gerhard Skrobek once again following an original drawing by Sister M.I. Hummel, is the seventh special edition issued for members of the Goebel Collectors' Club (now the M.I. Hummel Club). The usual redemption card was required for purchase of this figurine at $90.

What Now? Stands, 5-1/4" high, and since May 31, 1985, has been available only on the secondary market. It carries a 1981 incised copyright date and blue decal with special inscription: "EXCLUSIVE SPECIAL EDITION No. 7 FOR MEMBERS OF THE GOEBEL COLLECTORS' CLUB."

There are no variations that affect this figure's value.

Hum No.	Basic Size	Trademark	Current Value
422	5-1/4"	TMK-6	$350-$400

What Now?, Hum 422, with the matching M.I. Hummel exclusive miniature as a pendant. This M.I. Hummel Club exclusive figurine carries TMK-6 and 1981 incised copyright date.

Hum 423: Horse Trainer

Horse Trainer, which was designed by master sculptor Gerhard Skrobek in 1980, was added to the line in 1990 at a suggested retail price of $155. It carries a 1981 incised copyright date. There are no variations that affect this value.

Horse Trainer, Hum 423, in TMK-6 with 1981 copyright date.

Hum No.	Basic Size	Trademark	Current Value
423	4-1/2"	TMK-6	$265-$270
423	4-1/2"	TMK-7	$260-$265
423	4-1/2"	TMK-8	$268

Photo courtesy Goebel of North America.

Today's variation (TMK-8) of Horse Trainer, Hum 423.

Hum 424: Sleep Tight

A 1990 release, this piece was first crafted in 1980 by master sculptor Gerhard Skrobek. It bears an incised 1981 copyright date and has no significant variation affecting value.

Hum No.	Basic Size	Trademark	Current Value
424	4-1/2"	TMK-6	$265-$270
424	4-1/2"	TMK-7	$260-$265
424	4-1/2"	TMK-8	$255

The TMK-6 version of Sleep Tight, Hum 424, with 1981 copyright date.

Sleep Tight, Hum 424, in today's TMK-8.

Photo courtesy Goebel of North America.

Hum 425: Pleasant Moment (Possible Future Edition)

This 4-1/2" figure, the design of master sculptor Gerhard Skrobek in 1980, has two seated girls. One holds flowers in her left hand, while the other reaches down with her right hand toward a yellow butterfly. It carries a 1981 incised copyright date. At this time, it is a possible future edition only.

Hum 426: Pay Attention

Listed in the last edition of this book as a possible future edition, this figurine has since been placed into production, but not in the original 5-3/4" size. A 4-1/4" size (Hum 426/3/0), crafted by master sculptor Helmut Fischer in 1997, was released in 1999.

First modeled by master sculptor Gerhard Skrobek in 1980, the figurine depicts a girl sitting on a fence while holding flowers and a basket. She is looking away from a crowing blackbird perched on the fence post behind her. The original pieces carry an incised 1981 copyright date, while the newer, smaller pieces have a 1997 copyright date. The original 1999 issue price was $175. The 5-3/4" size, bearing TMK-6, is now considered an early sample.

Pay Attention, Hum 426.

Hum No.	Basic Size	Trademark	Current Value
426	5-3/4"	TMK-6	$1,500-$2,000
426/3/0	4-1/2"	TMK-7	$180-$185
426/3/0	4-1/2"	TMK-8	$190

Hum 427: Where Are You?

Listed in the last edition of this book as a possible future edition, this figurine has since been placed into production, but not in the original 5-3/4" size. A 4-1/4" size (Hum 427/3/0), crafted by master sculptor Helmut Fischer in 1997, was released in 1999.

In this figurine, a boy sits on a fence and holds a bouquet of flowers while a bird is perched on a fence post. It was originally designed in 1980 by master sculptor Gerhard Skrobek and those larger pieces carry a 1981 incised copyright date. The 5-3/4" size, bearing TMK-6, is now considered an early sample.

The newer, smaller pieces carry TMK-7 and a 1997 copyright date. The original 1999 issue price was $175.

Where Are You?, Hum 427.

Hum No.	Basic Size	Trademark	Current Value
427	5-3/4"	TMK-6	$1,500-$2,000
427/3/0	4-1/2"	TMK-7	$180-$185
427/3/0	4-1/2"	TMK-8	$190

Hum 428: Summertime Surprise

Again listed in the last edition of this book as a possible future edition under the name "I Won't Hurt You," this figurine has since been placed into production, but not in the original 5-3/4" size. A 3-1/2" size (Hum 428/3/0) was released in 1997.

In it, a boy with a hiking staff in his left hand looks down at a ladybug in his right hand. Master sculptor Gerhard Skrobek was responsible for the original design of this piece in 1980. This 5-3/4" size, bearing TMK-6 and a 1981 incised copyright date, is now considered an early sample.

The newer, smaller pieces, which were the redesign of master sculptor Helmut Fischer, carry an incised 1989 copyright date and TMK-7. The original 1997 price was $140.

Summertime Surprise, Hum 428.

Hum No.	Basic Size	Trademark	Current Value
428	5-3/4"	TMK-6	$2,000-$3,000
428/3/0	3-1/2"	TMK-7	$155-$160
428/3/0	3-1/2"	TMK-8	$160

Hum 429: Hello World

This piece was released in 1989 as an exclusive edition available to members of the Goebel Collectors' Club (now the M.I. Hummel Club) with redemption cards bearing the expiration date of May 31, 1990. It was designed in 1980 by master sculptor Gerhard Skrobek and carries an incised 1983 copyright date in addition to either TMK-6 or TMK-7. It further carries the special club "EXCLUSIVE EDITION" inscription on a blue decal.

There are already two variations to be found. In 1989, the club changed from the Goebel Collectors' Club to the M.I. Hummel Club. Apparently a few figures were released with the old special edition backstamp before the error was discovered. All those subsequently released bear the M.I. Hummel Club backstamp.

Hum No.	Basic Size	Trademark	Current Value
429	5-1/2"	TMK-6	$350-$400
429	5-1/2"	TMK-7	$300-$350

Hello World, Hum 429, in TMK-6 with 1983 copyright date.

Hum 430: In D Major

This 1989 release, originally designed by master sculptor Gerhard Skrobek in 1980, carries a 1981 copyright date incised beneath the base, and was released at $135. There is a "K B" on the boundary stone the little boy is sitting on that can be seen only by looking at the back. This is a reference to "Koenigreich Bayern," which translated to English means "Kingdom of Bavaria."

There are no significant variations to affect the value, although the piece was temporarily withdrawn from production on June 15, 2002.

Hum No.	Basic Size	Trademark	Current Value
430	4-1/4"	TMK-6	$245-$250
430	4-1/4"	TMK-7	$240-$245
430	4-1/4"	TMK-8	$250

In D Major, Hum 430, with TMK-6 and 1981 copyright date.

Hum 431: The Surprise

This figure, introduced in 1988, is the 12th special edition for members of the Goebel Collectors' Club (now M.I. Hummel Club). The expiration date on the redemption card was May 31, 1990.

The Surprise bears the incised copyright date of 1981 as well as the same date in decal beneath TMK-7. This figure, which was first modeled by master sculptor Gerhard Skrobek in 1980, is the first to also bear the little bumblebee that is to appear on all special editions for club members. It further carries on blue decal the inscription: "EXCLUSIVE SPECIAL EDITION No. 12 FOR MEMBERS OF THE GOEBEL COLLECTORS' CLUB."

It exists in TMK-6 as both an early sample and the exclusive member piece, but the sample is worth significantly more than the club piece. There is no club inscription on the sample piece.

Hum No.	Basic Size	Trademark	Current Value
431	4-1/4" to 5-1/2"	TMK-6	$2,000-$3,000
431	4-1/4" to 5-1/2"	TMK-6	$300-$350

TMK-6 variation of The Surprise, Hum 431, which bears a 1981 copyright date.

Many newer figurines come as part of Collector's Sets that include both a figurine and appropriate Hummel-Scape. Shown here is All Aboard, Hum 2044, with its free Homeward Bound Scape.

For Me?, Hum 2067/B, and Sweet Treats, Hum 2067/A, are coupled together here as part of the Gingerbread Lane Collector's Set.

Pretzel Boy, Hum 2093, shown here as part of a Collector's Set, which pairs the 4¼" figurine with matching Scape.

In 1994, Goebel announced production of the first M.I. Hummel figurine to feature an adult. Modeled by Goebel team of artists in 1993, At Grandpa's, Hum 621, was introduced in a limited edition of 10,000 sequentially numbered pieces for exclusive sale to members of the M.I. Hummel Club. A companion piece, A Story From Grandma, Hum 620, was released the following year with the same number of pieces and club exclusivity. Each of these pieces today is worth at least $1,500.

The spirit of Holy Year 2000 lives on with Millennium Madonna, Hum 855, which was released at the turn of the new century. It was a special limited edition of 7,500 numbered pieces worldwide. It carries the "First Issue 2000" backstamp, as well as TMK-8. It comes in a special, hinged, velvet-lined case. Now listed as a closed edition, it is worth $515.

Shown here are examples of some of the newest ornament variation in bas-relief. They are from left, beginning top left: St. Nicolas Day, Hum 2099/A; Ring In the Season, Hum 2129/A; Heavenly Angel, Hum 876/A; Sleep Tight, Hum 878/A; Christmas Song, Hum 879/A; Hear Ye, Hear Ye, Hum 880/A; Christmas Delivery, Hum 2110/A; Ride Into Christmas, Hum 877/A; Making New Friends, Hum 2111/A; and Cymbals of Joy, Hum 2098/C, which is actually part of an annual ornament series, explaining why the year is printed on the front while the others shown here do not have years on them.

ecently, jumbo versions of several figurines were released. hown here is Sweet Music with the jumbo 12½" piece Hum 186/III) on the left and the regular 5" edition (Hum 186) on e right. The jumbo piece is worth $1,550, whereas the regular MK-8 piece is $235.

Kids Club Collector's Set, which is made up of Love In Bloom, Hum 699; Practice Makes Perfect, Hum 771; and Heart's Delight, Hum 698.

The latest version of the annual M.I. Hummel calendar series is the 2003 edition and features Little Fiddler and Heart's Delight on the cover and then various other figurines for the monthly photos. A complete calendar listing can be found in Chapter Four.

wo examples of Shrine by Janet Robson. Each bears the Three ine Mark (TMK-4), mold number ROB 422 incised and inked in, dicating they are Mother Mold pieces. Both have the incised 961 copyright date and measure 5¼".

English/Beswick pieces. Left to right with their incised mold numbers: Meditation (910), Trumpet Boy (903), and Puppy Love (909).

A one-of-a-kind copy of one of the Internationals, Hum 851 in Hungarian dress. It was hand-made for personal enjoyment by a talented artist many years ago.

The unique Goose Girl with bowl, discovered in 1989.

Little Fiddler, Hum 4. The left piece is the doll face variation. Note the very pale face and hands, the completely different head position, and the lack of a neck kerchief. Each has the decimal point mold number designation 4. and the Crown Mark (TMK-1). Both are 5⅛".

Rear view of Sensitive Hunter, Hum 6, showing the "H" and "X" suspenders configuration discussed in Chapter Three.

A comparison between the normal skin coloration of Bookworm, Hum 8, at left and the pale coloration on the doll face piece at right. Both measure 4¼". The left bears a Stylized Bee (TMK-3) and the other has Double Crown Mark (TMK-1).

Two variations of Little Gardener, Hum 74. The one on the left carries the decimal point designator 74., incised Crown Mark (TMK-1), split base, and measures 4⅜". Note the height of the flower. The one at right is a TMK-6 piece and measures 4½".

The rear view of Globe Trotter, Hum 79, shows the different basket weave patterns discussed in Chapter Three. The older figure is on the left.

Happy Traveler, Hum 109/0. At left is a Full Bee piece (TMK-2) with black "Germany," doughnut base, and the normal green color coat. The other is a doll face Hum 109/0 with a blue plaid coat. It has no apparent base markings. Both measure 5".

Special edition of Auf Wiedersehen on a wooden base with the porcelain Airlift Memorial replica piece. It is made up of a 7½" wall piece and 5½" Hum 153/0 figurine. Both have special backstamp and were limited to 25,000.

Madonna plaque, Hum 222, with no apparent marks other than the mold number. Measures 4" x 5". The wire frame is detachable.

The Final Edition of Come Back Soon, Hum 291, which was issued in 1995 and completed the 25-plate series that began in 1971.

Whitsuntide, Hum 163. The piece at left carries an incised Crown Mark (TMK-1) and red candle in angel's hand. The variation on the right bears the Last Bee (TMK-5) and has no candle. Both measure 6¾".

Prototype of Concentration, Hum 302, with TMK-2. It has yet to be put into regular production.

Arithmetic Lesson, Hum 303, another TMK-2 prototype shown here that is currently listed as a possible future edition.

The Artist, Hum 304. The variation at left carries TMK-6 and incised 1955 copyright date. The other piece has an inked-in incised mold number indicating that it is a Master Mold piece. It bears a stamped Full Bee (TMK-2) and "© by W. Goebel, 1955." Note the paint drip on the base; this feature has never made it to the production piece.

Sunny Morning, Hum 313, with inked-in incised 313 mold number, Full Bee (TMK-2) in an incised circle, 1955 copyright date, "© by W. Goebel, 1956," and measuring 4¼".

Color Gallery

Relaxation, Hum 316, as a prototype piece at left with TMK-2 and as a M.I. Hummel Club exclusive at right with TMK-8.

Photos courtesy Goebel of North America.

The Art Critic, Hum 318, as a 5¼" demonstration piece with only the flesh tones and brown base color on the coat painted. It carries TMK-7, First Issue backstamp, and incised 1955 copyright date.

A Master Mold variation of The Professor, Hum 320. Note the red line around the base.

Two Three-Line (TMK-4) variations of Doll Bath, Hum 319. The one on the left has an incised 1956 copyright date and the other has an copyright date from the 1970s (impossible to discern the final digit).

In the wake of the terrorist attacks on the World Trade Center and Pentagon on September 11, 2001 and the resulting American military effort, Goebel alerted its M.I. Hummel Club chapters that it would make a commitment to donate appropriately themed figurines to local chapters to be used as raffle prizes. Any proceeds from such fund-raising events went to benefit the families of the victims. Seven figurines, including Call to Glory, Hum 739/I (above), were selected as appropriate due to their patriotic or firefighter/police/medical personnel themes.

At the Fence, Hum 324, has yet to be put into regular production. This is a sample piece (as indicated by the red line around the base) that carries TMK-2. Today, it is worth $4,000-$5,000.

Another TMK-2 sample, Helping Mother, Hum 325, is currently listed as a possible future edition. Because the figurine shown here is merely a prototype, it is currently worth $4,000-$5,000.

Two variations of Lucky Boy are shown here. The one on the left is a factory sample, Hum 335, with 1956 copyright date and height of 5¾". The other is a special 2½" limited edition carrying mold number 335/0, an incised 1989 copyright date, and 60th Anniversary backstamp.

Behave!, Hum 374, is shown at right in two variations. The one near right is a factory sample of the piece and is currently worth $4,000-$5,000. The other is the M.I. Hummel Club exclusive piece, which was released in 1996 for those marking 20 years membership. It carries TMK-7 and is currently worth $450-$500.

Birthday Present, Hum 341. The figurine on the left is an early factory sample measuring 5¼" and bearing the Stylized Bee (TMK-3). The one on the right is the smaller (4") TMK-7 piece with a 1989 copyright date.

An early factory sample of Morning Stroll, Hum 375.

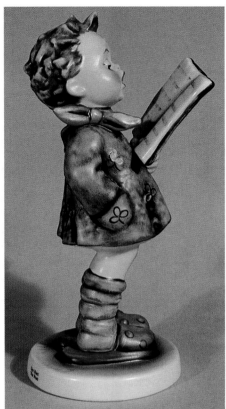

Shepherd Boy, Hum 395/0, was released in 1996 at 4⅞". The first year's figures will be marked with a combination "First Issue 1996" and "125th Anniversary Goebel" backstamp, TMK-7, and an incised 1972 copyright date. These TMK-7 pieces are worth $310-$315.

The Poet was released in 1994 in a 6" size. Those produced in 1994 bear the "First Issue" backstamp, are marked with Hum 397/I mold number, and are currently worth $250-$260. This variation was temporarily withdrawn from production on June 15, 2002.

Come Back Soon, Hum 545, is shown here with TMK-6 (left) and TMK-7 (right).

Rock-A-Bye, Hum 574, was the "Century Collection" piece for 1994. Today, it is worth $1,400-$1,600.

Star Gazer, Hum 132, was temporarily withdrawn from production on June 15, 2002. It is currently worth $245.

Looking Around, Hum 2089/A, was a M.I. Hummel Club exclusive first available in 2001 and retired on May 31, 2002. It is the first installment in the "Clowning Around" series, carries special "EXCLUSIVE EDITION" inscription, and is worth $230 today.

Another exclusive for club members only, Lucky Fellow, Hum 560, is 3⅝" tall and bears TMK-7, the special M.I. Hummel Club backstamp, and an incised 1989 copyright date.

Nimble Fingers, Hum 758, shown here at 4¾" high with 1993 incised copyright date and "First Issue 1995" backstamp. The other figurine is To Keep You Warm, Hum 759, which is the companion piece.

Welcome Spring, Hum 635, was the 1993 "Century Collection" figurine. Production was limited to that one year during the Twentieth Century. The 12¼" figurine is marked so on the base and comes with a certificate of authenticity. The decal inscription on underside of the base reads: "M.I. HUMMEL CENTURY COLLECTION 1993 XX."

This TMK-7 variation of Making New Friends, Hum 2002, carries the "First Issue 1996" and "125th Anniversary" backstamps. In 1997, it was the highest mold number utilized. That is no longer the case today.

We Wish You the Best, Hum 600, was the sixth figurine in the Century Collection, so it was produced as a limited edition for one year in 1991. It has an incised 1989 copyright date and circular inscription on a blue decal reading: "M.I. HUMMEL CENTURY COLLECTION 1991 XX."

Although not produced by Goebel, these ball ornaments do carry Hummel model numbers (the highest to date) and are featured in M.I. Hummel price lists and sales literature. Each measures 3" in diameter, features the design of one of the M.I. Hummel figurines, and retails for $49.

Celestial Musician, Hum 3012.

Christmas Angel, Hum 3015.

Angel Serenade, Hum 3017.

Christmas Song, Hum 3018.

Angel Duet, Hum 3016.

Festival Harmony With Flute, Hum 3019.

Festival Harmony With Mandolin, Hum 3020.

Heavenly Angel, Hum 3021.

There are two types of Nativity Sets, one small and one large determined by the size of figurines. The small one, Hum 214, is shown above, and the other, Hum 260, is shown below.

Wonder of Christmas Collector's Set, which pairs the Hum 2015 figurine with a Steiff bear. It was released in 1998 as a worldwide limited and numbered edition of 20,000. The set is worth $1,105 today.

Toyland Express, Hum 2018, and My Favorite Pony, Hum 2019, were made available only during special "Toyland Events" held in 2002. Each carried a "SPECIAL EVENT" backstamp and TMK-8 and came with a handmade Goebel porcelain pin.

Hummele, Hum 365, perched on top of a HummelScape here, was issued as a M.I. Hummel Club exclusive to commemorate the company's 90th anniversary in 1999.

Photo courtesy Goebel of North America.

Honey Lover, Hum 312/I, was released as a special M.I. Hummel Club exclusive in 1991. It is available to members after the 15th anniversary of their club membership.

Photo courtesy Goebel of North America.

Ring Around the Rosie, Hum 348, was first released in 1960 for the 25th anniversary of M.I. Hummel figurines and continues in the line today, shown here in TMK-8. They all bear a 1957 copyright date. It is one of the more valuable pieces with even the current-use pieces like this one selling for $3,200.

Photo courtesy Goebel of North America.

Harmony In Four Parts, Hum 471, was the 1989 addition to the Century Collection and therefore produced in that year only. The stamp on this figure is 1989 underlined, with the Roman numeral "XX" beneath it in the center of a circle made up of the M.I. Hummel signature and the words "CENTURY COLLECTION." Released at $850, this piece is now worth at least $2,000.

Photo courtesy Goebel of North America.

Adventure Bound, Hum 347, is one of the more complicated figurines since it quite large (7¼" x 8") and features multiple figures. It is this fine and detailed craftsmanship that makes it one of the more valuable pieces, ranging from $4,350 for a TMK-8 variation all the way up to $15,000 for a TMK-2 piece.

Photo courtesy Goebel of North America.

Originally released in 1991, The Guardian, Hum 455, was one of the first four Hummel figurines made available for personalization in 1996 as part of the "Personal Touch" series.

Another figurine in the "Personal Touch" figurine series began i 1996, Latest News, Hum 184, is able to be personalized perhap with a couple's last name and their wedding date as shown here

Photo courtesy Goebel of North America.

Shown here are two 25th Anniversary M.I. Hummel Club commemorative figurines: left is Picture Perfect, Hum 2100, and right is Camer Ready, Hum 2132. Considered companion pieces, both carry special "25th Anniversary" commemorative backstamps. The difference is th Picture Perfect was a sequentially numbered worldwide limited edition of 2,500 pieces and is therefore worth $3,495 in comparison t Camera Ready's current value of $525.

Four examples of the color variations of the Angels of Christmas ornament series, from left: Heavenly Angel, Hum 575; Festival Harmony With Mandolin, Hum 576; Festival Harmony With Flute, Hum 577; and Celestial Musician, Hum 578.

In 1992, Goebel made the Angels of Christmas ornament series available, but the finish is different. These small ornaments appear to have been made from the same molds as the Danbury Mint pieces, but they are rendered in white overglaze with only their eyes and lips painted in color. The wing tips are flashed in 14-karat gold. Each is worth $40.

Hello, Hum 788/A, and Sister, Hum 788/B, are the two perpetual calendars in the collection.

Ba-Bee Rings, Hum 30/A and 30/B, are two pieces that have been in continuous production since the original collection was released in 1935. The plaques shown here are the current-production pieces (TMK-8).

Soap Box Derby, Hum 2121, is the first edition in the "Moments in Time" series, which celebrates childhood. First available in the fall of 2002, the piece bears the "First Issue 2002" and "Moments in Time" backstamps, along with 2001 incised copyright date and TMK-8. This piece was limited to one year of production only and is worth $1,250.

These plates were part of the "Four Seasons" series that ran in consecutive years beginning in 1996. Each is 7½" in diameter and unique in that the design elements are three-dimensional rather than figural or bas-relief. They are, from top left: Winter Melody, Hum 296; Springtime Serenade, Hum 297; Summertime Stroll, Hum 298; and Autumn Glory, Hum 299. Each is worth $195-$200 today.

Little Scholar doll, Hum 522.

Apple Tree Girl doll, Hum 950.

Apple Tree Boy doll, Hum 951.

Ride Into Christmas doll, Hum 960.

Some of Sister M.I. Hummel's most beautiful pieces—and those perhaps most evident of her strong religious beliefs—are holy water fonts like the ones shown here, from left: Angel Duet, Hum 164; Angel Cloud, Hum 206; White Angel, Hum 75; and Guardian Angel, Hum 29.

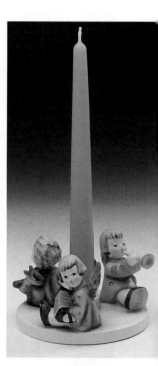

Not only are Hummel pieces beautiful, but many also serve utilitarian purposes, just as these candleholders do. Shown are, from left: Angel Lights, Hum 241, with its ability to hold four taper candles; Little Band, Hum 388/M, which not only holds a small taper candle, but also can be wound to play music; Birthday Cake, Hum 338, a single figurine with place to hold tiny candle; and Little Band, Hum 388, which is essentially the same as the other shown here but without the music box base.

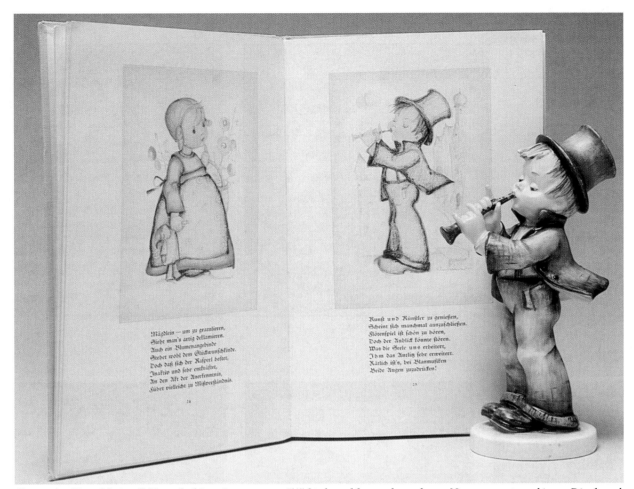

Serenade, Hum 85, in all blue clothing. It measures 7½" high and has a donut base. No apparent markings. Displayed here with a like illustration from a German book illustrating Hummel drawings. It is likely a prototype that never made it into routine production.

This particular variation of *Extra! Extra!*, Hum 2113, reflects the spirit of patriotism that arose in the wake of the September 11, 2001 terrorist attacks on the World Trade Center Towers and Pentagon.

Shown here are several pieces in the unique series of miniature Bavarian Village structures made of ceramic and electrically lit from the inside. They are not produced by Goebel, but each bears an M.I. Hummel facsimile signature and is listed in Goebel price lists and literature. As detailed in Chapter Six, there are 16 designs presently available and each is worth $60-$65.

Photo courtesy Goebel of North America.

Village Bakery.

Photo courtesy Goebel of North America.

Warm Winter Wishes.

Photo courtesy Goebel of North America.

Scholarly Thoughts.

Photo courtesy Goebel of North America.

Practice Makes Perfect.

Photo courtesy Goebel of North America.

Tending the Geese.

Photo courtesy Goebel of North America.

Apple Tree Cottage.

Photo courtesy Goebel of North America.

Village Pharmacy.

Photo courtesy Goebel of North America.

Clock Shop.

Tuneful Trio, Hum 757, is the first edition in the "Trio Collection" series. Issued on a hardwood base in 1996 in a limited edition of 20,000, each figure bears a "125th Anniversary" backstamp, as well as incised 1993 copyright date. The others in the series are A Trio of Wishes, Hum 721, and Traveling Trio, Hum 787.

Goose Girl anniversary clock, Hum 750, is one of the most unique—and most beautiful—pieces in the collection today. The TMK-8 piece shown here is worth $225.

Various plaques have been produced over the years to mark special occasions or to honor particular groups of people, including those shown here: Merry Wanderer authorized retailer plaque, Hum 900; Soldier Boy special military plaque, Hum 726; Puppy Love display plaque, Hum 767, which marked the 60th Anniversary of the making of Hummel figurines; and The Artist plaque, Hum 756, which marked the opening of the M.I. Hummel Museum in New Braunfels, Texas.

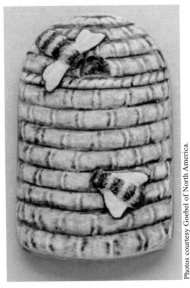

Shown here, from left, are three examples of handmade porcelain pins produced by Goebel recently: Basket of Flowers, Beehive, and Flying Goebel Bee.

In 1991, Goebel began producing Hummel figurines in 24% lead crystal. They each bore the incised M.I. Hummel signature, although the signature, TMK-6, and the year date 1991. Shown here is the entire collection. See Chapter Four for a complete description.

From left: Mother's Darling, Hum 175. Far left: Crown Mark (TMK-1), the bag in the right hand is pinkish and the upper part of her dress very light; Hum 175, Stylized Bee (TMK-3), bag in right hand is blue and the upper part of the dress very dark. Soldier Boy, Hum 332. Both of these bear the Three Line Mark (TMK-4). The one on the far right has the red cap medallion found on the earlier, more desirable pieces for collectors.

From left: Weary Wanderer, Hum 204. Both of these bear the Full Bee (TMK-2). The one on the left is probably the older of the two (the Full Bee is incised) and is referred to as the Blue eyes variation. Lost Sheep, Hum 68. Bears an incised Full Bee (TMK-2). It is the brown pants variation found on the older pieces. Far right: Last Bee (TMK-5) figurine illustrating the normal clothing colors.

From left: Kiss Me, Hum 311, with Three Line Mark (TMK-4), this is the older "socks on the doll variation," TMK-6 with the regular no socks version. Happy Birthday, Hum 176. Both are Crown Mark (TMK-1) pieces with the decimal designator "176."; however, the one on the far right also has a Full Bee (TMK-2). You can see that they are from different molds.

From left: Hello, Hum 124. The figure on the far left is the green pants, pink vest variation found on the older pieces. The Last Bee (TMK-5) figure to the right of the first one right is the norm for later releases. Next is Waiter, Hum 154, the older of the two figurines shown here, has an incised Crown Mark (TMK-1). It has gray pants. The right figurine has the brown pants found on the newer releases.

1990 Christmas Bells, Hum 776. The bell on the right is the normal color. The one on the left is the greenish yellow version made in limited edition for Christmas gift to company sales representatives.

Photo courtesy Goebel of North America.

Nutcracker Sweet, Hum 2130, was released in 2002 as part of a rather unique Collector's Set. This 6" figurine is a limited edition of 10,000 pieces and carries an incised 2000 copyright date. It is paired with an authentic Fritz von Nutcracker by Steinbach piece that measures 5" and was made exclusively for Goebel. The set is completed with an heirloom wooden chest.

Photos courtesy Goebel of North America.

Some of the newest additions to the line are trinket boxes in various shapes. Each carries an image of a figurine on top of its lid, as well as the M.I. Hummel signature. Shown here are: Umbrella Boy, Hum 688; Scamp, Hum 996; Pixie, Hum 997; and Sweet Greetings, Hum 686. Each is worth $50.

Madonna Holding Child, Hum 151. From left: Blue cloak and Full Bee (TMK-2); brown cloak with Crown and Full Bee marks; white overglaze with Double Full Bee (TMK-2).

Flower Madonna, Hum 10. From left: Normal color with Hum 10/III mold number and Stylized Bee (TMK-3); beige robe with orange piping, Hum 10/3 mold number, and Stylized Bee (TMK-3); white overglaze with Hum 10/III mold number and Stylized Bee (TMK-3).

Spring Cheer, Hum 72. Left to right: There is a Full Bee (TMK-2) piece, a small Stylized Bee piece, and a large Stylized Bee (TMK-3) piece. These three represent the major variations found in the older releases. The dress colors and the lack of flowers in the right hand are significant variations.

Sensitive Hunter, Hum 6. The left, mold number 6, is a Crown Mark (TMK-1) piece with the orange rabbit and "H" shaped suspenders on the back. The newer one on the right, Hum 6/0 with TMK-6, has the now common brown rabbit and "X" configuration of the suspenders.

Winter Adventure, Hum 2028, shown here as part of the Winter Adventure Collector's Set, which includes the Slalom Slopes Scape.

Ride Into Christmas, Hum 396. An interesting five-piece set from the Goebel factory illustrating an abbreviated version of the painting process.

Internationals. From left: Hungarian, Hum 853, with Crown Mark (TMK-1); Hungarian, Hum 852, with Crown Mark (TMK-1); Swedish, Hum 824; Swedish, Hum 824; and Swedish, Hum 824. Note the blue eyes.

Internationals. From left: Czechoslovakian, Hum 842, with Full Bee (TMK-2); Czechoslovakian, Hum 842, with Crown Mark (TMK-1); Country unknown, with Crown Mark (TMK-1); Serbian, Hum 913; and Serbian, Hum 913, with "(R)" marking.

Internationals. From left: Serbian, Hum 947/0, with Crown Mark (TMK-1); Serbian, Hum 947/0, with Double Crown Mark (TMK-1); Bulgarian, Hum 810, with Double Crown Mark (TMK-1); and Bulgarian, Hum 810, with Crown Mark (TMK-1).

Internationals. From left: Bulgarian, Mel. 9, with Double Crown Mark (TMK-1); Bulgarian, Bul. 2, with Crown Mark (TMK-1); Serbian, Hum 904, with Full Bee (TMK-2); and Bulgarian, Hum 811, with Double Crown Mark (TMK-1).

Internationals. From left: Country unknown, no apparent markings; Slovak dress, with an incised 82 or 89, but known to be Hum 831; and probably Serbian, Hum 806.

In 1971, Schmid began issuing annual Christmas plates with Hummel motifs. The following year, the annual Mother's Day plates began. Shown here are the plates for 1988: Cheerful Cherubs (Christmas, $65-$70) and Young Reader (Mother's Day, $85). A complete listing of the plates and their current values can be found in Chapter Six.

Released in 2002, The Final Sculpt, Hum 2180, is a sequentially numbered limited edition of 8,000 pieces and available only at selected retailers (those involved in former master sculptor Gerhard Skrobek's 2002 Farewell Tour). Each piece is signed by Skrobek, has a special backstamp, carries an incised 2001 copyright date, and comes with a Skrobek silhouette commemorative medallion. To date, it is the highest mold number for a regular Hummel figurine.

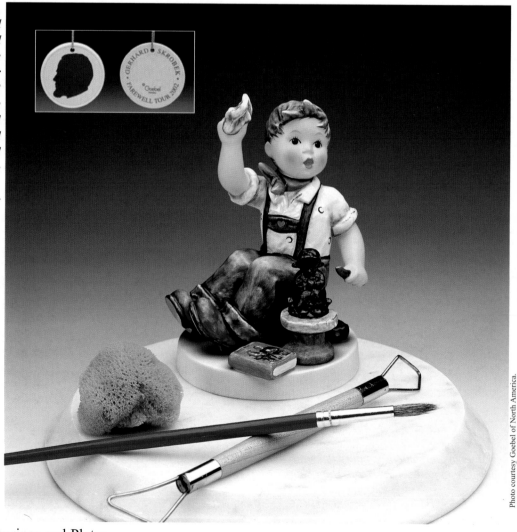

Hum 432: Knit One, Purl One

This figurine, the design of master sculptor Gerhard Skrobek in 1982, was a new addition to the line in 1983. It was made to go with the 1982 annual bell "Knit One" of the same motif (Hum 705). The figurine has an incised 1982 copyright date and no base. It was originally issued at $52.

There are no significant variations to affect collector values.

Hum No.	Basic Size	Trademark	Current Value
432	3"	TMK-6	$150-$155
432	3"	TMK-7	$145-$150
432	3"	TMK-8	$155

Knit One, Purl One, Hum 432, with TMK-6 and 1982 copyright date.

TMK-8 variation of Knit One, Purl One, Hum 432.

Photo courtesy Goebel of North America.

Hum 433: Sing Along

Released in 1987 at $145, this figure bears an incised copyright date of 1982 and was made to go with the 1986 annual bell of the same name and motif (Hum 708). Master sculptor Gerhard Skrobek first modeled it in 1981.

There are no variations to affect the collector value, but it has been temporarily withdrawn from production since January 1999.

Hum No.	Basic Size	Trademark	Current Value
433	4-1/2"	TMK-6	$330-$340
433	4-1/2"	TMK-7	$310-$320

Sing Along, Hum 433, in TMK-6 and carrying a 1982 copyright date.

TMK-7 version of Sing Along, Hum 433, which has been temporarily withdrawn.

Photo courtesy Goebel of North America.

Hum 434: Friend or Foe?

This 4" figure, released in 1991 at a $190 suggested retail price, bears an incised 1982 copyright date. Master sculptor Gerhard Skrobek first designed the piece in 1981.

There are no variations to affect the price of the normal production pieces, although it was temporarily withdrawn from production on June 15, 2002.

Hum No.	Basic Size	Trademark	Current Value
434	4"	TMK-6	$265-$270
434	4"	TMK-7	$260-$265
434	4"	TMK-8	$255

Three examples of Friend or Foe?, Hum 434, shown from left: TMK-6 piece with incised 1982 copyright date and "First Issue" backstamp dated 1991; a demonstration piece, worth $500, with only flesh tones and dress painted, TMK-7, incised 1982 copyright date, and measuring 3-7/8"; and today's variation (TMK-8) at 4" and worth $255.

Hum 435: Delicious

Originally made by master sculptor Gerhard Skrobek in 6" samples bearing a TMK-6, this figurine was not released until 1996 in a 3-7/8" size (Hum 435/3/0). It has an incised 1988 copyright date and two special backstamps: the "First Issue 1996" and the "125th Anniversary Goebel." Both appear only on those pieces produced in 1996. The issue price was $155 in the year of release, but the early samples are now worth significantly more than those released since.

This piece (435/3/0) was temporarily withdrawn from production on June 15, 2002.

Hum No.	Basic Size	Trademark	Current Value
435	6"	TMK-6	$2,000-$3,000
435/3/0	3-7/8"	TMK-7	$170-$175
435/3/0	3-7/8"	TMK-8	$175

Today's variation (TMK-8) of Delicious, Hum 435/3/0.

Delicious, Hum 435.

Hum 436: An Emergency (Possible Future Edition)

This 5-1/2" figurine, crafted by master sculptor Gerhard Skrobek in 1981, is a boy with a bandage on his head. He is about to push the button on the doctor's gate. At this time, it is a possible future edition only.

Hum 437: Tuba Player

This figurine, the 1982 design of master sculptor Gerhard Skrobek, was released in the winter of 1989. It carries a 1983 copyright date. Suggested retail price in 1989 was $160.

There are no variations to affect the value, but it was temporarily withdrawn from production on June 15, 2002.

Hum No.	Basic Size	Trademark	Current Value
437	6-1/4"	TMK-6	$335-$345
437	6-1/4"	TMK-7	$325-$335
437	6-1/4"	TMK-8	$320

Tuba Player, Hum 437, in TMK-6 with 1983 copyright date.

Today's variation (TMK-8) of Tuba Player, Hum 437.

Photo courtesy Goebel of North America.

Hum 438: Sounds of the Mandolin

This 3-3/4" figure was released in 1988 for $65 as one of three musical angel pieces. The other two were Song of Praise (Hum 454) and The Accompanist (Hum 453). First sculpted by master sculptor Gerhard Skrobek in 1982, it carries an incised 1984 copyright date and was first called "Mandolin Serenade."

There are no variations to affect that value; however, it was temporarily withdrawn from production on June 15, 2002.

Hum No.	Basic Size	Trademark	Current Value
438	3-3/4"	TMK-6	$160-$165
438	3-3/4"	TMK-7	$155-$160
438	3-3/4"	TMK-8	$160

Sounds of the Mandolin, Hum 438, in TMK-6 with incised 1984 copyright date.

The most recent variation (TMK-8) of Sounds of the Mandolin, Hum 438.

Photo courtesy Goebel of North America.

Hum 439: A Gentle Glow (Candleholder)

Released in 1987 at $110, this piece is a small standing child originally modeled by master sculptor Gerhard Skrobek in 1982. The candle receptacle appears to be resting on greenery that the child holds up with both hands. It carries a 1983 incised copyright date.

The figurine is found only in TMK-6 and TMK-7 as it was temporarily withdrawn from production in January 1999. There are no variations to affect the collector value.

Hum No.	Basic Size	Trademark	Current Value
439	5-1/4" to 5-1/2"	TMK-6	$240-$250
439	5-1/4" to 5-1/2"	TMK-7	$235-$240

A Gentle Glow candleholder, Hum 439, with TMK-6.

Hum 440: Birthday Candle (Candleholder)

This 5-1/2" candleholder, which was designed by master sculptor Gerhard Skrobek following an original M.I. Hummel drawing, is the 10th exclusive edition available to members of the Goebel Collectors' Club (now the M.I. Hummel Club). It bears a 1983 copyright date and the following inscription on blue decal: "EXCLUSIVE SPECIAL EDITION No. 10 FOR MEMBERS OF THE GOEBEL COLLECTORS' CLUB." It was released at $95, and the redemption card cut-off date was May 31, 1988. The figure was released in conjunction with the 10th anniversary celebration of the founding of the club. This piece is found in TMK-6 only. There are no variations affecting value.

Hum No.	Basic Size	Trademark	Current Value
440	5-1/2"	TMK-6	$350-$400

Birthday Candle candleholder, Hum 440, in TMK-6 with incised 1983 copyright date.

Hum 441: Call to Worship (Clock)

Introduced in 1988, this is only the second clock ever made from a Hummel design. First crafted by master sculptor Gerhard Skrobek in 1982, it stands 13" tall and chimes every hour. You can choose from two tunes by moving a switch beneath the figure. The tunes are "Ave Maria" and the "Westminster Chimes."

This is the second offering in what Goebel calls the Century Collection, a group of pieces produced in the 20th century with a one-year limited production. Figures in the collection bear the Roman numeral "XX" on their bases. The suggested retail price in 1988 was $600. These figures can be found in TMK-6 only with an incised 1983 copyright date.

There are no variations that affect value.

Hum No.	Basic Size	Trademark	Current Value
441	13"	TMK-6	$1,400-$1,500

Call to Worship clock, Hum 441, with TMK-6 and 1988 incised copyright date; part of the Century Collection, 1988.

Hum 442: Chapel Time (Clock)

This is the first clock to be put into production and released by Goebel. It was limited to one year of production (1986) and could not be made again in the 20th century. Included with the artist's mark and date on the bottom is the Roman numeral "XX," indicating the 20th century. The base also bears TMK-6, incised 1983 copyright date, and a blue M.I. Hummel signature with the inscription "The Love Lives On."

The original design of master sculptor Gerhard Skrobek in 1982, there are several variations of this piece, mostly having to do with the windows in the chapel building. So far the most common version has all windows closed and painted except for the four in the belfry. The rarest is a version with all windows closed and painted. According to Goebel, this version was a pre-production run numbering 800 to 1,000 pieces. Reportedly a few of these have been found with the two small round windows in the gables open. A third version has the gable and the belfry windows all open. There are other variations with regard to the base and size of the hole in the bottom (no replace battery), but these are not presently considered significant.

The following is a breakdown of the values of the three variations:

Hum No.	Basic Size	Trademark	Current Value
442	11-1/2"	TMK-6	$1,750-$2,000
(belfry and gable windows open)			
442	11-1/2"	TMK-6	$2,000-$2,500
(painted windows variation)			
442	11-1/2"	TMK-6	$2,500-$3,000
(belfry windows open, gable painted)			

Chapel Time clock, Hum 442, in TMK-6 with 1983 incised copyright date.

Hum 443: Country Song (Clock, Possible Future Edition)

This 8" figurine, modeled by master sculptor Gerhard Skrobek in 1982, is a boy blowing the horn. He is seated on a flower-covered mound. Blue flowers are used instead of numbers on the clock face. The piece bears a 1983 copyright date. At this time, it is a possible future edition only.

Hum 444 and 445: Unknown

Hum 446: A Personal Message (Possible Future Edition)

First designed by master sculptor Gerhard Skrobek in 1983, this 3-3/4" figure is a girl on her knees using a large pen to write on paper. There is an inkwell to her left. This pieces looks somewhat like Hum 309 (With Loving Greetings). At this time, it is a possible future edition only.

Hum 447: Morning Concert

This figurine, first sculpted by master sculptor Gerhard Skrobek from an original Hummel drawing, is the 11th exclusive special edition piece made and offered exclusively for members of the Goebel Collectors' Club (now the M.I. Hummel Club). They were available to members until the expiration date of May 31, 1989.

Morning Concert has a copyright date of 1984 incised beneath the base and the special edition club backstamp in decal underglaze. It carries the following inscription on blue decal: "EXCLUSIVE SPECIAL EDITION No. 11 FOR MEMBERS OF THE GOEBEL COLLECTORS' CLUB." It was available to members for $98.

There are no significant variations.

There are no apparent marks on this Morning Concert figurine, other than an incised copyright date of 1984. It is from the TMK-6 period and is a M.I. Hummel Club exclusive.

Hum No.	Basic Size	Trademark	Current Value
447	5-1/4"	TMK-6	$250-$300

Hum 448: Children's Prayer (Possible Future Edition)

This is an 8-1/4" figure of a boy and girl standing, looking up at a roadside shrine of Jesus on the cross. It was modeled by master sculptor Gerhard Skrobek in 1983 and has a 1984 incised copyright date. At this time, it is a possible future edition only.

Hum 449: The Little Pair

In 1990, the M.I. Hummel Club began offering special figures to those members who had passed certain milestones in their membership. This particular piece was made available by redemption card to only those members who attained or surpassed their 10th year of membership. Each carried a special backstamp commemorating the occasion. This piece was retired in May 2000 and is now only available on the secondary market.

Hum No.	Basic Size	Trademark	Current Value
449	5" to 5-1/4"	TMK-6	$350-$400
449	5" to 5-1/4"	TMK-7	$220-$225
449	5" to 5-1/4"	TMK-8	$225

Today's version (TMK-8) of The Little Pair, Hum 449.

Photo courtesy Goebel of North America.

Available exclusively to M.I. Hummel Club members who had attained 10 years membership, The Little Pair, Hum 449, is shown here with TMK-6 and incised 1985 copyright date.

Hum 450: Will It Sting?

Listed as a possible future edition in the previous edition o f this book, this figurine has since been released as an exclusive special edition to M.I. Hummel Club members to mark their 24th year. Released in 2000, the exclusive figure (Hum 450/0) was designed by master sculptor Helmut Fischer at a smaller size than the earlier TMK-6 sample that was crafted by master sculptor Gerhard Skrobek in 1984, which was 5-3/4".

The figure, a girl looking at a bee perched on a plant at her feet, carries the inscription applied as a blue decal on the bottom: "EXCLUSIVE EDITION 2000/01 M.I. HUMMEL CLUB." Like other club exclusives, a redemption card is necessary, and the issue price in 2000 was $260.

Hum No.	Basic Size	Trademark	Current Value
450	5-3/4"	TMK-6	$2,000-$3,000
450/0	5"	TMK-8	$260

Will It Sting?, Hum 450/0, is the M.I. Hummel Club exclusive for 2000-01 (TMK-8).

Hum 451: Just Dozing

Released in 1995, this figure was first modeled by master sculptor Gerhard Skrobek in 1984 and has an incised 1984 copyright date. Those produced in 1995 bear the "First Issue 1995" backstamp. It was originally released at $220.

Hum No.	Basic Size	Trademark	Current Value
451	4-1/4"	TMK-7	$255-$260
451	4-1/4"	TMK-8	$268

Just Dozing, Hum 451, shown here in TMK-7.

Today's rendition (TMK-8) of Just Dozing, Hum 451.

Hum 452: Flying High

This is the first in a series of hanging ornaments. It is not, however, the first Hummel hanging ornament. The first was the Flying Angel (Hum 366), commonly used with the nativity sets. Flying High was modeled by master sculptor Gerhard Skrobek in 1984 and introduced as the 1988 (first edition) ornament at $75. It has a 1984 incised copyright date.

There are three variations with regard to additional marks. When first released, there were no additional markings; these undated pieces are the most sought-after. The second variation is the appearance of the 1988 date as well as a decal reading "First Edition" beneath the skirt. The third is the appearance of "1988" painted on the back of the gown and no "First Edition."

Hum No.	Basic Size	Trademark	Current Value
452	4-1/2" x 2-3/4"	TMK-6	$250-$300
(no marks)			
452	4-1/2" x 2-3/4"	TMK-6	$175-$200
("First Edition")			
452	4-1/2" x 2-3/4"	TMK-6	$175-$200
("1988")			

TMK-6 version of Flying High, Hum 452, which was the 1988 Christmas ornament and carries no apparent markings. The one shown here is an early undated piece.

Hum 453: The Accompanist

This piece, along with Hum 454 (Song of Praise) and Hum 438 (Sounds of the Mandolin), was introduced in 1988 as a trio of angel musicians. It was released at $39.

The figurine, which was designed by master sculptor Gerhard Skrobek in 1984, measures 3-1/4" high and has an incised copyright date of 1984. It is not found with any earlier trademark than TMK-6.

Hum No.	Basic Size	Trademark	Current Value
453	3-1/4"	TMK-6	$125-$130
453	3-1/4"	TMK-7	$120-$125
453	3-1/4"	TMK-8	$135

The Accompanist, Hum 453, in TMK-6 with incised 1984 copyright date.

The TMK-8 variation of The Accompanist, Hum 453.

Photo courtesy Goebel of North America.

Hum 454: Song of Praise

This piece was one of three angel musician figures introduced in 1988. The others were Hum 453 (The Accompanist) and Hum 438 (Sounds of the Mandolin). It was released at $39.

Song of Praise, which was modeled by master sculptor Gerhard Skrobek in 1984, stands 3" high and has an incised copyright date of 1984. It is not found with any earlier trademark than TMK-6.

Hum No.	Basic Size	Trademark	Current Value
454	3"	TMK-6	$125-$130
454	3"	TMK-7	$120-$125
454	3"	TMK-8	$135

Song of Praise, Hum 454, with TMK-6 and 1984 copyright date.

Today's variation (TMK-8) of Song of Praise, Hum 454.

Hum 455: The Guardian

A 1991 release, The Guardian was first crafted by master sculptor Gerhard Skrobek in 1984. It bears an incised copyright date of 1984, and those made in 1991 bear the "First Issue 1991" backstamp dated 1991. These are not found in trademarks earlier than TMK-6. The suggested retail price at the time of release was $145.

In 1996, Goebel announced "Personal Touch" figurines. There were four figurines in the line at the time that lent themselves well to this application. The Guardian was one of these. The other three were Bird Duet (Hum 69), Latest News (Hum 184), and For Father (Hum 87). A permanent personalization of choice could be fired onto the piece. (The bird is removed for the inscription.)

Hum No.	Basic Size	Trademark	Current Value
455	2-3/4" x 3-1/2"	TMK-6	$195-$200
455	2-3/4" x 3-1/2"	TMK-7	$190-$195
455	2-3/4" x 3-1/2"	TMK-8	$200

Three examples of The Guardian, Hum 455, shown from left: TMK-6 piece with 1985 copyright date and "First Issue" backstamp dated 1991; a personalized piece, part of the "Personal Touch" sereis, which carries a child's name and date of birth; and today's TMK-8 rendition.

Hum 456: Sleep, Little One, Sleep (Possible Future Edition)

This 4-1/4" figurine, which was the design of master sculptor Gerhard Skrobek in 1984, depicts an angel standing beside a baby in a cradle, apparently rocking the child to sleep. At this time, it is a possible future edition only.

Hum 457: Sound the Trumpet

This figure, which was first modeled by master sculptor Gerhard Skrobek in 1984, was introduced in 1988 at a price of $45. It has an incised copyright date of 1984. The piece is not found in trademarks earlier than TMK-6 and was temporarily withdrawn from production on June 15, 2002.

Hum No.	Basic Size	Trademark	Current Value
457	3"	TMK-6	$135-$140
457	3"	TMK-7	$130-$135
457	3"	TMK-8	$128

Sound the Trumpet, Hum 457, with TMK-6 and 1984 copyright date.

Today's variation (TMK-8) of Sound the Trumpet, Hum 457.

Photo courtesy Goebel of North America.

Hum 458: Storybook Time

This piece was introduced as new for 1992 in the fall 1991 issue of Insights, the M.I. Hummel Club newsletter, with the name "Story Time." It was first crafted by master sculptor Gerhard Skrobek in 1984 and carries an incised 1985 copyright date. The release price was $330.

Hum No.	Basic Size	Trademark	Current Value
458	5-1/4"	TMK-7	$465-$475
458	5-1/4"	TMK-8	$490

Carrying the Hummel Mark (TMK-7) is Storybook Time, Hum 458, with incised 1985 copyright date and "First Issue" backstamp dated 1992.

Hum 459: In the Meadow

This figurine, which was the original work of master sculptor Gerhard Skrobek in 1984, was released in 1987 as one of five 1987 releases. The release price was $110. It has an incised copyright date of 1985 beneath the base.

In the Meadow was temporarily withdrawn from production on June 15, 2002.

Hum No.	Basic Size	Trademark	Current Value
459	4"	TMK-6	$245-$250
459	4"	TMK-7	$240-$245
459	4"	TMK-8	$250

In the Meadow, Hum 459, in TMK-6 with 1985 copyright date.

Today's variation (TMK-8) of In the Meadow, Hum 459.

Photo courtesy Goebel of North America.

Hum 460: Tally (Dealer Plaque)

This dealer plaque was introduced in 1986. Many assumed it was to replace the Hum 187 (Merry Wanderer) dealer plaque that had been used since the 1940s, but in 1990, the Merry Wanderer style was reissued. When Tally was first introduced, there was apparently a shortage and dealers were limited to one figure each, but the shortage was soon alleviated. The boy on the plaque is, as you can see, very similar to the center figure in School Boys (Hum 170). The base of the plaque bears an incised copyright date of 1984.

Grouping of Tally retail dealer plaques, from the following countries, starting to the left: United States, Great Britain, Germany, France, and Spain.

There are no structural, size (all are 5" x 6"), or color variations presently known, but there are variations in the language used on the front of the plaque. German, Swedish, French, Italian, Spanish, Dutch, and Japanese are used on the plaques. The Japanese variation was issued in 1996. In addition, there is a version for British dealers and one for the American market, for a total of nine different versions. The plaque was released as $85 in the U.S. The U.S. variation was closed in December 1989, and the others were temporarily withdrawn from production in January 1999.

Hum No.	Variation	Trademark	Current Value
460	Dutch	TMK-6	$900-$1,500
460	Dutch	TMK-7	$300-$500

Hum No.	Variation	Trademark	Current Value
460	English/U.S.	TMK-6	$200-$225
460	English/Britain	TMK-6	$500-$750
460	English/Britain	TMK-7	$300-$500
460	French	TMK-6	$750-$1,000
460	French	TMK-7	$300-$500
460	German	TMK-6	$750-$1,000
460	German	TMK-7	$300-$500
460	Italian	TMK-6	$900-$1,500
460	Italian	TMK-7	$300-$500
460	Japanese	TMK-7	$500-$750
460	Spanish	TMK-6	$900-$1,500

Hum No.	Variation	Trademark	Current Value
460	Spanish	TMK-7	$300-$500
460	Swedish	TMK-6	$750-$1,000
460	Swedish	TMK-7	$300-$500

The retail dealer plaque, Tally, Hum 460, shown from left in Italian, Swedish, and Dutch.

Hum 461: In the Orchard (Possible Future Edition)

This 5-1/2" figurine, which was first modeled by master sculptor Gerhard Skrobek in 1984, depicts a girl standing next to an apple tree sapling that is tied to a wooden post for support. The child has an apple in her left hand and a shovel in the other. At this time, it is a possible future edition only.

Hum 462: Tit For Tat (Possible Future Edition)

This 3-3/4" figurine, designed by master sculptor Gerhard Skrobek in 1984, depicts a boy sitting next to a bird perched on a wooden post. The boy has a feather in his right hand and the bird is tugging at a lock of the boy's hair in retaliation. At this time, this piece is a possible future edition only.

Hum 463: My Wish is Small

This piece is a M.I. Hummel Club exclusive offering for the 16th club year available only in TMK-7, although early samples do exist bearing TMK-6. Such samples, which have a square base instead of the round base of the regular production figurines, are worth significantly more than the pieces made since.

The figure, which was modeled by master sculptor Gerhard Skrobek in 1985, was available exclusively to members with redemption cards for $170. It bears an incised 1985 copyright date, TMK-7, and special inscription on blue decal: "EXCLUSIVE EDITION 1992/93 M.I. HUMMEL CLUB."

This piece was permanently retired on May 31, 1994, and the mold was destroyed.

Hum No.	Basic Size	Trademark	Current Value
459	5-1/2"	TMK-6	$2,000-$2,500
459	5-1/2"	TMK-7	$250-$300

A M.I. Hummel Club exclusive, My Wish is Small, Hum 463/0, is shown here with TMK-7, incised 1985 copyright date, and special club backstamp.

Hum 464: Young Scholar (Possible Future Edition)

According to Goebel Factory records, master sculptor Gerhard Skrobek modeled this 5-1/8" figurine in 1985. It is a boy wearing a hat and jacket while sitting on a wooden bench reading a book. A basket rests beside him on the bench at his left. At this time, it is listed as a possible future edition only.

Hum 465: Where Shall I Go? (Possible Future Edition)

Sculpted by master sculptor Gerhard Skrobek in 1985, this figurine is approximately 4-1/4" and depicts a boy kneeling while holding a toy train. There is no base. At this time, it is a possible future edition only; however, Robert and Ruth Miller own the original drawing of Jochen Edinger (the inspiration for the figurine).

Hum 466: Do Re Mi (Possible Future Edition)

This 5-1/2" figurine, modeled by master sculptor Gerhard Skrobek in 1985, depicts two girls standing beside one another in short dressing singing joyfully. At this time, it is listed as a possible future edition only.

Hum 467: The Kindergartner

A new release at $100 in 1987, this figurine was first crafted by master sculptor Gerhard Skrobek in 1985. It bears a copyright date of 1986 incised beneath the base. This figure is not found with trademarks earlier than TMK-6 and it remains in production today.

Hum No.	Basic Size	Trademark	Current Value
467	5-1/4"	TMK-6	$245-$250
467	5-1/4"	TMK-7	$240-$245
467	5-1/4"	TMK-8	$250

The Kindergartner, Hum 467, with TMK-6 and 1985 copyright date.

Today's rendition (TMK-8) of TheKindergartner, Hum 467.

Photo courtesy Goebel of North America.

Hum 468: Come On (Possible Future Edition)

This 5-1/4" figurine, modeled by master sculptor Gerhard Skrobek in 1986, depicts a little boy walking, with a stick in his right hand and a lamb tugging at his jacket on his left. At this time, it is listed as a possible future edition only.

Hum 469: Starting Young (Possible Future Edition)

This 4-3/4" figurine, first designed by master sculptor Gerhard Skrobek in 1986, depicts two girls: one sewing and one knitting. At this time, it is listed as a possible future edition only.

Hum 470: Time Out (Possible Future Edition)

This 4-1/2" figurine, first crafted by master sculptor Gerhard Skrobek in 1986, is of a boy apparently taking a rest, sitting with one shoe off and his mandolin tucked under his left arm. At this time, it is a possible future edition only.

Hum 471: Harmony In Four Parts

This piece was the 1989 addition to the Century Collection. These pieces are limited to one production year and were not produced again in the 20th century. They bear a special backstamp indicating such. The stamp on this figure is 1989 underlined, with the Roman numeral "XX" beneath it in the center of a circle made up of the M.I. Hummel signature and the words "CENTURY COLLECTION." The copyright date is 1987, and it was released at $850.

Designed by master sculptor Gerhard Skrobek in 1986, the lamppost was originally made of the same fine earthenware used to render Hummel pieces, but it was soon noted that the post was very easily broken. To alleviate this problem, Goebel began using a metal post. Although there is presently no difference in the value of the figures, it is reasonable to assume that the earthenware post version may become uncommon and thus more desirable to serious collectors and more valuable. Only time will tell.

Hum No.	Basic Size	Trademark	Current Value
471	9-3/4"	TMK-6	$2,000-$2,500

Harmony in Four Parts, Hum 471, in TMK-6 with 1987 copyright date and belonging to the Century Collection, 1989.

Hum 472: On Our Way

This unusual piece, which was first crafted by master sculptor Gerhard Skrobek in 1986, was introduced as new for 1992 in the fall 1991 issue of Insights, the M.I. Hummel Club newsletter. On Our Way was the Century Collection piece for 1992, which means its availability was limited by the number produced during the one year of production.

The figures bear a special identifying backstamp and are accompanied by a certificate of authenticity. In addition to an incised 1987 copyright date, the piece also carries a special inscription on a blue decal: "M.I. HUMMEL CENTURY COLLECTION 1992 XX." The release price was $950.

Early samples exist in TMK-6 and are worth more than the figures made since.

Hum No.	Basic Size	Trademark	Current Value
472	8" to 8-1/4"	TMK-6	$2,000-$3,000
472	8" to 8-1/4"	TMK-7	$1,200-$1,500

On Our Way, Hum 472, shown here in TMK-7 with incised 1987 copyright date and belonging to the Century Collection, 1992.

Hum 473: Ruprecht (Knecht Ruprecht)

This figurine was produced in 1987 as a limited edition of 20,000 sequentially numbered pieces. It was modeled by master sculptor Gerhard Skrobek in 1986 and carries a 1987 incised copyright date. Early samples, which were then called "Father Christmas," do exist in TMK-6 and are worth significantly more than the figures made since.

This piece is considered a companion to Saint Nicholas Day (Hum 2012), which was released the same year with matching edition numbers. Both pieces were offered at a reduced M.I. Hummel Club price of $1,000 per set.

Hum No.	Basic Size	Trademark	Current Value
473	6"	TMK-6	$2,000-$3,000
473	6"	TMK-7	$500-$600

Ruprecht, Hum 473, which is a limited edition produced in TMK-7 only.

Hum 474: Gentle Care (Possible Future Edition)

This 6" figurine was first modeled by master sculptor Gerhard Skrobek in 1986. It shows two girls, both of who are wearing long dresses and handkerchiefs in their hair. One girl carries a lamb, while the other holds a basketful of apples. At this time, it is listed as a possible future edition only.

Hum 475: Make a Wish

This piece was a new release in 1989 and bears a 1987 incised copyright date. The original design of master sculptor Gerhard Skrobek in 1986, these figures cannot be found with trademarks earlier than TMK-6. The original issue price was $135.

Make a Wish was temporarily withdrawn from production in 1999.

Hum No.	Basic Size	Trademark	Current Value
475	4-1/2"	TMK-6	$240-$250
475	4-1/2"	TMK-7	$225-$230

Make a Wish, Hum 475, with TMK-6 and 1987 copyright date.

Hum 476: A Winter Song

This figurine, which was modeled by master sculptor Gerhard Skrobek in 1987, was a 1988 release and was priced at $45 when introduced. It bears an incised copyright date of 1987 and appears with TMK-6 or later trademarks. There are no significant variations affecting collector value.

Hum No.	Basic Size	Trademark	Current Value
476	4"	TMK-6	$145-$150
476	4"	TMK-7	$140-$145
476	4"	TMK-8	$145

A TMK-6 version of Winter Song, Hum 476, with incised copyright date of 1987.

Today's variation (TMK-8) of Winter Song, Hum 476.

Photo courtesy Goebel of North America.

Hum 477: A Budding Maestro

The work of master sculptor Gerhard Skrobek in 1987, this piece was released in 1988 at $45 and is found with TMK-6 or later trademarks. It carries an incised 1987 copyright date.

There are no significant variations; however, it was temporarily withdrawn from production in January 1999.

Hum No.	Basic Size	Trademark	Current Value
477	4"	TMK-6	$130-$135
477	4"	TMK-7	$120-$125

A Budding Maestro, Hum 477, with TMK-6 and incised 1987 copyright date.

Hum 478: I'm Here

I'm Here was released in 1989 as a new addition to the line. First modeled by master sculptor Gerhard Skrobek in 1987, it carries a 1987 incised copyright date. The price at release was $50. This piece is not found with trademarks earlier than TMK-6.

There are no significant variations, but the piece was temporarily withdrawn from production on June 15, 2002.

Hum No.	Basic Size	Trademark	Current Value
478	3"	TMK-6	$140-$145
478	3"	TMK-7	$135-$140
478	3"	TMK-8	$140

I'm Here, Hum 478, with TMK-6.

Hum 479: I Brought You a Gift

On June 1, 1989, the 4" bisque plaque with the Merry Wanderer motif, which had been given to every new member of the Goebel Collectors' Club, was officially retired. On the same date, the club became the M.I. Hummel Club, and a new membership premium, I Brought You a Gift, was introduced. At the time of transition, each renewing and new member was given the new premium.

Crafted by master sculptor Gerhard Skrobek in 1987, I Brought You a Gift has the incised copyright date of 1987 on the underside of the base. There are two variations with regard to the club special edition backstamp. If you will look at the accompanying photograph of the base, you will note one old club name underneath the bumblebee. This is found on the early examples. Newer ones have the M.I. Hummel Club name on them.

This figurine was permanently retired on May 31, 1996.

Hum No.	Basic Size	Trademark	Current Value
479	4"	TMK-6	$150-$175
479	4"	TMK-7	$125-$150

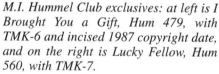

M.I. Hummel Club exclusives: at left is I Brought You a Gift, Hum 479, with TMK-6 and incised 1987 copyright date, and on the right is Lucky Fellow, Hum 560, with TMK-7.

I Brought You a Gift, Hum 479, bearing TMK-6, incised 1987 copyright date, and the special club exclusive backstamp, which all can be seen on the base photo (above right). Note the club name is the old "Goebel Collectors Club" name instead of the current M.I. Hummel Club moniker.

Hum 480: Hosanna

Released in 1989, this figurine was first modeled by master sculptor Gerhard Skrobek in 1987 and therefore carries a 1987 copyright date incised under the base. The suggested retail price at the time of the release was $68. Hum 480 is not found with trademarks earlier than TMK-6.

Hosanna was temporarily withdrawn from production on June 15, 2002.

Hum No.	Basic Size	Trademark	Current Value
480	4"	TMK-6	$135-$140
480	4"	TMK-7	$130-$135
480	4"	TMK-8	$135

Hosanna, Hum 480, from left: TMK-6 variation with 1987 copyright date and today's TMK-8 figurine.

Hum 481: Love From Above (1989 Christmas Ornament)

This ornament is the second edition in the hanging ornament series that began with the 1988 Flying High (Hum 452). The design of master sculptor Gerhard Skrobek in 1987, it bears a 1987 incised copyright date and TMK-6. It was released at $75.

The 1989 Christmas ornament, Love From Above, Hum 481, is shown here with TMK-6 and 1987 copyright date.

Hum No.	Basic Size	Trademark	Current Value
481	3-1/4"	TMK-6	$125-$150

Hum 482: One For You, One For Me

This piece was a new release in 1989. It was first crafted by master sculptor Gerhard Skrobek in 1987 and thereby carries a 1987 incised copyright date. It was originally priced at $50.

The 3" figurine is not found with trademarks earlier than TMK-6 and it was temporarily withdrawn from production on June 15, 2002.

A 2-3/4" piece was introduced in 1996 as part of the "Pen Pals" figurines line, which is a series of personalized name card decorations. That piece was temporarily withdrawn in January 1999.

Hum No.	Basic Size	Trademark	Current Value
482/5/0	2-3/4"	TMK-7	$55
482	3"	TMK-6	$135-$140
482	3"	TMK-7	$130-$135
482	3"	TMK-8	$135

One For You, One For Me, Hum 482. No apparent markings of any sort, 3-3/16".

Photo courtesy Goebel of North America.

The most recent variation (TMK-8) of One For You, One For Me, Hum 482.

Hum 483: I'll Protect Him

New in 1989, this figure was designed by master sculptor Gerhard Skrobek in 1987 and bears an incised copyright date of 1987 on the underside of the base. The release price was $55. It is not found with trademarks earlier than TMK-6 and was temporarily withdrawn from production on June 15, 2002.

I'll Protect Him, Hum 483, shown in TMK-6 with 1987 copyright date.

Hum No.	Basic Size	Trademark	Current Value
483	3-3/4"	TMK-6	$110-$115
483	3-3/4"	TMK-7	$105-$110
483	3-3/4"	TMK-8	$110

Today's variation (TMK-8) of I'll Protect Him, Hum 483.

Photo courtesy Goebel of North America.

Hum 484: Peace On Earth (1990 Christmas Ornament)

The third in an annual series of M.I. Hummel Christmas ornaments, this one was released in 1990 at a suggested retail price of $80. It was modeled by master sculptor Gerhard Skrobek in 1987 and carries a 1987 incised copyright date. It is found only in TMK-6.

Hum No.	Basic Size	Trademark	Current Value
484	3-1/4"	TMK-6	$125-$150

Peace On Earth, Hum 484. 1990 Christmas ornament, TMK-6.

Hum 485: A Gift From a Friend

This little fellow, crafted by master sculptor Gerhard Skrobek in 1988, was offered exclusively to members of the M.I. Hummel club in the club year 1991-92. Its availability to members at $160 with redemption card was subject to the cutoff date of May 31, 1993. It carries a 1988 incised copyright date and special decaled club inscription: "EXCLUSIVE EDITION 1991/92 M.I. HUMMEL CLUB." A large, black bumblebee is located on the bottom.

This figurine is found in both TMK-6 and TMK-7, but the older mark is slightly more valuable than the new. There are no significant variations.

Hum No.	Basic Size	Trademark	Current Value
485	5"	TMK-6	$300-$330
485	5"	TMK-7	$250-$300

A Gift From A Friend, Hum 485, produced in TMK-7 as a M.I. Hummel Club exclusive offer.

Hum 486: I Wonder

This piece, which was first modeled by master sculptor Helmut Fischer in 1988, was a club exclusive offered only to members of the M.I. Hummel Club during the club year of June 1, 1990, to May 31, 1991. The figurines were offered by way of a redemption card at $140. Each piece bears the bumblebee club backstamp, as well as 1988 incised copyright date and special decaled club inscription: "EXCLUSIVE EDITION 1990/91 M.I. HUMMEL CLUB." It is found in both TMK-6 and TMK-7, but the older mark is slightly more valuable than the new.

I Wonder, Hum 486. TMK-6, incised 1988 copyright date, 5-1/4".

Somehow, an estimated 300 of these escaped the factory with the erroneous year date "1991/92" on the backstamp, according to Goebel. Only time will tell if this variation becomes significant.

Hum No.	Basic Size	Trademark	Current Value
486	5-1/4"	TMK-6	$300-$330
486	5-1/4"	TMK-7	$250-$300

I Wonder, Hum 486. Demonstration piece with only flesh tones painted. It has TMK-7, M.I. Hummel Club special backstamp, and incised 1988 copyright date.

Hum 487: Let's Tell the World

First crafted by master sculptor Gerhard Skrobek in 1987 and released in 1990 as part of the Century Collection, Let's Tell the World was limited to one year (1990) and the edition was listed as closed in the 1992 Goebel price list. The actual number of figures produced is not known.

Each piece bears a special backstamp commemorating the 55th anniversary of M.I. Hummel figurines and an incised 1988 copyright date. A blue decal was also applied with special inscription: "M.I. HUMMEL CENTURY COLLECTION 1990 XX" and "1935-1990 – 55 Years of M.I. Hummel Figurines." Released at $875, they are available only in TMK-6.

Hum No.	Basic Size	Trademark	Current Value
487	10-1/2" x 7"	TMK-6	$1,500-$1,800

Let's Tell the World, Hum 487. TMK-6, 1988 copyright date, 8" x 10-7/16" high. Century Collection dated 1990, "1935-1990 55 Years of M.I. Hummel Figurines."

Hum 488: What's That?

This figurine, modeled by master sculptor Helmut Fischer in 1988, was produced in 1997 as an exclusive preview edition for members of the M.I. Hummel Club. It carries an incised 1988 copyright date, as well as TMK-7. A decal on the underside of the base reads, "EXCLUSIVE EDITION 1997/98 M.I. HUMMEL CLUB." It was originally issued to collectors at $150.

What's That is a companion to One, Two, Three (Hum 555).

Hum No.	Basic Size	Trademark	Current Value
488	4"	TMK-7	$175-$195

What's That?, Hum 488, was an M.I. Hummel Club exclusive and exists in TMK-7 only.

Hum 489: Pretty Please

This figurine, which was introduced in 1996, is part of an informal series of paired pieces called "Cozy Companions." The piece paired with this one is No Thank You (Hum 535).

Pretty Please, which was crafted by master sculptor Helmut Fischer in 1988, has an incised copyright date of 1988 and bears both the "First Issue 1996" and the "125th Anniversary" backstamps during the initial year of production. The issue price was $120.

Temporarily withdrawn from production on June 15, 2002.

Hum No.	Basic Size	Trademark	Current Value
489	3-1/2"	TMK-7	$130-$135
489	3-1/2"	TMK-8	$135

Pretty Please, Hum 489, shown here in TMK-7. It is part of an informal series called "Cozy Companions" in which it is paired with No Thank You, Hum 535.

The most recent rendition (TMK-8) of Pretty Please, Hum 499, which was temporarily withdrawn from production in June 2002.

Hum 490: Carefree

Another in the informal annual series called "Cozy Companions," Carefree is paired with Free Spirit (Hum 564).

First designed by master sculptor Helmut Fischer in 1988, Carefree bears an incised copyright date of 1988.

Those released in the first year of production have the "First Issue 1997" backstamp. The release price was $120.

Hum No.	Basic Size	Trademark	Current Value
490	3-1/2"	TMK-7	$130-$135
490	3-1/2"	TMK-8	$135

Carefree, Hum 490, in TMK-7.

Today's rendition (TMK-8) of Carefree, Hum 490, which is worth $135.

Photo courtesy Goebel of North America.

Hum 491, 492: Open Numbers

Hum 493: Two Hands, One Treat

This special 4" figurine, the design of master sculptor Helmut Fischer in 1988, is a M.I. Hummel Club exclusive. It was made available as a renewal premium, a gift, to those members renewing their membership in the club year 1991-92. The club placed a $65 value on the piece at that time.

These figures, which carry an incised 1988 copyright date, are found only with TMK-7. A special decaled club inscription reads: "M.I. HUMMEL CLUB." There is also the black flying bumblebee to signify a club piece.

Hum No.	Basic Size	Trademark	Current Value
493	4"	TMK-7	$125-$150

Two Hands, One Treat, Hum 493, with TMK-7 and incised 1988 copyright date.

Hum 494: Open Number

Hum 495: Evening Prayer

Introduced in the fall 1991 at $95, this figurine was first modeled by master sculptor Helmut Fischer in 1988. It has an incised 1988 mold induction. There are no significant variations to affect collector value, although it is noteworthy to mention that the girl is similar to Doll Mother (Hum 67).

Hum No.	Basic Size	Trademark	Current Value
495	3-3/4"	TMK-7	$130-$135
495	3-3/4"	TMK-8	$135

Evening Prayer, Hum 495, in TMK-7 with incised 1988 copyright date and "First Issue" backstamp dated 1992.

Today's rendition (TMK-8) of Evening Prayer, Hum 495.

Photo courtesy Goebel of North America.

Hum 496, 497: Open Numbers

Hum 498: All Smiles

This 4" figurine, modeled by master sculptor Helmut Fischer in 1988, was released in 1997 as a sequentially numbered limited edition of 25,000 pieces. The original retail price was $175.

The piece carries a 1988 incised copyright date and is similar to the girl from Telling Her Secret (Hum 196), except with no pigtails and a longer dress.

Hum No.	Basic Size	Trademark	Current Value
498	4"	TMK-7	$200-$225

All Smiles, Hum 498, was released 1997 as a limited edition. It exists in TMK-7 only.

Photo courtesy Goebel of North America.

Hum 499: Open Number

Hum 500: Flowers For Mother
(Mother's Day Plate, Possible Future Edition)

This plate was listed in the index of the M.I. Hummel: The Golden Anniversary Album. It was not illustrated, however, and little else is known about why it has never been issued.

Hum 501-511: Doll Parts

These mold numbers were utilized to identify the heads, arms, and legs of the eight porcelain dolls released by Goebel, starting in 1984. There were eight different heads and the left and right hands were the same on each doll, which accounts for the 10 mold numbers used. Hum 501 through 508 were doll heads; Hum 509 and 511 were arms and legs; and Hum 510 was an actual doll (Carnival Doll).

Hum 512-524: Dolls

These are the mold numbers used to identify the dolls made by the Danbury Mint, as well as two produced by Goebel. Since the early 1950s, Hummel dolls have been produced. These dolls were originally produced with rubber heads, but changed to vinyl in 1964. Later, in 1983, the porcelain-style of doll was introduced.

Originally, the dolls were 16" tall and had the "M.I. Hummel" signature incised on the back of the neck. In 1961, however, the dolls were downsized to 10", and today, they range in size from 10" to 16". Each Hummel doll is worth between $200 and $250.

Hum 512	Umbrella Girl Doll
Hum 513	Little Fiddler Doll
Hum 514	Friend or Foe? Doll
Hum 515	Kiss Me Doll
Hum 516	Merry Wanderer Doll
Hum 517	Goose Girl Doll
Hum 518	Umbrella Boy Doll
Hum 519	Ride Into Christmas Doll
Hum 520	Possible Future Edition
Hum 521	School Girl Doll (by Goebel Retailers)
Hum 522	Little Scholar Doll (by Goebel Retailers)
Hum 523	Possible Future Edition
Hum 524	Valentine Gift Doll
Hum 950	Apple Tree Girl Doll (by Goebel Retailers)
Hum 951	Apple Tree Boy Doll (by Goebel Retailers)
Hum 960	Ride Into Christmas Doll (by Goebel Retailers)

Just a few of the dolls in the line are shown here, from left: School Girl, Hum 521; Little Scholar, Hum 522; and Valentine Gift, Hum 524. While School Girl and Little Scholar are among the dolls produced by Goebel retailers, Valentine Gift is by Danbury Mint.

Hum 525-529: Open Numbers

Hum 530: Land In Sight

This large, complicated piece is very special. The design of master sculptor Gerhard Skrobek in 1988, Land in Sight is a sequentially numbered limited edition of 30,000 worldwide, released in the fall of 1991 to commemorate Columbus' discovery of America. It carries a 1988 incised copyright date and special inscription that reads: "1492 – The Quincentennial of America's Discovery." A medallion accompanies the figurine. These pieces, which were priced at $1,600 at time of release, are found only in TMK-7.

Hum No.	Basic Size	Trademark	Current Value
530	9" x 9-1/2"	TMK-7	$1,800-$2,250

Land In Sight, Hum 530, with TMK-7 and incised 1988 copyright date. This is #1,112 of 30,000. The medallion that accompanies the figure is hanging from the mast. It is not attached.

Hum 531, 532: Open Numbers

Hum 533: Ooh, My Tooth

This figurine was modeled by master sculptor Gerhard Skrobek in 1988 and first issued in 1995 with a "SPECIAL EVENT" backstamp, as it was available at district manager promotions and in-store events. It also carries an incised 1988 copyright date and those pieces issued the first year carry the "First Issue 1995" backstamp. The original retail price was $110.

Temporarily withdrawn from production on June 15, 2002.

Hum No.	Basic Size	Trademark	Current Value
533	3"	TMK-7	$145-$150
533	3"	TMK-8	$145

Ooh, My Tooth, Hum 533.

Photo courtesy Goebel of North America.

Hum 534: A Nap

This piece was introduced as new for 1991 in the fall issue of the M.I. Hummel Club newsletter, Insights. It was modeled by master sculptor Gerhard Skrobek in 1988 and bears an incised 1988 copyright date. A Nap was originally released at $100.

Hum No.	Basic Size	Trademark	Current Value
534	2-1/4"	TMK-6	$145-$150
534	2-1/4"	TMK-7	$140-$145
534	2-1/4"	TMK-8	$150

A Nap, Hum 534, shown here in TMK-6 with 1988 copyright date and "First Issue" paper sticker.

Today's variation (TMK-8) of A Nap, Hum 534.

Photo courtesy Goebel of North America.

Hum 535: No Thank You

This piece is part of an informal series of paired figurines called "Cozy Companions." Its companion piece is Pretty Please (Hum 489).

The 1996 release carried the "125th Anniversary" and "First Issue 1996" backstamps. Modeled by master sculptor Helmut Fischer in 1988, it therefore has an incised 1988 copyright date. The issue price was $120.

Hum No.	Basic Size	Trademark	Current Value
535	3-1/2"	TMK-7	$130-$135
535	3-1/2"	TMK-8	$130

Photo courtesy Goebel of North America.

Today's No Thank You, Hum 535, (TMK-8) is part of an informal series called "Cozy Companions." It is paired with Pretty Please, Hum 489.

Hum 536: Christmas Surprise

This figurine, modeled by master sculptor Helmut Fischer in 1988, was produced in a limited edition of 15,000 pieces and was sold exclusively by QVC, the Home Shopping Network, in 1998. It bears a 1988 incised copyright date, as well as TMK-7. Original issue price was $139.50. It came with HummelScape Musikfest display for a Collector's Set. The figurine was introduced, retired, and mold broken all on the same day.

An ornament variation also exists as 536/3/0/0 at 3-1/4" in TMK-8.

Hum No.	Basic Size	Trademark	Current Value
536/3/0	4"	TMK-7	$175-$200
536/3/0/0	3-1/4"	TMK-8	$80

Photo courtesy Goebel of North America.

The ornament variation of Christmas Surprise, Hum 536/3/0/0.

Hum 537: Open Number

Hum 538: School's Out

School's Out, Hum 538, in TMK-7.

First crafted by master sculptor Helmut Fischer in 1988, this was a new piece for 1997. It is 4" and has a 1988 incised copyright date. The first year of production has the "First Issue 1997" oval decal on the bottom. The original suggested retail price was $170. There are no significant variations to affect collector values.

Hum No.	Basic Size	Trademark	Current Value
538	4"	TMK-7	$190-$200
538	4"	TMK-8	$190

Photo courtesy Goebel of North America.

Today's variation (TMK-8) of School's Out, Hum 538.

Hum 539: Good News

This figurine, modeled by master sculptor Helmut Fischer in 1988 and thereby carrying a 1988 incised copyright date, was first released at the 1996 M.I. Hummel Club Convention in Coburg, Germany. It was issued to the U.S. market in 1997 at a retail price of $180.

Good News is a part of the Goebel Company's Personalization Program, whereby two letters or two numbers can be permanently applied by a Goebel authorized artisan.

Hum No.	Basic Size	Trademark	Current Value
539	4-1/2"	TMK-7	$210-$220
539	4-1/2"	TMK-8	$210

Good News, Hum 539, shown here in current-use TMK-8. This piece can be personalized with two letters or two numbers, which are permanently applied by a Goebel authorized artisan.

Hum 540: Best Wishes

Modeled by master sculptor Helmut Fischer in 1988 and carrying an incised 1988 copyright date, this figurine was first released at the 1996 M.I. Hummel Club Convention in Coburg, Germany, and later released in the U.S. in 1997. It originally retailed for $180.

Again part of Goebel's "Personal Touch" program, Best Wishes could have two letters or two numbers applied by a Goebel authorized artisan. It was also a 1997 "SPECIAL EVENT" piece with a flying bumblebee decal applied to the flowers.

Hum No.	Basic Size	Trademark	Current Value
540	4-5/8"	TMK-7	$200-$210
540	4-5/8"	TMK-8	$200

Another in the company's Personalization Program, Best Wishes, Hum 540, can be personalized with two letters or two numbers. It is shown here in TMK-8.

Hum 541: Sweet As Can Be

Modeled by master sculptor Helmut Fischer in 1988, a special preview edition of this figure was offered only to members of the M.I. Hummel Club for the 17th club year. The figures were given the standard club exclusive backstamp for 1993 and were put into regular production with the regular trademark afterward.

Goebel placed a value of $125 on the figure in the spring of 1993. Each carried a 1988 incised copyright date, black club bumblebee, and special decaled inscription: "EXCLUSIVE EDITION 1993/94 M.I. HUMMEL CLUB."

The M.I. Hummel Birthday Sampler Set was released in 1998 and features Sweet As Can Be along with a sensational Happy Birthday HummelScape.

Hum No.	Basic Size	Trademark	Current Value
541	4-1/8"	TMK-7	$170-$180
541	4-1/8"	TMK-8	$170

Sweet As Can Be, Hum 541. 1993/94 club exclusive "Preview Edition."

Sweet As Can Be, Hum 541, shown here in TMK-7 as part of the Birthday Sampler.

Hum 542: Open Number

Hum 543: I'm Sorry (Possible Future Edition)

Figurine modeled by master sculptor Gerhard Skrobek in 1988 and carries an incised copyright date of 1988. It depicts a little boy, eyes cast downward and arms behind his back looking quite apologetic. At this time, it is listed as a possible future edition only.

Hum 544: Open Number

Hum 545: Come Back Soon

This figure, which was first designed by master sculptor Helmut Fischer in 1989, was first released in 1995. In the first year of production, each figure was given the special "First Issue 1995" oval decal on the bottom. These pieces have a 1989 copyright date and the TMK-7. The original issue price was #135.

For some inexplicable reason, those produced after the first year are a very slightly different style from an obviously different mold. These bear a 1988 copyright date and the earlier TMK-6. It appears that Goebel produced many of the regular figurines in advance of the "First Issue" pieces released in 1995.

This figurine matches the 25th and final installation in the annual plate series.

Come Back Soon was temporarily withdrawn from production on June 15, 2002.

Hum No.	Basic Size	Trademark	Current Value
545	4-1/4"	TMK-6	$300-$500
545	4-1/4"	TMK-7	$180-$190
545	4-1/4"	TMK-8	$180

Come Back Soon, Hum 545. Left: The regular production figure with TMK-6. Right: The 1995 "First Issue" version with TMK-7.

Today's version (TMK-8) of Come Back Soon, Hum 545.

Photo courtesy Goebel of North America.

Bases of the Hum 545 showing the trademarks and backstamps.

Hum 548: Flower Girl

In 1990, this special figure became available only to members of the M.I. Hummel Club and then only upon or after the fifth anniversary of their membership. It was modeled by master sculptor Helmut Fischer in 1989 and bears a special "EXCLUSIVE EDITION" backstamp to indicate its unique status. As with any of the club anniversary exclusives, members attained this piece by way of a redemption card. The original price was $105.

Flower Girl was retired on May 31, 2000.

Hum No.	Basic Size	Trademark	Current Value
548	4-1/2"	TMK-6	$175-$225
548	4-1/2"	TMK-7	$150-$175
548	4-1/2"	TMK-8	$150

Today's variation (TMK-8) of Flower Girl, Hum 548.

Photo courtesy Goebel of North America.

Flower Girl, Hum 548, shown here in TMK-6 with incised 1989 copyright date, 4-1/2". A M.I. Hummel Club exclusive offer.

M.I. Hummel Club™ Exclusive
Flower Girl
5 Year Member Offer

Hum 549: A Sweet Offering

Modeled by master sculptor Helmut Fischer in 1992, this piece is a M.I. Hummel Club exclusive for members only. Free to members renewing their membership for club year 1993-94, it carries the mold number 549/3/0 and has a basic size of 3-1/2". It has a 1992 copyright date and carries the inscription: "M.I. HUMMEL CLUB Membership Year 1993/94." Goebel valued the piece originally at $80.

Hum No.	Basic Size	Trademark	Current Value
549/3/0	3-1/2"	TMK-7	$100-$125

A Sweet Offering, Hum 549/3/0. 1993-94 club renewal gift, 3-1/2".

Hum 550, 551, 552: Open Numbers

Hum 553: Scamp

The design of master sculptor Helmut Fischer in 1989, this figurine was a new figure in 1992. It has a basic size of 3-1/2" and an incised copyright date of 1989. The original suggested retail price was $95. It is considered a companion piece to Pixie (Hum 768) as part of the "Cozy Companion" series.

There are no known significant variations, but it is interesting to note the similarity to the "Max" boy in Hum 123.

Hum No.	Basic Size	Trademark	Current Value
553	3-1/2"	TMK-7	$140-$150
553	3-1/2"	TMK-8	$135

Scamp, Hum 553, with TMK-7, incised 1989 copyright date, and "First Issue 1992" backstamp.

Hum 554: Cheeky Fellow

This figure, which was modeled by master sculptor Helmut Fischer in 1989 and similar to the "Moritz" boy in Hum 123, was offered in a special preview edition exclusively to members of the M.I. Hummel Club for the 1992-93 club year. Figures produced in that year were given the standard club exclusive backstamp. Those produced later became regular production pieces and no longer had the special marking. Each carries a 1989 incised copyright date. Goebel placed a value of $120 on the figure when released.

Hum No.	Basic Size	Trademark	Current Value
554	4-1/8"	TMK-7	$150-$160
554	4-1/8"	TMK-8	$145

Cheeky Fellow, Hum 554. Incised 1989 copyright date, 4-1/8".

The present-day variation of Cheeky Fellow, Hum 554, is paired with Little Helper, Hum 73, to create the Treehouse Treats Collector's Set.

Photo courtesy Goebel of North America.

Left: Cheeky Fellow, Hum 554, with TMK-7, incised 1989 copyright date, and measuring 4-1/8". Right: My Wish Is Small, Hum 463/0, with TMK-7, incised 1985 copyright date, and measuring 5-1/2".

Hum 555: One, Two, Three

This small figurine, modeled by master sculptor Helmut Fischer in 1989, was released in 1996. It is an exclusive edition available to members of the M.I. Hummel Club only and therefore carries special club backstamp and the following inscription on a blue decal: "EXCLUSIVE EDITION 1996/97 M.I. HUMMEL CLUB." It has an incised copyright date of 1989. One, Two, Three was released at $145. The 1997 companion piece is What's That? (Hum 488).

Hum No.	Basic Size	Trademark	Current Value
555	3-7/8"	TMK-7	$150-$175

One, Two, Three, Hum 555.

Hum 556: One Plus One

This figurine was first made available in a limited form. Although it was released in 1993, it was not made available through normal channels, but rather only at authorized dealer promotions that were billed as a "district manager promotion" in the United States and a "Canadian artist promotion" in Canada. The figures were made available for purchase by anyone interested, on a first-come, first-served basis.

These pieces, which were first crafted by master sculptor Helmut Fischer in 1989, bear a "SPECIAL EVENT" backstamp, along with the regular markings (1989 incised copyright date), to indicate they were part of the promotion.

They sold for $115 at these events, were in regular production for a time, and are now temporarily withdrawn from production.

Hum No.	Basic Size	Trademark	Current Value
556 (special event)	4"	TMK-7	$180-$200
556	4"	TMK-7	$170-$180
556	4"	TMK-8	$165

Today's TMK-8 variation of One Plus One, Hum 556.

Photo courtesy Goebel of North America.

Hum 557: Strum Along

Strum Along was first issued in 1995 to members of the M.I. Hummel Club. Modeled by master sculptor Helmut Fischer in 1989, this figurine has a 1989 incised copyright date. It carries the inscription: "EXCLUSIVE EDITION 1995/96 M.I. HUMMEL CLUB." Issue price in 1995 was $135.

Strum Along was later reintroduced as an open edition without "exclusive edition" wording on the backstamp.

Hum No.	Basic Size	Trademark	Current Value
557	3-7/8"	TMK-7	$160-$175
557	3-7/8"	TMK-8	$155

Strum Along, Hum 557, shown here in TMK-8.

Photo courtesy Goebel of North America.

Hum 558: Little Troubadour

Released in 1994, this figurine, modeled by master sculptor Helmut Fischer in 1989, has an incised 1989 copyright date. It was an exclusive edition reserved for members of the M.I. Hummel Club, and it bears the special club backstamp and special decaled inscription: "EXCLUSIVE EDITION 1994/95 M.I. HUMMEL CLUB." The original issue price was $130.

Hum No.	Basic Size	Trademark	Current Value
558	4-1/8"	TMK-7	$150-$160
558	4-1/8"	TMK-8	$145

Little Troubadour, Hum 558. The figurine on the left is TMK-7 and the other is today's TMK-8 rendition.

HHum 559: Heart and Soul

This figurine, which was first designed by master sculptor Helmut Fischer in 1988, is part of an informal annual series of paired figurines called "Cozy Companions." It is paired with From the Heart (Hum 761).

Released in 1996, Heart and Soul has an incised copyright date of 1989. Those produced in 1996 will bear both the "First Issue 1996" and the "125th Anniversary" back stamps. The suggested retail price at release was $120.

Hum No.	Basic Size	Trademark	Current Value
559	3-5/8"	TMK-7	$140-$150
559	3-5/8"	TMK-8	$135

Heart and Soul, Hum 559. The variation on the left is TMK-7 and carries the special 125th Anniversary backstamp, while the right figurine is today's TMK-8.

Hum 560: Lucky Fellow

Modeled by master sculptor Helmut Fischer in 1989, this figure was given free to members who renewed their membership in the club year 1992-93. Lucky Fellow carries a 1989 copyright date and the inscription: "M.I. HUMMEL CLUB." Goebel valued it at $75 when first released.

Hum No.	Basic Size	Trademark	Current Value
560	3-5/8"	TMK-7	$100-$120

Lucky Fellow, Hum 560. A M.I. Hummel Club exclusive offering. It is 3-5/8" tall, bears TMK-7, the special club backstamp, and an incised 1989 copyright date.

Hum 561: Grandma's Girl

Modeled by master sculptor Helmut Fischer in 1989, this piece was first released in 1990. It carries a 1989 incised copyright date and is essentially a smaller version of the same girl as the one on Going Home (Hum 383). The original price at time of release was $100.

In 1993, on the day after the First Annual M.I. Hummel Club Convention, a special meeting was held for local chapter members from all over the United States and Canada. Each member of the 650 attending was given either a Hum 561 (Grandma's Girl) or a Hum 562 (Grandpa's Boy). On the side of the each base was the inscription "1993 – M.I. Hummel Club Convention." Goebel master sculptor Gerhard Skrobek also signed each figurine.

Hum No.	Basic Size	Trademark	Current Value
561	4"	TMK-6	$190-$200
561	4"	TMK-7	$180-$190
561	4"	TMK-8	$180

Grandma's Girl, Hum 561, showing the convention inscription.

Grandma's Girl, Hum 561, TMK-6, 1989 copyright date incised, 4". Has the "First Issue" backstamp dated 1991.

Photo courtesy Goebel of North America.

Grandma's Girl in current production TMK-8.

Hum 562: Grandpa's Boy

Modeled by master sculptor Helmut Fischer in 1989, this piece was first released in 1990. It carries a 1989 incised copyright date and is essentially a smaller version of the same boy from Going Home (Hum 383). The original price at time of release was $100.

In 1993, on the day after the First Annual M.I. Hummel Club Convention, a special meeting was held for local chapter members from all over the United States and Canada. Each member of the 650 attending was given either a Hum 561 (Grandma's Girl) or a Hum 562 (Grandpa's Boy). On the side of the each base was the inscription "1993 – M.I. Hummel Club Convention." Goebel master sculptor Gerhard Skrobek also signed each figurine.

Hum No.	Basic Size	Trademark	Current Value
562	4-1/4"	TMK-6	$190-$200
562	4-1/4"	TMK-7	$180-$190
562	4-1/4"	TMK-8	$180

Grandpa's Boy, Hum 562, with TMK-6, 1989 copyright date incised, and "First Issue 1991" backstamp.

Grandpa's Boy, Hum 562, showing the convention inscription.

Photo courtesy Goebel of North America.

Grandpa's Boy shown here in today's TMK-8.

Hum 563: Little Visitor

This figure, modeled by master sculptor Helmut Fischer in 1991, has the mold number 563/0, indicating that another size might be in the offering. This one measures 5-1/8" and has an incised 1991 copyright date.

Little Visitor was a M.I. Hummel Club exclusive, available only to club members. It was released in 1994 and bears the special club backstamp, as well as the inscription: "EXCLUSIVE EDITION 1994/95 M.I. HUMMEL CLUB." The original price to members was $180.

Little Visitor, Hum 563.

Hum No.	Basic Size	Trademark	Current Value
563/0	5-1/8"	TMK-7	$200-$225

Hum 564: Free Spirit

Free Spirit is part of the "Cozy Companions" informal annual series of paired figurines. The pair for this piece is Carefree (Hum 490).

Free Spirit, modeled by master sculptor Helmut Fischer in 1988, has an incised copyright date of 1988 and a "First Issue 1997" backstamp. Both this figure and Carefree were released in the fall of 1996, Free Spirit then priced at $120.

Hum No.	Basic Size	Trademark	Current Value
564	3-1/2"	TMK-7	$140-$150
564	3-1/2"	TMK-8	$135

Free Spirit, Hum 564, shown at left in TMK-7, which was the M.I. Hummel Club exclusive piece, and then at right in TMK-8, which is part of the "Cozy Companions" series when paired with Carefree, Hum 490.

Hum 565: Open Number

Hum 566: The Angler

Modeled by master sculptor Gerhard Skrobek in 1989, this figure was released in 1995 at $320. It measures nearly 6" and bears a 1989 incised copyright date. Each figure produced during 1995 will be found bearing the "First Issue 1995" backstamp.

Hum No.	Basic Size	Trademark	Current Value
566	5-7/8"	TMK-7	$400-$420
566	5-7/8"	TMK-8	$395

The Angler, Hum 566, shown here in TMK-7. First issued in 1995, this piece today is worth $400-$420.

The TMK-8 variation of The Angler, Hum 566.

Photo courtesy Goebel of North America.

Hum 567, 568: Open Numbers

Hum 569: A Free Flight

This figure was released in 1993 and carries a 1989 incised copyright date. Modeled by master sculptor Gerhard Skrobek in 1989, this piece was issued with a "First Edition 1993" oval decal on the underside. Retail price when issued was $185.

A special Canadian piece was produced with the words "O Canada" on the front of the base and a maple leaf appeared on the front of the boy's paper. The retail price for this special edition was about $200.

A Free Flight was temporarily withdrawn from production on June 15, 2002.

Hum No.	Basic Size	Trademark	Current Value
569	4-3/4"	TMK-7	$220-$230
569	4-3/4"	TMK-8	$215

A Free Flight, Hum 569, shown here in TMK-7.

Today's variation (TMK-8) of A Free Flight, Hum 569.

Photo courtesy Goebel of North America.

Hum 570: Open Number

Hum 571: Angelic Guide (1991 Christmas Ornament)

This figurine, modeled by master sculptor Gerhard Skrobek, was released in 1991 with an incised copyright date of 1989. This ornament was the fourth in the annual series of M.I. Hummel figural ornaments. It has a metal ring atop the angel's head for hanging as an ornament. Issue price in 1991 was $95.

Angelic Guide, Hum 571. 1991 Christmas ornament, TMK-6 mark, 1989 copyright date, 3-1/2".

Hum No.	Basic Size	Trademark	Current Value
571	4"	TMK-6	$150-$200
571	4"	TMK-7	$125-$150

Hum 572: Country Devotion (Possible Future Edition)

Modeled by Gerhard Skrobek in 1989, this figurine has a 1989 copyright date incised. It depicts a boy and girl standing at the foot of a country shrine. The girl has her head bowed and hands folded in prayer while a basket of flowers hangs from her left arm. The boy, who is signifi-cantly smaller, holds his hat in his hands while he gazes upward. A small coniferous tree and wooden fence also adorn the base next to the shrine. At this time, it is still listed as a possible future edition.

Hum 573: Open Number

Hum 574: Rock-A-Bye

This figurine is the "Century Collection" piece for 1994, the ninth piece in the series. Production in the 20th century was limited to only that one year. The figure has a special Century Collection backstamp, incised 1991 copyright date, TMK-7, and special decaled inscription: "M.I. HUMMEL CENTURY COLLECTION 1994 XX." Modeled by master sculptor Helmut Fischer in 1991, the original 1994 issue price was $1,150.

Rock-a-Bye, Hum 574.

Hum No.	Basic Size	Trademark	Current Value
574	7-1/2"	TMK-7	$1,400-$1,600

Hum 575-582, 585, 586: Angels of Christmas (Christmas Ornament Series)

This series of ornaments was modeled by master sculptor Helmut Fischer in 1988 and made by Goebel in 1990 for mail-order distribution by Danbury Mint. The figures were made in full color for Danbury. Each carries an incised "M.I. Hummel" signature and TMK-6, but no incised model number.

In 1992, Goebel made these pieces available as the Christmas Angels, but the finish is different. These small ornaments appear to have been made from the same molds as the Danbury Mint pieces, but they are rendered in white overglaze with only their eyes and lips painted in color (in the same fashion as the Expressions of Youth series). The wing tips are flashed in 14-karat gold.

Hum No.	Design	Size	Current Value (color)	Current Value (white)
Hum 575	Heavenly Angel	3"	$45-$50 (TMK-6)	$40 (TMK-7)
Hum 576	Festival Harmony With Mandolin	3"	$45-$50 (TMK-6)	$40 (TMK-7)
Hum 577	Festival Harmony With Flute	3"	$45-$50 (TMK-6)	$40 (TMK-7)
Hum 578	Celestial Musician	3"	$45-$50 (TMK-6)	$40 (TMK-7)
Hum 579	Song of Praise	2-1/2"	$45-$50 (TMK-6)	$40 (TMK-7)
Hum 580	Angel With Lute	2-1/2"	$45-$50 (TMK-6)	$40 (TMK-7)
Hum 581	Prayer of Thanks	3"	$45-$50 (TMK-6)	$40 (TMK-7)
Hum 582	Gentle Song	3"	$45-$50 (TMK-6)	$40 (TMK-7)
Hum 585	Angel In Cloud	2-1/2"	$45-$50 (TMK-6)	$40 (TMK-7)
Hum 586	Angel With Trumpet	2-1/2"	$45-$50 (TMK-6)	$40 (TMK-7)

Cover versions of several of the Angels of Christmas ornament series, from left: Heavenly Angel, Hum 575; Festival Harmony With Mandolin, Hum 576; Festival Harmony With Flute, Hum 577; and Celestial Musician, Hum 578. See Color Gallery section also.

Color versions of the remaining ornaments in the series, from left: Song of Praise, Hum 579; Angel With Lute, Hum 580; Prayer of Thanks, Hum 581; Gentle Song, Hum 582; Angel In Cloud, Hum 585; and Angel With Trumpet, Hum 586.

A Christmas tree adorned with Angels of Christmas ornaments in white overglaze.

Hum 596: Thanksgiving Prayer (Christmas Ornament)

Modeled by master sculptor Helmut Fischer in 1995, this ornament was first released in 1997 without an incised copyright date. It does, however, have an incised model number of 596, as well as an oval "First Issue 1997" sticker on the lower part of the gown. Issue price in 1997 was $120.

Hum No.	Basic Size	Trademark	Current Value
596	3"	TMK-7	$130-$140

Thanksgiving Prayer Christmas ornament, Hum 596.

Hum 597: Echoes of Joy (Christmas Ornament)

Master sculptor Helmut Fischer modeled this ornament in 1996. Listed as an "open number" in the last edition of this book, the piece was first released in 1997 with a "First Issue 1998" sticker attached. Incised "M.I. Hummel" signature appeared on the backside. Issue price was $120 in 1997.

This ornament was temporarily withdrawn from production on June 15, 2002, as were the Echoes of Joy figurines (Hum 642/0 and 642/4/0).

Hum No.	Basic Size	Trademark	Current Value
597	2-3/4" to 3"	TMK-7	$130-$140

Echoes of Joy Christmas ornament, Hum 597.

Photo courtesy Goebel of North America.

Hum 598: Joyful Noise (Christmas Ornament)

Master sculptor Helmut Fischer modeled this ornament in 1995. Listed as an "open number" in the last edition of this book, the piece was first released in 1998 with a "First Issue 1999" oval sticker. An incised "M.I. Hummel" signature appears on the backside. Issue price was $120 in 1998.

Temporarily withdrawn from production on June 15, 2002.

Hum No.	Basic Size	Trademark	Current Value
598	2-3/4" to 3"	TMK-7	$130-$140

Joyful Noise Christmas ornament, Hum 598.

Photo courtesy Goebel of North America.

Hum 599: Light the Way (Christmas Ornament)

Modeled by master sculptor Helmut Fischer in 1995 and listed as an "open number" in the last edition of this book, this ornament was first released in 2000 with a "First Issue 2000" oval sticker. An incised "Hummel" signature appeared on the backside. Issue price was $120 in 1999.

This ornament was temporarily withdrawn from production on June 15, 2002, as were both sizes of the Light the Way figurine (Hum 715/4/0 and 715/0).

Hum No.	Basic Size	Trademark	Current Value
599	2-3/4" to 3"	TMK-7	$130-$140

Light the Way Christmas ornament, Hum 599.

Hum 600: We Wish You the Best

Modeled by master sculptor Helmut Fischer in 1989, this piece was the sixth figurine in the "Century Collection," so it was produced as a limited edition for one year. It has an incised 1989 copyright date and circular inscription on a blue decal reading: "M.I. HUMMEL CENTURY COLLECTION 1991 XX." Issue price in 1991 was $1,300.

Hum No.	Basic Size	Trademark	Current Value
600	8-1/4" x 9-1/2"	TMK-6	$1,900-$2,100
600	8-1/4" x 9-1/2"	TMK-7	$1,700-$1,900

Hum 601-607: Open Numbers

Hum 608: Blossom Time

A 1996 release, this piece has the "125th Anniversary" and the "First Issue 1996" backstamps. Modeled by master sculptor Helmut Fischer in 1989, it measures 3-1/8" and has an incised copyright date of 1990. The release price was $155.

Blossom Time, Hum 608, shown here in TMK-7.

Hum No.	Basic Size	Trademark	Current Value
608	3-1/8"	TMK-7	$175-$180
608	3-1/8"	TMK-8	$175

Blossom Time, Hum 608, at left is the TMK-7 version and the other is today's variation with TMK-8. Both are the same size at 3-1/8".

Hum IV/608: Blossom Time (Music Box)

Modeled by master sculptor Helmut Fischer, this music box was issued in 1999 at $250. It carried a 1999 incised copyright date and was produced in a limited edition of only 500 pieces that were sold exclusively through the former Hummel Museum in New Braunfels, Texas. The box played "Edelweiss."

Hum No.	Basic Size	Trademark	Current Value
IV/608	5-1/2"	TMK-7	$300-$400

Photo courtesy Goebel of North America.

Blossom Time music box, Hum IV/608, which exists in TMK-7 only.

Hum 609: Open Number

Hum 610: April Shower (Possible Future Edition)

Master sculptor Helmut Fischer modeled April Shower in 1989 as a 9-3/8" figure. Goebel lists this item as a possible future edition only at this time. It carries a 1990 incised copyright date and depicts a boy and girl huddled beneath an umbrella while sitting on a wooden fence.

Hum 611: Sunny Song (Possible Future Edition)

Modeled by master sculptor Helmut Fischer in 1989 as a 5-1/8" figurine, it is a girl singing and holding flowers while a boy sits next to her playing a horn. It bears a 1990 incised copyright date. At this time, it is listed as a possible future edition only.

Hum 612: Lazybones (Possible Future Edition)

Modeled by master sculptor Helmut Fischer in 1989 as a 3-7/8" figurine with an incised 1990 copyright date, Goebel lists this item as a possible future edition. It is a boy lying on his stomach gazing at a bird perched on a plant.

Hum 613: What's Up? (Possible Future Edition)

Modeled by master sculptor Helmut Fischer in 1989 as a 5-1/2" figure, this piece depicts a boy sitting casually on a bench. It carries a 1990 incised copyright date. At this time, Goebel lists this item as a possible future edition only.

Hum 614: Harmonica Player (Possible Future Edition)

This figurine, modeled by master sculptor Helmut Fischer in 1989, depicts a boy playing a harmonica. It is a 5-1/2" figurine with a 1990 incised copyright date and is currently listed as a possible future edition only.

Hum 615: Private Conversation

Modeled by master sculptor Helmut Fischer in 1989, this figurine was listed has an "open number" in the last edition of this book but has since been put into production as an exclusive edition for members of the M.I. Hummel Club. This figurine has a 1990 incised copyright date and decal inscription: "EXCLUSIVE EDITION 1999/2000 M.I. HUMMEL CLUB." Issue price was $260, and it was not available after May 2000.

Hum No.	Basic Size	Trademark	Current Value
615	4-1/2"	TMK-7	$260-$280

Private Conversation, Hum 615, was an exclusive edition for the M.I. Hummel Club, which is available only in TMK-7.

Hum 616: Parade of Lights

This 6" figurine, released in 1993, seems to be a cousin of Carnival (Hum 328). Designed by master sculptor Helmut Fischer, it has an incised copyright date of 1990 and "First Issue 1993" backstamp the first year it was released. The original issue price was $235.

Hum No.	Basic Size	Trademark	Current Value
616	6"	TMK-7	$290-$300
616	6"	TMK-8	$285

Parade of Lights, Hum 616, at left with TMK-7 and the other with current-production TMK-8.

Hum 617: Open Number

Hum 618: A Basket of Gifts

Listed as an "open number" in the last edition of this book, this piece has since been put into production. Master sculptor Helmut Fischer modeled the piece in 1990. Released in 2002, it carries a "First Issue 2002" backstamp, 1990 incised copyright date, and TMK-8.

Hum No.	Basic Size	Trademark	Current Value
618	5-1/4"	TMK-8	$375

Hum 619: Open Number

Basket of Gifts, Hum 618, was new for 2002 with a retail price of $375.

Hum 620: A Story From Grandma

Goebel introduced this relatively large, complicated 8" figurine as a M.I. Hummel Club exclusive in 1995. It was a companion piece to At Grandpa's (Hum 621), which was introduced a year earlier. If you bought At Grandpa's, you were given the opportunity to reserve A Story from Grandma with the same sequential limited edition number as the first. Once these reserved pieces were sold, the figurine was released to the general membership of the club. Like Hum 621, Hum 620 was limited to 10,000 pieces worldwide. Modeled by Goebel team of artists in 1993, it carries an incised copyright date of that year. It was released at $1,300.

A Story From Grandma, Hum 620.

Hum No.	Basic Size	Trademark	Current Value
620	8"	TMK-7	$1,500-$1,600

Hum 621: At Grandpa's

In 1994, Goebel announced production of the first M.I. Hummel figurine to feature an adult. Modeled by Goebel team of artists in 1993, Hum 621 was introduced in a limited edition of 10,000 sequentially numbered pieces for exclusive sale to members of the M.I. Hummel Club. The edition was limited in sale "from June 1, 1994 until May 31, 1995, or unless the edition is sold out." Each bears the club exclusive backstamp, incised 1993 copyright date, and was released at $1,300.

A companion piece, A Story From Grandma (Hum 620), was released the following year.

At Grandpa's, Hum 621.

Hum No.	Basic Size	Trademark	Current Value
621	9"	TMK-7	$1,500-$1,600

Hum 622: Light Up the Night (1992 Christmas Ornament)

This is another in the annual series of ornaments. Modeled by master sculptor Gerhard Skrobek in 1990, it was released in 1992 as the fifth edition to the series. It has an incised 1990 copyright date and was issued at $95.

Hum No.	Basic Size	Trademark	Current Value
622	3-1/4"	TMK-7	$125-$150

Light Up the Night, Hum 622. 1992 Christmas ornament. Hummel Mark (TMK-7), 1990 copyright date, 3-1/4".

Hum 623: Herald On High (1993 Christmas Ornament)

This is another in the annual series of ornaments. Modeled by master sculptor Gerhard Skrobek in 1990, the piece was released in 1993 as the sixth and final issue in the series. The figurine has a "Final Issue" decal. The issue price in 1993 was $155.

Hum No.	Basic Size	Trademark	Current Value
623	2-3/4" x 4-1/2"	TMK-7	$180-$200

Herald On High, Hum 623. 1993 Christmas ornament.

Hum 624: Open Number

Hum 625: Goose Girl (Vase)

Listed as an "open number" in the last edition of this book, this piece has since been put into production. It was modeled by master sculptor Helmut Fischer and released in 1997 in combination with the small size 47/3/0 Goose Girl figurine.

This porcelain vase features a bas-relief design of the Goose Girl motif and has a 1989 copyright date. Issue price for the combination figurine and vase was $200, including $15 value for the vase.

Hum No.	Basic Size	Trademark	Current Value
625	4" x 3-1/2"	TMK-7	$50-$75

Photo courtesy Goebel of North America.

Goose Girl vase, Hum 625, shown here along with the small size Goose Girl figurine. The two were sold as a set for $200 at the time of release.

Hum 626: I Didn't Do It

This figurine, modeled by master sculptor Helmut Fischer in 1992 with a basic size of 5-1/2", was the M.I. Hummel Club exclusive offering for the club year 1993-94. It was available for $175 to members with redemption cards. It has the special club exclusive backstamp, 1992 incised copyright date, and inscription on decal under the base that reads: "EXCLUSIVE EDITION 1993/94 M.I. HUMMEL CLUB."

Hum No.	Basic Size	Trademark	Current Value
626	5-1/2"	TMK-7	$200-$225

I Didn't Do It, Hum 626. 1993/94 club exclusive. The object he holds behind himself is an archery bow.

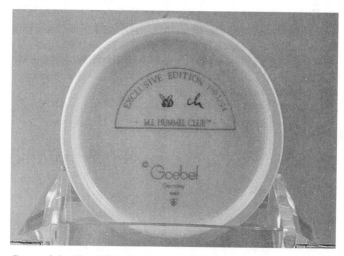

Base of the Hum 626 showing the M.I. Hummel Club special backstamp.

Hum 627: Open Number

Hum 628: Gentle Fellowship

Modeled by master sculptor Helmut Fischer in 1992, this was released in 1995 as the third and final figurine issued in the "UNICEF Commemorative Series." This piece bears the special UNICEF backstamp and has an incised 1992 copyright date. It is the only M.I. Hummel figurine to date that depicts two black African children. The design was taken from a drawing made during the 1930s when the Siessen Convent was beginning to develop missionary work in Africa.

The figurine was limited in production to 25,000 sequentially numbered pieces. The suggested retail price at release was $550.

As with the two previous figures in the series, for each one sold, a $25 donation was made to the United States Committee for UNICEF.

Hum No.	Size	Trademark	Retail Value
628	5-3/4"	TMK-7	$600-$625

Gentle Fellowship, Hum 628.

Base of Hum 628 showing the special backstamp.

Hum 629: From Me To You

This figurine, which was modeled by master sculptor Helmut Fischer in 1992, was given to each member of the M.I. Hummel Club who renewed their membership for the 1995-96 club year. It measures 3-1/2" and has a 1992 incised copyright date. At the time of release, the club valued it at $85. It bears the special inscription applied by decal that reads: "M.I. HUMMEL CLUB Membership Year 1995/96."

Hum No.	Size	Trademark	Current Value
629	3-1/2"	TMK-7	$100-$125

From Me to You, Hum 629.

Hum 630: For Keeps

Modeled by master sculptor Helmut Fischer in 1992, this figurine measures 3-1/2" and bears an incised copyright date of 1992. It was the renewal premium given free to members of the M.I. Hummel Club when they renewed their membership for the club year 1994-95. It has the special inscription: "M.I. HUMMEL CLUB Membership Year 1994/95."

Hum No.	Size	Trademark	Current Value
630	3-1/2"	TMK-7	$100-$125

For Keeps, Hum 630.

Hum 631: Open Number

Hum 632: At Play

Listed as an "open number" in the last edition of this book, this piece has since been put into production. Modeled by master sculptor Helmut Fischer in 1990, At Play was released in 1998 exclusively for members of the M. I. Hummel Club. Special decal on the underside reads: "EXCLUSIVE EDITION 1998/99 M.I. HUMMEL CLUB." Issue price in 1998 was $260. Goebel now lists this figurine as a closed edition.

Hum No.	Size	Trademark	Current Value
632	3-1/2"	TMK-7	$280-$300

At Play, Hum 632, is was released in 1998 as a M.I. Hummel Club exclusive and therefore exists only in TMK-7 with special "Exclusive Edition" backstamp.

Photo courtesy Goebel of North America.

Hum 633: I'm Carefree

Modeled by master sculptor Helmut Fischer in 1990 and released in 1994, this figure carries an incised copyright date of 1990.

When the piece was first released, the M.I. Hummel signature was located on the rear of the wagon. Later, the signature was moved to the backside of the piece, beneath the bird. It is thought that fewer than 1,000 of these were produced with the signature on the rear end of the wagon and this "rear signature" variation brings a premium on the secondary market.

All those figurines produced in 1994 will bear the "First Issue 1994" backstamp. Issue price was $365.

I'm Carefree was temporarily withdrawn from production on June 15, 2002.

Hum No.	Size	Trademark	Current Value
633 (rear signature)	4-3/4" x 4-1/4"	TMK-7	$800-$1,000
633 (side signature)	4-3/4" x 4-1/4"	TMK-7	$440-$450
633	4-3/4" x 4-1/4"	TMK-8	$440

I'm Carefree, Hum 633, shown here in TMK-7.

The TMK-8 version of I'm Carefree, Hum 633.

Photo courtesy Goebel of North America.

Hum 634: Sunshower

Listed as an "open number" in the last edition of this book, Hum 634 has since been placed into production. Modeled by master sculptor Helmut Fischer in 1990, Sunshower was produced as a limited edition of 10,000 pieces to commemorate the 60th anniversary of Hum 71, Stormy Weather. It carries a 1990 incised copyright date. It was released as Hum 634/2/0 in 1997 at an issue price of $360.

Hum No.	Size	Trademark	Current Value
634/2/0	4-1/2"	TMK-7	$380-$400

Sunshower, Hum 634/2/0, was made as a limited edition to mark the 60th Anniversary. It was released in 1997 and exists in TMK-7 only.

Hum 635: Welcome Spring

This is the 1993 "Century Collection" piece. It was modeled by master sculptor Helmut Fischer in 1990 and therefore bears an incised 1990 copyright date. Production was limited to that one year during the 20th century. The figure is marked so on the base and comes with a certificate of authenticity. The decal inscription on underside of the base reads: "M.I. HUMMEL CENTURY COLLECTION 1993 XX." The release price was $1,085.

Hum No.	Size	Trademark	Current Value
635	12-1/4"	TMK-7	$1,600-$1,800

Hum 636, 637: Open Numbers

Welcome Spring, Hum 635, shown here with TMK-7. It is the 1993 Century Collection piece.

Hum 638: The Botanist (Vase)

Listed as an "open number" in the last edition of this book, this piece has since been put into production. Modeled by master sculptor Helmut Fischer, it is a porcelain vase with bas-relief image of The Botanist (Hum 351). The vase was sold in combination with The Botanist figurine in 1998 for $210. The vase has a fired decal with a 1997 copyright date and incised "M.I. Hummel" signature.

Hum No.	Size	Trademark	Current Value
638	4" x 3-1/2"	TMK-7	$50-$75

The Botanist vase, Hum 638, which exists in TMK-7 only.

Hum 639, 640: Open Numbers

Hum 641: Thanksgiving Prayer

Modeled by master sculptor Helmut Fischer in 1991 and 1995. This is a miniature-size figurine with the mold number 641/0. Several pieces are released each year, each with the same theme, to form a Christmas group consisting of a mini-figurine, a Christmas tree ornament, a bell, and a plate. This mini-size figurine measures 5", has a 1991 copyright date, and if produced during the first year, it will bear the 1995 Limited Issue backstamp. (Compare to Hum 596.) A second, even smaller size was later introduced and numbered 641/4/0. Both sizes were first sold in the U.S. in 1997. Original issue prices were $180 for the large size (641/0) and $120 for the smaller size (641/4/0).

Both sizes were temporarily withdrawn from production on June 15, 2002.

Hum No.	Size	Trademark	Current Value
641/4/0	3-1/4"	TMK-7	$130-$140
641/4/0	3-1/4"	TMK-8	$130
641/0	5"	TMK-7	$200-$210
641/0	5"	TMK-8	$200

Thanksgiving Prayer is shown here in the larger 5" size at left with it's TMK-7 and 641/0 mold number and the smaller 3-1/4" size in TMK-8 with its 641/4/0. Note the difference in bases: one square, the other round. Both sizes of this figurine were temporarily withdrawn from production in June 2002.

Hum 642: Echoes of Joy

Listed as an "open number" in the last edition of this book, this piece has since been put into production in two sizes. Modeled by master sculptor Helmut Fischer in 1991 and 1995, both sizes were introduced to the U.S. market in 1997 and have a "First Issue 1998" decal fired on the under-side of the base. Original issue prices were $180 for the large size (642/0) and $120 for the smaller size (642/4/0).

Both sizes were temporarily withdrawn from production on June 15, 2002, as was the Echoes of Joy ornament (Hum 597).

Hum No.	Size	Trademark	Current Value
642/4/0	3-1/8"	TMK-7	$130-$140
642/4/0	3-1/8"	TMK-8	$130
642/0	5-1/8"	TMK-7	$200-$210
642/0	5-1/8"	TMK-8	$200

Echoes of Joy, Hum 642/0, is the larger variation at 5-1/8". It was temporarily withdrawn from production in June 2002, along with the smaller 642/4/0 version and the ornament of the same name, Hum 597.

Hum 643: Joyful Noise

Listed as an "open number" in the last edition of this book, this piece has since been put into production in two sizes. Modeled by master sculptor Helmut Fischer in 1991 and 1996, both sizes were introduced in the U.S. market in 1999 and have a "First Issue 1999" decal fired on the under-side of the base. Original issue prices were $180 for the large size (643/0) and $120 for the smaller (643/4/0) size.

Both sizes were temporarily withdrawn from production on June 15, 2002, as was the Joyful Noise ornament (Hum 598).

Hum No.	Size	Trademark	Current Value
643/4/0	3"	TMK-7	$130-$140
643/4/0	3"	TMK-8	$130
643/0	5"	TMK-7	$200-$210
643/0	5"	TMK-8	$195

Joyful Noise, Hum 643/0, was first issued in 1999, along with a smaller 3" size with mold number 643/4/0. Both sizes, along with the ornament variation of the same name (Hum 598) were temporarily withdrawn from production in June 2002.

Hum 644: Open Number

Hum 645: Christmas Song (Annual Ornament)

Modeled by master sculptor Helmut Fischer in 1991, this ornament is part of the "Annual Ornament" series. It matches a miniature figurine and Christmas plate in the same design. It carries an incised "Hummel" signature on rear side and "125th Anniversary Goebel" on the lower part of the angel's gown. Original issue price was $115 in 1996.

Hum No.	Size	Trademark	Current Value
645	3-1/4"	TMK-7	$130-$140

Christmas Song, Hum 645, 1996 Annual Christmas Ornament.

Hum 646: Celestial Musician (Annual Ornament)

Modeled by master sculptor Gerhard Skrobek in 1991, this ornament is part of the "Annual Ornament" series. It matches a miniature figurine and Christmas plate in the same design. Original issue price was $90 in 1993. It carries an incised "Hummel" signature on rear side.

Hum No.	Size	Trademark	Current Value
646	2-7/8"	TMK-7	$130-$140

Celestial Musician, Hum 646, 1993 Annual Christmas Ornament.

Hum 647: Festival Harmony With Mandolin (Annual Ornament)

Modeled by master sculptor Helmut Fischer in 1991, this ornament is part of the "Annual Ornament" series. It matches a miniature figurine and Christmas plate in the same design. It carries an incised "Hummel" signature on the rear side. Original issue price was $95 when first released in the U.S. in 1994.

Hum No.	Size	Trademark	Current Value
647	2 "	TMK-7	$130-$140

Festival Harmony With Mandolin, Hum 647, 1994 Annual Christmas Ornament.

Hum 648: Festival Harmony With Flute (Annual Ornament)

Modeled by master sculptor Helmut Fischer in 1991, this ornament is part of the "Annual Ornament" series. It matches a miniature figurine and Christmas plate in the same design. It carries an incised "Hummel" signature on the rear side. Original issue price was $100 when issued in 1995.

Hum No.	Size	Trademark	Current Value
648	2-3/4"	TMK-7	$130-$140

Festival Harmony With Flute, Hum 648, 1995 Annual Christmas Ornament.

Hum 649: Fascination

Listed as an "open number" in the last edition of this book, Hum 649 has since been put into production. Modeled by master sculptor Helmut Fischer in 1990, it was produced as a limited edition of 25,000 sequentially numbered pieces to commemorate Goebel's 125th anniversary. It was released in a quantity of 15,000 pieces in the U.S. for a retail price of $190 in 1996.

Hum No.	Size	Trademark	Current Value
649/0	4-3/4"	TMK-7	$200-$225

Fascination, Hum 649/0, was a limited edition released in 1996 to commemorate Goebel's 125th Anniversary. It exists only in TMK-7.

Hum 650-657: Open Numbers

Hum 658: Playful Blessing

Listed as an "open number" in the last edition of this book, Hum 658 has since been placed into production. Modeled by master sculptor Helmut Fischer in 1992, it was produced as an exclusive edition for members of the M.I. Hummel Club and introduced in 1997. Playful Blessing has an incised 1992 copyright date and inscription: "EXCLUSIVE EDITION 1997/98 M.I. HUMMEL CLUB." Issue price in 1997 was $260.

Hum No.	Size	Trademark	Current Value
658	3-1/2"	TMK-7	$280-$300

Playful Blessing, Hum 658, was a M.I. Hummel Club exclusive and exists in TMK-7 only.

Hum 659: Open Number

Hum 660: Fond Goodbye

This is the 12th piece in the "Century Collection." Modeled by master sculptor Helmut Fischer in 1991, it was released in the U.S. in 1997. During the 20th century, the edition was limited to those produced in 1997. The figures are marked with the Century Collection backstamp and accompanied with a certificate of authenticity. The decaled inscription on the underside of the base read: "M.I. HUMMEL CENTURY COLLECTION 1997 XX." The suggested retail price at the time of release was $1,450.

Hum No.	Size	Trademark	Current Value
660	6-7/8" x 11"	TMK-7	$1,600-$1,800

Hum 661: Open Number

Hum 662: Friends Together

This figurine was released in the summer of 1993 in two basic sizes. The smaller of the two, Hum 662/0 at 4", is the regular production figure. It bears a special Commemorative Edition backstamp. The larger size, Hum 662/1 (6") is a limited edition of 25,000 worldwide. This is the first of three cooperative fund-raising efforts between Goebel and the U.S. Committee for UNICEF, the United Nations Children's Fund. The art from which the figurine is taken was done by Sister Maria Innocentia Hummel in connection with Siessen Convent and its African missionary work during the 1930s.

Friends Together, Hum 662/I, was released in 1993 exclusively to M.I. Hummel Club members as a limited edition of 25,000 pieces. This 6" size exists in TMK-7 only and is worth $600-$650 today.

Fond Goodbye, Hum 660.

The figurines were not released to the public until September 3, 1993, but were available exclusively to members of the M.I. Hummel Club on a first-come, first-served basis for roughly one month prior to the general release. These figures were not marked with the special club exclusive backstamp and are not considered club pieces. The suggested retail price for the 4" size at release was $260. The release price for the limited edition, 6" size, was $475, with $25 of that amount contributed to UNICEF.

Hum No.	Size	Trademark	Current Value
662/0	4-1/4"	TMK-7	$350-$400
662/0	4-1/4"	TMK-8	$350
662/I	6"	TMK-7	$600-$650

The smaller variation (4-1/4") of Friends Together, Hum 662/0, shown here in TMK-8.

Hum 663-666: Open Numbers

Hum 667: Pretty As a Picture (Possible Future Edition)

Modeled by master sculptor Gerhard Skrobek in 1992, Pretty As A Picture (7-1/8") has an incised 1992 copyright date. It depicts a boy and girl standing beside one another as subject for an aspiring young boy photographer who kneels down to view the two through his camera, which is propped on a wooden tripod. Listed by the Goebel factory as a possible future edition.

Hum 668: Strike Up the Band

This figurine, modeled by master sculptor Helmut Fischer in 1993 and released in 1995, is the 10th piece in the "Century Collection." All figures in the Century Collection are limited in number to those produced in one designated year of the 20th century. This piece has an incised copyright date of 1992 and special decaled inscription on base underside that reads: "M.I. HUMMEL CENTURY COLLECTION 1995 XX." The suggested retail price was $1,200 when released.

Hum No.	Size	Trademark	Current Value
668	7-3/8"	TMK-7	$1,400-$1,600

Fond Goodbye, Hum 660.

Hum 669-674: Kitchen Moulds

Modeled by master sculptor Helmut Fischer in 1989, six kitchen moulds were distributed exclusively by the Danbury Mint in the U.S. and were released in 1991. One mould was released every three months. Each bears an incised "M.I. Hummel" signature and either a TMK-6 or TMK-7. Price at issue was $99 each.

Hum No.	Size	Design	Trademark	Current Value
669	7-1/2"	Baking Day	TMK-6 or 7	$170-$190
670	7-1/2"	A Fair Measure	TMK-6 or 7	$170-$190
671	7-1/2"	Sweet As Can Be	TMK-6 or 7	$170-$190
672	8"	For Father	TMK-6 or 7	$170-$190
673	8"	Supper's Coming	TMK-6 or 7	$170-$190
674	8"	Baker	TMK-6 or 7	$170-$190

The entire set of kitchen moulds, which were released by Danbury Mint, clockwise from top left: Sweet As Can Be (Hum 671), Baking Day (Hum 669), Supper's Coming (Hum 673), For Father (Hum 672), Baker (Hum 674), and A Fair Measure (Hum 670).

Hum 675: Open Number

Hum 676, 677: Apple Tree Girl and Apple Tree Boy (Candleholders)

These candleholders were modeled by master sculptor Helmut Fischer in 1988 and distributed exclusively in the U.S. by the Danbury Mint in 1989. Each has a 1988 incised copyright date. Retail price at issue was $142.50 each.

Hum No.	Size	Trademark	Current Value
676	6-3/4"	TMK-6 or 7	$200-$250
677	6-3/4"	TMK-6 or 7	$200-$250

Photo courtesy Goebel of North America.

Apple Tree Girl (Hum 676) and Apple Tree Boy (Hum 677) candleholders.

Hum 678, 679: She Loves Me, She Loves Me Not and Good Friends (Candleholders)

Modeled by master sculptor Helmut Fischer in 1989 and distributed exclusively in the U.S. by the Danbury Mint in 1990. Each has an incised 1989 copyright date. Retail price at issue was $142.50 each.

Hum No.	Size	Trademark	Current Value
678	6-1/4"	TMK-6 or 7	$200-$250
679	6-1/4"	TMK-6 or 7	$200-$250

Good Friends (Hum 679) and She Loves Me, She Loves Me Not (Hum 678) candleholders.

Photo courtesy Goebel of North America.

Hum 680-683: Open Numbers

Hum 684: Thoughtful (Trinket Box)

Modeled by master sculptor Helmut Fischer in 2001 and released in 2002, this 3-1/2"-diameter round box bears the image of the figurine with the same name (Hum 415) on top of the lid, along with "M.I. Hummel" signature. Small train images embellish the sides of the box.

Hum No.	Size	Trademark	Current Value
684	3-1/2"	TMK-8	$50

Thoughtful trinket box, Hum 684.

Hum 685: Book Worm (Trinket Box)

Released in 2002, this 3-1/2"-diameter round box is another design by master sculptor Helmut Fischer in 2001. It carries the image of the figurine with the same name (Hum 8) on top of the lid, along with "M.I. Hummel" signature. Small duck images (like those in her book) embellish the sides of the box.

Hum No.	Size	Trademark	Current Value
685	3-1/2"	TMK-8	$50

Book Worm trinket box, Hum 685.

Hum 686: Sweet Greetings (Trinket Box)

Modeled by master sculptor Helmut Fischer in 2001and released in 2002, this 3-1/5" x 3-1/4" heart-shaped box bears the image of the figurine with the same name (Hum 352) on top of the lid, along with "M.I. Hummel" signature. Small heart images embellish the sides of the box.

Hum No.	Size	Trademark	Current Value
686	3-1/2" x 3-1/4"	TMK-8	$50

Sweet Greetings trinket box, Hum 686.

Hum 687: She Loves Me, She Loves Me Not (Trinket Box)

Released in 2002, this 3-1/4" x 3-3/4" heart-shaped box bears the image of the figurine with the same name (Hum 174) on top of the lid, along with "M.I. Hummel" signature. Small bird images embellish the sides of the box. It was modeled in 2001 by master sculptor Helmut Fischer.

Hum No.	Size	Trademark	Current Value
687	3-1/4" x 3-3/4"	TMK-8	$50

She Loves Me, She Loves Me Not trinket box, Hum 687.

Hum 688: Umbrella Boy (Trinket Box)

Modeled by master sculptor Helmut Fischer in 2001 and released in 2002, this 5"-diameter round box bears the instantly recognizable Umbrella Boy image on top of the lid, along with "M.I. Hummel" signature. Small images of kites blowing in the wind embellish the sides of the box.

Umbrella Boy trinket box, Hum 688.

Hum No.	Size	Trademark	Current Value
688	5"	TMK-8	$60

Hum 689: Umbrella Girl (Trinket Box)

Released in 2002, this 5"-diameter round box is the same in size and shape as Hum 689 except that it has the Umbrella Girl image on top of the lid, along with "M.I. Hummel" signature. Small images of kites blowing in the wind embellish the sides of the box. Like the other trinket boxes released that year, it was designed by master sculptor Helmut Fischer in 2001.

Umbrella Girl trinket box, Hum 689.

Hum No.	Size	Trademark	Current Value
689	5"	TMK-8	$60

Hum 690: Smiling Through (Wall Plaque)

Modeled by master sculptor Gerhard Skrobek from an original Sister M.I. Hummel drawing, this is the second special edition produced in 1978 exclusively for members of the Goebel Collectors' Club (now M.I. Hummel Club). It was available through membership in the club only. Members received a redemption certificate upon receipt of their annual dues, and they could purchase the piece for $55 through dealers who are official representatives of the club. The figure bears TMK-5 and carries a decaled inscription that reads: 'EXCLUSIVE SPECIAL EDITION No. 2 HUM 690 FOR MEMBERS OF THE GOEBEL COLLECTORS' CLUB." As of May 31, 1984, it was no longer available as a redemption piece.

Smiling Through plaque, Hum 690, in the optional frame. Last Bee, 5-3/4" diameter. M.I. Hummel Club exclusive.

Hum No.	Size	Trademark	Current Value
690	5-3/4"	TMK-5	$50-$75

Hum 691: Open Number

Hum 692: Christmas Song (1996 Annual Christmas Plate)

Modeled by master sculptor Helmut Fischer in 1994, this plate has a 1994 copyright date and an incised "M.I. Hummel" signature on the front. It was issued in 1996 as part of the "Annual Christmas Plate" series at $130.

Hum No.	Size	Trademark	Current Value
692	5-7/8"	TMK-7	$40-$80

A Christmas Song grouping for 1996 comprising the mini-figurine, Hum 343/0, the plate and the ornament, Hum 645.

Hum 693: Festival Harmony With Flute (1995 Annual Christmas Plate)

Modeled by master sculptor Helmut Fischer in 1994, this piece was issued in 1995 as part of the "Annual Christmas Plate" series at $125. The plate has a 1994 copyright date and an incised "M.I. Hummel" signature on the front of the plate.

Hum No.	Size	Trademark	Current Value
693	5-7/8"	TMK-7	$50-$75

Festival Harmony With Flute. Christmas grouping for 1995 comprising the mini-figurine, Hum 173/4/0, the plate and the ornament, Hum 647.

Hum 694: Thanksgiving Prayer (1997 Annual Christmas Plate)

Modeled by master sculptor Helmut Fischer in 1994, this piece was issued in 1997 as part of the "Annual Christmas Plate" series at $40. The plate has a 1995 copyright date and an incised "M.I. Hummel" signature on the front of the plate.

Hum No.	Size	Trademark	Current Value
694	5-7/8"	TMK-7	$50-$75

Thanksgiving Prayer, Hum 694, annual Christmas plate for 1997.

Hum 695: Echoes of Joy (1998 Annual Christmas Plate)

Listed in the last edition of this book as an "open number," Hum 695 has since been put into production as one in the "Annual Christmas Plate" series. Modeled by master sculptor Helmut Fischer in 1996, this piece was issued in 1998 at $145. The plate has a 1996 copyright date and an incised "M.I. Hummel" signature on the front of the plate.

Hum No.	Size	Trademark	Current Value
695	5-7/8"	TMK-7	$75-$100

Echoes of Joy, Hum 695, annual Christmas plate for 1998.

Hum 696: Joyful Noise (1999 Annual Christmas Plate)

Listed in the last edition of this book as an "open number," Hum 696 has since been put into production as one in the "Annual Christmas Plate" series. Modeled by master sculptor Helmut Fischer in 1995, this piece was issued in 1999 at $145. The plate has a 1996 copyright date and an incised "M.I. Hummel" signature on the front of the plate.

Hum No.	Size	Trademark	Current Value
696	5-7/8"	TMK-7	$75-$100

A Joyful Noise, Hum 696, annual Christmas plate for 1999.

Hum 697: Light the Way (2000 Annual Christmas Plate)

Light the Way, Hum 697, annual Christmas plate for 2000.

Listed in the last edition of this book as an "open number," Hum 697 has since been put into production as one in the "Annual Christmas Plate" series. Modeled by master sculptor Helmut Fischer in 1995, this piece was issued at $145 in 2000. The plate has a 1996 copyright date and an incised "M.I. Hummel" signature on the front of the plate. The design is based on the figurine of the same name (Hum 715).

Hum No.	Size	Trademark	Current Value
697	5-7/8"	TMK-7	$75-$100

Hum 698: Heart's Delight

Listed in the last edition of this book as an "open number," Hum 698 has since been put into production. Modeled by master sculptor Helmut Fischer in 1996, this figurine was issued in 1998 as $220. It has an incised copyright date of 1996. The figurine sits on a small wooden chair.

This piece is considered a part of the Kid's Club Collector's Set, which was first offered in 2002 and also included

Practice Makes Perfect (Hum 771) and Love in Bloom (Hum 699). The set retailed for $650.

Hum No.	Size	Trademark	Current Value
698	4"	TMK-7	$250-$260
698	4"	TMK-8	$245

Kids Club Collector's Set. The set is made up of, from left to right: Love In Bloom, Hum 699; Practice Makes Perfect, Hum 771; and Heart's Delight, Hum 698.

Heart's Delight, Hum 698, with its red wooden chair.

Hum 699: Love In Bloom

Listed in the last edition of this book as an "open number," Hum 699 has since been put into regular production. Modeled by master sculptor Helmut Fischer in 1996, this figurine was issued in the U.S. in 1997 at a retail price of $220, including a wooden wagon the figurine sits on. It has an incised copyright date of 1996.

Love In Bloom is considered a part of the Kid's Club Collector's Set, which was first offered in 2002 and also included Practice Makes Perfect (Hum 771) and Heart's Delight (Hum 698). The set retailed for $650.

Hum No.	Size	Trademark	Current Value
699	4-1/4"	TMK-7	$250-$260
699	4-1/4"	TMK-8	$245

Love In Bloom, Hum 699, with its wooden wagon.

Annual Bells (left to right): 1978, 1979, 1980, 1981, and 1982.   *Annual Bells (left to right): 1983, 1984, 1985, 1986, and 1987.*

Annual Bells (left to right): 1988, 1989, 1990, 1991, and 1992.

Hum 700-714: Annual Bells

First began in 1978, the company issued annual bells through 1992, all in 6" size with bas-relief image on the front.

Hum No.	Design	Year	Trademark	Current Value
700	Let's Sing	1978	TMK-5	$25-$50
701	Farewell	1979	TMK-5	$20-$30
702	Thoughtful	1980	TMK-6	$25-$30
703	In Tune	1981	TMK-6	$25-$50
704	She Loves Me, She Loves Me Not	1982	TMK-6	$30-$40
705	Knit One, Purl One	1983	TMK-6	$30-$40
706	Mountaineer	1984	TMK-6	$30-$40
707	Girl With Sheet Music	1985	TMK-6	$30-$40
708	Sing Along	1986	TMK-6	$40-$75
709	With Loving Greetings	1987	TMK-6	$40-$75
710	Busy Student	1988	TMK-6	$40-$75
711	Latest News	1989	TMK-6	$40-$75
712	What's New?	1990	TMK-6	$40-$75
713	Favorite Pet	1991	TMK-6	$40-$75
714	Whistler's Duet	1992	TMK-6	$40-$75

Hum 715: Light the Way

Modeled by master sculptor Helmut Fischer in 1995, this piece was first released at a retail price of $120 in 1999, for the 715/4/0 size. The larger size, 715/0, was released at $180. Both carry the "First Issue 2000" backstamp, with the larger piece bearing a 1995 copyright date and the smaller an incised 1996 copyright date.

Both sizes were temporarily withdrawn from production on June 15, 2002, as was the Light the Way ornament (Hum 599).

Hum No.	Size	Trademark	Current Value
715/4/0	3"	TMK-8	$130
715/0	5"	TMK-8	$190

Light the Way, Hum 715/0.

Hum 716: Open Number

Hum 717: Valentine Gift (Display Plaque)

This plaque was a M.I. Hummel Club exclusive to celebrate the 20th anniversary of the club. It is 5-1/4" high and utilizes the first club exclusive figurine design, Valentine Gift (Hum 387). It was available to any member from March 1996 through December of the same year for $250. For an extra $20, the purchaser could have it personalized.

The piece carries an incised 1995 copyright date and incised "M.I. Hummel" signature diagonally on the back.

Hum No.	Size	Trademark	Current Value
717	5-1/4" x 6-1/2"	TMK-7	$300-$350

Valentine Gift display plaque, Hum 717, was a M.I. Hummel Club exclusive and exists in TMK-7 only.

Hum 718: Heavenly Angels

Modeled by master sculptor Helmut Fischer in 1996, the Hum 718 figurines were released in the U.S. in 1999 at the retail price of $90 each. They were sold exclusively through the Danbury Mint, which added in a hardwood display case at no additional charge.

Hum No.	Design	Trademark	Current Value
718/A	Let It Shine	TMK-7	$100-$110
718/B	Hush-A-Bye	TMK-7	$100-$110
718/C	Holy Offering	TMK-7	$100-$110
718/D	Join In Song	TMK-7	$100-$110
718/E	Peaceful Sounds	TMK-7	$100-$110
214/D/0	Angel Serenade	TMK-7	$100-$110

Heavenly Angels (Hum 718) shown here clockwise from top left: Peaceful Sounds, Hush-A-Bye, Let It Shine, Holy Offering, Join In Song, and Angel Serenade (Hum 214/D/0).

Hum 719: Open Number

Hum 720: On Parade

Modeled by master sculptor Helmut Fischer in 1994, Hum 720 was issued in the U.S. in 1998. It carries an incised 1995 copyright date and "First Issue 1998" decaled backstamp in the first year of production. The retail price at time of issue was $165.

Hum No.	Size	Trademark	Current Value
720	4-3/4"	TMK-7	$180-$200
720	4-3/4"	TMK-8	$180

On Parade, Hum 720, shown here in TMK-7.

Hum 721: Trio of Wishes

This is the second (1997) in a series of three called the "Trio Collection." Modeled by master sculptor Helmut Fischer in 1995, Trio of Wishes was released at $475 suggested retail price. It has an incised 1995 copyright date and comes with a hardwood display base. Production was limited to 20,000 sequentially numbered pieces. The other two figurines in the series are Tuneful Trio (Hum 757) and Traveling Trio (Hum 787).

Hum No.	Size	Trademark	Current Value
721	4-1/2"	TMK-7	$550-$600

A Trio Of Wishes, Hum 721.

Hum 722: Little Visitor (Plaque)

Modeled by master sculptor Helmut Fischer in 1995, Hum 722 carries an incised 1995 copyright date. Produced for purchase at the Visitors Center at the Goebel factory in Rodental, Germany, it was available with personalization at a price of approximately $120.

Hum No.	Size	Trademark	Current Value
722	4-3/4" x 5"	TMK-7	$140-$160
722	4-3/4" x 5"	TMK-8	$120

Little Visitor plaque, Hum 722, was released in TMK-7 as a piece available only at the Visitors Center at the Goebel factory.

Hum 723: Silent Vigil (Possible Future Edition)

Modeled by master sculptor Helmut Fischer in 1995, this piece bears an incised 1995 copyright date. The 6-3/4" figurine depicts a scene first used on a postcard drawing of Mary and Joseph watching over the Baby Jesus. Mary is seated on a wooden stool on one side of the baby cradle, while Joseph stands on the other. Goebel lists this piece as a possible future edition.

Hum 724, 725: Open Numbers

Hum 726: Soldier Boy (Plaque)

Modeled by master sculptor Helmut Fischer in 1996, this plaque bears an incised 1996 copyright date. It was released in 1996 exclusively by the U.S. Military post exchanges as a limited edition of 7,500 pieces. Original issue price was $140.

Hum No.	Size	Trademark	Current Value
726	5-1/2" x 6-3/4"	TMK-7	$200-$250

Soldier Boy plaque, Hum 726, was released in 1996 exclusively by U.S. Military post exchanges in a limited edition of 7,500 pieces.

Hum 727: Garden Treasures

Modeled by master sculptor Helmut Fischer in 1996, this figurine was released in the U.S. as the free gift for renewing membership in the M. I. Hummel Club for the 1998-99 membership year. In addition to a black flying bumblebee on the bottom, the piece also carries the inscription: "M.I. HUMMEL CLUB Membership year 1998/99."

Hum No.	Size	Trademark	Current Value
727	3-1/2"	TMK-7	$90-$100

Garden Treasures, Hum 727, is a M.I. Hummel Club exclusive and exists in TMK-7 only.

Hum 728: Open Number

Hum 729: Nature's Gift

Modeled by master sculptor Helmut Fischer in 1996, this figurine was released in the U.S. as the free gift for renewing membership in the M. I. Hummel Club for the 1997-98 membership year. It carries a black flying bumblebee on the bottom, as well as the inscription: "M.I. HUMMEL CLUB Membership Year 1997-1998."

Hum No.	Size	Trademark	Current Value
729	3-1/2"	TMK-7	$90-$100

Nature's Gift, Hum 729.

Hum 730: Just Resting (1985 Anniversary Bell)

Although this piece was announced and listed in the index of the *M.I. Hummel: Golden Anniversary Album*, it has never been produced for release to the general public. The original intention was to release it as a companion piece for a plate in the Anniversary Plate Series, but since the series was cancelled, apparently so went the bell. Modeled by master sculptor Gerhard Skrobek in 1978, what are likely samples are known to exist in several private collections.

Photo courtesy Goebel of North America.

Just Resting, Hum 730, the 1985 anniversary bell.

Hum No.	Size	Trademark	Current Value
730	7-1/8" x 4"	TMK-6	$1,500-$2,000

Hum 731: Best Friends (Possible Future Edition)

Modeled by master sculptor Helmut Fischer in 1992, this 5-1/2" figurine bears a 1992 incised copyright date. It depicts two girls walking arm in arm as one carries flowers and the other has a book/book strap slung over her shoulder. Goebel records list this piece as a possible future edition.

Hum 732: For My Sweetheart (Possible Future Edition)

Modeled by master sculptor Helmut Fischer in 1992, this 5-3/4" figurine carries an incised 1993 copyright date. It depicts a boy wearing long pants and a hat with guitar slung over his shoulder while he looks at a flower in his hand. Goebel lists this figurine as a possible future edition.

Hum 733, 734: Open Numbers

Hum 735-738: Celebration Plate Series

A series of four 6-1/4" plates was made available exclusively to members of the Goebel Collectors' Club (now the M.I. Hummel Club) to celebrate the club's 10th anniversary. One plate was released each year, starting in 1986. Modeled by master sculptor Gerhard Skrobek in 1985, each plate was originally sold only by redemption card to members of the M. I. Hummel Club one at a time. Each has an incised "M.I. Hummel" signature and special decal inscription on the back that reads: 'EXCLUSIVELY FOR MEMBERS OF THE GOEBEL COLLECTORS' CLUB."

Hum No.	Design	Year	Current Value
735	It's Cold	1989	$50-$60
736	Daisies Don't Tell	1988	$50-$60
737	Valentine Joy	1987	$50-$60
738	Valentine Gift	1986	$50-$60

Celebration Plate Series (left to right): It's Cold, Daisies Don't Tell, Valentine Joy, and Valentine Gift.

Hum 739/I: Call to Glory

This figurine was released in 1994. All pieces produced that year bear the "First Issue 1994" backstamp. The figure has an incised copyright date of 1992, measures 5-3/4", and comes with three flags: the German, the European Common Market, and the U.S. The suggested retail price at time of release was $250. A special edition of this figurine was made for attendees of the M.I. Hummel Club Convention in Orlando, Florida.

In the wake of the terrorist attacks on the World Trade Center and Pentagon on September 11, 2001 and the resulting American military effort, Goebel alerted its M.I. Hummel Club chapters that it would make a commitment to donate appropriately themed figurines to local chapters to be used as raffle prizes. Any proceeds from such fund-raising events would then go to benefit the families of the victims. Seven figurines, including this one, were selected as appropriate due to their patriotic or firefighter/police/medical personnel themes.

Photo courtesy Goebel of North America.

Call to Glory, Hum 739/I, shown here in TMK-7.

Today's rendition (TMK-8) of Call to Glory, Hum 739/I.

Hum No.	Size	Trademark	Current Value
739/I	5-3/4"	TMK-7	$300-$325
739/I	5-3/4"	TMK-8	$295

Hum 740: Open Number

Hum 741-744: Little Music Makers (Mini-Plate Series)

This is a four-plate series of 4" diameter plates. At the time the plates were issued, small figurines in matching motifs were also issued. All were modeled by master sculptor Gerhard Skrobek in 1982. The plates were limited in number to the amount produced during each year of the release. They are all found with TMK-6. There is no explanation for the nonsequential mold number/year of release situation.

Hum No.	Design	Year	Collector Value
741	Serenade	1985	$25-$30
742	Band Leader	1987	$25-$30
743	Soloist	1986	$25-$30
744	Little Fiddler	1984	$25-$30

Little Music Makers Plate Series (left to right): Serenade, Band Leader, Soloist, Little Fiddler. Plates are accompanied by the corresponding figurines.

Hum 745-748: Little Homemakers (Mini-Plate Series)

This four-piece mini-plate series began in 1988. The plates are 4" in diameter, and a small matching figurine was issued every year along with each plate. Master sculptor Gerhard Skrobek modeled all of them in 1986. Each plate was limited to the number produced in the year of issue. All but the last one in the series bear TMK-6. The last one, produced in 1991, is found with TMK-7.

Hum No.	Design	Year	Current Value
745	Little Sweeper	1988	$25-$30
746	Wash Day	1989	$25-$30
747	A Stitch in Time	1990	$25-$30
748	Chicken-Licken	1991	$25-$30

Little Homemakers Plate Series, from left: Little Sweeper, Wash Day, Stitch in Time, and Chicken-Licken. The corresponding figurines accompany plates.

Hum 749: Open Number

Hum 750: Goose Girl (Anniversary Clock)

This is one of the most unusual Hummel items ever produced. Modeled by master sculptor Helmut Fischer in 1993, it was first issued in U.S. in 1995. The face of the clock, which carries an incised "M.I. Hummel" signature, is approximately 4" in diameter and is the Goose Girl rendered in bas-relief. The overall height, including the dome, is 12". The release price was $200.

Hum No.	Trademark	Current Value
750	TMK-7	$230-$275
750	TMK-8	$225

Today's rendition (TMK-8) of the Goose Girl anniversary clock.

Hum 751: Love's Bounty

Hum 751 is the 11th piece in the "Century Collection." Production of this figure was limited to one year only in the 20th century. This particular piece is in commemoration of Goebel's 125th anniversary and each figure is so marked with special "125th Anniversary" backstamp. In addition, they each bear the Century Collection backstamp and special decal inscription: "M.I. HUMMEL CENTURY COLLECTION 1996 XX." It has an incised copyright date of 1993. Modeled by master sculptor Helmut Fischer in 1993, Love's Bounty was released in 1996 at a retail price of $1,200.

Love's Bounty, Hum 751.

Hum No.	Size	Trademark	Current Value
751	6-1/2" x 8-1/2"	TMK-7	$1,600-$1,800

Hum 752: Open Number

Hum 753: Togetherness (Possible Future Edition)

Modeled by master sculptor Helmut Fischer in 1993, this piece bears a 1994 copyright date. It depicts a boy and girl, each sitting on wooden stools on either side of a table-cloth-draped table. The girl is sewing, while the boy reads a book that is resting on the tabletop. A cat plays at their feet while a candle burns on the tabletop. Listed by Goebel as a possible future edition.

Hum 754: We Come In Peace

We Come In Peace, Hum 754.

This figurine, released in 1994, is a special commemorative UNICEF piece. Modeled by Helmut Fischer in 1993, it is quite similar to Hum 31 and Hum 113, but was redesigned especially for this release. It has a 1993 copyright date and a special backstamp identifying it as a UNICEF piece. The price at release was $350.

A $25 donation was made to the United States Committee for UNICEF for each figurine sold.

Hum No.	Size	Trademark	Current Value
754	3-1/2" x 5"	TMK-7	$385-$400

Hum 755: Heavenly Angel (Tree Topper)

Heavenly Angel tree topper, Hum 755.

This is another very unusual M.I. Hummel item. The familiar Heavenly Angel (Hum 21) theme has been rendered as a topmost ornament for a Christmas tree. It is open from the bottom so that it may be placed at the tree-top, or it can be slipped over a wood base for display.

The figure, modeled by master sculptor Helmut Fischer in 1992, was released in 1994. Those produced during that first year have the "First Issue 1994" backstamp. It has a copyright date of 1992 and was issued at $450.

Goebel temporarily withdrew this piece from production in January 1999.

Hum No.	Size	Trademark	Current Value
755	7-3/4"	TMK-7	$480-$500

Hum 756: The Artist (Display Plaque)

In 1993, Goebel released The Artist (Hum 304) in display plaque form to commemorate the opening of the former M.I. Hummel Museum in New Braunfels, Texas. At the time, it sold for $260. It was available with the "Grand Opening" wording in 1993 only. Thereafter, it was made without that inscription. The museum had used the plaque as its logo on letterhead and more, but has since ceased to operate.

Modeled by master sculptor Helmut Fischer in 1993, there are two more The Artist display plaques, both produced for German consumption and in very limited quantities. Each has a 1993 copyright date (see accompanying photo).

Hum No.	Size	Trademark	Current Value
756	5" x 6-3/4"	TMK-7	$400-$500

Three variations of The Artist display plaque, Hum 756, from left: piece to mark the 1993 opening of the M.I. Hummel Museum in New Braunfels, Texas, and two other pieces that were released in the German market only for events there in the 1990s.

Hum 757: Tuneful Trio

This is the first edition in a series called the "Trio Collection." Issued on a hardwood base in 1996 in a limited edition of 20,000, each figure bears a "125th Anniversary" backstamp, as well as incised 1993 copyright date. The figurine, modeled by master sculptor Helmut Fischer in 1993, had a suggested retail price at release of $450. The second in the series is A Trio of Wishes (Hum 721) and the third is Traveling Trio (Hum 787).

Hum No.	Size	Trademark	Current Value
757	4-7/8"	TMK-7	$480-$500

Tuneful Trio, Hum 757.

Hum 758: Nimble Fingers

Modeled by master sculptor Helmut Fischer in 1993, this is the second figurine in the collection to be fashioned so it must be seated. It came with a separate wooden bench. Seen in the photos here with its companion piece To Keep You Warm (Hum 759), which came out a year before, it has a 1993 copyright date. Those made in 1996, the year of release, bear the "First Issue 1996" backstamp. The release price was $225.

Hum No.	Size	Trademark	Current Value
758	4-1/2"	TMK-7	$260-$275
758	4-1/2"	TMK-8	$250

Left: Nimble Fingers, Hum 758, in TMK-7 with 1993 incised copyright date. First Issue 1995. Right: To Keep You Warm, Hum 759, also shown in TMK-7.

Today's variation (TMK-8) of Nimble Fingers, Hum 758.

Photo courtesy Goebel of North America.

Hum 759: To Keep You Warm

Modeled by master sculptor Helmut Fischer in 1993 and released in 1995, this is the first M.I. Hummel figurine to be fashioned so that it must be seated. As you can see from the photo, a wooden chair was provided with the figure. It bears a 1993 copyright date. It will have both the "First Issue 1995" and the "125th Anniversary" backstamps if made during 1995. Issued at a retail price of $195.

Nimble Fingers (Hum 758) was issued the following year and considered a companion piece.

Hum No.	Size	Trademark	Current Value
759	5"	TMK-7	$260-$275
759	5"	TMK-8	$258

To Keep You Warm, Hum 759. First Issue and 125th Anniversary backstamps (TMK-7).

Today's rendition (TMK-8) of To Keep You Warm, Hum 759.

Photo courtesy Goebel of North America.

Hum 760: Country Suitor

This figurine was released in 1995 as a M.I. Hummel Club exclusive. Modeled by master sculptor Helmut Fischer in 1993, it has an incised copyright date of 1993. It carries the black club flying bumblebee, as well as decal inscription: "EXCLUSIVE EDITION 1995/96 M.I. HUMMEL CLUB." The release price was $195.

Hum No.	Size	Trademark	Current Value
760	5-1/2"	TMK-7	$200-$225

Country Suitor, Hum 760.

Hum 761: From the Heart

This figurine is part of an informal annual series of paired figurines called "Cozy Companions." The other figurine in this pair is Heart and Soul (Hum 559). Both were released in 1996.

From the Heart was modeled by master sculptor Helmut Fischer in 1993 and has an incised 1993 copyright date. Those produced in 1996 bear both the "First Issue 1996" and the "125th Anniversary" backstamps. It was released at a suggested retail price of $120.

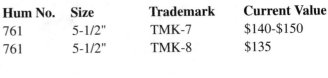

Hum No.	Size	Trademark	Current Value
761	5-1/2"	TMK-7	$140-$150
761	5-1/2"	TMK-8	$135

From the Heart, Hum 761, in TMK-7, which was released in 1996 and bears the 125th Anniversary backstamp.

Today's variation (TMK-8) of From the Heart, Hum 761.

Photo courtesy Goebel of North America.

Hum 762: Roses Are Red

Modeled by master sculptor Helmut Fischer in 1993, this piece carries a 1993 incised copyright date. It was first released in the U.S. in 1997 at the retail price of $120. There are no significant variations to affect collector values.

Hum No.	Size	Trademark	Current Value
762	3-7/8"	TMK-7	$140-$150
762	3-7/8"	TMK-8	$135

Roses Are Red, Hum 762, in today's TMK-8.

Hum 763: Happy Returns (Possible Future Edition)

Modeled by master sculptor Gerhard Skrobek in 1993, this 7-1/8" figurine has an incised copyright date of 1994. The piece shows a boy and girl standing side by side while a dog stands at their feet. The boy is holding a birthday cake, while the girl clutches a potted flower plant with bird perched atop. Listed by Goebel as a possible future edition.

Hum 764: Mission Madonna (Possible Future Edition)

Modeled by master sculptor Helmut Fischer in 1993, this 10-1/2" piece depicts a Madonna holding a Caucasian child while two African-American children play at her feet: one standing with a flower and the other seated. Listed by Goebel as a possible future edition.

Hum 765: First Love (Possible Future Edition)

Modeled by master sculptor Helmut Fischer in 1993, this figurine bears a 1994 incised copyright date. It features a boy similar to She Loves Me, She Loves Me Not (Hum 174) and a girl from the Hummel drawing "He Loves Me?" seated next to each other near a wooden fence. Each has a flower in his/her hand and two birds rest on the fence on either side of them, appearing interested in their activities. Listed by Goebel as a possible future edition.

Hum 766: Here's My Heart

Here's My Heart, Hum 766.

Modeled by master sculptor Helmut Fischer in 1994, this figurine was issued as the 1998 "Century Collection" release and was produced for only one year as a limited edition. It bears an incised 1994 copyright date, as well as decal inscription: "M.I. HUMMEL CENTURY COLLECTION 1998 XX." Issue price was $1,375.

Hum No.	Size	Trademark	Current Value
766	10-3/4"	TMK-7	$1,500-$1,600

Hum 767: Puppy Love (Display Plaque)

Modeled by master sculptor Helmut Fischer in 1993, this plaque is a special edition created to celebrate the 60th anniversary of the making of Hummel figurines. It features Puppy Love, the first in the series of original figurines released in 1935. The plaque in the accompanying photograph has a 1993 copyright date and "Special Edition 1995" backstamp in German and English. Available only during 1995, the original issue price was $240.

Hum No.	Size	Trademark	Current Value
767	4-1/2" x 7-1/4"	TMK-7	$300-$350

60-Year Anniversary display plaque, Hum 767.

Hum 768: Pixie

This figurine, modeled by master sculptor Helmut Fischer in 1994, was released in 1995. Each piece made that year had the "First Issue 1995" backstamp. It has an incised 1994 copyright date. The suggested retail price for Pixie in 1995 was $105.

Pixie is part of an informal series of paired figurines called "Cozy Companions." Its companion piece is Scamp (Hum 553).

Hum No.	Size	Trademark	Current Value
768	3-1/2"	TMK-7	$140-$150
768	3-1/2"	TMK-8	$140

Pixie, Hum 768, shown here in TMK-7.

Today's rendition (TMK-8) of Pixie, Hum 768.

Photo courtesy Goebel of North America.

Hum 769, 770: Open Numbers

Hum 771: Practice Makes Perfect

Modeled by master sculptor Helmut Fischer in 1994, this piece is one of only a few figures in the collection that is fashioned so as to be seated on something. In this case, a rocking chair is supplied with the figurine. It has an incised 1994 copyright date and was released in the U.S. in 1997. The first year of production bears the "First Issue 1997" backstamp. Suggested retail price at time of issue was $250.

This piece is considered a part of the Kid's Club Collector's Set, which was first offered in 2002 and also included Love In Bloom (Hum 699) and Heart's Delight (Hum 698). The set retailed for $650.

Practice Makes Perfect was temporarily withdrawn from production on June 15, 2002.

Hum No.	Size	Trademark	Current Value
771	4-3/4"	TMK-7	$280-300
771	4-3/4"	TMK-8	$280

Practice Makes Perfect, Hum 771, in TMK-7.

Today's version (TMK-8) of Practice Makes Perfect, Hum 771.

Photo courtesy Goebel of North America.

Photo courtesy Goebel of North America.

Practice Makes Perfect, Hum 771, shown here as part of the Kids Club Collector's Set. The set is made up of, from left to right: Love In Bloom, Hum 699; Practice Makes Perfect, Hum 771; and Heart's Delight, Hum 698.

Hum 772-774: Open Numbers

Hum 775-786: Christmas Bell Series

Christmas bells were released in three four-year series: 1989-1992, 1993-1996, and 1997-2000. The bells have pinecone-shaped clappers and all measure 3-1/4" in height.

Master sculptor Helmut Fischer modeled all the bells between 1987 and 1996. Issue prices at the time of release were: $35 in 1989, $37.50 in 1990, $39.50 in 1991, $45 in 1992, $50 in 1993 and 1994, $55 in 1995, $65 in 1996, $68 in 1997, $70 in 1998, 1999, and 2000. With the exception of Hum 775 and 776, which carry TMK-6, and Hum 786, which bears TMK-8, the rest of the bells carry TMK-7.

The only significant variation to be found is with regard to color. Some 250 to 300 of the 1990 bell, Ride Into Christmas, were made in greenish-yellow color and given to company representatives as a Christmas present from Goebel.

Hum No.	Year	Design	Current Value
775	1989	Ride Into Christmas	$30-$40
776	1990	Letter to Santa Claus	$30-$40
777	1991	Hear Ye, Hear Ye	$30-$40
778	1992	Harmony in Four Parts	$30-$40
779	1993	Celestial Musician	$25-$35
780	1994	Festival Harmony With Mandolin	$25-$35
781	1995	Festival Harmony With Flute	$25-$35
782	1996	Christmas Song	$25-$35
783	1997	Thanksgiving Prayer	$70-$75
784	1998	Echoes of Joy	$70-$75
785	1999	Joyful Noise	$70-$75
786	2000	Light the Way	$70-$75

Christmas Bells, left to right: 1989, Hum 775, Ride Into Christmas; 1991, Hum 777, Hear Ye, Hear Ye; 1992, Hum 778, Harmony in Four Parts.

1990 Christmas Bells. The one on the right is the reverse side of the regular 1990 bell. Letter to Santa Claus, in a soft pastel blue color. The bell on the left is rendered in a greenish-yellow color in a limited edition of 295.

Celestial Musician, Hum 779, the 1993 Christmas bell, which was dark green in color.

Celestial Musician bell showing the location of the markings in the bells.

The 1994, 1995 and 1996 Christmas bells: Festival Harmony With Mandolin, Festival Harmony With Flute and Christmas Song. They are colored lavender, yellow and pink, respectively.

Photo courtesy Goebel of North America.

From left: Thanksgiving Prayer, Hum 783, the 1997 Christmas bell, which was pale blue in color; Echoes of Joy, Hum 784, 1998's greenish-yellow bell; A Joyful Noise, Hum 785, the 1999 bell, which was pink; and Light the Way, Hum 786, the 2000 bell, which was the same hue of blue as the 1990 bell.

Hum 787: Traveling Trio

Listed as an "open number" in the last edition of this book, this piece has since been put into production as the third edition in a series called the "Trio Collection." Modeled by master sculptor Helmut Fischer in 1995 and issued in 1997 in a limited edition of 20,000 sequentially numbered figurines, Hum 787 bears a 1995 incised copyright date. The figurine measures 5-1/4". The suggested retail price at release was $490. First in the series was Tuneful Trio (Hum 757) and second in the series was A Trio of Wishes (Hum 721).

Photo courtesy Goebel of North America.

Traveling Trio, Hum 787, is the third addition to the "Trio Collection" series, which also includes Tuneful Trio, Hum 757, and A Trio of Wishes, Hum 721. It is available in TMK-7 only.

Hum No.	Size	Trademark	Current Value
787	5-1/4"	TMK-7	$500-$550

Hum 788/A: Hello and Hum 788/B: Sister (Perpetual Calendars)

Modeled by master sculptor Helmut Fischer in 1995 and released that summer, both of these pieces bear an incised 1995 copyright date. Each has wooden holder for calendar cards in which the month is written in both English and German. Both were released at a suggested retail price of $295 and both were temporarily withdrawn from production on June 15, 2002.

Hum No.	Size	Trademark	Current Value
788/A	7-1/2" x 6-1/8"	TMK-7	$300-$350
788/B	7-1/2" x 5-5/8"	TMK-7	$300-$350

Hello perpetual calendar, Hum 788/A.

Sister perpetual calendar, Hum 788/B.

Hum 789: Open Number

Hum 790: Celebrate With Song

This unusual figurine, modeled by master sculptor Helmut Fischer in 1994, was issued in 1996 as an exclusive M.I. Hummel Club piece. Sold only to those with redemption certificates from the club, it celebrates the 20th anniversary of the club. Valid redemption period ended May 31, 1998. It has an incised 1994 copyright date and the decal inscription: "EXCLUSIVE EDITION 1996/97 M.I. HUMMEL CLUB 1977 (20) 1997." It was priced at $295 at the time of release.

Hum No.	Size	Trademark	Current Value
790	5-7/8"	TMK-7	$300-$325

Celebrate With Song, Hum 790, was a M.I. Hummel Club member exclusive.

Hum 791: May Dance

Modeled by master sculptor Helmut Fischer in 1996, this figurine bears a "SPECIAL EVENT" decal since it was produced for sale only at "Mai Fest" celebrations during the year 2000. It also carries a 1996 incised copyright date. Original issue price was $199.

Hum No.	Size	Trademark	Current Value
791	7"	TMK-8	$199

Hum 792: Open Number

Photo courtesy Goebel of North America.

May Dance, Hum 791, a special event piece to coincide with "Mai Fest" celebration during 2000 (TMK-8).

Hum 793: Forever Yours

Forever Yours, modeled by master sculptor Helmut Fischer in 1994, bears a 1994 incised copyright date. It was the renewal gift for members of the M.I. Hummel Club who renewed their membership for the club year 1996-97. The figure has the special club backstamp, as well as the "First Issue 1996/97" backstamp and medallion. The inscription reads: "M.I. HUMMEL CLUB." Issue price was a $60 value as the gift with membership.

Hum No.	Size	Trademark	Current Value
793	4-1/8"	TMK-7	$80-$100

Forever Yours, Hum 793, was a renewal gift for M.I. Hummel Club members.

Hum 794: Best Buddies (Possible Future Edition)

Modeled by master sculptor Helmut Fischer in 1995, this 3-1/2" figurine has an incised 1996 copyright date. It depicts a boy sitting next to a black cat and is similar to the Being Punished Wall Plaque (Hum 326). Goebel lists this figurine as a possible future edition.

Hum 795: From My Garden

From My Garden, modeled by master sculptor Helmut Fischer in 1994, has a mold number of 795/0, which suggests that there may be another size in the offering. It has a copyright date of 1994 and bears the "First Issue 1997" backstamp. Original release price was $180.

Hum No.	Size	Trademark	Current Value
795/0	4-7/8"	TMK-7	$200-$220
795/0	4-7/8"	TMK-8	$200

From My Garden, Hum 795/0, in TMK-7.

Today's variation (TMK-8) of From My Garden, Hum 795/0.

Photo courtesy Goebel of North America.

Hum 796: Brave Voyager (Possible Future Edition)

Modeled by master sculptor Helmut Fischer in 1994, this 3-7/8" figurine has an incised 1994 copyright date. It depicts a boy holding a horn and sitting in a little Viking ship, just like the postcard drawing of the same name. At this time, Goebel lists this as a possible future edition only.

Hum 797: Rainy Day Bouquet (Possible Future Edition)

Modeled by master sculptor Helmut Fischer in 1994, this 5-1/8" figurine is listed as a possible future edition. It has an incised 1995 copyright date and depicts a girl standing under an umbrella while holding a bouquet of flowers in her right hand.

Hum 798: Open Number

Hum 799: Vagabond (Possible Future Edition)

Modeled by master sculptor Helmut Fischer in 1994, this 5-7/8" figurine has an incised 1995 copyright date. It portrays a boy holding a walking stick in his right hand and mandolin strung to his back. A bird sits atop the end of the instrument. Goebel lists it as a possible future edition only.

Hum 800: Proud Moments

Modeled by master sculptor Helmut Fischer in 1998, this figurine has an incised 1998 copyright date along with a "First Issue 2000 MILLENNIUM" oval decal and the TMK-8. It was first released in the U.S. in the fall of 1999 at an original issue price of $300.

Hum No.	Size	Trademark	Current Value
800	3-5/8"	TMK-8	$320

Proud Moments, Hum 800.

Photo courtesy Goebel of North America.

Hum 801: Open Number

Hum 802: Brave Soldier (Possible Future Edition)

Listed as a possible future edition only at this time, Brave Soldier was modeled by master sculptor Helmut Fischer in 1996 and has an incised 1997 copyright date. This 5-1/8" figurine depicts a boy holding a gun.

Hum 803, 804: Open Numbers

Hum 805: Little Toddler (Possible Future Edition)

Modeled by master sculptor Helmut Fischer in 1996, this 2-3/4" figurine is of a toddler lying on his stomach while pushing up on his toddler arms. It has an incised 1997 copyright date. Goebel lists this piece as a possible future edition.

Hum 806-813, 824, 825, 831, 832, 834, 841, 842, 851-854, 904, 913, 947 and 968: International Figurines

All international figurines were modeled by master sculptors Arthur Moeller or Reinhold Unger in 1940. Since 1976, several duplicates of some models and new variations of others have been found, usually selling in the $10,000 to $15,000 price range. See Chapter Five for more information on these unique figurines, as well as photographs.

They are as follows:

Hum No.	Description
806	Bulgarian Boy
807	Bulgarian Girl
808	Bulgarian Boy
809	Bulgarian Girl
810(A)	Bulgarian Girl
810(B)	Bulgarian Girl
811	Bulgarian Boy
812(A)	Serbian Girl
812(B)	Serbian Girl
813	Serbian Boy
824(A)	Swedish Boy
824(B)	Swedish Boy
825(A)	Swedish Girl
825(B)	Swedish Girl
831	Slovak Boy

Hum No.	Description
832(B)	Slovak Girl
832	Slovak Boy
834	Slovak Boy
841	Czech Boy
842(A)	Czech Girl
842(B)	Czech Girl
851	Hungarian Boy
852(A)	Hungarian Girl
852(B)	Hungarian Girl
853(A)	Hungarian Boy
853(B)	Hungarian Boy
854	Hungarian Girl
904	Serbian Boy
913	Serbian Girl
947	Serbian Girl
968	Serbian Boy

Hum 814: Peaceful Blessing

Modeled by master sculptor Helmut Fischer in 1997, this piece has an incised 1997 copyright date along with the "First Issue 1999" oval decal backstamp and TMK-7. It was first released in U.S. in the fall of 1998 at an original issue price of $180. It remains in production today.

Hum No.	Size	Trademark	Current Value
814	4-1/2"	TMK-7	$195-$200
814	4-1/2"	TMK-8	$195

Peaceful Blessing, Hum 814.

Hum 815: Heavenly Prayer

Modeled by master sculptor Helmut Fischer in 1997, this figurine was first released in the fall of 1998 for 1999. It has an incised 1997 copyright date, along with the TMK-7, and the "First Issue 1999" oval decal. Official issue price was $180 in 1999.

Hum No.	Size	Trademark	Current Value
815	4-7/8"	TMK-7	$195-$200
815	4-7/8"	TMK-8	$195

Heavenly Prayer, Hum 815.

Hum 816-819: Open Numbers

Hum 820: Adieu (Plaque)

Modeled by master sculptor Helmut Fischer in 1997, this piece has an incised 1997 copyright date. It was first released in Cayman Islands British West Indies in 1999 in a limited edition of approximately 300 pieces. It was sold exclusively (by Kirk Freeport Plaza, Ltd.) with 10 other models of M.I. Hummel figurines with a special floral backstamp and the words "Caribbean Collection." Issue price was $127 plus shipping/handling.

Hum No.	Size	Trademark	Current Value
820	3-3/4" x 6"	TMK-7	$160-$200

Adieu, Hum 820, was a special "Caribbean Collection" plaque.

Hum 821: Open Number

Hum 822: Hummelnest (Plaque)

Modeled by master sculptor Helmut Fischer in 1997, this figurine was first released in the fall of 1997 as the new visitors' plaque that can be personalized for visiting the Goebel factory in Rödental, Germany. Original issue price was DM195 (approximately $100 U.S.). It has an incised 1997 copyright date, along with the TMK-7.

Hum No.	Size	Trademark	Current Value
822	5-1/4" x 4-3/8"	TMK-7	$125

Hum 823: Open Number

Hum 824, 825: Swedish Figurines

See Hum 806: International Figurines.

Hummelnest, Hum 820, was a "special visitor's plaque" available only at the Goebel Germany Information Center.

Hum 826: Little Maestro

First issued in 2000, this figurine came as part of a limited-edition Gift Set. The set, which was limited to 20,000 numbered pieces worldwide, included the 5-3/4" figurine and a 5-1/4" Steiff teddy bear. The bear had a consecutively numbered white ear tag and button-in-ear and wore a medallion at its neck that depicted the figurine image.

Hum No.	Size	Trademark	Current Value
826 (Set)	5-3/4"	TMK-8	$425

Little Maestro, Hum 826, shown here as part of a set that also features a Steiff teddy bear.

Hum 827: Daydreamer (Plaque)

Modeled by master sculptor Helmut Fischer in 1998, this piece has an incised 1998 copyright date along with the TMK-7 and the "First Issue 2000 MILLENNIUM" oval decal backstamp. It was first released in 1999 as the new visitors plaque to those visiting the Goebel factory in Rödental, Germany. Official issue price was $140.

Hum No.	Size	Trademark	Current Value
827	3-1/2" x 4-3/8"	TMK-7	$150-$160
827	3-1/2" x 4-3/8"	TMK-8	$150

Daydreamer plaque, Hum 827, in today's TMK-8. The German phrase on the front translates to "The dear Mama."

Hum 828: Over the Horizon (Plaque)

Released in the U.S. in 2000, this piece was originally only available during artist promotions. Modeled by master sculptor Helmut Fischer, it carries a 1998 copyright date. The original retail price was $140.

Hum No.	Size	Trademark	Current Value
828	3-1/4"	TMK-8	$140

Over the Horizon plaque, Hum 828. The German phrase on the front translates to "For Daddy."

Hum 829: Where To Go?

Modeled by master sculptor Helmut Fischer, this special limited-edition figurine was part of a four-piece set that was released in 1999 through U.S. Military Post Exchanges in Europe to mark the 10-year anniversary of the fall of the Berlin Wall. Similar to Crossroads (Hum 331), the Hum 829 carries an incised 1999 copyright date.

The Enduring Glow of Freedom Set consists of two figurines: Where To Go? (Hum 829) and Happy Traveler (Hum 109). The piece was limited to 5,000 sequentially numbered pieces worldwide. It came with a wooden base that had an engraved brass plaque on the front that read: "Commemorating the 10 Year Anniversary of the Fall of the Berlin Wall and the Sweet Glow of Freedom for all of Germany. 1989 – November – 1999." The colorful "rainbow" is made of plastic and fits firmly in a slot on the wooden base. The set originally sold for $358.

Hum No.	Size	Trademark	Current Value
829 (Set)	6-1/2"	TMK-7	$375

Enduring Glow Of Freedom Set, a limited edition set that consisted of Hum 829 and Hum 109 as well as wooden base.

Hum 830: Open Number

Hum 831-834: Slovak Figurines

See Hum 806: International Figurines.

Hum 835: Garden Splendor

Released in 2000, this piece was first modeled by master sculptor Helmut Fischer and carries a 1998 incised copyright date as well as "First Issue 2000" special backstamp in the first year of production. This figurine also is the subject of a plate by the same name (Hum 921).

Hum No.	Size	Trademark	Current Value
835	3-1/4"	TMK-8	$155

Garden Splendor, Hum 835.

Hum 836: Afternoon Nap

Released in 2001, this piece was first modeled by master sculptor Helmut Fischer in 1999 and carries a 1999 incised copyright date as well as "First Issue 2001" special backstamp in the first year of production. This figurine also is the subject of a plate by the same name (Hum 922).

Hum No.	Size	Trademark	Current Value
836	3-1/2"	TMK-8	$225

Afternoon Nap, Hum 836.

Hum 837: Bumblebee Friend

This figurine, released in 2002, was first modeled by master sculptor Helmut Fischer in 2000. It carries a 2000 incised copyright date, as well as "First Issue 2002" backstamp in the first year of production. The same motif was used for the 2002 annual plate that carries the same name (Hum 923).

Hum No.	Size	Trademark	Current Value
837	5-1/4"	TMK-8	$260

Bumblebee Friend, Hum 837.

Hum 838: Christmas By Candlelight

This piece, released in 2001, was modeled by master sculptor Helmut Fischer in 2000. It measures 7-1/2" and carries TMK-8 and an incised 2000 copyright date, as well as a special "First Issue 2001" backstamp in the first year of production.

Hum No.	Size	Trademark	Current Value
838	7-1/2"	TMK-8	$215

Christmas By Candlelight, Hum 838.

Hum 839, 840: Open Numbers

Hum 841, 842: Czech Figurines

See Hum 806: International Figurines.

Hum 843-850: Open Numbers

Hum 851-854: Hungarian Figurines

See Hum 806: International Figurines.

Hum 855: Millennium Madonna

On Christmas Eve 1999, Pope John Paul II opened the holy doors at St. Peter's Basilica in Rome to mark the beginning of Jubilee 2000, the Holy Year. Jubilee 2000 ended on Epiphany 2001, when the Supreme Pontiff sealed the doors of St. Peter's, marking the closing of the Holy Year. But the spirit of Holy Year 2000 lives on with this beautiful piece, which was released in 2000 to mark this wonderful event. It was a special limited edition of 7,500 numbered pieces worldwide. Modeled by master sculptor Helmut Fischer, it carries the "First Issue 2000" backstamp, as well as TMK-8. It comes in a special, hinged, velvet-lined case. Now listed as a closed edition.

Hum No.	Size	Trademark	Current Value
855	10-1/4"	TMK-7	$515

Photo courtesy Goebel of North America.

Hum 856-859: Open Numbers

An exquisite limited edition, Millennium Madonna (Hum 855) was released in 1999 to mark the coming change of centuries.

Hum 860-874: Miniature Bells

Ten miniature bells were released in January 2000 and another five were released in 2001. Modeled by master sculptor Helmut Fischer in 1999, each miniature bell is a reproduction of the larger Annual Bells and originally retailed for DM 49 (about $24.50 apiece). Wooden display racks in two different finishes—"Countrystyle" and "Light Brown"—were also available for DM 95 (about $47.50). All measure 3-3/4", carry TMK-8, and are currently worth $25.

Hum No.	Design
860	Let's Sing
861	Farewell
862	Thoughtful
863	In Tune
864	She Loves Me, She Loves Me Not
865	Knit One, Purl One
866	Mountaineer
867	Girl With Sheet Music
868	Sing Along
869	With Loving Greetings
870	Busy Student
871	Latest News
872	What's New?
873	Favorite Pet
874	Whistler's Duet

Photo courtesy Goebel of North America.

All 15 pieces in the miniature bell series, shown here in the light brown display rack in sequential order of Hum number from left to right, beginning with the top row.

Hum 875: Open Number

Hum 876/A: Heavenly Angel (Ornament)

This bell-shaped bas-relief Christmas ornament, measuring 3-1/4" with an incised "M.I. Hummel" signature on the front, was released in 1999 as part of what is now a series of nine decorative ornaments. In addition to this piece (Hum 876/A), the series, which was modeled by master sculptor Helmut Fischer in 1999, included the following: Hum 877/A, Hum 878/A, Hum 879/A, Hum 880/A, Hum 2099/A, Hum 2110/A, Hum 2111/A, and Hum 2129/A.

Hum No.	Size	Trademark	Current Value
876/A	3-1/4"	TMK-7	$20

Heavenly Angel ornament, Hum 876/A.

Hum 877/A: Ride Into Christmas (Ornament)

Released in 1999, this decorative bas-relief Christmas ornament is in the shape of a Christmas tree and was the design of master sculptor Helmut Fischer in 1999. It measures 4-1/4" and has an incised "M.I. Hummel" signature on the front. It is another in the series of similar ornaments (see Hum 876/A).

Hum No.	Size	Trademark	Current Value
877/A	4-1/4"	TMK-7	$20

Ride Into Christmas ornament, Hum 877/A.

Hum 878/A: Sleep Tight (Ornament)

This decorative bas-relief Christmas ornament in the shape of a ball ornament with bow was modeled by master sculptor Helmut Fischer in 1999. Measuring 3-1/2" with an incised "M.I. Hummel" signature on the front, it was released in 1999 as part of what is now a series of similar ornaments (see Hum 876/A).

Hum No.	Size	Trademark	Current Value
878/A	3-1/2"	TMK-7	$20

Sleep Tight ornament, Hum 878/A.

Hum 879/A: Christmas Song (Ornament)

This bas-relief ornament is in the shape of a candlestick and was released new for 2002. Designed by master sculptor Helmut Fischer in 1999, it has an incised "M.I. Hummel" signature on the front. It is another in the series of similar decorative ornaments (see Hum 876/A).

Hum No.	Size	Trademark	Current Value
879/A	3-1/2"	TMK-8	$20

Photo courtesy Goebel of North America.

Christmas Song ornament, Hum 879/A.

Hum 880/A: Hear Ye, Hear Ye (Ornament)

Released new for 2002, this bas-relief Christmas ornament is in the shape of a lantern. Master sculptor Helmut Fischer modeled it in 1999. It has an incised "M.I. Hummel" signature on the front. It is another in the series of similar decorative ornaments (see Hum 876/A).

Hum No.	Size	Trademark	Current Value
880/A	4-1/4"	TMK-8	$20

Photo courtesy Goebel of North America.

Hear Ye, Hear Ye ornament, Hum 880/A.

Hum 881-884: New Baby Gifts

Released new for 2003, the New Baby Gift Set features four pieces, all of which display The Guardian (Hum 445) motif. The pieces are: Baby's First Christmas ornament (Hum 881/A); an earthenware framed picture (Hum 882/A); earthenware birth certificate/storybook with pen (Hum 883/A); and The Guardian round trinket box (Hum 884).

Hum No.	Basic Size	Trademark	Current Value
881/A	3-1/2"	TMK-8	$22.50
882/A	5-1/2"	TMK-8	$75
883/A	5-1/2"	TMK-8	$50
884	4"	TMK-8	$50

Hum 885: Open Number

Hum 886-899: Century Collection Mini Plates

The Century Collection Miniature Plates feature each of the limited edition M.I. Hummel figurines on a single plate. Each plate measures 4" diameter and is worth $30. A wall display in walnut was available for $100.

Hum No.	Design	Year
886	Chapel Time	1986
887	Pleasant Journey	1987
888	Call to Worship	1988
889	Harmony In Four Parts	1989
890	Let's Tell the World	1990
891	We Wish You the Best	1991
892	On Our Way	1992
893	Welcome Spring	1993
894	Rock-A-Bye	1994
895	Strike Up the Band	1995
896	Love's Bounty	1996
897	Fond Goodbye	1997
898	Here's My Heart	1998
899	Fanfare	1999

Chapel Time mini plate, Hum 886, released in 1986.

Pleasant Journey mini plate, Hum 887, released in 1987.

Call to Worship mini plate, Hum 888, released in 1988.

Harmony in Four Parts mini plate, Hum 889, released in 1989.

Let's Tell the World, mini plate, Hum 890, released in 1990.

We Wish You the Best mini plate, Hum 891, released in 1991.

On Our Way mini plate, Hum 892, released in 1992.

Welcome Spring mini plate, Hum 893, released in 1993.

Rock-A-Bye mini plate, Hum 894, released in 1994.

Strike Up the Band mini plate, Hum 895, released in 1995.

Love's Bounty mini plate, Hum 896, released in 1996.

Fond Goodbye mini plate, Hum 897, released in 1997.

Here's My Heart mini plate, Hum 898, released in 1998.

Fanfare mini plate, Hum 899, released in 1999.

Hum 900: Merry Wanderer (Plaque)

Modeled in 1998 by master sculptor Helmut Fischer, this piece was a M.I. Hummel Club exclusive. It has an incised 1998 copyright date, along with the TMK-8 and "Original Goebel archival plaque ca. 1947" incised on the back of the Collectors' Club plaque only. First released in U.S. in the fall of 1999 at $195, with the member's redemption card.

Hum No.	Size	Trademark	Value
900	4" x 5-3/4"	TMK-8	$195 (Retailer Plaque)
900	4" x 5-3/4"	TMK-8	$195 (Collector's Plaque)

Merry Wanderer plaque, Hum 900.

Hum 901-903: Open Numbers

Hum 904:Serbian Boy

See Hum 806: International Figurines.

Hum 905-912: Open Numbers

Hum 913: Serbian Girl

See Hum 806: International Figurines.

Hum 914-919: Open Numbers

Hum 920: Star Gazer (Annual Plate)

Modeled by master sculptor Helmut Fischer in 1990, this plate has an incised 1999 copyright date along with TMK-8. It is a part of the "Millennium" plate series, bears a special "60th Anniversary" backstamp honoring Hum 132 (Star Gazer). Official issue price was $198 in 2000.

Hum No.	Size	Trademark	Value
920	7-1/2"	TMK-8	$198

Star Gazer, Hum 920, is the annual plate for 2000. It uses the design of the figurine of the same name (Hum 132).

Hum 921: Garden Splendor (Annual Plate)

With the design of the figurine of the same name (Hum 835), this plate was introduced new in 2000 as that year's edition in the annual plate series.

Hum No.	Size	Trademark	Current Value
921	7"	TMK-8	$198

Garden Splendor plate, Hum 921, which utilizes the design of the figurine of the same name (Hum 835).

Hum 922: Afternoon Nap (Annual Plate)

The 2001 installment in the annual plate series, Afternoon Nap is adorned with the image of the figurine of the same name (Hum 836). Master sculptor Helmut Fischer modeled it in 1999.

Hum No.	Size	Trademark	Current Value
922	7"	TMK-8	$198

Afternoon Nap, Hum 922, is the annual plate for 2001. It uses the design of the figurine of the same name (Hum 836).

Hum 923: Bumblebee Friend (Annual Plate)

Carrying the image of the figurine with the same name (Hum 837), Bumblebee Friend is the 2002 edition in the annual plate series. It was modeled by master sculptor Helmut Fischer in 1999.

Hum No.	Size	Trademark	Current Value
923	7"	TMK-8	$198

Bumblebee Friend, Hum 923, is the annual plate for 2002 and is shown here with the figurine of the same name (Hum 837).

Hum 924: The Florist (Annual Plate)

The most recent addition to the annual plate series is The Florist, which is new for 2003. It is paired with the 5-1/4" figurine of the same name (Hum 349/0).

Hum No.	Size	Trademark	Current Value
924	7"	TMK-8	$215

The Florist, Hum 924, is the annual plate for 2003.

Hum 925-946: Open Numbers

Hum 947: Serbian Girl

See Hum 806: International Figurines.

382   Luckey's Hummel Figurines and Plates

Hum 948, 949: Open Numbers

Hum 950: Apple Tree Girl (Doll)

Released in 1998, this doll was a companion to the Apple Tree Boy doll, Hum 951, and is Goebel's continuation of the doll series began by Danbury Mint (see Hum 512-524). This doll is costumed by world-renowned doll designer Bette Ball and is seated in its own tree display stand, detailed with apples, apple blossoms, and even a friendly bird. Master sculptor Marion Huschka modeled it in 1996.

Hum No.	Size	Trademark	Current Value
950	13"	TMK-7	$250

Apple Tree Girl doll, Hum 950, shown here in TMK-7 with its tree display stand.

Hum 951: Apple Tree Boy (Doll)

The companion to Hum 950, this Apple Tree Boy doll was also released in 1998 and is Goebel's continuation of the doll series began by Danbury Mint (see Hum 512-524). Like Apple Tree Girl doll, this doll is costumed by world-renowned doll designer Bette Ball and is seated in its own tree display stand, detailed with apples, apple blossoms, and even a friendly bird. Master sculptor Marion Huschka modeled it in 1996.

Hum No.	Size	Trademark	Current Value
951	13"	TMK-7	$250

Apple Tree Boy doll, Hum 951, was released in 1998 as a companion to the Apple Tree Girl doll, Hum 950.

Hum 952-959: Open Numbers

Hum 960: Ride Into Christmas (Doll)

Released in 1999, Ride Into Christmas is another addition to the doll series began by Danbury Mint (see Hum 512-524). It was modeled by master sculptor Helmut Fischer in 1997 and measures 11".

Hum No.	Size	Trademark	Current Value
960	11"	TMK-7	$200

Ride Into Christmas doll, Hum 960.

Hum 961-967: Open Numbers

Hum 968: Serbian Boy

See Hum 806: International Figurines.

Hum 969, 970: Open Numbers

Hum 971-995: M.I. Hummel Miniature Plate Series

Each plate in this 25-piece series has a 1995 copyright date as part of the TMK-7 applied by blue decal on the back. Each measures 3-1/4" as is a reproduction of the larger Annual Plates with the same names.

They were produced in 1995 for the European market only, but have since been made available in the U.S. though Danbury Mint. They retail at $19.95 each. A custom wooden wall display is also available for $19.95.

Hum No.	Design	Year
971	Heavenly Angel	1997
972	Hear Ye, Hear Ye	1997
973	Happy Traveler	1997
974	Goose Girl	1997
975	Ride Into Christmas	1997
976	Apple Tree Girl	1997
977	Apple Tree Boy	1997
978	Happy Pastime	1997
979	Singing Lesson	1997
980	School Girl	1997
981	Umbrella Boy	1997
982	Umbrella Girl	1997
983	Postman	1998
984	Little Helper	1998
985	Chick Girl	1998
986	Playmates	1998
987	Feeding Time	1998
988	Little Goat Herder	1998
989	Farm Boy	1998
990	Shepherd's Boy	1998
991	Just Resting	1998
992	Wayside Harmony	1998
993	Doll Bath	1998
994	Doctor	1998
995	Come Back Soon	1998

The entire M.I. Hummel Miniature Plate Series, Hum 971-995, displayed in wooden wall rack crafted especially for the collection.

Hum 996: Scamp (Trinket Box)

Released in 2002, this 4" x 3" oval box was modeled by master sculptor Helmut Fischer in 2001. It bears the image of the figurine with the same name (Hum 553) on top of the lid, along with "M.I. Hummel" signature. Small cattail-like images embellish the sides of the box.

Hum No.	Size	Trademark	Current Value
996	4" x 3"	TMK-8	$50

Scamp trinket box, Hum 996.

Hum 997: Pixie (Trinket Box)

Modeled by master sculptor Helmut Fischer in 2001 and released in 2002, this 4" x 3" oval box bears the image of the figurine with the same name (Hum 768) on top of the lid, along with "M.I. Hummel" signature. Small rural homestead images embellish the sides of the box.

Hum No.	Size	Trademark	Current Value
997	4" x 3"	TMK-8	$50

Pixie trinket box, Hum 997.

Hum 998-1998: Open Numbers

Hum 1999: Fanfare

The 14th and final figurine in the "Century Collection," Fanfare was released in 1999 and was produced for this one year only in the 20th century. This was attested by a certificate of authenticity and a special stamp on the bottom of the figurines. The inscription read: "M.I. HUMMEL 1999 XX FINAL EDITION—CENTURY COLLECTION." Modeled by master sculptors Helmut Fischer and Marion Huschka in 1993, the piece bears an incised 1993 copyright date. An incised "M.I. Hummel" signature appears on the back. It came with a hardwood base with brass plaque that read: "CENTURY COLLECTION 1999 LETZTE AUSGABE – FINAL EDITION."

Hum No.	Size	Trademark	Current Value
1999	11"	TMK-7	$1,275-$1,300

Fanfare, Hum 1999, which in 1999 was the final installment in the "Century Collection."

Hum 2000: Worldwide Wanderers

This gorgeous figurine was modeled by master sculptors Helmut Fischer and Tamara Fuchs in 1998 and released in the U.S. in 1999. A worldwide limited and numbered edition of 2,000 pieces, it has an 1998 incised copyright date, special "Year 2000 Millennium" backstamp, and TMK-8. It comes with velvet-covered base and porcelain certificate of authenticity. The original issue price was $4,500. Closed edition.

Hum No.	Size	Trademark	Current Value
2000	8"	TMK- 8	$4,500

Hum 2001: Open Number

Hum 2002: Making New Friends

Released in September 1996, this figurine was modeled by master sculptor Helmut Fischer and has a 1996 copyright date. Those produced in 1996 have the "First Issue 1996" and the "125th Anniversary" backstamps applied to the bottom on blue decal. The original issue price was $595.

Hum No.	Size	Trademark	Current Value
2002	6-1/2"	TMK-7	$595-$600
2002	6-1/2"	TMK-8	$625

Worldwide Wanders, Hum 2000, displayed here on special wooden base and with "Millennium" medallion.

Making New Friends, Hum 2002.

Hum 2003: Dearly Beloved

Modeled by master sculptor Helmut Fischer in 1997, this figurine was first released in 1998. It bears a 1997 incised copyright date, and those released in that first production year carry "First Issue 1998" special backstamp. The piece came with a neutral brass plaque affixed to wooden base, which could be engraved by a specialist. The original issue price was $450.

Hum No.	Size	Trademark	Current Value
2003	6-5/8"	TMK-7	$475-$500
2003	6-5/8"	TMK-8	$510

Dearly Beloved, Hum 2003, shown here in TMK-7.

Hum 2004: Pretzel Girl

This figurine, modeled by master sculptor Helmut Fischer in 1996, was first released in the U.S. in 1999. Pieces produced that year will carry a "First Issue 1999" backstamp. It has an incised 1996 copyright date and an original release price of $185. It is considered a companion piece to Pretzel Boy (Hum 2093).

Several Special Event Collector's Set pieces were issued, including two with "Germany" backstamps, one with "Two Flags, USA," and another with "M.I. Hummel Club Convention, Germany." Although listed as a closed edition in the U.S., the piece is available in other world markets.

Hum No.	Size	Trademark	Current Value
2004	4"	TMK-7	$185-$200

Pretzel Girl, Hum 2004.

Hum 2005, 2006: Open Numbers

Hum 2007: Tender Love

Modeled by master sculptor Helmut Fischer in 1996, this 4-1/4" figurine was issued as a limited edition in 1998 for the Spring Open House event at participating U.S. retailers. Production consisted of a worldwide limited and numbered edition of 25,000 pieces. It has an incised copyright date of 1996, and its original retail price was $198. Closed edition.

Hum No.	Size	Trademark	Current Value
2007	4-1/4"	TMK-7	$200

Tender Love, Hum 2007, was a limited edition released in 1998 and exists in TMK-7 only.

Frisky Friends, Hum 2008, was released in 1997 as a limited edition of 25,000 pieces and therefore exists in TMK-7 only.

Hum 2008: Frisky Friends

This 4-1/4" figurine, modeled by master sculptor Helmut Fischer in 1996, was issued as a limited edition in 1997 for the Fall Open House event at participating U.S. retailers. Production consisted of a worldwide limited and numbered edition of 25,000 pieces. It has an incised copyright date of 1996, and its original retail price was $198. Closed edition.

Hum No.	Size	Trademark	Current Value
2008	4-1/4"	TMK-7	$195-$200

Hum 2009, 2010: Open Numbers

Hum 2011: Little Landscaper

Sold first as part of the limited-edition Little Landscaper Collector's Set on QVC in March 2002, this figurine was later available at authorized M.I. Hummel retailers for $200. The set features the 4-1/4" figurine, which was modeled by master sculptor Helmut Fischer in 1996, and the Bountiful Garden HummelScape. It carries a "First Issue 2002" backstamp and TMK-8.

Hum No.	Size	Trademark	Current Value
2011	4-14"	TMK-8	$200

Little Landscaper, Hum 2011.

Little Landscaper, Hum 2011, as part of the Collector's Set, which includes a complimentary HummelScape.

Hum 2012: Saint Nicholas Day

Another limited edition, Saint Nicholas Day was modeled by master sculptor Helmut Fischer in 1996 and released in the U.S. in 1997. This 6-3/4" figurine, with a copyright date of 1996 and TMK-7, was distributed worldwide in a limited and numbered edition of 20,000 pieces. It is considered a companion piece to Ruprecht (Hum 473, formerly called "Father Christmas"), and was sold as a matching-numbered set originally for $1,000. On its own, the piece was originally priced at $650. Closed edition.

Hum No.	Size	Trademark	Current Value
2012	6-3/4"	TMK-7	$650-$700

St. Nicholas Day, Hum 2012, was released in 1997 as a limited edition of 20,000.

Hum 2013: Surprise Visit

This figurine became available for the first time in July 2002 as part of the QVC's 14th year of hosting M.I. Hummel shows. The piece carries a "First Issue 2003" backstamp and TMK-8. It was sold as part of the Surprise Visit Collector's Set, which also included musical Bee Happy display that plays "In the Good Old Summertime." The set was available on QVC only through September 1, 2002, and then available separately at retailers beginning in December 2002.

Hum No.	Size	Trademark	Current Value
2013	4"	TMK-8	$225

Surprise Visit, Hum 2013, was a special offer first available on QVC in July 2002.

Hum 2014: Christmas Delivery

First released in 1997 in a 5-3/4" size (Hum 2014/I), this piece was also produced in a smaller 4-1/4" size (Hum 2014/2/0), beginning in 2000. In the first years of production, each figure carries the "First Issue" backstamps. Modeled by master sculptor Helmut Fischer, this design is a combination of Ride Into Christmas (Hum 396) and Sleep Tight (Hum 424).

Hum No.	Size	Trademark	Current Value
2014/I	5-3/4"	TMK-7	$495-$500
2014/I	5-3/4"	TMK-8	$530
2014/2/0	4-1/4"	TMK-8	$285

Christmas Delivery, Hum 2014/I, displayed alone in TMK-7.

The smaller present-day (TMK-8) variation of Christmas Delivery, Hum 2014/2/0, which is 4-1/4" and worth $285.

Christmas Delivery, Hum 2014, is produced today (TMK-8) in two sizes: 5-3/4" (2014/I, shown here) and 4-1/4" (2014/2/0). The figurine is displayed here as a Gift Set, which includes Winter Wonderland Scape and retails for $495.

Hum 2015: Wonder of Christmas

Modeled by master sculptor Helmut Fischer in 1997, this 7" figure was first released in 1998 in a worldwide limited and numbered edition of 20,000. It carries an incised 1997 copyright date and TMK-7.

Hum 2015 is also available in a Wonder of Christmas Collector's Set, which pairs the figurine with a Steiff teddy bear. The set's bear is a worldwide limited and numbered edition of 20,000. The backstamp contained a "First Issue" marking in the year it was released, 1998. The original price of the set was $575.

Hum No.	Size	Trademark	Current Value
2015	7"	TMK-7	$575
Set		TMK-7	$1,105

Limited-edition Wonder of Christmas Collector's Set shown here with the 7" figurine (Hum 2015, TMK-7) and the special Steiff Teddy Bear. This set is worth $1,105.

Hum 2016, 2017: Open Numbers

Hum 2018: Toyland Express

Introduced in the summer of 2002, this figurine was made available only during special "Toyland Events" held from September 1 through December 31, 2002. The piece, which was modeled by master sculptor Helmut Fischer in 1998, carries a special "Little Town Train" backstamp and came with a free handmade Goebel beehive pin. It is considered a companion to the spring 2002 Toyland Event figurine, My Favorite Pony (Hum 2019).

Hum No.	Size	Trademark	Current Value
2018	4-1/4"	TMK-8	$225

Toyland Express, Hum 2018.

Hum 2019: My Favorite Pony

This figurine was made available only during special "Toyland Events" held in the spring of 2002, from March 1 through June 30. The piece, which was modeled by master sculptor Helmut Fischer in 1998, carried a "SPECIAL EVENT" backstamp and TMK-8 and came with a handmade Goebel basket of flowers porcelain pin. It is considered a companion to the fall 2002 Toyland Event figurine, Toyland Express (Hum 2018).

A variation of this piece was made available in March 2002 through QVC (Home Shopping Network). Called Darling Duckling, the figurine was essentially the same as My Favorite Pony, except that in place of the pony, a wooden duck was affixed. Since the girl figurine and the size is the same for both pieces, Darling Duckling carries the same model number—2019—as My Favorite Pony along with an "EXCLUSIVE EDITION" backstamp. QVC sold the figurine as part of the Towne Square Collector's

My Favorite Pony, Hum 2019.

Set, which also included a musical HummelScape. Despite the variation between duck and pony, Darling Duckling is priced the same as the regular variation of My Favorite Pony.

Hum No.	Size	Trademark	Current Value
2019	4-1/4"	TMK-8	$200

Offered by QVC in March 2002, Darling Duckling is a variation of My Favorite Pony but carries the same model number (Hum 2019). Note the only difference between the two pieces is the change in the small wooden accessory—from pony to baby duck—attached to the base.

Hum 2020: Riding Lesson

Modeled by master sculptor Helmut Fischer, this 4-1/2" figurine was first released in the U.S. in 2001. It carries a "First Issue 2001" special backstamp in the first year of production, along with TMK-8. It is considered an unofficial companion piece to Cowboy Corral (Hum 2021).

Hum No.	Size	Trademark	Current Value
2020	4-1/2"	TMK-8	$200

Released in 2001, Riding Lesson, Hum 2020, is worth $200.

Hum 2021: Cowboy Corral

This 4-1/4" figurine, modeled by master sculptor Helmut Fischer, was first released in the U.S. in 2001. An unofficial companion piece to Riding Lesson (Hum 2020), it carries a "First Issue 2001" special backstamp in the first year of production, along with TMK-8. It is one of two M.I. Hummel figurines that won *Collector Editions* magazine Awards of Excellence for 2001; the other was Scooter Time (Hum 2070).

Hum No.	Size	Trademark	Current Value
2021	4-1/4"	TMK-8	$200

Cowboy Corral, Hum 2021, actually depicts a cowgirl on a rocking horse, rather than a cowboy as its name suggests.

Hum 2022-2024: Open Numbers

Hum 2025/A: Wishes Come True

Modeled by master sculptor Helmut Fischer in 1997, this 6-1/2" figurine is the exclusive annual edition for members of the M.I. Hummel Club in club year 2000-2001. It carries an incised 1997 copyright date, as well as the club exclusive backstamp and TMK-8. As with any of the club exclusives, it was received by way of a redemption card. This original issue price was $695.

Hum No.	Size	Trademark	Current Value
2025/A	6-1/2"	TMK-8	$695

Wishes Come True, Hum 2025/A, was the club exclusive for M.I. Hummel Club members in 2000-01 and is therefore only in existence in TMK-8.

Hum 2026: Open Number

Hum 2027: Easter's Coming

Modeled by master sculptor Helmut Fischer, this 4" figurine was first released in the U.S. in 2001. It carries a "First Issue" special backstamp in the first year of production, along with TMK-8.

Hum No.	Size	Trademark	Current Value
2027	4"	TMK-8	$245

Easter's Coming, Hum 2027, shown here as part of the Easter Basket Gift Set.

Hum 2028: Winter Adventure

This 4-1/4" figurine, modeled by master sculptor Helmut Fischer, was first released in the U.S. in 2001. It carries a "First Issue" special backstamp in the first year of production, along with TMK-8. It came as part of a Collector's Set, which included the figurine and the Slalom Slopes HummelScape.

Hum No.	Size	Trademark	Current Value
2028	4-1/4"	TMK-8	$225

Winter Adventure, Hum 2028, shown here as part of the Winter Adventure Collector's Set, which includes the Slalom Slopes Scape.

Hum 2029: Open Number

Hum 2030: Firefighter

Modeled by master sculptor Helmut Fischer in 1997, this 4-1/4" figurine was first released in the U.S. in late-1999. It carries a "First Issue 2000 Millennium" special backstamp in the first year of production, along with TMK-8. It comes with a complimentary HummelScape, To the Rescue.

In the wake of the terrorist attacks on the World Trade Center and Pentagon on September 11, 2001 and the resulting American military effort, Goebel alerted its M.I. Hummel Club chapters that it would make a commitment to donate appropriately themed figurines to local chapters to be used as raffle prizes. Any proceeds from such fund-raising events would then go to benefit the families of the victims. Seven figurines, including this one, were selected as appropriate due to their patriotic or firefighter/police/medical personnel themes.

Hum No.	Size	Trademark	Current Value
2030	4-1/4"	TMK-8	$250

Firefighter, Hum 2030, shown here as part of a Collector's Set, which pairs the 4-1/4" figurine with a complimentary HummelScape, To the Rescue.

Firefighter, Hum 2030.

Photo courtesy Goebel of North America.

Hum 2031: Catch of the Day

This 4-1/4" figurine, modeled by master sculptor Helmut Fischer, was first released in the U.S. in 2000. It carries a "First Issue" special backstamp in the first year of production, along with TMK-8. A complimentary Fisherman's Feast HummelScape is included to form a Collector's Set.

Hum No.	Size	Trademark	Current Value
2031	4-1/4"	TMK-8	$255

Catch of the Day, Hum 2031, shown here within its complimentary Fisherman's Feast Scape.

Photo courtesy Goebel of North America.

Hum 2032: Puppy Pause

This 4-1/4" figurine, modeled by master sculptor Marion Huschka in 1997, was first released in the U.S. in 2001. It carries a "First Issue 2001" special backstamp in the first year of production, along with TMK-8. It is to dog lovers what Kitty Kisses (Hum 2033), which was released at the same time, is to cat lovers.

Hum No.	Size	Trademark	Current Value
2032	4-1/4"	TMK-8	$195

Puppy Pause, Hum 2032, is 4-1/4" and worth $195.

Hum 2033: Kitty Kisses

First issued in 2001, this figurine was modeled by master sculptor Marion Huschka in 1997. It carries a "First Issue 2001" special backstamp in the first year of production, as well as TMK-8. It is to cat lovers what Puppy Pause (Hum 2032), which was released at the same time, is to dog lovers.

Hum No.	Size	Trademark	Current Value
2033	4-1/4"	TMK-8	$195

Kitty Kisses, Hum 2033, is the perfect 4-1/4" piece for cat lovers.

Hum 2034: Good Luck Charm

This figurine, which was first released in 2001, carries the special "First Issue 2001" backstamp in the first year of production. Modeled by master sculptor Marion Huschka in 1998, it is 4-1/2" and the original suggested retail price was $190.

Hum No.	Size	Trademark	Current Value
2034	4-1/2"	TMK-8	$190

Good Luck Charm, Hum 2034.

Hum 2035: First Snow

Modeled by master sculptor Helmut Fischer in 1997, this figurine was first released with its companion piece Let It Snow, Hum 2036, in the U.S. in 1999. It carries a "First Issue" special backstamp in the first year of production, along with TMK-7. The two figurines were part of the "Frosty Friends" Collector's Set, which also contained a white Steiff snowman-like bear. The set, which is worth $598, was released as a worldwide limited and sequentially numbered edition of 20,000.

Hum No.	Size	Trademark	Current Value
2035	5-1/2"	TMK-7	$318

First Snow, Hum 2035, and Let It Snow, Hum 2036, shown here as part of the Frosty Friends Collector's Set, which also includes a white Steiff snowman-like bear.

Hum 2036: Let It Snow

Modeled by master sculptor Helmut Fischer in 1997, this figurine, along with its companion piece First Snow, Hum 2035, was first released in the U.S. in 1999. It carries a "First Issue" special backstamp in the first year of production, along with TMK-7. The two figurines were part of the "Frosty Friends" Collector's Set, which also contained a white Steiff snowman-like bear. The set, which is worth $598, was released as a worldwide limited and sequentially numbered edition of 20,000.

Hum No.	Size	Trademark	Current Value
2036	5"	TMK-7	$280

Hum 2037: Open Number

Hum 2038: In the Kitchen

Released in late-1999, In the Kitchen was modeled by master sculptor Helmut Fischer in 1998 and carries a 1998 copyright date. Sold on QVC, it bears TMK-8 and the "First Issue 2000 MILLENNIUM" backstamp. Like Hum 2030, it too came with a free HummelScape, Painting Pals.

Hum No.	Size	Trademark	Current Value
2038	4-1/2"	TMK-8	$255

In the Kitchen, Hum 2038.

Hum 2039: Halt!

First designed by master sculptor Helmut Fischer in 1997, this figurine was released in 2000. It carries a 1998 copyright date, as well as the "First Issue 2000" special backstamp in the first year of production. It is one of the figurines in the "Off to Work" series. As part of a Collector's Set, the figurine is sold with a complimentary Duck Crossing HummelScape. The issue price of this piece was $250.

In the wake of the terrorist attacks on the World Trade Center and Pentagon on September 11, 2001 and the resulting American military effort, Goebel alerted its M.I. Hummel Club chapters that it would make a commitment to donate appropriately themed figurines to local chapters to be used as raffle prizes. Any proceeds from such fund-raising events would then go to benefit the families of the victims. Seven figurines, including this one, were selected as appropriate due to their patriotic or firefighter/police/medical personnel themes.

Hum No.	Size	Trademark	Current Value
2039	4-3/4"	TMK-8	$255

As a Collector's Set, Halt!, Hum 2039, features a 4-3/4" figurine and complimentary HummelScape, Duck Crossing.

Hum 2040: One Coat or Two?

First issued in 2000, this piece is the work of master sculptor Helmut Fischer, who modeled it in 1998. It carries a 1998 incised copyright date and the special "First Issue 2000" backstamp in the first year of production. The figurine was available as part of a Collector's Set with HummelScape. Original issue price was $250.

Hum No.	Size	Trademark	Current Value
2040	4-1/2"	TMK-8	$255

One Coat or Two?, Hum 2040.

Hum 2041-2043: Open Numbers

Hum 2044: All Aboard

Another piece in the "Off to Work" series, this figurine was modeled by master sculptor Helmut Fischer is 1996. It carries an incised 1997 copyright date. Those pieces made in the first year of production carry the special "First Issue" backstamp. The Homeward Bound HummelScape is included as part of a Collector's Set. The original issue price was $250.

Hum No.	Size	Trademark	Current Value
2044	5"	TMK-8	$255

All Aboard, Hum 2044, is displayed here with its free Homeward Bound HummelScape.

Hum 2045-2048: Open Numbers

Hum 2049/A: Cuddles

Modeled by master sculptor Helmut Fischer in 1997, this piece was first issued as a 3-1/2" figurine in 1998 at $80. Hum 2049/A carries the special "First Issue 1998" backstamp in the first year of production, along with incised 1997 copyright date and TMK-7. It is considered an unofficial companion to My Best Friend (Hum 2049/B).

A smaller 3-1/4" ornament variation of this piece was issued later with model number 2049/A/0 and TMK-8.

Hum No.	Size	Trademark	Current Value
2049/A	3-1/2"	TMK-7	$90-$95
2049/A/0	3-1/4"	TMK-8	$95

The ornament variation of Cuddles, Hum 2049/A/0.

Hum 2049/B: My Best Friend

First issued as a 3-1/2" figurine in 1998 at $80, Hum 2049/B carries the special "First Issue 1998" backstamp in the first year of production, an incised 1997 copyright date, and TMK-7. Master sculptor Helmut Fischer first modeled this piece in 1997. It is considered an unofficial companion to Cuddles (Hum 2049/A), which was issued the same year.

A smaller 3-1/4" ornament variation of this piece was issued later with model number 2049/B/0 and TMK-8.

Hum No.	Size	Trademark	Current Value
2049/B	3-1/2"	TMK-7	$90-$95
2049/B/0	3-1/4"	TMK-8	$95

The ornament variation of My Best Friend, Hum 2049/B/0.

Hum 2050/A: Messages of Love

First issued in 1999, this piece was modeled by master sculptor Helmut Fischer in 1997. It carries an incised 1997 copyright date, a "First Issue 1999" special backstamp in the first year of production, and TMK-7. Newer pieces now carry TMK-8. It is considered a companion piece to Be Mine (Hum 2050/B), which was issued the same year.

In 1999, some pieces will also carry a special edition backstamp "Hummel, Bumble Bee" for an event held in the U.S. These special editions were available for one year only and are now listed as closed editions.

Hum No.	Size	Trademark	Current Value
2050/A	3-1/4"	TMK-7	$90-$95
2050/A	3-1/4"	TMK-8	$95

Messages of Love, Hum 2050/A.

Hum 2050/B: Be Mine

First issued in 1999, this 3-1/2" piece was modeled by master sculptor Helmut Fischer in 1997. It carries a "First Issue 1999" special backstamp in the first year of production, incised 1997 copyright date, and TMK-7. Newer pieces now carry TMK-8. It is considered a companion piece to Messages of Love (Hum 2050/A), which was issued the same year.

Hum No.	Size	Trademark	Current Value
2050/B	3-1/2"	TMK-7	$90-$95
2050/B	3-1/2"	TMK-8	$95

Be Mine, Hum 2050/B.

Hum 2051/A: Once Upon a Time

This figurine, the design of master sculptor Helmut Fischer in 1997, was first released in 1998 and any of those pieces issued in the first year of production will carry the special "First Issue 1998" backstamp, incised 1997 copyright date, and TMK-7. Newer pieces will carry TMK-8. The original issue price was $80. Once Upon a Time is considered a companion piece to Let's Play (Hum 2051/B).

There are two editions of this figurine that carry special backstamps. One was issued in 1998 as a promotional piece for the "Miller's Expo" in the U.S., and the other in 2000 for an event in Germany. Pieces carrying these special backstamps were issued only for one year and are now considered closed editions.

Hum No.	Size	Trademark	Current Value
2051/A	3-1/2"	TMK-7	$90-$95
2051/A	3-1/2"	TMK-8	$95

Once Upon a Time, Hum 2051/A, shown here in TMK-7.

Hum 2051/B: Let's Play

First issued in 1998, this figurine was crafted by master sculptor Helmut Fischer in 1997 and therefore carries a 1997 incised copyright date. Those pieces issued in the first year of production carry "First Issue 1998" with special backstamp and TMK-7. Newer pieces carry TMK-8. The original issue price was $80.

Hum No.	Size	Trademark	Current Value
2051/B	3-1/2"	TMK-7	$90-$95
2051/B	3-1/2"	TMK-8	$95

Let's Play, Hum 2051/B, shown here with "First Issue" backstamp 1998 and TMK-7.

Hum 2052: Pigtails

This figurine, which was modeled by master sculptor Helmut Fischer in 1998, was released in 1999 as the free exclusive renewal figurine for members of the M.I. Hummel Club in club year 1999-2000. It carries an incised copyright date of 1998, special club bumblebee marking, TMK-7, and decal inscription: "MI.I. HUMMEL CLUB Membership Year 1999/2000." It is a companion piece to Lucky Charmer (Hum 2071).

Hum No.	Size	Trademark	Current Value
2052	3-1/2"	TMK-7	$90-$100

Photo courtesy Goebel of North America.

Pigtails, Hum 2052, was produced in a limited edition of 25,000 pieces in TMK-7 only.

Hum 2053: Playful Pals

Modeled by master sculptor Helmut Fischer in 1997, this figurine was issued in 1998 as a limited and numbered edition of 25,000 pieces worldwide. It has an incised 1997 copyright date and TMK-7, but does not carry a "First Issue" backstamp. It came with a free Autumn Frolic HummelScape. It is now listed as a closed edition.

Hum No.	Size	Trademark	Current Value
2053	3-1/2"	TMK-7	$198

Playful Pals, Hum 2053.

Photo courtesy Goebel of North America.

Hum 2054-2057: Open Numbers

Hum 2058/A: Skating Lesson

Modeled by master sculptor Helmut Fischer in 1998, this winter-themed figurine was first issued in 2000 along with its companion piece, Skate In Stride (Hum 2058/B). Those released in the first year of production carry the special "First Issue 2000" backstamp, incised 1998 copyright date, and TMK-8. The two figurines together make up the Icy Adventure Collector's Set, which retailed for $375 and included the Icy Adventure HummelScape.

Photo courtesy Goebel of North America.

Skating Lesson, Hum 2058/A, and Skate In Stride, Hum 2058/B, are shown here paired together in the Icy Adventure Collector's Set.

Hum No.	Size	Trademark	Current Value
2058/A	3-1/4"	TMK-8	$155

Photo courtesy Goebel of North America.

Skating Lesson, Hum 2058/A.

Hum 2058/B: Skate In Stride

Modeled by master sculptor Helmut Fischer in 1998, this winter-themed figurine was first issued in 2000 along with its companion piece, Skating Lesson (Hum 2058/A). Those released in the first year of production carry the special "First Issue 2000" backstamp, incised 1998 copyright date, and TMK-8. The two figurines together make up the Icy Adventure Collector's Set, which retailed for $375 and included the Icy Adventure HummelScape.

Hum No.	Size	Trademark	Current Value
2058/B	3"	TMK-8	$155

Hum 2059: Open Number

Skating In Stride, Hum 2058/B.

Hum 2060: European Wanderer

This 3-1/2" figurine came as part of a three-piece set released in 1999. The set, which included the figurine, a ceramic globe, and a black hardwood base, was modeled by master sculptors Helmut Fischer and Tamara Fuchs in 1998 and therefore carries an incised 1998 copyright date and TMK-8. An oval decal backstamp reads "First Issue 2000 MILLENNIUM." The original issue price was $250. This regular open edition was temporarily withdrawn from production on June 15, 2002.

Several editions of Hum 2060 were issued with special backstamps in 1999, including U.S. Military pieces and figurines made available in Australia and the Caribbean. These special edition pieces are closed.

In total, there were five similar figurines issued in 1999 and depicting the continents of Australia, Asia, Europe, America, and Africa (Hum 2060-2064). Together, these pieces were available in a "Millennium Collection" Set that included a black pentagonal wooden base for display. The original issue price of the set was $1,250. It is considered a closed edition.

Hum No.	Size	Trademark	Current Value
2060	3-1/2"	TMK-8	$260

European Wanderer, Hum 2060.

The Wanderer figurines (Hum 2060-2064) were part of a special "Millennium Collection" set that included a black pentagonal wooden base for displaying all five pieces.

Hum 2061: American Wanderer

This 4-1/4" figurine came as part of a three-piece set released in 1999. The set, which included the figurine, a ceramic globe, and a black hardwood base, was modeled by master sculptors Helmut Fischer and Tamara Fuchs in 1998 and therefore carries an incised 1998 copyright date and TMK-8. An oval decal backstamp reads "First Issue 2000 MILLENNIUM." The original issue price was $250. This regular open edition was temporarily withdrawn from production on June 15, 2002.

Several editions of Hum 2061 were issued with special backstamps in 1999, including U.S. Military pieces and figurines made available in Canada and Germany. These special edition pieces are closed.

In total, there were five similar figurines issued in 1999 and depicting the continents of Australia, Asia, Europe, America, and Africa (Hum 2060-2064). Together, these pieces were available in a "Millennium Collection" Set that included a black pentagonal wooden base for display (see Hum 2060 for photo of the set). The original issue price of the set was $1,250. It is considered a closed edition.

American Wanderer, Hum 2061.

Hum No.	Size	Trademark	Current Value
2061	4-1/4"	TMK-8	$260

Hum 2062: African Wanderer

This 3-1/2" figurine came as part of a three-piece set released in 1999. The set, which included the figurine, a ceramic globe, and a black hardwood base, was modeled by master sculptors Helmut Fischer and Tamara Fuchs in 1998 and therefore carries an incised 1998 copyright date and TMK-8. An oval decal backstamp reads "First Issue 2000 MILLENNIUM." The original issue price was $250. This regular open edition was temporarily withdrawn from production on June 15, 2002.

A U.S. Military edition of Hum 2062 was issued in 1999 with special backstamp. These special edition pieces are closed.

In total, there were five similar figurines issued in 1999 and depicting the continents of Australia, Asia, Europe, America, and Africa (Hum 2060-2064). Together, these pieces were available in a "Millennium Collection" Set that included a black pentagonal wooden base for display (see Hum 2060 for photo of the set). The original issue price of the set was $1,250. It is considered a closed edition.

African Wanderer, Hum 2062.

Hum No.	Size	Trademark	Current Value
2062	3-1/2"	TMK-8	$260

Hum 2063: Asian Wanderer

This 4" figurine came as part of a three-piece set released in 1999. The set, which included the figurine, a ceramic globe, and a black hardwood base, was modeled by master sculptors Helmut Fischer and Tamara Fuchs in 1998 and therefore carries an incised 1998 copyright date and TMK-8. An oval decal backstamp reads "First Issue 2000 MILLENNIUM." The original issue price was $250. This regular open edition was temporarily withdrawn from production on June 15, 2002.

A U.S. Military edition of Hum 2063 was issued in 1999 with special backstamp. These special edition pieces are closed.

In total, there were five similar figurines issued in 1999 and depicting the continents of Australia, Asia, Europe, America, and Africa (Hum 2060-2064). Together, these pieces were available in a "Millennium Collection" Set that included a black pentagonal wooden base for display (see Hum 2060 for photo of the set). The original issue price of the set was $1,250. It is considered a closed edition.

Asian Wanderer, Hum 2063.

Photo courtesy Goebel of North America.

Hum No.	Size	Trademark	Current Value
2063	4"	TMK-8	$260

Hum 2064: Australian Wanderer

This 3-1/2" figurine came as part of a three-piece set released in 1999. The set, which included the figurine, a ceramic globe, and a black hardwood base, was modeled by master sculptors Helmut Fischer and Tamara Fuchs in 1998 and therefore carries an incised 1998 copyright date and TMK-8. An oval decal backstamp reads "First Issue 2000 MILLENNIUM." The original issue price was $250. This regular open edition was temporarily withdrawn from production on June 15, 2002.

A U.S. Military edition of Hum 2064 was issued in 1999 with special backstamp. These special edition pieces are closed.

In total, there were five similar figurines issued in 1999 and depicting the continents of Australia, Asia, Europe, America, and Africa (Hum 2060-2064). Together, these pieces were available in a "Millennium Collection" Set that included a black pentagonal wooden base for display (see Hum 2060 for photo of the set). The original issue price of the set was $1,250. It is considered a closed edition.

Australian Wanderer, Hum 2064.

Photo courtesy Goebel of North America.

Hum No.	Size	Trademark	Current Value
2064	3-1/2"	TMK-8	$260

Hum 2065: Open Number

Hum 2066: Peaceful Offering

Modeled by master sculptor Helmut Fischer in 1998, this figurine was released in 1999 as a limited and numbered edition of 25,000 pieces. It carries an incised 1998 copyright date and TMK-7, but does not have a "First Issue" backstamp. The figurine came as a Collectors Set with free Friendship In Bloom HummelScape. This piece is a closed edition.

Hum No.	Size	Trademark	Current Value
2066	4-1/4"	TMK-7	$200

Peaceful Offering, Hum 2066.

Hum 2067/A: Sweet Treats

Modeled by master sculptor Helmut Fischer in 1998, the ornament variation (2067/A/0) of this piece was released in 1999 in the U.S. only as a limited and numbered edition of 25,000 pieces. It carries a stamped 1998 copyright date and TMK-7 on its feet and a small brass ring on the head for hanging as an ornament. It could either be obtained for $75 in 1999 or as a free gift to members of the M.I. Hummel Club who had redemption cards and purchased $150 in Hummel products.

The figurine (Hum 2067/A) was issued in 2000 and carries an incised 1998 copyright date, TMK-8, and "First Issue 2000" special backstamp in the first year of production.

Hum No.	Size	Trademark	Current Value
2067/A	3-1/4"	TMK-8	$95
2067/A/0	3-1/4"	TMK-7	$95

Sweet Treats, Hum 2067/A, is 3-1/4" and was released in 2000.

Hum 2067/B: For Me?

Just as its companion piece (2067/A), For Me? exists in both an ornament and figurine form.

Modeled by master sculptor Helmut Fischer in 1998, the ornament variation (2067/A/0) of this piece was released in 2000 in the U.S. only as a limited and numbered edition of 25,000 pieces. It carries a stamped 1998 copyright date and TMK-8 on its feet and a small brass ring on the head for hanging as an ornament.

The figurine (Hum 2067/A) was issued in 2000 and carries an incised 1998 copyright date, TMK-8, and "First Issue 2000" special backstamp in the first year of production.

Hum No.	Size	Trademark	Current Value
2067/B	3-1/2"	TMK-8	$95
2067/B/0	3-1/4"	TMK-8	$95

For Me?, Hum 2067/B, was released in 2000 and measures 3-1/2".

The ornament variation of For Me?, Hum 2067/B/0.

For Me?, Hum 2067/B and Sweet Treats, Hum 2067/A, coupled together as part of the Gingerbread Lane Collector's Set.

Hum 2068, 2069: Open Numbers
Hum 2070: Scooter Time

From the "Wonder of Childhood" collection, this piece is the second edition in the series. It is a M.I. Hummel Club members' exclusive presented for club year 25, which means it was retired on May 31, 2002. Modeled by master sculptor Helmut Fischer, it comes with a wooden base bearing an engraved brass plaque and special club "EXCLUSIVE EDITION" backstamp. It is one of two M.I. Hummel figurines that won Collector Editions magazine Awards of Excellence for 2001; the other was Cowboy Corral (Hum 2021).

Hum No.	Size	Trademark	Current Value
2070	6-3/4"	TMK-8	$695

Presented to M.I. Hummel Club members with 25 years membership, Scooter Time, Hum 2070, comes with a special wooden base.

Hum 2071: Lucky Charmer

Modeled by master sculptor Helmut Fischer in 1999, this figurine was released in 1999 as an exclusive annual edition for members of the M.I. Hummel Club in club year 1999-2000. It has an incised 1999 copyright date, as well as special club bumblebee symbol and decal inscription that reads: "M.I. HUMMEL CLUB Membership Year 1999/2000." The official issue price is $90 in 1999 with redemption card. This figurine was retired May 31, 2000.

Hum No.	Size	Trademark	Current Value
2071	3-1/2"	TMK-7	$90

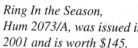

Lucky Charmer, Hum 2071, was an annual exclusive edition for M.I. Hummel Club members in 1999/2000. It exists in TMK-7 only.

Hum 2072: Open Number

Hum 2073/A: Ring In the Season

Modeled in 1999 and carrying that year's incised copyright date, this 4" figurine was released in 2001. Pieces produced in 2001 bear the special "First Issue 2001" backstamp and TMK-8. This holiday piece is a companion to Christmas Carol (Hum 2073/B), which was issued the same year.

Hum No.	Size	Trademark	Current Value
2073/A	4"	TMK-8	$145

Ring In the Season, Hum 2073/A, was issued in 2001 and is worth $145.

Hum 2073/B: Christmas Carol

Modeled in 1999 and carrying that year's incised copyright date, this 4" figurine was released in 2001. Pieces produced in 2001 bear the special "First Issue 2001" backstamp and TMK-8. This holiday piece is a companion to Ring in the Season (Hum 2073/A).

Hum No.	Size	Trademark	Current Value
2073/B	4"	TMK-8	$145

Another holiday figurine released in 2001, Christmas Carol, Hum 2073/B, is worth $145.

Hum 2074/A: Christmas Gift

The design of master sculptor Helmut Fischer in 1998, this piece was released first as a 3-1/4" ornament (Hum 2074/A/0) in 1998 and then as a 3-1/2" figurine (Hum 2074/A) in 1999.

The ornament was available in the U.S. only as a free gift when $150 of Hummel merchandise was purchased from participating retailers.

The figurine was released with 1998 incised copyright date, TMK-7, and "First Issue 1998" backstamp the first year of production. Newer pieces bear TMK-8. The original issue price was $90.

Hum No.	Size	Trademark	Current Value
2074/A	3-1/2"	TMK-7	$90-$95
2074/A	3-1/2"	TMK-8	$95
2074/A/0	3-1/4"	TMK-7	$80-$90

Christmas Gift, Hum 2074.

Hum 2075: Comfort and Care

Originally crafted in 1998, this piece was released in 2000 as part of the "Off to Work" series. The 4-1/4" figurine, which carried special "First Issue 2000" backstamp in the first year of production and incised 1998 copyright date, came with the Healing Hands HummelScape included.

In the wake of the terrorist attacks on the World Trade Center and Pentagon on September 11, 2001 and the resulting American military effort, Goebel alerted its M.I. Hummel Club chapters that it would make a commitment to donate appropriately themed figurines to local chapters to be used as raffle prizes. Any proceeds from such fund-raising events would then go to benefit the families of the victims. Seven figurines, including this one, were selected as appropriate due to their patriotic or firefighter/police/medical personnel themes.

Hum No.	Size	Trademark	Current Value
2075	4-1/4"	TMK-8	$255

Comfort and Care, Hum 2075, is shown here with its complimentary Healing Hands HummelScape, which completes this Collector's Set.

Hum 2076: Open Number

Hum 2077/A: First Bloom

Master sculptor Helmut Fischer modeled this figurine in 1999, and it therefore carries an incised copyright date with that year. It was released in the fall of 1999 at select retailers only with other retailers added in by early 2000. Pieces produced in the first year of production bear the "First Issue 2000" special backstamp, along with TMK-8. The original issue price was $85. First Bloom is considered a companion to A Flower For You (Hum 2077/B), which was released the same year.

An ornament variation (Hum 2077/A/0) was released the same year. It was available exclusively in the U.S.

Hum No.	Size	Trademark	Current Value
2077/A	3-1/4"	TMK-8	$90
2077/A/0	3"	TMK-8	$90

The ornament variation of First Bloom, Hum 2077/A/0.

Hum 2077/B: A Flower For You

Modeled by master sculptor Helmut Fischer in 1999, this figurine carries an incised copyright date with that year. It was a new release for 2000. Pieces produced in the first year of production bear the "First Issue 2000" special backstamp, along with TMK-8. The original issue price was $85. A Flower For You is considered a companion to First Bloom (Hum 2077/A), which was released the same year.

An ornament variation (Hum 2077/B/0) was released the same year. It was available exclusively in the U.S.

Hum No.	Size	Trademark	Current Value
2077/B	3-1/4"	TMK-8	$90
2077/B/0	3"	TMK-8	$90

The ornament variation of A Flower For You, Hum 2077/B/0.

Hum 2078: Open Number

Hum 2079/A: All By Myself

A new release for 2003, this piece measures 3-3/4" and is a companion piece to Hum 2079/B, Windy Wishes.

Hum No.	Size	Trademark	Current Value
2079/A	3-3/4"	TMK-8	$140

All By Myself, Hum 2079/A.

Hum 2079/B: Windy Wishes

This figurine is the companion to All By Myself, Hum 2079/A. It is slightly bigger at 4". It, too, is a new release for 2003.

Hum No.	Size	Trademark	Current Value
2079/B	4"	TMK-8	$140

Windy Wishes, Hum 2079/B.

Hum 2080-2084: Open Numbers

Hum 2085: Little Farm Hand

A 1999 release, Little Farm Hand was a limited and numbered edition of 25,000 pieces worldwide. First designed by master sculptor Helmut Fischer in 1998, it carries a 1998 incised copyright date, as well as TMK-8. Because it is a limited edition, it does not carry the "First Issue" backstamp. The figurine came with a free Millennium Harvest HummelScape. The original issue price was $198.

This piece, which is a companion to Spring Sowing (Hum 2086), is now considered a closed edition.

Hum No.	Size	Trademark	Current Value
2085	4-3/4"	TMK-8	$198

Little Farm Hand, Hum 2085.

Hum 2086: Spring Sowing

Modeled by master sculptor Helmut Fischer in 1999, this figurine was released in 2000 as a limited and numbered edition of 25,000 pieces. It carries an incised 1999 copyright date, as well as TMK-8. Because it is a limited edition, it does not have a "First Issue" backstamp. The figurine came as a Collector's Set with free Seeds of Friendship HummelScape. The original issue price was $198.

This piece is a companion to Little Farm Hand (Hum 2085).

Hum No.	Size	Trademark	Current Value
2086	3-1/2"	TMK-8	$198

Spring Sowing, Hum 2086.

Hum 2087/A: Sharpest Student

Released in the spring of 2000, this figurine was an exclusive edition for members of the M.I. Hummel Club in club year 2000-2001. Master sculptor Helmut Fischer modeled this piece in 1999, so it therefore carries an incised 1999 copyright date along with TMK-8 and club exclusive backstamp. The original issue price was $95.

Sharpest Student is considered a companion to Honor Student (Hum 2087/B).

Hum No.	Size	Trademark	Current Value
2087/A	4"	TMK-8	$95

Sharpest Student, Hum 2087/A.

Hum 2087/B: Honor Student

Modeled by master sculptor Helmut Fischer in 1999, this figurine was the free gift for members of the M.I. Hummel Club renewing in club year 2000-2001. It was released in 2000 and carries a 1999 incised copyright date, as well as TMK-8 and exclusive club backstamp.

Hum No.	Size	Trademark	Current Value
2087/B	3-3/4"	TMK-8	$85-$100

Photo courtesy Goebel of North America.

Honor Student, Hum 2087/B.

Hum 2088/A: Playing Around (Possible Future Edition)

Expected to be released in May 2003 for M.I. Hummel Club year 27, this 4" figurine will be the third in the "Clowning Around" series. Like the others in the series, it is slated for release to club members only and will be retired after one year. See Hum 2088/B, Hum 2089/A, and Hum 2089/B for the other series pieces.

Photo courtesy Goebel of North America.

Playing Around, Hum 2088/A, is expected to be released in May 2003 as an M.I. Hummel Club exclusive that is part of the "Clowning Around" series.

Hum 2088/B: Rolling Around

The second installment in the "Clowning Around" series, this piece was introduced in 2002. It is a M.I. Hummel Club exclusive and therefore bears the special club backstamp and "EXCLUSIVE EDITION 2002/2003" inscription in addition to TMK-8. As a club year 26 exclusive, Rolling Around will be retired on May 31, 2003.

Hum No.	Size	Trademark	Current Value
2088/B	3-1/4"	TMK-8	$230

Rolling Around, Hum 2088/B, part of the "Clowning Around" series and a M.I. Hummel Club exclusive.

Photo courtesy Goebel of North America.

Hum 2089/A: Looking Around

This piece is a M.I. Hummel Club exclusive available for the 2001-2002 club year only. It is the first installment in the "Clowning Around" series, which also includes Hum 2088/B. It carries a special club backstamp, TMK-8, and the inscription: "EXCLUSIVE EDITION 2001/2002 M.I. HUMMEL CLUB." It was retired on May 31, 2002.

Hum No.	Size	Trademark	Current Value
2089/A	4-1/4"	TMK-8	$230

Looking Around, Hum 2089/A, is a M.I. Hummel Club exclusive and part of the "Clowning Around" series.

Hum 2089/B: Waiting Around (Possible Future Edition)

Expected to be released in May 2004 for M.I. Hummel Club year 28, this 4-3/4" figurine will be the fourth and final piece in the "Clowning Around" series. Like the others in the series, it is slated for release to club members only and will be retired after one year. See Hum 2088/A, Hum 2088/B, and Hum 2089/A for the other series pieces.

Hum 2090: Open Number

Hum 2091: Maid To Order

Modeled in 1999, this figurine was issued in 2001 as another piece in the "Off to Work" series. Those issued in the first year of production carry a special "First Issue 2001" backstamp, along with TMK-8 and incised 1999 copyright date. The 4" figurine came with Strudel Haus HummelScape included.

Hum No.	Size	Trademark	Current Value
2091	4"	TMK-8	$255

Waiting Around, Hum 2089/B, is slated for a May 2004 as an M.I. Hummel Club exclusive that is part of the "Clowning Around" series.

Maid to Order, Hum 2091, comes as a Collector's Set with the Strudel Haus Scape included.

Hum 2092: Make Me Pretty

Another piece in the "Off to Work" series, this figurine was modeled in 1999 and released in 2001. Those made in the first year of production carry special "First Issue 2001" backstamp plus TMK-8 and incised 1999 copyright date. This 4-1/4" figurine came with Day of Beauty HummelScape included.

Hum No.	Size	Trademark	Current Value
2092	4-1/4"	TMK-8	$255

Make Me Pretty, Hum 2092, is paired with the Day of Beauty HummelScape to complete a Collector's Set.

Hum 2093: Pretzel Boy

This figurine, which was modeled by master sculptor Helmut Fischer in 1998, was released in 1999 as a companion to Pretzel Girl (Hum 2004). It has a 1998 incised copyright date, TMK-8, and "First Issue 2000 MILLENNIUM" backstamp in the first year of production.

A special edition of this figurine was issued in 2000 for the M.I. Hummel Club Convention in Germany. It was also part of a Collector's Set, which included a free Bavarian Bier Garten HummelScape.

Hum No.	Size	Trademark	Current Value
2093	4-1/4"	TMK-8	$190

Pretzel Boy, Hum 2093, shown here as a Collector's Set, which pairs the 4-1/4" figurine with a HummelScape.

Hum 2094: Christmas Wish

Modeled by master sculptor Helmut Fischer in 1999, this piece came as both a figurine (Hum 2094) and an ornament (Hum 2094/0). The 4" figurine was released in 1999 as a limited edition of 20,000 pieces sold exclusively on QVC on November 17, 1999. It carries a 1999 incised copyright date, along with TMK-7 and special "Exclusive Edition" backstamp. The figurine came as a Collector's Set with free Musikfest HummelScape. It has been temporarily withdrawn from production.

The ornament variation was released later in a smaller, 3-1/4" size with TMK-8.

Hum No.	Size	Trademark	Current Value
2094	4"	TMK-7	$150-$200
2094/0	3-1/4"	TMK-8	$80

The ornament variation of Christmas Wish, Hum 2094/0.

Hum 2095: Open Number

Hum 2096: Angel Symphony

This is a series of lively little angels that began in 1999 and continues to grow with each passing year. Modeled by master sculptors Helmut Fischer and Marion Huschka between 1999 and 2000, the pieces vary in size from 3-3/4" up to 4-1/2". Depending on the year of release, they may carry either a TMK-7 or TMK-8 and incised copyright dates of either 1999 or 2000.

Angelic Conductor, Hum 2096/A.

Celestial Drummer, Hum 2096/C.

Hum No.	Size	Year	Name	Current Value
2096/A	4-1/4"	1999	Angelic Conductor	$135
2096/C	4-1/4"	1999	Celestial Drummer	$135
2096/D	4-1/4"	1999	String Symphony	$135
2096/E	4"	1999	Heavenly Rhapsody	$135
2096/F	4"	1999	Celestial Strings	$135
2096/G	4-1/4"	2000	Celestial Reveille	$135
2096/H*	4-1/2"	2000	Millennium Bliss	$140
2096/J	4"	1999	Heavenly Horn Player	$135
2096/K*	4-1/2"	2001	Joyful Recital	$140
2096/L	3-3/4"	2001	Heavenly Harmony	$135
2096/M	4-1/4"	2002	Divine Drummer	$135
2096/N	3-1/4"	2002	Zealous Xylophonist	$135
2096/P	4-1/4"	2002	Heavenly Hubbub	$135
2096/Q	4"	2002	Heaven and Nature Sing	$135
2096/R	4-1/4"	2002	Seraphim Soprano	$135
2096/S	3-1/4"	2002	Triumphant Trumpeter	$135
2096/U*	4"	2002	Cymbals of Joy	$140
2096/V	4"	2002	Bells on High	$135

*These pieces are part of the Annual Angel series and come with dated wooden bases.

String Symphony, Hum 2096/D.

Heavenly Rhapsody, Hum 2096/E.

Celestial Strings, Hum 2096/F.

Celestial Reveille, Hum 2096/E.

Heavenly Horn Player, Hum 2096/J.

Joyful Recital,
Hum 2096/K.

Heavenly Harmony,
Hum 2096/L.

Divine Drummer,
Hum 2096/M.

Zealous Xylophonist,
Hum 2096/N.

Heavenly Hubbub,
Hum 2096/P.

Heaven and Nature Sing,
Hum 2096/Q.

Seraphim Soprano,
Hum 2096/R.

Triumphant Trumpeter,
Hum 2096/S.

Cymbals of Joy,
Hum 2096/U.

Bells on High,
Hum 2096/V.

Hum 2097: Open Number

Hum 2098: Annual Ornament Series

This is a series of what are currently three annual ornaments that began in 2000 with the release of Millennium Bliss (Hum 2098/A) and has been added to in 2001 with Joyful Recital (Hum 2098/B) and 2002 with Cymbals of Joy (Hum 2098/C). Each is 3-1/2" and shaped like a six-pointed star. TMK-8 appears on the front of the ornaments.

Hum No.	Size	Year	Design	Trademark	Current Value
2098/A	3-1/2"	2000	Millennium Bliss	TMK-8	$20
2098/B	3-1/2"	2001	Joyful Recital	TMK-8	$20
2098/C	3-1/2"	2002	Cymbals of Joy	TMK-8	$20

Millennium
Bliss,
Hum 2098/A,
the annual
ornament for
2000.

Joyful Recital,
Hum 2098/B,
the annual
ornament for
2001.

Cymbals of
Joy,
Hum 2098/C,
the annual
ornament for
2002.

Hum 2099/A: Saint Nicholas Day (Ornament)

This boot-shaped bas-relief Christmas ornament, measuring 3-1/4" with an incised "M.I. Hummel" signature on the front, was released in 2000 as part of a series of what are now nine decorative ornaments (see Hum 876/A). Those released in the first year of production carry a "First Issue 2000" indicator.

Hum No.	Size	Trademark	Current Value
2099/A	3-1/4"	TMK-8	$20

Photo courtesy Goebel of North America.

St. Nicolas Day ornament, Hum 2099/A, a boot-shaped Christmas tree ornament issued in 2000.

Hum 2100: Picture Perfect

Modeled by master sculptor Helmut Fischer in 2000, this is the 25th Anniversary Club Commemorative figurine for M.I. Hummel Club members only. It carries an incised 2000 copyright date, as well as "25th Anniversary" commemorative backstamp. It comes with wooden base and porcelain plaque. Sequentially numbered worldwide limited edition of 2,500 pieces. A companion piece is Camera Ready (Hum 2132).

Hum No.	Size	Trademark	Current Value
2100	8-1/4"	TMK-8	$3,495

Picture Perfect, Hum 2100, is a 25th Anniversary commemorative figurine.

Photo courtesy Goebel of North America.

Hum 2101/A: A Girl's Best Friend

Modeled in 1999, this figurine was new for 2001. Those produced in the first year of production carry special "First Issue 2001" backstamp, along with incised 1999 copyright date and TMK-8. A Girl's Best Friend is considered a companion piece to A Boy's Best Friend (Hum 2101/B), which was released at the same time.

Hum No.	Size	Trademark	Current Value
2101/A	4"	TMK-8	$20

A Girl's Best Friend, Hum 2101/A.

Hum 2101/B: A Boy's Best Friend

This figurine, a companion to A Girl's Best Friend (Hum 2101/A), was also modeled in 1999 and released in 2001. Those produced in the first year of production carry special "First Issue 2001" backstamp, along with incised 1999 copyright date and TMK-8.

Hum No.	Size	Trademark	Current Value
2101/B	4"	TMK-8	$20

A Boy's Best Friend, Hum 2101/B.

Hum 2102/A: My Heart's Desire

Modeled by master sculptor Helmut Fischer in 2000, this piece was introduced in the summer of 2002. It carries a "First Issue 2002" backstamp, as well as incised copyright date of 2000 and TMK-8. It is considered a companion piece to Secret Admirer (Hum 2102/B).

Hum No.	Size	Trademark	Current Value
2102/A	3-3/4"	TMK-8	$140

My Heart's Desire, Hum 2102/A.

Hum 2102/B: Secret Admirer

Another design by master sculptor Helmut Fischer 2000, this piece was introduced in the summer of 2002. It carries an incised 2000 copyright date and "First Issue 2002" backstamp, as well as TMK-8. It is considered a companion piece to My Heart's Desire (Hum 2102/A).

Hum No.	Size	Trademark	Current Value
2102/B	4"	TMK-8	$140

Secret Admirer, Hum 2102/B.

Hum 2103/A: Puppet Princess

Puppet Princess, which was modeled by master sculptor Marion Huschka in 1999, is a companion piece to Puppet Prince (Hum 2103/B). It was offered as a gift to new 2001-2002 members of the M.I. Hummel Club who were joining for the first time or renewing membership, and therefore bears the special club backstamp in addition to TMK-8 and an incised 1999 copyright date. It was retired May 31, 2002.

Hum No.	Size	Trademark	Current Value
2103/A	3-3/4"	TMK-8	$90

Puppet Princess, Hum 2103/A, a M.I. Hummel Club exclusive for 2002.

Hum 2103/B: Puppet Prince

Modeled by master sculptor Marion Huschka in 1999, Puppet Prince is a companion piece to Puppet Princess (Hum 2103/A). It was released in 2001 as a M.I. Hummel Club exclusive to new members who joined in that year and therefore bears the special club backstamp and incised 1999 copyright date, along with TMK-8. It was retired May 31, 2002.

Hum No.	Size	Trademark	Current Value
2103/B	4"	TMK-8	$100

Puppet Prince, Hum 2103/B, a M.I. Hummel Club exclusive for 2001.

Hum 2104: Sunflower Friends

Modeled in 1999, this figurine is a M.I. Hummel Club exclusive issued to members as a loyalty piece upon their fifth year of personal membership. Issued in 2001, it carries an incised 1999 copyright date, TMK-8, and special club backstamp

Hum No.	Size	Trademark	Current Value
2104	3-1/2"	TMK-8	$195

Sunflower Friends, Hum 2104, is offered to M.I. Hummel Club members after five years membership.

Hum 2105: Miss Beehaving

Modeled in 1999, this figurine is a M.I. Hummel Club exclusive issued to members as a loyalty piece upon their 10th year of personal membership. Issued in 2001, it carries an incised 1999 copyright date, TMK-8, and special club backstamp.

Hum No.	Size	Trademark	Current Value
2105	2-3/4"	TMK-8	$240

Miss Beehaving, Hum 2105, is the figurine marking 10 years membership in the M.I. Hummel Club.

Hum 2106: Christmas Time

This piece, which was modeled by master sculptor Helmut Fischer in 1999, was released first as a 3-1/4" ornament in 2001 and later as a 4" figurine. The ornament carries mold number 2106/0, whereas the figurine is simple Hum 2106. The figurine bears an incised 1999 copyright date and TMK-8. It came with special holiday-themed HummelScape.

Hum No.	Size	Trademark	Current Value
2106	4"	TMK-8	$180
2106/0	3-1/4"	TMK-8	$80

Christmas Time, Hum 2106, shown here in the figurine variation as a Collector's Set with HummelScape. There is also an ornament variation (Hum 2106/0).

Hum 2107/A: Bee Hopeful

Modeled in 1999, this figurine was released in 2000 as a limited and numbered edition of 25,000 pieces. It carries a 1999 incised copyright date, TMK-8, and backstamp to indicate a limited edition. It is considered a companion piece to Little Knitter (Hum 2107/B), which was released the following year.

Hum No.	Size	Trademark	Current Value
2107/A	4"	TMK-8	$198

Bee Hopeful, Hum 2107/A, shown here as part of a Collector's Set.

Hum 2107/B: Little Knitter

Modeled in 1999, this figurine was released in 2001 as the companion piece to Bee Hopeful (Hum 2107/A), which was released the year before. Like its companion, Little Knitter was a limited and numbered edition of 25,000 pieces. It carries 1999 incised copyright date, TMK-8, and special backstamp.

Hum No.	Size	Trademark	Current Value
2107/B	4"	TMK-8	$198

Little Knitter, Hum 2107/B, shown here as part of a Collector's Set, which includes a HummelScape.

Hum 2108/A: Musik Please

Offered in the spring of 2002 as part of the Musik Please Collector's Set, this piece is the work of master sculptor Helmut Fischer, who designed it in 1999. The set features a 4-1/4" Bavarian girl figurine with an incised 1999 copyright date and a Volkfest display in a limited edition of 15,000 pieces. It is considered a companion piece to Alpine Dancer (Hum 2108/B).

Hum No.	Size	Trademark	Current Value
2108/A	4-1/4"	TMK-8	$198

Musik Please, Hum 2108/A.

Hum 2108/B: Alpine Dancer

Offered in the fall of 2001 as part of the Alpine Dancer Collector's Set, this piece is the work of master sculptor Helmut Fischer, who crafted it in 1999. It features a 4-1/4" Bavarian boy figurine with an incised 1999 copyright date and a display. It is considered a companion piece to Musik Please (Hum 2108/A).

Hum No.	Size	Trademark	Current Value
2108/B	4-1/4"	TMK-8	$198

Alpine Dancer, Hum 2108/B, and Musik Please, Hum 2108/A, are paired together with a HummelScape to create a Collector's Set.

Hum 2109: Open Number

Hum 2110/A: Christmas Delivery (Ornament)

This star-shaped bas-relief Christmas ornament, measuring 3-1/2" with an incised "M.I. Hummel" signature on the front, was released in 1999 as part of what is now a series of nine decorative ornaments (see Hum 876/A). Modeled by master sculptor Helmut Fischer in 1999, those issued the first year of production carry a "First Issue 1999" indicator and TMK-7, as well as an incised 1999 copyright date. The newer pieces carry TMK-8.

Hum No.	Size	Trademark	Current Value
2110/A	3-1/2"	TMK-7	$20
2110/A	3-1/2"	TMK-8	$20

Christmas Delivery ornament, Hum 2110/A, measures 3-1/2" and was first issued in 1999 (TMK-7).

Hum 2111/A: Making New Friends (Ornament)

Released in 1999, this snowflake-shaped bas-relief Christmas ornament, measuring 3-1/2" with an incised "M.I. Hummel" signature on the front, is part of what is now a series of nine decorative ornaments (see Hum 876/A). Modeled by master sculptor Helmut Fischer in 1999, each carries an incised 1999 copyright date. Those issued the first year of production carry a "First Issue 1999" indicator and TMK-7. The newer pieces carry TMK-8.

Hum No.	Size	Trademark	Current Value
2111/A	3-1/2"	TMK-7	$20
2111/A	3-1/2"	TMK-8	$20

Making New Friends ornament, Hum 2111/A, measures 3-1/2" and was released in 1999 (TMK-7).

Hum 2112: Open Number

Hum 2113: Extra! Extra!

Available in several variations, including special exclusive limited-edition USO pieces as well as "America: We Stand Proud" pieces to commemorate the September 11 tragedy, this figurine was modeled by master sculptor Helmut Fischer in 1999 and released in 2001. It carries an incised 1999 copyright date and "First Issue" backstamp in the first year of production.

In the wake of the terrorist attacks on the World Trade Center and Pentagon on September 11, 2001 and the resulting American military effort, Goebel alerted its M.I. Hummel Club chapters that it would make a commitment to donate appropriately themed figurines to local chapters to be used as raffle prizes. Any proceeds from such fundraising events would then go to benefit the families of the victims. Seven figurines, including this one, were selected as appropriate due to their patriotic or firefighter/police/medical personnel themes.

Extra! Extra!, Hum 2113.

Hum No.	Size	Trademark	Current Value
2113	5-1/2"	TMK-8	$265

Special edition of Extra! Extra!, Hum 2113, exclusively for members of the M.I. Hummel Club. Note that instead of holding a newspaper, the boy holds the clubs' newsletter, "Insights."

Hum 2114, 2115: Open Numbers

Hum 2116/A: One Cup of Sugar

Modeled in 2000, this figurine was released new for 2001. It bears a 2000 copyright date and TMK-8. Those made in the first year of production also carry the special "First Issue 2001" backstamp. It is a companion piece to Baking Time (Hum 2116/B), which was released in the same year.

Hum No.	Size	Trademark	Current Value
2116/A	3-3/4"	TMK-8	$145

One Cup of Sugar, Hum 2116/A, stands 3-1/4" and bears TMK-8.

Hum 2116/B: Baking Time

This figurine was modeled in 2000 and released in 2001. It bears a 2000 copyright date and TMK-8. Those made in the first year of production also carry the special "First Issue 2001" backstamp. It is a companion piece to One Cup of Sugar (Hum 2116/A), which was released in the same year.

Hum No.	Size	Trademark	Current Value
2116/B	4"	TMK-8	$145

Baking Time, Hum 2116/B, is a 4" companion piece to One Cup of Sugar, Hum 2116/A.

Hum 2117-2120: Open Numbers

Hum 2121: Soap Box Derby

Soap Box Derby, Hum 2121, is the first edition in the "Moments in Time" series, which celebrates childhood. Modeled by master sculptor Marion Huschka in 2001 and first available in the fall of 2002, the piece bears the "First Issue 2002" and "Moments in Time" backstamps, along with 2001 incised copyright date. This piece was limited to one year of production only.

Hum No.	Size	Trademark	Current Value
2121	7" x 6-1/2" x 9-1/2"	TMK-8	$1,250

Soap Box Derby, Hum 2121.

Hum 2122, 2123: Open Numbers

Hum 2124: Summer Adventure

First available in 2002, this piece is the third and final edition in the "Wonder of Childhood" collection. It was modeled by master sculptor Helmut Fischer in 2001 and therefore carries an incised 2001 copyright date. It comes with a wooden base with an attached engraved brass plaque (total height with wooden base is 6-1/2") and carries special club inscription, bumblebee stamp, and TMK-8. It was an exclusive edition for M.I. Hummel Club members only, offered in club year 26, which runs from June 1, 2002 through May 31, 2003. As a club year 26 exclusive, Summer Adventure will be retired on May 31, 2003.

Hum No.	Size	Trademark	Current Value
2124	5-3/4"	TMK-8	$695

Summer Adventure, Hum 2124, is the final piece in the "Wonder of Childhood" collection.

Hum 2125: Teacher's Pet

Modeled by master sculptor Helmut Fischer in 2000 and released in 2002, this figurine is similar to Little Scholar (Hum 80/2/0), except that it is a girl student rather than a boy. It carries an incised 2000 copyright date, "First Issue 2002" special backstamp, and TMK-8.

Hum No.	Size	Trademark	Current Value
2125	4-1/4"	TMK-8	$175

Teacher's Pet, Hum 2125.

Hum 2126-2128: Open Numbers

Hum 2129/A: Ring In the Season (Ornament)

This pinecone-shaped bas-relief Christmas tree ornament was modeled by master sculptor Helmut Fischer in 2001 and released in 2002 as part of what is now a series of nine decorative ornaments (see Hum 876/A). It measures 3-1/2" and carries an incised "M.I. Hummel" signature on the front and TMK-8 on the back.

Hum No.	Size	Trademark	Current Value
2129/A	3-1/2"	TMK-8	$20

Ring In the Season, Hum 2129/A, is a nice addition to the bas-relief ornaments with its interesting pinecone shape.

Hum 2130: Nutcracker Sweet

The design of master sculptor Marion Huschka in 2000 and released in 2002 as part of a Collector's Set, this 6" figurine is a limited edition of 10,000 pieces. The figurine carries an incised 2000 copyright date. It is paired with an authentic Fritz von Nutcracker by Steinbach piece that measures 5" and was made exclusively for Goebel. The set is completed with an heirloom wooden chest.

Hum No.	Size	Trademark	Current Value
2130	6"	TMK-8	$375

Nutcracker Sweet Collector's Set, Hum 2130.

Hum 2131: Open Number

Hum 2132: Camera Ready

This figurine, which was modeled by master sculptor Helmut Fischer in 2000, is the 25th Anniversary M.I. Hummel Club commemorative figurine. It carries an incised 2000 copyright date, along with a commemorative backstamp. It was available for only one year (2002) and is a companion piece to Picture Perfect (Hum 2100). It features a unique fabric bow around the teddy bear's neck.

Hum No.	Size	Trademark	Current Value
2132	5-1/2"	TMK-8	$525

Camera Ready, Hum 2132, is a special 25th Anniversary commemorative figurine.

Hum 2133: Bashful Serenade

This figurine was first available in January 2002. Modeled by master sculptor Marion Huschka in 2000, it carries an incised 2000 copyright date, "First Issue 2002" special backstamp in the first year of production, and TMK-8.

Hum No.	Size	Trademark	Current Value
2133	5-1/4"	TMK-8	$475

Bashful Serenade, Hum 2133.

Hum 2134: Wintertime Duet

This figurine, a 2002 new release, was first introduced on QVC and later made available through regular retailers. Crafted by master sculptor Helmut Fischer in 2000, it is 4" tall, carries an incised 2000 copyright date and special "First Issue 2002" backstamp. The original suggested retail price was $175.

Hum No.	Size	Trademark	Current Value
2134	4"	TMK-8	$175

Wintertime Adventure, Hum 2134.

Hum 2135: Open Number

Hum 2136: The Cat's Meow

A new release for 2003, this 3-1/2" figurine became instantly more collectible within months after the release when Goebel announced that its team of artisans had inadvertently painted the cat on the "First Issue 2003" piece the wrong color. Factory officials said less than 5,000 of these figurines had been painted with a black cat when in fact the cat was supposed to be gray. This error in color variation is expected to make those pieces with the black cat more rare and therefore more valuable in future years.

This figurine is considered a companion piece to Proud Moments, Hum 800, which was released in 2000.

The Cat's Meow, Hum 2136.

Hum No.	Size	Trademark	Current Value
2136	3-1/2"	TMK-8	$310

Hum 2137-2142: Open Numbers

Hum 2143/A: Season's Best

The design of master sculptor Helmut Fischer in 2001, this figurine was introduced in the summer of 2002. It carries an incised 2001 copyright date, "First Issue 2002" backstamp, and TMK-8. It was sold along with a cold cast porcelain ice rink display and is considered a companion to Let's Take To the Ice (Hum 2143/B).

Hum No.	Size	Trademark	Current Value
2143/A	3-3/4"	TMK-8	$220

Season's Best, Hum 2143/A.

Hum 2143/B: Let's Take To the Ice

Let's Take To the Ice, Hum 2143/B.

Introduced in the summer of 2002, this figurine was modeled by master sculptor Helmut Fischer in 2000. It carries a 2000 incised copyright date, "First Issue 2002" backstamp in its first year of production, and TMK-8. Like its companion piece, Season's Best (Hum 2143/A), it was sold along with a cold cast porcelain ice rink display.

Hum No.	Size	Trademark	Current Value
2143/B	4"	TMK-8	$220

Hum 2144-2147: Open Numbers

Hum 2148/A: Wait For Me

Modeled by master sculptor Helmut Fischer, this figurine was introduced in 2002 as a M.I. Hummel Club exclusive. As such, it carries a special club inscription and bumblebee. It is considered a companion piece to First Mate, the club renewal premium for club year 26. As a club year 26 exclusive, Wait For Me will be retired on May 31, 2003.

Hum No.	Size	Trademark	Current Value
2148/A	4-1/4"	TMK-8	$100

Wait For Me, Hum 2148/A, was an M.I. Hummel Club exclusive for club year 26 and will therefore be retired on May 30, 2003.

Hum 2148/B: First Mate

Introduced in 2002 as the M.I. Hummel Club exclusive renewal piece for club year 26, this piece was modeled by master sculptor Helmut Fischer. It was offered free to club members renewing or new to members from June 1, 2002 to May 31, 2003, at which point it will be retired. It is considered a companion to Wait For Me (Hum 2148/A).

Hum No.	Size	Trademark	Current Value
2148/B	4"	TMK-8	$90

Another M.I. Hummel Club exclusive for club year 26, First Mate, Hum 2148/B, is a companion to Wait For Me, Hum 2148/A.

Hum 2149-2151: Open Numbers

Hum 2152/A: Dearly Beloved (Trinket Box)

Released new for 2003, this heart-shaped trinket box is part of the Bridal Gift Set, which includes three other pieces all featuring the Dearly Beloved (Hum 2003) motif. The other three pieces are: Couple's First Christmas ornament (Hum 2163/A); earthenware framed picture (Hum 2178/A); and earthenware marriage license/storybook (Hum 2179/A).

Hum No.	Basic Size	Trademark	Current Value
2152/A	3-1/4"	TMK-8	$50

Hum 2153: Big Announcement

A limited-edition 2003 special event piece, this 4-1/2" figurine features a boy carrying a sandwich board that reads "Happy Birthday." It will only be available at participating retailers nationwide, which are detailed on the mihummel.com Web site calendar of events. It carries "SPECIAL EVENT" and "First Issue 2003" backstamps and is referred to as a "tailor-made figurine."

Hum No.	Basic Size	Trademark	Current Value
2153	4-1/2"	TMK-8	$230

Hum 2154-2162: Open Numbers

Hum 2163/A: Dearly Beloved (Ornament)

Released new for 2003, this "Couple's First Christmas" ornament is part of the Bridal Gift Set, which includes three other pieces all featuring the Dearly Beloved (Hum 2003) motif. The other three pieces are: Dearly Beloved trinket box (Hum 2152/A); earthenware framed picture (Hum 2178/A); and earthenware marriage license/storybook (Hum 2179/A).

Hum No.	Basic Size	Trademark	Current Value
2163/A	3-1/2"	TMK-8	$22.50

Hum 2164: Me and My Shadow

This special figurine, which was modeled by master sculptor Marion Huschka in 2001, was issued in 2002 along with a limited-edition Steiff as a commemorative Collector's Set in honor of the 100th birthday of the teddy bear. The Hummel piece carries an incised 2001 copyright date, commemorative backstamp, and TMK-8. The bear, with white numbered limited-edition button-in-ear tag, was made exclusively for Goebel and has a commemorative porcelain medallion attached to its neck bow. The set was limited to 10,000 worldwide.

Me and My Shadow, Hum 2164, shown here with special edition Steiff bear to commemorate the 100th birthday of the teddy bear in 2002.

Photo courtesy Goebel of North America.

Hum No.	Size	Trademark	Current Value
2164	6"	TMK-8	$450

Hum 2165: Farm Days

Released new for 2003, this detailed 7-1/2" figurine modeled by master sculptor Helmut Fischer is the second edition in the "Moments in Time" series, which celebrates childhood. It joins Soap Box Derby (Hum 2121). Farm Days features four children experiencing the joy and wonder of feeding a young calf with a bottle. It bears the "First Issue 2003" and "Moments in Time" backstamps and will be limited to one year of production only.

Hum No.	Size	Trademark	Current Value
2165	7-1/2"	TMK-8	$1,200

Hum 2166–2177: Open Numbers

Hum 2178/A and Hum 2179/A: Bridal Gifts

Released new for 2003, this earthenware framed picture (Hum 2178/A) and earthenware marriage license/storybook (Hum 2179/A) are part of the Bridal Gift Set, which includes two other pieces all featuring the Dearly Beloved (Hum 2003) motif. The other pieces are: Dearly Beloved trinket box (Hum 2152/A) and Dearly Beloved ornament (Hum 2163/A).

Hum No.	Basic Size	Trademark	Current Value
2178/A	7-1/4"	TMK-8	$75
2179/A	5-1/2"	TMK-8	$50

Hum 2180: The Final Sculpt

Modeled by master sculptor Gerhard Skrobek in 2001 exclusively for his Farewell Tour in 2002, this piece is the last Skrobek completed before retiring from touring at the age of 80. It is a depiction of Skrobek's fond memories at Goebel—specifically his recollection of modeling The Botanist figurine (Hum 351).

Gerhard Skrobek

Photo courtesy Goebel of North America.

Released in 2002, The Final Sculpt is a sequentially numbered limited edition of 8,000 pieces and available only at selected retailers (those involved in Skrobek's Farewell Tour). Each piece is signed by Skrobek, has a special backstamp, carries an incised 2001 copyright date, and comes with a Skrobek silhouette commemorative medallion.

The Final Sculpt, Hum 2180, shown here along with the special medallion and a close-up of the special markings on its base.

Photo courtesy Goebel of North America.

Hum No.	Size	Trademark	Current Value
2180	5-1/4"	TMK-8	$350

Hum 3012, 3015-3021: Ball Ornaments

Although not produced by Goebel, these ball ornaments do carry Hummel model numbers (the highest to date) and are featured in M.I. Hummel price lists and sales literature.

Each measures 3" in diameter, features the design of one of the M.I. Hummel figurines, and retails for $49.

Hum No.	Size	Design	Trademark	Current Value
3012	3"	Celestial Musician	TMK-8	$49
3015	3"	Christmas Angel	TMK-8	$49
3016	3"	Angel Duet	TMK-8	$49
3017	3"	Angel Serenade	TMK-8	$49
3018	3"	Christmas Song	TMK-8	$49
3019	3"	Festival Harmony With Flute	TMK-8	$49
3020	3"	Festival Harmony With Mandolin	TMK-8	$49
3021	3"	Heavenly Angel	TMK-8	$49

Christmas Song ball ornament.

Festival Harmony With Flute ball ornament.

Festival Harmony With Mandolin ball ornament.

Heavenly Angel ball ornament.

Celestial Musician ball ornament.

Christmas Angel ball ornament.

Angel Duet ball ornament.

Angel Serenade ball ornament.

Chapter Four

Other

Hummel

Collectibles

The M.I. Hummel Club Exclusives

When the club was founded under Goebel sponsorship and management, part of the benefits of membership were pieces the company produced that were available only through the club. There were two types of these pieces. One was in the form of a membership renewal premium. For the past several years, these have been figurines. The other type was a redemption card(s) given to members each year, subsequent to renewal. The card(s) allowed the member to purchase that year's exclusive offerings. They were available only through officially sanctioned dealers representing the club. Where practical, until early in 1989, each of these exclusive pieces bore the following inscription:

"EXCLUSIVE SPECIAL EDITION

No. (1,2,3, etc) FOR MEMBERS OF THE GOEBEL COLLECTORS' CLUB"

Concurrent with the transition from the old Goebel Collectors' Club to the M.I. Hummel Club came a change in the club exclusive backstamp. The backstamp incorporated a black and yellow Hummel bee within a lined half-circle with "M.I. Hummel" beneath the half-circle.

With only one exception, each of the redemption pieces had been based on an original M.I. Hummel drawing or painting. The exception was the redemption piece offered in the third year, a bust of Sister M.I. Hummel (Hu 3) designed by Goebel master sculptor Gerhard Skrobek and illustrated here.

M.I. Hummel Bust, Hu 3. Although not a Hummel piece, this 5-3/4" bust does carry TMK-5 and an incised 1978 copyright date.

A most unusual club piece was offered in addition to the figurine for the 1983-84 club exclusive. This was a miniature of the first exclusive club piece, Valentine Gift. It was a tiny 1/2" figurine mounted in a 14-karat gold-plated cage on a chain to be worn as a necklace. The figurine could be easily removed from the cage for display as a free-standing piece.

In 1986, a second M.I. Hummel minia-

Base of Hum 479 (I Brought You a Gift) showing the new special club backstamp.

ture, What Now?, was introduced as an exclusive piece available to members.

For the club year 1991-92, Goebel created another miniature figurine exclusive for the club. This one was a 1" freestanding figurine titled Morning Concert. It was supplied with an earthenware Bavarian Bandstand setting and a protective glass display dome and base. The release price was $175.

In 1984, Goebel announced that from that point forward, there would be a cut-off date for use of the redemption certificates, after which the pieces would no longer be available and the molds destroyed.

Following is a list of each of the exclusive club pieces and their respective cut-off dates. Those that do not bear regular Goebel Hummel mold numbers are illustrated and discussed at their appropriate location within the collection listing. The others are illustrated in this section.

Pins given to members of the M.I. Hummel Club (formerly the Goebel Collectors' Club) to commemorate the fifth, 10th, 15th, and 20th anniversaries of their membership.

Release Date	Name	Mold No.	Cut-off Date
1977-78	Valentine Gift	387	5/31/84
1978-79	Smiling Through (plaque)	690	5/31/84
1979-80	M.I. Hummel Bust	HU-3	5/31/84
1980-81	Valentine Joy	399	5/31/84
1981-82	Daisies Don't Tell	380	5/31/85
1982-83	It's Cold	421	5/31/85
1983-84	What Now?	422	5/31/85
1984-85	Valentine Gift (Miniature)	—	12/31/84
1984-85	Coffee Break	409	5/31/86
1985-86	Smiling Through	408	5/31/87
1986-87	What Now? (Miniature)	—	5/31/88
1986-87	Birthday Candle	440	5/31/88
1986-87**	Valentine Gift (6" plate)	738	5/31/88
1987-88	Morning Concert	447	5/31/89
1987-88**	Valentine Joy (6" plate)	737	5/31/89
1988-89	The Surprise	431	5/31/90
1988-89**	Daisies Don't Tell (6" plate)	736	5/31/90
1988-89	Daisies Don't Tell	380	5/31/90
1989-90*	I Brought You a Gift	479	5/31/91
1989-90**	It's Cold (6" plate)	735	5/31/91
1989-90	Hello World	429	5/31/91
1990-91	I Wonder	486	5/31/92
	Merry Wanderer (sterling silver pendant)	—	5/31/92
1991-92	Morning Concert (miniature with display in dome)	—	5/31/93
1991-92	Two Hands, One Treat	493	5/31/93
1992-93	My Wish is Small	463/0	5/31/94
1992-93*	Lucky Fellow	560	5/31/94
1993-94	I Didn't Do It	626	5/31/95
1993-94*	A Sweet Offering	549/3/0	5/31/95
1993-94***	Sweet As Can Be	541	5/31/95
1994-95*	For Keeps	630	5/31/96
1994-95	Little Visitor	563/0	5/31/96
1994-95***	Little Troubadour	558	5/31/96
1994-95	Honey Lover (miniature on a gold chain)	—	531/96
1994-95	At Grandpa's	621	5/31/95
1995-96	A Story from Grandma	620	5/31/96
1995-96*	From Me to You	629	5/31/97
1995-96	Country Suitor	760	5/31/97
1995-96***	Strum Along	557	5/31/97
1996-97*	Forever Yours	793	5/31/98
1996-97	Valentine Gift Display Plaque (personalized)	717	5/31/98
1996-97***	One, Two, Three	555	5/31/98
1996-97	What's New?	418	5/31/97

4" plaque given to members upon joining until May 31, 1989.

What Now? pendant.

Valentine Gift pendant.

The club membership gift for 1990-91, a sterling silver pendant.

The club published a calendar for members each year for a while.

*Special edition pieces given to all old members who renewed. New members got the figure for the year they first joined.

**Four-plate series called the Celebration Plate Series.

***Preview Edition. This figure was offered to members exclusively, with the club backstamp, for two years. Thereafter it was a regular production figure with regular markings.

Miniature Morning Concert, GMS 269-P. This M.I. Hummel Club exclusive is shown in the optional display dome and bandstand setting and also with the Goebel English-language miniature studio display plaque to the left. Note the dime on the right for scale.

Since 1997, the number of M.I. Hummel Club exclusive pieces has been too numerous to even attempt to list in the space allotted here. The existing list is representative of the types of pieces that have been produced for club members in recent years. In terms of the exclusive figurines, please refer to the description text for each figurine in Chapter Three where it is noted whether a piece was issued as a club exclusive.

M.I. Hummel Dolls

The first Hummel dolls were made in 1950. At that time, they were made outside the Goebel factory by another company. The first dolls had rubber heads and soft, stuffed bodies, stood 16" tall, and were delivered to the Goebel factory to be dressed in handmade clothing. Very shortly thereafter (1951), the composition of the body was changed to rubber. Only six dolls were produced at first. In 1952, Goebel brought the entire production of the dolls in-house and added a smaller 10" size.

Over the years, it became apparent that the rubber used in the dolls was unstable and the compound would sometimes break down. This breakdown was evident in the overall deterioration of the head and body, with areas sinking in or collapsing, cracking, or a combination of any or all. According to the company's advertising at the time, by 1963 or 1964, Goebel changed the composition to rubber and vinyl. The bodies were then all made of soft, durable material that is a type of polyvinylchloride (PVC).

There were about 12 different dolls of this type produced in a 10" (26 cm) size until 1983. At that point,

Goebel introduced a completely new line. These are discussed on later pages.

Name	Similar to:
Bertl	Little Shopper
Gretl	Sister
Hansel	Little Hiker
Felix	Chimney Sweep
Radi-Bub	For Father
Mariandl	None
Liesl	None
Max	Max and Moritz
Seppl	Boy With Toothache
Rosl	School Girl
Peterle	School Boy
Seppl	None

Over the years, the company called the dolls by different names and also made an 8" version of some. A 1976 catalog advertised the 8" dolls as:

Name	Similar to:
Vroni	Meditation
Rudi	Home From Market
Seppl	Boy With Toothache
Mariandi	None
Jackl	Happy Traveler (somewhat)
Rosl	Little Sweeper (somewhat)

The 1976 catalog also listed and illustrated a 10" baby doll in two different costumes (boy and girl), although it was not completely clear whether or not they were Hummel dolls. The nine 10" dolls in production up until the introduction of the new line in 1983 were:

Name	Similar to:
Felix	Chimney Sweep
Ganseliesl	Goose Girl
Gretl	Sister
Hansel	Brother
Peterle	School Boy
Radibub	For Father
Rosi	School Girl
Striekliesl	A Stitch In Time (somewhat)
Wanderbub	Merry Wanderer

All the heads and limbs of the girls and boys were the same (two styles only). It was the costumes and accessories that made them different. Identification of the above Hummel dolls is made relatively easy by the presence of an incised M.I. Hummel signature and Goebel trademark found on the back of the neck.

Current Production Dolls

In 1983, Goebel announced a completely new line of M.I. Hummel dolls. The heads, hands, and feet of the new dolls were made of the same or similar ceramic-type material as the figurines. The bodies were still of a soft, stuffed material.

The new dolls were readily identifiable by the material of the heads, hands, and feet, but there were additional unmistakable identifying characteristics. They were 15-3/4" in height, and each had the M.I. Hummel signature and production year. The bodies also carried a label containing the production date along with identifying remarks. The first four to be released were: Postman, On Holiday, boy from Birthday Serenade, and girl from Birthday Serenade. They were released at a suggested retail price of $175 each and production was limited to the year 1984.

The dolls limited in production to the year 1985 were: Lost Sheep, Easter Greetings, Signs of Spring, and Carnival.

New dolls were released in 1996 and 1997. Little Scholar, 14" tall, was released in 1996 and School Girl in 1997. Each

came with a wooden stand. They had the usual porcelain head and limbs. They were released at about $200. Please turn to the Danbury Mint section for more on dolls.

Birthday Serenade girl doll.

On Holiday doll.

Lost Sheep doll.

Postman doll.

Carnival doll.

Easter Greetings doll.

Signs of Spring doll.

Birthday Serenade boy doll.

Expressions of Youth

During factory tours or promotional tours (where a Goebel artist demonstrated the painting of a figure), Goebel officials noticed that people were drawn to the figurines in the pure white, glazed stage of production. Something about the shiny pure white figurine was intriguing to them. Over the years, collectors have also been drawn to the white overglaze pieces in the collection. Goebel decided to create a small collection of the white pieces with only the eyes, eyebrows, and the lips rendered in color. Below are the seven earliest pieces in that collection:

Name	Design	Size
Hum 2/I	Little Fiddler	7-1/2"
Hum 7/I	Merry Wanderer	7"
Hum 13/V	Meditation	13-1/2"

Name	Design	Size
Hum 15/II	Hear Ye, Hear Ye	7-1/2"
Hum 21/II	Heavenly Angel	8-3/4"
Hum 47/II	Goose Girl	7-1/2"
Hum 89/II	Little Cellist	8"

These figurines were produced as an open edition, but methods of production and the extraordinary quality control required in their production limited the number available. Each was identified beneath the base with the inscription "Expressions of Youth" in red, in addition to the trademark and other normal marks.

Today, such whiteware pieces are also available in what is called a "Work In Progress" Collector's Set, which began in 2002 and was available on QVC only. The series featured the figurine in three stages: one whiteware, one partially painted, and one complete. The set includes an authentic brush used by a Goebel painter and wooden display base. Hear Ye, Hear Ye (Hum 15/0) and On Holiday (Hum 350) were offered in such sets. These were limited editions of 500 sequentially numbered pieces.

The Crystal Collection

In 1991, Goebel began producing 12 Hummel figurines in 24% lead crystal. They each bore the incised M.I. Hummel signature, although the signature is not visible in any of the accompanying photographs. They also bore TMK-6 and the year date 1991.

Apple Tree Girl	3-3/4"
Apple Tree Boy	3-3/4"
The Botanist	3-1/8"
For Mother	2-7/8"
Little Sweeper	2-1/8"
March Winds	2-7/8"
Meditation	3-1/2"
Merry Wanderer	3-1/2"
Postman	3-7/8"
Sister	3-7/8"
Soloist	3"
Village Boy	3"
Visiting an Invalid	3-1/4"

The observant among you may have counted the above and found 13 figurines, not 12 as previously stated. In 1995, Goebel offered a special where if you bought the 141/3/0 and 142/3/0 sizes of Apple Tree Boy and Apple Tree Girl, you would receive a matching crystal figurine free. Somewhere along the line, Goebel decided to add the crystal version of Apple Tree Boy to go along with the girl version. Please turn to the color section to this book to see the crystal variations of Apple Tree Boy and Girl.

Yet more in the Crystal Collection, left to right: The Botanist, Merry Wanderer, and Apple Tree Girl.

Three pieces of the Crystal Collection, left to right: Postman, Meditation, and Visiting an Invalid.

Five more Crystal Collection pieces, left to right: Little Sweeper, Soloist, For Mother, Sister, Village Boy, and March Winds.

Busts of M.I. Hummel

Only three Hummel busts have been produced. The first was large, 15" high, and fashioned in a white bisque finish.

These were made primarily as display pieces for authorized dealers and were given to them. The number made is not known, but is likely to be fairly limited. First made in 1965, they had the incised mold number "HU 1" and the Three Line Mark (TMK-4).

The second one to be made was a smaller version. The one in the photograph here measured 6-5/8" high. It had an incised mold number of "HU 2." As you can see, it bore the incised signature on the base at front. Not visible is "1967 Skrobek" on the back of the base. It can be found in both the Three Line Mark (TMK-4) and the Last Bee (TMK-5) mark.

This is the "Hu 2" bisque finish bust of M.I. Hummel made for sale through dealers. This particular one was taken to a commercial mold ceramic operation, sprayed, and fired, giving it this white overglaze finish. These were never produced by Goebel in white overglaze.

The third version appeared to be the same as the "HU 2," but had the incised mold number "HU 3" and was painted in colors. It was limited to one year of production (1979-1980), during which it was an exclusive offering to the Goebel Collectors' Club (now M.I. Hummel Club). It bore the Last Bee (TMK-5) mark. It is shown here.

M.I. Hummel Bust, Hu 3. Although not a Hummel piece, this 5-3/4" bust does carry TMK-5 and an incised 1978 copyright date.

Wooden Music Boxes

A series of four music boxes was announced in late-1986. This was the first officially authorized hand-carved M.I. Hummel design in wood. Designed by Goebel and made in cooperation with the Anri Workshop carvers in Italy, the four designs were rendered in relief on the covers of the boxes. Each music box was accompanied by a sequentially numbered ceramic medallion made by Goebel. Each of the four was limited in production to 10,000. The four motifs are:

Year	Design	Release Price
1987	Ride Into Christmas	$389.95
1988	Chick Girl	$400
1989	In Tune	$425
1990	Umbrella Girl	$450

Wooden music boxes: 1987 (Ride Into Christmas) and 1988 (Chick Girl).

Two more wooden music boxes: 1989 (In Tune) and 1990 (Umbrella Girl).

Example of the ceramic medallion that accompanied each Goebel music box.

Plaques, Patches, and Pins

Many collectors like to add related articles, sometimes called ephemera, to their collections. Various items made by Goebel, as well as by other companies (with and without Goebel's knowledge and permission), have been made to commemorate events in the world of M.I. Hummel collecting. There are probably more than are listed here as this goes on constantly. There are a few unauthorized items that are too localized and small in number to precipitate a reaction from the company and probably others that are unknown to them for the same reasons. Whatever the case, the following lists and illustrations give you a good idea of the type of thing collectors may find.

Plaques

Year	Design	Event
none	Merry Wanderer	Free to each visitor to the Goebel factory, 1977-May 31, 1989
none	Merry Wanderer	Free to each new member of the Goebel Collectors' Club, states membership
1979	Merry Wanderer	Hummel Festival, Eaton, Ohio
1980	Meditation	Hummel Festival, Eaton, Ohio
1981	Little Fiddler	Hummel Festival, Eaton, Ohio
1982	Goose Girl	Hummel Festival, Eaton, Ohio
1983	Little Fiddler (head)	Dealer Festival, January 6, 1983
1983	Merry Wanderer	South Bend Plate Collectors Convention, Goebel Facsimile Factory Display, South Bend, Indiana
1983	Confidentially	M.I. Hummel Fiesta, Misty's Gift Gallery, Sierra Vista, Arizona
1983	Merry Wanderer	Archive Tour Spenser-Zaring, Ltd., Carefree, Arizona
1983	Merry Wanderer	Archive Tour Carol's Gift Shop, Artesia, California
1983	Merry Wanderer	Archive Tour, Henri's, Belmont, California
1985	Jubilee	Free to factory visitors
1985	Little Fiddler Head	Golden Anniversary Gala, January 6, 1985
1989	Rose	World's Fair of Hummels, Rosemont, Illinois, 1989
1991	text only	Commemorates the new M.I. Hummel backstamp (TMK-7)
1993	text only (back)	German language plaque celebrating open house for club members at the factory September 4, 1993
1997	Valentine Gift	Given to charter members of the M.I. Hummel Club commemorating the 20th anniversary

1998 to present: The number of special event plaques issued since 1997 is too numerous to even attempt to list. Those shown here are representative, however, of the types of events in which such plaques were issued.

Many small plaques like these were prepared by the factory for Goebel-sanctioned events. Above left is the front of the plaques while the other photo shows the reverse of the same two plaques with their special inscriptions.

Three of the plaques made especially for the U.S. tour of the Goebel Facsimile Factory and the Goebel Archive Tour. There were many more than just these three.

These 4-1/8" plaques were given to those who visited Goebel in Rodental. What is not generally known is the existence of the Golden Anniversary version shown on the right. Normally printed in blue, the special version was printed in gold and given to visitors during 1985. The background shows the front of the plaque with Jubilee, Hum 416.

A special plaque commemorating the creation of the new Goebel trademark for exclusive use on Goebel M.I. Hummel collectibles. It came in a blue velvet presentation pouch.

Patches

Year	Design	Event
1977	Merry Wanderer	Hummel Festival, Eaton, Ohio
1978	Merry Wanderer	Hummel Festival, Eaton, Ohio
1978	Silent Night With Black Child, Hum 31	Hummel Festival, Eaton, Ohio
1979	Mountaineer	Hummel Festival, Eaton, Ohio
1979	Singing Lesson	Collector's Exposition, Rosemont, Illinois (plate)
1980	Meditation	Hummel Festival, Eaton, Ohio
1981	Little Fiddler	Hummel Festival, Eaton, Ohio
1982	Goose Girl	Hummel Festival, Eaton, Ohio
--	text only	"Goebel Collectors' Club" (Local Chapter Member Name)
1983	Confidentially	M.I. Hummel Fiesta, Sierra Vista, Arizona
1988	Puppy Love	Bavarian Summer Festival, Eaton, Ohio
1988	text only	World's Fair of Hummels, Rosemont, Illinois

These two patches commemorated festivals held in Eaton, Ohio.

From left: Patch for 1982 M.I. Hummel Festival in Eaton, Ohio, and a patch for the 1983 M.I. Hummel Fiesta in Sierra Vista, Arizona.

Patches from M.I. Hummel Festivals in Eaton, Ohio, from left: 1979, 1980, and 1981.

Patch to commemorate the World's Fair of Hummels in Rosemont, Illinois, in 1989.

Second annual Eaton, Ohio Hummel Festival patch.

The first patch issued in honor of the Hummel Festival in Eaton, Ohio, which began in 1977.

Pins

Year	Design	Event
—	Merry Wanderer	Five-year membership pin for members of the Whitier, California chapter
1983	Confidentially	M.I. Hummel Fiesta, Misty's Gift Gallery Sierra Vista, Arizona
1982	text only	Five-year membership pin for members of the Goebel Collectors' Club
1987	text only	10-year membership pin for members of the Goebel Collectors' Club
1988	Home From Market	Hummel Festival Volksmarsch, Eaton, Ohio
1988	Friends	Hummel Festival Volksmarsch, Eaton, Ohio
1989	Latest News	Hummel World's Fair Volksmarsch, above without the Volksmarsch banner
1989	Bumblebee on Rose	Created for the 1989 Chicago Show
1991	Crossroads	Hummel Expo '91, Dayton, Ohio
1992	Land In Sight	Miller's Hummel Expo '92, Dayton, Ohio (large badge)
1992	Merry Wanderer	15-year membership pin for members of the M.I. Hummel Club
1997	Merry Wanderer	(from 20-year membership pin shoulders up) M.I. Hummel Club members

1998 to present: The number of special event pins issued since 1997 is too numerous to even attempt to list. Those shown here are representative, however, of the types of events in which such pins were issued.

Button given to attendees at the 1993 M.I. Hummel Club Convention.

Examples of cloisonne pins made to commemorate events in the Hummel collecting world. These have become increasingly expensive and scarce.

Metal Hum 472 (On Our Way) cast for the Miller's Expo '92 in Dayton, Ohio.

Metal pins with Hummel designs produced for occasions of note.

Button from the Miller's Expo '92 in Dayton, Ohio.

Shown here are three examples of handmade porcelain pins produced by Goebel recently and issued along with figurines at special events. They are: Beehive, Basket of Flowers, and Flying Goebel Bee.

Photo courtesy Goebel of North America.

Year	Design	Event
1986	Commemorative plaque	Goebel Fest (DeGrazia figure) Las Vegas, Nevada
1986	Mug (Chapel Time)	Goebel Fest, Las Vegas, Nevada
1992	On Our Way	Miller's Expo '92, Dayton, Ohio (metal in figure)
1993	Museum Building	Opening of the new Hummel Museum, New Braunfels, Silver Plate Medallion, Texas

Metal Hum 472 (On Our Way) cast for the Miller's Expo '92 in Dayton, Ohio.

Base of the metal Hum 472 (On Our Way).

Jewelry

In past years, from time to time an individual or a company has produced jewelry utilizing M.I. Hummel design motifs. Goebel keeps tight control of licensing these days, but in the earlier years there were some who took advantage. One such effort turned into the Goebel Miniatures division of the company (see Chapter Five). Refer also to the section on the M.I. Hummel Club exclusives for pictures of the pendants offered to the membership.

Valentine Gift pendant.

Most of the items are in the form of pins or brooches. Probably in excess of 50 of these have been produced. Quality has ranged from pot metal to silver and gold.

A few examples of brooches you may find are: Little Hiker, For Mother, Retreat to Safety, and Umbrella Boy. There are many more.

Calendars

Goebel published the first calendar in 1951 in German only. The following year, the first English language version was published, and until 1975, when the German version illustrated the 1975 plate on the cover, the English calendar used the design from the previous year's German edition. In 1975, the cover of the German calendar was the 1975 Annual Plate, so the next year's English edition illustrated the 1976 plate. The practice reverted to the German language design preceding the English edition after that, with the exception of 1964 and 1965. In 1989, the format of the calendars changed completely.

Goebel published a special calendar in 1985 to celebrate the 50th anniversary of M.I. Hummel figurines. This was apart from the annual series of calendars.

Another special edition calendar was published for 1987. This one was in commemoration of the 10th anniversary of the founding of the Goebel Collectors' Club (now the M.I. Hummel Club). This calendar was apart from the annual series of Hummel calendars.

The M. I. Hummel Annual Calendar Listing

Year	Design	
1951	German	Goose Girl
1952	English	Vacation Time
1953	German	Heavenly Protection
1954	English	
1954	German	Festival Harmony With Flute
1955	English	
1955	German	Candle Light candleholder
1956	English	
1956	German	School Girls
1957	English	
1957	German	School Boys
1958	English	
1958	German	Meditation
1959	English	
1959	German	Stormy Weather
1960	English	
1960	German	Book Worm
1961	English	
1961	German	Flower Madonna
1962	English	
1962	German	Telling Her Secret
1963	English	
1963	German	Little Tooter
1964	English	
1964	German	Saint George
1965	English	Goose Girl
1965	German	Spring Dance
1966	English	
1966	German	School Girls
1967	English	
1967	German	Duet
1968	English	
1968	German	The Mail is Here
1969	English	
1969	German	Ring Around the Rosie
1970	English	
1970	German	To Market
1971	English	
1971	German	Stormy Weather (detail)
1972	English	
1972	German	Adventure Bound
1973	English	
1973	German	Umbrella Boy
1974	English	
1974	German	Happy Days
1975	English	
1975	German	1975 Annual Plate
1976	English	1976 Annual Plate
1976	German	The Artist

Year	Design	
1977	English	
1977	German	Follow the Leader
1978	English	
1978	German	Happy Pastime
1979	English	
1979	German	Smart Little Sister
1980	English	
1980	German	School Girl
1981	English	
1981	German	Ring Around the Rosie
1983	English	
1983	German	Happy Days
1984	English	
1984	German	Merry Wanderer
1985	English	
1985	German	Thoughtful
1986	English	
1986	German	Auf Wiedersehen
1987	English	
1987	German	In Tune

(Note: From 1988 on the format was changed)

1988	English	In Tune
1988	German	Be Patient and Barnyard Hero

A Goebel calendar from 1978.

Year	Design		Year	Design	
1989	English		1996	Both variations	She Loves Me, She Loves Me Not and In the Meadow
1989	German	Crossroads	1997	Both variations	Sweet Music and Tuba Player
1990	English		1998	Both variations	The Little Pair
1990	German	Ring Around the Rosie	1999	Both variations	From My Garden
1991	English		2000	Both variations	Star Gazer and Millennium Grouping
1991	German	Home From Market and Globe Trotter	2001	Both variations	The Baker and In the Kitchen
1992	English		2002	Both variations	Be Patient
1992	German	A Fair Measure and Kiss Me	2003	Both variations	Little Fiddler and Heart's Delight
1993	Both variations	Going to Grandma's			
1994	Both variations	Book Worm			
1995	Both variations	Bath Time			

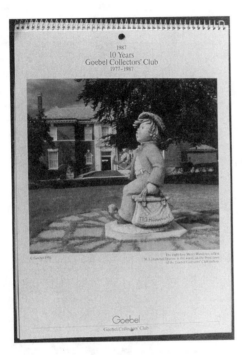

Goebel's 1987 calendar, a special edition in celebration of the 10th anniversary of the Goebel Collectors' Club (now M.I. Hummel Club).

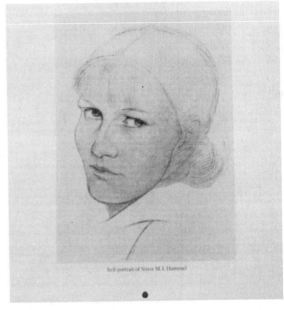

Goebel's 1985 calendar, in celebration of 50 years of Hummel figurines.

2001 M.I. Hummel annual calendar.

The most recent annual calendar, 2003. The cover (above) features Little Fiddler and Heart's Delight figurines and the inside (at right) features different figurines for each month.

Chapter Five

The Rare and the Unusual

The Rare and the Unusual

This section is devoted to the rare and the not-so-rare-but-unusual items. The most well-known of these is, of course, the International Collection. There are some others that are difficult to classify in the normal divisions of derivations of M.I. Hummel art and so they are placed here.

Still others that could be placed with their respective normal production piece counterpart are more appropriately placed here because of a perceived special status. In some cases, they will appear in both places, and in other cases, they will be cross-referenced.

Earthenware

Faience or "Doll Face" Pieces

In 1986, a U.S. Army officer stationed in Germany discovered a most unusual Little Fiddler with the incised M.I. Hummel signature and the Crown trademark (TMK-1) in a German flea market. It was painted differently, with brighter colors than normal. Even more unusual was the china white face, hands, and base, and the very shiny glaze.

Subsequent investigation not only authenticated the piece as genuine, but uncovered some new and interesting information with regard to the early history of the development of M.I. Hummel figurines. It seems that early on, while experimenting with different mediums, glazed porcelain was used. As far as is known, Goebel did not mass-produce the porcelain pieces, for it was found that the fine earthenware with a matte finish was more amenable to the true reproduction of the soft pastel colors used by M.I. Hummel in her artwork.

What we do know is that they were produced in sufficient numbers for many to end up in private collections. Models and colors vary widely, but the majority reflects the normal colors. The piece the officer found had a bright blue coat, a red kerchief instead of the normal blue, and a brown hat instead of black. The

The two unusual Crown Marks shown here are often found incised on the underside of the base of the Doll Face pieces. The reason for the odd devices over the mark is as yet unexplained.

accompanying photo illustrates the difference between the normal and the faience pieces of the same era, but the difference can be more readily seen if you will turn to the examples shown in the color section. The faience variation can be found on Hum 1 through Hum 15. If found, these are valued about 20% higher than their Crown Mark (TMK-1) counterparts. It is unusual, but the faience pieces have been found bearing Full Bee and Stylized Bee marks as well. The difference between them is more readily seen in the color section.

How They Came to Be

Porcelain was used in early experiments with the media and paints in which to render three-dimensional Hummel figures. In the long run, it was found that the inherent "whiteness" of fired porcelain didn't lend itself to the rendering of the rosy cheeks so typical of M.I. Hummel's children in the paintings and drawings. They did, however, cast, paint, and fire the first 15 of the designs in porcelain and took them along with the earthenware figures to the Leipzig Fair.

When they displayed the original 46 figurines at the Leipzig Fair in 1935, they displayed the porcelain ones also. At the end of the fair, it was the now-familiar earthenware pieces that proved the most popular. The porcelain pieces apparently languished in some storage area or

The Little Fiddler figurine on the left is the faience piece. Note the very pale look to the face compared to the normal figure on the right. It has an incised Crown Mark (TMK-1) that has been colored with green ink. The figure has a doughnut base and measures 10-15/16".

another, but they obviously somehow made their way into the market. The individual faience pieces are identified with their respective designs in the Goebel figurine listing.

The Terra Cotta Pieces

When Goebel displayed the original 46 figurines, they also displayed a number of figures rendered in terra cotta, a brownish red unglazed earthenware. As with the porcelain pieces, the terra cotta figurines did not prove to be popular, and subsequently, production was abandoned. There is no way of knowing how many designs and how many of each of the designs were made.

What we do know is that they were apparently severely limited in number. For example: an unquestionably genuine terra cotta Puppy Love has been found with an incised "T 1" mold number and the M.I. Hummel signature, but it is the only one known to be in a private collection.

All known terra cotta pieces are individually identified in the Goebel collection listing with their respective designs.

International Figurines

One of the most interesting and exciting aspects of collecting Hummel figurines and other related pieces is the omnipresent chance to discover a relatively uncommon or significantly rare piece. This fortuitous circumstance has happened many times. It has often occurred as a result of painstaking research and detective work, but more often, it is pure chance.

One such example is the story of the "Hungarians." A knowledgeable and serious collector of Hummel collectibles, Robert L. Miller, regularly advertises in various collector periodicals around the world that he will buy original Hummel pieces. As a result, he received a postcard from Europe describing some Hummels an individual had for sale. After he obtained photographs of a few figurines, it was obvious that some were familiar Hummel designs, but some were apparently in Hungarian costume. Miller had told Carl Luckey that he felt at first that they were probably not real Hummel pieces, but were attractive and he thought they might make a nice Christmas present for his wife. He sent a check, and after some thought, he called the factory to inquire as to their possible authenticity. He was informed that they knew of no such figures.

By the time the pieces arrived, however, he had begun to think they might be genuine. Upon opening and examining them, he saw that each bore the familiar M.I. Hummel signature! He again called the factory and was told again they knew nothing of them but would investigate. A short time later, Miller received a letter from Goebel stating that the eight figurines were indeed produced by the factory as samples for a dealer in Hungary before the war and the company believed them to be the only eight ever produced.

Two International Figurines, from left: 5" piece that has no identifying marks in terms of country or mold number and a 5-1/4" Bulgarian girl with stamped Crown (TMK-1) and MEL 9. mold number.

Two Bulgarian pieces in the line of Internationals: The girl, which is 5-1/4" tall, carries Hum 811 mold number and a Double Crown Mark (TMK-1) and the boy, which is 5" tall, carries an incised "Bul. 2." and incised Crown Mark (TMK-1). The mold number on the boy example is not evident, but it is known to be Hum 807.

Examples of more Bulgarian pieces, from left: Both boys are Hum 808 with the left boy carrying 808. mold number and Double Crown Mark (TMK-1) and the right boy displaying no apparent markings. The left boy has a doughnut base and measures 5", while the right boy is slightly smaller at 4-15/16". The two girls are Hum 810 and both have Double Crown Marks (TMK-1) and measure 5-1/8".

Although similar in costume and pose, these two Hum 812 Serbian girl figurines are obviously from different molds. Both have doughnut bases and measure 5-3/4".

The base of one of the two Hum 812 pieces shown in the previous photo, showing the markings.

As most of us are aware now, many more have turned up since Miller's discovery. In fact, something like 26 or more different designs have been found, representing many different countries. In the beginning, they were thought to be unique and each of them commanded a price of $20,000. The old law of supply and demand came very much into play as more and more were found, however, Today, their value ranges from as low as about $7,500 to as high as about $15,000 for the very scarce and rare examples.

For several years, these superb figures were erroneously referred to as "the Hungarians," but they are now known as the Internationals because as time went, by more and more were found wearing costumes from countries other than Hungary, including: Bulgaria, Serbia, Hungary, Czech

Markings beneath the base of Hum 813, Serbian boy.

Republic, Slovakia, and Sweden. There may yet be others found. The photos of the International figures here are also found in the color section.

So far, there have been at least 26 unique models found. Counting variations and those figures that are different but bear the same mold number, there are at least 36. When considering numbers missing in the sequence of those found so far, a conservative estimate of those left unfound would be 25 to 35, but there is a distinct—however remote—possibility that upwards of 100 may yet be out there.

Hum 813, Serbian boy. Left: Incised Crown Mark (TMK-1), 5-3/4". Right: No apparent trademark, 5-3/4". There are some color decoration variations between the two.

This example of the Hum 825 Swedish girl has an incised Crown Mark (TMK-1) and a stamped Full Bee (TMK-2) trademark, black "Germany," and measures 5".

Hum 824, Swedish boys, shown here at 4-5/8" and 4-3/4". Both obviously inspired by the Merry Wanderer, the one on the right is really stepping out!

The following is a list of the different designs that have so far been found.

Hum No.	Nationality	Description
806	Bulgarian	Similar to Serenade.
807	Bulgarian	Entirely different from other known Hummel designs. Could be a redesign of Feeding Time.
808	Bulgarian	Similar to Serenade.
809	Bulgarian	Similar to Feeding Time. Has also been found with the MEL 9 designator.
810	Bulgarian	Entirely different from other known Hummel designs. There are four distinct paint variations to be found.
810	Bulgarian	Similar to Serenade.
811	Bulgarian	Entirely different from other known Hummel designs.
812	Serbian	Entirely different from other known Hummel designs.
813	Serbian	Entirely different from other known Hummel designs.
824	Swedish	Similar to Merry Wanderer. The 824 has also been found with the "MEL 24" designator.
825	Swedish	Similar to Meditation.
831	Slovak	Similar to Serenade.
832	Slovak	Similar to Meditation.
833	Slovak	Similar to Serenade, but with a different instrument.
841	Czech	Similar to Lost Sheep.
842	Czech	Similar to Goose Girl.
851	Hungarian	Similar to Little Hiker.
852	Hungarian	Entirely different from other known Hummel designs.
853	Hungarian	Similar to Not For You.
853	Hungarian	Entirely different from other known Hummel designs. Boy with derby hat and flowers.
854	Hungarian	Similar to the girl on the right in Happy Birthday.
904	Serbian	Similar to Little Fiddler.
913	Serbian	Similar to Meditation.
947	Serbian	Similar to Goose Girl.
968	Serbian	Similar to Lost Sheep.

International versions of Serenade and Lost Sheep, from left: 5-5/8" boy in Slovak dress, with no apparent mold number, but it is known to be Hum 831; 5" tall boy in Bulgarian dress with mold number 806; 5-3/4" Czech boy and sheep with mold number 841 and stamped Crown Mark (TMK-1); and 5-1/2" Serbian boy and sheep with mold number 968, stamped Full Bee (TMK-2), and black "Germany."

Hum 832, Slovak girl with incised Crown Mark (TMK-1) colored in blue. Measures 5-7/16".

Hum 842, Czechoslovakian girls from two obviously different molds. Left: 842, stamped Crown Mark (TMK-1), 5-5/8". Right: 842, Full Bee (TMK-2), black "Germany," 5-1/2".

Hum 852, 5" Hungarian girl with incised Crown (TMK-1) and Full Bee (TMK-2) marks.

One-of-a-kind copy of one of the Internationals, Hum 851, in Hungarian dress. It was handmade for personal enjoyment by a talented artist many years ago.

Hum 851, two 5-1/4" Hungarian boy figurines, with the one at left carrying Double Crown Mark (TMK-1) and the one on the right bearing an incised Crown Mark (TMK-1), stamped Full Bee (TMK-2) mark, and black "Germany."

Three Hungarian boys, from left: Hum 853, which measures 5", has a doughnut base, and carries an incised Crown Mark (TMK-1); Hum 851 at 5-1/4" with Double Crown Mark (TMK-1); and another 5-1/4" Hum 851 with Crown Mark (TMK-1), stamped Full Bee (TMK-2) and black "Germany."

Hum 854, Hungarian girl with Double Crown Mark (TMK-1).

Three Hungarian boys, from left: Hum 853, which measures 5", has a doughnut base, and carries an incised Crown Mark (TMK-1); Hum 851 at 5-1/4" with Double Crown Mark (TMK-1); and another 5-1/4" Hum 851 with Crown Mark (TMK-1), stamped Full Bee (TMK-2) and black "Germany."

It was not generally known, but there was a tentative plan in the works to reissue 30 of the international designs in a larger size than the originals. It got as far as the sample phase, but the plan was reconsidered and finally scrapped. Dealers and collectors lauded the decision to cancel the plan, as there was much speculation that such an issue would have a negative effect on one of the most exciting aspects of collecting M.I. Hummel items, i.e. the value of those known Internationals and those yet to be uncovered.

The Internationals were never part of the regular production line. Because they were never produced and released in large quantities, but only as a very limited number of sample pieces, they are quite rare.

The MEL Pieces

At least seven of a possible 24 or more of these interesting pieces are known to exist today. Some are more common than others but only on a relative basis. They are all scarce.

Generally speaking, the rule of identification is that each of the pieces have the three-letter prefix "MEL" incised along with the mold number. It is now known that these were produced as samples only and marked with the last three letters of Hummel to identify them as such. Only two of these so far have been found with the M.I. Hummel incised signature, and they are unique. The remaining pieces do not have the signature and therefore cannot be considered original Hummel pieces in the strictest sense. Their claim to authenticity otherwise is obvious.

MEL 6, Child in Bed candy dish.

Those positively identified as MEL pieces are:

MEL No.	Design	Current Value
MEL 1	Girl With Nosegay	$300
MEL 2	Girl With Fir Tree	$300
MEL 3	Boy With Horse	$300
MEL 4	Candy dish or box with a boy on the lid	$6,500-$7,500
MEL 5	Candy dish or box with a girl on the lid	$6,500-$7,500
MEL 6	Child In Bed candy dish or box	$2,500-$3,000
MEL 7	Child (sitting on lid of candy dish)	$6,500-$7,500
MEL 9	International figurine (Bulgarian, Hum 809)	
MEL 24*	International figure (Swedish, Hum 824)	

*This particular MEL piece bears the incised M.I. Hummel signature. The only one known is in a private collection.

Three MEL pieces, from left: MEL 1, MEL 2, and MEL 3. Each also has a black "Germany" beneath the base.

Of all these, the first three are the most commonly found. It is a matter of interest that these three (MEL 1 through MEL 3) have subsequently been released as HUM 115, 116, and 117. The other MEL piece with the signature is only assumed to be so through an old Goebel catalog listing, for it does not have the MEL prefix in the mold number. It is unique, and the only one known is in a private collection.

Some information suggests there may be more of these pieces to be found. For instance, there are missing numbers between nine and twenty-four, and factory records recount the modeling of MEL 4 and MEL 5, both candy dishes, one with a boy on top and the other with a girl.

Metal Figurines

Bronze or Brass

Pictured here are four metal Hummel figurines. In actuality, they are the casting pieces from which the molds for the crystal figurines were cast. They are unique and a realistic secondary market value is impossible to assign. How they got into a private collection is unknown. As there are 14 crystal pieces in this one collection, there is the possibility, however unlikely, that 12 more of these will be found. See the Crystal Collection in Chapter Four.

Bronze casting pieces used for the crystal figurine molds.

The Miniature Collection

There is another division of Goebel, based in California, called Goebel Miniatures. They are the sole producers of the painted bronze miniature renditions of M.I. Hummel figurines.

There is an interesting story behind the formation of Goebel Miniatures. A few years before the division existed, a talented artist named Robert Olszewski produced several miniature replicas of Hummel figurines in gold, innocently unaware of the need to obtain permission to do so. It is unlikely that the company would have allowed it and that's what makes the story interesting. Prior to Goebel finding out about Olszewski's work and stopping him, he produced

Goebel Miniatures, from left: We Congratulate, Stormy Weather, Apple Tree Boy, School Boy, Little Sweeper, and Merry Wanderer. Note how they compare in size to a U.S. dime.

Goebel Miniatures, from left: Little Tooter, Waiter, Accordion Boy, Little Fiddler, Baker, and Goose Girl. Note the U.S. dime for scale.

Goebel Miniatures compared in size to a dime, from left: a German-language miniature display plaque, Visiting an Invalid, Postman, and Ride into Christmas.

Goebel Miniatures, from left: Doll Bath, a U.S. dime for scale, and Busy Student.

The Mail is Here miniature in clock tower display vignette. The clear protective dome has been removed.

miniatures of each of the following five figurines: Barnyard Hero, Stormy Weather, Kiss Me, Ring Around the Rosie, and Ride Into Christmas.

Olszewski had also fashioned a very small number of solid gold bracelets with each of the above miniatures attached. Those bracelets and the unauthorized miniatures have since become highly sought and, if sold, can command extraordinarily high prices.

Out of this incident came Goebel's recognition of Olszewski's talent and the fact that there was a market for the miniature figurines. It resulted in his association with Goebel and the creation of Goebel Miniatures with Olszewski as its head.

Goebel Miniatures has produced many other miniatures for Goebel, but our interest is in the series of miniatures of the M.I. Hummel figurines.

The series is enhanced by the introduction of six separate little Bavarian buildings and settings that were connected by bridges. They were made to the same scale as the miniatures for their display. The settings are known as Kinder Way.

The following is a list of all the miniatures produced:
• Accordion Boy
• Apple Tree Boy
• Baker
• Busy Student
• Doll Bath
• Dealer Display Plaque (English language)
• Dealer Display Plaque (German language)
• Goose Girl
• Honey Lover (with pendant cage and chain)
• Little Fiddler
• Little Sweeper
• Little Tooter
• The Mail is Here (display vignette with dome)
• Merry Wanderer

The Rare and the Unusual 🐝 451

Ring Around the Rosie miniature on musical display. The clear protective dome has been removed.

Morning Concert Miniature, GMS 269-P, shown in the optional display dome and bandstand setting and also with the Goebel English-language miniature studio display plaque to the left. Note the dime on the right for scale. M.I. Hummel Club exclusive.

- Morning Concert (M.I. Hummel Club exclusive, display with dome)
- Postman
- Ride Into Christmas
- Ring Around the Rosie (musical display vignette with dome)
- School Boy
- Stormy Weather
- Valentine Gift (M.I. Hummel Club exclusive)
- Visiting an Invalid
- Waiter
- Wayside Harmony
- We Congratulate
- What Now? (M.I. Hummel Club exclusive)

The Kinder Way Displays are: Market Square Flower Stand, Countryside School, Wayside Shrine, Bavarian Cottage, and Bavarian Village.

Goebel announced in early 1992 that the Kinder Way Bavarian Village settings would be permanently retired, but more importantly, it announced that production of the M.I. Hummel figurine miniatures would be suspended indefinitely as of the end of 1992. The company further

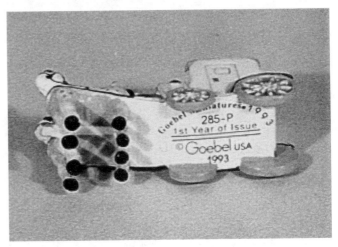

The underside of the Mail is Here miniature shows the markings.

stated in the announcement (*Insights*, Vol. 15, No. 4, page 8): "Though the figurine miniatures have not yet been formally retired, there are currently no plans to resume production." There have been at least three produced since then as special editions. They are Ring Around the Rosie, The Mail is Here, and Honey Lover.

Plaques and Plates

The Jumbo Wooden Display Plaque

At least seven of these plaques have been found in recent years. They are each magnum-sized (34" x 23", 20 pounds), carved from wood, and beautifully painted, duplicating the Hum 187 Display Plaque in a jumbo size.

The only identifying mark that could be found on the plaque was a curious "A" within a circle. The crossbar in the "A" appeared to be a bolt of lightening.

For several years, the origin of this plaque remained elusive, giving rise to much speculation regarding the circle-A mark. The "A" gave rise to the theory that the plaques were produced in the famous Anri workshop in Italy. The character of the carving and painting seemed to match the style and quality of the famed woodcarvers.

Some of the circle-A marks were placed upside-down on the back of the plaques and not rendered very clearly. This anomaly made the mark resemble the Goebel "Vee and Bee" trademark, giving rise to yet another theory that it might have been a Goebel product.

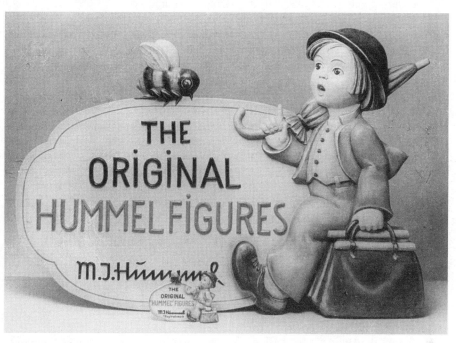

Oversize Wooden Display Plaque. Its genuine Hummel normal-sized Merry Wanderer Display Plaque counterpart is placed in the foreground for size comparison.

Both of these theories were discredited when the origin of the plaques was finally traced. It seems that the manufacturer was a furniture company quite close to the Goebel factory in Oeslau (now Rodental), Germany. In fact, Goebel had the plaques made by the furniture company and painted by Goebel artists. When queried about them, the furniture company said it did indeed produce the plaques, but have not done so for more than 30 years. It seems there was some sort of changeover in the type of production facility, which resulted in the company no longer employing the woodcarvers necessary to produce these plaques. No doubt Goebel would take a dim view of this endeavor these days in any case.

There is no record of how many plaques were made, but they are in short supply. They have been found both in Europe and the United States. Secondary market value is around $5,000-$6,000.

The Factory Workers' Plate

This plate was produced for distribution to the Goebel factory workers involved in plate production, in commemoration of the 10th (1980) annual plate. Obviously, it would have been produced in extremely low numbers

The 1971-1980 Factory Workers Plate.

since it was never intended for general distribution and retail sales. The quantity is reported to be 60 to 100. It is not rendered in bas-relief, as are all the other Goebel plates, but was made by utilizing the decal method. The design depicts the 10 plates in miniature in a counterclockwise circle with the 1971 plate in the 12 o'clock position.

There are apparently three authorized and one unauthorized versions of this plate. The three legitimate versions are an uncolored plate, a single-color wash on the illustrated plate, and a single-color illustrated plate with the inscription in a black rectangular box. The collector value of these three is $1,200-$1,800.

Of some interest is the unauthorized version of this plate. It seems that someone produced a few of the plates in full color. When Goebel found out about this, it quickly put a stop to it. Some collectors place a value of about $300 on these color versions, but most are uninterested because they were not produced by or under the auspices of W. Goebel Porzellanfabrik.

The Goebel Employee Service Plaque

This unique piece is quite similar to the Hum 187 display plaque, but it does not have the usual "Original Hummel Figures" inscription. On the occasion of an individual's 25th, 40th, and 50th anniversaries of employment with the company, one of these plaques was presented and personalized with the employee's name and the date of the anniversary. A very small number of these pieces have surfaced in private collections. They are valued at $1,000-$2,000.

The Local Chapter Plaque

Pictured here is an example of a display plaque many collectors are not aware of. It is a modified Hum 187 Display Plaque that was made available for a short time to members of local chapters of the Goebel Collectors' Club (now the M.I. Hummel Club). It was personalized with the name of the member and the local chapter name.

The Goebel Employee Service Plaque.

The Artist Display Plaque

The mold number for this display plaque is Hum 756. It was originally produced to commemorate the 1993 grand opening of the M.I. Hummel Museum in Texas, as you can see in the accompanying photo. Subsequent to that event, the plaque had been issued to commemorate at least two other events: one in 1994 and one in 1995, both in Germany.

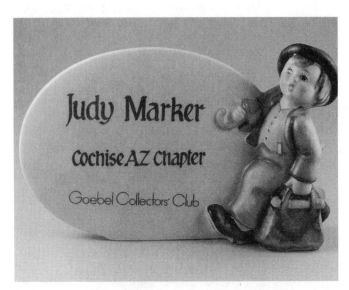

Goebel Collectors' Club Chapter Plaque.

Little Artist Display Plaque.

Special edition Puppy Love Display Plaque.

Special Edition Puppy Love Display Plaque

This display plaque bore the Hummel mold number 767 and a 1993 copyright date. As you can see from the accompanying photo, the front carries the M.I. Hummel signature and TMK-7, as well as "60" and "1935-1995." It was issued in 1995 to commemorate 60 years of Hummel figurine production. It features Puppy Love, the first in the series of original figurines released in 1935. Available only during 1995, the original issue price was $240. Today, it is worth $300-$350.

1948 Christmas Plate

This plate was never put into production, but obviously a few managed to make their way into private hands. Perhaps this happened through samples given to sales representatives or inadvertent loss at trade shows. It measured 7-1/4" in diameter and the reverse side of the plate had three concentric raised circles, the center of which had the hand-inked words: "Entw. A. Moller Ausf. H. Sommer nach Hummel". The collector value range is in the mid-five figures.

The 1948 Christmas plate.

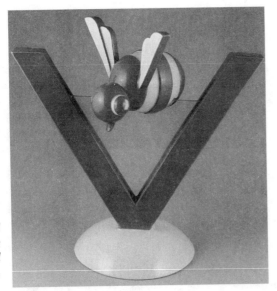

Goebel Flying Bee promotional piece.

Miscellaneous

The Goebel Flying Bee

Goebel changed its trademark (backstamp) from the Crown Mark (TMK-1) to the Full Bee (TMK-2) in 1950. This large promotional display piece was made to depict the new mark. There are two sizes to be found. The one in the photo here is the larger size. It is thought to be a prototype because there are many more of the smaller size out there. The secondary market value for any of them is $2,000-$2,500.

Unidentified Holy Water Font

This is a beautiful little font with an incised M.I. Hummel signature but no other apparent markings whatsoever. It has not been found listed or illustrated in any references. The globe is colored a beautiful deep blue with white stars. The piece is unique and there is no record of trading on the secondary market, therefore no valuation is attempted.

A holy water font that is unidentified except by incised M.I. Hummel signature.

Figure identified only as Goebel mold number HS 1, possibly related to Hum 88, Heavenly Protection.

Unidentified Goebel "Hs 1"

This piece is thought by some to be the forerunner to the Hum 88, Heavenly Protection. The two are quite similar, but the connection has not yet been proven. It could simply have been inspired by the Heavenly Protection figurine or the painting from which it was derived. The final conclusion must be made by the individual collector until some evidence is found to support or refute the theory.

Another possibility is that it is the Hum 108 prototype. The piece may have been a M.I. Hummel design that was not approved for production. See Heavenly Protection, Hum 88.

Goose Girl With Bowl

This mysterious piece was uncovered in Germany around 1989. It has an incised Crown Mark (TMK-1). It is a 4-3/4" Goose Girl with an attached bowl. Upon close examination, it appears that they were joined before firing, lending legitimacy to the presumption that it was fashioned at the factory. The bowl is a Double Crown piece with an incised mold number "1."

There have been at least two more of these unusual pieces found. They are Hum 13, Meditation, and Hum 17, Congratulations. The attached pots are different from the one in the picture here. The pots are round, slightly tapered from the bottom to a larger diameter at the top, and have four ridges around the main body. These are sample pieces that were not approved by the convent and never placed into production.

The collector value range is $6,000-$7,000.

The unique Goose Girl With Bowl, discovered in 1989.

The limited-edition gold gift base Little Fiddler, Hum 2/1.

Limited Edition Little Fiddler

Little-known about in the U.S. is the limited production of a 7-1/2" Little Fiddler (Hum 2/I) with a gilded base. According to company promotional literature, only 50 of these were made, and they were part of a Goebel contest giveaway in Germany. This is probably one of the most severely limited production figures Goebel ever produced. The collector value is about $1,700-$2,000. Please see Chimney Sweep (Hum 12) for another gilded base figurine.

The underside of the base of the gold base Hum 2/1, showing the trademark and the German-language Golden Jubilee backstamp. It reads: "50 JAHRE M.I. HUMMel-FIGUREN 1935-1985."

A piece of German promotional material for this special Little Fiddler.

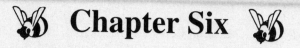

Chapter Six

Hummel Collectibles by Others

The Ars Edition, Inc./ARS AG Collectibles

The company Ars Sacra Josef Müller, Munich, Germany (now Ars Edition GmbH) has had a long association with M.I. Hummel art.

In March 1933, the company received a letter from the Siessen Convent that said: "Enclosed please find three proof sheets of the newest sketches of our young artist B. Hummel. We beg to inquire whether and under what conditions an edition of devout pictures in black and white, and later on in color, would be possible."

This modest beginning gave rise to many years of fruitful collaboration, and up to now, the publishing house has printed more than 300 Hummel motifs in the form of pictures for wall decoration, prayer books, postcards, and books. Over the years, it was possible for the publisher to procure most of these originals from the convent.

From 1981 through 1983, a number of products under the name of Ars Edition, Inc. have been put on the market. In 1983, ARS AG, Zug/Switzerland was founded and obtained exclusive rights for the two-dimensional reproduction of original artwork and figurines on various products, such as limited editions for commemorative spoons and bells, stained glass, thimbles, note card assortments, candles, books, clocks, boxes, and so on.

While most of the items you will see listed and illustrated here are no longer produced, the company is still in business. There is another company, Fink Verlag in Stuttgart, Germany, that also has also published prints and is still in business today publishing prints, postcards, calendars, gift boxes, and greeting cards.

The reason for listing the various products is to inform the collector about what is out there. Few of these products are assigned a collector value because there is no organized secondary market trading in most of them. Where possible, the original price and year will be given. As the years go by, an organized secondary market will likely evolve. It is you, the collector, who will dictate values as activity in the market expands.

There may be more products than are listed here. The catalogs and other material researched did not provide as much detail and dating as hoped, so keep your eyes open.

The Prints

They range in size from postcards at about 2-3/4" x 4-1/4" to approximately 10" x 14". They were not all available in all sizes. Some were sold framed.

There are also some limited-edition prints, larger in size. The company cataloged all of the pictures by title or subject, assigning "H" numbers beginning with H 101 for Hello There! and ending with H 626, A Gift for Jesus, for example. There are several groups of consecutive numbers not used and a couple of single numbers not used. There is no explanation. Perhaps the numbers are assigned to drawings or paintings not published or were meant to be assigned elsewhere. In many of the catalogs, these numbers are referenced no matter what the product.

In 1982, Ars Edition, Inc. published a full-color booklet/catalog, The Hummel Collection, copyright 1981, Ars Edition, Inc. That publication illustrated 292 M.I. Hummel artworks along with illustrations of details of 24 of them. It is with the kind permission of ARS AG that we reproduce them for you here, that you may finally have a reference of much of the artwork that is the basis for the many figurines and other collectibles.

Note: All photos are reproductions of postcards. The inscription in the four photos marked with an asterisk (*) is in the original art in German.

Twelve different matted and framed prints. Size: 3-3/4" x 4-1/2".

H 101 Hello There!

H 102 Blessed Event

H 103 Good Morning

H 104 What's New?

H 105 Loves Laughing

H 106 My Baby
Bumblebee

H 107 Nature's Child

H 108 Sunflower Shade

H 109 Baby and
the Spider

H 110 Baby and the Bee

H 111 Innocence

H 112 The Unexpected
Guest

H 113 Friend of
the Flowers

H 114 Sleepy Time

H 116 Honey Lovers

H 118 The Song Birds

H 120 Slumber Time

H 121 Wishing Time

H 122 Morning Light

H 123 Daisy Duet

*H 124 Sunrise
Shepherd*

H 125 Springtime Joys

H128 Daisy

H 132 Dandelion

*H 133 My Wish
Is Small*

H 134 Heidi

H 135 First Portrait

*H 136 Portrait of
a Little Girl*

H 137 Curiosity

H 138 Discovery

H 139 Spring Basket

H 140 The Flower Girl

H 141 Out of Tune

*H 142 Child of
the Heart/I*

H 143 Young Crawler

*H 144 Meeting in the
Meadow (In Tune)*

*H145 Meeting
on the Mountain
(Whistler's Duet)*

*H 178 The Opinion/II
(Sing Along)*

H 147 Tit-for-Tat

H150 Carefree

H 151
Grandma's Story

H 152
Grandpa's Helper

H 153 On the
Other Side

H 154 Cinderella

H 156 Hold Your Head
High and Swallow Hard

H 157 Feathered
Friends

H 158 Retreat to Safety

H 159 On Tiptoes

H 160 Behind the Fence

H 162 Summertime

H 163 Little Thrifty

H 164 Doll Mother

H 165
Prayer Before Battle

H 166
The Golden Rule

H 167 Let's Sing/I

H 191 School Girl

H 192 Little Scholar

H 193 Little Brother's
Lesson

H 194 School Chums

H 195
Knit One, Purl Two

H 197 School Girls

H 198 School Boys

H 200 Captive

H 201
Mother's Helper

H 202
Little Bookkeeper

H 203
The Mountaineer

H 204 Ring Around
the Rosie

H 205 The Goat Girl
(Good Friends)

H 206 Vacation Time

H 207 Rosebud

H 208
The Flower Vendor

H 209 Blue Belle

H 210 Bye-Bye!

H 214 Adventure
Bound

H 216
The Globe Trotter

H 217
Hansel and Gretel

H 218 The Runaway

H 231 Kiss Me

H 232 Washday

H 234
The Little Sweeper

H 235 The Little Goat Herder

H 236 Feeding Time

H 237 The Fisherman (Just Fishing)

H 238 Good Hunting

H 239 The Boss (Hello)

H 240 The Professor

H 241 Little Pharmacist

H 242 The Stargazer

H 243 The Baker

H 244 The Waiter

H 245 Latest News

H 246 The Postman

H 237 Too Short to Read

H 248 The Conductor/I

H 249 The End of the Song

H 250 Little Cellist

H 251 The Artist

H 252 The Art Crittic

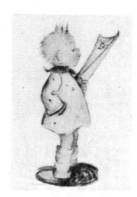

H 253 The Poet

H 254 Confidentially

H 255 Little Boots

H 256 The Doctor

*H 257 The Toothache
(Boy With Toothache)*

H 258 The Little Tailor

*H 260
The Photographer*

H 261 Chimney Sweep

*H 262 The Draftsman
(The Little Architect)*

H 271 Just For You

*H 273 Mountain's
Peace (Forest Shrine)*

H 276 Prayer Time

H 278 Resting

H 282 Spring's Return

*H 283 The Birthday Gifts
(We Wish You the Best)*

H 284 Quartet

H 287 Sunny Weather

H 288 Stormy Weather

*H 289
Wayside Harmony*

H 290 Just Resting

*H 291
Telling Her Secret*

H 292 Not for You!

H 297 Apple Tree Boy   *H 298 Apple Tree Girl*   *H 299 Girl on Fence/I*   *H 300 Boy on a Fence*   *H 301 For Mother*

H 302 For Father   *H 303 Off to Town*   *H 304 Looks Like Rain*   *H 305 His Happy Pastime*   *H 306 Her Happy Pastime*

H 307 Happy John   *H 308 Coquettes*   *H 310 Farewell*   *H 311 Evening Tide*   *H 312 Twilight Tune*

H 313 The Work Is Done   *H 314 Homeward Bound*   *H 316 Winter Fun (Ride Into Christmas)*   *H 317 March Winds*   *H 333 This Heart Is Mine*

H 334 Catch My Heart

*H 335 I Like You Boy
(Valentine Gift)*

*H 336 I Like You Girl
(Valentine Joy)*

H 337 Take Me along

H 338 The Strummers

*H 339 To Market,
to Market*

H 342 Serenade

H 346 Boys Ensemble

H 347 Girls Ensemlble

H 348 Special Gift

H 349 Special Delivery

H 350 Bashful

H 352 Max and Moritz

*H 354 A Smile is
Your Umbrella*

*H 355
Begging His Share*

H 371 Chick Girl

H 372 Playmates

H 374 a Little Hare

H 375 Favorite Pet

H 376 Chicken-Licken

H 377 Children
on the Church Road

H 378
The Shepherd's Tune

H 379
Easter Playmates

H 380 Easter Basket

H 381 And One
Makes a Dozen

H 382 Return
to the Fold

H 383 In Full
Harmony (Eventide)

H 384 Praise to God

H 385 Alleluja

H 386 The Easter Lamb

H 401
In Guardian Arms

H 402 Deliver Us
from Evil

H 404 The
Guardian Angel

H 405 Guardian Angel
Preserve Us

H 406 The Renewal

H 407
Boy's Communion

H 408
Girl's Communion

H 409 Angel/Trumpet

H 410 Tender Watch

H 411 Angel Duet

H 412 Candle Light

H 435 Angel/Horn

H 436 Angelic Care

H 437 Light of the
World (Merry
Christmas, Plaque)

H 438 Guiding Angel

H 441 Celestial
Musician

H 442 Bearing
Christmas Gifts
(Christmas Angel)

H 444 The Littlest
Candle

H 448 Angel/Harp
(Song of Praise)

H 449 Angel/Mandolin

H 451 Watchful Angel

H 453 Guiding Light

H 454 Angel and Birds

H 471 Trinity

H 475 Alleluja Angel

H 477 Silent Night,
Holy Night
(Whitsuntide)

H 479
Joyous Christmas

H 480 Flying Angel

H 481 Jubliation

H 482 Prince of Peace

H 483
Merry Christmas and
Happy New Year

H 484 Love and Luck

H 485 Glory to God
in the Highest

H 486 Bless Your Soul
on Christmas

H 487 Joyous Holidays

H 488 Good Luck
in the New Year

*H 490 For All Men

*H 492 God Is Born

H 494 May You Sing

*H 496 We Wish
the Very Best

H 497 Town Crier
(Hear Ye, Hear Ye)

H 500
The Good Shepherd

H 520 Queen of May

H 521 Mary;
Queen of May

H 522
Fruit of the Vine

H 523 Mother of God

H 524 Mary Mother,
Queen Maid

H 525 Immaculata

H 526 Mother
at the Window

H 527 Mother of Christ

H 528
Queen of the Rosary

H 529 Nativity

H 530
At Mary's Knee

H 531 Mary Take
Us into Your Care

H 532
Madonna in Green

H 533 Loving Mother
and Child

H 537 Born in
Bethlehem

H 538 Blessings

H 539 Virgin Mother

H 540 Christ
Child Sleeping

H 543 Christ is Born

H 615 Crossroads

H 616 Teach Me to Fly

H 617 Mail is Here

H 619 Sunrise

H 620
Sing to the Mountains

H 622 Hard Letters

H 623 Easy Letters
(With Loving Greetings)

H 624 Gift Bearers

H 625 Angel's Music

H 626 A Gift for Jesus

Limited-Edition Prints

There are at least two prints identified as limited editions by ARS AG. They are from what is called the "Hummel Gallery" and are limited to 799 hand-numbered prints.

Carefree: Limited to 799 hand-numbered copies, this print is 27" x 24-1/2".

Alleluia: Limited to 799 hand-numbered copies, this print is 24-3/8" x 21-3/8".

Calendars

There are four types of calendars that were produced by the company, two of which are the traditional month by month. Another is the Advent Calendar. The fourth is a linen wall-hanging type.

The company has produced a couple of large calendars annually for many years. The older ones are 10-1/2" x 16" at first, then approximately 12" x 16" for a time and spiral bound. They can be found in French, English, and German. It is unclear in which years the French version was published. There were format changes in 1984 and a significant change in 1989 to a larger 13" x 12" format. In 1984, Ars began producing the calendar for Goebel.

There is also a small postcard calendar at 4-1/2" x 9-1/2" that features prints that can be easily detached for framing, etc.

Advent Calendars

The Advent Calendars are a tradition. They have windows for each of the 24 days before Christmas and are a traditional part of European children's and many American children's Christmases. Each day, one window is opened, revealing a piece of Hummel art with a religious theme. Each year, the central Hummel picture is different. In 1986 the format was changed and from that year on, four different designs were offered. The picture was a depiction of a winter scene utilizing actual M.I. Hummel figurines. The size of these new calendars was given as 15" x 11".

For at least two years, Ars Edition produced a 16" x 21"(16" x 22-3/4" including wood) "Collector's Limited Edition Calendar" printed on linen and fitted with a

This is the old style of Advent Calendar.

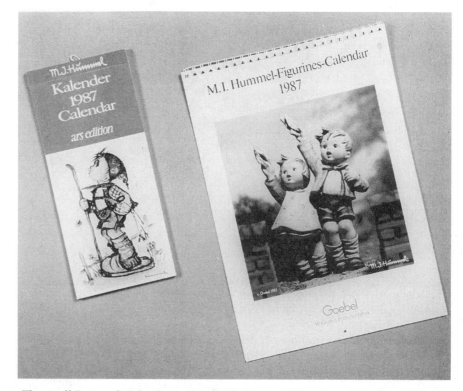

The 1985 linen calendar by Ars Edition.

wooden bar across the top and bottom. The first edition was released in 1981 and the theme was Sunny Weather (H 287), a drawing much like Stormy Weather except the children face right and there is no rain in the picture. For the second edition, the 1982 calendar, the theme was Not For You. The next catalog available for study was from 1985 and there was no such calendar listed, but, as you can see from the illustration, the 1985 calendar was produced. The limit of the edition was 15,000 individually numbered calendars.

Wall Plaques

Wall plaques are available in several sizes and styles. The prints are mounted on wood and a hard finish is applied, making them very durable and attractive. They are square, rectangular, or round, and here are 27 of them to be found. There are many others made by other companies as the prints have been readily available and easy to apply to many types of objects.

The small Postcard Calendar and the M. I. Hummel-Figurines-Calendar 1987

Musical Wall Plaques

There are 12 designs of musical wall plaques. Six of them have red ribbon hangers, and the others have a hanger on their backs. They are 4" round wooden framed prints mounted with a music box movement. Pulling a round wooden knob on a string mounted at the bottom activates the music box.

Music Boxes

Several different styles and sizes of music boxes have been available from Ars Edition, Inc. A licensee from ARS AG, Zug/Switzerland, the Art Decor Company (now Ercolano s.r.l.) in Sorrento, Italy, produces the music boxes marketed by H & G Studios. There were about 25 different motifs, five sizes, and two basic styles at the time. See the section below on current-production music boxes.

The boxes are made of furniture-grade wood with a fine finish and turned brass feet on each corner. You can barely see the feet in the accompanying photograph of four. These sold for $55 in 1986. A slightly larger size in this style that has a lock and key sold for $79 in 1986.

The rest of the music boxes were simple rectangular boxes and ranged in price from about $30 to $40 in the mid-1980s. Today, these pieces sell for about $10 to $20 on the secondary market. The double-lid larger pieces sell for between $35 and $50. Sizes found are as follows:

- 10-1/4" x 8-1/4"
- 8-1/4" x 5-3/4"
- 7-1/4" x 6"
- 6" x 4-1/2"
- 5" x 4-5/8"

This is a double-lid music box measuring 5-3/4" x 8-1/4".

Six Hummel jewelry music boxes featuring original art.

Another style of jewelry music boxes featuring original art. It measures 7-1/4" x 6".

Four Hummel jewelry music boxes featuring scenes with Hummel figurines.

Jigsaw Puzzles

There are at least eight of these to be found. The four older puzzles can be identified by their yellow boxes with red printing. The newer ones have the art printed in full color on the boxes.

Books

Ars Edition has published at least 10 small books in English and possibly a few earlier in German. Most are very small, about 4" x 6". One not illustrated here is Ride Into Christmas, a book of pictures of figurines and hints for celebrating the Christmas season. It is 8" x 8-1/2". Also, there are the six assorted little 3" x 4" address books and the book, The Hummel.

My Memory Book, produced by Ars Edition.

My M.I. Hummel Collection, yet another book put out by Ars Edition.

The Hummel, another Ars Edition book.

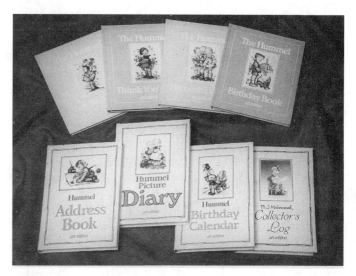

More examples of Hummel books by Ars Edition.

Wall Clocks

In all, there are nine wall clocks in the Ars Edition, Inc. catalogs, in two styles. There are three quartz movement square clocks with a round print in the center. The designs are Umbrella Boy, Telling Her Secret, and Meeting in the Meadow.

The other style is a small, pendulum movement clock found in at least 12 different designs: Mother's Helper; Follow the Leader; Umbrella Girl; Coquettes; Resting; Little Bookkeeper; Sunny Weather; School Girl; School Boys; School Chums; Globe Trotter; and School Girls.

Generally, these clocks sell for only $15 to $25 on the secondary market.

Silk Carpets

A 1988 ARS AG catalog offered a "First Edition" silk carpet, limited to 99 carpets worldwide. The carpet was described as having been made by hand-knotting 120 knots per square inch. The design was Celestial Musician and the size was listed as 31-1/2" x 42".

In the spring 1990 issue of Insights, the M.I. Hummel Club newsletter, another of these silk carpets was offered in a worldwide limited edition of 50. It was similarly described and offered at $1,800. No mention of Ars Edition was made, but it can probably be safely assumed that it was a subsequent edition. The design of this tapestry was Umbrella Girl and the size was 35-1/4" x 26-1/2".

The Ars Edition "First Edition" silk carpet.

Candles

There is a wide variety of candles in two sizes in the catalogs. They are a high-quality candle. One catalog listing described their cream-colored paraffin as the ideal color for placing the art on. Though it is quite rare to find one of these candles in mint condition (unburned), the values on the secondary market are not usually more than $5 apiece.

Gift Wrap and Gift Cards

There are 18 designs of the gift card. They are 2-1/4" x 2-1/4" and come with envelopes. Gift tags have also been offered. One gift wrap illustrates a variety of M.I. Hummel artworks, all separated by bright red borders.

Candles with Hummel designs.

Note Cards

A 1982 edition of an Ars Edition, Inc. catalog is the only one to mention note cards. Only three were illustrated, but the text accompanying stated that the "...notes featured many of the illustrations found in this booklet." There were at least 300 illustrations, so there are probably several dozen different designs of note cards out there.

They are listed only as "slightly oversized." Included were colored envelopes with lining featuring the Hummel signature. They were sold in boxes of 20.

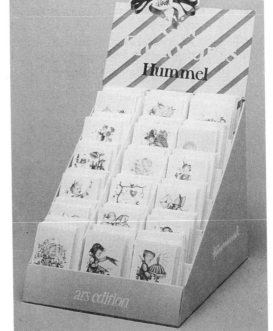

A display of Hummel cards offered by Ars Edition.

Leaded Glass Panels

At least three of these painted leaded glass panels were available through ARS AG. The three known designs are Ring Around the Rosie (1986), Postman (1987), and one similar to Stormy Weather called Sunny Weather (1988).

The size of these is 6-1/4" x 8-1/4". They were limited to 2,500 pieces worldwide and are individually numbered. The release price in 1986 was $65. Others have been produced by a different company. They may or may not be from the same source.

Metal Trays

Two metal trays were offered in the early 1980s. The designs were Apple Tree Boy and Apple Tree Girl. They were oval in shape and measure 11-1/2" x 14-1/2". Both designs were numbered TR-H298 and carry a 1982 copyright date. Today, these pieces sell for $10 to $30 apiece.

Placemats and Coasters

These are found in sets of six coasters and sets of four placemats.

There are a total of 14 pieces to be found. They consist of two sizes of four placemats, 12" x 9" and 15-3/4" x 11-7/8". The illustrations are photographs of actual Goebel M.I. Hummel figurines in models of life-like settings.

There are six coaster designs measuring 4" square. They are made in England and cork-backed hard board with a heat resistant acrylic finish. The designs consist of photographs of figurines in realistic settings.

A leaded glass panel painted with the Hummel design Ring Around the Rosie.

Christmas Ornaments

Ars Edition, Inc./ARS AG has offered at least 40 different ornaments over the years. The styles are widely varied. In 1982, the company introduced a gold satin ball as a "First Edition." In 1983, however, the design was changed to a more traditional glass ball, with the First Edition rendered in glass.

This is the fourth edition glass Christmas ornament, Merry Christmas (Hum 323).

Pillboxes

There are four motifs to be found on the tops of these little 1-5/8" x 1-1/2" oval metal pillboxes: Wayside Harmony, Chick Girl, Easy Letters (With Loving Greetings, Hum 309), and Playmates.

They were no longer in the catalog in 1988. They sold for about $18 in the mid-1980s and have not appreciated significantly in value on the secondary market since.

Pillboxes decorated with Hummel motifs.

Collector Spoons

In 1982, Ars Edition, Inc. began an annual collector spoon series with a 12-piece set of silver-plated 5" spoons with shield-like enamel finials each bearing a different M.I. Hummel design. The backs of the spoons bear the company name, the year of the edition, and the M.I. Hummel signature. The series ended with the third set. Through many circumstances, the sets may have been broken up so they may be found singly. The lists on the following page specify the designs in each set.

Six Ars Edition silver collector spoons.

First Edition	Second Edition	Third Edition
Sunny Weather	Hello	The Renewal
School Girl	Rosebud	Innocence
Farewell	On the Other Side	Just Resting
Wayside Harmony	Blessed Event	Behind the Fence
Chick Girl	Little Bookkeeper	My Dolly
Stormy Weather	Feeding Time	Star Gazer
School Boy	Slumber Time	Boy's Communion
Not For You	Little Sweeper	Postman
Girl on Fence	Little Cellist	Confidentially
Playmates	Mother's Helper	Serenade
	Little Goat Herder	Baker
	Springtime Joys	Goat Girl (Good Friends)

Christmas Spoon, Bell, and Thimble

1981	Christmas Angel
1982	Guiding Angel
1983	Prayer of Adoration
1984	Heavenly Duo
1985	Guiding Light
1986	Celestial Musician
1987	Candle Light
1988	Angelic Guide

In 1986, a set of six 4-3/8" spoons began a new annual series. The finial shape had changed to round. These were also issued for three years and are listed here by edition in case the sets were broken up, to aid the collector in identifying them. They each bear the company name, the year of issue, and the M.I. Hummel signature.

First Edition	Second Edition	Third Edition
His Happy Pastime	Sleepy Time	She Loves Me, She Loves Me Not
Her Happy Pastime	My Wish is Small	He Loves Me, He Loves Me Not
Discovery	School Girl	
Tit-For-Tat	Little Scholar	We Wish You the Best
Sunny Weather	Off to Town	Special Gift
Stormy Weather	Looks Like Rain	Harmony In Four Parts
		Special Delivery

There are as many as seven Mother's Day Spoons to be found beginning in 1982 and continuing through 1988. They are 25-karat gold-plated and have an enamel finial with the design on it. The length is 4-3/8" and each of them has "For Mother" engraved in the bowl.

There was also an Annual Christmas Spoon, Thimble, and Bell Series. These began in 1981. They are all engraved with the year and "Christmas" in the bowl of the spoon and on the body of the bell. Those missing from the list were not found in the catalogs of the corresponding year.

Christmas Spoon, Bell, and Thimble Series

1981	Christmas Angel
1982	Guiding Angel
1983	Prayer of Adoration
1984	Heavenly Duo
1985	Guiding Light
1986	Celestial Musician
1987	Candle Light
1988	Angelic Guide

In terms of value for any of these collector spoons, there does not currently appear to be heavy secondary market interest in Hummel-related spoons. Most sell for not more than $5 apiece.

Shown here are the 1986 Christmas Spoon and Bell (Celestial Musician) and the 1986 Annual Bell (Apple Tree Boy).

Annual Bells

The Annual Bell Series wasn't begun until 1983. They are silver-plated and measure 3-1/2" high. Each had the year and design engraved on the body of the bell. When they were first issued, they cost about $20. Recent secondary market sales show limited interest in these bells with most selling for not more than $10 apiece.

Year	Design
1983	Ring Around the Rosie
1984	Telling Her Secret
1985	Quartet (Harmony In Four Parts)
1986	Apple Tree Boy
1987	Follow the Leader
1988	Max and Moritz

Pendants

At one time, the finial portion of the bells was made into pendants. It is not known how many different designs there were. Sunny Weather and Honey Lover are two known examples. They came with a 24" rope chain, but may be found with any other or no chain at all. They were $10 in the early 1980s. Recent secondary market prices for the Honey Lover pendant, for example, have it priced between $120 and $150.

Thimbles

The series of six annual editions of six assorted thimbles each began in 1983. These thimbles are silver-plated and are 1" high. The back of each has the "Hummel" signature, "ars edition," copyright symbol with year, and "limited edition." "W. Germany" and "silverplated" appear inside each. Recent secondary market sales indicate a fair amount of interest in these pieces, but they tend to sell for not more than $10 to $12 apiece.

First Edition	Second Edition	Third Edition	Fourth Edition	Fifth Edition
Book Worm	Hello There	Helping Mother	Apple Tree Girl	Chick Girl
Doll Mother	Baby and Spider	Little Bookkeeper	Little Goat Herder	Playmates
Prayer Before Battle	His Happy Pastime	Sunny Weather	Off to Town	Ring Around the Rosie
Knit One, Purl One	Her Happy Pastime	Stormy Weather	Apple Tree Boy	Harmony In Four Parts
Umbrella Boy	Discovery	Special Gift	Goat Girl (Friends)	Wayside Harmony
Umbrella Girl	Tit-For-Tat	Special Delivery	Happy John	Coquettes

Little Bookkeeper
Annual Thimble.

Sunny Weather Annual Thimble.

Special Gift Annual Thimble.

Helping Mother
Annual Thimble.

Stormy Weather Annual Thimble.

Special Delivery
Annual Thimble.

Annual Christmas Plates, 1987-1990.

Annual Christmas Plates

This is a four-plate series that began in 1987. The beautiful porcelain plates are in full color and decorated with 24-karat gold. Made by Goebel and marketed by ARS AG, they are 7-1/2" in diameter and limited worldwide to 20,000 sequentially numbered plates. Each was made of porcelain with 24-karat gold embellishments. The original retail price was $65; however, the secondary market interest in such plates is quite low so they typically do not sell today for more than $10 apiece.

Miniature Annual Plates

This is a series of six miniature plates (1") that are replicas of the first six plates in the Goebel Annual Plate Series, 1971 through 1976. The total production is 15,000 sets worldwide. The complete set, released in 1986, was offered at $150 including a wooden oval display frame designed for the set.

There is a second set depicting the 1977 through the 1982 plates. The series was planned but never produced.

The Reutter Collection

M.W. Reutter Porzellan GmbH, a German porcelain firm, was first licensed in 1996 to begin production of Hummel-related items for the consumer and collector. The market began primarily in Europe, but today, the products can be found in the United States and Canada either through regular retail outlets, mail-order gift catalogs, or on the Internet (www.reutterporcelain.com or www.reutterporzellan.com). The products are primarily tea or coffee services, but they also make a several other items. A sample list of its products follows:

- Plate, 3-3/4" round porcelain with gold rim
- Mug
- Money bank
- Vase (two types)
- Pillbox, approximately 1-1/2" x 2-1/4"
- Box, 3-3/4" round with lid
- Dish, 4" x 7" oval with pierced work border
- Dish, 3" round with pierced work border
- Dish, 5" round with pierced work border
- Coffee set for two
- Coffee set for four
- Miniature coffee set, 2" high teapot
- Doll coffee set

Miniature Annual Plates: Limited-edition (15,000) miniature replicas of the 1971 through 1976 plates in an oval wooden frame.

Reutter Coffee Set for two.

Miniature Coffee Set by Reutter.

Reutter Collection pieces, from left: 3" bowl, 5" bowl, 4" x 7" oval bowl, pillbox, and 3-3/4" box.

The company began making items in just three Hummel designs: He Loves Me, He Loves Me Not (H 127), Lily of the Valley (H 130), and Hansel and Gretel (H 217). It has since expanded its offerings to include Umbrella Girl, Follow the Leader, and The Guiding Angel.

The Danbury Mint Collection

This well-known division of the Norwalk, Connecticut company MBI has been in the business of offering fine collectibles for many years. Its Hummel products are either made by the Goebel company or licensed by ARS AG, Zug, Switzerland to have items bearing M.I. Hummel artwork made for them. ARS AG has very exacting standards and monitors the process to insure the highest quality. The collection is extensive and some items are appearing on the secondary market. There is not yet sufficient trade data, however, to establish realistic collector values for them except where noted. All Danbury Mint products are sold by mail-order subscription only. The collector is never obligated to purchase the entire series and is given the right to cancel the subscription at any time. It is possible that not all of the editions of the following collectible are sold out, especially some of the later ones. To find out what may still be available, call them at 1-800-243-4664.

Where possible, the year of release and release price including shipping and handling will be quoted. The fol-

Among the many beautiful Hummel-related collectible made by Danbury Mint are plates like the one shown here, Come Back Soon.

lowing is a list of known items produced by the Danbury Mint and/or related divisions of MBI.

- Books, Bible (Easton Press) and diary
- Christmas ornaments, porcelain
- Christmas ornaments, gold (The Christmas Ornament Collectors Club)
- Clocks
- Cookie jars
- Cup and saucer collection
- Eggs, porcelain
- First Day Covers
- Kitchen canisters
- Music boxes
- Plates, collector
- Salt-and-pepper shakers
- Spice jars
- Stamps, postage (Postal Commemorative Society)
- Tea sets
- Thimbles (Thimble Collectors Club)

Spice Jars

A collection of 24 porcelain spice jars bearing reproduction of original artwork and 23-karat decoration was offered by subscription, beginning in January 1993. They were delivered to the collector at the rate of two every other month for $19.75 plus $1 shipping for each piece, for a total cost of $498. A wooden spice rack was also included for displaying the jars. Today, these jars can be purchased on the secondary market for about $15 to $20 apiece.

Kitchen Canisters

A set of four canisters was offered in 1991. They were decorated with pictures of M.I. Hummel figurines with an appropriate Bavarian scene for a background. They were offered for $239.40, including shipping in six monthly installments. Today, the set in mint condition would probably sell for about the same amount as its original issue price, or about $45 for each individual canister. They came in four different sizes as listed below:

Size	Volume	Design
5"	12 oz.	Timid Little Sister, Hum 394
6-1/2"	24 oz.	Barnyard Hero, Hum 195
7-1/2"	48 oz.	In Tune, Hum 414
8-1/2"	60 oz.	Little Goat Herder, Hum 200

The First Hummel Gold Christmas Ornament Collection

In 1988, Danbury offered a set of double-sided Hummel prints laminated in round form and surrounded by matching 24-karat gold-finished decorative filigreed elements. There are 36 different designs measuring 2-3/4" in diameter. The ornaments were available by subscription at $18 each, including shipping and handling. You could cancel your subscription at any time, but if you completed the collection the total would have been $648.

The Hummel "School Children" Collector Thimbles

The Thimble Collectors Club offered this series in 1993. It is a series of 28 gold-plated thimbles, each bearing a Hummel artwork depicting a child connected in some way to school. With the series came a very nice wooden wall display with a brass identification plaque in the center. The thimbles cost $17 each with $1.50 shipping and handling. The completed collection amounted to a total of $518.

Each thimble measured about 1" high and carried a "M.I. Hummel" signature on the back with "ars/TCC" and "Made in W. Germany" on the inside. Today, these golden thimbles receive a fair amount of interest on the secondary market and generally sell for $20 to $25 apiece.

Plates

Calendar Plate Collection

Hummel company literature from 1993 calls this plate a double first. It was the first time the Hummel calendar scene Maypole appeared on a plate and it was "...also the first issue in the M.I. Hummel Calendar Plate Collection!" The design consists of the figurine Maypole in a realistic setting. A flyer promoting the plate states: "'Maypole is forever limited to an edition size of 75 firing days." The collection consisted of 12 plates, each 8-1/4" in diameter.

The original issue price was $29.95 plus $2.95 shipping and handling, for a total of $32.90. Today, because of a very limited interest in collector plates, these plates sell for not more than $10 apiece on the secondary market.

Playmates Collector Plate

In 1993, Danbury offered this 8-1/4" plate for $29.50 plus $2.95 shipping and handling, for a total of $32.45. It was limited in edition number to those produced in 25 firing days. The design is the figurine placed on the cobblestone stoop in front of the door to a Bavarian home. Recent secondary market information lists the value of this plate at $30 to $35.

Private Parade, one of the various collector plates produced by Danbury Mint.

Number	Design Theme
1	Apple Tree Boy and Apple Tree Girl
2	Stormy Weather
3	Tender Loving Care
4	Squeaky Clean
5	Little Explorers
6	Surprise
7	Little Musicians
8	Budding Scholars
9	Hello Down There
10	Come Back Soon
11	Country Crossroads
12	Private Parade

Land In Sight Collector Plate

This plate was issued in 1992. It is a large plate, 10-1/2" in diameter, and came with a handsome polished mahogany display base with identifying brass plaque. The design is surrounded with a 3/4"-wide band of 24-karat gold. The design is the figurine Land In Sight in an extremely well-rendered realistic sea setting. The number in the edition was not revealed, but limited to the number produced in $75 firing days. The original cost was $87 plus $2.85 shipping and handling, for a total of $89.85. With limited interest in collector plates, secondary market prices for this piece today are $20 to $35.

We Wish You the Best Century Plate

This plate was issued in 1993. It was a large plate, 10-1/2" in diameter, and came with a handsome polished mahogany display stand with a brass identifying plaque. The design in the center is surrounded by a 3/4" wide band of 24-karat gold. The design featured is the Hummel figurine We Wish You the Best Century Collection piece placed in a realistic setting. The number in the edition was not revealed, but limited to the number produced in a $75 firing day period. The cost was $87 plus $2.85 shipping and handling, for a total of $89.85. Today, it sells on the secondary market for $20 to $35.

Little Companions Plate Series

In 1990, Danbury issued a series of limited production collector plates. The plate designs are figurines photographed in realistic settings and applied to an 8-1/2" porcelain plate rimmed in 23-karat gold. The edition size was not revealed, but literature promoting the series states that the edition sized will be "...forever limited to the production capacity of 14 full firing days." Available by mail-order, the release price was $32.45, including shipping and handling costs. This makes the total price $389.40 for the completed series, which included a nice display rack. Today, these pieces sell for $20 to $30 each on the secondary market.

Hummel Mold
Hum 141, Hum 142

Hum 71
Hum 376 (Little Nurse)
Hum 412 (Bath Time)
Hum 16 (Little Hiker) and Hum 49, (To Market, girl only)
Hum 94
Hum 150 (Happy Days)
Hum 415 (Thoughtful) and Hum 418 (What's New?)
Hum 394 (Timid Little Sister)
Hum 545
Unknown
Hum 86 (Happiness) and Hum 240 (Little Drummer)

Gentle Friends Plate Series

In 1991, Danbury issued a series of limited-edition production plates. The designs are photographs of Hummel figurines in realistic settings applied to 8-1/2" porcelain plates rimmed in 23-karat gold. The number in the edition is not revealed, but literature promoting the series states the edition size will be "...forever limited to the production capacity of 14 full firing days". Available by mail-order subscription, the price for each including shipping and handling was $32.45 for the first five in the series and $32.73 for the last seven (apparently shipping and handling costs went up), for a total of $391.36 for the completed series, which included a nice display rack. Today, these plates sell for $20 to $35 apiece.

Number	Theme	Hummel Mold
1	Favorite Pet	Hum 361
2	Feathered Friends	Hum 344
3	Let's Sing	Hum 110
4	Playmates	Hum 58
5	Farm Boy	Hum 66
6	Lost Sheep	Hum 68
7	Feeding Time	Hum 199
8	Cinderella	Hum 337
9	Friends	Hum 136
10	Goose Girl	Hum 47
11	Strolling Along	Hum 5
12	Little Goat Herder	Hum 200

Porcelain Egg Collection

This collection of 12 eggs was offered in 1995. Each egg depicts a Hummel figurine in a realistic vignette and is approximately 3-3/8" high by 2-1/2" wide and came with an attractive hardwood base. They sold for $19.95 each, plus $2.95 shipping and handling, for a total of $22.90 each. Today, these eggs generally sell for $5 to $8 on the secondary market.

Porcelain Cup and Saucer Collection

This collection was offered in 1995. It consists of 12 demitasse cups (mugs) and saucers. M.I. Hummel figurines were depicted on the 2" high cups and saucers were decorated with a thematic border to match the figurine somehow or a design element on the figure itself. For example, apples were used to match Apple Tree Boy and raindrops to match Umbrella Girl. They were offered for $39.50 plus $1.75 shipping and handling, for a total of $41.25 each. The cost for the completed collection was $495. A nice display fixture was included at no extra charge. Today, these pieces sell for $10 to $20 apiece (cup with saucer) on the secondary market. The designs are listed following:

- Apple Tree Girl
- Little Fiddler
- Apple Tree Boy
- Stormy Weather
- Postman
- Goose Girl
- Umbrella Girl
- Happy Pastime
- Umbrella Boy
- Merry Wanderer
- Blessed Event
- Kiss Me

Other

The Holy Bible

The Easton Press division of MBI made this beautiful leather-bound, gold-tooled Bible available to collectors in 1996. It is profusely illustrated using full-color M.I. Hummel artwork, and it is the first time her art has been used to illustrate a Bible. It was available in two versions: the New King James version for Protestants and the New American Bible, the official version recognized by the Roman Catholic Church. The original cost was $49, plus $5 shipping and handling, for a total of $54.

Needlework

If you are handy with cross-stitch, crewelwork, embroidery, and other needle arts, you may benefit from the treasure trove of M.I. Hummel designs available in needlework. Some of the designs that are listed have been discontinued, but they still arise, still in kit form, from time to time in antique shops and the like. Finished kits also surface in the same places and at garage and estate sales.

At least three companies have produced the kits: JCA, Inc., 35 Scales Lane, Townsend, MA 01469; Jenson Designs from Denmark; and Paragon Needlecraft from the National Paragon Corporation of New York. JCA is still very much in business and producing dozens of kits for the aficionado. Paragon and Jenson Designs, however, are no longer in business.

There are round, oval, and square needlework shapes, and they are also made up for bell pulls and pillows. If you are really talented, you are limited only by your imagination. And if you make your own from a Hummel design, it's perfectly all right as long as it is for your own private use.

School Mates pair of cross-stitch projects.

JCA, Inc.

Following are JCA's Hummel needlecraft products on the market as of October 1996.

Cross-Stitch Leaflets

84022	The Hikers (pair): Off to Town and Little Hiker
84023	Carefree Days (pair): Meeting in the Meadow and Meeting on the Mountain
84024	Little Friends (pair): Chick Girl and Playmates
84025	School Mates (pair): School Girl, Little Scholar
84034	Land In Sight: Hum 530
84035	Blessed Event: Hum 333
84036	The Apple Tree (pair): Apple Tree Girl, Apple Tree Boy
84037	Playtime (pair): Knit One, Purl One, Book Worm
84038	Ready For Rain (pair): Umbrella Boy and Umbrella Girl
84039	Alpine Afternoon (pair): Bashful and Globe Trotter
84042	The Birthday Gifts: We Wish You the Best
84043	Wee Three: Three standing girls in front of fence

Needle Treasures Kits (Cross-Stitch Kits)

02607	Sunny Weather
02608	Ring Around the Rosie
02609	Not For You
02610	Telling Her Secret
02633	Wash Day
02634	Postman
02641	Stormy Weather
02642	Hansel and Gretel
02649	Sunny Weather (afghan)
04217	Blessed Event (baby quilt)
02662	Follow the Leader
02672	Max and Moritz
02675	Bashful: (banner)
02676	The Globe Trotter (banner)

02677	Feeding Time		04628	Coquettes
02678	Little Goat Herder		04629	Blessed Event
02687	The Strummers		04636	Blue Belle
02688	He Loves Me, He Loves Me Not (pillow)		04644	Little Flower Girl
02689	She Loves Me, She Loves Me Not (pillow)		06613	The Doctor (needlepoint)

04600 Merry Wanderer
04601 Little Fiddler
04607 Lily of the Valley (pillow)
04609 Daisy (cushion)
04619 Brother's Lesson

What's New? Counted cross-stitch.

Christmas Kits (Counted Cross-Stitch)
02864 Christmas Angel
02865 Candle Light
02874 Letter to Santa Claus
02882 Silent Night (Hum 54)
02891 Celestial Musician (Hum 188)
02897 Skier (Christmas stocking)
02927 Angel Duet
02954 Angel With Horn

Weekenders (Miniature Needlecraft, 5"x7")
00750 Chicken-Licken (stitchery)
02755 Cinderella
02762 Sleepy Time
02775 Looks Like Rain
02802 What's New?
03513 Little Sweeper

Cross-Stitch Greeting Cards
02410 Off to Town
02411 Little Hiker
02412 Wash Day
02413 School Girl
02414 Little Scholar
02415 Not For You
02416 Postman
02417 The Doctor
02418 Looks Like Rain
02501 Celestial Musician
02502 Candle Light
02503 Letter to Santa
02504 Angel With Trumpet

Toy Truck

What will we find next? Yes, as you can see by the accompanying photograph, this is a M.I. Hummel truck. It was authorized by ARS AG and marketed through a toy company. It is a high-quality, highly detailed model about 6" long. Everybody needs a Hummel 18-wheeler for their collection. Not everybody will get one, however, because although the number manufactured is not presently known, it is small. They were selling for about $35 for a few years, but when word got around recently that a dealer had a few in stock, they disappeared from the shelves rapidly.

Unauthorized M.I. Hummel toy truck.

Examples of cigar bands using M.I. Hummel designs.

Cigar Bands (Unauthorized product)

Believe it or not, there are cigar bands—many of them. One collector suggests that they might be gum or candy wrappers. They may very well be, but they do look like cigar bands, too.

At one point, an antique dealer sent Carl Luckey a set of 15 mint-condition bands, asking if he knew anything about them. He did not, but arranged to buy the set. When they arrived, he couldn't believe how beautiful they were. They were high-quality, full-color photographic reproductions of Hummel figurines in realistic settings. Several are reproduced here for you to see the style. Each band has the notation "T.S.H. HIPPO."

Similar bands surfaced after Carl had found the initial set. Some depict M.I. Hummel art, rather than figurines. Each of the styles also has the word "Hummelbeelden" on the reverse side of each of the bands.

Others have black-and-white photo reproductions of the figurines. The smaller ones are framed in gold color ink and they are found in one of five colors: red, yellow, green, blue, or white (no color). The small ones measure 2-1/2" (6.4 cm) and come in sets of 48. As you can see, each is clearly identified, even down to the mold number, although the company that produced them got the mold numbers wrong in a couple of instances. The larger band measures 4" (10 cm). They are found in sets of 12. Both styles are clearly numbered so you may know when you have obtained a complete set.

These, at least some of them, have to be of fairly recent vintage as one of them depicts Hum 416, Jubilee, which was issued in 1985.

Umbrella Girl Tapestry

In the spring 1990 issue of Insights, the newsletter of the M.I. Hummel Club, a tapestry was offered. Only 50 were made worldwide. They were hand-knotted of pure silk with 120 lines of knots per foot. They were made in Beijing, China, and measure 25-1/4"x 26-1/2". The initial offering was for $1,800. Although the newsletter entry did not mention Ars Edition, it is very likely that the company was behind its production. There was another, very similar item offered by Ars in the mid-1990s. The descriptions are strikingly alike. See the Ars Edition, Inc./ARS AG section for this similar piece.

Postage Stamps and First Day Covers

Stamps

A number of First Day Covers and foreign stamps depict Hummel art. They are not all covered here, as it is difficult to ascertain just what and how many have been produced.

The first ones were released in 1990 by the island country of St. Vincent in the Caribbean. From then until 1992, six more countries joined St. Vincent by issuing stamps. The stamps are all full-color and similar in design. Each features a photograph of a different Hummel figurine as the central design. There are at least 100 to be collected, but only 86 of them are identified here as follows:

A few examples of Hummel postage stamps.

Antigua and Barbuda:
Crossroads (Hum 331)
Flower Vendor (Hum 381)
Globe Trotter (Hum 79)
Good Hunting (Hum 307)
Homeward Bound (Hum 334)
Just Resting (Hum 112)
Little Hiker (Hum 16)
Mountaineer (Hum 315)

Cambodia:
Adventure Bound (Hum 347)
Doll Bath (Hum 319)
Doll Mother (Hum 67)
Pleasant Journey (Hum 406)
Prayer Before Battle (Hum 20)
Ring Around the Rosie (Hum 348)
Volunteers (Hum 50)
Kiss Me! (Hum 311)

Commonwealth of Dominica:
Celestial Musician (Hum 188)
Festival Harmony With Flute (Hum 173)
Festival Harmony With Mandolin (Hum 172)
Flying High Christmas Ornament (Hum 452)
Heavenly Angel (Hum 21)
Joyous News (Hum 27)
Merry Christmas (Hum 323)
Searching Angel (Hum 310)

Gambia:
Auf Wiedersehen (Hum 153)

Coquettes (Hum 179)
Daddy's Girls (Hum 371)
Going Home (Hum 383)
Max and Moritz (Hum 123)
Stormy Weather (Hum 71)
Telling Her Secret (Hum 196)
Vacation Time (Hum 125)

Ghana:
Autumn Harvest (Hum 355)
Bashful (Hum 377)
Chick Girl (Hum 57)
Easter Greetings (Hum 378)
Farewell (Hum 65)
Favorite Pet (Hum 361)
Playmates (Hum 58)
The Run-A-Way (Hum 327)

Grenada and the Grenadines (Christmas Stamps):
Angel Duet (Hum 193)
Christmas Angel (Hum 301)
Christmas Song (Hum 343)
Good Shepherd (Hum 42)
Hosanna (Hum 480)
Heavenly Lullaby (Hum 262)
Silent Night (Hum 54)
Watchful Angel (Hum 194)

Guyana:
Baker (Hum 128)
Begging His Share (Hum 9)
Congratulations (Hum 17)

Follow the Leader (Hum 369)
My Wish is Small (Hum 463)
Valentine Gift (Hum 387)
Valentine Joy (Hum 399)
We Wish You the Best (Hum 600)
Maldives:
Thoughtful (Hum 415)
Little Bookkeeper (Hum 306)
Little Scholar (Hum 80)
School Boys (Hum 170)
School Girl (Hum 81)
School Girls (Hum 177)
Smart Little Sister (Hum 346)
With Loving Greetings (Hum 309)
Saint Kitts and Nevis:
Apple Tree Boy (Hum 142)
Apple Tree Girl (Hum 141)
The Botanist (Hum 351)
For Father (Hum 87)
March Winds (Hum 43)
Ride Into Christmas (Hum 396)
Umbrella Boy (Hum 152A)
Umbrella Girl (Hum 152B)
Saint Vincent:
The Artist (Hum 304)
Boots (Hum 143)
Chimney Sweep (Hum 12)
Hello (Hum 124)
Little Pharmacist (Hum 322)
Postman (Hum 119)
The Photographer (Hum 178)
Waiter (Hum 154)
Tanzania:
Close Harmony (Hum 336)

Happiness (Hum 86)
Happy Days (Hum 150)
In D Major (Hum 430)
Serenade (Hum 85)
Whitsuntide (Hum 163)
Uganda:
Big Housecleaning (Hum 363)
Happy Pastime (Hum 69)
Harmony In Four Parts (Hum 471)
Hear Ye, Hear Ye (Hum 15)
Little Cellist (Hum 89)
Little Sweeper (Hum 171)
Little Tailor (Hum 308)
Let's Sing (Hum 110)
Mischief Maker (Hum 342)
Mother's Helper (Hum 133)
Singing Lesson (Hum 63)
Star Gazer (Hum 132)
Tuba Player (Hum 437)
Wash Day (Hum 321)

Some or all of the stamps are also known to have been issued in commemorative blocks of one and four.

First Day Covers

For you non-philatelists, a First Day Cover is an envelope with a new stamp that is postmarked the first day of issue of that stamp. Many countries will create a special postmark to be used on that particular First Day Cover on that day alone. Often, there is a special privately printed envelope bearing some art or other decoration commemorating whatever the stamp design was intended to honor.

The First Day Cover depicted in this section is not strictly a Hummel First Day Cover, but is interesting

Example of a First Day Cover, created for the now-defunct M.I. Hummel Museum of New Braunfels, Texas.

because of the special postmark created for it. As you can see by the return address, it was a special-event post office branch set up at the former museum in Texas.

The Postal Commemorative Society of Norwalk, Connecticut (its address is the same as the Danbury Mint) is likely to have had an important role in the issuance of all the foreign country M.I. Hummel postage stamps discussed earlier. In 1991, the society issued a series of First Day Covers utilizing the same stamps. They produced 100 covers. Each bore a stamp depicting a figurine and a full-color reproduction of the original Hummel art from which the figurine was modeled. They were issued by subscription at $7.75 per cover. Included was a very nice loose-leaf display album.

Research has also brought forth a Swiss company that has produced First Day Covers. The company is originally known as Verlag Groth AG. It is now simply called Groth AG and has the following address: Gewerbestrasse19, P.O. Box 167, CH-6314 Unterageri, Switzerland. The phone number is 0041-41-750-45-72 and e-mail is info@groth.ch. You can also find some information at www.groth.ch.

Since 1989, there has been a First Day Cover issued from Rodental, Bavaria, Germany each year. These each bear a different Hummel design and a Hummel design cancellation mark. Sponsored by Goebel, these First Day Covers commemorate the change from the old name "Oeslau" to Rodental where W. Goebel Porzellanfabrik is located. The stamps are not designs from M.I. Hummel artwork. The first seven designs were:

- Postman (1989)
- The Mail Is Here (1990)
- Chimney Sweep (1991)
- Hear Ye, Hear Ye (1992)
- Baker (1993)
- Boots (1994)
- The Artist (1995)
- The Photographer (1996)
- Waiter (1997)

Stationery, Memo Pads, Note Cards, Christmas Cards, Gift Wrap, Calendars, and More

Several companies are licensed to produce these items. More information on cards, gift wrap, etc. is listed on the following pages. Some of the companies are:

- Case Stationery Company, Yonkers, New York
- Deluxe Corporation, Shoreview, Minnesota
- Goebel of North America, Pennington, New Jersey
- CPS Corporation, Franklin, Tennesee
- Emil Fink Verlag, Stuttgart, Germany
- Ars Edition, Munich, Germany

The Case Stationery Company Products

Case apparently created its initial Hummel paper line based on the following 11 different M.I. Hummel figurines: Adventure Bound; Apple Tree Girl; Happy Pastime; Hello; Merry Wanderer; Postman; School Boys; Telling Her Secret; Umbrella Girl; We Congratulate; and Worship.

These designs such products as desk caddies (150 sheets), memo cubes (700 sheets), memo books, stationery (6" x 8" in 11 designs), envelopes, folded note cards (6" x 8" unfolded size), and magnetic memo pads (3-1/4" x 6-1/2").

Case also produced some decorated metal storage tins. Four of them are filled with a packet of the stationery and envelopes mentioned earlier. The boxes measure 9-1/8" x 6-7/8" x 2-1/4". The designs are Adventure Bound, Apple Tree Girl, School Boys, and We Congratulate. All of these were photographed in realistic vignettes.

Case also produced another decorated box the same size, but without decorated stationery. The design is oriented horizontally and utilizes the Angel Duet candleholder flanked by Festival Harmony With Flute and Festival Harmony With Mandolin. This design is called

Decorated storage tin and stationary from the Case Stationary Company.

Power of Faith, which is emphasized by a stained glass window behind each design.

Case also made five smaller tins. They were white with gold trim. Each is decorated with color photographs of several figurines according to a theme.

Design	Size	Style
Come Out and Play	5-1/8" diameter	Round
Special Editions	3-1/2" diameter	Round
Seasons	4-1/4"	Square
Home Sweet Home	3-3/4" "	Oval
Merry Sounds of Music	4-1/4" "	Octagonal

Note cards from the Case Stationary Company.

More examples of decorated tins from the Case Stationary Company.

Deluxe Corporation Products

Deluxe is the largest check printer in the world, so naturally, much of its Hummel-related items are those related to checks. The following are some of the company's Hummel products, but you can obtain more information by logging onto the Web site at www.deluxe.com:

M.I. Hummel check and checkbook from the Deluxe Corporation.

- Checks (four M.I. Hummel scenes represented)
- Checkbook cover (burnished leather decorated with a medallion with the Merry Wanderer motif)
- Checkbook cover (has facsimile of an M.I. Hummel signature)
- Personalized note cards (figurines in realistic vignettes)
- Personalized stationery (four lines of personalization with a Hummel decoration in the lower left corner)
- Peel-and-stick address labels (up to three lines of personalization; comes with a dispenser.)

CPS Corporation Products

CPS offers gift wrap in three different designs and colors, gift tags, Christmas cards, note cards, and a two-year planner. The company can be reached by phone at (615) 794-8000 or by writing to its address: 1715 Columbia Avenue, Franklin, TN 37064.

Emil Fink Calendars

This company, also a publisher of prints and postcards, publishes four styles of calendars each year for the German-speaking public. It is not known how many have been published over the years. They are all fairly small, about the size of a postcard or slightly larger. Three of the four are typically decorated with very familiar M.I. Hummel drawings and paintings. The other utilizes watercolor paintings that are much less familiar.

A detail of one of the gift wrap designs from CPS Corporation.

A gift tag from CPS Corporation.

Display of three-dimensional greeting cards from Rococo.

Card Name	Mold No.	Hummel Name
Little Bookkeeper	Hum 306	same
Kiss Me	Hum 311	same
Our Secret	Hum 317	Not For You
	Hum 459	In the Meadow
Wash Day	Hum 321	same
Blessed Event	Hum 333	same
Sweet Greetings	Hum 352	same
Christmas Choir	Hum 2	Little Fiddler
	Hum 85	Serenade
	Hum 336	Close Harmony
	Hum 471	Harmony In Four Parts
Hear Ye, Hear Ye	Hum 15	same
Holy Children	Hum 18	Christ Child
	Hum 83	Angel Serenade With Lamb
	Hum 238C	Angel With Trumpet
	Hum 359	Tuneful Angel
Christmas Blessing	Hum 42	Good Shepherd
	Hum 54	Silent Night
	Hum 454	Song of Praise
Bird Duet	Hum 169	same
Little Angels	Hum 194	Watchful Angel
	Hum 357	Guiding Angel
	Hum 438	Sounds of the Mandolin
	Hum 571	Angelic Guide
The Mail is Here	Hum 226	same
Angel Duet	Hum 261	same
Merry Christmas	Hum 323	same
Letter to Santa Claus	Hum 340	same
Ride Into Christmas	Hum 396	same

Greeting Cards

Rococo is a line of everyday and Christmas pop-up cards made in England and distributed in the U.S. by Marian Heath Greeting Cards. Contact the company by phone at (508) 291-0766, online at www.marianheath.com or by mail at: 9 Kendrick Road, Wareham, MA 02571. Rococo designs are ingenious cards that are mailed flat, but when you open them up, they become three-dimensional. There are 20 different designs, of which two are religious and nine Christmas cards. The designs are:

Card Name	Mold No.	Hummel Name
Barnyard Hero	Hum 195	same
Feeding Time	Hum 199	same
Birthday Serenade	Hum 218	same

Christmas Cards

The M.I. Hummel Club offered five different Christmas cards through its newsletter mailings in 1993 and 1994. The company producing these was Brett Forer. They came in boxes of 18 with envelopes. The themes were:

1993

A Gift for Jesus	H 626
Celestial Musician	H 441, Hum 188
Candle Light	H 412, Hum 192

1994

A Gift for Jesus	H 626
Tender Watch	H 410
Quartet	Hum 134

Happy Pastime, Joyful, and Book Worm all depicted on postcard #156-514 by Classico.

Postcards

Over the years, a number of companies have produced postcards of M.I. Hummel art. The first of these were published in 1933 by Ars Sacra, Josef Müller in Munich, Germany. The company is now known as Ars Edition. These first cards are the ones that inspired the idea of creating figurines from the art.

Of interest to collectors of the postcards are the following publishers:
Ars sacra Josef Müller
Ars Edition

Telling Her Secret, postcard #62.1291 by Ars Edition.

In the center is a 1991 promotional postcard from Goebel.

The cards are of two basic types: a photo of a figurine(s), usually in a realistic vignette, or a reproduction of M.I. Hummel art.

There is a third type, produced by Goebel for promotional purposes only. The card is usually a color photo of one or more figurines in an arrangement of related material or decorations suitable to the promotion.

A few postcards were published by other companies about 20 years ago, before the convent, Goebel, and their agents tightened the reins on rights. Many larger gift shops and similar operations had their own cards made for promotional purposes.

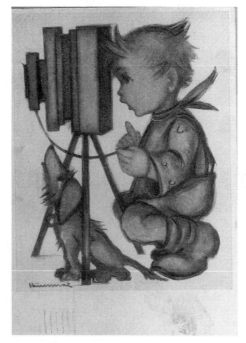

The Photographer, postcard #4767 by Verlag Joseph Mueller.

Perched on a Fence, postcard #815 by Emil Fink Verlag.

Metal Tins

These tins, which were filled with traditional German cookies and gingerbread, are produced by Lebkuchen Schmidt GmbH & Co. KG, Zollhausstr. 30, 90469 Nuremberg, Germany. They are very attractive, approximately 11" x 7" x 4" deep metal containers decorated with M.I. Hummel art (vignettes of children). The company can be reached by phone at + 49 (0) 911-89 66 0, at the address listed above, or on the Internet at ww2.lebkuchen-schmidt.com/htm/index.html.

Refrigerator Magnets (Unauthorized product)

About 1994, a gift shop offered what was described in its mail-order catalog as "New! Goldtone Framed 'HUMMEL PICTURES'."

The entry went on to say you could hang these pieces as pictures or use them as magnets. They are 2-1/2" in diameter and the designs are M.I. Hummel art. There are at least eight different designs, four of which are depicted in the accompanying photo. They were offered at about $15 for a set of four. The catalog entry states they were imported from Germany.

Hummel refrigerator magnets.

Jigsaw Puzzles

The F.X. Schmid Company of New Hampshire, which is now owned by Ravensburger of Germany, offered at least eight M.I. Hummel jigsaw puzzles. Two of them have 1,000 pieces and measure 29" x 23" when completed. The designs consist of figurines placed in realistic surroundings. One is called Springtime and contains Coquettes and Easter Time. The other is called Good Friends and contains Friends and Playmates. They originally sold for about $20.

The company also offered a selection of at least six miniature puzzles that had 100 pieces and measured 7" x 7" when completed. The designs are the figurines: School Boys, Ring Around the Rosie, Blessed Event, Playmates, In Tune, and Feathered Friends.

More information can be obtained online at: www.mystery-games.com/ravjigpuz.html.

Snack Trays

A mail-order gift catalog listed these as available off and on from around 1993. They are illustrated by figurines photographed in realistic settings. Three designs are illustrated: Home From Market, Hansel and Gretel, and Be Patient.

They are made of Melamine, measure 5-3/4" x 9-1/4", and have small holes should you wish to hang them as decoration. They are worth $25 for a set of three today.

"Moments To Remember" Pocket Watches

Gruen Watches of Exeter, Pennsylvania, produces a series of six different watches on 28" watch chains. The purchase includes a display dome on a wooden base. There are two different styles of watch case: a plain smooth case and one with a scalloped rim around the back and a fancy twisted rope-style loop at the winder. The watches are 1-1/2" in diameter and are 23-karat gold-plated. The back features a photo of a figurine, and the watch face has the name of the figurine and a facsimile M.I. Hummel signature. The movement is quartz. They originally sold for about $65, but today, they only sell for about $15 on the secondary market.

There are at least eight different designs, including: Umbrella Girl (Hum 152/B); Mountaineer (Hum 315); Ring Around the Rosie (Hum 348); Spring Dance (Hum 353); Follow the Leader (Hum 369); In the Meadow (Hum 459); Ride Into Christmas (Hum 396); and Little Fiddler (Hum 4).

Ride Into Christmas pocket watch, front and back.

Wooden Music Boxes

Made by Ercolano s.r.l. of Sorrento, Italy, for H & G Studios, Inc. of West Palm Beach, Florida, these are high-quality handmade boxes with a print of a figurine in a realistic setting applied to the top. The prints are covered with a high-grade protective coating, making it appear as part of the top. There is a Swiss musical movement inside each, chosen to complement the image on the box.

The boxes are made in two sizes. Large (7-1/2" x 6-1/2"), which originally sold for $139 and small (5-1/4" x 4-3/4"), which originally sold for $99. Each size is 2-7/8" deep. The list on the following pages specifies the design, size, and musical tune on each.

MBH516
Ring Around The Rosie
7 1/2"x 6 1/2"x 2 7/8"
Tune: *Alouette*

MBH514
Feathered Friends
7 1/2"x 6 1/2"x 2 7/8"
Tune: *Swan Lake*

MBH535
Strolling Along
5 1/4"x 4 3/4"x 2 7/8"
Tune: *My What A Happy Day*

MBH534
Happiness
5 1/4"x 4 3/4"x 2 7/8"
Tune: *Hi Lili, Hi Lo*

MBH531
School Boys
5 1/4"x 4 3/4"x 2 7/8"
Tune: *That's What Friends Are For*

MBH532
The Skier
5 1/4"x 4 3/4"x 2 7/8"
Tune: *Edelweiss*

MBH533
Coquettes
5 1/4"x 4 3/4"x 2 7/8"
Tune: *I Love You Truly*

Wooden music boxes made by Ercolano s.r.l. in Sorrento, Italy.

Design	Size	Tune
Doll Mother	small	"Rock-A-Bye Baby"
Stormy Weather	both sizes	"Raindrops Keep Falling on My Head"
Serenade	small	"The Sound of Music"
For Mother	small	"Always"

Design	Size	Tune
Ride Into Christmas	both sizes	"Jingle Bells"
Apple Tree Boy and	large	"It's a Small World"
Apple Tree Girl		
Little Fiddler	large	"If I Were a Rich Man"
Eventide	large	"A Whole New World"
Merry Wanderer	large	"Take Me Home, Country Roads"
Feathered Friends	large	"Swan Lake"
Ring Around the Rosie	large	"Alouette"
School Boys	small	"That's What Friends Are For"
Skier	small	"Edelweiss"
Coquettes	small	"I Love You Truly"
Happiness	small	"Hi Li, Hi Lo"
Strolling Along	small	"My What a Happy Day"
Farewell	large	"Auf Wiedersehen"
The Mail Is Here	large	"Chariots of Fire"

Bavarian Village

Housed in Niles, Illinois, the Hawthorne Collection is a unique series of miniature Bavarian Village structures made of ceramic. Each is electrically lit from the inside. Each represents a different structure and in the windows or doors of these structures is an M.I. Hummel design backlit by the interior light. Each bears an M.I. Hummel facsimile signature. There are 16 designs presently available. They are listed below.

Name	Size	Current Value
All Aboard	4-3/4"	$60
Angel's Duet	8-1/4"	$60
Apple Tree Cottage	6"	$65
Christmas Mail	5-1/2"	$60
Clock Shop	6"	$65
Company's Coming	5-1/4"	$60

Name	Size	Current Value
Heavenly Harmony	9"	$60
Off For the Holidays	5-1/2"	$60
Practice Makes Perfect	6-3/4"	$65
Scholarly Thoughts	6-1/2"	$65
Shoe Maker Shop	5-1/4"	$60
Tending the Geese	4-1/4"	$65
Village Bakery	5-1/2"	$60
Village Pharmacy	6-1/2"	$65
Warm Winter Wishes	6-1/4"	$65
Winter's Comfort	5-1/2"	$60

Additionally, there are a number of non-Hummel design accessories that you can buy to set up a little winter village. Those include the items listed on the following page.

Angel's Duet.

Village Bakery.

Warm Winter Wishes.

Name	Size	Current Value
Bench/Pine Tree Set	1-1/4"	$30
Evergreen Tree Set	2-1/4"	$30
Holiday Fountain	2-3/4"	$35
Holiday Lights (2)	3-1/2"	$20
Horse With Sled	6"	$35
Mailbox	2-1/2"	$20
Sled/Pine Tree Set	1-3/4"	$30
Village Bridge	2-1/4"	$30
Wishing Well	2-1/4"	$30

Tending the Geese.

Scholarly Thoughts.

Practice Makes Perfect.

Clock Shop.

Apple Tree Cottage.

Village Pharmacy.

Metal canisters from the Olive Can Company.

Canisters

At least seven different sizes and designs of metal canisters were made by the Olive Can Company of Elgin, Illinois, when the last edition of this book was published in 1997. It is unclear as to how many more have been produced since, but the company's Web site (www.olive-can.com) does list M.I. Hummel as one of the brands that it still has licensing for. The company provided the photograph shown here for the last edition of this publication, and it is the same photograph that appears on the company Web site today for its M.I. Hummel licensed products, so it is possible that no new Hummel designs have been licensed for production since these initial designs. The company can be reached by phone at (847) 468-7474 or by mail at: Olive Can Company, 1111 Bowes Road, Elgin, IL 60123. Several e-mail addresses for specific inquiries also can be found on the company Web site.

The Schmid/Berta Hummel Collection

The history of the Schmid company's association with the art of M.I. Hummel goes all the way back to when the first figurines were put on the market in Germany in 1935. The Schmid Brothers noticed them, arranged to buy a few, and ended up being the Goebel company's U.S. distributor. Its association with Goebel first ended in 1968. About the same time, Schmid began offering a selection of Hummel collectibles of its own manufacture or from other sources, and in 1971, Schmid offered a Christmas plate utilizing the same original Hummel art as the Goebel 1971 first annual Christmas plate. As you might expect, the companies ended up in court.

Berta Hummel, as she was known before taking her vows as a Franciscan nun, had created a large body of work before entering the convent. All that work had become the property of the family—her mother Viktoria Hummel in particular—after her death. Schmid made an agreement with Mrs. Hummel allowing the company to produce decorative items and other collectibles inspired by or using this early work of the artist.

Over the years, Schmid produced a number of Berta Hummel collectibles, as they called them. At one point,

A self-portrait with an image size that measures 9-5/8" x 13-1/4'

Goebel and Schmid entered into another agreement whereby Schmid once again became the U.S. distributor. In 1994, distribution was again taken over by Goebel of North America. By 1996, Schmid Brothers was no longer operating. This section enumerates the Schmid Berta Hummel Collection, illustrating many of the pieces. There are no secondary market values (Collector Value) given for most of the items, as there has not yet been a market established for most. Many collectors are not even aware of them or, if aware, pay little attention to them. This will change over the years because none of the items are or have been in production for many years.

Limited-Edition Prints and Berta Hummel Art

There have been roughly 130 small, framed lithographic prints (reproductions) offered over the years. Schmid took these existing prints and had them framed in quantities sufficient to wholesale to the trade.

By far the most important of the prints by Schmid are the following described and illustrated limited-edition issues.

Hummel's sensitive self-portrait, rendered in sepia tone, was released in 1981 in a limited edition of 525. Each print is sequentially numbered and signed by the artist's brother,

Poppies.

Adolph Hummel. The print was issued at $125 and is valued at $500 on the secondary market today.

The print of flowers was issued in 1980-81. The colors are rich earth tones with a cheerful red-orange poppy. The edition was limited to 450 and each was signed by the artist's brother, Adolph Hummel. The release price was $125, and it is presently valued at $750 on the secondary market.

A Time to Remember was issued in 1980-81 in an edition limited to 900. It is a color print depicting a boy with three children on a sled. There is a snow-covered fir tree in the background. Each of the prints is signed by Adolph Hummel, brother of the artist. There is penciled inscription in German around the border on 180 of the prints. The inscription translates: "Seasons Greetings from the Hummel family home in Massing, Bavaria, West Germany. The Hummel family wishes you and yours a Merry Christmas and a very happy and prosperous New Year." The picture depicts a Hummel family Christmas tradition of going into the woods to pick out a tree. The regular prints were released originally at $150 and are now valued at $500. The 180 copies with the Christmas inscription are worth about $1,500.

A Time to Remember.

Moonlight Return is a pastel Berta Hummel did to depict an incident in her brother Adolf's boyhood. He signed the limited-edition issue of this print. The edition issue quantity was 900, and the release price was $150. It is now valued at $1,000-$1,200 on the secondary market.

The Angelic Messenger print was issued in an edition of 600 and each print was signed by the artist's brother, Adolph Hummel. Two hundred of the

Moonlight Return.

prints are numbered as usual, but the other 400 were given inscriptions in German. The inscriptions began on the left border and went over the top and down the right border. They are translated: "May the angel of Christmas abide with you, at Advent, and all year through." This edition is valued at $750, and the one with the 75th anniversary inscription is valued at about $1,000. The regular edition is about $500.

Angelic Messenger.

The Birthday Bouquet print is thought to be the only self-portrait Berta Hummel ever did of herself as a young child. It seems that the Hummel children always picked flowers from their garden for their mother on her birthday. The story goes that Berta Hummel was away at art school and unable to come home for her mother's birthday, so she painted this portrait and sent it home to her mother. It was issued in 1985 in three editions for a total quantity of 520. The Birthday Greeting Edition was limited to 195 signed and numbered prints. They were signed and inscribed by Adolf Hummel as follows: "The Hummel family of Massing, Germany wishes you a very happy birthday." This edition was issued at $450 and is now worth at least $750. The Heirloom Edition is limited to 225 and bears the written inscription by Adolf Hummel: "A child's loving gift is a remembrance, that lives like a bouquet in our hearts." It was originally issued at $375 and is now worth about $500. The Regular Edition was limited to 100 prints that were signed and numbered by Adolf Hummel. This edition was issued at $195 and worth about $350.

Birthday Bouquet.

Paperweight

This was called the "Sister Berta Hummel Visage Paperweight" in promotional literature. It is a beautiful French sulfide crystal paperweight measuring 2-1/4" in diameter and 1-7/8" high. It was limited in production to 4,000. Each is individually etched with the number on the bottom of the piece.

Side view of the Schmid Berta Hummel paperweight.

Top view of the Schmid Berta Hummel crystal paperweight.

Coffee Service

About 1970, Schmid released a 21-piece coffee service for six. It consisted of six cups and saucers, six cake plates, a sugar, creamer, and coffeepot, each with a different Berta Hummel design. They were apparently short-lived and disappeared from the market soon after. The assorted designs used on the pieces in the set are all artwork accomplished after Berta Hummel joined the convent. This could be part or all of the reason they were removed from the market.

There is no way of knowing how many sets were produced and sold, but they are in short supply. The photos accompanying were furnished by a collector. As you can see, the cake plates are missing, so it is unclear as to what the designs were. The production of the set was authorized by the Hummel family and is so noted on the backstamp. Other coffee and tea service pieces were mentioned earlier in this chapter.

Pieces from Schmid's Hummel-inspired coffee service.

"Tranquility" and "Serenity" Plate Series

The first of this two-plate series was Tranquility, released in 1978. The second, Serenity, was issued in 1982. Each of these is about 10" in diameter. The edition quantities were limited to 15,000 for each plate. The plate is hand-painted museum-quality porcelain with an application of 24-karat gold. The resulting soft glowing finish was achieved by a unique technique that required six separate kiln firings.

Tranquility. Limited edition of 15,000.

Serenity. Limited edition of 15,000.

Annual Christmas Plate Series

Beginning in 1971, Schmid started issuing annual Christmas plates. In 1972, a matching bell was added to accompany the annual Christmas plate. In 1974, the matching ornament was added in and in 1975, the matching mug. You might notice that the values listed here are no different than in the last edition of this book. That is because the secondary market for these pieces—plates, especially—has hit a plateau that has resulted in stagnation in values during the last few years. Until interest in collectible plates and the like goes back up, the values will remain the same and it is highly possible that sales on the secondary market will not even reach what a piece is currently worth—if there is any buyer interest at all.

Year	Plate Design	Plate Value	Bell	Cup	Ornament
1971	Angel With Candle	$20-$25	no	no	no
1972	Angel With Flute	$15-$20	yes	no	no
1973	Nativity	$75-$95	yes	no	no
1974	Guardian Angel	$10-$15	yes	no	yes
1975	Christmas Child	$15-$20	yes	yes	yes
1976	Sacred Journey	$10-$15	yes	no	yes
1977	Herald Angel	$10-$15	yes	no	yes
1978	Heavenly Trio	$10-$15	yes	no	yes
1979	Starlight Angel	$10-$15	yes	no	yes
1980	Parade Into Toyland	$15-$20	yes	yes	yes
1981	A Time to Remember	$25-$30	yes	no	yes

Year	Plate Design	Plate Value	Bell	Cup	Ornament
1982	Angelic Procession	$30-$35	yes	no	yes
1983	Angelic Message	$25-$30	yes	no	yes
1984	A Gift From Heaven	$35-$40	yes	no	yes
1985	Heavenly Light	$30-$35	yes	no	yes
1986	Tell the Heavens	$40-$45	yes	no	yes
1987	Angelic Gifts	$35-$40	yes	no	yes
1988	Cheerful Cherubs	$65-$70	yes	no	yes
1989	Angelic Musician	$45-$50	yes	no	yes
1990	Angel's Light	$40-$45	yes	no	yes
1991	Message From Above	$40-$45	yes	no	yes
1992	Sweet Blessings	$40-$45	yes	no	yes
1993	Silent Wonder	$40-$45	yes	no	yes

Angel With Candle,
1971 Schmid Christmas Plate.

Angel With Flute,
1972 Schmid Christmas Plate.

Nativity,
1973 Schmid Christmas Plate.

The Guardian Angel,
1974 Schmid Christmas Plate.

Christmas Child,
1975 Schmid Christmas Plate.

Sacred Journey,
1976 Schmid Christmas Plate.

Herald Angel,
1977 Schmid Christmas Plate.

Heavenly Trio,
1978 Schmid Christmas Plate.

Starlight Angel,
1979 Schmid Christmas Plate.

Parade Into Toyland,
1980 Schmid Christmas Plate.

A Time to Remember,
1981 Schmid Christmas Plate.

Angelic Procession,
1982 Schmid Christmas Plate.

Heavenly Light,
1985 Schmid Christmas Plate.

Tell the Heavens,
1986 Schmid Christmas Plate.

Cheerful Cherubs,
1988 Schmid Christmas Plate.

Message From Above,
1991 Schmid Christmas Plate.

Sweet Blessings,
1992 Schmid Christmas Plate.

Silent Wonder,
1993 Schmid Christmas Plate.

Silent Wonder, 1993 Ornament.

Heavenly Melody, 1994 Ornament.

God's Littlest Messenger Series

This is a four-year series that began in 1991. The plates had a release price of $60 and the production was limited to 15,000 pieces. The matching bells were limited to 5,000 and the original price was $58. There were also a miniature plate, thimble, cup, and ornament in the series. The designs for each year are as follows:

- 1991: A Message From Above
- 1992: Sweet Blessings
- 1993: Silent Wonder
- 1994: Heavenly Melody

God's Little Messenger Series: Sweet Blessings. Plate: 7-1/2", limited edition of 15,000. Miniature Plate: 4-1/4". Thimble: 1" high. Ornament: 3-1/4". Bell: 4-1/2" high, limited edition of 5,000. Cup: 2-1/2" high.

God's Little Messenger Series: A Message From Above. Plate: 7-1/2", limited edition of 15,000. Miniature Plate: 4-3/4". Thimble: 1" high. Ornament: 3-1/4". Bell: 4-1/2" high, limited edition of 5,000. Cup: 2-1/2" high.

God's Little Messenger Series: Heavenly Melody. Plate: 7-1/2", limited edition of 15,000. Miniature Plate: 4-3/4". Thimble (not shown): 1" high. Ornament (not shown): 3-1/2". Bell: 4-1/2" high, limited edition of 5,000. Cup: 2-1/2" high.

God's Little Messenger Series: Silent Wonder. Plate: 7-1/2", limited edition of 15,000. Miniature Plate: 4-3/4". Thimble (not shown): 1" high. Ornament (not shown): 3-1/2". Bell: 4-1/2" high, limited edition of 5,000. Cup: 2-1/2" high.

Annual Mother's Day Plates, Bells, and Cups

Beginning in 1972, Schmid produced a series of 7-1/2" plates. In 1976, the company began producing matching bells at 6-1/2" high and cups at 2-1/2" high. Inexplicably, there is also a matching cup to be found for the year 1974. The series ended with the 1990 plate. From 1981 through 1984, other matching pieces were made. Intermittently these were eggs, thimbles, and trinket boxes. These will be covered later. Once again, the secondary market for such pieces has been quite flat during the last few years, so values mirror those in the previous edition.

Playing Hooky, 1972
Schmid Mother's Day Plate.

The Little Fisherman, 1973
Schmid Mother's Day Plate.

The Bumblebee, 1974
Schmid Mother's Day Plate.

Message of Love, 1975
Schmid Mother's Day Plate.

Devotion For Mothers, 1976
Schmid Mother's Day Plate.

Moonlight Return, 1977
Schmid Mother's Day Plate.

Afternoom Stroll, 1978
Schmid Mother's Day Plate.

Cherubs Gift, 1979
Schmid Mother's Day Plate.

Mother's Helpers, 1980
Schmid Mother's Day Plate.

Playtime, 1981
Schmid Mother's Day Plate.

The Flower Basket, 1982
Schmid Mother's Day Plate.

Young Reader, 1988
Schmid Mother's Day Plate.

Year	Plate Design	Plate Value	Bell	Cup
1972	Playing Hooky	$20	no	no
1973	The Little Fisherman	$40	no	no
1974	The Bumblebee	$30	no	yes
1975	Message of Love	$25	no	no
1976	Devotion For Mothers	$20	yes	yes
1977	Moonlight Return	$30	yes	yes
1978	Afternoon Stroll	$20	yes	yes
1979	Cherub's Gift	$30	yes	yes
1980	Mother's Helpers	$30	yes	no
1981	Playtime	$25	yes	yes
1982	The Flower Basket	$45	yes	yes
1983	Spring Bouquet	$35	yes	yes
1984	A Joy to Share	$30	yes	no
1985	A Mother's Journey	$40	yes	no
1986	Home From School	$40	yes	no
1987	Mother's Little Learner	$60	no	yes
1988	Young Reader	$85	yes	no
1989	Pretty As a Picture	$80	yes	no
1990	Mother's Little Athlete	$80	yes	no

Annual Cups

The Annual Cup Series (12 in the series) was introduced in 1973 with an untitled design. The art was of a baby in a basket with a bird and flowers. This cup was not a match to any other piece in the collection.

The next year, the design matched the 1974 Mother's Day Plate, and in 1975, the cup design matched that of the same year's Christmas Plate.

The cup design reverted to match the Mother's Day Plate in 1976 for four more years when in 1980, it once again was made to match the Christmas Plate. This was the last change, for after this, the cups matched the Mother's Day design until the Annual Cup Series ended with the 12th edition in 1984.

Annual Bells

The Annual Bell Series got under way in 1976 and matched the design of the 1976 Mother's Day Plate, Devotion For Mothers. Each year thereafter, a bell was always produced to go along with that year's plate. For some unknown reason, however, a bell was not produced in 1987. These bells had the same shape and general look as the annual Christmas Bells.

1982 Annual Cup, 2-1/2" diameter, 2-1/2" high, 10th edition.

1982 Mother's Day Bell, 6-1/4" high, seventh edition.

Stained Glass

For three years, Schmid issued a 6"-diameter round stained-glass decoration. The design was applied to the glass. It is framed in lead in the traditional manner of stained glass and a chain hanger is provided. Six were found cataloged, two each year matching the Christmas and the Mother's Day motifs.

Year	Christmas Design	Mother's Day Design
1976	Sacred Journey	Devotion For Mothers
1977	Herald Angel	Moonlight Return
1978	Heavenly Trio	Afternoon Stroll

Schmid stained glass decoration, 1976 Mother's Day.

Schmid stained glass decoration, 1977 Mother's Day.

Thimbles

The original series of three porcelain thimbles began in 1982. They are 1" high, and the designs matched the corresponding designs for the Mother's Day Plates. They were originally issued at $10.

Designs were:
   • The Flower Basket (1982)
   • Spring Bouquet (1983)
   • A Joy to Share (1984)

Trinket Boxes

At the same time the collector porcelain egg was introduced, a three-piece series of porcelain trinket boxes with lids was started. These are 2-1/2" in diameter and sold for $20 at release. Designs were the same during the three years of production (1982-1984) as the thimbles (see previous heading).

Schmid stained glass decoration, 1978 Christmas.

Collector Eggs

The original series of four porcelain eggs began in 1981. They are 3" high when placed on the base that came with them. They were issued at $35 retail price and are not worth anymore than that today. Each design was the same as the corresponding year of the Mother's Day Plate:
- Playtime (1981)
- The Flower Basket (1982)
- Spring Bouquet (1983)
- A Joy to Share (1984)

The Flower Basket, 1982 egg, 3" high with base. Second edition.

Statuette Ornaments

In 1983, Schmid released the first in a series of what were called statuette ornaments. These were little 4-1/2" figures with bases for standing up and provisions for hanging on the Christmas tree.

The first edition (1983) was called Hark the Herald and was a boy with a trumpet tucked under his right arm and his left hand stuck in his pocket.

The second edition, 1984, was called Sweetheart and is similar to the figurine Little Shopper (Hum 96). No more were found in the catalogs and literature studied, but it is known that a third edition, Alpine Boy, was released. See accompanying photographs. The retail price at the time was about $18 and does not sell for more than that on the secondary market today.

Hark the Herald statuette ornament. First edition, 1983.

Sweetheart statuette ornament. Second edition, 1984

Alpine Boy statuette ornament. Third edition, 1985.

Base of Hark the Herald.

Hark the Herald statuette-theme collection.

"Hark the Herald" Statuette-Theme Collection

In 1984, Schmid introduced this group of items to commemorate the 75th year since Berta Hummel's birth. Apparently inspired by the 1984 statuette ornament Sweetheart, each of these items consisted of either a three-dimensional figure or a bas-relief incorporated into its design. The following is a list of the items and its 1984 retail price.

Type of Piece	Size	Issue Price
Plate	7" diameter	$40
Medallion Ornament	2-7/8" diameter	$10
Bell	5-1/4" high	$20
Mug	3-1/4" high	$15
Thimble	1" high	$10
Music Box	5-1/4" high	$30
Trinket Box	3-1/2" diameter	$15

At least 70 different music boxes have been offered by Schmid over the years. A few other musical items can be found, such as round wall music boxes, musical jewelry boxes, musical key chains, musical bookends, and even a musical cube with designs on all four sides and the top.

Limited-Edition Music Box

In 1981, Schmid introduced what its brochure described as a: "first limited edition inlaid Sorrento wooden music box..." The motif for the box was Devotion. The edition was limited to 5,000 sequentially numbered music boxes at $150. There may be more boxes in this issue, but they are not found in the catalogs and other literature available for study.

Schmid limited-edition music box, introduced in 1981.

Annual Music Boxes

Although seldom cataloged, there were annual, year-dated music boxes made in the same design as the annual releases of the Christmas and Mother's Day plates beginning in 1974. Although Carl Luckey found them referenced in 1976 and 1977 only in catalogs and other promotional literature, they were presumably offered every year. The ones found referenced were 4" x 5-1/4" x 2" high. They sold for $20 to $25 in the 1970s and are likely worth about the same on the secondary market today.

Other Music Boxes

There are at least 42 Berta Hummel design music boxes in varying shapes and sizes. All are made of wood. The shapes and sizes are listed here.

Number of Designs	Shape	Size
42	Rectangular	4-1/4" x 3" x 2-1/4" high
12	Rectangular	5-3/4" x 3-7/8"x 2" high
3	Heart	5-1/4" x 6-1/4"x 1-3/4" high
4	Oval	4-1/4" x 6-1/4"x 1-3/4" high

Musical Wall Pictures (Round)

There are six of these to be found. They are round, wooden, 5-1/4" in diameter, and are activated by a pull cord on the bottom.

Musical Wall Pictures (Shadow Box)

At one point, Schmid offered these in four sizes. There were actually only two sizes of shadow box pictures. They were available with or without musical movements. At least three of them had what appears to be drawers at the bottom. This concealed the movement and made the pictures larger as a result.

Musical Jewelry Boxes

Fifteen of these can be found, in two sizes and shapes. They are footed metal boxes with a satin top bearing the Berta Hummel artwork.

There six different designs found on two sizes of rectangular boxes: 3" x 2-1/2" x 2-1/4" high and 3-3/4" and 4-3/4 x 2" high. The other three are heart-shaped and their sizes are 4-1/2" x 6-1/4" x 2" high.

Assorted Hummel items from a Schmid catalog.

Miscellaneous Other Musical and Non-musical Items

- Six different musical key chains, 1-1/2" x 1-1/4".
- One pair of musical bookends, 6-1/4" wide x 7-1/4" high.
- One pair of bookends with assorted prints, 3-7/8" wide x 6" high.
- Musical cube with five different prints, 4" square.

- Wall-mount key rack with print.
- 1975 linen calendar, 17-1/2" x 30". The design matches the Mother's Day Plate of the same year.
- Needlepoint kit of the same design as above, 18" square.

Candles

Some dated candles were made to match the various limited annual plates, cups, bells etc. There are otherwise dozens of candles in various sizes bearing Berta Hummel art.

The company also offered a wide variety of candle stands made of metal and wood, some of which were even musical. None of these had any Berta Hummel designs on them.

New England Collectors Society

Apparently the New England Collectors Society was established at some time in the late-1970s or very early 1980s and came under the ownership of Reed and Barton Silversmiths soon thereafter. The first product was probably a collector spoon produced in 1981. Then came a bell and a pendant in 1982. Each of these three were made by Reed and Barton and rendered in Damascene, which they describe as "a rich blend of pure gold, silver, copper, and bronze." The NECS advertising flyers all named Reed and Barton Silversmiths as the maker of these items. The following an attempt at a complete listing of the NECS products with as much detail as is available. All items listed were available by mail-order subscription only.

Christmas Spoons

For two years, Christmas spoons were issued in silver plate and Damascene. They measure 6-1/8" long.

Year	Design	Release Price
1981	Herald Angel	$14.50 plus $1.50 shipping and handling
1982	Joyful Trumpeter	$14.50 plus $1.75 shipping and handling

Spoons

In 1982, NECS issued a set of 12 spoons. The artwork was rendered in Damascene, and the remainder of the spoon in silver plate. Each was sold for $14.50 plus $1.50 shipping and handling. That totals $192 total outlay at release price, for the completed collection. This included a nice display rack. The designs are:

- Lighting the Way
- Heavenly Child
- A Child's Gift
- Moonlight Journey
- Starlight Angel
- Baker's Helper
- Evening Walk
- Spring Delight
- Cherubs Gift
- A Child's Treasures
- Christmas Morning
- Barefoot Boy

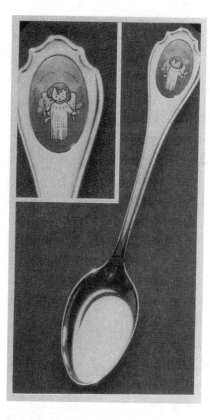

The Herald Angel Christmas Spoon.

Pendants

There are two 24-karat gold-plated and Damascene pendants and neck chains, both issued in 1982.

Occasion	Design Theme	Release Price
Mother's Day	Devotion For Mother	$19.50 plus $1.75 shipping and handling
Christmas	Starlight Angel	$19.50 plus $1.75 shipping and handling

The Starlight Angel pendant.

Christmas Bells

There were two Christmas bells released by the NECS. The 1982 bell is 5" tall and made of silver plate and Damascene, while the 1983 bell is 4" tall and made of porcelain.

Year	Design Theme	Release Price
1982	Heavenly Gifts	$19.50 plus $1.75 shipping and handling
1983	Angelic Procession	$14.50 plus $1.75 shipping and handling

New England Collectors Society Heavenly Gifts Christmas Bell.

New England Collectors Society Angelic Procession Christmas Bell.

Plates

The New England Collectors Society issued two sets of 12 mini-plates each. Each plate measures 4" in diameter. The first set corresponded with Schmid's full-size Mother's Day or Christmas plates. In the second set, only a few of the designs corresponded with the full-size Schmid Christmas or Mother's Day plates.

The mini-plates were produced under Schmid's auspices. Each plate in each set was sold for $12.50 plus $1.75 shipping and handling. This totals $171 for each set of 12.

Plate Set Number One

No.	Design Theme	Year Issued	Corresponding Schmid Plate
1	Cherub's Gift	1978	1979 Mother's Day
2	Starlight Angel	1979	1979 Christmas
3	Parade Into Toyland	1979	1980 Christmas

No.	Design Theme	Year Issued	Corresponding Schmid Plate
4	A Time to Remember	1980	1981 Christmas
5	Afternoon Stroll	1977	1978 Mother's Day
6	Playtime	1980	1981 Mother's Day
7	Heavenly Trio	1977	1978 Christmas
8	Mother's Helpers	1979	1980 Mother's Day
9	Herald Angel	1979	1977 Christmas
10	Christmas Child	1974	1975 Christmas
11	Devotion For Mother	1975	1976 Mother's Day
12	Sacred Journey	1975	1976 Christmas

Plate Set Number Two

No.	Design Theme	Year Issued	Corresponding Schmid Plate
1	Angelic Messenger	1982	1983 Christmas
2	Flower Basket	1981	1982 Mother's Day
3	Spring Bouquet	1982	1983 Mother's Day
4	Story Time	—	not applicable
5	Tidings From on High	—	not applicable
6	Evening Serenade	—	not applicable
7	Unknown	—	not applicable
8	Angelic Caroler	—	not applicable
9	Heavenly Caroler	—	not applicable
10	Radiant Gifts	—	not applicable
11	Heaven's Offerings	—	not applicable
12	Guardian Angels	1973	1974 Christmas

The 4" plates and 2-1/2" boxes with lids.

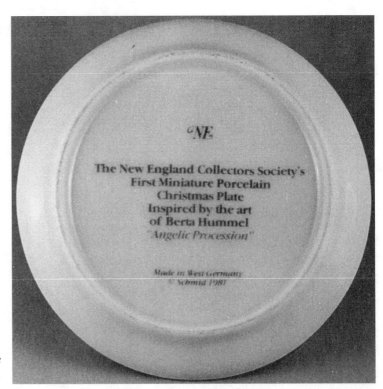

Several examples of the New England Collectors Society mini-plates.

Berta Hummel Museum Collection

In German, this museum is called "Das Berta Hummel Museum Im Hummel Haus." Translated this means "The Berta Hummel Museum in the Hummel House." The museum is located in Massing, Germany, in the home where Berta Hummel was born. (See Chapter 1 for a description of the museum and its contents, as well as photos.)

Berta's nephew Albert Hummel, son of her brother Adolf, is the director of the museum. He provided photographs of the museum and some of its offerings. The museum owns the rights to all Hummel artwork done prior to her entering the convent and license others to use it on collectibles from time to time. One example is the collection of mini-plates produced by the Schmid Brothers for the New England Collectors Society. The museum offers a similar set of these plates. There are six of them, along with matching pillboxes.

They also offer a large array of candles in three sizes, postcards of pre-convent M.I. Hummel art and eight beautiful full-color posters.

Three sizes of candles available from the Berta Hummel Museum.

The label sometimes found on older Berta Hummel Museum collectibles.

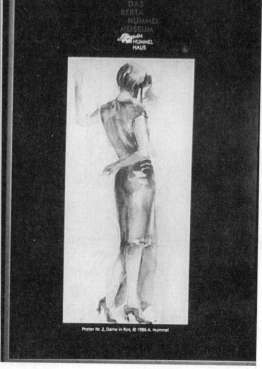

Poster No. 5, Poster No. 2.

Poster No. 3, Poster No. 4.

Poster No.6, Poster No. 8.

Luckey's Hummel Figurines and Plates

Poster No. 9, Poster No. 7.

Berta Hummel Throw

This is a 100% cotton blanket measuring 66" x 48" with fringe around the perimeter. It is colored in mute greens, blues, reds, and yellows. The theme is Joyous Celebration, a manger scene.

Goebel Products From Danbury Mint and Others

Porcelain Dolls

Danbury introduced a doll series in 1988 with the Umbrella Girl. The doll's heads, arms, and legs were cast and hand-painted in the traditional manner by the artisans at W. Goebel Porzellanfabrik, maker of the M.I. Hummel figurines. The dolls bear the signature and the Goebel trademarks on the back of the neck. Although they are cataloged at Goebel by mold number, the dolls do not bear the number. The dolls were released at $250 and are listed with current pricing information in Chapter 3 under the Hum 512 listing.

Kitchen Moulds

Six of these were offered by subscription beginning in 1991. Danbury shipped them to the collector one every three months at $103.50 each, including shipping and handling, for a total of $621. These were made by Goebel and they are cataloged by a Goebel mold number, but the pieces do not bear the number. They do bear the incised signature. The six are listed with current pricing information in Chapter 3 under the Hum 669 listing.

Angels of Christmas Ornament Series

This is a series of full-color decorated Christmas ornaments made by Goebel for Danbury for subscription distribution beginning in 1990. They were issued one every other month at $42 each, including $2.50 shipping and handling, for a total of $420. Goebel cataloged them according to mold number, but did not place this number on the figures. Goebel also utilized the same molds to release another series of ornaments. For a complete listing of names, mold numbers, sizes, and current values, see the Hum 575 listing in Chapter 3.

Candleholders

The Danbury Mint issued four candleholders made for them by Goebel. The first two were released three months apart in 1989 and the next two were released likewise in 1990. They each cost $145.50 including shipping and handling. Goebel catalogs the molds with mold numbers, but the pieces do not bear those numbers. They are listed with current pricing information in Chapter 3 under the Hum 676 and Hum 678 listings.

Goose Girl Figurine

In the mid-1990s, Danbury released this famous figurine in white overglaze with just the eyes, eyebrows, and lips of the girl and the eyes of the geese painted. These are made by Goebel from the Hummel mold Hum 47/II, 7-1/2" size for the Danbury Mint. It should be noted here that Goebel announced its Expressions of Youth Series in the summer 1992 issue of Insights, the M.I. Hummel Club newsletter. There were six figurines in the series including this one. The cost of the Danbury Mint Goose Girl was $199 plus $6 shipping and handling, for a total of $205. Today, it is worth $400.

Paper Products

The M.I. Hummel Club (Goebel Collectors Club at that time) gave members a box of note paper and envelopes with round gold seals as a renewal premium in the 1984-85 Club Year. There were two designs: Coffee Break and What Now? Folded, they measure 5" x 3-3/4".

Paperweight

This consists of a delicate lacework by Abbey Lace of Bath, England, in a design reminiscent of Umbrella Girl set against a velour background and placed in a clear glass paperweight. It is 3-1/2" in diameter. Assembled in England. The collector value is about $25.

The Glass Goose Girl

Many collectors are familiar with this interesting piece, but before Lawrence Wonsch's guide Hummel Copycats, few, if any, knew the history behind it. Wonsch goes into great detail about the historical background and the company L.E. Smith Glass Company, which originated the piece in 1937. The previous edition of this book stated the company was still making this piece in 1997, but a search of the company Web site (www.lesmithglass.com) did not yield any mention of this piece today.

Inspired by the M.I. Hummel Goose Girl, this hollow figurine can be found in 33 distinct variations according to color, size, base variations, and some other characteristics detailed in Wonsch's book. Those with a plain glass base are pre-1970 vintage, and those with the textured wheat straw base, as in the accompanying photograph, were produced from 1970 on. Some of the colors are amber, blue, and green, but there are others. The collector value ranges from $25 to $75.

Note paper issued by the Goebel Collectors Club (now M.I. Hummel Club).

The Glass Goose Girl, created by the L.E. Smith Company.

The Avon Collectibles

All of you have heard of the Avon Lady, and not that long ago, she delivered M.I. Hummel collectibles. Avon began a series of crystal collectors' pieces in 1994. Each is a Christmas item made of 24% lead crystal and features a

Year	Item	Size
1993	Trinket Box	4"
1994	Bell	5-3/4"
1995	Candleholders	3-1/2"
1996	Plate	8-1/2"

The Trinket Box sold for $39.95 in 1994 and is presently bringing about $100 among Avon collectors.

In 2002, Berta Hummel produced an Avon exclusive Christmas ornament called Perfect Fit. The ornament is the first such piece manufactured by Goebel. It is a bisque porcelain piece with bas-relief design of a child showing delight in finding the perfect hat for her snowman. Beneath the design on the front is the year 2002. The piece is 3-1/4" x 2-3/4" and originally sold for $19.99.

figurine as the theme. The first one has gained some recognition on the secondary market, so there is the possibility that the others will also. The four in the series to date are listed below.

Corresponding Hummel Design
Hum 239A, Girl With Nosegay
Hum 135, Soloist
Hum 454, Song of Praise
Hum 194, Watchful Angel

Avon crystal trinket box with Hummel design.

Avon crystal bell with Hummel design.

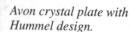

Avon crystal plate with Hummel design.

There are two very good reasons for taking good photographs of your collection. The most important is to have a record of what you had in the unfortunate event of a theft, fire or any other disaster that may result in the loss or destruction of your collection. Insurance companies are loathe to take your word that you had a Hum 1, Puppy Love worth 10 times the normal value just because its head was titled in a different direction. A photograph would prove it. In the case of theft you have little chance of identifying your collection in the event of a recovery in some instances. Law enforcement authorities often recover stolen property that can't be identified as to owner. If you have photographs of marks, etc., they can help you detailed descriptions of marks, etc., they can help you positively identify what is yours. The second reason for this section is to help you also, but it is to help me as well. I get hundreds of photos each year, most of which are useless. You send me the photograph(s) with your questions and all I can see is what looks like a scarecrow out in the middle of a four acre field or a fuzzy Feathered Friends figurine due to its being out of focus. Can't help you much there. So, ready for your photography lesson?

This will be simple and fun for most of you. It won't make you America's next Ansel Adams, but it will make you a better photographer of figurines. You experts and pros can move on to the next section now.

The Camera

The two most common cameras most of us use today are the 35mm single lens reflex (SLR) and the automatic "point and shoot" cameras that use the mini negative disc or regular 35mm film. The method for taking the kind of photographs we are looking for here differs between the types so we will go through the basic set-up to get your figurines ready to shoot and then describe the method for each of the camera types.

Setting

I employ a light blue or gray paper background normally that starts flat on a table top and is rolled up behind the figurine forming a curved background so there is no horizontal line to distract from the figure. You probably won't want to get that elaborate so go out and get a sheet of poster board. I recommend a light gray, pale blue or

beige for a neutral background. First try to set it up as I described before, rolling it up. If you are not successful that way, try cutting it in half, putting one piece flat on the table top and the other propped up somehow behind it as in the diagram. The diagram is overly simple and out of scale, but illustrates the idea.

If this set-up is more than you want to try, a simple tabletop or any flat surface will suffice. Try to avoid any with a patterned surface.

Lighting

There are two types of light: natural (or available) light and artificial light.

Natural Light

The simplest and best light is natural light outdoors, on an overcast day or in the shade on a bright sunshiny day.

This eliminates harsh shadows. You can get almost the same light indoors if you shoot your picture at a large window that is admitting much light but not letting direct sunlight in.

Artificial Light

If you wish to shoot inside under artificial light you can do so in a bright, well-lighted room. You must be careful, however, about the type of light you have. Fluorescent lighting will produce pictures with a decidedly greenish cast. Incandescent lighting, ordinary light bulbs, will cause your pictures to come out with a yellowish or red cast. This is true when using ordinary, daylight color film designed for use outdoors or with a flash. Most modern photo processing labs can filter this color distortion out, but you must tell them about the type of light you used beforehand.

Using a flash is the third possibility, but under ordinary circumstances produces a severe, flat picture with harsh shadows.

If you can devise a way of filtering the flash, diffusing it or bouncing it off the ceiling or any other reflector you can devise, results are generally much more satisfying. The best use of flash is for "fill light" when shooting outdoors. It fills in shadows, eliminating them if done right.

Choice of Film

Film comes in different speeds (ASA ratings). The higher the ASA the faster the speed. The faster the speed, the less light needed to take a good photograph. There is a trade-off, however. The faster the speed the grainier the picture. This should not be of concern to you unless you are going to enlarge the picture or submit it for publications. I recommend that you use film with an ASA or 100 or 200, but if you have a poor light situation the ASA 400 would give you satisfactory pictures. Those of you with the modern automatic cameras shouldn't need to worry about switching these ASA's because your camera will automatically adjust to the ASA. Be sure to read your manual about this (You did read your manual didn't you?). Those of you with the more complicated SLR's know what to do.

General Techniques

First, you have a choice of methods. If you are shooting the pictures for instance purposes you may choose to make a gang shot; that is shooting of two or three or more at the same time, or shooting your display cabinets or shelves (if there is a glass door, be sure to open it first). The latter is less desirable because you lose the detail you may need for identification later. If you don't wish to shoot each individual piece, then shoot them in groups of no more than three or four and try to match sizes as best you can.

When you take your pictures get in as close as you can, filling the frame with the figures. Try to hold the camera as low and level with the pieces as you can unless this causes a hand or some other part of the figure to obscure or cast a shadow on a face or other important features. Sometimes adjusting the position of the figure can alleviate this problem. Remember, you want to show it at its best. If your camera is capable of close-up photography or there is a close-up lens attachment for it, take shots of the underside of the base of each piece or at least of the most valuable ones. These close-up attachments are usually quite inexpensive and come in sets of three lens.

Technique for Automatic Cameras

Most of the automatic cameras of today come with a fixed focus lens or an automatic focus feature. Some even have a "macro" feature allowing you to get a little closer than normal to your subject. This feature allows somewhat nicer close-up portraiture, but is not of much use for our purposes here. Most automatic cameras will not allow you to get any closer than three feet from your subject. Any closer and everything will be out of focus. The field of view at three feet will be about 20" x 24". If you put one 6" figurine in the middle of that, take the picture and process it, you will get a photo about 4" x 5" in size and the figurine will be less than 1-1/4" tall, a lonesome trifling tidbit in the center. (Remember the scarecrow in the 40-acre field?). It would be of little use in identification. A few of these cameras have close-up attachments available so check your manual to see if yours is one of them. If not then you will at best, only be able to make group pictures. You might want to experiment with one roll of film. Some of the automatic cameras will do much more than others and some will do better than the manual indicates. If your experiment is a failure, I suggest you prevail upon a friend or relative who has a better camera to help you out. Better yet, go out and buy one. The single lens reflex cameras are not nearly as complicated to use as they appear, and some of the new, electronic ones make it almost impossible to take a bad picture.

Technique for Single Lens Reflex Camera

Chances are many of you who have SLRs have never tried to do macro work. That is what small object photography is called. If you have perfected that art, you have permission to skip the rest of this section.

Macrophotography is a big word for a relatively simple technique, the results of which can be quite rewarding. In fact many of the photos in this book were shot with a Honeywell Pentax SLR with a standard 55mm lens that I bought many years ago. Many of you will probably have much newer and better cameras than mine. Your camera should do as well as the one I have. Mine will focus down to about 13" from the subject with a 5" x 7" field of view and with a set of inexpensive close-up lens (less than $25), you can get spectacular close-ups. Remember though, the more magnification you get, the less depth of field is available. I may have lost some of you there. Depth of field is simply the area in front of the camera that will photograph with acceptable sharpness. Said another way, it is the difference between the nearest and the furthest point of acceptable sharpness or focus in the scene to be photographed.

Focusing and Depth of Field

The depth of field you will be connected with here is a function of the F-stop for the photograph and to a lesser extent, the distance from the lens to the subject. Simply put, the higher the F-stop selected, the more depth of field you have. It varies with the lens but the depth of field on my camera at F-16 is about 3" when it is focused as close as possible. When I focus on a figurine I try to focus about midway into its depth. This is entirely sufficient to keeping all parts of the figurine in focus in most cases. You may be able to do a little better or a little worse depending on your lens. Although you will likely be working as close to the subject as you can get, you should know that the further you get from the subject, the more the depth of field.

Shutter Speeds and F-stops

We have already noted that you will want to use a high F-stop number, F-11 or higher. Well the higher the F-stop, the smaller the aperture (the hold through which the reflected light passes on its way to the film). The smaller that hole is the longer it takes enough light reflected from your subject to form a good image on the film. So it follows that the smaller the hole the longer the shutter must remain open. Since we want enough depth of field so that all of a figurine is in focus, we'll have to trade off for time. That means the shutter speed will be too slow for you to hand hold your camera. That is why you will need to buy or borrow a tripod. Some folks are clever enough to jury-rig one. It would also be a good idea to have a cable release to insure that you do not shake the camera when tripping the shutter. They are inexpensive and available anywhere good cameras are sold.

Shooting the Picture

Here is a typical set-up in sufficient light to take your pictures:

Film speed	**ASA 100 to 200**
Shutter speed	**1/8 to 1/30**
F-stop	**F-11 to F-16**
Focal distance	**14" to 18"; as close as you can or need to be.**

You will likely need to experiment a little until you are happy with the results. There are 12 print rolls of film available if you don't wish to waste film. The best way to find the ideal set-up for your light conditions is to shoot at different F-stops, leaving everything else constant, and place a piece of paper with your subject with the setting written on it or do the same thing varying any setting you want. You then will have a set of photos from which to pick the best and have the best camera setting right there in the picture.

Some Final Notes

Now you have your photograph(s). First, especially if this is an insurance inventory, you should have two sets of photographs. One set for you to keep at home to work with when you need to and the other in a safe deposit box or a separate location in case of fire or other happenstance resulting in the loss of your photographs. Second, you should have a written record either on the back of the photos or separate from them, of the date of purchase, the amount of the purchase, where or from whom you obtained it, the size, the trademark and every other mark to be found on the piece. This data along with the photo can leave no doubt as to ownership. This is especially true when, as in the case of Hummel, each piece is hand painted therefore slightly different from any other like piece; same as people. One last comment: If you are photographing the piece to send to me—give me thesame information.

🐝 Appendix B 🐝

Current Price List

This listing is taken from the Suggested Retail Price List issued by Goebel in 2002. It is the published suggested retail price for the figures and other items that bear the trademark presently being used by the company (TMK-8). The appearance of a particular piece on this list is not necessarily an indication that it is available from dealers. Few dealers have the wherewithal to pick their stock and even fewer have the ability to have a large, comprehensive stock.

The abbreviation "TW" in the place of a retail price means that the item has been "Temporarily Withdrawn" from current production with no stated date for reinstatement. Other pieces may be absent from the list. Those have been removed from production or retired.

Figurines

Name	Mold Number	Size*	Price**
Accompanist, The	453	3-1/4"	$135
Adoration	23/I	6-1/4"	$430
Adventure Bound	347	7-1/2" x 8-1/4"	$4,350
Afternoon Nap	836	3-1/2"	$225
All By Myself	2079/A	3-34"	$140
An Apple a Day	403	6-1/4"	$350
Angel Duet	261	5"	$270
Angel Serenade	214/D/I	3"	$110
Angel Serenade With Lamb	83	5-1/2"	$270
Angel With Accordion	238/B	2"	$72.50
Angel With Lute	238/A	2"	$72.50
Angel With Trumpet	238/C	2"	$72.50
Angelic Song	144	4"	$185
Angler, The	566	6"	$395
Apple Tree Boy	142/3/0	4"	$180
Apple Tree Boy	142/I	6"	$350
Apple Tree Boy	142/V	10"	$1,495
Apple Tree Boy	142/X	32"	$26,550
Apple Tree Girl	141/3/0	4"	$180
Apple Tree Girl	141/I	6"	$350
Apple Tree Girl	141/V	10"	$1,495
Apple Tree Girl	141/X	32"	$26,550
Artist, The	304	5-1/2"	$305
Autumn Harvest	355	4-3/4"	$250
Baker	128	4-3/4"	$250
Baking Time	2116/B	4"	$145
Band Leader	129/4/0	3"	$130
Band Leader	129/0	5"	$250
Barnyard Hero	195/2/0	4"	$205
Bashful	377	4-3/4"	$250
Bashful Serenade	2133	5-1/4"	$475
Basket of Gifts, A	618	5-1/4"	$375
Bath Time	412	6"	$535
Be Mine	2050/B	3-1/2"	$95
Be Patient	197/2/0	4-1/4"	$250

Name	Mold Number	Size*	Price**
Best Wishes (personalized)	540	4-1/2"	$200
Big Announcement	2153	4-1/2"	$230
Bird Duet	169	4"	$185
Bird Watcher	300	5-1/4"	$270
Birthday Present	341/3/0	4"	$180
Birthday Serenade	218/2/0	4-1/4"	$210
Blessed Event	333	5-1/2"	$400
Blossom Time	608	3"	$175
Book Worm	8	4"	$270
Book Worm	3/I	5-1/2"	$380
Botanist, The	351	4-1/2"	$215
Boy With Accordion	390	2-1/4"	$105
Boy With Horse	239/C	3-1/2"	$72.50
Boy With Toothache	217	5-1/2"	$250
Boy With Toothache (50th Anniversary Edition, 2002)	217	5-1/2"	$250
Boy's Best Friend, A	2101/B	4"	$145
Brother	95	5-1/2"	$250
Builder, The	305	5-1/2"	$305
Bumblebee Friend	837	5-1/4"	$260
Busy Student	367	4-1/4"	$200
Call to Glory	739/I	5-3/4"	$295
Camera Ready (Commemorative Edition)	2132	5-1/2"	$525
Carefree	490	3-1/2"	$135
Cat's Meow, The	2136	3-1/2"	$310
Celestial Musician	188/4/0	3"	$130
Celestial Musician	188/0	5-1/2"	$267.50
Cheeky Fellow	554	4"	$145
Chick Girl	57/2/0	3-1/4"	$185
Chick Girl	57/0	3-1/2"	$205
Chicken-Licken	385/I	4-3/4"	$350
Chimney Sweep	12/2/0	4"	$150
Christmas Angel	301	6-1/4"	$310
Christmas Carol	2073/B	4"	$145
Christmas Delivery	2014/2/0	4-1/4"	$285
Christmas Delivery	2014/I	5-3/4"	$530
Christmas Gift	2074/A	3-1/2"	$95
Christmas Song	343/4/0	3-1/2"	$135
Christmas Song	343/I	6-1/2"	$270
Cinderella	337	4-1/2"	$355
Close Harmony	336	5-1/2"	$375
Come Back Soon	545	4-1/4"	$180
Cowboy Corral	2021	4-1/4"	$200
Crossroads	331	6-3/4"	$510
Cuddles	2049/A	3-1/2"	$95
Culprits	56/A	6-1/4"	$365
Daddy's Girls	371	4-3/4"	$275
Dearly Beloved (with wood base/ engraveable plaque)	2003	6-1/2"	$510
Delicious	435/3/0	3-3/4"	$175
Doctor	127	4-3/4"	$190

Name	Mold Number	Size*	Price**
Doll Bath	319	5"	$355
Doll Mother	67	4-3/4"	$257.50
Easter Time	384	4"	$300
Echoes of Joy (mini)	642/4/0	3"	$130
Echoes of Joy	642/0	4-3/4"	$200
Evening Prayer	495	4"	$135
Extra! Extra!	2113	5-1/2"	$240
Extra! Extra! (personalizable)	2113	5-1/2"	$240
Extra! Extra! (We Stand Proud)	2113	5-1/2"	$265
Farm Boy	66	5"	$290
Feathered Friends	344	4-3/4"	$350
Feeding Time	199/0	4-1/4"	$250
Festival Harmony With Flute	173/4/0	3"	$130
Festival Harmony With Mandolin	172/4/0	3"	$130
Firefighter	2030	4-1/4"	$205
First Bloom	2077/A	3-1/4"	$95
Florist, The	349/0	5-1/4"	$300
Flower For You, A	2077/B	3-1/4"	$95
Flower Vendor	381	5-1/4"	$305
For Father (personalization)	87	5-1/2"	$270
For Father (downsized)	87/2/0	4-1/4"	$190
For Me?	2067/B	3-1/2"	$95
For Mother	257/2/0	4"	$155
For Mother	257/0	5"	$250
Free Flight, A	569	4-3/4"	$215
Free Spirit	564	3-1/2"	$135
Friend or Foe?	434	3-3/4"	$267.50
Friends	136/I	5"	$260
Friends Together	662/0	4"	$350
Friends Together (Limited Edition)	662/I	6"	$560
From My Garden	795/0	4-3/4"	$200
From the Heart	761	3-1/2"	$135
Garden Splendor	835	3-1/4"	$195
Gay Adventure	356	5"	$245
Girl With Doll	239/B	3-1/2"	$72.50
Girl With Fir Tree	239/0	3-1/2"	$72.50
Girl With Nosegay	239/A	3-1/2"	$72.50
Girl With Sheet Music	389	2-1/4"	$110
Girl With Trumpet	391	2-1/4"	$110
Girl's Best Friend, A	2101/A	4"	$145
Going Home	383	4-3/4"	$395
Going To Grandma's	52/0	4-3/4"	$305
Good Friends	182	4-1/4"	$250
Good Hunting	307	5"	$300
Good Luck Charm	2034	4-1/2"	$190
Good News	539	4-1/2"	$210
Goose Girl	47/3/0	4"	$205
Goose Girl	47/0	4-3/4"	$290
Grandma's Girl	561	4"	$180
Grandpa's Boy	562	4"	$180
Guardian, The	455	2-3/4"	$200
Guardian, The (personalized)	455	2-3/4"	$200

Name	Mold Number	Size*	Price**
Guiding Angel	357	2-3/4"	$110
Happiness	86	4-3/4"	$170
Happy Birthday	176/0	5-1/2"	$280
Happy Days	150/2/0	4-1/4"	$210
Happy Traveler	109/0	5"	$185
Hear Ye, Hear Ye	15/2/0	4"	$190
Heart and Soul	559	3-1/2"	$135
Heart's Delight (with chair)	698	4-3/4"	$245
Heavenly Angel	21/0	4-3/4"	$160
Heavenly Angel	21/0/5	6"	$270
Heavenly Prayer	815	5"	$195
Heavenly Protection	88/I	6-3/4"	$540
Hello (2001 Final Issue)	124/0	6"	$255
Home From Market	198/2/0	4-3/4"	$190
Horse Trainer	423	4-1/2"	$267.50
Hosanna	480	3-3/4"	$135
I'll Protect Him	483	3-1/4"	$110
I'm Carefree	633	4-3/4"	$440
I'm Here	478	3"	$140
In D Major	430	4-1/4"	$250
In the Meadow	459	4"	$250
Is It Raining?	420	6"	$340
Joyful Noise	643/0	5"	$195
Joyful Noise (mini)	643/4/0	3"	$130
Just Dozing	451	4-1/4"	$267.50
Just Resting	112/3/0	4"	$185
Kindergartner, The	467	5-1/4"	$250
Kiss Me	311	6"	$355
Kitty Kisses	2033	4-1/4"	$195
Knit One, Purl One	432	3"	$155
Latest News	184	5"	$360
Let's Play	2051/B	3-1/2"	$160
Let's Sing	110/0	3"	$160
Letter to Santa Claus	340	7-1/4"	$400
Light the Way	715/0	5"	$190
Light the Way (mini)	715/4/0	3"	$130
Little Architect, The	410/I	6"	$365
Little Bookkeeper	306	4-3/4"	$355
Little Cellist	89/I	6"	$270
Little Drummer	240	4-1/4"	$185
Little Fiddler	4	4-3/4"	$250
Little Fiddler	2/0	6"	$270
Little Gardener	74	4"	$150
Little Goat Herder	200/0	4-3/4"	$250
Little Guardian	145	4"	$185
Little Helper	73	4-1/4"	$150
Little Hiker	16/2/0	4"	$145
Little Landscaper	2011	4-1/4"	$200
Little Nurse	376	4"	$295
Little Pharmacist	322	6"	$300
Little Scholar	80/2/0	4-1/4"	$175
Little Scholar	80	5-1/2"	$270

Name	Mold Number	Size*	Price**
Little Shopper	96	5-1/2"	$180
Little Sweeper	171/0	4-1/4"	$185
Little Tailor	308	5-1/2"	$305
Little Thrifty	118	5"	$195
Little Tooter	214/H/1	4"	$155
Little Troubadour	558	4"	$145
Lost Stocking	374	4-1/4"	$185
Love In Bloom (with wagon)	699	4-3/4"	$245
Mail is Here, The	226	4-1/2"	$655
Making New Friends	2002	6-3/4"	$625
March Winds	43	5"	$190
March Winds	43/0	5-1/4"	$425
(Limited Edition Progression Set)			
Max and Moritz	123	5"	$270
Merry Wanderer	11/2/0	4-1/4"	$180
Merry Wanderer	7/0	6-1/4"	$350
Merry Wanderer	7/X	32"	$26,550
Messages of Love	2050/A	3-1/2"	$95
Millennium Revival (Limited Edition)		7"	$1,750
Morning Stroll	375/3/0	3-3/4"	$215
Mother's Helper	133	5"	$257.50
Mountaineer	315	5"	$270
My Best Friend	2049/B	3-1/2"	$150
Nap, A	534	2-1/2"	$150
Nimble Fingers (with wooden bench)	758	4-1/2"	$250
No Thank You	535	3-1/2"	$135
Not For You	317	6"	$300
On Parade	720	4"	$180
On Secret Path	386	5-1/4"	$300
Once Upon a Time	2051A	3-1/2"	$95
One Cup of Sugar	2116A	4"	$145
One For You, One For Me	482	3"	$135
One Plus One	556	4"	$165
Ooh, My Tooth	533	3"	$145
Out of Danger	56/B	6-1/4"	$365
Parade of Lights	616	6"	$305
Pay Attention	426/3/0	4"	$190
Peaceful Blessing	814	4-1/2"	$195
Photographer, The	178	5"	$355
Pixie	768	3-1/2"	$140
Playmates	58/2/0	3-3/4"	$185
Playmates	58/0	4"	$205
Poet, The	397/I	6"	$280
Postman	119/2/0	4-1/2"	$180
Postman	119/0	5"	$250
Practice Makes Perfect	771	4-3/4"	$280
(with wooden rocker)			
Prayer Before Battle	20	4-1/4"	$205
Pretty Please	489	3-1/2"	$135
Professor, The	320/0	4-3/4"	$257.50
Proud Moments	800	3-1/2"	$320
Puppy Pause	2032	4-1/4"	$195

Name	Mold Number	Size*	Price**
Retreat to Safety	201/2/0	4"	$200
Ride Into Christmas	396/2/0	4-1/4"	$290
Ride Into Christmas	396/I	5-3/4"	$530
Riding Lesson	2020	4-1/2"	$200
Ring Around the Rosie	348	6-3/4"	$3,200
Ring In the Season	2073/A	4"	$145
Roses Are Red	762	3-1/2"	$135
Ruprecht (Limited Edition)	473	6"	$470
Saint Nicholas Day (Limited Edition)	2012	6-1/2"	$650
Scamp	553	3-1/2"	$135
School Boy	82/2/0	4"	$180
School Boys	170/I	7-1/2"	$1,480
School Boys (Limited Edition)	170/III	9-3/4"	$2,750
School Girl	81/2/0	4-1/4"	$180
School Girls	177/I	7-1/2"	$1,480
School Girls (Limited Edition)	177/II	9-1/2"	$2,750
School's Out	538	4"	$190
Sensitive Hunter	6/0	4-3/4"	$250
Serenade	85/4/0	3"	$130
Serenade	85/0	4-3/4"	$170
Serenade	85/III	12-1/2"	$1,550
She Loves Me, She Loves Me Not	174	4-1/2"	$257.50
Shepherd Boy	395/0	4-1/4"	$280
Shepherd's Boy	64	5-1/2"	$330
Shining Light	358	2-3/4"	$110
Singing Lesson	63	2-3/4"	$155
Sister	98/2/0	4-3/4"	$180
Skate In Stride	2058/B	3"	$155
Skating Lesson	2058/A	3-1/4"	$155
Skier	59	5"	$250
Sleep Tight	424	4-1/2"	$267.50
Smart Little Sister	346	4-3/4"	$300
Soloist	135/4/0	3"	$135
Soloist	135	4-3/4"	$170
Soloist	135/III	13"	$1,550
Song of Praise	454	3"	$135
Sound the Trumpet	457	3"	$135
Sounds of the Mandolin	438	3-3/4"	$160
Spring Dance	353/0	5-1/4"	$395
Star Gazer	132	4-3/4"	$257.50
Stormy Weather	71/2/0	4-3/4"	$365
Stormy Weather	71/I	6-1/4"	$540
Storybook Time	458	5"	$490
Street Singer	131	5"	$245
Strum Along	557	3-3/4"	$155
Summertime Surprise	428/3/0	3-1/2"	$160
Sunny Morning	313/0	3-1/2"	$300
Sunshower	634/2/0	4-1/2"	$385
Surprise	94/3/0	4"	$190
Sweet Greetings	352	4-1/4"	$215

Name	Mold Number	Size*	Price**
Sweet Music	186	5"	$250
Sweet Treats	2067/A	3-1/4"	$95
Teacher's Pet	2125	4-1/4"	$175
Telling Her Secret	196/0	5"	$375
Thanksgiving Prayer (mini)	641/4/0	3-1/4"	$130
Thanksgiving Prayer	641/0	4-3/4"	$200
Thoughtful	415	4-1/2"	$270
Timid Little Sister	394	6-3/4"	$530
To Keep You Warm (with wooden chair)	759	5"	$257.50
To Market	49/3/0	4"	$195
To Market	49/0	5-1/2"	325
True Friendship	402	5-1/4"	$365
Tuba Player	437	6"	$340
Tuneful Angel	359	2-3/4"	$110
Umbrella Boy	152/A/2/0	3-1/2"	$300
Umbrella Boy	152/A/0	4-3/4"	$715
Umbrella Boy	152/A/II	8"	$1,750
Umbrella Girl	152/B/2/0	3-1/2"	$300
Umbrella Girl	152/B/0	4-3/4"	$715
Umbrella Girl	152/B/II	8"	$1,750
Village Boy	51/3/0	4"	$150
Village Boy	51/2/0	5"	$185
Volunteers	50/2/0	5"	$265
Volunteers	50/0	5-1/2"	$375
Volunteers (50th Anniversary Edition, 2002)	52/2/0	5"	$265
Waiter	154/0	6"	$270
Wash Day	321/I	6"	$365
Watchful Angel	194	6-3/4"	$365
Wayside Devotion	28/II	7-1/2"	$510
Wayside Harmony	111/3/0	4"	$185
We Congratulate	214/E/I	3-1/2"	$195
We Congratulate	220	4"	$200
We Congratulate (50th Anniversary Edition, 2002)	214/E/I	3-1/2"	$195
What's New?	418	5-1/4"	$350
Where Are You?	427/3/0	4"	$190
Whistler's Duet	413	4-1/4"	$350
Winter Song	476	4-1/4"	$145
Wintertime Duet	2134	4"	$175
Worship	84/0	5"	$200

2002 Annual Angel

Name	Mold Number	Size	Price
Cymbals of Joy (2002, with dated wooden base)	2096/U	4"	$140

2002 Special Event Editions

Name	Mold Number	Size	Price
My Favorite Pony (Limited Edition)	2019	4-1/4"	$225
Toyland Express (Limited Edition)	2018	4-1/4"	$225

Angel Symphony

Name	Mold Number	Size	Price
Angelic Conductor	2096/A	4-1/4"	$135
Bells on High	2096/V	3-1/2"	$135
Celestial Drummer	2096/C	4-1/4"	$135
Celestial Reveille	2096/G	4-1/4"	$135
Celestial Strings	2096/F	4"	$135
Divine Drummer	2096/M	4-1/4"	$135
Heaven and Nature Sing	2096/Q	4"	$135
Heavenly Harmony	2096/L	3-3/4"	$135
Heavenly Hornplayer	2096/J	4"	$135
Heavenly Hubbub	2096/P	4-1/4"	$135
Heavenly Rhapsody	2096/E	4"	$135
Seraphim Soprano	2096/R	4-1/4"	$135
String Symphony	2096/D	4-1/4"	$135
Triumphant Trumpeter	2096/S	3-1/4"	$135
Zealous Xylophonist	2096/N	3-1/4"	$135
Bavarian Church Display	-	12" x 10" x 10"	$15

Annual Plate Series

Name	Mold Number	Size	Price
Bumblebee Friend (2002)	923	7"	$198
Florist, The (2003)	924	7"	$215

Baby Gifts***

Name	Mold Number	Size	Price
Baby's First Christmas Ornament	881/A	3-1/2"	$22.50
Round Trinket Box	884	4"	$50
Earthenware Birth Certificate/ Storybook (with pen)	883/A	5-1/2"	$50
Earthenware Framed Picture	882/A	5-1/2"	$75
The Guardian (Figurine)	445	2-3/4"	$200
New Baby 4-Piece Set (Large)	-	-	$197.50

***All baby gift pieces feature The Guardian motif.

Ball Ornaments

Name	Mold Number	Size	Price
Angel Duet	3016	3"	$49
Angel Serenade	3017	3"	$49
Celestial Musician	3012	3"	$49
Christmas Angel	3015	3"	$49

Name	Mold Number	Size	Price
Christmas Song	3018	3"	$49
Festival Harmony With Flute	3019	3"	$49
Festival Harmony With Mandolin	3020	3"	$49
Heavenly Angel	3021	3"	$49

Bas-Relief Christmas Ornaments

Name	Mold Number	Size	Price
Christmas Delivery Star	2110/A	3-1/2"	$20
Christmas Song Candlestick	879/A	3-1/2"	$20
Hear Ye, Hear Ye Lantern	880/A	3-1/2"	$20
Heavenly Angel Bell	876/A	3-1/4"	$20
Making New Friends Flake	2111/A	3-1/2"	$20
Ride Into Christmas Tree	877/A	4-1/4"	$20
Ring In the Season Pinecone	2129/A	3-1/2"	$20
Sleep Tight Ball	878/A	3-1/2"	$20
Saint Nicholas Day Boot	2099/A	3-1/4"	$20

Bavarian Village Collection

Houses

Name	Mold Number	Size	Price
All Aboard	-	4-3/4"	$60
Angel's Duet	-	8-1/4"	$60
Apple Tree Cottage	-	6"	$65
Christmas Mail	-	5-1/2"	$60
Clock Shop	-	6"	$65
Company's Coming	-	5-1/4"	$60
Heavenly Harmony	-	9"	$60
Off For the Holidays	-	5-1/2"	$60
Practice Makes Perfect	-	6-3/4"	$65
Scholarly Thoughts	-	6-1/2"	$65
Shoemaker Shop	-	5-1/4"	$60
Tending the Geese	-	4-1/4"	$65
Village Bakery	-	5-1/2"	$60
Village Pharmacy	-	6-1/2"	$65
Warm Winter Wishes	-	6-1/4"	$65
Winter's Comfort	-	5-1/2"	$60

Accessories

Name	Mold Number	Size	Price
Bench and Pine Tree Set	-	1-1/4"	$30
Evergreen Tree Set	-	2-1/4"	$30
Holiday Fountain	-	2-3/4"	$35
Holiday Lights (2)	-	3-1/2"	$20
Horse with Sled	-	6"	$35
Mailbox	-	2-1/2"	$20
Sled and Pine Tree Set	-	1-3/4"	$30
Village Bridge	-	2-1/4"	$30
Wishing Well	-	2-1/4"	$30

Bridal Gifts****

Name	Mold Number	Size	Price
Couple's First Christmas Ornament	2163/A	3-1/2"	$22.50
Heart Trinket Box (with ring cushion)	2152/A	3-1/4"	$50
Earthenware Marriage License/ Storybook (with pen)	2179/A	5-1/2"	$50
Earthenware Framed Picture	2178/A	7-1/4"	$75
Dearly Beloved (Figurine)	2003/2/0	4-1/4"	$200
Bridal 4-Piece Set (Large)	-	-	$197.50

****All bridal gift pieces feature Dearly Beloved motif.

Calendars/Perpetual

Name	Mold Number	Size	Price
2003	-	9-1/2" x 12-1/2"	$15
Hello	788/A	6-1/4"	$310
Sister	788/B	6-1/4"	$310

Candleholders

Name	Mold Number	Size	Price
Angel With Accordion	I/32/0	2"	$72.50
Angel With Lute	I/38/0	2"	$72.50
Angel With Trumpet	I/40/0	2"	$72.50
Boy With Horse	117	3-1/2"	$72.50
Girl With Fir Tree	116	3-1/2"	$72.50
Girl With Nosegay	115	3-1/2"	$72.50

Century Collection Mini-Plates

Name	Mold Number	Size	Price
Call to Worship ('88)	888	4"	$31.50
Chapel Time ('86)	886	4"	$31.50
Fanfare ('99)	899	4"	$31.50
Fond Goodbye ('97)	897	4"	$31.50
Harmony In Four Parts ('89)	889	4"	$31.50
Here's My Heart ('98)	898	4"	$31.50
Let's Tell the World ('90)	890	4"	$31.50
Love's Bounty ('96)	896	4"	$31.50
On Our Way ('92)	892	4"	$31.50
Pleasant Journey ('87)	887	4"	$31.50
Rock-A-Bye ('94)	894	4"	$31.50
Strike Up the Band ('95)	895	4"	$31.50
We Wish You the Best ('91)	891	4"	$31.50
Welcome Spring ('93)	893	4"	$31.50
Walnut Display Unit	-	25-1/2" x 14" x 2-1/4"	$100

Clocks

Name	Mold Number	Size	Price
Goose Girl	750	12"	$225

Display Plaques

Name	Mold Number	Size	Price
Daydreamer (personalizable)	827	3-1/2"	$150
Over the Horizon (personalizable)	828	3-1/4"	$150

Figural Ornaments

Name	Mold Number	Size	Price
Boy With Horse	239/C/0	3-1/2"	$72.50
Christmas Surprise	536/3/0/O	3-1/4"	$85
Christmas Time	2106	3-1/4"	$85
Christmas Wish	2094/0	3-1/4"	$85
Cuddles	2049/A/O	3"	$85
First Bloom	2077/A/O	3"	$85
Flower For You, A	2077/B/O	3"	$85
For Me?	2067/B/O	3-1/4"	$85
Girl With Doll	239/B/0	3-1/2"	$72.50
Girl With Fir Tree	239/D/0	3-1/2"	$72.50
Girl With Nosegay	239/A/0	3-1/2"	$72.50
My Best Friend	2049/B/O	3"	$85

Fonts

Name	Mold Number	Size	Price
Angel Facing Left	91/A	4-3/4"	$57.50
Angel Facing Right	91/B	4-3/4"	$57.50
Angel Shrine	147	5"	$67.50
Angel Sitting	22/0	3-1/2"	$57.50
Angel With Bird	167	4-3/4"	$67.50
Child With Flowers	36/0	4"	$57.50
Good Shepherd	35/0	4-3/4"	$57.50
Heavenly Angel	207	4-3/4"	$67.50
Holy Family	246	4-3/4"	$67.50
Madonna and Child	243	4"	$67.50
Worship	164	4-3/4"	$67.50

Gift/Collector's Sets

Name	Mold Number	Size	Price
All Aboard Collector's Set	2044	5"	$255
Baked With Love Cookie Press (with functional cookie press)	239/A	3-1/2"	$99
Catch of the Day Collector's Set	2031	4-1/4"	$255
Christmas Delivery Gift Set	2014/I	5-1/2" x 8-3/4"	$530
Comfort and Care Collector's Set	2075	4-1/4"	$255
Easter Basket Gift Set	2027	4"	$245
For Mother Gift Set	257/2/0	4-1/2"	$180
Gingerbread Lane Collector's Set	2067/A/B	3-1/4"/3-1/2"	$240
Goose Girl Sampler	47/3/0	4"	$210
Guardian Gift Set	455	4-1/4"	$200
Halt! Collector's Set	2039	2-1/2"	$255
Icy Adventure Collector's Set	2058/A/B	3-1/2"/3-3/4"	$385
In the Kitchen Collector's Set	2038	4-1/2"	$255

Name	Mold Number	Size	Price
Kid's Club Collector's Set	-	-	$680
Little Landscaper Collector's Set	2011	4-1/4"	$250
Little Maestro Collector's Set	826/I	5-1/2"	$435
Maid to Order Collector's Set	2091	4-1/4"	$255
Make Me Pretty Collector's Set	2092	4-1/4"	$255
Nutcracker Sweet Collector's Set	2130	6"	$375
One Coat or Two? Collector's Set	2040	4-1/2"	$255
Pretzel Boy Collector's Set	2093	4"	$190
Ride Into Christmas Gift Set	396/I	6" x 8-1/2"	$530
Saint Nicholas Day/Ruprecht	2012/473	6"	$1,120
Swaying Lullaby Collector's Set	165	4-1/2" x 5-1/4"	$345
Sweet As Can Be Birthday Sampler	541	4"	$170
Sweet Treats Holiday Baking Set	2067/A	3-1/4"	$99
Treehouse Treats Collector's Set	73/554	4-1/4" x 4"	$345
Tuneful Goodnight	180	6-1/4" x 6-1/2"	$305
We Congratulate Gift Set	220	4"	$200
Winter Adventure Collector's Set	2028	4-3/4"	$230
Vacation Time Plaque/Display	125	4-3/4"	$445

Madonnas

Name	Mold Number	Size	Price
Madonna With Halo, Color	45/I/6	12"	$160
Millennium Madonna (Limited Edition)	855	10-1/4"	$495

M.I. Hummel Club Exclusive Collectibles

Anniversary Figurines (prices subject to change)

Name	Mold Number	Size	Price
Sunflower Friends (5-Year Figurine)	2104	3-1/2"	$195
Miss Beehaving (10-Year Figurine)	2105	2-3/4"	$240
Honey Lover (15-Year Figurine)	312/I	3-3/4"	$235
Behave (20-Year Figurine)	339	5-1/2"	$360
Relaxation (25-Year Figurine)	316	3-3/4"	$390

Club Figurines (available to current members only)

Name	Mold Number	Size	Price
Looking Around	2089/A	4-1/4"	$230
Picture Perfect	2100	8-1/4"	$3,495
Puppet Prince	2103/B	3-3/4"	$100
Scooter Time	2070	6-3/4"	$695
Rolling Around	2088/B	3-1/4"	$230
Summer Adventure	2124	5-3/4"	$695
Wait For Me	2148/A	4-1/4"	$100
Extra! Extra! (25th Anniversary)	2113	5-1/2"	$240

M.I. Hummel Pins

Name	Mold Number	Size	Price
Basket of Flowers Pin	-	1"	$25
Beehive Pin	-	1"	$25
Bumblebee Pin	-	1"	$20
Heart Pin	-	1"	$25
Palette Pin	-	1"	$25

Millennium Collection

Name	Mold Number	Size	Price
African Wanderer	2062	4-1/4"	(TW) $260
American Wanderer	2061	5"	(TW) $260
Asian Wanderer	2063	4-1/2"	(TW) $260
Australian Wanderer	2064	4-1/4"	(TW) $260
European Wanderer	2060	4-1/4"	(TW) $260

Millennium Love Collection

Name	Mold Number	Size	Price
Band Leader	129/III	13-1/2"	$1,550
Little Fiddler	2/III	12-1/2"	$1,550
Serenade	85/III	12-1/2"	$1,550
Soloist	135/III	13"	$1,550
Sweet Music	186/III	13"	$1,550

Moments In Time Series

Name	Mold Number	Size	Price
Soap Box Derby	2121	6-1/2"	$1,250
Farm Days	2165	7-1/2"	$1,200

Nativity Figurines

Name	Mold Number	Size	Price
Virgin Mary	214/A/M/0	5-1/4"	$165
St. Joseph	214/B/0	6"	$165
Infant Jesus	214/A/K/0	1" x 2-3/4"	$57.50
Flying Angel	366/0	3"	$132.50
King Kneeling	214/M/0	4-1/4"	$175
King Kneeling With Box	214/N/0	4"	$170
King, Moorish	214/L/0	6-1/4"	$185
Little Tooter	214/H/0	3"	$122.50
Shepherd Kneeling	214/G/0	4"	$150
Shepherd Standing	214/F/0	5-1/2"	$185
Small Camel Standing	-	6-3/4" x 7"	$230
Small Camel Lying	-	3-1/4" x 6-3/4"	$230
Small Camel Kneeling	-	4" x 7-1/4"	$230

Name	Mold Number	Size	Price
Donkey	214/J/0	4"	$62.50
Lamb	214/O/0	1-1/2" x 1"	$27.50
Ox	214/K/0	2-3/4" x 5"	$62.50
Heirloom Chest	-	-	$400
Virgin Mary	214/A/M/I	6-1/2"	$210
St. Joseph	214/B/I	7-1/2"	$210
Infant Jesus	214/A/K/I	3-1/2" x 1-1/2"	$80
Angel Serenade	214/D/I	3"	$110
Flying Angel	366/I	3-1/2"	$160
Good Night	214/C/I	3-1/2"	$110
King Moorish	214/L/I	8-1/4"	$215
King Kneeling	214/M/I	5-1/2"	$210
King Kneeling With Box	214/N/I	5-1/2"	$195
Little Tooter	214/H/I	4"	$155
We Congratulate	214/E/I	3-1/2"	$195
Shepherd With Sheep (1-Piece)	214/F/I	7"	$210
Shepherd Boy	214/G/I	4-3/4"	$165
Camel Standing	-	8-1/2" x 7-3/4"	$285
Camel Kneeling	-	9-1/4" x 5-1/2"	$285
Camel Lying	-	8-1/4" x 4-1/4"	$285
Donkey	214/J/I	5"	$87
Lamb	214/O/I	2" x 1-1/2"	$27.50
Ox	214/K/I	6-1/2" x 3-1/2"	$87

Nativity Sets

Name	Mold Number	Size	Price
Holy Family, (3 Pieces Color, Stable)	214/A/M/0,B/0, A/K/0	-	$387.50
Holy Family (3 Pieces Color)	214/A/M/I,B/I, A/K/I	-	$500
Holy Family	-	-	$387.50
Holy Family (3 Pieces White)	214/A/M/0, B/0, A/K/0		$225
12 -Piece Set With Free Stable and Heirloom Chest (smaller size)	-	-	$1,940
12 -Piece Set Figurines Only Color (larger size)	214/A/M/I, B/I, A/K/I, F/I, G/I, J/I, K/I, L/I, M/I, N/I, O/I, 366/I		$1,856.50
16 -Piece Set Figurines Only Color (larger size)	214/A/M/I, B/I, A/K/I, C/I, D/I, E/I, F/I, G/I, H/I, J/I, K/I, L/I, M/I, N/I, O/I, 366/I		$2,426.50

Nativity Stables

Name	Mold Number	Size	Price
Stable Only, to fit 3-Piece Hum 214 Set	214/S11	13-1/2" x 8-1/2" x 6-1/4"	$52.50
Stable Only, to fit 12-or 16-Piece Hum 214/11 Set	214/S1	23-1/2" x 12" x 9-1/4"	$125
Stable Only, to fit 16-Piece Hum 260 Set	260/S	31-1/2" x 12-1/2" x 23-1/4"	$480

Ornament Gift Cards

Name	Mold Number	Size	Price
Celestial Musician	578/FD	3-1/2"	$27.50
Festival Harmony With Flute	577/FD	3-1/4"	$27.50
Festival Harmony With Mandolin	576/FD	3-1/4"	$27.50
Heavenly Angel	575/FD	3-1/4"	$27.50

Trinket Boxes

Name	Mold Number	Size	Price
Pixie (Oval)	997	4"	$50
Scamp (Oval)	996	4"	$50
Sweet Greetings (Heart)	686	3-3/4"	$50
Umbrella Boy (Round)	688	5"	$60
Umbrella Girl (Round)	689	5"	$60

HummelScapes

Name	Mold Number	Size	Price
A Wish For Mother (tune: "I Just Called To Say I Love You")	-	4-1/4" x 5-1/2"	$50
Christmas Frolic	-	6" x 8-1/2"	$75
Going to Church	-	5-3/4" x 6-1/2"	$75
Heavenly Harmonies	-	7-1/2" x 6"	$100
Icy Adventure	-	4-1/2" x 6"	$125
Strolling Through the Park	-	6-1/4" x 7-1/2"	$75
Tannenbaum Display	-	8-1/2" x 6-1/2"	$50
We Congratulate Trellis	-	4-3/4" x 6"	$40
Winter Wonderland	-	5-1/2" x 8-3/4"	$75

Wall Plaques

Name	Mold Number	Size	Price
Ba-Bee Ring (Boy)	30/A	4-3/4" x 5"	$85
Ba-Bee Ring (Girl)	30/B	4-3/4" x 5"	$85
Child In Bed	137	2-1/2" x 2-3/4"	$60
Flitting Butterfly	139	2-1/2" x 2-1/2"	$60
Merry Christmas	323	5-1/4"	$120
Searching Angel	310	4-1/8" x 3-3/8"	$115

Other Items

Name	Mold Number	Size	Price
Charm Bracelet	-	7-1/2"	$295
Collector's Catalog	-	8-1/2" x 11"	$29.95
In the Land of Hummel Book	-	8-1/2" x 11"	$35
In the Land of Hummel Book		8-1/2" x 11"	$65
Deluxe Edition Luckey's Hummel Book 12th edition		8-1/2" x 11"	$27.95
Miller's Price Guide 8th Edition	-	-	$24.95
Nativity Chest	-	-	$400

*SIZES INDICATED ARE ONLY APPROXIMATE
**PRICES SUBJECT TO CHANGE WITHOUT NOTICE

Recommended Books for Collectors

Aaseng, Nathan. *The Unsung Heroes: Unheralded People Who Invented Famous Products.* Lerner Publications Co., Minneapolis, MN 55401. Eight people are included in this book for young readers. Among them are the inventors of Coca Cola, McDonald's hamburgers, and vacuum cleaners. "Sister Maria Innocentia's Gift, M.I. Hummel Figurines" is the relevant chapter.

Arbenz, Pat. *Hummel Facts.* Misty's Gift Gallery, 228 Fry Blvd., Sierra Vista, AZ 85635. A reprint collection of all Mr. Arbenz' columns for Plate Collector magazine. Indispensable to the collector. Although inexpensive, it is out of print and difficult to find. You might try contacting Arbenz: he may have a few copies.

Armke, Ken. *Hummel: An Illustrated Handbook and Price Guide.* Published by Wallace-Homestead, c/o Krause Publications, 700 E. State St., Iola, WI 54990. 1995. This full-color guide is of much practical use to the collector. Well researched, well written, and interesting.

ArsEdition. *The Hummel.* Verlag Ars Sacra Josef Mueller, Munich, Germany, 1984. A 78-page, full-color hardcover book, full of illustrations by Sister M.I. Hummel and light verse.

Authentic Hummel Figurines. Copyright by W. Goebel, Rodental, Germany. An illustrated catalog that was for many years published by the company. Out of print.

Ehrmann, Erich and Robert L. Miller (special contributor). *Hummel, The Complete Collector's Guide and Illustrated Reference.* Portfolio Press Corporation, Huntington, NY 11743. 1976. Ehrmann, publisher of *Collectors Editions* magazine, and Miller, acknowledged expert and owner of one of the world's largest Hummel collections, collaborated to present this large work. As a reference it is invaluable to collectors.

Ehrmann, Erich W., Robert L. Miller and Walter Pfeiffer. *M.I. Hummel: The Golden Anniversary Album.* Portfolio Press Corporation, Huntington, NY 11743. 1984. A beautiful book full of color photos and much good information for collectors.

Guide for Collectors. Copyright by W. Goebel, Rodental, Germany. Available through the M.I. Hummel Club, P.O. Box 11, Pennington, NJ 08534-0011. A beautiful, large-format, full-color catalog of the current Goebel M.I. Hummel collection including closed editions. It is updated periodically.

Hotchkiss, John. *Hummel Art.* 3rd edition. Wallace-Homestead Book Co., c/o Krause Publications, 700 E. State St., Iola, WI 54990. 1982. A full-color handbook that essentially updates the first and second editions. Out of print.

Hummel, Berta and Margarete Seeman. *The Hummel Book.* 17th edition. W. Goebel, Rodental, Germany, 1992. This copyright is today with ARS AG, Zug, Switzerland.

Hummel, Maria Innocentia. *Hummel: The Original Illustrations of Sister Maria Innocentia Hummel.* Courage Books. 1998. 144 pages.

Hunt, Dick. *Goebel Miniatures of Robert Olzewski.* 595 Jackson Ave., Satellite Beach, FL. Hunt's Collectibles.

Koller, Angelica. *The Hummel.* Released by ArsEdition in 1995, this book describes Berta Hummel's childhood and her life as a nun. It also explains her theory of art and includes many full-color reproductions of her art. Hardcover, 141 pages. Available through your dealer or the M.I. Hummel Club.

Luckey, Carl F. (edited by Dean A. Genth). *Luckey's Hummel Figurines and Plates.* 12th edition. Krause Publications, 700 E. State St., Iola, WI 54990. 2002. The most comprehensive collector's reference on the market today. Not only does it cover all of the W. Goebel Porzellanfabrik three-dimensional M.I. Hummel figurines and related items, but also all of the hundreds of other available Hummel collectibles. Chock full of great pictures and useful and fascinating information. 550 pages. Available at most booksellers.

M.I. Hummel Album. Portfolio Press Corporation, Huntington, NY 11743. 1992. A beautiful full-color reference showing most of the figurines ever made. Of particular interest is the illustration of many possible future editions (PFE). A Goebel publication. See your dealer or contact the M.I. Hummel Club.

Miller, Robert L. *Hummel.* Portfolio Press Corporation, Huntington, NY 11743. 1979. This is a supplement to the original Hummel, the Complete Collector's Guide and Illustrated Reference by Ehrmann and Miller.

Miller, Robert L. *M.I. Hummel Figurines, Plates, More ...* 8th edition. Portfolio Press Corporation, Huntington, NY 11743. 2000. A well-organized and handy reference by this noted collector.

Miller, Robert L. *Hummels 1978-1998: 20 Years of "Miller on Hummel" Columns.* From Collector's News.1998. 246 pages.

Plaut, James S. *Formation of an Artist, The Early Works of Berta Hummel.* Schmid Brothers, Inc., Randolph, MA,

1980. This softbound book is actually a catalog of the 1980-82 tour of an exhibition of paintings, drawings, photographs, and a tapestry from the collection of the Hummel family.

Saal, Kathleen *In the Land of Hummel: Traditional Bavarian Life*. Portfolio Press Corporation, Huntington, NY 11743. 1999. 160 pages. Photographer Walter Pfeiffer.

Schwatlo, Wolfgang. *M.I. Hummel Collector's Handbook*. Schwatlo GMBH, D65522 Niedernhausen, Postfach 1224, Germany, 1994. This full-color handbook is of great value to the collector. It concentrates on the many variations that can be found and includes color photographs. A must for the serious collector.

Schwatlo, Wolfgang. *M.I. Hummel Collector's Handbook with Prices*. Schwatlo GmbH, D-65522 Niedernhausen, Postfach 1224, Germany, 1996. An update of Schwatlo's 1994 book. This edition has been expanded to include many other related collectibles. It is full-color and bilingual. A very useful book for the serious collector.

Struss, Dieter. *M.I. Hummel Figuren*. Weltbild Verlag GmbH, Augsburg, Bavaria, Germany, 1993. A full-color hardbound collector's guide (in German).

Wiegand, Sister M. Gonsalva, O.S.F. *Sketch Me Berta Hummel*. Reprinted by Robert L. Miller and available at most dealers or from Miller at P.O. Box 210, Eaton, OH 45320.

Wonsch, Lawrence L. *Hummel Copycats*. Wallace-Homestead, c/o Krause Publications, 700 E. State St., Iola, WI 54990. 1987. A superb treatment of the hundreds of copies of M.I. Hummel figurines over the years and around the world.

Videotapes

A Hummel Christmas. Cascom International, Inc., 806 4th Ave. So., Nashville, TN 37210. 1995. An enchanting production about 30 minutes long, this video boasts a masterful blend of rare figurines, original M.I. Hummel art, special effects, and Christmas music. This is a must-have video for the Christmas season for any lover of Hummel figurines and art.

M.I. Hummel Marks of Distinction. A historical look at the progression of M.I. Hummel backstamps from the beginning to the current mark. Available from the M.I. Hummel Club.

The Insider's Guide to M.I. Hummel Collecting. Bottom Line Productions, Inc., 1994. This one-hour video features M.I. Hummel Club spokesperson Gwen Toma in an excellent presentation of the various marks and backstamps found on the figurines and related items. An excellent overview of how they are produced, as well as an explanation of how the figurines are painted by Goebel Master Artist Sigrid Then. The greatest part of the video is given over to a charming sequence by Bob and Ruth Miller, who give you a personal tour of some of the more rare and interesting pieces in their famous collection. Available from the M.I. Hummel Club.

The Life of Sister M.I. Hummel. Produced by W. Goebel. This is a striking 25-minute treatment of Berta Hummel's life. Available from the M.I. Hummel Club.

Periodicals

The following is a list of periodicals you may find useful in collecting Hummel figurines.

Antiques Journal (monthly)
P.O. Box 1046
Dubuque, IA 52001
Has occasional articles about Hummel collecting and ads for buying and selling Hummels.

The Antique Trader Weekly (weekly)
700 E. State St.
Iola, WI 54990
Occasional Hummel articles and extensive ads for buying and selling Hummel items.

Collector Editions (quarterly)
170 Fifth Avenue
New York, NY 10010
Has occasional Hummel column.

Collectors Journal (weekly)
Box 601
Vinton, IA 52349
Has ads for Hummel buying and selling.

Collectors Mart (bimonthly)
700 E. State St.
Iola, WI 54990

Collectors News (monthly)
606 8th Street
Grundy Center, IA 50638
Has ads for Hummel buying and selling and occasional Hummel articles.

Collectors' Showcase (bimonthly)
P.O. Box 6929
San Diego, CA 92106

The Tri-State Trader (weekly)
P.O. Box 90
Knightstown, IN 46148
Has ads for Hummel buying and selling.

Clubs and Organizations

There are a few dealers and manufacturers who sponsor "collector's clubs." They are designed to market their products to a target audience. This is a good marketing technique that doubles as a means of educating collectors as to what artists and manufacturers are presently doing. The collector of M.I. Hummel items is lucky to have a couple of these. They are unique in that they are very large

Plaque given to charter members of the M.I. Hummel Club.

Plaque given to charter members of the club on the occasion of their 20th consecutive year of membership.

organizations and are very serious about keeping collectors informedition. Both organizations offer a very valuable member figurine sales and wanted list. Membership in both is highly recommendedition.

The Hummel Collector's Club, Inc.

1261 University Drive
P.O. Box 157
Yardley, PA 19067
(888) 5-HUMMEL (toll-free)

This club was established in 1975 by Dorothy Dous. She and her husband developed the club into a very valuable organization for collectors of Hummel collectibles. Mrs. Dous (Dottie) writes an interesting quarterly newsletter that is lengthy, easy to read, and crammed with information. The newsletter also includes a long list of members' for-sale, trade, or wanted lists. The club acts as a gratis go-between for its members. Any collector would benefit by becoming a member of this organization.

The M.I. Hummel Club

Goebel Plaza
P.O. Box 11
Pennington, NJ 08534-0011
(609) 737-8777, (800) 666-2582 (toll-free)
www.mihummel.com

This club was founded by the W. Goebel firm in 1976 as the Goebel Collectors' Club and became the M.I. Hummel Club in the spring of 1989. The club publishes a beautiful and very informative full-color quarterly newsletter, *Insights*, which no collector should be without. Another advantage of membership is the renewal gifts each year, usually a figurine, and the chance to buy figures that are offered exclusively to members and are specially marked with the club backstamp. They also maintain a referral list

of members' items for sale or wantedition. In 2002, the M.I. Hummel club celebrated its 25th anniversary. Check the website for current exclusive offerings and events.

Local Chapters of the M.I. Hummel Club

At least 143 local chapters of the M.I. Hummel Club were active in 41 states and 4 provinces in Canada as of October 1996. There is even an International Chapter for members with the name "Hummel" as their surname or maiden name. If you are interested in joining a local chapter or starting one of your own, call or write the club in Pennington, New Jersey (information listed earlier in this chapter).

United States

Arizona

Roadrunner (Phoenix)
Yuma

Arkansas

Arkansas Traveler (Magnolia)

California

Camarillo
Central Coast (Lompoc)
Fresno
Heart of the Redwoods (Eureka)
Orange County
Pleasant Valley (Camarillo)
San Bernardino (Yucaipa)
San Diego County
San Francisco East Bay

The old local chapter patch. The new ones read "M.I. Hummel Club." Many have their own custom patches made to more personally identify their chapter.

San Gabriel (Covina)
Silicon Valley (San Jose)
Whittier (West Hills)

Colorado

Gateway to the Rockies (Aurora)
Loveland Sweetheart (Fort Collins)
Mile Hi (Denver)
Pikes Peak (Colorado Springs)

Connecticut

Central (Plantsville)
Rose City (Norwich)

Florida

Daytona Beach
Delray Beach
Fivay
Ft. Lauderdale (Closed)
Greater Zephryhills
Jacksonville
Leesburg
Ocala
Orlando Area
Palm Beach
Seven Rivers (Beverly Hills)
Suncoast (Palm Harbor)
Tampa Area (Closed)
The Villages of Lady Lake

Georgia

Augusta (Evans)
Metro Atlanta (Dallas)

Illinois

Batavia Travelers
Gateway East (Belleville)

Greater Peoria Area
Illiana (Valpariso)
LaGrange Park (Bridgeview)
McHenry County
Northern Illinois (Crystal Lake)
N.W. Suburban (Palatine)

Indiana

Danville (Avon)
Hoosier Connection (Russiaville)

Kansas

Mo-Kan (Kansas City)
North Central Kansas (Salina)
Sunflower (McPherson)

Louisiana

Cajun Collectors (Baton Rouge)

Maine

Nor'Easter (Auburn)

Maryland

Eventide (Easton)
Pleasant Journey (Crownsville)
Silver Spring

Massachusetts

Cape Cod (Sandwich)
Neponset Valley (Dedham)
Pioneer Valley (West Springfield)
Quabbin (Ludlow)

Michigan

Adventurous Anglers (Tipton) (Closed)
Dearborn
Great Lakes (Dearborn)
Niles Saginaw Valley (Bay City)

Missouri

St. Louis Spirit of the River (Ballwin)

Montana

Big Sky (Great Falls)
Yellowstone (Billings)

Nebraska

Cinderella (Lincoln)
Huskers (Lincoln)
Omaha

Nevada

High Sierra

New Hampshire

Graniteer (Manchester)

New Jersey

Friendly Hands (NJ and NY)
Jersey Cape (Absecon)
Ocean Pines (Forked River)

New Mexico

Albuquerque

New York

Great South Bay (Massapequa)
Nassau-Suffolk (New Hyde Park)
Northern Catskills (Hunter)
Paumanok (Closed)
Rochester (Hilton)
Tonawanda Valley (Attica)
Western NY (Getzville)

North Carolina

Carolina Mountain Region (Flat Rock)
Hornet's Nest (Concord)

Ohio

Firelands Area (Sandusky)
Greater Cleveland
Miami Valley (Beavercreek)
Stark County Hall of Fame (N. Canton)
Toledo (Archbold)
Queen City (Cincinnati)
Youngstown/Hubbard

Oklahoma

OK Chapter (Oklahoma City)

Oregon

Cascade (Eugene)
Portland (Tigard)

Pennsylvania

Antietam Valley (Waynesboro)
Berks County (Kutztown)
Bux-Mont (Bucks & Montgomery Countys)
Central (Mifflinburg)
Schuylkill County (Hamburg)
York County (Spring Grove)

South Carolina

Piedmont Carolinas (Charlotte)

Tennessee

Knoxville (Friendsville)

Texas

Alamo (San Antonio)
Brazosport (Lake Jackson)
Dallas Metroplex (Frisco)
Fort Worth
Gulf Coats (Houston)
Hill County Hummeles

Utah

Beehive
Cache Bridgerland

Vermont

Burlington (Essex Junction)

Virginia

Gentle Care (West Springfield) (Closed)
Northern Virginia (Springfield)
Tidewater Area (Chesapeake)
West Richmond (Glen Allen)

Washington

Bellevue (Closed)
Puget Sound (Marysville)
Seattle-Tacoma (Edmonds)

West Virginia

Almost Heaven (Morgantown)

Wisconsin

Fox Valley (Fond du Lac)
Mad City West (Middleton)
Milwaukee

Canada

Alberta

Calgary
Calgary (Alberta)
Edmonton (Sherwood Park)

British Columbia

Greater Vancouver (Langley)

Saskatchewan

Saskatoon

International

Club members with "Hummel" as their surnames or maiden names. There is also a group of International M.I. Hummel Clubs in Europe.

✺ *Index* ✺